国家重点学科华东政法大学法律史学科建设项目（学科代码：03102）

比较法文丛

何勤华 主编

42

20世纪以来英美国家的古希腊法律史研究

胡骏 著

法律出版社
LAW PRESS·CHINA
北京

图书在版编目(CIP)数据

20世纪以来英美国家的古希腊法律史研究 / 胡骏著.
-- 北京:法律出版社,2023
(比较法文丛 / 何勤华主编)
ISBN 978-7-5197-1003-3

Ⅰ.①2… Ⅱ.①胡… Ⅲ.①法制史-研究-古希腊
Ⅳ.①D954.59

中国版本图书馆CIP数据核字(2017)第122568号

20世纪以来英美国家的古希腊法律史研究
20 SHIJI YILAI YING-MEI GUOJIA DE GUXILA FALÜSHI YANJIU

胡 骏 著

策划编辑 沈小英
责任编辑 刘晓萌
装帧设计 李 瞻

出版发行 法律出版社
编辑统筹 法治与经济出版分社
责任校对 王晓萍
责任印制 吕亚莉
经 销 新华书店

开本 710毫米×1000毫米 1/16
印张 22.75 **字数** 437千
版本 2023年3月第1版
印次 2023年3月第1次印刷
印刷 北京虎彩文化传播有限公司

地址:北京市丰台区莲花池西里7号(100073)
网址:www.lawpress.com.cn
投稿邮箱:info@lawpress.com.cn
举报盗版邮箱:jbwq@lawpress.com.cn
销售电话:010-83938349
客服电话:010-83938350
咨询电话:010-63939796

书号:ISBN 978-7-5197-1003-3
定价:138.00元
凡购买本社图书,如有印装错误,我社负责退换。电话:010-83938349

总　序

自1978年改革开放以来，我国在外国法或西方法的研究方面取得了重大成就。这方面的系列丛书可谓琳琅满目，其中，影响较大的有：商务印书馆的“汉译世界学术名著丛书”（法学部分，1981年）及“法学译丛”（2004年）、中国大百科全书出版社的“外国法律文库”（1991年）、中国政法大学出版社的“当代法学名著译丛”（1990年）及“美国法律文库”（2001年）、北京大学出版社的“比较法学丛书”（1998年）、中国法制出版社的“西方法哲学文库”（2001年）、清华大学出版社的“比较法学丛书”（2001年）、上海人民出版社的“世界法学名著译丛”（2001年）、北京大学出版社的“外国法与比较法文库”（2008年），等等。

然而，在上述众多的系列丛书中，真正冠以“比较法”字样的丛书还不是很多。的确，在20世纪80年代到90年代，我国也先后出版了诸如：茨威格特和克茨的《比较法总论》（贵州人民出版社1992年版）、勒内·达维德的《当代主要法律体系》（上海译文出版社1984年版）、梅利曼的《大陆法系》（知识出版社1984年版）、大木雅夫的《比较法》（法律出版社1999年版）等比较法方面的经典。但是，出版这些著作大多都是当时一种零星的、偶尔的出版行为，并非系统策划的比较法系列丛书。

众所周知，21世纪的中国已步入法制建设的攻坚阶段。今后，对于外国法的吸收、借鉴和移植将是我国一项大量的、经常性的任务。要顺利完成这一任务，离不开发达的比较法研究。而当下我国比较法著作缺乏出版途径的现状已严重制约了比较法研究的繁荣和发展。因此，加强比较法方面的研究和出版，成为我国学界和出版界一项刻不容缓的工作。

鉴于此，法律出版社高瞻远瞩，勇挑重担，与华东政法大学共同策划、出版一套“比较法文丛”，以期为我国比较法的研究和出版开辟一个新的途径。本文丛以扶植中青年学者，尤其是法学博士、博士后，为这些法学新秀提供一个出版的平台为目的。为此，特选择一批国内最新且富有特色的比较法著作进行出版，同时，也可容纳部分纯粹的外国法方面的译著、专著。

本文丛的主要原则和特色是：在百花齐放、百家争鸣的前提下，坚持质量第一，宁缺毋滥，不定期出版的原则。具体将体现为以下三点特色：第一，本文丛的著作，应属国内学术界没有涉及的课题，具有填补法学研究空白的特色；第二，本文丛的著作，应是国内学术界都很感兴趣，但还没有系统研究或未及时挖掘的课题；第三，本文丛的著作，应具有比较高的文献史料价值，能为学术界进一步研究提供基础性的资料。我相信，“比较法文丛”的出版，一定会为我国比较法研究的进步与发展作出新的贡献。

本文丛的出版，得到了法律出版社沈小英分社长的全力支持和帮助，也得到了华东政法大学外国法与比较法研究院的建设经费资助。在此，特表示诚挚的谢意。

何勤华

于华政人可居

2010年9月19日

Contents

目录

导 论

古代希腊作为西方文明的发源地之一,近代西方哲学、美学、医学、文学、数学、天文学以及论理学等,无不发端于此地。正如哲学家黑格尔所言:“一提到希腊这个名字,在有教养的欧洲人心中……自然会引起一种家园之感。”①英国诗人雪莱则毫不掩饰地在其抒情歌剧《希腊》的前言中写道:“我们全部是希腊人——我们的法律,我们的文学,我们的宗教,我们的艺术,根源都在希腊。如非希腊,罗马这个引导者、征服者和我们祖先的母城就无法以她的武力传播文化,我们可能仍然是野蛮人和偶像崇拜者;或者更糟……进入一个停滞和悲惨的状态。”②恩格斯也曾经说过:“在希腊哲学的多种多样的形式中,几乎可以发现以后的所有观点的胚胎、萌芽。”③而作为近代西方文明重要组成部分的政治与法律制度也在很大程度上受益于古希腊时期确立的民主、法治思想。虽然能否将西方法律传统的源头追溯至古希腊还有待学者的进一

① [德]黑格尔:《哲学演讲录》(第1卷),贺麟、王太庆译,商务印书馆1981年版,第157页。

② Shelley, *Shelley's Poetry and Prose Selected and Edited by Donald H. Reiman and Sharon B. Powers*, W. W. Norton and Company Inc. ,1977, pp. 406 – 440.

③ 《马克思恩格斯选集》(第4卷),人民出版社1995年版,第287页。

步研究,[①]然而毫无疑问的是:在西方法律传统乃至整个人类法律文明的历史长河中,古希腊世界的法律制度是值得也应该引起我们重视并加以深入研究的。[②]

事实上,近代西方英美法系中的衡平法、大陆法系中"公法"与"私法"的区分以及我们所熟知的西方法律传统中的陪审法庭、法庭辩论等法律制度的产生都可追溯到古典时代的雅典城邦。[③] 而最为后人所称道的罗马法的制定也曾受到古希腊法律,尤其是雅典法律的很大影响。据记载,在罗马《十二铜表法》制定之前,罗马人就"开始派遣一个特使团去雅典学习梭伦的法律和其他希腊城邦的制度"。[④] 伟大的罗马律师小普利尼也以钦佩的口吻谈到希腊人。他的朋友克西姆斯于公元前2世纪初去希腊,在特拉真皇帝手下担任执行官,小普利尼写了如下一段话来告诫临行前的克西姆斯:"记住你被派往真正的希腊,礼貌和学识的国度……记住一点,他们把法律给予了我们。记住你要去雅典和斯巴达,剥夺这样

---

① 一般认为,西方法学诞生于古代罗马,而非希腊。See E. Ehrlich, *Fundamental Principles of the Sociology of Law*, translated by W. L. Moll, Transaction Publishers, 1962, p. 247; Hans Julius Wolff, *Roman Law, An Historical Introduction*, University of Oklahoma Press, 1951. p. 92. 不过英国法律史学家梅因(Henry Sumner Maine, 1822～1888年)则认为"《十二铜表法》的公布并不能作为我们开始研究法律史的最早起点"。参见[英]梅因:《古代法》,沈景一译,商务印书馆1959年版,第1页。

② 所谓"古希腊世界",并不是一个统一的国家,而是一个地理和文化概念。从地理上讲,它以爱琴海地区为中心,包括希腊半岛,爱琴海诸岛屿以及小亚细亚西部沿海地区、意大利南部及西西里岛东部沿岸地区(比现在的希腊共和国略大一些);从文化上讲,它还包括希腊化时代在希腊本土之外建立的希腊化国家。从旧石器时代开始,希腊半岛就有人类居住,公元前2000年左右,从北方陆续迁入印欧语族的亚加亚人、爱奥尼亚人、伊奥利亚人和多利亚人,逐渐分居于希腊各地,古希腊民族的萌芽初步形成。在希腊本土的半岛地区,没有宽广的平原,也没有浩瀚的大江,这里山脉纵横,河道交叉,土地贫瘠,不适宜农耕。但它与海洋紧密的联系,养成了古希腊人"两栖类式的生活,使他们能够随心所欲地凌波往来,无异于陆上行走"([德]黑格尔:《历史哲学》,王造时译,生活·读书·新知三联书店1956年版,第272页)。这种近海的地理环境,不仅造就了古希腊人勇敢、探求与多思的民族性格,而且非常有利于他们通商航海和吸收他国文化的先进成果。古希腊法律文明正是在上述优越的人文和地理环境中茁壮成长起来的。由于在希腊历史和希腊文明领域内并不存在能够管辖全希腊境内的最高政治权力,因此并不存在能够统一适用于整个希腊全境内的法律体系;但同时由于城邦的分裂繁殖和殖民模式,使得在整个希腊城邦之间,始终存在互相联系的纽带:他们通过语言和文化的亲和性辨识其共享的希腊民族性。因此本书所涉及的古希腊法并不是一个国家法的概念,而是就其地域范围而言的,泛指存在于古代希腊世界所有法律规范的总称。

③ 古代希腊的历史大致分为五个阶段:(1)爱琴文明或克里特、迈锡尼文明时代(公元前20世纪～公元前12世纪);(2)荷马时代(公元前11世纪～公元前9世纪);(3)古风时代(公元前8世纪～公元前6世纪);(4)古典时代(公元前5世纪～公元前4世纪);(5)马其顿统治时代(公元前4世纪晚期～公元前2世纪中期)。参见吴于廑、齐世荣主编:《世界史·古代史编》(上卷),高等教育出版社1994年版,第90～91页。

④ [意]朱塞佩·格罗索:《罗马法史》,黄风译,中国政法大学出版社1994年版,第77页。

的人民的自由权是野蛮、残酷、不人道的。”①因此，深入探究古代希腊的法律制度能使我们更好地理解西方法律文明的内在精神与后世传承。

近年来，我国法律史学者对古希腊法律史的研究取得了可喜的成果，②但在英美国家古希腊法律史的学说史研究方面一直没有学者涉足，最新的研究也还停留在对亚里士多德、柏拉图相关法学论述进行解读的传统研究阶段。对英美国家学者从事古希腊法律史研究的学术历程进行回顾和总结，是一项开拓性的新课题。作为罗马法诞生前一个影响空前的法律体系，古希腊法律史研究的重要地位一直被人忽视。古希腊法持续时间久远（从公元前 11 世纪的荷马时期至公元前 30 年希腊化时期结束）、适用地域广阔（包括巴尔干半岛的希腊、马其顿，南欧的意大利，西亚的土耳其、叙利亚，北非的埃及、利比亚等），其本身是一个独立完整的法律体系，且承上（近东法）启下（罗马法），是世界法律发展史中的重要一环，古希腊法律史的研究对于我们认识“法律如何成长、何种因素引发和促进其成长”等法学基本问题具有重要意义。而对英美国家古希腊法律史研究的学术史进行梳理总结是深入开展古希腊法律史研究的一个必要准备。

通过对英美国家古希腊法律史研究的演变历史、基本范式、研究资料和最新研究趋势等的总结介绍，特别是对相关历史时期英美国家社会政治发展背景对学者研究方向影响的分析，本书试图揭示法律史研究与现实社会发展之间的规律性联系，诚如克罗齐所言“一切历史都是当代史”。同时，本书也试图为国内学者后续对古希腊法基本制度的研究提供新的路径。古希腊各城邦经历了各种政治与法律制度的演变与试验，贵族寡头制与平民民主制的斗争一直贯穿于其各个历史发展时期，伴随其中的法律制度演变也多种多样，法治思想如何诞生于此，如何影响至今，唯有深入加以考察才会真正理解。英美国家古希腊法律史研究的学术史

① [美]约翰·赞恩：《法律的故事》，刘昕、胡凝译，江苏人民出版社 1998 年版，第 95 页。

② 目前国内古希腊法律史研究主要包括五个路径：一是介绍性述评（叶秋华，1999 年；贺卫方、任强，2004 年）；二是古希腊自然法的研究（陈金全，1992 年；汪太贤，2004 年）；三是古希腊宪政制度的研究（刘艺工、张卫良，2001 年；程汉大，2009 年）；四是司法制度的研究（蔡连曾，1997 年；肖厚国，2011 年；阴元涛，2012 年），主要对雅典陪审法庭展开了深入的研究；五是古希腊私法制度的研究（易继明，1999 年；何勤华，2007 年），主要观点是大陆法系私法的源头应该源于古希腊的雅典城邦法。尽管现有古希腊法律史研究关注的重点已经由早期的法学理论拓展到具体法律制度的研究，但研究资料的匮乏决定了现有研究的局限：(1)研究视角上主要采用罗马法学为代表的现代法学概念研究古希腊法律现象，忽略了前罗马时期不同地区的语言和文化差异；(2)研究内容上主要关注古希腊本身的法律现象，对欧洲大陆国家古希腊法律史研究的学说史研究相对缺乏；(3)研究方法上多采用外国学者论述的二次文献，直接引证原始资料相对缺乏；(4)时间跨度上多关注古典时期的雅典城邦，忽略了希腊化时期马其顿王国及其衍生国家的法制发展，而后者恰恰是文献资料保留下来最完整的历史时期。

在某种意义上也是西方法学家探寻法治发展道路的路径再现,追寻这一路径也许可以为我们现今的法治化道路争议提供一些新的思考方向。

目前,国内学术界以"20世纪以来英美国家的古希腊法律史研究"为研究对象的法律史论著还未出现,只有少数以古希腊历史和学说史为研究内容的论著,以及在考察古希腊政治与社会制度方面涉及西方学者对古希腊政治法律制度的论述,这些论述对本书研究有重要参考价值。其中,《古代希腊土地制度研究》介绍了西方学者对古希腊土地法律制度的研究概况;①《古典历史研究史》(上、下卷)提及了多位英美学者对古希腊法的研究。② 在英美国家,针对古希腊法律史的研究起步较早,但系统化、学术化的研究成果则出现于19世纪工业革命以后,时至今日已经形成了一个完整的研究体系。不过对欧洲和英美国家古希腊法律史研究的学术史进行专题研究的外文学术著作还未出现,仅有少数学者以论文形式对古希腊法的研究价值、研究方向与研究方法提出了自己的见解,如德国学者沃尔夫的论文《古希腊法律史:它的功能和可能性》③、《古希腊法学:任务、问题和可能性》④、《作为古希腊遗产重要组成部分之一的古希腊法》⑤、《古希腊法律史思想史研究的意义》⑥等。纵观近代以来欧美国家(包括欧洲大陆国家)的古希腊法律史研究,对本书有重要参考价值的著作主要包括如下几个方面。

1. 在对古希腊法律思想和法学理论进行论述时涉及前人相关研究成果的介绍,例如,对古希腊法律思想史研究的学说回顾(艾瑞克:《古希腊法律思想史》,1950~1970年)、对古希腊自然法理念的学说回顾(彭斯:《亚里士多德和自然法理论》,2011年)、对民主制与法治关系的学说回顾(哈瑞斯:《古典雅典的民主制与法治》,2006年)。

2. 在对古希腊法进行整体研究时涉及前人研究成果的总结:(1)关于古希腊

① 参见黄洋:《古代希腊土地制度研究》,复旦大学出版社1995年版。

② 参见晏绍祥:《古典历史研究史》(上卷),北京大学出版社2013年版;晏绍祥:《古典历史研究史》(下卷),北京大学出版社2013年版。

③ Hans Julius Wolff(1975b),"Greek Legal History-Its Functions and Potentialities",Washington University Law Quarterly,395 – 408(= Revista de Estudios Historico-Juridicos 1(1976)136 – 148).

④ Hans Julius Wolff(1975a),"Juristische Gräzistik-Aufgaben, Probleme, Möglichkeiten", in Symposion 1971,1 – 22.

⑤ Hans Julius Wolff(1973c),"Das Recht als Komponente des griechischen Erbes",in Gehrig,H.(ed)Der Lebenswert des Griechischen,29 – 41,Karlsruhe(Veröffentlichungen der Katholischen Akademie der Erzdioezese Freiburg 29)(= Opuscula,1 – 13).

⑥ Hans Julius Wolff(1973b),"Zur Bedeutung der altgriechischen Rechtsgeschichte für die Rechtswissenschaft",in Xenion Zeppos,757 – 763.

法律史研究的回顾(罗茨等:《古希腊各城邦的立法》,1997 年;加加林等:《剑桥古希腊法指南》,2005 年);(2)关于雅典法律的研究回顾(哈里森:《雅典法:家庭和财产法/程序法》,1968 ~ 1971 年;麦克道威尔:《古典时期雅典的法律》,1986 年;贾斯特斯:《雅典法律和司法程序》,1905 年);(3)关于早期希腊法的研究(加加林:《早期希腊法》,1989 年);(4)关于雅典帝国法律的研究(巴尔塞:《雅典关于 Chalkis 城邦的立法:雅典帝国法研究》,1978 年);(5)关于马其顿时期的希腊法研究[Karakostas:《亚历山大到奥古斯特的希腊法律》(公元前 323 年 ~ 公元 14 年),2002 年];(6)关于希腊化埃及法律研究的回顾(拉夫尔:《希腊罗马时期埃及的纸莎草纸法》,1955 年;沃尔夫:《托勒密时期纸莎草纸记录的希腊法》,2002 年);(7)关于欧洲法源于希腊的研究(巴塔:《希腊:欧洲法律的起源》,2010 年)。

3. 在对古希腊专门法律制度进行论述时涉及该制度的学说史研究,例如,对雅典公私法的整体研究(穆佩罗特:《雅典共和国的私法和公法》,1867 年;博谢:《雅典共和国私法史》,1897 年)、对雅典宪法的研究资料和成果进行介绍(希格奈特:《雅典宪法史》,1958 年)、对斯巴达财产法律制度的研究回顾(皮卡特等:《斯巴达财产制度研究》,1880 年)、对雅典战神山议事会司法职能研究的学说回顾(华莱士:《战神山议事会研究》,1985 年)、对雅典公民大会研究的总结(罗茨:《雅典公民大会》,1972 年)、对古希腊司法行政研究的回顾(博纳:《从荷马到亚里士多德的司法行政》,1930 年;琼斯:《宙斯的司法》,1971 年)、对雅典杀人法研究的回顾(麦克道威尔:《演说家时代的雅典杀人法》,1963 年;斯特劳德:《德拉古杀人法》,1968 年)、对性犯罪研究的回顾(科恩:《法律与性:古希腊道德的执行》,1991 年)、对僭越犯罪研究的回顾(菲舍:《僭越》,1992 年)、对涉及女性法律问题的研究(贾思特:《雅典法律与社会生活的妇女》,1989 年;拉斐尔:《古希腊的妇女与法律》,1990 年)、对希腊宗教法研究的回顾(鲁普:《希腊宗教法》,2009 年)。

4. 在对古希腊演说家法庭演说词进行汇编总结时涉及相关法律制度研究的回顾,例如,对伊萨乌斯法庭演说的研究(琼斯:《伊萨乌斯有关雅典财产继承法的演说集》,1779 年)、对德摩斯梯尼法庭演说的研究(凯瑞:《德摩斯梯尼演说词选编》,1985 年)、对伊索格拉底法庭演说的研究(《雅典的伊索格拉底》,1862 年)、对雅典法律演说的研究(安德鲁:《民主雅典的法律演说》,1965 年)。

5. 在对古希腊铭文资料进行汇编总结时,对涉及法律内容进行归类总结或加以研究评述(伊万:《雅典法律汇编》,1868 年;梅格思和刘易斯:《希腊铭文选》,

1969年;兰伯特:《公元前352/1～322/1雅典法律法令汇编》,2012年)。

6. 学术年会论文集对研究大师的介绍、对离世学者的纪念文集和纪念性文章等。欧洲古希腊及希腊化法研究会自1971年定期出版《古希腊及希腊化时期法律研究论文集》,至今已出版16卷,其中包括了众多对离世学者的生平介绍和学术评价文章,这些文章具有重要的参考意义。

7. 学术用语及研究资料目录的总结。这方面主要包括古希腊法律专业术语的介绍(托德:《雅典法律的形状》,1993年)以及古希腊法律的立法方式(加加林:《写古希腊法》,2008年),另外还有少量的参考书目类书(詹姆斯:《古希腊法书目参考》,1927年;桑达:《新古希腊法书目参考》,2011年)。

此外,还有数量众多的古希腊法律史研究论文散见于各种历史学科的期刊和论文集中,这些资料的参考价值也是不容忽视的。

本书以20世纪至今英美国家的古希腊法律史研究为主要研究对象,[①]主要包括如下内容:

第一章　欧美国家古希腊研究与古希腊法律史研究的兴起

第二章　英国的古希腊法律史研究

第三章　美国的古希腊法律史研究

第四章　欧美国家古希腊法律史研究的专业刊物与资料汇编

附　录　附录一:古希腊语法律术语(古希腊语、英语对照)

附录二:古希腊法律史研究外文参考书目

通过上述对英美国家古希腊法律史研究的概括与描述,本书力图展现20世纪以来英美国家古希腊法律史研究的主要成果,探讨英美国家古希腊法律史研究的主要研究方法及研究趋势,并揭示古希腊法对西方法治理念形成的基础性影响,此外,试图完成完整的英美国家学者古希腊法律史研究成果目录。

在对英美国家古希腊法律史研究展开全面论述之前,有必要对英美国家古希腊法律研究相关的史料来源和古希腊法的法律术语做一个简要的介绍。

一、史料来源

一般而言,涉及古希腊法律制度的基本史料主要包括诉讼演说词、历史学著

---

① 英美国家学者对古希腊法律史的研究包括了古希腊荷马时期至希腊化时期希腊语系人种所适用的一系列法律制度,以公元前5世纪～公元前4世纪雅典人的法律制度为主,同时也包括了希腊化时期马其顿王国及其衍生的希腊化国家统治下的北非、西亚、中亚等地区的法律制度。

作、经典作家文集残篇、铭文、纸莎草纸文献等。

(一)诉讼演说词

古希腊保存至今的与诉讼有关的演说词共103篇,其中以吕西阿斯和德摩斯梯尼两个人的作品居多。

1. 艾斯西尼斯①

在艾斯西尼斯流传下来的手稿中,主要包括3篇演说词,即《反提玛库斯》《论出使》《反塞提斯丰》。

2. 安多西底斯②

由于其他人对亚西比德亵渎神灵行为的检举,演讲家安多西底斯卷入一系列诉讼中。在他的4篇演说词中,2篇和上述事件有直接关系,还有1篇控诉返回雅典的亚西比德,剩下1篇主要论述雅典对斯巴达的政策,与我们研究古希腊的法律的关系不大。

3. 安提丰③

传说安提丰的演说词共有35篇,但是保存到今天的演说词只有15篇,“洛易布丛书”收录了其6篇私人演说词以及一些残篇。这些演说词主要涉及谋杀和意外伤亡等方面的法律诉讼案件。

4. 达玛德斯④

“洛易布丛书”收录了达玛德斯1篇演说词。虽然它不是关于诉讼的演讲,但是在内容上多少也涉及一些雅典的法律。

---

① 艾斯西尼斯(Aeschines)生于公元前390年,40岁时在政治领域中已经举足轻重,坚定支持保守派,曾经多次作为雅典的代表参加希腊城邦间政治会议,并一度与德摩斯梯尼关系密切。

② 安多西底斯(Andochides)大约生于公元前440年,可能和苏格拉底比较熟悉。他在政治上倾向于寡头政治,曾遭受两次流放。第二次流放后,人们就不知其所终了。

③ 安提丰(Antiplzon)大约生于公元前480年,死于公元前411年。他的一生目睹了雅典帝国的兴衰。人们在研究希腊文化时通常愿意把目光聚集在他身上,他给那些需要在法庭或者民众大会上发言的人写演说词,凭借这种本领,在公元前430年前后,他已经声名显赫。安提丰参与了公元前411年政变,同年被控叛国,法庭辩护失败后被处死。

④ 达玛德斯(Demades)生于雅典,但不知道具体的年月,只是在公元前319年被处死的时候,人们知道他年龄很大了。他是政治老手,习惯于两面三刀,还是无耻之徒,接受几乎所有党派的贿赂;并且极端放纵口腹之欲,虽然他是亲马其顿派,但是马其顿人讽刺他:“在年老时就只剩下舌头和胃了。”在拉米阿(lamia)战役结束后,他一方面与新当权的寡头结合在一起,处死了很多民主派;另一方面秘密和民主派通信。在公元前319年,他给民主派的信笺暴露,他和儿子一起被寡头政权处死了。

5. 德摩斯梯尼①

德摩斯梯尼的演说词共有61篇，包括私人诉讼演讲29篇（有7篇是其他人作品而归于他的名下）和公共演讲32篇。其中，第1～17篇演说是在公民大会上的辩论，第18～26篇演说是政治审判的演说，这些是最有史料价值的。德摩斯梯尼的演说词深刻地揭示了雅典生活与社会的状况。

6. 第那库斯②

第那库斯的3篇演说都与一件非常重要的案件有关，即公元前323年一批雅典显贵因收受马其顿贵族的贿赂而受到审判。"洛易布丛书"还收录了一些第那库斯演说词残篇。

7. 海泊瑞底斯③

"洛易布丛书"收录了海泊瑞底斯的6篇演说词，其中包括2篇辩护词（内容关于通奸诉讼、贿赂等）、3篇控诉词（内容多是控诉亲马其顿派人物）和1篇葬礼演说。此外，《洛易布丛书》还收录一些海泊瑞底斯的演说词残篇。

8. 伊撒乌斯④

伊撒乌斯的演说词大约有60篇，但是保留下来的只有11篇。其中，有4篇演说词的年代可以确定：第5篇为公元前390年；第6篇为公元前364年；第7篇为公元前355年；第2篇为公元前350年。所有篇目都涉及遗产继承等方面。例

① 德摩斯梯尼（Demosthenes）生于公元前384年左右。他的父亲早亡，给他留下14塔兰特财产，但是，由于监护人管理不当，德摩斯梯尼成年的时候只收到原来财产的1/10。为了使自己有把握起诉监护人，他跟随伊撒乌斯（Isaeus）学习修辞学。伊撒乌斯是继承案件的专家。在案件结束后，他为其他诉讼人写法庭演说词。我们手中流传下来私人演说词大部分写于公元前363年到公元前354年。在30岁的时候，德摩斯梯尼开始担任公职，此后，他在城邦政治旋涡中呼风唤雨。德摩斯梯尼于公元前324年遭受流放，公元前322年去世。

② 第那库斯（Dinarchus）公元前361年生于科林斯城邦。他在青年时代移居雅典。作为外邦人侨民，他没有资格参加城邦政治，但是，依靠为别人写演说词，第那库斯获得了名声。当亚历山大逝世和雅典的德摩斯梯尼被流放的时候，他的事业达到顶峰。公元前307年，为了避免支持寡头政治的嫌疑，第那库斯卖掉雅典的财产搬到优卑亚岛。公元前292年，第那库斯被允许回到雅典。但是，当他寄居在朋友家里时，朋友家失窃。由于这一笔钱他卷入诉讼之中，以后的事情人们就不清楚了。

③ 海泊瑞底斯（Hypereides）公元前390年生于雅典，公元前322年被处死。年轻时他跟随柏拉图和伊索克拉底学习，从事为别人写诉讼演说词的职业。在参与公共政治后，海泊瑞底斯积极反对马其顿，不时控诉雅典的亲马其顿派。公元前323年亚历山大去世后，他到伯罗奔尼撒半岛鼓动那里的城邦反对马其顿。次年，雅典无条件屈服于马其顿，雅典宪法被修改，寡头派当权，人民在演讲家达玛德斯的鼓动下，将海泊瑞底斯和德摩斯梯尼等人判处死刑。

④ 伊撒乌斯（Isaeus）生于公元前420年。他向吕西阿斯学习过，并教授过德摩斯梯尼。他的演说词主要集中在财产的纠葛方面，这也反映出他是这方面的专家。德摩斯梯尼也曾经跟随伊撒乌斯学习财产诉讼演说训练，目的是控诉自己的监护人。

如,《克列尼穆斯的财产》涉及妇女财产继承,《门尼克里斯的财产》涉及养子继承,《派瑞扈斯的财产》涉及遗产继承。相对于其他人的演讲来说,伊撒乌斯的演说是研究雅典社会遗产继承关系的基本材料。

9. 伊索克拉底①

伊索克拉底共有 21 篇演说词和 9 封信件流传下来。其中有 6 篇诉讼演说词,内容主要涉及遗产继承、侵吞财产、借贷纠纷、伤害等诉讼。

10. 来库古斯②

流传下来的只有 1 篇来库古斯的演说词。这篇演讲大概发表于公元前 330 年,在演说中,他对 1 位雅典公民的叛国罪行进行了控诉。

11. 吕西阿斯③

根据《名哲言行录》的记录,吕西阿斯的演说词共达 230 篇之多,但是,实际上"洛易布丛书"中只收录有 34 篇,形成于公元前 403 年 ~ 约公元前 380 年。这些演说词除了 1 篇葬礼演说外,基本都是为私人写的诉讼词。吕西阿斯的诉讼演讲主要涉及伤害、通奸、临阵脱逃和商业纠纷。其中,较为著名的有两篇,一篇是吕西阿斯为 1 位残疾人争取补助金而作的诉讼演说,另一篇是吕西阿斯为自己写的诉讼演讲。多佛尔撰写的《吕西阿斯及吕西阿斯全集》对吕西阿斯及其演说词进行了深入的研究。④

(二)历史学著作

1. 希罗多德(公元前 480 年 ~ 公元前 420 年)的《历史》。希罗多德的描述以四处扩张的波斯帝国为中心,其中简略叙述了公元前 440 年和公元前 430 年波斯

---

① 伊索克拉底(Isocrates)生于公元前 436 年,死于公元前 338 年。在青年时代,伊索克拉底或许受到高尔吉亚的影响,但现代的学者对这一点表示怀疑。在伯罗奔尼撒战争中,伊索克拉底丧失了全部财产,依靠授业收取报酬勉强度日,也为别人写诉讼演说词,后来他在雅典开办了一所学园,大获成功。在马其顿崛起后,他与民主派发生了政见分歧,而有亲马其顿的嫌疑。

② 来库古斯(Lycurgus)大概和德摩斯梯尼同年,公元前 384 年生于雅典,死于公元前 324 年。来库古斯年轻时曾经跟随柏拉图和伊索克拉底学习过。在 50 岁的时候,他开始参与公共生活,并成为雅典政治舞台上的显赫人物,掌管雅典的财政长达 12 年之久,在担任公职期间,他致力驱逐雅典的腐败现象与反马其顿事业。

③ 吕西阿斯(Lysias)的父亲是一个富有的武器制造商、叙拉古移民。公元前 430 年左右,他父亲作为侨民定居在雅典。吕西阿斯排行老二,大概出生于公元前 458 年,死于公元前 380 年。公元前 440 年,吕西阿斯跟随西西里的修辞学家学习。直到公元前 412 年,他才回到雅典。在伯罗奔尼撒战争诡谲起伏的年代里,吕西阿斯坚定支持民主制度,因此他被授予了雅典公民权;在一次控诉中,由于违反法律程序,吕西阿斯又被剥夺了公民权。此后,他专职为人撰写诉讼演说词。

④ K. J. Dover, *Lysias and the Corpus Lysiacum*, University of California Press, 1968.

帝国边陲的希腊城邦政治发展，包括雅典在民主制度草创时期的主要事件，这些资料有助于我们了解雅典城邦早期政治状况。虽然《历史》中关于法律的直接记录寥寥无几，但是，仍有与法律相关联的事件，如关于梭伦的传说和关于雅典妇女丧失投票权的神话等内容。

2. 修昔底德（公元前454年～公元前390年以后）的《伯罗奔尼撒战争史》。这部著作的主题与《历史》相同，都是记录战争，其第1卷是有关公元前478年～公元前432年希腊史实的基本史料，第2～8卷是对公元前431年～公元前411年的军事行动进行了非常细致的记述。但是，在对战争过程的描述以外，修昔底德还穿插大量刻意雕琢的演讲和对历史的回顾，如放逐地米斯托克利与亚西比得案件、伯里克利在葬礼上的演讲、关于处置密提林的辩论等。在这些演讲和回顾中，我们可以发掘到许多有关古希腊法律的信息。

3. 色诺芬（公元前425年～约公元前355年）的《希腊史》。作者的目的在于续写修昔底德所记录的历史。《希腊史》主要记载了公元前411年到公元前362年的历史，其中，对雅典的政治生活描述颇多。应该说，这部作品属于当时人的记录。色诺芬作为典型的希腊绅士兼职业军人、业余历史学家，对文化和政治的追求足以让他以生动而令人愉悦的笔调撰写不同问题的论述，包括雅典税收和苏格拉底的事迹。由于作者倾向于贵族政治，所以在描述中夹杂了个人好恶，但这也在情理之中。

4. 狄奥多鲁斯（活跃于公元前60年～公元前36年）的《通史》。作者作为西西里的希腊人，著有《通史》一书，卷11～20提供了从公元前478年～公元前302年地中海世界（主要是希腊）历史的较完整叙述。其中，对公元前362年～公元前336年的记载是现存仅有的记叙，对于其他时段的记载，《通史》保存了不同于修昔底德和色诺芬的较早记叙。

5. 普鲁塔克（约公元46年～公元120年）的《名人传》。《名人传》是作者为研究人物性格而作，是其道德著述的一部分。尽管这部诞生于罗马帝国鼎盛时期的历史作品无疑离雅典古典时代已经相当遥远，但普鲁塔克对个性的兴趣及其关于历史和其他文献的渊博知识，使《名人传》成为我们了解事件、引文和古人如何解释事物的珍贵史料。在《名人传》中几个希腊历史人物深刻影响雅典生活的方方面面，我们研究古希腊与雅典城邦法律自然也没有办法绕开这部著作。

（三）经典作家文集

1. 柏拉图（公元前428年～公元前348年）。其大量的哲学著述是研究他那个时代以及公元前5世纪思想史的基本史料，其间对于雅典苏格拉底圈子的社会生活的速写及其关于希腊历史与制度雄辩的个人化观点极其具有史料价值。柏拉图的作品包括传世的25篇对话、13封信件和1篇辩护词,其中比较重要的有关于苏格拉底案件的4篇记述、《理想国》和《法律篇》等。无论是研究古希腊人——上层和下层——法律思想,还是研究古希腊法律实践,这些都属于重要材料。

2. 亚里士多德(公元前384年~公元前322年)。亚里士多德是最为著名的古希腊哲学家和博学之士,就古希腊法律而言,最有帮助的亚里士多德的著作是《政治学》《雅典政制》《修辞学》《尼各马科伦理学》。其中,《政治学》包含了希腊早期法律发展的材料,也包含了雅典具体的法律条文;《雅典政制》是一部雅典法律发展简史,现存文本的第1~41章简略概述从传说时代到公元前403年雅典政体的历史,第42~69章描述公元前320年雅典政体的结构,其对于雅典立法、司法审判、法庭选举等制度层面的叙述是研究雅典法律最重要的材料;《修辞学》中作者对雅典法庭的演讲、法庭的证据进行了研究;《尼各马科伦理学》对研究雅典法律思想有所裨益。

3. 色诺芬。他的著作主要包括《论雅典的收入》《苏格拉底的辩护》《回忆苏格拉底》《拉客第梦人的政体》,以及上面提到的《希腊史》等。在这些著作中,既有对雅典公民大会、议事会、法庭的描述,也有对苏格拉底案件的回忆。关于色诺芬对斯巴达政体的描述,基本是站在寡头的立场,同情和支持寡头政治。

(四)残篇①

古代希腊人所撰写的大量各种著述业已全部散失,或者仅仅通过后人引述的短语或段落保存少许。许久以来,学者们致力于收集这种"残篇"并试图重视其原作的总体结构。本书最经常引用的两部残篇集为FGH和DK。前者为F.雅科比所编的《希腊历史残篇》(F. Jacoby, Die Fragmente der griechischen Historiker, Berlin, 1922)。全书文本为希腊文原文,辅以德文或英文评注,但没有译文。它收集了大部分希腊历史学家的残篇(尚未全部完成)。就古典时期而言,其著作已丢失的两位最重要的历史学家是埃弗罗斯(约公元前405年~约公元前330年)和特奥庞波斯(约公元前379年~公元前323年以后)。前者出生于小亚细亚的库迈(Kyme),是伊索克拉底的弟子,其著作共计30卷,记叙了自从作者移民小亚细亚直至公元前341年的希腊历史。其虔诚的态度、狄奥多鲁斯对他的利用以及

① 此处"残篇"和下面的"铭文"部分参考了黄洋、晏绍祥著的《古希腊史研究入门》(北京大学出版社2009年版)的相关论述。

其影响都使他很重要,但我们须对他对希腊史学史的影响进行新的研究,以取代 G. L. 巴贝尔的《历史学家埃弗罗斯》(G. L. Barber, *The Historian Ephorus*, Cambridge University Press,1935)。克俄斯的特奥庞波斯和色诺芬一样,撰写了续写修昔底德的《希腊史》(*Hellenika*),但他接着又撰写了一部当代史,而且使用了《腓力浦志》这个重要的题目。其两部著作似乎都滥用评论,以贬低大国(尤其是雅典)的自我标榜,这是因为他对它们不抱好感。参见 W. R. 科内尔的《特奥庞波斯和公元前5世纪的雅典》(W. R. Connor, *Theopompus and Fifth-Century Athens*, Centre for Hellenic Studies,1968)以及 G. S. 希林普顿的《历史学家特奥庞波斯》(G. S. Shrimpton, *Theopompus the Historian*, McGill-Queen's U. P. ,1991)。

约公元前400年之前的哲学家的残篇收入 DK,即 H. 迪尔斯和 W. 克兰兹编的《前苏格拉底哲学家残篇》(H. Diels and W. Kranz, Die Fragmente der Vorsokratiker,第6版,柏林1951年版)。该书收录希腊文原文,并有德文译文。英译本见 K. 弗里曼的《前苏格拉底哲学家残篇》(K. Freeman, *Ancilla to Pre-Socratic Philosophers*, Blackwell, 1947)及乔纳森·巴恩斯的《早期希腊哲学》(Jonathan Barnes, *Early Greek Philosophy*, Penguin, 1987)。

(五)铭文

标准的铭文集,从理论上说包括所有希腊铭文的是柏林学术院从1873年开始编著至今仍在进行的《希腊铭文集成》(*Inscriptiones Graecae*,简称 IG)。然而,许多文件引自更晚近的版本和选集,特别是下列各种:

ML,即 R. 梅格斯和 D. M. 刘易斯编《至公元前5世纪末的希腊历史铭文选》(R. Meiggs and D. M. Lewis, *A Selection of Greek Historical Inscriptions to the End of the Fifth Century BC*,牛津大学出版社1969年版,1988年修订版)。

SEG,即《希腊铭文补遗》(*Supplementum Epigraphicum Graecum*)。

TOD,即 M. N. 托德:《希腊历史铭文选·第3卷:自公元前403至公元前323年》(M. N. Tod, *A Selection of Greek Historical Inscriptions*, *Vol. Ⅲ*: *From* 403 *to* 323 *BC*,牛津大学出版社1948年版)。所收铭文均有英文译文。

直到近些年,一直很少有铭文的译本,现在则更易于得到。ML 收录的大部分铭文要么见于《希腊罗马文书选择》(*Translated Documents of Greece and Rome*, eds. by E. Badian and R. K. Sherk)这一译丛的第1卷,题为《古风时代至伯罗奔尼撒战争结束》(*Archaic Times to the End of the Pelopnnesian War*, C. W. Fornara 编译,约翰·霍普金斯大学出版社1977年版,1983年第2版),要么见于 LACTOR 第1种:《雅典帝国》(*The Athenian Empire*, R. W. J. Clayton 编,1970年第2版)。

公元前4世纪则收录于LACTOR第9种:《公元前359~公元前323年的希腊历史铭文选译》(P. J. Rhodes, *Greek Historical Inscriptions* 359–323 *BC*, 1971), J. 魏克山和G. 维布鲁格所编《公元前4世纪的希腊历史文书》(J. Wickersham and G. Verbrugghe, *Greek Historical Documents: The Fourth Century BC*, Hakkert, 1973),还有《希腊罗马文书选译》第2卷《从伯罗奔尼撒战争结束至伊普苏斯之战》(*From the End of the Peloponnesian War to the Battle of Ipsus*, P. Harding 编译,剑桥大学出版社1985年版)。

(六)纸莎草纸文献

近年来出土的大量纸莎草纸文献对于英美国家研究古希腊法,特别是希腊化时期埃及托勒密王朝的法律制度具有举足轻重的地位。纸莎草纸源于古代埃及,是古代埃及人为人类文明做出的重要贡献之一。英语中的纸莎草纸一词"papyrus"源于希腊语"papyros",最早出现于思想家和历史学家托普拉斯图斯(Tboprastus,约公元前4世纪~公元前3世纪)的著作中。公元前8世纪前后,纸莎草纸制作方法经由地中海东岸的港口城市巴比罗斯(Byblos)传到古代希腊和罗马,著名古典作家希罗多德以该城的名字来命名纸莎草。在希腊语中关于纸莎草纸的单词的原始含义是"pa—per-aa,属于国王的",由此揭示出希腊化时代纸莎草纸的生产很有可能是被王室垄断的。①

埃及托勒密王朝时期(约公元前323年~公元前30年),纸莎草纸的产量增加,质量改善。纸莎草纸源源不断供应,使托勒密王朝的亚历山大城成了一个官僚文牍盛行的城市。一份公元前258年至公元前257年的单据显示,财务大臣的衙门在33天里共收下434卷纸莎草纸文件。也正是因为同样的原因,亚历山大城的书籍要比地中海世界的其他任何地方都多,当时亚历山大城号称拥有世界上最大的图书馆。公元前250年之后,古罗马向东方大举扩张,在欣羡于希腊文化成就的同时,把大量的纸莎草纸文献藏书搬运回罗马。② 公元前168年,希腊马其顿王朝末代国王佩尔修斯战败之后,罗马保民官保卢斯把佩尔修斯的图书馆整体搬到了罗马。苏拉此前已把提亚斯的阿波林图书馆迁至罗马,还把亚里士多德和泰奥弗拉斯托斯的著作从雅典运回罗马。西塞罗的朋友阿提库斯(Atticus)则以

---

① [苏联] B. A. 伊斯特林:《文字的产生和发展》,左少兴译,北京大学出版社1987年版,第82页。

② W. H. P. Hatch, *The Principal Uncial Manuscriptof the New Testament*, The University Chicago Press, 1939, p. 5.

私人的身份从希腊搜求纸莎草纸文献，积累了大量藏书，成为著名的出版商。

1880年，学者在埃及进行考古时首次发现了纸莎草纸文献，此后，成千上万的纸莎草纸文献相继出土，但由于许多阿拉伯国家当时处于外国统治时期，大部分纸莎草纸文献流失到世界各地。随着埃及等阿拉伯国家的纸莎草纸文献大量散入世界各地，[①]世界各国都开展了对纸莎草纸文献的研究，"纸莎草纸文献学"也随之兴起。尤其是欧美国家高度重视对纸莎草纸文献的保护、编目、考证和出版工作，并设立了专门的研究院系，定期编辑出版最新的纸莎草纸文献研究成果。

二、古希腊法的法律术语[②]

（一）agoranomos（Greek：ἀγορανόμος，ἀγορανόμοι）[③]

市场监管员，是指古希腊监管市场（或集市）的专门官员，一城邦通常设置多个市场监管员。

他们的职责包括：制定某些商品价格、证明货物重量和规模、控监管货币交换。此外，管理城邦的粮食供应是其重要功能之一。在管理奸商方面，市场监管员有权对非自由民施加体罚，对自由公民则处以罚款。市场监管员也负责监督市场周边的寺庙。

随着时间的推移，市场监管员也成为一种荣誉称号，被誉为公共恩人，意为公共机构提供捐助的人。

（二）aidesis（Greek：αἴδεσις）[④]

赦免，在古希腊刑法中，杀人犯罪属于自诉案件，受害者的亲属作为起诉人在某些情况下可以给予杀人者赦免。一旦作出赦免，杀人者就被免除进一步的起诉。该术语的出现比较模糊，可以确定它跟动词"aideomai"（感到羞耻，敬畏或尊

---

① 陈建民：《纸莎草纸与"文明"的流失》，载《阿拉伯世界》2002年第2期。

② 以下所附英文解释文本可能与笔者所述内容有所差别，供参考。

③ Agoranomos，agoranomoi · Lit. "agora-regulator(s)"：public officials attested in a large number of Greek poleis；their duties consisted of supervising the commercial aspects of the agora.

④ Aidesis · Because homicide in Athenian law was a matter for private prosecution，the relatives of the dead man，as prosecutors，were under certain circumstances permitted or expected to grant pardon (aidesis) to his killer. Once this had been done，the killer was immune from further prosecution. The derivation of the term is unclear：it is certainly connected with the verb aideomai "to feel shame，awe or respect"；LSJ notes that the verb can be used to mean "to respect another's misfortune" and thus "to be reconciled to him"；but unlike English "reconciliation"，aidesis is only used to denote the action of the wronged party.

敬)相关,有学者认为这个动词被用来表示尊重他人的不幸,但又心存不甘。不同于英语中的“和解”,该词仅用来表示冤屈(受害者)一方的行为。

该制度的出现与德拉古刑法改革密切相关,德拉古对雅典刑法的改革之一就是明确在杀人案件中区分故意与过失。在过失杀人案件中,受害人亲属就可以选择使用赦免行为。

(三)anakrisis(Greek:ἀνάκρισις)①

预审,在法院(陪审法庭)进行正式审判前进行的一次审查,不同于大陆法系国家的纠问制度,雅典公共官员(执政官)在进行预审时受到严格的限制,也不同于仲裁员,他的职能并不是裁判案件。在预审过程中,涉案双方向执政官提交各自的证据,执政官不作判决,而是决定是否将案件提交陪审法庭审理。

(四)antidosis(Greek:ἀντίδοσις)②

财产交换法,雅典城邦为了保证公益捐制的顺利实行,制定了交换法。如果被指定为捐助者的富有公民 A 不愿意提供捐助,可以提出由没有被指定为捐助者的更为富有的公民 B 提供捐助。双方往往诉诸法庭,分别将两人的财产列出清单,呈交法庭。公民 B 面临两个选择:要么承认自己更为富有,并自愿承担捐助;要么否认自己更为富有,那么公民 A 就可以要求与公民 B 互换财产之后自己承担捐助。“交换法”鼓励富人之间的相互猜疑,同时可以避免富人阶层与城邦的对立,使公益捐助更为制度化。公益捐助的实质则是富人财产的公益化——既调控富人财产,又使更多的公民从公益活动中直接受益。根据历史记载,尽管有数起涉及交换法的诉讼案件,但并没有出现财产交换被完成的结果。

---

① Anakrisis · A preliminary hearing before the public official within whose court a case will later be heard(for the role of the presiding official within a lawcourt, see sv. arkhon). Lit. “examination”, but it should not be equated with the inquisitorial instruction of civil-law systems: an Athenian public official had very restricted discretion; and unlike an arbitrator(see sv. diaitetes), his function was not to settle the case.

② Antidosis · Lit. “a giving in exchange”. A man who was nominated to perform a liturgy could avoid this duty if he could name another citizen who was richer and better qualified to perform the task. If the man challenged agreed that he was richer, he had to take over the liturgy; if he claimed to be poorer, then the challenger could insist on an exchange of all their property to test the claim—in which case the challenger would himself perform the liturgy as the new owner of the(putatively) greater estate. This process of exchange was called antidosis. The advantage of the system from the viewpoint of the democracy was that it encouraged the rich to be suspicious of each other, instead of being hostile towards the state; but although we know of several challenges, there is no attested case in which the exchange was completed.

(五) apagoge (Greek: ἀπαγωγή)①

即时判决(原意为拖走)。雅典法律规定,对某些犯罪(如盗窃和抢劫),如果犯罪嫌疑人被当场抓获并以红色标志移交至执政官面前,在被告认罪的情况下,执政官可以立即对其判决并马上执行,只有当犯罪嫌疑人声称自己是无辜的,才会选择进行正式审判。

(六) apographe (Greek: ἀπογραφή)②

书面目录,拖欠国家债务的公民个人的财产目录(部分或全部),目录上的财产并没有被国家没收,它看上去是留给个人或本地区官员备用的。该术语常被用于拖欠国家债务案件的庭审中。

(七) apophasis (Greek: ἀπόφασις)③

报告或申明,是公元前4世纪中期新出现的一个程序。战神山议事会可以自己(或应公民大会要求)调查涉及公众安全的任何事项,并向公民大会移交这样的报告,在其中建议采取特别行动,如起诉特定的公民个人。这样的报告或声明只适用于公民阶层(存疑)。

(八) apragmon (Greek: ἀπράγμων, ἀπράγμονες; ἀπραγμοσύνη)④

不参与商业活动的人或不参加公共事务的人。该词同时具有积极或消极的属性,主要取决于使用者的态度。

---

① Apagoge, pl. apagogai · Lit. "dragging away", i. e., to the appropriate magistrate. Summary arrest was permitted against certain categories of criminal, such as thieves and highwaymen, if they were caught ep'autophori—red handed. If the accused admitted his guilt before the magistrate he was promptly executed; only if he claimed to be innocent was he put on trial. See also sv. Ephegesis.

② Apographe · Lit. "a (written) list": a catalogue of some or all of the property of a man in debt to the state. The state took no initiative in the confiscation of property: this was left either to private individuals or else, it appears, to local deme's officials. The term apographe is used to describe the list itself, the process of denunciation, and any judicial hearing arising out of the case. See also sv. phasis.

③ Apophasis · Lit. "a showing forth, declaration". A procedure newly instituted around the middle of the fourth century: either on the invitation of the ekklesia or on its own initiative, the Areiopagos could investigate any matter involving public security and present a report (apophasis) to the ekklesia, recommending particular action, for instance the prosecution of a named individual. Apophasis is the subject of a Demos article.

④ Apragmon, pl. apragmones (adj.); apragmosune (abstract noun) · Lit. "one who does not conduct business": a person who refrains from taking part in public affairs. It can be either a positive or a negative characteristic, depending on the attitude of the speaker ("philosophical contemplation" or "political irresponsibility"). For the opposite characteristic, see sv. Polupragmon.

（九）Areiopagos（Greek：Ἄρειος πάγος；Ἄρεος πάγος）[①]

战神山议事会，由雅典城邦早期的贵族议事会演变而来，成员由退任的九执政官组成。战神山议事会起初拥有广泛的司法权力，但经过埃菲阿尔特斯在公元前460年的改革后其权力已经大幅削弱，仅留下杀人案件的司法管辖权，但在公元前4世纪其权力又有所增加，最典型的如前述"apophasis"，即向公民大会的报告和建议权。

（十）arkhon（Greek：ἄρχων，ἄρχοντες）[②]

执政官，在雅典城邦有三层含义：第一，泛指雅典的公共官员；第二，九执政官之一；第三，作为一个整体来描述九执政官。公元前682年起，雅典年年公布执政官名单。到公元前7世纪中叶，行政权便掌握在9个执政官手中，由他们分担过去由国王1人独揽的宗教、军事和司法职责。名年执政官是主要的民政和司法官员，负责审理家庭和继承案件，可能兼任500人会议和公民大会主席，并且以他的名字命名在职年份。军事执政官在战争中担任统帅，在涉及债务案件、外国人的诉讼案件中担任法官。王者执政官是主要的宗教官职，并在贵族会议承审杀人案件时担任首席。最后还有6名民事法官，处理琐细的司法问

---

① Areiopagos · The ancient and originally aristocratic council of Athens; its membership comprised those who had completed a term as one of the nine archons. Its powers had been severely restricted by the democratic reforms of Ephialtes in the 460s BCE, which left it as little more than the main court for cases of homicide; in the fourth century however other powers were added, most notably apophasis.

② Arkhon, pl. arkhontes (participle acting as a noun), Eng. archon or arkhon · Lit. "one who is in authority". Used in three senses: loosely, to refer to any Athenian public official; more strictly (usually a collective plural) to describe the "nine arkhons"; specifically, as the title of the senior of the nine arkhonships. These were still the titular chief magistrates of Athens, but their real authority had been severely restricted ever since they began to be appointed by lot, apparently in the 480s. They retained however an honorific position, particularly in the administration of justice: or instance, former arkhons became members of the Areiopagos for life; and during their year of office they processed the litigation presented to the most important of the dikasteria, and presided over trials held there, although in this capacity they were by now little more than non-voting (and non-speaking) chairmen. The three senior arkhons each had a specific title and competence: the arkhon (the eponymous official of Athens who gave his name to the civil year) heard cases involving family and inheritance matters of citizens; the arkhon basileus (lit. "king arkhon") presided over religious matters, including sacrilege and homicide; the polemarkhos (lit. "war arkhon," but by now all his military functions had been handed over to the strategoi) dealt with family and inheritance cases involving metics and apparently cases involving certain other privileged foreigners also. The other six arkhons were called thesmothetai (sing. thesmothetes: originally perhaps "establisher of judgements" rather than "maker of laws"); they heard those public cases, and perhaps also some private ones, which did not fall within the competence of the three senior arkhons or of other named officials.

题。执政官原先只能由贵族出身的人担任,而且是终身制。最后任期减为10年,又减为1年,任期结束不再当选,但可以成为贵族会议的终身议员。大约在公元前594年,梭伦规定财产最多和次多的两个阶级均可当选执政官,以前贵族垄断的情况才告中断。根据《克利斯提尼宪法》规定,执政官直接由公民大会选出;后来则由500名事先选出的候选人抽签产生。之后,被选举权扩大到第三个、第四个阶级。到公元前480年,执政官权力大减,尽管其仍然是雅典名义上的首席裁判官,但其真正的权威受到严重限制,因为他们中的很多人开始被任命产生。不过,卸任执政官可以成为战神山议事会的法定成员,仍享有崇高的地位,战神山议事会拥有向公民大会提出诉讼建议的权力,并在重大案件中主持审判。

(十一)astunomos(Greek:ἀστυνόμος,ἀστυνόμοι)①

十一人委员会。其职能包括监管监狱,还监督对诸如盗窃、绑架、抢劫神庙等普通刑事犯的执行,负责对如苏格拉底那样被判死刑的人行刑。十一人委员会的职能类似于警察,但他们不承担犯罪侦查、逮捕、判决等责任。

(十二)atimia[Greek:ἀτιμία(loss of τιμή)]②

丧失公民权。在古代雅典,该词意味着放逐,并被剥夺全部权利,任何人都可以杀死丧失公民权者而不被起诉或遭受血亲复仇。到古典时期,丧失公

① Astunomos, pl. astunomoi · Lit. "one who regulates (affairs within) the astu (the built-up area of Athens)". A board of public officials charged with the general supervisory duties which we associate with the police. Unlike the police, however, they did not undertake the investigation of crime. Nor were they much concerned with the arrest or punishment of accused or convicted criminals: this role was played by the Eleven.

② Atimia (abstract noun) · Lit. "loss of time, honour". In early archaic Athens, atimia seems to have meant outlawry, the total deprivation of all rights, such that a citizen could kill an atimos (pl. atimoi: person suffering from atimia) without committing an offence or apparently incurring blood-guilt. Well before the classical period, however, atimia had already been restricted in its scope to mean the loss of some or all of a man's active rights as a citizen. Such atimia could be partial or total; it could be imposed permanently by a court, or it could be the (theoretically) temporary result of an unpaid debt to the state, a condition which would automatically terminate if the debt were ever paid off. A man subject to total atimia could not appear in certain public places, could not take part in public life, and could not appear in court. If he broke any of these bans, he was liable to apagoge and death. But he did retain his private rights as a citizen: to kill him would be murder; he was not formally exiled; and he continued to own his property—though his lack of the capacity to sue may have made it difficult procedurally to defend these rights, and many may have found life under such restrictions so intolerable that voluntary exile seemed preferable. A man subject to partial atimia lost either a particular right or rights, or else the power to exercise his rights in a particular situation: for instance, the ability to bring certain types of prosecution.

民权的范围已经被严格限制,仅为丧失部分公民权或丧失全部政治权利,并分为法院判决的永久丧失公民权和因未偿付公共债务而暂时丧失公民权。全部丧失公民权的人不得出现在公共场所,不得参与政治活动(某种程度上成为政治斗争的工具),不得出现在法院(参加诉讼)。如果违反了上述限制,行为人将被立即执行死刑,任何人都可以将其杀死。在丧失部分公民权的情况下,杀死丧失部分公民权的人将被以谋杀罪起诉。丧失部分公民权的人并不意味着被正式排除在社会生活之外,他仍拥有自己的财产,尽管无法以诉讼形式保护自己的财产权利。但是,许多丧失部分公民权的人可能会发现那样的权利限制可能是无法忍受的,以至于自愿流放可能是更可取的。丧失部分公民权意味着缺乏某些权利或缺乏行使某些权利的资格,如丧失提起某些类型诉讼的权利。

(十三)basileus(Greek:βασιλεύς)①

王者执政官。参见前述"执政官"条,字面意思是"王",即所谓宗教执政官,负责城邦的祭祀、宗教事务、国家大典等事项。

(十四)boule(Greek:βουλή)②

议事会,即500人议事会,由选举产生的年满30岁的公民担任,并有严格的任职条件。议事会的主要职能是为公民大会准备议程,承担日常的行政工作,在某些情况下承担一定的司法功能,如涉及城邦安全、孤儿案件等,议事会也有权决定是否将案件提交公民大会或陪审法庭审理。

(十五)(ho)boulomenos(Greek:ὁ βουλόμενος)③

自愿起诉者,字面意思为"任何想起诉的人"。在雅典,某些案件只能由受害人一方提起,但在其他一些案件如"graphe"和公共案件,任何未丧失公民权的公民都有资格提起,该种情形下提起诉讼的无关联公民被称为自愿起诉者。

---

① Basileus See sv. arkhon.

② Boule · Lit. "council". The democratic council of 500 men, appointed annually by lot from among citizens aged at least thirty, and with severe restrictions on repeated membership. Its chief function was to prepare the agenda for meetings of the ekklesia, and to undertake certain routine administrative duties, in particular that of co-ordinating the activities of numerous boards of minor officials; but it had also certain independent judicial powers, mainly but not only in cases of limited importance: in some cases of eisangelia, the boule could decide whether to refer the trial to the ekklesia or to a dikasterion.

③ (Ho) Boulomenos · Lit. "anyone who wishes". Whereas prosecution in a dike could only be brought by the aggrieved party, in a graphe or other public case it could be brought by any qualified person (which normally meant any Athenian citizen who was not himself atimos).

(十六) diadikasia (Greek: διαδικασία) ①

判决,意为涉及两方纠纷的判决,双方诉求相同,尤其是在有关继承问题的争议中。

(十七) diaitetes (Greek: διαιτητής, διαιτηταί) ②

仲裁员。在整个雅典法律史中,一直承认基于私人基础上为争议各方提供私人仲裁员的制度:从理论上讲,一个私人仲裁员的裁定是有约束力的,大概是因为当事人自愿签约接受它。公元前400年雅典引入公共仲裁制度,每一个现役士兵(或可能是每一个公民),在59岁不再有资格服兵役时,转而成为公众仲裁员。每一个社区都抽签选举产生一名仲裁员,来尝试在正式的审判前解决纠纷。在这种情况下,仲裁是强制性的(当事人被迫参加),但结果不具约束力,不满的当事人可以拒绝接受判决。根据亚里士多德的记载,仲裁员的工作(私人或公众)主要有以下几个方面:在强加解决方案之前,应该尽量让双方和解;有权在当事人提出的诉讼请求中作出中间性或中立性的裁决;裁决应该更加着眼于公平而不是法律规定。

(十八) diamarturia (Greek: διαμαρτυρία) ③

"diamarturia"为雅典城邦针对证人的一种特定诉讼,因为先前该证人的证词已经推动公共官员作出了某项决定。公元前400年随着"paragraphe"诉讼方式的产生,"diamarturia"诉讼方式的使用范围已经大为缩窄,特别是公元前380年以后

---

① Diadikasia · Lit. "judgement (contested) between": a dispute between two people who each claim the same thing, in particular a contested inheritance.

② Diaitetes, pl. diaitetai · An arbitrator. Throughout the history of Athenian law, it had always been open for litigants to arrange arbitration (diaita) on a private basis: in theory, the decision of a private arbitrator was binding, presumably because the litigants had voluntarily contracted to accept it. There was also, however, a system of public arbitration, introduced c. 400 BCE: every hoplite (or possibly every citizen), in the year that he ceased to be eligible for military service at the age of 59, had to serve as public arbitrator; and every dike (private dispute) was allocated by lot to one of them for an attempt at preliminary resolution. In such cases arbitration was compulsory (litigants were obliged to attend) but it was not binding (a dissatisfied litigant could refuse to accept the verdict: see sv. ephesis). According to Aristotle, the job of the arbitrator (private or public) is unlike that of the dikastes in several respects: he should try to reconcile the parties before imposing a solution; he has the discretion to bring in a decision mid-way between the demands of the litigants; and in his judgement he should look to epieikeia ("equity", but see further sv. epieikeia) rather than to dike ("justice").

③ Diamarturia · A formal presentation of a witness (martus) whose evidence serves to compel the public official before whom it is presented either to act in a certain way, or (more commonly) to desist from so acting. As a result of the introduction of paragraphe around 400 BCE, the scope of diamarturia was soon rapidly restricted: after 380 BCE, its only attested use is in inheritance cases, where a legitimate son could have a claim by a more remote relative quashed on the grounds that the case was not actionable; to re-open the case, the rival claimant would have successfully to prosecute the witness by dike pseudomarturion.

仅适用于继承案件。在继承案件中,作为法定继承人的儿子想要起诉一名获得继承权的远方亲戚,在提起诉讼之前,必须首先通过"diamarturia"诉讼方式起诉证明远方亲戚有继承权的那名证人。

(十九) dike(Greek:δίκη,δίκαι)①

"dike"是一个范围广泛的概念:"正义""良好秩序""判决",但也被表述为一个公正的判决的诉讼过程,如"法律诉讼""审判""某人提起诉讼的一个案件""某人应该承受的一种惩罚"。"dike"可以用于一般意义上的任何类型的起诉书,也可以表示在某些技术意义上的诉讼,如旧的"私人诉讼"(其中只有受害方或其亲属或亲近人员代表可以提起诉讼),而不能表示较新的"公共诉讼"(graphe),它可以由任何良好公民提起。

(二十) diomosia(Greek:διωμοσία)②

"diomosia"为凶杀案件采取的一项特殊的宣誓(证明),在其他案件中只需当事人独自针对对方发誓即可,称为"antimosia"宣誓(两方相互之间的宣誓)。但在凶杀案中所有证人必须参加自己所支持一方的宣誓,因为这个原因该种宣誓被称为"diomosia"(双方都有两个以上的人之间的誓言)。

(二十一) dokimasia(Greek:δοκιμασία,δοκιμασίαι)③

"dokimasia"为一种资格审查诉讼,由执政官代表公民大会主持审查诉讼,目

---

① Dike,pl. dikai · A concept of wide scope:"justice","good order","judgement". But it can also refer to the process by which a just settlement is determined,thus "a lawsuit","a trial",and even "the case which one pleads" or "the penalty which one has to pay". In the sence of "lawsuit",dike can be used either generically,to refer to any type of indictment,or else(more commonly)in a semi-technical sense,to denote the older "private suit" (which only the aggrieved party or his immediate or his immediate personal representatives could bring)as opposed to the newer "public suit"(graphe),which could be brought by any citizen in good standing.

② Diomosia · A special oath taken in cases of homicide:in all other cases the litigants alone swore the antimosia(lit. "oath [of two people] against each other");in homicide cases all the witnesses had to join in the oath of their principals, which was for this reason known as the diomosia lit. "oath between [more than two people]".

③ Dokimasia,pl. dokimasiai · An investigation held either by the boule or in a court,to test whether a man was formally qualified either to hold the public office to which he had been appointed or else to exercise a privilege to which he was laying claim. Dokimasiai were of various types,and were for the most part held in advance:no public official,whether elected or appointed by lot,could hold office without having passed his dokimasia;and newly enrolled citizens,whether by birth or by naturalisation(uncommon),were among those similarly tested. In these cases a man who was rejected suffered disqualification but no further penalty;a public speaker however(see sv. rhetor)could be challenged to undergo a retroactive dokimasia before a court,and this had more of the nature of a regular trial,in that if convicted he would apparently be punished.

的在于确认雅典居民是否具有担任某种公共官职的资格，以及个人是否具有享有某种权利的资格，如公民资格及服兵役的资格等。“dokimasia”包括多种类型，一般采取事先审查模式，公共官员在被选举或抽签任命前必须通过相应类型的“dokimasia”审查；新登记的公民，包括出生或归化两种形式，都必须通过“dokimasia”资格审查。通常情况下没有通过资格审查的人不会被判处进一步的刑事处罚，但是如果公共演说者在法院被提起一个有溯及力的“dokimasia”资格审查时，这种资格审查诉讼就具有了更多的效力，如果没有通过资格审查，同时还会被判决处以相应的刑罚。

（二十二）eisangelia（Greek：εἰσαγγελία，εἰσαγγελίαι）①

检举告发，意为“公告，发布信息”，是一种类似于美国弹劾制度的公诉方式。它通常适用于检举告发现任或离任官员（审判期间将被中止一切公共职务），也可针对发表公共言论的政治领导人。该类案件将首先被提交给公民大会或500人议事会，最终的审判将由公民大会负责，在公元前360年以后，则通常由陪审法庭负责审理。

（二十三）ekdosis（Greek：ἔκδοσις）②

“ekdosis”是雅典婚姻形式中的一种，意为“发表，发布”。在该婚姻的仪式中未婚女子由其监护人（父亲或其他监护人）交给她的新任丈夫。在雅典法律中，规定了两种婚姻形式，一种是由担保人和监护人负责的婚姻，另一种是在未婚女子的父亲去世，并且父亲的财产无其他继承人时，那么该女子必须与同一家族的男性结婚以保有去世父亲的财产，同时其遗产继承也必须由女继承人向执政官申请无遗嘱的遗产占有令状来实现。

（二十四）ekklesia（Greek：ἐκκλησία）. Athens③

公民大会是古希腊各城邦的最高权力机关，雅典的公民大会由所有成年男性

---

① Eisangelia, pl. eisangeliai · Lit. “public announcement, laying of information”: a form of public indictment broadly corresponding to impeachment in the USA. It was available for use against any public official during or after his term of office (he would normally be suspended from office for the duration of the trial) or against any political leader who had made a public proposal. It seems that the case could be brought either directly to the ekklesia or else to the boule, and that the final hearing would take place either before the ekklesia or (more commonly, and in every known case after 360 B. C.) before a dikasterion.

② Ekdosis · Lit. “giving forth”: the ceremony at which the kurios of a betrothed bride gave her into the hand of her new husband. Marriage in Athenian law took one of two forms, either by engue and ekdosis or else (if a man died leaving his daughter with no kurios to give her away, and no heir to his property) by the epidikasia of the epikleros.

③ Ekklesia · The public assembly of Athens, held usually on the Pnyx, at which all adult male citizens were formally entitled to attend, vote, and speak.

公民组成,通过投票方式决定城邦一切重大问题。

(二十五)(the) Eleven(Greek:οἱ Ἕνδεκα)[①]

十一人委员会,负责掌管雅典的监狱,并负责绝大部分"apagogai"(涉及杀人)案件的审理,同时也负责执行死刑。

(二十六) emporike(Greek:ἐμπορικὴ δίκη,ἐμπορικαὶ δίκαι)[②]

"emporike"为雅典的一种特殊诉讼程序,涉及该程序的案件主要是涉及一些进口到雅典的特殊商品(尤其是指进口到雅典的急需谷物)。这些涉及紧急商品交易的案件中,雅典法律规定了快速和特殊的法庭起诉途径。传统观点认为这些特殊程序包括案件必须在1个月内审理完毕;最新的观点则认为,每个月仅有1次提起这样案件诉讼的机会。这种诉讼程序可能仅仅适用于夏天或冬天的某些月份,并且在这类案件中也存在运用其他特殊规则的可能性。

(二十七) endeixis(Greek:ἔνδειξις,ἐνδείξεις)[③]

"endeixis"是与"apagoge"紧密相关的一个诉讼程序,其准确含义还存在争议。传统观点认为,该程序适用于弹劾案件,但在某些案件中也可能作为提起"apagoge"诉讼的一个自选前置程序被原告使用。

---

① The Eleven; Gk. hoi hendeka · A board of public officials responsible for the state prison of Athens. The majority of apagogai were brought before them, and they were in charge of all executions.

② Attica. emporike dike., pl. emporikai dikai · A case involving emporoi, traders who import goods (especially the extra grain which was needed to feed the population of Attica). Because of the urgency of the trade, such cases had rapid and privileged access to the courts; but it is not clear whether the term emmenos, commonly used to describe them, should be interpreted to mean that the case must be completed within a month (the traditional view), or (as has recently been argued) that there was an opportunity every month to initiate such cases; it is uncertain also whether such litigation could take place only during the summer months or only during the winter months. It is possible that other special rules may have applied in these cases.

③ Endeixis, pl. endeixeis · A procedure closely related to apagoge. The precise significance of the term is disputed: traditionally it was thought to be a denunciation made before a public official who would then himself arrest the culprit; but it may instead have been used by the plaintiff in some cases as a voluntary preliminary to apagoge.

（二十八）engue（Greek：ἐγγύη，ἐγγύαι；ἐγγυητής）①

“engue”意为担保物（复数为“enguai”），“enguetes”则表示担保人。古希腊的担保制度适用于如下情况：保证支付罚款或保证被告（特别是外国人）如期出席法庭审判；作为包税人向国家支付税金或商人支付采矿特许权费用的押金；作为雅典“ekdosis”婚姻中订婚的担保。

（二十九）ephesis（Greek：ἔφεσις）②

“ephesis”是雅典城邦一种类似于现代上诉制度的诉讼制度，但又具有自己的一些特点。具体而言，“ephesis”意味着当事人拒绝承认行政官员的决定或法院的判决，并同时向上一级机构提出重新解决争议的请求。梭伦在公元前590年创建了向陪审法庭提起“上诉”的“ephesis”制度，用以抑制政府官员的简易案件管辖权，从公元前400年开始，这项制度也适用于公共仲裁员作出的裁定。与现代司法制度中的上诉制度“一审中败诉的被告提出上诉，并负责说服上诉法庭采纳自己诉讼请求，以推翻原审判决”不同，雅典的“ephesis”诉讼在某些情况可能发生于一审判决作出之前，并且要由原告承担向二审法院证明自己诉讼主张的责任，这是因为此时的二审法院是重新审理该案而不考虑审查先前一审作出的判决。需要指出的是，梭伦创建的“ephesis”诉讼制度可能意味着“上诉”行为是自动启动的，并不以诉讼双方当事人发起该诉讼行为为前提条件。

---

① Engue, pl. enguai; enguetes · A surety: the engue is the thing which is pledged as security, and the enguetes the person who pledges or commits himself as a pledge. Such sureties were used in a range of legal contexts: to guarantee the payment of a fine or the appearance of a defendant (particularly a foreigner) in court; and as a deposit payable to those who contracted from the state the right to collect taxes or to operate mining concessions. But the most notable use of engue was as the necessary prelude to ekdosis in the regular Athenian form of marriage, corresponding to (but much stronger than) the modern engagement.

② Ephesis · Refusal to accept the decision of an official or a court of first instance, combined with a demand for the dispute to be resolved by a higher authority. For instance, Solon in the 590s is said to have introduced "ephesis to the dikasterion" as a curb on the summary jurisdiction of public officials; and from their introduction in c. 400 B. C., the decisions of public arbitrators were similarly subject to ephesis. Ephesis is traditionally translated "appeal", but this can have misleading connotations. An appeal in English law is brought on the initiative of a dissatisfied litigant (in criminal cases, a convicted defendant) after the court of first instance has decided against him/her; it is his/her duty to persuade the appellate court to reverse the decision, and s/he becomes in a sense the plaintiff in the process. In Athens, there were at least some situations in which ephesis could take place before the lower authority had reached a decision; it was the duty of the original plaintiff, not of the dissatisfied litigant, to persuade the court to act (that it, the court was retrying the case from scratch and not reviewing a decision already made); and it is possible that in the case of Solonian ephesis, this referral was automatic and did not depend on an initiative taken by one of the two litigants.

（三十）epieikeia（Greek：ἐπιείκεια）①

古希腊法中的"epieikeia"制度与现代英美法中的衡平观念类似。"epieikeia"最早源于亚里士多德的论述，他认为法官和陪审员应该依据法律进行审判，而仲裁员则应依据"epieikeia"进行裁决。"epieikeia"意味着衡平，即公正或自然争议，以与法律规则的严格执行相区分。不过需要注意的是衡平在英美法国家中还意味着大法官法院所适用的衡平法体系（英美普通法系的一种法律形式），这种衡平法律体系与亚里士多德所说的"epieikeia"显著不同。在雅典的现实生活中，亚里士多德提出的"epieikeia"即衡平学说并没有获得较多的承认，当一位雅典公民在诉讼中试图运用"自然正义"的观念为自己的诉讼主张提供支持时，他通常使用"dike"一词，而不是亚里士多德所说的"epieikeia"。

（三十一）epikleros（Greek：ἐπίκληρος，ἐπικληρώτη）②

女继承人（制度），是指一位雅典男性公民如果在去世后仅有一个女儿，而没有其他男性继承人，那么尽管该女子不能作为继承人，但是她可以通过婚姻形式占有父亲的土地等不动产。这一继承方式也被称为女继承人制度。

---

① Epieikeia · Aristotle says that it is the function of the dikastes（juror/judge）to judge according to dike（"justice"），but that the diaitetes（arbitrator）should make his decision according to epieikeia. It is conventional therefore to translate epieikeia as "equity"，since this is a standard and convenient way to describe "fairness" or "natural justice" as opposed to the strict application of legal rules. There are however certain problems here. "Equity" in English law can mean simply "fairness"，but it is also the name given to the system of law developed originally by the Court of Chancery（the Lord Chancellor's court），to provide relief in cases where to apply the rules of the common law would have seemed manifestly unfair. "Equity" in this sense is itself a body of rules；it is found only in countries which base their legal system on the common law；and it is clearly not what Aristotle is talking about. It should indeed be noted that Aristotle's statement of theory receives little acknowledgment in Athenian practice：when a litigant in an extant speech pleads for the application of natural justice in his favour，he characteristically describes this as dike and not as epieikeia.

② Epikleros（fem. adj. acting as noun），epiklerote（abstract noun） · An epikleros was the daughter of a man who died leaving no male heir；she was not his heiress，but possession of his estate went together with her hand in marriage. This system of inheritance is described as the epiklerate：for further details，see sv. inheritance；and for comparison，see sv. engue and sv. ekdosis. The etymology of epikleros is unclear：it may possibly mean "one to whom the property pertains"，but more likely is "one who pertains to the property".

(三十二)euthune(Greek:εὐθύνη,εὔθυναι)①

“euthune”是雅典城邦的一项离职审查制度。按照雅典法律的规定,任何公共官员在任期届满后都必须接受对自己任职期间所有行为的审查。如果该官员负责财政资金事务,他必须提供所有账目;在其他情形下,被审查的官员也必须对自己行使权力的正当性提供适当证明。离职审查由专门设置的离职审查委员会负责,但是任何公民都有权在审查的任何一个阶段对被审查的官员提出质询或控告。

(三十三)exegetes(Greek:ἐξηγητής,ἐξηγηταί)②

法律解释官,主要职能是在涉及特殊宗教法律问题的案件中负责阐述,提供适当的诉讼程序。法律解释官的职能还体现在所有杀人案件中,以及在任何案件中作为个人(而非专家证人)对案件的当事人在法庭上提出的法律质询进行回应。在一些案件中,法律解释官还会主动建议诉讼当事人一些事项,这暗示他们的职能可能远远不止法律解释这一通常的功能。

(三十四)graphe(Greek:γραφή,γραφαί)③

“graphe”是雅典城邦公共诉讼程序的一种,由执政官梭伦在公元前590年创设。它的主要特点在于:相对于雅典旧的诉讼程序规定只能由受害一方当事人提起诉讼,“graphe”诉讼可以由任何一位合格公民提起。并且“graphe”诉讼和其他

---

① Euthune, normally pl. euthunai · Lit. “the action of setting straight”. Every public official at Athens had to undergo at the end of his term an examination of his conduct in office. If he had handled public money, he had to present his accounts(logoi, pl.); in all cases he had to seek approval of the way he had used his powers(euthunai properly so called, but the term euthunai came also to be applied to the whole process of audit, logoi included). The examination was conducted by boards of logistai(pl.) and euthunoi(pl.), as appropriate; but any private citizen could bring a charge at any stage during the proceedings.

② Exegetes, pl. exegetai · Lit. “interpreter”. A group of officials who expound the proper procedure in situations which raise unusual questions of religious law. Their activity is attested in several cases, all of homicide; and in each case they are responding to an inquiry by an individual by an individual rather than as expert witnesses before a court. In one case they offer also to advise a litigant, implying that this was something more than their regular function of interpreting the law.

③ Graphe, pl. graphai · Lit. “a writing”; hence, “a written indictment”, cf. Eng. “writ.” This was the name given to the new “public” form of ordinary prosecution introduced apparently by Solon in the 590s. Its characteristic was that the indictment could be brought by any qualified citizen(ho boulomenos), whereas the older dike procedure could be brought only by the injured party. Graphai and other public procedures appear to have given rise to higher penalties, and thus to have rewarded a successful plaintiff much more heavily than did dikai; but they were also considerably more risky: a plaintiff in a public suit who failed to obtain 20 per cent of the votes of the jury could expect to suffer a heavy fine and possibly also other penalties(e. g. at least partial atimia).

新设的公共程序都没有加重对提起诉讼者的处罚(如系诬告),相反却是较早先的法律规定而言增加了对成功起诉者的奖励。需要指出的是,提起"graphe"的公民也需要承担相应的惩罚风险,如果提起公共诉讼者没有获得陪审法庭20%以上的投票支持,他将被判处较重的罚金,并且会被判处其他刑罚(如被判决丧失部分公民权)。"graphe"又可具体分为多种程序,如"Hybreos Graphe"(ὕβρεως γραφή),即涉及殴打或任何形式的个人暴力的刑事起诉,根据该程序可以判处直至死刑在内的多种刑罚,涉及该诉讼的案件由"Heliastic"法院审理。

(三十五)klepsudra(Greek:κλεψύδρα)[①]

水钟,在雅典城邦通常被用来在诉讼案件中控制诉讼每一阶段的时间。它是一个基座有一个小孔,上部是一个盛满水的碗的装置,小孔可以根据需要打开或关闭,通常由两个碗并在一起使用,这样一个碗中的水可以流空到另一个碗中,反之亦然(类似今天的漏斗装置),从而用来控制诉讼各个阶段的时间。在案件审理中,每个发言者都被分配到一个水钟,但是在陈述法律内容和证人证词时,水钟中的水将被停止流出,即不计入发言者的发言时间。

(三十六)kurios(Greek:κύριος)[②]

主人。古希腊妇女在法律交易中必须被一名男性亲属代理从事法律行为,该男性亲属即为主人。主人的范围包括:未婚女性或回到娘家的寡妇,主人通常是她的父亲或哥哥、叔伯(父亲缺位时),也可能是寡妇的成年儿子;已婚妇女的主人是她的丈夫,但是她的父系亲属似乎仍保留一定的权利,如索回嫁妆。主人有时也被用来表示财产的主人或家庭的主人,这在一些情况存在法律上的冲突,如

---

① Klepsudra · Lt. "water-stealer". A water-clock, used to regulate the length of the proceedings in legal cases. It consisted of a bowl of water with a small hole near the base, such that the hole could be stopped or opened as desired: normally two such bowls were used, the one being allowed to empty its contents into the other, and then vice versa, to measure the passage of time. In any category of case, a set number of bowls-full was allocated to each speaker, but the flow of water was stopped for the reading of laws and the testimony of witness.

② Kurios · Lit. "master", "lord", or in certain contexts "sovereign". An Athenian woman had to be represented in legal transactions by a male relative, who was described as her kurios: in the case of an unmarried girl or widow who had returned to the house of her family, this would normally be her father or (failing him) her brother or paternal uncle, but it could even be her adult son. A married woman was represented by her husband, but it appears that her agnatic kurios did retain certain rights: for instance, the reversion of her dowry. Confusingly, the term kurios was also used to denote the owner of property or the master of a household, and there are contexts in which the two uses might conflict: a married son, for instance, would be kurios of his wife; but his father may still be kurios of his household.

结婚的儿子是自己妻子的主人,但同时他的父亲也可能仍然是他的家庭的主人。

(三十七)logographos(Greek:λογογράφος,λογογράφοι)①

法庭演说词写作家,在雅典城邦专指帮助诉讼者撰写演说词的人。最新的观点认为法庭演说词写作家在帮助诉讼者准备演说词时并没有做出太多的贡献,当然这种观点还存疑。

(三十八)nomos(Greek:νόμος,νόμοι)②

"nomos"在雅典法律体系中包含法律和惯例两层含义。在雅典人的思想体系(尤其是公元前5世纪时),"nomos"是与"自然"相对应的范畴,后者代表了现实基础,前者则是表示人们采用的用以表示后者的某种类型概念。在这种意义上,"nomos"通常被翻译为公约、惯例。

(三十九)nomothesia(Greek:νομοθεσία; νομοθέτης,νομοθέται)③

"nomothesia"是雅典制定法令和永久立法程序中的一个前置程序。在公元前403年以后,该前置立法程序从公民大会转移到"nomothesia",目的在于对鲁莽立法进行充分审查。"nomothesia"程序的内容曾经在公元前4世纪进行了多次修正。但可以确认的是,"nomothesia"由符合条件的陪审员抽签产生,主要职能在于听取(支持或反对)某一立法动议的争论,并(讨论,非必要条件)作出最终的权威决定(同意提交立法或否)。当且仅当公民大会提出相关立法审查要求时,"nomothesia"才能应邀进行相关审查。

① Logographos, pl. logographoi · Lit. "speech-writer": specifically, a professional writer of speeches for litigants to deliver in court. It has recently been argued that the logographos did not normally write the speech so much as help the litigant to prepare it, but this view is contested.

② Nomos, pl. nomoi · Lit. a "norm", in the sense both of "custom" and of "law". Nomos is often contrasted, especially in fifth-century Greek thought, with phusis (lit. "nature"); the latter represents underlying reality, and the former denotes the patterns by which men try to shape this. In this sense nomos is normally translated "convention".

③ Nomothesia, nomothetes, pl. nomothetai · Nomothesia is the process of enacting laws (of general and/or permanent validity). After 403 BCE, this was taken out of the hands of the ekklesia and given to the nomothetai, in order to provide a check on the passage of reckless legislation. The precise arrangements for the process seem to have been revised several times during the fourth century; but it is notable that the nomothetai were a body selected by lot from among the panel of eligible dikastai. Their function was to hear in detail (but not apparently to discuss) the arguments for and against any proposed legislative change, and to make a final and authoritative decision. They could however only act when requested to do so on the initiative of the ekklesia.

（四十）nothos（Greek：νόθος，νόθοι）①

“nothos”意指私生子。在古典时代，雅典公民权获得的前提是父母双方必须同时具有雅典公民权，因此，雅典公民和非公民的未婚私生子不享有雅典公民权和继承权。但是雅典公民与公民间的未婚私生子的法律地位则不甚明确，一般而言，他们不具有继承权，至于是否具有公民权还存在争议。此外，“nothos”还被用来表示某些情况下（如公元前450年前）混合婚姻所诞下的子女，这种混合婚姻被雅典法律承认，并且所涉及的子女也很可能具有雅典公民权和继承权。

（四十一）oikos（Greek：οἶκος）②

家庭，家族。在古希腊语中，“oikos”可以被用来表示一个家族，也用来单独表示家族成员、家族财产（包括奴隶）或房屋，亦可三者都包含在内。该词很少出现于雅典正式的法律条文中，但在雅典的家庭生活和身份法律的适用方面起到了非常重要的作用。

（四十二）paragraphe（Greek：παραγραφή）③

“paragraphe”是雅典城邦的一种反诉程序。根据该反诉程序，被告可以控告原告对自己提起的是一个非法诉讼。这一诉讼程序产生（或重新修订）于公元前400年，目的在于帮助那些受到（因违反特赦规定而被）指控的人们。这些人曾经被置于斯巴达监管之下，目的是保护三十僭主（存在于公元前404年/前403年的

---

① Nothos，pl. nothoi · Lit. “a bastard”. In the classical period，Athenian citizenship was confined to those born of citizen parents on both sides. The child of an unmarried union between citizen and non-citizen was clearly illegitimate，and had rights neither of inheritance nor of citizenship. The status of the child of unmarried citizen parents is less clear：such a person was clearly a nothos without rights of inheritance，but it is disputed whether s/he was or was not a citizen. It is possible，though less certain，that the word nothos was used to describe the child of a mixed marriage even in those contexts（e. g. before 450 BCE）where such a marriage was legally permissible，even though such a child might have full rights to inheritance as well as to citizenship.

② Oikos · A household：the word can be used to describe people or family property or a building，or all three together. The term is rarely used in the formulation of Athenian statutes，but the concept seems to play an important rôle not only in family but in citizenship law：see svv. kurios，nothos.

③ Paragraphe · A counter-indictment，in which the defendant charges the plaintiff with bringing an illegal prosecution. The procedure was invented（or possibly re-organised）around 400，to help those threatened with charges which broke the Amnesty：the latter had been imposed under Spartan supervision to protect former supporters of the Thirty Tyrants，the oligarchic junta of 404/3 which had been overthrown by the democratic restoration of 403/2. Paragraphe，however rapidly extended its scope：for the defendant，it seems to have had the advantage that it was itself a prosecution；whereas the older procedure of diamarturia simply served to block a particular claim by the plaintiff，paragraphe enabled the defendant to turn the tables，becoming himself the prosecutor and（if successful）imposing a penalty on his opponent.

寡头政治集团，于公元前403年/前402年被民主派推翻）的支持者。该反诉程序产生后，不久就扩大了使用范围，使反诉者不仅可以反对针对自己的诉讼请求，阻止针对自己的特定索赔，还可以针对原告请求判处相应刑罚。

（四十三）(graphe) paranomon (Greek：γραφὴ παρανόνων)①

"paranomon"是雅典城邦的一种公共诉讼程序，针对的是新法令的提议者，主要审查其提出的立法建议是否符合基本法律或者说是否合宪。起诉者运用该程序时通常采用的理由是该立法建议没有履行必要的手续，但更多的此类诉讼是针对（授予某人）荣誉立法，提出的理由主要是某人不值得拥有此项荣誉。提出该项诉讼的时间可以在公民大会审查该项立法建议之前或之后。公元前403年之前，该诉讼可以同时适用于审查法令和审查法律两种情况，而此后，旧的"graphe paranomon"诉讼只适用于审查法令类的立法建议，一种新的类似于"graphenomon"的诉讼形式专门用于审查法律的立法建议。

（四十四）phasis (Greek：φάσις)②

"phasis"是雅典城邦的一种诉讼程序，用于告发非法侵占国家财产的人。不同于与之相类似的"apographe"程序，"phasis"程序直接针对的是人而非财产。

（四十五）polupragmon (Greek：πολυπράγμων, πολυπράγμονες)③

"polupragmon"意为一个忙碌的人，从事了过多事情的人。在演说家的眼里

---

① (Graphe) Paranomon · A public indictment against the proposer of a new psephisma (decree), charging that his proposal is unconstitutional (lit. "against the law"): One of the most extensively documented of all Athenian legal procedures, and one of the most overtly political: the prosecutor might claim for instance that the bill had been proposed without the necessary formalities; but many of the extant graphai paranomon are directed against honorary decrees, and in these the prosecutor regularly bases his case on the claim that the honour is itself undeserved. The procedure could be employed against proposals both before and after they had been voted on by the ekklesia. Until 403 B. C., it was apparently used without discrimination against both nomoi (laws) and psephismata; but in that year a formal distinction was for the first time drawn between the two types of statute (see sv. nomos, Legislation). The old procedure of graphi paranomon was retained for use against psephismata; but a new parallel procedure, the graphi nomon me epitedeion theinai, was felt to be required for use against unconstitutional (lit. "inexpedient") nomoi.

② Phasis · Lit. "a showing forth, declaration": denunciation of a man who is illegally withholding property which belongs to the state. Unlike the related (and much better attested) procedure of apographe, phasis was apparently directed against the person rather than the property.

③ Polupragmon, pl. polupragmones (adj.); polupragmosune (abstract noun) · Lit. "one who conducts much business", i. e. "too much". Usually pejorative in the eyes of the speaker. The fifth-century Athenian empire was according to its opponents the product of cooperative Athenian polupragmosune; on an individual level, the term has overtones of "officious" and "busybody".

该词通常是贬义的。公元前5世纪雅典帝国的成立就被雅典城邦的对手认为是雅典人多管闲事的产物;在个人层面上,这个词有“多管闲事”和“爱管闲事”的色彩。

(四十六) probole (Greek: προβολή, προβολαί) ①

“probole”是雅典城邦的一种诉讼程序,意为初步指控。在该诉讼程序中原告可以在公民大会提起,而不是直接到陪审法庭提起诉讼。公民大会针对该诉讼的投票结果没有法律上的效果:它没有强制要求(成功)原告继续向法庭上提出诉讼,也显然没有阻止(失败)原告向法庭提出诉讼,它没有强加任何处罚于原告或被告身上。该诉讼的潜在含义在于对(成功)原告施以援手,即经过民意测验的方式,表明社会舆论究竟于哪一方更为有利。“probole”诉讼主要适用于出现于节日的争议案件以及针对用花言巧语谄媚者、对民众作出虚假承诺的政治领袖。

(四十七) (dike) pseudomarturion (Greek: δίκη ψευδομαρτυριῶν) ②

“pseudomarturion”为雅典城邦的一种诉讼程序,意为对错误证人的私人诉讼。“pseudomarturion”从其性质而言属于二次诉讼,它起诉的是在前一次诉讼中作出错误证明或非法证明的证人。

(四十八) sukophantes (Greek: συκοφάντης, συκοφάνται; συκοφαντεῖν) ③

“sukophantes”意为一个爱管闲事的诉讼当事人,多为贬义,也被译为溜须拍马者。现在英语中的形容词“阿谀奉承”为该词在后古典时代的发展引申。

---

① Probole, pl. probolai · Lit. “a throwing forward”. A preliminary accusation, which an intending plaintiff could bring before the ekklesia (Assembly) rather than directly to a dikasterion (court). This vote of the ekklesia had no formal effect: it did not bind a successful plaintiff to continue his action in court, nor apparently did it prevent him from doing so if unsuccessful; it imposed no penalty either on plaintiff or on defendant. It did however strengthen the hand of the successful plaintiff: after the manner of a straw poll, it showed which way the wind was blowing. We hear of probole being used in disputes which arise at festivals, and also against sycophants and against political leaders (presumably) who have allegedly deceived the people with false promises.

② Pseudomarturion · Lit. “(prosecution concerning) false witness”: a private indictment against a martus (“witness”). This is by its nature a secondary action, brought against a man who has been a witness in previous legal proceedings, and charging him with having given a false or illegal testimony.

③ Sukophantes, pl. sukophantai (noun); sukophantein (verb) · A term of disputed etymology and disputed meaning, used pejoratively to describe an officious litigant. Conventionally transliterated as “sycophant” or “sykophant”, but the English adjective “sycophantic” derives from a later, post-classical development in the meaning of the word.

(四十九)sunegoros(Greek:συν ήγορος,συν ήγοροι)①

"sunegoros"意为代理人,负责跟随诉讼当事人出席庭审并代表其在法庭上发表意见。尽管在理论上雅典城邦法律不允许代理人在法庭上代表当事人,但是"sunegoros"在某种程度上是受到国家承认的支持诉讼的演说人。"sunegoros"也被用来表示受到任命代表国家出庭(负责公共诉讼案件)的检察官,但是在雅典城邦绝大多数公共诉讼案件都可以由个人发起。

① Sunegoros, pl. sunegoroi · Most commonly, a person who appears in court to speak on behalf of a litigant. Lit "speaker together with", thus at least in theory preserving the rule that litigants could not be represented by advocates: the sunegoros was officially the supporting speaker. The word is also used to describe a speaker appointed to represent the state, normally as prosecutor; but the overwhelming majority even of public prosecutions were brought by private individuals.

第一章　欧美国家古希腊研究与古希腊法律史研究的兴起

与欧洲大陆国家相似，英美国家的古希腊研究与古希腊法律史研究的兴起也得益于14～17世纪首先兴起于意大利的欧洲文艺复兴运动，特别是受到18世纪中后期以来以德国为代表的西欧知识界对古希腊文化展开大规模研究的称为“Hellenism”（古典希腊理想化）文化运动的巨大影响。在“Hellenism”文化思潮中，欧洲学者试图以理想的古典希腊抒发、寄托现代欧洲的精神，[①]并以理想化的希腊文化来形塑和表述当时欧洲的现代性思潮。英美国家的古希腊法律史研究正是在这一文化思潮的主导下兴起，并在20世纪前后开始逐渐兴盛起来。

第一节　欧美国家古希腊研究的兴起

在近代，欧洲经过千年的中世纪“黑暗时代”之后，在公元14～17世纪掀起了以“人文主义”为口号的文艺复兴运动，意图复兴古代希腊、罗马时期的辉煌成就。近代欧洲的文艺复兴运动首先兴起于公元14世纪的意大利，原因有三：其一，意大利资本主义萌芽出现较早，资本阶级凭借强大的经济实力在很大程度上掌握了城市国家的

① 参见黄洋：《古典希腊理想化：作为一种文化现象的Hellenism》，载《中国社会科学》2009年第2期。

统治权，有研究古典文化的物质与社会政治基础；其二，当时的意大利城市国家在政治经济制度、社会文化等方面与古代的城邦国家存在很大的相似性；其三，意大利的地中海沿岸自治城市在历史上就曾经是古希腊的殖民城邦或位于其相邻地区，更是其后罗马国家的本土组成部分之一，并且由于地理位置的优势与中世纪长期存在的东方拜占庭帝国存在密切的联系。上述因素的长期综合影响在14世纪终于引发意大利率先扛起复兴古典文化的旗帜，掀起了一场波及全欧洲的以"人文主义"为口号文艺复兴运动。

在文艺复兴运动中，欧洲的人文主义者在研究古希腊文学、艺术的同时，对古希腊史和古希腊法的研究也不断深入，也许近代最早的古希腊史著作是苏格兰王室历史学家格利斯（John Gillies）1786年出版的2卷本《古代希腊史》①（*History of Ancient Greece*）。这本书首先从希腊人的祖先赫伦（Hellen）写起，一直写到亚历山大大帝去世，帝国分裂而结束。英国古希腊史专家格罗特（G. Grote）也写有12卷本的《希腊史》②（*A History of Greece*），该书从古代希腊的传说开始至公元前301年止。在这部希腊史著作中，作者以公元前776年作为希腊信史的开端。③公元19世纪的大部分古希腊史著作喜欢以亚历山大的去世作为古希腊史的结束，或者至多写到公元前146年科林斯的灭亡，希腊地区最终成为罗马帝国的一部分。只有一部分古希腊史著作包括了从亚历山大去世到托勒密王朝灭亡这一时期的历史，西方学者在写作古希腊史时之所以没有把希腊化时代的历史写入其中，也许是由于西方学者"雅典中心主义"的情怀以及这一时期的历史错综复杂、难于把握，并且相关史料非常稀少，多数又残缺不全的缘故。④另一个原因为，自公元前3世纪以后，罗马帝国开始向东地中海地区扩张，因此很多罗马史的学者倾向于把这一时期的历史作为罗马帝国征服史的一部分。

然而德国史学家德罗伊森却不这样认为，他对亚历山大去世到奥古斯都之间这一段希腊—马其顿人统治的历史首次作出了界定，在古典希腊与古典罗马之间架起了一座桥梁。他在1836年首先提出了"希腊化"的概念，开创了从亚历山大去世到埃及托勒密王朝灭亡这一历史时期的研究，并把这一时期称为"希腊化时代"，用德语词"Hellenismus"来表示。德罗伊森认为在这一时期，希腊的政治、经

---

① 中文版可参见［英］J. B. 伯里：《希腊史》，晏绍祥导读，北京大学出版社2009年版，第1页。

② G. Grote, *A History of Greece*, Volume I, London: J. M. Dent & Co., 1918.

③ 陈恒：《希腊化研究》，商务印书馆2006年版，第1页。

④ 同上书，第2页。

济、文化等各方面向东方传播，并与当地文化相融合，这种融合为基督教的产生铺平了道路。在德罗伊森的笔下，亚历山大为希腊化时代的到来奠定了基础，他也倾向于把亚历山大描写为受波斯暴政压迫之下诸民族的解放者，而且是把希腊启蒙思想传播到亚洲世界的中介者。在其《希腊化史》一书中，东西方的冲突与融合是一个重要思想。[①] 继德罗伊森开创了"希腊化时代"的研究以来，"随着考古学革命和对希腊化时代历史的不断评估"，从 19 世纪晚期到 20 世纪早期出现了诸多希腊化史方面的专家和研究成果，这其中希腊化法研究也取得了长足的发展，特别是大量一手出土资料（如埃及纸莎草纸文献）的获得，在很大程度上弥补了希腊古典时期法律研究中实证资料不足的缺陷。

18 世纪在欧洲出现的"Hellenism"文化思潮将欧洲大陆国家对古希腊的研究推向了最高潮。"Hellenism"与德语词"Hellenismus"一样都是希腊语"Ἑλληνισμός"拉丁化的结果，其本意是"对希腊语言、希腊生活的模仿"。"Hellenism"有多种含义，在《牛津英语词典》[②]中这个词有四种含义：(1)希腊语言的特点，古希腊语中的习语、语言表达、语言的构成；(2)采纳希腊人的说话方式和思想观念，对希腊语言的模仿，如分散各地的犹太人对古希腊语的模仿及后来的罗马人对古希腊语的模仿，及遵循希腊人的原则；(3)希腊人的民族特征或希腊精神，古希腊文化；(4)希腊的民族性，希腊式的竞赛或作为一个政治实体的世界。而且这本词典指出，"Hellenism"在 1609 年已出现，"为 Philemon Holland (1552～1637 年)于1609 年翻译 Ammianus Marcellinus 的 Roman Histories 时使用了该词"。[③] 18 世纪在欧洲出现的"Hellenism"文化思潮则"包含了更为丰富的内涵，不仅表达了一系列的文化与政治思想，而且体现出强烈的对古典希腊理想化的色彩，以理想的古希腊抒发、寄托现代欧洲的精神"，[④]这一文化思潮兴起于 18 世纪中期的德国，发起人为德国人温克尔曼，代表人物有洪堡、康德、沃尔夫、拜伦、莱辛等。

作为"Hellenism"文化思潮的发起人，1755 年温克尔曼出版了标题为《对于模

---

① 陈致宏：《德国史家朵尔森(J. G. Droysen)的历史思想与现实意识》，载《台湾大学丛刊》2002 年，第 55 页。该文中的朵尔森(J. G. Droysen)即本书中的德罗伊森(J. G. Droysen)。

② J. A. Simpson and E. S. C. Weiner, *The Oxford English Dictionary*, Second Edition, Oxford: The Clarendon Press, 1989, p. 121.

③ 陈恒：《希腊化研究》，商务印书馆 2006 年版，第 30 页。

④ 黄洋：《古典希腊理想化：作为一种文化现象的 Hellenism》，载《中国社会科学》2009 年第 2 期。

仿希腊绘画和雕塑的思考》[①]的小册子，对当时欧洲盛行的审美和文化观念提出了颠覆性的观点："我们变得伟大，如果可能的话，伟大得无可比拟的唯一方式，就是模仿古代人。"[②]他认为希腊人关于美的观念虽然源于自然，但"高出于自然"，"是完全出自心灵之理想的自然"。因此，现代艺术如果要具有创造性，要达到纯粹的美，就应该模仿古典希腊艺术，而不是模仿自然。希腊艺术是单纯、完美与和谐的典范，代表了"高贵的单纯，静穆的伟大"（Edle Einfachheit und heitere Größe）。温克尔曼的这一论断打破了自从文艺复兴以来就一直存在的欧洲艺术"模仿自然"的崇高信条，从根本上改变了欧洲艺术价值观念的历史走向。温克尔曼还进一步指出，希腊充满阳光而温和的气候、希腊人对于体育竞技的热爱、他们的生活习性，造就了一个最为健美的民族，也是最会欣赏美的民族。最为重要的是，完美的希腊艺术是充满自由和欢乐的文明的产物。1764年温克尔曼又出版了《古代艺术史》一书，更为系统地阐发了他在《对于模仿希腊绘画和雕塑的思考》中提出的思想，认为艺术史不再是以对于单个艺术家及其作品的细致描绘为中心，而是基于对艺术作品赖以产生的历史与社会环境的把握，艺术作品被看作特定时代、特定地域的文化表达。[③]温克尔曼的著作很快被翻译成英语、法语等欧洲主要语言，他对古典希腊的推崇在全欧洲范围内都产生了巨大影响，更开启了德国新人文主义时代。[④]

温克尔曼提倡模仿希腊艺术的目的并不全然是回到古代希腊，他的根本目的是再造现代艺术和现代文化。在温克尔曼之前，主导欧洲文学艺术的是文艺复兴所建立起来的以罗马为核心的人文主义以及继之而起的法国古典主义，在艺术领域的主要表现形式是颓废的洛可可和巴洛克风格。温克尔曼反叛了这个主导性的传统，他在希腊艺术中看到了一种单纯、极致的美。在温克尔曼看来，艺术作品不仅表现了希腊人外表的美，还表达了他们高贵的思想和情操，反映了他们美满和谐的生活世界。因此，单纯和极致的美是希腊文化的内涵，艺术不过充分地表现了这种美，但它同样也体现在希腊文学作品之中。[⑤] 希腊艺术已经不纯粹是艺

---

① Johann Joachim Winckelmann, Gedanken über die Nachahmung der Griechischen Werke der Malerei und Bildhauerkunst, 1755.

② Winckelmann, *Reflections on the Imitation of Greek Works in Painting and Sculpture*, p. 5.

③ Winckelmann, *History of the Art of Antiquity*, trans. by Harry Francis Mallgrave, Los Angeles: Getty Publications, 2006.

④ K. J. Dover, ed., *Perceptions of the Greeks*, Oxford and Cambridge, Mass., Basil Blackwell Ltd., 1992, chapter 8: "Germany 1750 – 1830", by Joachim Wohlleben, pp. 170 – 202.

⑤ Winckelmann, *Reflections on the Imitation of Greek Works in Painting and Sculpture*, pp. 37 – 39.

术,它代表和反映的是一个理想的文化世界。现代艺术、现代文化的发展都必须以此来衡量。温克尔曼所谓的模仿,已经不是指形式上的模仿,而是呼唤学习古代人的创造精神,追求纯粹的、极致的美,创造一个超越古代人的绚丽的现代人的文化。与此同时,温克尔曼还在很大程度上塑造了德意志的民族和文化精神,通过抛弃以罗马为中心的法国古典主义,将希腊确立为榜样,温克尔曼实际上不仅结束了罗马人文主义及其法定后继者法国古典主义的文化主导性,给德意志带来了思想上的独立,而且将人们关注的重心从政治带向了文化领域。德意志作为文化民族的观念,在很大程度上发端于温克尔曼。①

温克尔曼在18世纪中后期对古代希腊艺术的阐述,引发了近代欧洲特别是德国学者关于现代性的思考。通过树立一个完美的古代文化的榜样,温克尔曼提出了对于现代性的拷问。② 18世纪后期乃至19世纪欧洲现代性意识的核心问题是:面对古代文化的最高成就,现代人应该如何超越呢?温克尔曼本人对此的回答是通过学习古代文化的精髓,以达到超越它的目的。此后,赫尔德接受和发展了温克尔曼对于希腊文化的阐述,认为尽管希腊文化可以作为现代人的榜样,但无论多么辉煌,仍是古代历史的产物,已经一去不复返了。但这并不意味着古典希腊失去了它的意义,恰恰相反,它是现代人借以创造自己的不可缺少的"兄弟",是创造现代性的路径。③

歌德在温克尔曼之后对德国人的希腊观产生了决定性影响。歌德于1786年发表的《伊菲革涅亚在陶里斯》通过希腊的题材表现启蒙时期的理想,寻找现代人的精神源泉。在歌德看来,现实问题的根源恰恰在于人们教化和文明的程度不够,以希腊文化的理想教化现代人,才是解决现实问题的根本出路。④ 而对于希腊理想的理论总结则要等到洪堡来完成,他在1792年撰写的《论古代研究尤其是古代希腊研究》一文中,对于为什么要学习希腊文化以及如何学习希腊文化进行了专门论述,指出教育的目的是培养完善的人格,而古代希腊人是理想人格的体

---

① 参见黄洋:《古典希腊理想化:作为一种文化现象的Hellenism》,载《中国社会科学》2009年第2期。

② David S. Ferris, *Silent Urns: Romanticism, Hellenism, Modernity*, Stanford: Stanford University Press, 2000, chapter 1: "Greece and the Invention of Culture: Winckelmann", pp. 16 – 51.

③ Georg G. Iggers, *The German Conception of History: The National Tradition of Historical Thought from Herder to the Present*, Middletown, Wesleyan University Press, 1968, chapter Ⅱ, pp. 30 – 43.

④ Charles C. Grair, "Antiquity and Weimar Classicism", p. 77.

现,因而培养全面的人的唯一方式,就是学习希腊文化。①

正是在上述这股“Hellenism”热潮中,作为现代学科的古典学(包含古希腊和罗马研究)率先在德国建立和发展起来。1777 年一位名叫沃尔夫的学生进入哥廷根大学,要求注册学习“古典学”(studiosus philologiae),这标志着现代古典学正式确立。而洪堡在 1809 年被钦命为普鲁士教育部部长,得以进一步把他的“Hellenism”理论付诸实践。他改革普鲁士教育系统,建立起文科中学体系,推广以希腊文和拉丁文为核心的古典人文教育,并在 1810 年创建后来成为现代大学原型的柏林大学,亦使古典学成为人文学术的基础和核心。此后,古典教育深深植根于整个德意志的教育体系之中,这也成为此后德国学术界古希腊法律史研究居于世界前列的深层次原因。

“Hellenism”并非德国特有的文化思潮,而是席卷了整个欧洲的文化运动。在英国,斯图亚特(James Stuart)和里伏特(Nicholas Revett)通过两年对雅典古迹的实地考察,于 1762 年出版大型画册《雅典古迹》(*The Antiquities of Athens*)第一卷,将古代希腊建筑直接介绍给了英国人,从而开启了英国的“Hellenism”运动。②此后,温克尔曼等德国学者著作的英译本逐渐问世,对英国的“Hellenism”产生了深刻的影响。与德国的“Hellenism”主要基于文献和想象不同,英国“Hellenism”从一开始就带有朝圣的意味,更为注重寻访希腊的古迹和名胜,更为注重从考古发掘资料出发展开相关研究。

如前所述,18 世纪中期兴起的“Hellenism”运动席卷了欧美大多数国家,其目的在于借想象的希腊,阐述现代性的理想,探寻现代性的道路。其内在的逻辑在于,古典希腊文化被看作古代文明的高峰,是和谐、完善和完美人性的象征,是科学和理性、民主与自由的代表,也是现代欧洲文明直接的先驱、源泉。当然,学者也都认识到效法古典希腊并不是为了回到过去,而是为了学习其精神,为了超越这个过去的最高峰,建设一个前所未有的、全新的现代文明。现代性以古典希腊这个参照物而凸显自身,经由古典希腊而得以形成清晰的概念,并且通过希腊文化的理想而表达出来。欧洲“Hellenism”运动兴起的深层次原因在于 18 世纪随着工业化和启蒙运动的全面展开,西欧社会、经济和思想领域都出现了根本性的变化。面对这种前所未有的快速发展,西欧知识阶层发现,需要追寻自己的文化根

---

① Wilhelm von Humboldt, “ber das Studium des Altertums, und des Griechischen Insbesondere” (1792), see K. J. Dover, ed., *Perceptions of the Greeks*, p. 199.

② Richard Jenkyns, *The Victoria and Ancient Greece*, Basil Blackwell, 1980, pp. 1 – 7.

源,以理解现实的发展和把握未来的方向。基督教文明赖以产生的希伯来传统已经无助于理解这一新的发展了,它需要的是一个不同的传统,一个替代希伯来宗教文化的传统,一个和启蒙精神相合的世俗的、理性的传统。古典希腊文化由此全面进入了西欧知识界的视野之中。

如黄洋教授所言,"Hellenism"运动对欧洲古代希腊研究产生的影响主要包括两个方面:[①]其一,以完美的希腊理想为核心来构筑欧洲新的学术与教育体系,如理想希腊的最大推崇者洪堡就以理想希腊为核心来设计普鲁士新的教育与学术体制;其二,作为"Hellenism"的核心,纯粹的希腊文化应该是理性、秩序、自由和民主的化身,所以西方人理想的希腊是城邦时代的希腊。反映在古希腊历史研究中,城邦文明的兴起及兴盛就成为主导性的框架。前城邦时代体现出和城邦文明非常不同的特征,因而必定和城邦文明没有多少因承关系。沿着这样的逻辑,西方学者把看起来体现出专制王权特征的迈锡尼文明称为"东方式宫殿文明",而倾向于强调迈锡尼文明与希腊城邦文明之间的断裂以及公元前 8 世纪希腊文明的"新生"或者"复兴",进而确立了一个城邦兴起的范式,成为诸多研究的出发点和前提。[②]

相应地,"Hellenism"运动对英美国家早期的古希腊法律史研究也产生了两个方面的影响:其一,在古希腊法律史研究中英美早期学者多把古希腊法和其支撑的民主制度视为完美无缺的理想制度,忽视了早期法律文明发展阶段中一些基本的规律性认识,如学者大力颂扬的古希腊普通民众的权利保障和政治平等参与等所涉及的具体法律保障制度在事实上还没有那么完善。其二,英美早期学者的古希腊法律史研究多集中于城邦时期的雅典法律制度研究,忽视了迈锡尼文明等前城邦时期的法律制度,也忽视了希腊化时期希腊化国家(如埃及的托勒密王朝)的法律制度研究。

第二节 欧美国家古希腊法律史研究的兴起

在 19 世纪之前,欧美国家的古希腊法律史研究都处于萌芽和初创阶段。在

① 参见黄洋:《古典希腊理想化:作为一种文化现象的 Hellenism》,载《中国社会科学》2009 年第 2 期。

② 同上。

欧洲大陆,16世纪法国人纪尧姆出版了拉丁文版的《希腊语评注》(1529年),[①]最早对古希腊法的个别制度作出了详细具体的描述。17世纪德国法学家马夸特出版了拉丁文版的《战神山议事会判例集》(1615年),该书最早对古希腊法展开系统研究。同时期的法国胡格诺派牧师塞缪尔也在随后出版了拉丁文版著作《阿提卡法》(1635年),对雅典城邦所处的雅典半岛地区法律制度进行了总体性介绍。在笔者的知识范围内,后两部著作似乎是迄今为止欧美国家关于古希腊法律史研究最早的学术著作。19世纪前后,随着欧洲大陆古希腊研究在18世纪的知识积累和研究范围的扩大,德国法学者率先对古希腊法展开了系统性的研究,随后扩展到包括英美国家在内的欧美其他国家。

相对而言,欧洲大陆国家的古希腊法律史研究起步较早,19世纪以后逐渐进入成熟时期,而英美国家的古希腊法律史研究则起步较晚,20世纪以后才进入蓬勃发展期。同时,由于研究出发点的差异形成了两种不同的古希腊法律史研究风格:在欧洲大陆国家(尤其是德国),大多数法学家将雅典法律视为自己法律体系的历史渊源之一,采用法学方法进行研究;而在英美国家,由于普通法系在法律观念上并不以古希腊法为历史源头,因此早期从事相关研究的主要是历史学者,研究领域被归于古典学范畴,并且主要采用历史学和社会学的方法进行研究。进入20世纪以后,有更多的英美法律史学者投入古希腊法律史研究中,他们的研究在注重法学分析的同时,更注重逻辑分析、强调一手资料,对古希腊法律制度的相关论述独具特色,影响力也日益提高。

一、欧洲大陆国家的古希腊法律史研究

在欧洲大陆国家(尤其是德国),古希腊法律史研究属于法律史的研究范畴,古希腊法本身也被视为他们自己法律体系的历史渊源之一。欧洲大陆最早从事古希腊法律史研究的学者是部分历史学家,后来逐渐为专业化的法学家所取代,研究方法也主要采用法学方法进行研究。受到前述"Hellenism"文化运动影响,德国文学家席勒(Christoph Friedrich von Schiller,1759～1805年)早在18世纪晚期就撰写了描述斯巴达与雅典立法活动的专著《来库古与梭伦的立法》(Die Gesetzgebung des Lykurgus und Solon,1790年),并对梭伦立法所代表的雅典城邦立法大加颂扬,认为梭伦的立法是"动态的、有弹性的,有利于成长","因为梭伦'理解法律仅仅是一种文化的侍女,成年的民族需要的是不同于孩童的知道',时

① Guillaume Budé,Commentarii linguae Graecae,Paris,1529.

间证明梭伦的立法更有利于造就完整和全面的人"。[①] 从19世纪初期开始,德国的古希腊法律史研究在欧洲,甚至整个世界都处于领先的地位。德国古希腊法律史研究取得世界领先地位的原因主要包括三个:一是浪漫主义思潮和古典学研究传统的影响,使德国学者不自觉地把眼光投向过去,同时德国在拿破仑战争中的失败也刺激了德国的民族自尊心,研究古希腊史、罗马史成为德国学者借古讽今并为下一代提供学习古代榜样的有效途径;二是当时德国的各诸侯国统治者重视科学研究,并提供了大量的财政资助,典型的如普鲁士统治者不但创办了举世闻名的柏林大学,还通过普鲁士科学院大力资助学术著作的出版;三是当时德国的历史研究逐步摆脱了对神学与哲学的依附地位发展成为一门独立的学科,历史研究专业化程度的加强也间接推动了德国古典史研究的深入。[②]

其中,系统化的古希腊法律史研究也在德国古典史研究的蓬勃发展中逐渐发展成熟起来。19世纪前期德国最著名的古典史学家奥古斯特·博克(August Bockh)在研究雅典金融行政问题时,注意到雅典法律研究的重要性,由此把雅典法律程序设定为获奖论文的主题,随后奥古斯特·博克的两个弟子迈耶和朔曼合作出版了著名的《雅典诉讼程序》一书,这部作品获得柏林皇家学院的肯定与奖励,并于1883年至1887年由J. H.利普修多次修订,至今仍然是研究雅典法定程序的标准参考书。受奥古斯特·博克的影响,早期德国学者如迈耶和朔曼以及其后的贝洛赫(Karl Julius Beloch)都注重从经济和社会发展角度来研究历史发展进程的各种法律问题。布佐尔特(Georg Busolt,1850~1920年)则属例外,他更多地从德国传统政治史的角度研究古希腊的政治法律制度。尽管19世纪中后期,法国的古希腊法律史研究异军突起,在某些方面甚至超越了德国,但20世纪中后期至今,德国的古希腊法律史研究重回领先地位,代表性学者汉斯教授倡导创建了德国弗赖堡大学古希腊法律史研究中心,并发起成立了国际性的欧洲古希腊及希腊化法研究会,其研究对象广泛,不仅包括古典时期雅典的法律制度,如《古代雅典的婚姻和家庭组织法》(1944年)、《希腊人之间司法诉讼的起源》(1946年)、《作为一名律师的德摩斯梯尼》(1968年)、《雅典民主体制下的立法和司法》(1970年)、《古希腊法铭文集》(1973年),也包括了希腊化时期埃及的法律制度,

---

① Christoph Friedrich von Schiller, Die Gesetzgebung des Lykurgus und Solon, 1790; Jennifer Tolbert Roberts, *Athens on Trial*, Princeton University Press, 1997, p. 212.

② 历史研究最终成为一种职业,要求从事研究者必须经过专门训练才能胜任,这有利于古典史研究的深入发展。参见王晴佳:《近代德国的历史思想与实践》,载《世界历史》1990年第6期。

如《托勒密时期的司法体制》(1962 年)、《希腊化时期埃及纸莎草纸所反映的公共和私人生活的证据》(1978 年)等。同时期的德国代表性学者及作品还有莫罗教授的《柏拉图论古希腊法中的奴隶法》(1939 年),捷耐特教授的《古希腊的法律与社会》(1955 年),沃尔夫教授的《古希腊法律思想史》(4 卷,1950 ~ 1968 年),饶申布什教授的《梭伦法》(1966 年)、《雅典刑法研究》(1968 年)、《希腊法律史》(2004 年)等。

随着 17 ~ 18 世纪欧洲古典文献学的发展,18 世纪法国的古代史研究也逐渐兴盛起来,但是与德国学者重点关注古希腊史研究不同,法国人最为重视的是罗马史的研究,如孟德斯鸠就在《论法的精神》一书中将古希腊的法律制度一掠而过,将关注的重点落在罗马法律制度的讨论上。空想社会主义者马布里在其《希腊史论》一书中,也对雅典的民主与法律制度评价不高,认为“民主是所有制度中最坏的,而它恰恰是雅典的制度”。[①] 相应地,法国学者对古希腊法律史的系统研究也晚于德国,但是在 19 世纪中后期至 20 世纪初期法国学者的古希腊法律史研究渐入佳境,不仅在原有基础上加深了对古希腊公法的研究,如欧仁教授撰写的《古希腊立法者与宪法的历史》(1852 年),更是涌现出一大批从事古希腊私法制度研究的学者以及众多相关研究成果,如佩罗教授的《雅典共和国公法和私法论集》(1867 年)、《雅典市民权论集》(1867 年)、《雅典的政治和法律演讲集》(1873 年),卡梅耶(Caillemer)教授的《雅典法律典籍研究》(1870 年),鲁道夫教授的《雅典继承立法研究》(1879 年)等。法国学者的古希腊法律史研究呈现四个显著的特点:(1)注重跨学科的学术联系,善于综合运用人类学、社会学和古典学研究方法;(2)注重实证研究,相关研究成果较多倚重考古发掘资料;(3)注重学术传承,尤以古郎士学派、热内尔结构学派为典型代表;(4)研究方向更加细化,对古希腊单一法律制度、代表性法学家的研究逐渐深入,研究范围也从传统的雅典、斯巴达扩展到古希腊其他主要城邦。

一直以来,意大利的古希腊法律史研究都卓有成效。尽管由于资料所限,我们对于意大利 19 世纪的古希腊法律史研究知之甚少,但从 20 世纪意大利古希腊法律史研究的丰硕成果不难推测其长期以来深厚的学术积累。相比其他国家的学者而言,意大利学者对古希腊法的研究有着鲜明的地域特色,他们对古希腊时期在意大利的拓殖地法律制度展开了深入的研究,并在其他很多领域如古希腊女

---

① Abbe de Mably, *Observations on the Greeks*, 2nd ed., London, 1776, p. 76. 转引自晏绍祥:《古典历史研究史》(上卷),北京大学出版社 2013 年版,第 43 页。

性法律问题、柏拉图《法律篇》研究等方面取得了丰硕的研究成果。

由于近代以来希腊地区长期处于奥斯曼土耳其帝国的统治之下，希腊本土的古希腊法律史研究起步较晚，一直到20世纪初期希腊学者才开始展开相关研究。不过基于语言的同源性和希腊学者自身的巨大努力，希腊本土的古希腊法律史研究也取得了令人瞩目的成果。

欧洲大陆其他国家的古希腊法律史研究相对比较分散，比利时、丹麦、西班牙、葡萄牙、南斯拉夫等国家都有从事相关研究的重要学者。受到前述各主要国家研究流派与研究风格的巨大影响，上述学者对古希腊法的研究或注重在经济视野下解释法律现象，或从民主发展角度阐释法律制度的起源，或针对某一领域如海商法、军事法、奴隶法、联盟法展开深入研究，或凭借某一特定媒介如演说词、戏剧等分析具体法律问题，或集中于某一特定区域如格尔蒂、萨索斯岛等的法律制度研究。

二、英美国家的古希腊法律史研究

英国在17世纪之前的古希腊研究，远远落后于欧洲大陆国家。17～18世纪随着资本主义生产方式在英国逐渐占据统治地位，以及18世纪中期开始的英国工业革命的巨大成功，英国的自然科学和人文科学都得到了充分重视和快速发展。特别是在古典史研究领域，英国在18世纪出现了众多卓有影响的古希腊史著作，先后有托马斯·亨德（Thomas Hind，1683～1748年）的《希腊史》、威廉·罗伯逊（William Robertson，1705～1785年）的《古希腊史》、戈德史密斯（Oliver Goldsmith）的《古希腊史》、坦普尔·斯坦严（Temple Stanyan，1667～1752年）的《古希腊史》、格利斯（John Gillies，1747～1836年）的《古希腊史》、威廉·米特福德（William Mitford，1744～1827年）的8卷本《希腊史》等。19世纪上半叶，英国工业革命完成后，社会经济和政治环境日益稳定，历史学家的研究趋向也日渐由相对保守的古史观转向功利主义历史观，其中的代表性作品是格罗特（George Grote，1794～1871年）的《希腊史》。其研究的核心是自克里斯提尼改革以来的雅典民主制度，对古希腊法律制度也多有涉及。

19世纪后半期以来，英美两国先后成为世界霸主，从而也间接为英美国家的古典史研究提供了雄厚的经济基础以及广阔的发掘场所。特别是第二次世界大战期间，盟军为了作战需要，广泛运用空中侦查技术，获得了大量古典文明时期的历史地理资料，并发现了以前不太为人注意或在地面不易发现的一些遗址。战后，英美设在雅典、罗马的考古研究机构根据前述发现，运用先进的空中摄影与照相技术,在希腊、意大利、西西里、小亚细亚等地进行了广泛且具有系统性与科学性的考古发掘活动。有些英美大学还组织了专门的考古队从事某一特定遗址的考古发掘,如辛辛那提大学对希腊美塞尼亚西南部传说中的涅斯托耳的派罗斯王宫的发掘活动、芝加哥大学对科林斯进行的考古发掘、哈佛大学和康奈尔大学联合考古队对萨尔迪斯的发掘活动以及美国雅典研究院在雅典广场及卫城1931年开始持续至今的考古发掘活动。通过上述专业的考古发掘活动及其随后整理出版的大量考古报告,英美国家古希腊研究的研究基础大为扩展,加之碑铭、纸草文献、钱币学等辅助学科的进步,使英美国家的古希腊法研究突破了人们对古典文献的迷信,不再是对古代文献的摘编。

英美国家古希腊法系统研究的真正展开始于20世纪初,随后出现了一大批知名学者和重要作品。在美国,早期的代表人物包括:约翰逊教授对古希腊的司法行政制度进行了深入的研究,著有《雅典法律中的证据制度》(1905年)、《荷马时代的司法行政》(1911年)、《古代雅典的律师和立法者》(1927年)、《从荷马到亚里士多德的司法行政》(1930年)以及论文《雅典仲裁员的司法管辖权》(1907年);卡尔霍恩教授的研究重点则为古希腊法理学,著有《希腊法与现代法理学》(1923年)、《古希腊法律的研究材料》(1924年)、《古希腊刑法的成长》(1927年)、《古希腊法律科学》(1944年)等。近年来,美国学者加加林教授的古希腊法律史研究开始引起国际关注,他从研究古希腊演说家的法庭演说词入手对古希腊法展开了广泛的研究,代表作为专著《早期希腊法》(1989年)、主编《剑桥古希腊法指南》(2005年)等,以及大量专题论文。在英国,学者对古希腊法的研究更为系统全面,代表作为琼斯的《希腊人的法律与法律理论》(1956年),哈里森教授的《雅典法:家庭和财产法》(1968年)、《雅典法:程序法》(1971年)、《公元前4世纪雅典的法律审查法院》(1977年),麦克道威尔的《古典雅典的法律》(1978年)、《斯巴达法》(1995年)等。此外,也有深入的个案研究,如菲舍对僭越法律问题的研究等。

第二章　英国的古希腊法律史研究

随着英国在19世纪下半叶成为世界霸主以及随之而来的经济繁荣和庞大的殖民帝国带来的发掘场所，使包括古希腊法律史研究在内的英国古典史研究逐渐蓬勃发展起来。这一时期是大量收集整理资料、建立各种研究会和专业研究机构（如1886年英国雅典研究院的建立）的时代，也是碑铭学、纸草文献学、钱币学等辅助学科大发展的时代。尤为值得一提的是，英国学者利用英国在埃及殖民统治的便利，考古发掘出土了大量有关希腊罗马的草纸文献，这其中就包括《雅典政制》的发现以及据信是提奥庞普斯《希腊史》的残篇等一些鲜为人知的作品，还有希腊化时期托勒密王朝的大量法律文献。这些基础性工作的广泛开展，为20世纪英国古典学及古希腊法律史研究的系统展开提供了坚实的基础。

一、19世纪至20世纪初英国的古希腊法律史学者和作品

（一）乔治·格罗特（George Grote，1794～1871年）

格罗特是19世纪至20世纪初英国最著名的古希腊学者之一，他对雅典民主与宪法制度的深入探究为英国古希腊法律史研究的系统展开奠定了学术基础。格罗特出身于英国肯特郡的一个德国移民新教徒家庭，16岁中学毕业后，从父命进入银行工作。此后深受边沁功利主义哲学影响，认识到只有民主政治最能反映社会大多数

人的利益,因此积极参与英国的议会改革运动,并最终转向对古代民主政治制度的研究。1826~1830年,格罗特偕同穆勒、布鲁姆创办伦敦大学学院(University College London,UCL),历任该校委员、司库、主席,1862年晋升为副校长,直至去世,其间曾当选为国会议员。1842年格罗特游历意大利,归国后致力于古希腊史的研究工作。他著有《从远古时代到亚历山大大帝同辈人去世的希腊史》(12卷),上起传说时期,下迄马其顿国王亚历山大东征,该书史料翔实,结构严谨,是西方史学名著之一;另著有《柏拉图以及苏格拉底的其他学侣》(3卷)①、《亚里士多德》(2卷)②作为《希腊史》的续编和补充。此外,还有《议会改革问题探讨》《议会改革要义》③等著述。

格罗特所著的《希腊史》,起自传说时期,止于马其顿王亚历山大的军事扩张,取材丰富、条理清楚。格罗特落笔前曾收集了大量的资料,借鉴了前人的成果,构思20余年。这部巨著分12大卷,历时10年才出版完毕。格罗特继承启蒙时期欧洲史学家的优秀传统,把"理性主义"的精神贯彻在历史研究中,坚持历史著述必须是纪实,以公元前776年所举行的第一次奥林匹克竞技会作为希腊信史的开端。④ 约翰·穆勒在评价此部著作时曾说:"在他未重新作出论断以前,希腊历史上有许多重大的事都是暧昧不明的,而在这以后,一部希腊史便完全可以理解了。"该书的不足之处在于详于政事,略于社会经济;详于雅典,略于希腊其他各邦。不过格罗特所著的《希腊史》的上述不足之处恰恰成为其本人在雅典民主与法律制度研究方面做出重大贡献的前提条件。

格罗特在《希腊史》一书中把雅典历史作为整个希腊历史的中心与主要线索,并把自克里斯提尼以来的雅典民主史作为其研究的核心,认为克里斯提尼改革及其所建立的一系列制度奠定了雅典民主制度的基本框架,人民主权是雅典民主产生的根本原因。据此,否定了梭伦作为雅典民主政治建立者的一般观点,从而成功地将民主政治与僭主政治分离开来。众所周知,自古以来众多学者都将民主政治(梭伦倡导)的放纵与庇西特拉图僭主政治的建立联系起来,格罗特则认为,梭伦改革仅仅是雅典民主政治的前奏,公元前510年僭主被推翻后克里斯提

---

① George Grote(1865),*Plato,and the other Companions of Sokrates.*

② George Grote(1872),*Aristotle*(edited by Alexander Bain and G. Croom Robertson),Volume 1, Volume 2.

③ George Grote(1831),*Essentials of Parliamentary Reform.*

④ George Grote(1846 – 1856),*A History of Greece:From the Earliest Period to the Close of the Generation Contemporary with Alexander the Great.*

尼所推行的政治改革才真正建立了雅典的民主制度。格罗特还拿出较多篇幅对古典时期雅典民主政治研究的众多误区一一更正,特别是对雅典激进民主制、智者派哲学家的行为作出了强有力的辩护。格罗特进行这些研究的最终目的是昭示希腊人在政治和法律(宪法)制度方面的巨大成就,强调希腊人对当今世界的最大贡献是其所倡导的政治自由。从这个角度出发,格罗特对雅典僭主政治和马其顿的集权统治都采取负面评价态度。

格罗特对雅典民主和宪法制度的研究得到了后世广泛的赞誉,许多学者都围绕格罗特的论述对古希腊相关制度展开研究,如法国古希腊法学家索曼教授专门以《对格罗特〈希腊史〉中有关雅典宪政历史论述的评论》为题的专著形式对格罗特雅典宪法论述做出回应;①英国学者鲍桑葵也撰有《格罗特的〈雅典宪法〉》一文对格罗特的雅典民主研究做出较高评价。② 我国学者郭圣铭也认为格罗特《希腊史》体大精深,是19世纪英国史学家中最有成就的著作,③因而将其第46章《伯里克利时代雅典宪政和司法制度的变迁》译出,收入吴于廑主编的《外国史学名著选》。④

(二)爱德华·奥古斯·弗里曼(Edward Augustus Freeman,1832~1892年)

弗里曼1832年出生于英国伯明翰郊区,后就读于牛津大学三一学院,1884年任牛津大学讲座教授。在古代史研究方面,弗里曼撰有《雅典民主》《荷马与荷马时代》等论文,对雅典民主政治给予高度评价。弗里曼同时撰有《西西里史》⑤和《古希腊和意大利联邦政府史》⑥两本专著,前者对古希腊在西西里的殖民城邦叙拉古的僭主政治进行了深入的研究,后者对古代希腊的联邦政府如近邻同盟(Amphictyonic League)、比奥提亚同盟、阿凯亚同盟和埃托利亚同盟进行了详尽的分析,是第一部系统研究古希腊联邦法律制度的专著。

(三)詹姆斯·威克里夫·海德拉姆(James Wycliffe Headlam,1863~1929年)

海德拉姆于1863年出生于英国诺森伯兰的一个牧师家庭,先后就读于伊顿公学和剑桥大学,1894年至1900年任英国玛丽女王学院希腊史和古代史教授。

---

① Schömann G. F. (1854), Die Verfassungsgeschichte Athens nach Grote's History of Greece, Kritisch geprüft, Leipzig.

② Bosanquet B. (1877), "Grote on the Athenian Constitution", *The Academy* 12, pp. 220 - 221.

③ 郭圣铭:《西方史学史概要》,上海人民出版社1983年版,第164页、第166页。

④ 参见吴于廑主编:《外国史学名著选》(上),商务印书馆1986年版。

⑤ Edward Augustus Freeman (1891 - 1894), *History of Sicily*, 4 Vols, The Clarendon Press.

⑥ Edward Augustus Freeman (1863), *History of the Federal Government from the Foundation of the Archaian League to the disruption of the United States.*

海德拉姆教授在古希腊法律史研究方面的代表作有专著《雅典的抽签选举制度》[①]以及论文《格尔蒂出土铭文中的程序》[②]、《阿提卡法中的"proklesis eis basanon"》[③]、《对C. V. Thompson〈雅典奴隶侵权〉一文的回复》[④]等。在《雅典的抽签选举制度》一书中，海德拉姆认为抽签是雅典民主政治的基本标志，通过抽签制度可以保证人民真正行使统治权，因为雅典官员和近代选举产生的部长不同，"他们不是那种人民通过投票，把事务的最高管理权委托给他们的智慧和处置权的人，他们是被指定来执行人民的命令，并服从其命令的人"。[⑤]

（四）阿贝·尔亨迪·琼斯·格林尼奇（Abel Hendy Jones Greenidge，1865～1906年）

格林尼奇于1865年出生于巴巴多斯，先后于1891年和1904年获得牛津大学古典学硕士和博士学位，1892年开始任职于牛津大学哈特福学院，1906年英年早逝。格林尼奇在古希腊法律史研究方面的代表作是1896年出版的《古希腊宪政史手册》一书。[⑥]

（五）阿尔弗雷德·埃克哈德·齐默恩（Alfred Eckhard Zimmern，1879～1957年）

齐默恩曾于1930年到1944年担任牛津大学国际关系学教授，他在古希腊法律史方面的研究成果主要包括专著《希腊共和国》（1918年）[⑦]等，该书主要研究了公元前5世纪雅典的社会经济和法律制度，认为雅典不存在发达的商品经济，反对用现在的经济术语去理解和解释古代的经济。同时，齐默恩也认为，雅典民主的优势不在于其制度设计如何先进，而是雅典民主的整套制度更适合雅典人发挥他们的才能。换言之，雅典城邦的优势在于，它给每个公民创造的那种亲身参与政治运作的幸福感。

---

① James Wycliffe Headlam (1891), *Election by Lot at Athens*, Cambridge (Cambridge historical essays 4).

② James Wycliffe Headlam (1892 – 1893), "The Procedure of the Gortynian Inscription", *JHS* 13, pp. 48 – 69.

③ James Wycliffe Headlam (1893), "On the Proklesis eis Basanon in Attic Law", *CR* 7, pp. 1 – 5.

④ James Wycliffe Headlam (1894), "In Answer to C. V. Thompson's Article on Slave Torture in Athens", *CR* 8, pp. 136 – 137.

⑤ James Wycliffe Headlam (1991), *Election by Lot at Athens*, Cambridge, p. 27.

⑥ Abel Hendy Jones Greenidge (1914), *A handbook of Greek Constitutional History*, London.

⑦ Zimmern, A. E. (1924), *The Greek Commonwealth: Politics and Economics in Fifth-century Athens*, Oxford.

（六）阿诺德·威科姆·戈麦（Arnold Wycombe Gomme，1886～1959年）

戈麦早年毕业于英国剑桥大学三一学院，1911年至1957年任教于英国格拉斯哥大学，1947年任英国人文和社会科学学院院士。戈麦最重要的学术贡献是，完成了巨大篇幅的权威著作《修昔底德历史注疏》[①]，他在古希腊法律史研究方面的成果主要包括专著《公元前5世纪至公元前4世纪雅典的人口》[②]、《希腊历史和文化论集》[③]等，以及论文《伯利克里君主》[④]、《关于雅典公民身份法的两个问题》[⑤]等。戈麦对雅典人口问题的分析对研究雅典政治与法律制度具有重要意义，他从雅典军队数量、谷物供应与消费、德谟名单、议事会成员及铭文中收集有关资料，最后估计的雅典人口数据是：公元前431年阿提卡地区总人口约31万人，其中奴隶约11万人；公元前323年总人口为25万～26万人，奴隶约10万人。尽管戈麦的雅典人口统计数据未必准确，但可为后世分析雅典的选举制度与公民大会运作法律制度提供相对可行的人口数据参照物。

（七）凯瑟琳·弗里曼（Kathleen Freeman，1897～1959年）

弗里曼一直就读于英国南威尔士大学学院，于1940年获得该校文学博士学位，并自1919起任教于该校古典学专业。她在古希腊法律史研究方面的成果主要包括专著《梭伦的工作与生平》[⑥]、《谋杀赫罗德斯和雅典法庭的其他审判》[⑦]等以及论文《舞者之秘》[⑧]等。在《梭伦的工作与生平》一书中，弗里曼着重分析了梭伦改革的主要内容，认为梭伦对雅典先前的政治制度并未在宪法上进行大的变

---

① Gomme, A. W., *A Historical Commentary on Thucydides*. Vol. Ⅰ: Introduction and Commentary on Book Ⅰ, Oxford: Clarendon Press; Toronto: Oxford University Press, 1945. Vols. Ⅱ – Ⅲ: The Ten Years' War (Books Ⅱ – Ⅲ and Books Ⅳ – Ⅴ), Oxford: Clarendon Press; Toronto: Oxford University Press, 1956. Vol. Ⅳ: Books Ⅴ. 25 – Ⅶ (with A. Andrewes and K. J. Dover), Oxford: Clarendon Press, 1970. Vol. Ⅴ: Book Ⅷ (with A. Andrewes and K. J. Dover), Oxford: Clarendon Press, 1981.

② Gomme, A. W. (1933), *The Population of Athens in the Fifth and Fourth Centuries B. C.*

③ Gomme, A. W. (1937), *Essays in Greek History and Literature*, Oxford: Basil Blackwell.

④ Gomme, A. W. (1950), "Pericles monarchos", *JHS* 70, 77. (= Perikles und seine Zeit, 143, Darmstadt 1979 (Wege der Forschung 412)).

⑤ Gomme, A. W. (1934), "Two Problems on Athenian Citizenship Law", *CPh* 29, 123 – 140 (= *Essays in Greek History and Literature*, 67 – 86, Oxford 1937).

⑥ Freeman, K. (1926), *The Work and Life of Solon*, with a Translation of his Poems, Cardiff, University of Wales Press Board.

⑦ Freeman, K. (1946), *The Murder of Herodes and other Trials from the Athenian Law Courts*, London.

⑧ Freeman, K. (1952), "The Mystery of the Choreutes", in White, M. E. (ed), *Studies in Honour of G. Norwood*, 85 – 94, Toronto.

动,而是尽可能地运用原来的机构,只是在机构相互关系中充分运用了制衡原则,如公民大会制约400人议事会、民众法庭监管官员等,她还探讨了梭伦关于吸引外邦人到雅典定居的法律的真实性问题。

二、20世纪中后期至今英国的古希腊法律史学者和作品

(一)道格拉斯·莫里斯·麦克道威尔(Douglas Maurice MacDowell,1931～2010年)

麦克道威尔是20世纪英国著名的古希腊法律史学家,早年毕业于牛津大学贝利奥尔学院,曾任职于曼彻斯特大学、格拉斯哥大学,是爱丁堡皇家学会和英国皇家学会的资深会员。2010年格拉斯哥大学收到麦克道威尔教授240万英镑的遗嘱捐赠,这些资金被用来建立以他的名字命名的古希腊教授职位。麦克道威尔在古希腊法律史研究方面的代表作有专著《演说家时代的雅典杀人法》①、《古典时期雅典的法律》②、《斯巴达法》③等,还编辑出版了涉及古希腊法律的多部古典作品,包括《德摩斯梯尼:诉梅地亚斯》④、阿里斯托芬的《马蜂》⑤、《安多西德:On the Mysteries》⑥、《德摩斯梯尼:使团辞》⑦、《德摩斯梯尼:演说词27～38》⑧等。

麦克道威尔教授关于古希腊法律史研究的论文主要包括以下几个方面。

1. 在古希腊整体法律制度研究方面的成果主要包括《希腊法》⑨、《公元前4世纪雅典的立法》⑩、《公元前401年至公元前398年雅典演说年表和法律创新》⑪、《"德摩斯梯尼29(诉Aphobos Ⅲ)"作为认识雅典法律渊源的可靠性》⑫、

---

① MacDowell, D. M. (1963), *Athenian Homicide Law in the Age of the Orators*, Manchester.

② MacDowell, D. M. (1978), *The Law in Classical Athens*, London.

③ MacDowell, D. M. (1986), *Spartan Law*, Edinburgh (Scottish Classical Studies 1).

④ MacDowell, D. M. (1990), *Demosthenes: Against Meidias (Oration 21)*, Oxford.

⑤ MacDowell, D. M. (1971), *Aristophanes' Wasps*, Oxford.

⑥ MacDowell, D. M. (1962), *Andocides: On the Mysteries*, Oxford.

⑦ MacDowell, D. M. (2000a), *Demosthenes: On the False Embassy* (Oration 19), Oxford.

⑧ MacDowell, D. M. (2004a), *Demosthenes: Speeches* 27 – 38, Austin, Tx (The oratory of classical Greece 8).

⑨ MacDowell, D. M. (1988), "Greek law", in Grant, R. M. & R. Kitzinger (eds), *Civilisations of the ancient Mediterranean* Ⅰ, 589 – 605, New York.

⑩ MacDowell, D. M. (1975), "Law-making at Athens in the fourth century B. C.", *JHS* 95, 62 – 74.

⑪ MacDowell, D. M. (1971), "The Chronology of Athenian Speeches and Legal Innovations in 401 – 398 B. C.", *RIDA* 18, 267 – 273.

⑫ MacDowell, D. M. (1989), "The Authenticity of Demosthenes 29 (Against Aphobos Ⅲ) as a Source of Information about Athenian Law", in Symposion 1985, 253 – 263.

《爱与法律：米南德〈盾牌〉随笔》①、《阿里斯托芬和雅典法律》②等。

2. 在古希腊刑事法律研究方面的研究成果主要包括《雅典关于"epobelia"的刑罚》③、《雅典关于贿赂犯罪的法律》④、《〈希波吕托斯〉中的过失杀人》⑤、《雅典关于同性恋的法律》⑥、《雅典公民中的败类(混蛋)》⑦、《雅典的"Hybris"》⑧等。

3. 在古希腊程序法律研究方面的研究成果主要包括《演说家记载的雅典"dokimasia"程序》⑨、《雅典公共犯罪的审判期限》⑩、《阿里斯托芬和雅典法庭》⑪、《法西斯城雅典人的诉讼程序》⑫、《雅典关于合唱制度的法律》⑬等。

4. 在古希腊婚姻家庭法律研究方面的研究成果主要包括《阿里斯托芬记载的外国出生(人士)和雅典公民权》⑭、《雅典法律中的家族》⑮等。

5. 在古希腊经济民商事法律研究方面的研究成果主要包括《雅典法中的矿业案例》⑯、《凯里尼的财政盈余和雅典人的税收特权》⑰、《佩里安德关于捐助团的法律》⑱等。

---

① MacDowell, D. M. (1982), "Love Versus Law: An Essay on Menander's Aspis", *G & R* 29, 42 – 52.

② MacDowell, D. M. (2010), "Aristophanes and Athenian Law", in *Law and Drama in Ancient Greece*, 147 – 157.

③ MacDowell, D. M. (2009), "The Athenian Penalty of Epobelia", in Symposion 2007, 87 – 94.

④ MacDowell, D. M. (1983), "Athenian Laws about Bribery", *RIDA* 30, 57 – 78.

⑤ MacDowell, D. M. (1968), "Unintentional Homicide in the Hippolytos", *RhM* 111, 156 – 158.

⑥ MacDowell, D. M. (2000c), "Athenian Laws about Homosexuality", *RIDA* 47, 13 – 27.

⑦ MacDowell, D. M. (1976a), "Bastards as Athenian Citizens", *CQ* 26, 88 – 91.

⑧ MacDowell, D. M. (1976b), "Hybris in Athens", *G & R* 23, 14 – 31.

⑨ MacDowell, D. M. (2005), "The Athenian Procedure of Dokimasia of Orators", in Symposion 2001, 79 – 87 (with a reply by Gagliardi, L., 89 – 97).

⑩ MacDowell, D. M. (2000), "The Length of Trials for Public Offences in Athens", in *Polis and Politics*, 563 – 568.

⑪ MacDowell, D. M. (1992), "O Aristophanes kai ta Atheniaka dikasteria", in *Symboles* Ⅰ, 137 – 158.

⑫ MacDowell, D. M. (1991), "The Athenian Procedure of Phasis", in Symposion 1990, 187 – 98.

⑬ MacDowell, D. M. (1989a), "Athenian Laws about Choruses", in Symposion 1982, 65 – 78.

⑭ MacDowell, D. M. (1993), "Foreign Birth and Athenian Citizenship in Aristophanes", in Sommerstein A. H., Halliwell J., Henderson J. & B. Zimmermann (eds), *Tragedy, Comedy and the Polis*, 359 – 371, London.

⑮ MacDowell, D. M. (1989), "The Oikos in Athenian Law", *CQ* 39, 10 – 21.

⑯ MacDowell, D. M. (2006), "Mining Cases in Athenian Law", in Symposion 2003, 121 – 140.

⑰ MacDowell, D. M. (2004), "Epikerdes of Kyrene and the Athenian Privilege of Ateleia", *ZPE* 150, 127 – 133.

⑱ MacDowell, D. M. (1986), "The Law of Periandros about Symmories", *CQ* 36, 438 – 449.

(二)爱德华·M.哈里斯(Edward M. Harris)

哈里斯现为英国杜伦大学古代史教授,曾兼任美国普林斯顿大学高等研究院研究员和美国驻雅典古典研究院研究员。哈里斯教授的古希腊法律史研究主要集中于雅典的政治和法律制度,代表作有专著《斯基涅斯和雅典政治》①、《古希腊的法律与法庭》②、《古典雅典的民主与法治》③、《民主雅典下法治的实际运转》④等。哈里斯教授还翻译出版了《德摩斯梯尼:演说词20~22》⑤,并与他人编辑出版了《古希腊的法律和喜剧》⑥、《欧洲古希腊和希腊化法年会论文集(2007卷)》⑦等作品。

哈里斯教授关于古希腊法律史研究的论文主要包括以下几个方面。

1.在古希腊整体法律制度研究方面的成果主要包括《古希腊城邦的法治和军事组织》⑧、《雅典法律包括哪些:雅典成文法的实体法和程序法》⑨、《雅典民主制中的法治:基于司法宣誓的反思》⑩、《谁是雅典的执法者?》⑪、《梭伦与古希腊法律精神》⑫、《关于雅典法律开放性结构的进一步思考》⑬、《立法者迪庇第斯:基于

① Harris,E. M. (1995),*Aeschines and Athenian Politics*,New York and Oxford.

② Edward M. Harris & Lene Rubinstein(2004),*The Law and the Courts in Ancient Greece*,London.

③ Harris,E. M. (2006),*Democracy and the Rule of Law in Classical Athens*,Cambridge University Press.

④ Harris,E. M. (2013),*The Rule of Law in Action in Democratic Athens*,Oxford University Press.

⑤ Harris,E. M. (2008),*Demosthenes:Speeches* 20–22,Austin,Texas:University of Texas Press.

⑥ Harris,E. M., Leao, Delfim & Rhodes, Peter J. (2010), *Law and Drama in Ancient Greece*. London:Duckworth.

⑦ Harris,E. M. & Thür, G. (2009), Symposion 2007:Akten der Gesellschaft für griechische und hellenistisch Rechtsgeschichte(Durham,2–6 September 2007),Vienna.

⑧ Harris,E. M. (2010a),"The Rule of Law and Military Organization in the Greek Polis",in Thür, G. (ed)Symposion 2009,Vorträge zur griechischen und hellenistischen Rechtsgeschichte(Seggau,25. –30. August 2009),405–18,Wien.

⑨ Harris,E. M. (2009–2010),"What are the Laws of Athens about? Substance and Procedure in Athenian Statutes?",Dike 12–13,5–67.

⑩ Harris,E. M. (2007c),"The Rule of Law in Athenian Democracy, Reflections on the Judicial Oath",in Etica e politica/Ethics and Politics 9,55–74(=Dike 9(2006)157–181).

⑪ Harris,E. M. (2007a),"Who Enforced the Law in Classical Athens?",in Symposion 2005,159–176.

⑫ Harris,E. M. (2006a),"Solon and the Spirit of the Laws in Archaic and Classical Greece",in Solon of Athens,290–320(=Harris,Democracy and the rule of law,3–28).

⑬ Harris,E. M. (2004d),"More Thoughts on Open Texture in Athenian Law",in Nomos. Direito e sociedade,241–262.

阿里斯多芬〈云〉的研究》①、《雅典法律的开放性结构》②、《律师安提戈涅,抑或法律的模糊性》③、《雅典公民大会召开的频次如何?》④、《对5000人宪法的分析》⑤、《5000人大会的宪法》⑥、《法律和演说词》⑦等。

2. 在古希腊刑事法律研究方面的研究成果主要包括《俄狄浦斯有罪吗? 索福克勒斯和雅典杀人法》⑧、《希腊化时期的雅典是否存在强奸:涉及性暴力法律的进一步反思》⑨、《在阿提卡希腊如何实施凶杀:动词 kteinein 的语义及其对雅典杀人法的影响》⑩、《吕西阿斯(三)和雅典的复仇观念》⑪、《是否雅典人认为诱奸是比强奸更为严重的犯罪?》⑫等。

3. 在古希腊程序法律研究方面的研究成果主要包括《雅典法庭是否试图过实现一致性? ——雅典司法行政中的口头传统和书面记录》⑬、《欺骗还是法治? 古典雅典诉讼的性质》⑭、《"epieikeia"在雅典法庭中的作用》⑮、《雅典法律对轻率起

---

① Harris, E. M. (2002a), "Pheidippides the Legislator: A Note on Aristophanes' Clouds", *ZPE* 140, 3–5(= Harris, *Democracy and the Rule of Law*, 425–430).

② Harris, E. M. (2000), "Open Texture in Athenian Law", Dike 3, 29–79.

③ Harris, E. M. (2004b), "Antigone the Lawyer, or the Ambiguities of Nomos", in *The Law and the Courts*, 19–56(= Harris, *Democracy and the Rule of Law*, 41–80).

④ Harris, E. M. (1986), "How Often Did he Athenian Assembly Meet?", *Classical Quarterly* 36: 363–377.

⑤ Harris, E. M. (1997b), "A Note on the Constitution of the Five Thousand", *ZPE* 116, 300.

⑥ Harris, E. M. (1990a), "The constitution of the Five Thousand", *HSCP* 93, 243–280.

⑦ Harris, E. M. (1993a), "Law and oratory", in Worthington, I. (ed), *Persuasion: Greek Rhetoric in Action*, 130–152, London.

⑧ Harris, E. M. (2010b), "Is Oedipus Guilty? Sophocles and Athenian Homicide Law", in *Law and Drama in Ancient Greece*, 122–146.

⑨ Harris, E. M. (2004a), "Did Rape Exist in Hellenistic Athens? Further Reflections on the Laws about Sexual Violence", Dike 7, 41–83(= Harris, *Democracy and the Rule of Law*, 297–331).

⑩ Harris, E. M. (2001), "How to Kill in Attic Greek: The Semantics of the Verb(apo) Kteinein and Their Implications for Athenian Homicide Law", in Symposion 1997, 75–88(= Harris, *Democracy and the Rule of Law*, 391–404).

⑪ Harris, E. M. (1997a), "Lysias Ⅲ and the Athenian Beliefs about Revenge", *CQ* 47, 363–366.

⑫ Harris, E. M. (1990b), "Did the Athenians Regard Seduction as a Worse Crime than Rape?", *CQ* 40, 370–377(= Harris, *Democracy and the Rule of Law*, 283–296).

⑬ Harris, E. M. (2007b), "Did the Athenian Courts Attempt to Achieve Consistency? Oral Tradition and Written Records in the Athenian Administration of Justice", in *Politics of Orality*, 343–370.

⑭ Harris, E. M. (2005), "Feuding or the Rule of Law? The Nature of Litigation in Classical Athens: An Essay in Legal Sociology", in Symposion 2001, 125–141.

⑮ Harris, E. M. (2004c), "Le rôle de l'epieikeia dans les tribunaux athéniens", *RHDFE* 82, 1–13.

诉行为的处罚》①、《阿波罗多罗斯"控告提谟修斯演说词"的时间和它对雅典历史和法律程序的隐喻》②、《蒂马尔科斯的审判日期》③等。

4. 在古希腊婚姻家庭法律研究方面的研究成果主要包括《对收养和德谟注册关系的研究》④、《雅典社会的妇女和借贷:通过一个舞蹈的重申审视》⑤等。

5. 在古希腊经济民商事法律研究方面的研究成果主要包括《罗马法和古希腊法中的抵押权比较研究》⑥、《古典时期雅典的法律和经济:以德摩斯梯尼演说词"Against Dionysodorus"为中心》⑦、《梭伦是否废除了债务奴隶制》⑧、《对新谷物税法的研究》⑨、《对解负令之谜的最新答案》⑩、《Apotimema:适用于租赁和嫁妆协议的实物担保术语》⑪、《雅典法中商业伙伴的责任》⑫、《何时交易不再是交易?雅典不动产抵押品术语之谜的重新审视》⑬等。

---

① Harris, E. M. (1999b), "The Penalty for Frivolous Prosecutions in Athenian Law", Dike 2, 123 - 142 (= Harris, *Democracy and the Rule of Law*, 405 - 422).

② Harris, E. M. (1988a), "The Date of Apollodorus' Speech Against Timotheus and its Implications for Athenian History and Legal Procedure", *AJPh* 109, 44 - 52 (= Harris, *Democracy and the Rule of Law*, 355 - 364).

③ Harris, E. M. (1985), "The Date of the Trial of Timarchus", *Hermes* 113, 376 - 380.

④ Harris, E. M. (1996), "A Note on Adoption and Deme Registration", *Tyche* 11, 123 - 127 (= Harris, *Democracy and the Rule of Law*, 365 - 370).

⑤ Harris, E. M. (1992), "Women and Lending in Athenian Society: A Horos Re-examined", *Phoenix* 46, 309 - 321 (= Harris, *Democracy and the Rule of Law*, 333 - 346).

⑥ Harris, E. M. (2012), "Hypotheca in Roman Law and Hypotheke in Greek Law", in Legras, B. (ed) Transferts culturels et droits dans le monde grec et hellénistique (Actes du colloque international, Reims, 14 - 17 mai 2008), 433 - 441, Paris.

⑦ Harris, E. M. (2006b), "Law and Economy in Classical Athens: [Demosthenes] Against Dionysodorus", in Harris, *Democracy and the Rule of Law*, 143 - 162.

⑧ Harris, E. M. (2002b), "Did Solon Abolish Debt-bondage?", *CQ* 52, 415 - 430 (= Harris, *Democracy and the Rule of Law*, 249 - 270).

⑨ Harris, E. M. (1999a), "Notes on the New Grain-tax Law", *ZPE* 128, 269 - 272.

⑩ Harris, E. M. (1997c), "A New Solution to the Riddle of the Seisachtheia", in *The Development of the Polis*, 103 - 112.

⑪ Harris, E. M. (1993b), "Apotimema: Athenian Terminology for Real Security in Leases and Dowry Agreement", *CQ* 43, 73 - 95 (= Harris, *Democracy and the Rule of Law*, 207 - 240).

⑫ Harris, E. M. (1989), "The Liability of Business Partners in Athenian Law: The Dispute between Lycon and Megacleides ([Dem.] 52. 20 - 1)", *CQ* 39, 339 - 343 (= Harris, *Democracy and the Rule of Law*, 241 - 248).

⑬ Harris, E. M. (1988b), "When a Sale is Not a Sale? The Riddle of Athenian Terminology for Real Security Revisited", *CQ* 38, 351 - 381 (= Harris, *Democracy and the Rule of Law*, 163 - 206).

（三）阿利克·罗宾·沃尔沙姆·哈里森（Alick Robin Walsham Harrison，1900～1969年）

哈里森1900年出生于英国萨里的萨尔顿，后毕业于牛津大学默顿学院，1950年开始任教于牛津大学，1963年当选默顿学院院长。哈里森的主要研究方向为古代世界的法律制度，他在古希腊法律史研究方面的成果主要包括专著《雅典法》（卷1：《家庭和财产法》；卷2：《程序法》），以及论文《德拉古的"protos axon"》①、《公元前5世纪末雅典的法律制定》②、《雅典无遗嘱继承规则存在的问题》③等。

（四）彼得·约翰·罗德斯（Peter John Rhodes，1940年至今）

罗德斯是当代英国最著名的古典学者之一，现任杜伦大学古代史专业荣誉教授，主要研究方向为古希腊政治和法律制度。罗德斯早年就读于牛津大学瓦德汉学院，获古典文学方向博士学位，1965年任英国杜伦大学古典和古代史专业讲师，1977年晋升为高级讲师，1983年被任命为古代史教授，2005年退休成为该校荣誉教授，1987年任英国国家人文和社会科学学院院士，2005年任丹麦皇家学院外籍院士，2014年至2015年任英国古典协会主席。罗德斯教授在古希腊法律史研究方面的研究成果主要包括专著《雅典五百人议事会》④、《亚里士多德〈雅典政制〉评注》⑤、《雅典帝国》⑥、《希腊城邦国家》⑦、《古希腊各城邦国家法律》⑧等，以及论文《公民意识和公民权》⑨、《雅典铭文中的国家和宗教》⑩、《古希腊世界的条

---

① Harrison, A. R. W. (1961), "Drakon's Protos Axon", *CQ* 11, 3－5.

② Harrison, A. R. W. (1955), "Law-Making at Athens at the End of the Fifth Century B. C.", *JHS* 75, 26－35.

③ Harrison, A. R. W. (1947), "A Problem in the Rules of Intestate Succession at Athens", *CR* 61, 41－42.

④ Rhodes, P. J., (1972) *The Athenian Boule*, Oxford University Press, 1972.

⑤ Rhodes, P. J., *A Commentary on the Aristotelian Athenaion Politeia*, Oxford University Press, 1981.

⑥ Rhodes, P. J., *The Athenian Empire*, Oxford University Press, 1985.

⑦ P. J. Rhodes, *The Greek City States: A Source Book*, Groom Helm, London, 1986.

⑧ P. J. Rhodes and David M. Lewis, *The Decrees of the Greek States*, Clarendon Press, 1997.

⑨ Rhodes, P. J. (2009b), "Civic ideology and citizenship", in *Greek and Roman Political Thought*, 57－69.

⑩ Rhodes, P. J. (2009a), "State and Religion in Athenian Inscriptions", *G & R* 56, 1－13.

约制定和条约违背》[1]、《区域(管理行政区)》[2]、《政治生活中的宣誓》[3]、《梭伦的法律和改革:基于乐观的看法》[4]、《亚里士多德〈雅典政制〉中的雅典法律》[5]、《公元前4世纪雅典的陪审员会议》[6]、《雅典的寡头》[7]、《古希腊国家的公共文件》[8]、《再论德摩提昂族与德凯莱亚人(何为胞族)》[9]、《碑铭证据:法律和法令》[10]、《公元前4世纪雅典的司法程序:提升抑或简单改变》[11]、《涉及海帕波拉斯的陶片放逐》[12]、《古希腊城邦:德漠、城市和联盟》[13]、《公元前410年至前399年的雅典法典》[14]、《古典雅典的"Nomothesia"程序》[15]、《公元前4世纪雅典的"Nomothesia"程序》[16]、《斯巴达检察官的选举》[17]、《雅典的检举程序》[18]、《具有雅典公民身份的私生子》[19]等。

(五)保罗·卡特里奇(Paul Cartledge,1947年至今)

卡特里奇早年毕业于牛津大学,在约翰·博德曼(John Boardman)教授指导

---

① Rhodes, P. J. (2008), "Making and Breaking Treaties in the Greek World", in de Souza, Ph. & S. J. France (eds), *War and Peace in Ancient and Medieval History*, 6 - 27, Cambridge.

② Rhodes, P. J. (2007b), "Dioikesis", *Chiron* 37, 349 - 362.

③ Rhodes, P. J. (2007a), "Oaths in Political Life", in *Horkos*, 11 - 25.

④ Rhodes, P. J. (2006), "The Reforms and Laws of Solon: An Optimistic View", in *Solon of Athens*, 261 - 275.

⑤ Rhodes, P. J. (2004b), "The Laws of Athens in the Aristotelian Athenaion Politeia", in *Nomos. Direito e Sociedade*, 75 - 90.

⑥ Rhodes, P. J. (2003), "Sessions of Nomothetai in Fourth-century Athens", *CQ* 53, 124 - 129.

⑦ Rhodes, P. J. (2002), "Oligarchs in Athens", in *Alternatives to Athens*, 119 - 136.

⑧ Rhodes, P. J. (2001), "Public Documents in the Greek States: Archives and Inscriptions", *G & R* 48, 33 - 44; 136 - 153.

⑨ Rhodes, P. J. (1997), "Deceleans and Demotionidae Again", *CQ* 47, 109 - 120.

⑩ Rhodes, P. J. (1995b), "Epigraphical Evidence: Laws and Decrees", in *Hansen, Sources*, 91 - 112.

⑪ Rhodes, P. J. (1995a), "Judicial Procedures in Fourth-century Athens: Improvement or Simply Change?", in *Die Athenische Demokratie*, 303 - 320.

⑫ Rhodes, P. J. (1994), "The Ostracism of Hyperbolus", in *Ritual, Finance, Politics*, 85 - 98.

⑬ Rhodes, P. J. (1993), "The Greek Poleis: Demes, Cities and Leagues", in Hansen, M. H. (ed), *The Ancient Greek City-state*, 161 - 182, Copenhagen.

⑭ Rhodes, P. J. (1991), "The Athenian Code of Laws, 410 - 399 BC", *JHS* 111, 87 - 100.

⑮ Rhodes, P. J. (1987), "Nomothesia in classical Athens", in *L'educazione Giuridica* V(ii), 5 - 26.

⑯ Rhodes, P. J. (1984), "Nomothesia in Fourth-century Athens", *CQ* 35, 55 - 60.

⑰ Rhodes, P. J. (1981b), "The Selection of Ephors at Sparta", *Historia* 30, 498 - 502.

⑱ Rhodes, P. J. (1979), "Eisangelia in Athens", *JHS* 99, 103 - 114.

⑲ Rhodes, P. J. (1978), "Bastards as Athenian Citizens", *CQ* 28, 89 - 92.

下获得博士学位（论文主题为《斯巴达考古学》），后任职于都柏林三一学院等多所大学，1979 年转入剑桥大学任职，2008 年至 2014 年任剑桥大学 A. G. Leventis 希腊文化讲席教授。卡特里奇教授的主要研究方向为古典时代的雅典和斯巴达，①他在古希腊法律史研究方面的成果主要包括专著《古希腊实践中的政治思想》②，主编《Nomos：雅典法律、政治和社会论文集》③、《Kosmos：古典雅典的秩序、冲突与社区论文集》④，以及论文《古希腊的"权利"、个人和社区》⑤、《斯巴达人的正义抑或监察官国家》⑥、《制定城邦法》⑦、《萌芽状态的幼虫：古希腊奴隶制的异质性》⑧、《家禽游戏：古典雅典的离奇诉讼》⑨、《一个新的公元前 5 世纪斯巴达条约》⑩等。

（六）N. R. E. 费舍尔（N. R. E. Fisher）

费舍尔教授现任职于英国卡迪夫大学，主要研究方向集中于古希腊社会生活中的"hybris"（傲慢）问题，包括与之相关的荣誉与法律等诸方面课题，他在古希腊法律史研究方面的成果主要包括专著《傲慢：古希腊社会中荣誉与耻辱价值研究》⑪、编译《埃斯奇奈斯"控告提马尔霍斯"》⑫，以及论文《古希腊社会的公民、外

---

① 卡特里奇在斯巴达研究领域的成果主要包括以下几部专著：*Spartan Reflections, a Collection of Essays New and Revised* (Duckworth, 2001), ISBN 0 - 7156 - 2966 - 2; *Sparta and Lakonia* (2nd edn. 2002); *Hellenistic and Roman Sparta* (rev. edns 2002), (with A. Spawforth); *The Spartans: An Epic History* (2nd edn, 2003)。

② Cartledge, P. (2009), *Ancient Greek Political Thought in Practice*, Cambridge University Press.

③ Cartledge, P., Paul Millett & Stephen Todd eds. (1991), *Nomos: Essays in Athenian Law, Politics and Society*, Cambridge University Press.

④ Cartledge, P., Paul Millett & Sitta von Reden eds. (2002), *Kosmos: Essays in Order, Conflict and Community in Classical Athens*, Cambridge University Press.

⑤ Cartledge, P. (2009), "'Rights', Individuals and Communities in Ancient Greece", in *Greek and Roman Political Thought*, 149 - 163.

⑥ Cartledge, P. (2000), "Spartan justice? or 'the state of the Ephors'?", Dike 3, 5 - 26.

⑦ Cartledge, P. (1998), "Laying down Polis Law", *CR* 49, 465 - 469.

⑧ Cartledge, P. (1993), "Like a Worm i' the Bud?: A Heterology of Classical Greek Slavery", *G & R* 40, 163 - 180.

⑨ Cartledge, P. (1990), "Fowl Play: A Curious Lawsuit in Classical Athens", in *Nomos*, 41 - 62.

⑩ Cartledge, P. (1976), "A New 5th-century Spartan Treaty", *LCM* 1, 87 - 92.

⑪ Fisher, N. R. E. (1992), "Hybris: A Study in the Values of Honour and Shame in Ancient Greece", Warminster.

⑫ Fisher, N. R. E. (2001), *Aeschines: Against Timarchos*, Oxford.

邦人和奴隶》[①]、《身体虐待：埃斯基涅斯“控告提马尔霍斯”中傲慢的修辞运用》[②]、《古希腊城邦国家的傲慢、复仇和内讧》[③]、《古典雅典的暴力、男子气概和法律》[④]、《恶棍车间：古典雅典是否存在大量的有组织的犯罪？》[⑤]、《饮酒、傲慢和斯巴达的和谐提升》[⑥]、《雅典涉及“hybris”的法律》[⑦]、《傲慢和不名誉》[⑧]等。

（七）大卫·怀特海德（David Whitehead）

怀特海德现任英国曼彻斯特大学教授，他在古希腊法律史研究方面的成果主要包括专著《希佩里德斯法庭演说词》[⑨]、《雅典外邦人的思想意识》[⑩]等，以及论文《希佩里德斯诉“Timandros”：观察和建议》[⑪]、《军事公诉中的雅典陪审团》[⑫]、《古希腊演说中的盗窃》[⑬]、《雅典人的缺席：吕西阿斯诉斐洛和吕库古斯诉列奥克拉特》[⑭]、《斯巴达宪法中的埃乎鲁斯》[⑮]、《公元前 5 世纪晚期雅典的法律和诉讼》[⑯]、

---

① Fisher, N. R. E. (2006), "Citizens, Foreigners and Slaves in Greek Society", in Kinzl, K. H. (ed), *A Companion to the Classical Greek World*, 327 – 349, Oxford.

② Fisher, N. R. E. (2005), "Body-abuse: The Rhetoric of Hybris in Aeschines' Against Timarchos", in *La violence*, 67 – 89.

③ Fisher, N. R. E. (2000), "Hybris, Revenge and Stasis in the Greek City-states", in van Wees, H. (ed), *War and Violence in Ancient Greece*, 83 – 123, London.

④ Fisher, N. R. E. (1999), "Violence, Masculinity and the Law in Classical Athens", in Foxhall, L. & J. Salmon (eds) *When Men were Men: Masculinity, Power and Identity in Classical Antiquity*, 68 – 97, London.

⑤ Fisher, N. R. E. (1999), "Workshops of Villains: Was there much Organised Crime in Classical Athens?", in Hopwood, K. (ed), *Organised Crime in Antiquity*, 53 – 96, London.

⑥ Fisher, N. R. E. (1989), "Drink, Hybris and the Promotion of Harmony in Sparta", in Powell, A. (ed), Classical Sparta. *The Techniques Behind Her Success*, 26 – 50, London.

⑦ Fisher, N. R. E. (1987), "La Legge Sulla Hybris ad Atene", *AION* (archeol) 9, 99 – 115 (= "The Law of Hybris in Athens", in *Nomos*, 123 – 138).

⑧ Fisher, N. R. E. (1976 – 1979), "Hybris and Dishonour", *G & R* 23, 177 – 93 & 26, 32 – 47.

⑨ Whitehead, D. (2000), *Hypereides. The Forensic Speeches*, Oxford.

⑩ Whitehead, D. (1977), *The Ideology of the Athenian Metic*, Cambridge (Cambridge Philological Society Suppl. 4).

⑪ Whitehead, D. (2009b), "Hypereides' Timandros: Observations and Suggestion", *BICS* 52, 135 – 148.

⑫ Whitehead, D. (2009a), "Athenian Juries in Military Graphai", in Symposion 2007, 23 – 36.

⑬ Whitehead, D. (2007), "'Theft' in Greek Oratory", *CQ* 57, 70 – 76.

⑭ Whitehead, D. (2006), "Absentee Athenians: Lysias Against Philon and Lycurgus Against Leocrates", *MH* 63, 132 – 151.

⑮ Whitehead, D. (2005), "Ephorus on the Spartan Constitution", *CQ* 55, 299 – 300.

⑯ Whitehead, D. (2002), "Athenian Law and Lawsuits in the Late Fifth Century BC", *MH* 59, 71 – 96.

《斐洛的弹劾》①、《古希腊的公民规范》②、《公元前 4 世纪雅典的妇女和入:亚基布的例子》③、《雅典外邦人的思想意识:一些吊坠和重新评估》④、《阿提卡的德谟社区(约公元前 508 年或 507 年至公元前 250 年):一个政治和社会研究》⑤、《一千名新雅典人》⑥等。

(八)琳恩·鲁宾斯坦(Lene Rubinstein)

琳恩·鲁宾斯坦现担任英国伦敦大学皇家霍洛威学院古代史教授,她在古希腊法律史研究方面的成果主要包括专著《公元前 4 世纪雅典的收养制度》⑦、《诉讼与合作:古典雅典法庭中的辅助演说家》⑧。目前,她正在整理伊索克拉的"六个法庭演讲"(与 D. 怀特海德合作),并致力于研究雅典以外的中晚期古典希腊世界以及早期希腊化时期的法律和司法行政。鲁宾斯坦教授在古希腊法律史研究方面的其他作品还有论文《"Praxis":古典晚期和希腊化早期刑罚的执行》⑨、《希佩里德斯"控告""Timandros"中的法律论争》⑩、《免税授权及其在古典和早期希腊化时期的推行》⑪、《古典和希腊化时期希腊法中的"Arai"》⑫、《阿提卡演说

---

① Whitehead, D. (1995), "The Impeachment of Philon (Hypereides, Pro Euxenippos 1)", *AHB* 9, 64-67.

② Whitehead, D. (1991), "Norms of Citizenship in Ancient Greece", in Molho, A., Raaflaub, K. & J. Emlen (eds), *City-states in Classical Antiquity and Medieval Italy*, 135-154, Stuttgart.

③ Whitehead, D. (1986c), "Women and Naturalization in Fourth-century Athens: The Case of Archippe", *CQ* 36, 109-114.

④ Whitehead, D. (1986b), "The Ideology of the Athenian Metic: Some Pendants and a Reappraisal", *PCPS* 212, 145-158.

⑤ Whitehead, D. (1986a), "The Demes of Attica (508/7-ca. 250 B. C.): A Political and Social Study", Princeton.

⑥ Whitehead, D. (1984), "A thousand New Athenians", *LCM* 9, 8-10.

⑦ Rubinstein, L. (1993), "Adoption in IVth Century Athens", *Copenhagen* (Opuscula Graeco Latina 34).

⑧ Rubinstein, L. (2000), "Litigation and Cooperation: Supporting Speakers in the Courts of Classical Athens", Stuttgart (Historia Einzelschriften 147).

⑨ Rubinstein, L. (2010), "Praxis: The enforcement of Penalties in the Late Classical and Early Hellenistic Periods", in Thür, G. (ed) Symposion 2009. Vorträge zur griechischen und hellenistischen Rechtsgeschichte (Seggau, 25. -30. August 2009), 193-216, Wien (with a response by F. Mitthof).

⑩ Rubinstein, L. (2009b), "Legal Argumentation in Hypereides' Against Timandros", *BICS* 52, 149-160.

⑪ Rubinstein, L. (2009a), "Ateleia grants and their enforcement in the classical and early Hellenistic periods", in *Greek History and Epigraphy*, 115-144.

⑫ Rubinstein, L. (2007b), "Araiin Greek Laws in the Classical and Hellenistic Periods: Deterrence or Concession to Tradition?", in Symposion 2005, 269-286.

家源于先例的论争》①、《雅典法院的主要诉讼人和证人:程序性变化》②、《雅典法院中的差异修辞策略》③、《"Synêgoroi"及它们在雅典法律程序再造中的位置》④、《古希腊世界的自愿起诉者》⑤、《古典雅典的收养制度》⑥等。

(九)斯蒂芬·C. 托德(Stephen C. Todd)

斯蒂芬·C. 托德现任英国曼彻斯特大学古代史教授,早年获得剑桥大学硕士、博士学位,先后任教于基尔大学和曼彻斯特大学,并担任《希腊研究》杂志、Dike杂志的编辑委员会成员。托德教授在古希腊法律史研究方面的成果主要包括专著《雅典法律的形状》⑦、《〈吕西阿斯〉卷1~11评论》⑧,编译《吕西阿斯》⑨,以及论文《雅典的"dokimasia"程序》⑩、《雅典法律中关于性犯罪的规定》⑪、《雅典的法律和演说词》⑫、《古典雅典的法律、喜剧、修辞和民主》⑬、《吕西阿斯和流产

---

① Rubinstein, L. (2007a), "Arguments from Precedent in the Attic Orators", in *The Attic Orators*, 359 – 371.

② Rubinstein, L. (2005b), "Main Litigants and Witnesses in the Athenian Courts: Procedural Variations", in Symposion 2001, 99 – 120 (with a reply by G. Thür, 121 – 124).

③ Rubinstein, L. (2005a), "Differentiated Rhetorical Strategies in Athenian Courts", in *The Cambridge Companion*, 129 – 145.

④ Rubinstein, L. (2003b), "Synêgoroi: Their Place in Our Reconstruction of the Athenian Legal Process", in Symposion 1999, 193 – 208.

⑤ Rubinstein, L. (2003a), "Volunteer Prosecutors in the Greek World", Dike 6, 87 – 114.

⑥ Rubinstein, L. (1999), "Adoption in Classical Athens", in Corbier, M. (ed), Adoption et fosterage, 45 – 62, Paris.

⑦ Todd, S. C. (1993), *The Shape of Athenian Law*, Oxford.

⑧ Todd, S. C. (2007), *A Commentary on Lysias, Speeches* 1 – 11, Oxford.

⑨ Todd, S. C. (2000b), Lysias, Austin, Tx (The oratory of classical Greece 2).

⑩ Todd, S. C. (2010), "The Athenian Procedure(s) of Dokimasia", in Thür, G. (ed), Symposion 2009. Vorträge zur griechischen und hellenistischen Rechtsgeschichte (Seggau, 25. – 30. August 2009), 73 – 98, Wien (with a response by L. Gagliardi).

⑪ Todd, S. C. (2006), "Some Notes on the Regulation of Sexuality in Athenian Law", in Symposion 2003, 93 – 120.

⑫ Todd, S. C. (2005b), "Law and Oratory at Athens", in *The Cambridge Companion*, 97 – 111.

⑬ Todd, S. C. (2005a), "Law, Theatre, Rhetoric and Democracy in classical Athens", *European Review of History* 12, 63 – 79.

问题》①、《雅典法庭中的宣传、标志和印记》②、《古典雅典的法律语言》③、《在公元前4世纪的雅典如何起诉他人》④、《吕西阿斯"控告Nikhomakhos":雅典法律中专家的命运》⑤、《公元前4世纪雅典的身份和合同》⑥、《早期希腊的书写法律》⑦、《法律、社会和雅典》⑧、《雅典法庭中证据的目的》⑨、《查泰莱夫人的情人和雅典演说家:雅典陪审法庭的社会构成》⑩等。

(十)克里斯托弗·凯利(Christopher Carey)

凯利现任职于伦敦大学皇家霍洛威学院,他在古希腊法律史研究方面的成果主要包括专著《埃斯基涅斯》⑪、《古典雅典的审判》⑫、《阿波罗多罗斯诉奈阿依拉》⑬、《吕西阿斯演说词节选》⑭、《德摩斯梯尼:私人演讲节选》⑮等,以及论文《悲剧法律》⑯、《被忽视的涉及"Isaios"纸莎草纸》⑰、《安提丰的女儿》⑱、《雅典法

---

① Todd, S. C. (2003), "Lysias on abortion", in Symposion 1999, 235 - 256.

② Todd, S. C. (2002), "Advocacy, Logography and Erotesis in Athenian Lawcourts", in McKechnie, P. (ed), *Thinking Like a Lawyer, Essays on Legal History and General History for J. Crook on His Eightieth Birthday*, 151 - 166, Leiden. (Mnemosyne Suppl. 231)

③ Todd, S. C. (2000c), "The Language of Law in Classical Athens", in Coss, P. (ed), *The Moral World of the Law*, 17 - 36, Cambridge.

④ Todd, S. C. (2000a), "How to Execute People in Fourth-century Athens", in *Law and Social Status*, 31 - 51.

⑤ Todd, S. C. (1998), "Lysias Against Nikhomakhos: The Fate of the Expert in Athenian Law", in *Law in its Political Settng*, 110 - 31.

⑥ Todd, S. C. (1994), "Status and Contract in Fourth-century Athens", in Symposion 1993, 125 - 140. (with a reply by E. E. Cohen, 141 - 152)

⑦ Todd, S. C. (1992), "Writing the Law in Early Greece", *Polis* 11, 28 - 39.

⑧ Todd, S. C. (1990c), "Law, Society and Athens", in *Nomos*, 1 - 18.

⑨ Todd, S. C. (1990b), "The Purpose of Evidence in Athenian Courts", in *Nomos*, 19 - 40.

⑩ Todd, S. C. (1990a), "Lady Chatterley's Lover and the Attic Orators: The Social Composition of the Athenian Jury", *JHS* 110, 146 - 173. (= The Attic Orators, 312 - 358)

⑪ Carey, C. (2000a), *Aeschines, Austin, Tx.* (The oratory of classical Greece 3)

⑫ Carey, C. (1997), *Trials from Classical Athens*, London.

⑬ Carey, C. (1992), *Apollodorus Against Neaira*, Warminster.

⑭ Carey, C. (1989), *Lysias: Selected speeches*, Cambridge.

⑮ Carey, C. & R. A. Reid(1985), *Demosthenes: Selected Private Speeches*, Cambridge.

⑯ Carey, C. (2007), "Tragic law", *Dioniso* 6, 22 - 33.

⑰ Carey, C. (2005), "An overlooked Papyrus of Isaios", *BICS* 48, 15 - 26.

⑱ Carey, C. (2004), "Antiphon's Daughter", in *Law, Rhetoric, and Comedy*, 1 - 14.

中的额犯罪和程序》[①]、《雅典法律的形状》[②]、《阿提卡修辞和演说中的法律》[③]、《雅典法律中的通奸和强奸》[④]、《雅典法庭中证人的"exomosia"》[⑤]、《亚里士多德和演说家眼中的朴实证据》[⑥]、《说服的修辞学方法》[⑦]、《阿波罗多洛的母亲:在雅典获得选举权的外邦人的妻子们》[⑧]、《关于雅典凶杀案件中拷问的研究》[⑨]等。

(十一)里克·凯尔斯卡特(Urich Kahrstedt,1888～1962年)

凯尔斯卡特曾在英国爱丁堡大学学习法律,受到蒙森《罗马公法》影响立志在希腊法律史领域也写出类似作品,并最终取得很大成功。凯尔斯卡特在古希腊法律史研究方面的代表作包括专著《希腊国家法(一):斯巴达及其同盟》[⑩]、《雅典公法研究(一):雅典的政府和公民》[⑪]、《雅典公法研究(二):雅典法官》[⑫],以及论文《公元前411年雅典政变后的政府合法性》[⑬]、《雅典的立法和立法者》[⑭]等。

(十二)埃利亚斯·Arnaoutoglou(Ilias Arnaoutoglou)

Arnaoutoglou 毕业于希腊塞萨洛尼基市的亚里士多德大学法学专业,并获得英国格拉斯大学古典学博士学位,他的研究志趣集中于古希腊的立法和立法者以及其与现代法律制度的异同和对现今立法的重要意义。Arnaoutoglou 在古希腊

---

① Carey, C. (2004), "Offence and Procedure in Athenian Law", in *The Law and the Courts*, 111－136.

② Carey, C. (1998), "The Shape of Athenian Laws", *CQ* 48, 93－109.

③ Carey, C. (1996), "Nomos in Attic Rhetoric and Oratory", *JHS* 116, 33－46.

④ Carey, C. (1995), "Rape and Adultery in Athenian Law", *CQ* 45, 407－417.

⑤ Carey, C. (1995), "The Witness's Exomosia in the Athenian Courts", *CQ* 45, 114－119.

⑥ Carey, C. (1994), "'Artless' Proofs in Aristotle and the Orators", *BICS* 39, 95－106 (= The Attic Orators, 229－246).

⑦ Carey, C. (1994), "Rhetorical Means of Persuasion", in Worthington, I. (ed), *Persuasion: Greek Rhetoric in Action*, 26－45, London.

⑧ Carey, C. (1991), "Apollodoros' Mother: The Wives of Enfranchised Aliens in Athens", *CQ* 41, 84－89.

⑨ Carey, C. (1988), "A Note on Torture in Athenian Homicide Cases", *Historia* 37, 241－245.

⑩ Urich, Kahrstedt, Griechisches Staatsrecht Ⅰ: Sparta und seine Symmachie, Götingen, 1922.

⑪ Urich Kahrstedt, Studien zum öffentlichen Recht Athens Tl. 1: Staatsgebiet und Staatsangehörige in Athen, Stuttgart, 1934 (Göttinger Forschungen 4).

⑫ Urich Kahrstedt, Studien zum öffentlichen Recht Athens Tl. 2: Untersuchungen zur Magistratur in Athen, Stuttgart, 1936.

⑬ Urich Kahrstedt, "Staatsrechtliches zum Putsch von 411", Hermes 49, 1914, pp. 47－69.

⑭ Urich Kahrstedt, "Untersuchungen zu athenischen Behörden Ⅱ: Die Nomotheten und die Legislative in Athen", *Klio* 31, 1938, pp. 1－32.

法律史研究方面的代表作主要包括专著《古希腊法》[①]和《性和献祭：希腊化时期雅典的私人宗教团体》[②]，以及论文《专有名词学和法律》[③]、《古希腊法中的专有名词》[④]、《公元前 318 年雅典对"Phokion"的审判》[⑤]、《雅典政制中的基本权利》[⑥]、《古希腊法律对奴隶的震慑》[⑦]、《古希腊的口头法》[⑧]、《互联网中的古希腊法律资料》[⑨]、《在"koinon"和"idion"：法律和社会层面的雅典宗教组织》[⑩]、《古典雅典的谋杀和侮辱》[⑪]、《雅典杀人法中的"污染"》[⑫]等。

三、20 世纪中后期至今英国从事古希腊法律史研究的其他古典学者

（一）摩西·以色列·芬利（Moses Israel Finley，1912 ~ 1986 年）

芬利是 20 世纪西方最有影响力的古史学家之一，初名摩西·以色列·芬利斯坦因（Moses Israel Finkelstein），师从著名古史学家威斯特尔曼（William Linn Westermann，1873 ~ 1954 年）。1912 年芬利出生于美国一个中产阶级家庭，1927 年，在刚过 15 岁生日后不到 1 个月，从叙拉古大学心理学专业毕业并转入哥伦比亚大学研习公法，1929 年获得法学硕士，并参与哥伦比亚大学《社会科学百科全书》编写工作，后转向研究社会学、经济学。1954 年任教英国剑桥大学，1962 年正式成为英国公民，1970 年接替著名史学家琼斯任剑桥大学古代史讲席教授，1979

---

① Arnaoutoglou, I. (1998), *Ancient Greek laws: A Sourcebook*, London.

② Arnaoutoglou, I. (2003), "Thusias Heneka Kai Sunousias: Private Religious Associations in Hellenistic Athens", Athens (EHHD Par. 4).

③ Arnaoutoglou, I. (2010), "Onomastics and law: Dike and-dike Names", in Catling, R. W. V. & F. Marchand (eds), *Onomatologos. Studies in Greek Personal Names Presented to Elaine Matthews*, 582 – 600, Oxford.

④ Arnaoutoglou, I. (2009), "Onomastique Grecet Droit", in *Mythe et Justice*, 7 – 22.

⑤ Arnaoutoglou, I. (2008), "The Trial of Phokion, Athens 318 BC", *EHHD* 41, 21 – 39 (in Greek).

⑥ Arnaoutoglou, I. (2007), "Fundamental Rights in Athenaion Politeia?", *EHHD* 40, 9 – 28 (in Greek).

⑦ Arnaoutoglou, I. (2007), "Fear of Slaves in Ancient Greek Legal Texts", in *Fear of Slaves*, 133 – 144.

⑧ Arnaoutoglou, I. (2004), "Aspects of Oral Law in Archaic Greece", in *Law, Rhetoric, and Comedy*, 1 – 14.

⑨ Arnaoutoglou, I. (2003), "Ancient Greek Laws in the World Wide Web", *Imeros* 3, 181 – 188.

⑩ Arnaoutoglou, I. (1998), "Between Koinon and: Legal and Social Dimensions of Religious Associations in Ancient Athens", in *Kosmos*, 68 – 83.

⑪ Arnaoutoglou, I. (1993), "Miasma kai anthropoktonia sten klassike Athena", in Praktika tou 13ou Panhelleniou Historikou Sunedriou (Thessalonike, 29 – 31 Maiou 1992), 11 – 18, Thessaloniki.

⑫ Arnaoutoglou, I. (1993a), "Pollution in the Athenian Homicide Law", *RIDA* 40, 109 – 37.

年因自己杰出的学术贡献受封为爵士。芬利的主要研究领域是古代希腊史，但其著作更多以整个古典世界为研究对象，芬利涉及古希腊法律史方面的研究成果主要包括专著《古代奴隶制与近现代意识形态》①、《古代经济》②、《古代雅典的土地和信贷研究（公元前500年至公元前200年）：界碑铭文》③等，以及论文《古希腊土地的可转让性》④、《古希腊法的统一性问题》⑤、《古希腊的奴隶制》⑥、《荷马和迈锡尼：财产和任期》⑦、《荷马世界的婚姻、交易和礼物》⑧、《雅典法律中针对不动产的多项税费：来自Agora铭文的新证据》⑨、《古典雅典的土地、债务和有产者》⑩、《古希腊法的一些问题：关于普林斯海姆贸易观点的思考》⑪等。

（二）肯尼思·詹姆斯·多佛（Kenneth James Dover，1920～2010年）

多佛是英国最著名的古典学者之一，早年毕业于牛津大学，1976～1986年任牛津大学基督圣体学院主席，1978～1981年任英国人文和社会学院主席，1981～2005年任圣安德鲁斯大学校长。多佛在古希腊法律史研究方面的成果主要包括专著《古希腊同性恋》⑫、《古希腊在柏拉图和亚里士多德时代的大众道德》⑬，以

---

① Finley, M. I. (1980), *Ancient Slavery and Modern Ideology*, London.

② Finley, M. I. (1973), *The Ancient Economy*, Berkely.

③ Finley, M. I. (1952), *Studies in Land and Credit in Ancient Athens. 500 – 200 B. C: The Horoi Inscriptions*, New Brunswick, Princeton.

④ Finley, M. I. (1968), "The Alienability of Land in Ancient Greece", *Eirene* 7, 25 – 32(= Annales ESC 25(1970) 1271 – 1277 and Finley, The use, 153 – 160).

⑤ Finley, M. I. (1966), "The Problem of the Unity of Greek Law", in La storia del diritto nel quadro delle scienze storiche (Atti del primo Congresso Internazionale della Società Italiana di Storia del Diritto, Rome, December 1963), 129 – 142, Firenze(= Finley, The use, 134 – 152).

⑥ Finley, M. I. (1960), "The Servile Statuses of Ancient Greece", *RIDA* 7, 165 – 189 (= Finley, Economy, 133 – 149).

⑦ Finley, M. I. (1957), "Homer and Mycenae: Property and Tenure", *Historia* 6, 133 – 159.

⑧ Finley, M. I. (1954), "Marriage, Sale and Gift in the Homeric World", *Seminar* 12, 121 – 33 (= RIDA 2(1955) 167 – 194 and Finley, Economy, 233 – 248).

⑨ Finley, M. I. (1953b), "Multiple Charges of Real Property in Athenian Law: New Evidence from an Agora Inscription", in *Studi Arangio-Ruiz* 3, 473 – 491 (= "Mehrfache Belastung von Grundstückseigentum im attischen Recht. Neues Beweismaterial aus einer auf der Agora gefundenen Inschrift" in Zur griechischen Rechtsgeschichte, 534 – 558).

⑩ Finley, M. I. (1953a), "Land, Debt and the Man of Property in Classical Athens", *Political Science Quarterly Review* 68, 149 – 168(= Finley, Economy, 62 – 76).

⑪ Finley, M. I. (1951), "Some Problems of Greek Law: A Consideration of Pringsheim on Sale", *Seminar* 9, 72 – 91.

⑫ Dover, K. J. (1978), *Greek Homosexuality*, London.

⑬ Dover, K. J. (1974), *Greek Popular Morality in the Time of Plato and Aristotle*, Berkeley.

及论文《性爱和法律》①、《安德洛森论陶片放逐》②等。

(三)休·劳埃德－琼斯(Hugh Lloyd-Jones,1922～2009年)

劳埃德－琼斯是英国著名的古典学和希腊研究学者,早年毕业于牛津大学基督教学院,在第二次世界大战中参军,战后任教于剑桥大学,1951年回牛津大学任教,1961年任牛津大学钦定讲席教授。他对米南德和索福克勒斯的戏剧进行了深入研究,1966年当选英国人文和社会科学学院院士,先后被芝加哥、特拉维夫、哥廷根和塞萨洛尼基大学授予荣誉博士学位。劳埃德－琼斯在古希腊法律史方面的研究成果主要包括专著《宙斯的正义》③等。

(四)特雷弗·J.桑德斯(Trevor J. Saunders,1934～1999年)

桑德斯是当代英国知名的柏拉图研究学者,他在古希腊法律史方面的成果研究也与其柏拉图研究紧密相关,主要包括专著《柏拉图〈法律篇〉中的外邦人》④、《柏拉图的刑法典》⑤等,以及论文《柏拉图和雅典盗窃法》⑥、《普罗泰戈拉和柏拉图论刑罚》⑦、《柏拉图的发条橙》⑧、《柏拉图〈法律篇〉研究文献目录(1920年至1976年)》⑨等。

(五)罗伯特·帕克(Robert Parker)

帕克曾任牛津大学古代史Wykeham讲席教授(1996～2016年),主要研究方向为古希腊宗教,他在古希腊法律史研究方面的成果主要包括专著《Miasma:早期古希腊宗教中的污染与净化》⑩、《雅典的一神教和社会》⑪、《古希腊宗教》⑫等,

---

① Dover, K. J. (1964), "Eros and nomos", *BICS* 11, 31－42.

② Dover, K. J. (1963), "Androtion on Ostracism", *CR* 13, 256－257(= The Greeks and their legacy II, 83－85).

③ Lloyd-Jones, H. (1971), *The Justice of Zeus*, Berkeley.

④ Saunders, T. J. (1962), *The Metic in Plato's Laws*, diss. Cambridge.

⑤ Saunders, T. J. (1993), *Plato's Penal Code: Tradition, Controversy, and Reform in Greek Penology*, Clarendon Press.

⑥ Saunders, T. J. (1990), "Plato and the Athenian Law of Theft", in *Nomos*, 63－82.

⑦ Saunders, T. J. (1981), "Protagoras and Plato on Punishment", in Kerford, G. B. (ed), *The Sophists and Their Legacy*, 129－141, Wiesbaden.

⑧ Saunders, T. J. (1975－6), "Plato's Clockwork Orange", *Durham University Journal* 37, 113－17.

⑨ Saunders, T. J. (1979), *Bibliography on Plato's Laws*, 1920－1976, *with Additional Citations Through March* 1979, *History of Ideas in Ancient Greece*.

⑩ Parker, R. (1983), *Miasma: Pollution and Purification in Early Greek Religion*, Oxford.

⑪ Parker, R. (2005), *Polytheism and Society at Athens*, Oxford.

⑫ Parker, R. (2011), *On Greek Religion*, Ithaca, NY.

以及论文《法律和宗教》①、《何为神圣法》②、《雅典宗教的新问题:来自 Aixone 地区的神圣法》③等。

(六)丹尼尔·奥格登(Daniel Ogden)

奥格登现任职于英国埃克塞特大学,他在古希腊法律史研究方面的研究成果主要包括专著《古希腊的扭曲国王》④、《在古典和希腊化时期希腊的私生子》⑤、《希腊化王朝的一夫多妻制、妓女和死亡》⑥等,以及论文《古希腊的私生子和生父不明者》⑦、《“gynaikonomoi”:控制妇女服装》⑧、《古典雅典的强奸、通奸和血统保护》⑨、《古希腊和希腊化时代的妇女和私生子》⑩等。

(七)保罗·米利特(Paul Millett,1954 年至今)

米利特现为剑桥大学高级讲师、剑桥大学唐宁学院成员,曾于剑桥大学获得博士学位,指导老师为著名的古代史学家芬利教授(Moses I. Finley),主要研究方向为古代经济学和人类相互关系尤以古代希腊为关注重点,他在古希腊法律史研究方面的成果主要包括专著《古典雅典的借贷》⑪,以及论文《重新审视苏格拉底的审判》⑫、《雅典法制和社会中的贸易、信用和兑换》⑬、《公元前 4 世纪雅典的海

---

① Parker,R. (2005),“Law and Religion”,in *The Cambridge Companion*,61 - 81.

② Parker,R. (2004),“What are Sacred Laws?”,in *The Law and the Courts*,57 - 70.

③ Parker,R. (2010),“New Problems in Athenian Religion:The ‘Sacred Law’ from Aixone”,in J. 44 Dijkstra,J. Kroesen and Y. Kuiper (eds),*Myths,Martyrs,and Modernity:Studies in the History of Religions in Honour of Jan N. Bremmer*(Leiden),193 - 208.

④ Ogden,D. (1997),*The Crooked Kings of Ancient Greece*,London.

⑤ Ogden,D. (1996),*Greek Bastardy in the Classical and the Hellenistic Periods*,Oxford.

⑥ Ogden,D. (1999),*Polygamy,Prostitutes and Death:The Hellenistic Dynasties*,Duckworth and Classical Press of Wales,London.

⑦ Ogden,D. (2009),“Bastardy and Fatherlessness in Ancient Greece”,in Hübner,S. R. & D. M. Ratzan(eds),*Growing up Fatherless in Antiquity*,105 - 119,Cambridge.

⑧ Ogden,D. (2002),“Controlling Women's Dress:Gynaikonomoi”,in Llewellyn-Jones,L. (ed),*Women's Dress in the Ancient Greek World*,203 - 225,London.

⑨ Ogden,D. (1997b),“Rape,Adultery and the Protection of Bloodlines in Classical Athens”,in *Rape in Antiquity*,25 - 41.

⑩ Ogden,D. (1995),“Women and Bastardy in Ancient Greece and the Hellenistic World”,in Powell,A. (ed),*The Greek World*,219 - 244,London.

⑪ Millett,P. (1991),*Lending and Borrowing in Classical Athens*,Cambridge.

⑫ Millett,P. (2005),“The Trial of Socrates Revisited”,*European Review of History* 12,23 - 62.

⑬ Millett,P. (1990),“Sale,Credit and Exchange in Athenian Law and Society”,in *Nomos*,167 - 194.

商贷款和信贷结构》[1]、《对阿提卡界牌的重新审视：基于最近的考古发现》[2]、《法律、社会和雅典》[3]等。

（八）罗莎琳德·托马斯（Rosalind Thomas）

托马斯现任职于牛津大学贝利奥尔学院古代史专业，她在古希腊法律史研究方面的成果主要包括专著《古典雅典的口头传统和书面记载》[4]，以及论文《写作、法律和书面法律》[5]、《篆刻于石？自由、平等、口头法律和法律编纂》[6]、《雅典民主中的法律和立法者》[7]等。

（九）罗赞娜·Omitowoju（Rosanna Omitowoju）

Omitowoju 现任职于剑桥大学国王学院，主要研究方向为米兰德和公元前 5 世纪至前 4 世纪雅典文化史，她在古希腊法律史方面的研究成果主要包括专著《古典雅典的强奸和公认政治》[8]，以及论文《规制强奸：雅典法庭的肥皂剧和利己主义》[9]等。

（十）罗杰·贾斯特（Roger Just）

贾斯特现任职于澳大利亚墨尔本大学，曾获牛津大学博士学位，他在古希腊法律史方面的研究成果主要包括专著《雅典法律和社会生活中的妇女》[10]等。

（十一）大卫·M. 夏普斯（David M. Schaps）

夏普斯在古希腊法律史研究方面的代表作包括专著《古希腊妇女的经济权利》[11]，以及论文《雅典自由民妇女的自由为何物》[12]、《建筑商、承包商和城邦权

---

① Millett, P. (1983), "Maritime Loans and the Structure of Credit in Fourth-century Athens", in Garnsey, P. D. A., Hopkins, M. K. & C. R. Whittaker (eds), *Trade in the Ancient Economy*, 36 – 52, London.

② Millett, P. (1982), "The Attic Horoi Revisited in the Light of Recent Discoveries", *Opus* 1, 219 – 249.

③ Millett, P. & St. Todd (1990), "Law, Society and Athens", in *Nomos*, 1 – 18.

④ Thomas, R. (1989), *Oral Tradition and Written Record in Classical Athens*, Cambridge.

⑤ Thomas, R. (2005), "Writing, Law, and Written Law", in *The Cambridge Companion*, 41 – 60.

⑥ Thomas, R. (1998), "Written in Stone? Liberty, Equality, Orality and the Codification of Law", in *Law in its Political Setting*, 9 – 32 (= BICS 40 (1995) 59 – 74).

⑦ Thomas, R. (1994), "Law and Lawgiver in the Athenian Democracy", in *Ritual, Finance, Politics*, 119 – 33.

⑧ Omitowoju, R. (2002), *Rape and the Politics of Consent in Classical Athens*, Cambridge.

⑨ Omitowoju, R. (1997), "Regulating Rape: Soap Operas and Self-interest in the Athenian Courts", in *Rape in Anti-quity*, 1 – 24.

⑩ Just, R. (1989), *Women in Athenian Law and Life*, London.

⑪ Schaps, D. M. (1979), *Economic Rights of Women in Ancient Greece*, Edinburgh.

⑫ Schaps, D. M. (1998), "What was Free about a Free Athenian Woman", *TAPhA* 128, 161 – 188.

力：古希腊的融资和建设项目管理》①、《皮奥夏一个有争议的奴隶》②、《古希腊继承法中的妇女》③等。

（十二）J. 沃尔特·琼斯（J. Walter Jones）

琼斯在古希腊法律史方面的研究成果主要包括专著《古希腊的法律和法律理论》④等。

---

① Schaps, D. M. (1996), "Builders, Contractors, and Power: Financing and Administering Building Projects in Ancient Greece", in Katzoff, R., Petroff, Y. & D. Schaps (eds), *Classical Studies in Honor of D. Sohlberg*, 77 – 90, Ramat Gan.

② Schaps, D. M. (1976), "A Disputed Slave in Boeotia", *ZPE* 20, 63 – 64.

③ Schaps, D. M. (1975), "Women in Greek Inheritance Law", *CQ* 25, 53 – 57.

④ Jones, J. W. (1956), *The Law and Legal Theory of the Greeks*, Oxford.

第三章　美国的古希腊法律史研究

自18世纪末建国一直到19世纪下半叶，美国在古典学研究方面一直明显落后于欧洲大陆国家。但几个世纪以来，美国的古典教育一直在哈佛、耶鲁等著名大学中占据中心地位，特别是19世纪后半叶以来，美国文献学学会、美国古典学协会、美国考古研究所、美国雅典研究院的建立，以及一批专业古典杂志的诞生如《美国文献学杂志》《美国考古杂志》《哈佛古典文献学研究》的创办，都标志着美国的古典学研究开始走向成熟。

进入20世纪，经过两次世界大战，美国社会经济与科学技术势力大为增强，从而为包括古希腊法律史研究在内的古典学研究的深入提供了坚实的经济基础和优越的技术条件。20世纪初，美国学者大量参与了在希腊的考古活动，取得了一系列重要的考古成果。特别是第二次世界大战后美国雅典研究院又成为唯一可以在阿提卡从事考古活动的外国机构，美国学者充分利用这一有利条件，发掘了众多遗址，出版了大量考古报告与著作。其中，美国雅典研究院在雅典广场及卫城的发掘活动始于1931年，1953年开始以《雅典广场》（*The Athenian Agora*）为丛书总名出版相关研究成果，至2006年已出版到第33卷。每卷各有一个主题，第15～16卷对古希腊法律史研究的参考价值最大，前者为与雅典议事会成员有关的铭文，后者为雅典城邦颁布的各类法令，为之后学者的古希腊法律史研究提供了大量原始文献资料。美国的古希腊法律史研究开始于20世纪末,进入21世纪后出现了一大批知名学者和重要作品,以下试分别介绍之。

一、19世纪至20世纪中叶美国的古希腊法律史学者及其研究成果

(一)科尼利厄斯·康威·费尔顿(Cornelius Conway Felton,1807~1862年)

费尔顿1807年出生于美国马萨诸塞州,1827年毕业于美国哈佛大学,1829年开始任教于哈佛大学,1832年成为哈佛大学教授,1860年任美国哈佛大学校长。费尔顿是19世纪美国最著名的古典学家之一,代表作有专著《希腊:古代与现代》(曾出版到第9版)①。在该书中,费尔顿对公元前5世纪的雅典民主与法律制度大加赞赏,尤为推崇梭伦确立的人道与克里斯提尼确立的权力制衡制度,但费尔顿对雅典的陶片放逐制度因其无视个人自由权利而持批评态度,这反映出当时美国学术界对古希腊法律的爱憎态度。

(二)乔治·威利斯·博茨福德(George Willis Botsford,1862~1917年)

博茨福德曾任美国哥伦比亚大学希腊和罗马史教授,在古希腊法律史研究方面的成果主要包括专著《雅典政制的发展》②及论文《比奥提亚联盟创建至公元前387年的宪法和政治》③等。在《雅典政制的发展》一书中,博茨福德以当时新出现的《雅典政制》为基础,系统全面地论述了雅典政治制度在伯罗奔尼撒战争以前的演变情况,并对雅典曾经存在过的各种政治法律制度和政治人物一一点评。

(三)罗伯特·J.邦纳(Robert J. Bonner,1868~1946年)

罗伯特·J.邦纳1868年出生于加拿大安大略省的牛津郡。先后就读于多伦多大学(本科,1890年)、安大略大学法学院(硕士,1893年)和芝加哥大学(古典文献学博士,1904年)。此后,先后任教于斯泰森大学(佛罗里达州)、芝加哥大学,1927年被任命为芝加哥大学古典系主任,1928~1929年任美国中西部和南部古典协会主席,1932年后任职于加州大学伯克利分校,1937年都柏林大学授予他名誉博士学位。

邦纳教授的研究重点是古希腊的法律和司法实践。在该领域,他和他的学

---

① Felton, C. C. (1867), *Greece, Ancient and Modern* (2 Vols), Boston and New York: Houghton, Mifflin and Company (9th ed, 1893).

② Botsford, G. W. (1893), *The Development of the Athenian Constitution*, New York (Cornell Studies in Classical Philology 4).

③ Botsford, G. W. (1910), "The Constitution and Politics of the Boeotian League from its Origin to the Year 387 B. C.", *Political Science Quarterly* 25, 271–296.

生,包括乔治·米勒·卡尔霍恩、威廉·斯科特·弗格森、约翰·哈特利和格兰特·罗伯逊奥斯卡被称为研究希腊法律的邦纳学校。邦纳教授在古希腊法律史研究方面的代表作为专著《雅典法庭的证据》①、《古希腊和解制度》②、《古代雅典的律师和诉讼当事人》③、《从荷马到亚里士多德的司法行政》④、《雅典民主面面观》⑤等,以及论文《服食毒芹实行死刑的运用》⑥、《庇西特拉图时期的司法行政》⑦、《雅典法庭中的机智和幽默》⑧、《麦加拉法令》⑨、《伊索格拉底〈易物〉中的法律构想》⑩、《Apollodorus 诉 Phormio:刑事袭击》⑪、《雅典的仲裁员制度》⑫、《陶片放逐法的最低投票数》⑬、《战神山议事会的证据制度》⑭、《赫西奥德时代的司法行政》⑮、《荷马时代的司法行政》⑯、《皮奥夏联邦宪法》⑰、《柏拉图〈申辩篇〉的法律构想》⑱、《阿提卡印章的使用和实效》⑲、《雅典仲裁人的管辖权》⑳、《雅典妇女是否能够在凶杀案件中作证?》㉑、《皮奥夏的司法行政》㉒、《德尔斐同盟的司法

---

① Bonner, R. J. (1979), *Evidence in Athenian Courts*, Chicago, 1905, Nachdrucke New York (reprint, 2006).

② Bonner, R. J. (1903), *Greek Compositions*, Chicago.

③ Bonner, R. J. (1927), *Lawyers and Litigants in Ancient Athens: The Genesis of the Legal Profession*, Chicago.

④ Bonner, R. J. (1930 – 1938), *Gertrude Smith, Administration of Justice from Homer to Aristotle*, Zwei Bände, Chicago.

⑤ Bonner, R. J. (1933), *Aspects of Athenian Democracy*, Berkeley, 1933 (Sather Classical Lectures 11).

⑥ Bonner, R. J. (1940), "The Use of Hemlock for Capital Punishment", in *Athenian Studies Presented to W. S. Ferguson*, 299 – 302, Cambridge, Mass.

⑦ Bonner, R. J. (1924), "Administration of Justice under Pisistratus", *CPh* 19, 359 – 361.

⑧ Bonner, R. J. (1922), "Wit and Humor in Athenian Courts", *CPh* 17, 97 – 103.

⑨ Bonner, R. J. (1921), "The Megarian Decrees", *CPh* 16, 238 – 245.

⑩ Bonner, R. J. (1920), "The Legal Setting of Isocrates' Antidosis", *CPh* 15, 193 – 197.

⑪ Bonner, R. J. (1919), "Apollodorus vs. Phormio; Criminal Assault", *CPh* 14, 83 – 84.

⑫ Bonner, R. J. (1916), "The Institution of Athenian Arbitrators", *CPh* 11, 191 – 195.

⑬ Bonner, R. J. (1913), "The Minimum Vote in Ostracism", *CPh* 8, 223 – 225.

⑭ Bonner, R. J. (1912b), "Evidence in the Areopagus", *CPh* 7, 450 – 456.

⑮ Bonner, R. J. (1912a), "Administration of Justice in the Age of Hesiod", *CPh* 7, 17 – 23.

⑯ Bonner, R. J. (1911), "Administration of Justice in the Age of Homer", *CPh* 6, 12 – 36.

⑰ Bonner, R. J. (1910), "The Boeotian Federal Constitution", *CPh* 5, 405 – 417.

⑱ Bonner, R. J. (1908b), "The Legal Setting of Plato's Apology", *CPh* 3, 169 – 177.

⑲ Bonner, R. J. (1908a), "The Use and Effect of Attic Seals", *CPh* 3, 399 – 407.

⑳ Bonner, R. J. (1907), "The Jurisdiction of Athenian Arbitrators", *CPh* 2, 407 – 418.

㉑ Bonner, R. J. (1906), "Did Women Testify in Homicide Cases at Athens?", *CPh* 1, 127 – 132.

㉒ Bonner, R. J. & G. Smith (1945), "The Administration of Justice in Boeotia", *CPh* 40, 11 – 23.

行政》[1]、《斯巴达的司法行政》[2]等。

1926年出版的《古代雅典的律师和辩护人》是邦纳教授的早期作品之一，该书分析了雅典法律制度下辩护人阶层的演变及其辩护技巧。1930年出版的《从荷马到亚里士多德的司法行政》是邦纳教授在古希腊法律史研究方面的重要作品之一，该书尽管以司法演变为载体，但事实上是一部雅典公元前4世纪中叶以前的法律发展史，尤其侧重于民众法庭改革对雅典法律发展的引导作用。在1933年出版的《雅典民主面面观》一书中，作者从人民主权出发，分析了雅典公民大会享有的各项政治与法律权力，认为立法、司法、行政机构都由抽签选出的公民掌握，所以雅典人民是真正地行使国家主权。

（四）乔治·米勒·卡尔霍恩（George Miller Calhoun，1880～?）

卡尔霍恩曾任职于加利福尼亚大学，在古希腊法律史方面的研究成果主要包括专著《雅典人的政治和诉讼俱乐部》[3]、《古希腊法工作参考书目》[4]、《古希腊刑法的演变》[5]、《古希腊法学简介》[6]等，以及论文《古典雅典海事借贷的风险》[7]、《古希腊城邦的法律体系》[8]、《古希腊研究的资料》[9]、《古希腊法律和宪法法学》[10]、《古希腊犯罪和刑法的早期历史》[11]、《雅典法庭的口头和书面起诉（或辩

---

① Bonner, R. J. & G. Smith (1943), "Administration of Justice in the Delphic Amphictiony", *CPh* 38, 1–12.

② Bonner, R. J. & G. Smith (1942), "Administration of Justice in Sparta", *CPh* 37, 113–129.

③ Calhoun, G. M. (1913), *Athenian Clubs in Politics and Litigation*, Austin, Texas (University of Texas bulletin, No. 262; Humanistic series, no. 14).

④ Calhoun, G. M. & C. Delamere (1927), *A Working Bibliography of Greek Law*, Cambridge, Mass.

⑤ Calhoun, G. M. (1927), *The Growth of Criminal Law in Ancient Greece*, Berkeley.

⑥ Calhoun, G. M. (1944), *Introduction to Greek Legal Science*, Oxford.

⑦ Calhoun, G. M. (1930), "Risk in Sea Loans in Ancient Athens", *Journal of Economic and Business History* 2, 561–584.

⑧ Calhoun, G. M. (1924b), "The Jurisprudence of the Greek City", *Columbia Law Review* 94, 154–171.

⑨ Calhoun, G. M. (1924a), "The Materials for a Study of Greek Law", *California Law Review* 12, 463–480.

⑩ Calhoun, G. M. (1923), "Greek Law and Modern Jurisprudence", *California Law Review* 11, 295–312.

⑪ Calhoun, G. M. (1921b), "The Early History of Crime and Criminal Law in Greece", *Proceedings of the Classical Association of England* 18, 86–104.

护)》①、《雅典法官和特殊答辩》②、《科浓房产诉讼中卡利斯特拉托斯的身份》③、《雅典仲裁员们面对的伪证》④、《雅典诉讼中的文件欺诈》⑤等。在《雅典人的政治和诉讼俱乐部》一书中,卡尔霍恩分析了雅典政治小集团——俱乐部的起源,并着重分析了它在法庭诉讼以及政治斗争中的作用,认为在公民大会的投票,尤其是关于陶片放逐的投票中,这种俱乐部有时可以起很大的作用,直接影响投票结果。

(五)格伦·R.莫罗(Glenn R. Morrow,1895~1973年)

莫罗教授是20世纪中叶美国最知名的古希腊史学者之一,曾长期担任美国宾夕法尼亚大学学院院长(1944~1952年),并担任德语杂志《哲学史档案》(Archiv Fur Geschichte Der Philosophie)的美国共同编辑(1960~1968年)。莫罗教授1895年出生于美国密苏里州卡尔霍恩县,1918年获密苏里大学硕士学位,1921年获康奈尔大学博士学位后,前往巴黎、慕尼黑和维也纳继续从事研究工作。在1939~1965年任职宾夕法尼亚大学之前,莫罗先后任职于康奈尔大学(1922~1923年)、密苏里大学(1923~1929年)、伊利诺伊大学(1929~1939年)。莫罗教授在古希腊法律史研究方面的成果主要包括专著《柏拉图的克里特城邦:对〈法律篇〉的一个历史解读》⑥、《柏拉图的奴隶制法及其与古希腊法律的关系》⑦,以及论文《柏拉图〈法律篇〉中的夜间委员会》⑧、《柏拉图〈法律篇〉中的普通法庭》⑨、《柏拉图和自然法》⑩、《柏拉图和法治》⑪、《柏拉图〈法律篇〉中的部落法庭》⑫、《柏拉图〈法律篇〉中的外国人身份》⑬、《柏拉图和古希腊奴隶制》⑭等。

---

① Calhoun, G. M. (1919b), "Oral and Written Pleading in Athenian Courts", *TAPhA* 50, 177-193.

② Calhoun, G. M. (1919a), "Athenian Magistrates and Special Pleas", *CPh* 14, 338-350.

③ Calhoun, G. M. (1918a), "The Status of Callistratus in the Litigation over the Estate of Conon. Demosthenes xlviii, 31, 43 ff", *CPh* 13, 410-412.

④ Calhoun, G. M. (1915b), "Perjury before Athenian Arbitrators", *CPh* 10, 1-7.

⑤ Calhoun, G. M. (1914), "Documentary Frauds in Litigation at Athens", *CPh* 9, 134-144.

⑥ *Plato's Cretan City: A Historical Interpretation of the "Laws"*, Princeton University Press, 1960.

⑦ Morrow, G. R. (1939), *Plato's Law of Slavery and its Relation to Greek Law*, Urbana, Ⅲ.

⑧ Morrow, G. R. (1960), "The Nocturnal Council in Plato's Laws", *AGPh* 42, 229-246.

⑨ Morrow, G. R. (1951), "The Popular Courts in Plato's Laws", *Scientia* 86, 145-150.

⑩ Morrow, G. R. (1948), "Plato and the Law of Nature", in Konvitz, M. R. & A. E. Murphy (eds) *Essays in Political Theory Presented to G. H. Sabine*, 17-44, Ithaca.

⑪ Morrow, G. R. (1941), "Plato and the Rule of Law", *Philosophical Review* 50, 105-136.

⑫ Morrow, G. R. (1941), "On the Tribal Courts in Plato's Laws", *AJPh* 62, 314-321.

⑬ Morrow, G. R. (1941), "The Status of the Alien in Plato's Laws", *Scientia* 70, 38-43.

⑭ Morrow, G. R. (1939), "Plato and Greek Slavery", *Mind* 48, 196-201.

（六）艾尔弗雷德·保罗·Dorjahn（Alfred Paul Dorjahn）

Dorjahn曾任美国西北大学拉丁语和拉丁文化John Evans讲席教授，在古希腊法律史方面的研究成果主要包括专著《古代雅典的政治赦免：公元前403年的特赦》①，以及论文《雅典法庭中的拷问证据》②、《古希腊法中的奴隶证据》③、《雅典人的预审》④、《雅典法庭中的外在影响因素》⑤、《雅典法庭中的恐吓胁迫》⑥、《雅典法庭中的争论预期》⑦、《雅典法庭中可使罪行减轻的情况》⑧、《雅典法庭的法律程序》⑨、《雅典法庭中的诗歌艺术》⑩等。

（七）雅各布·拉森（Jakob Aall O. Larsen）

拉森曾任职于芝加哥大学，在古希腊法律史方面的研究成果主要包括专著《古希腊联邦国家：他们的机构和历史》⑪、《古希腊和罗马历史上的代议制政府》⑫等，以及论文《伊庇鲁斯人授予妇女公民权》⑬、《一个关于塞萨利同盟的新诠释》⑭、《Orchomenos和Beotian联盟的形成》⑮、《伯罗奔尼撒同盟宪法（Ⅱ）》⑯、《斯巴达和爱奥尼亚反抗：斯巴达外交政策和伯罗奔尼撒同盟成因研究》⑰等。

---

① Dorjahn, A. P. (1946), *Political Forgiveness in Old Athens: The Amnesty of* 403 *B. C.*, Evanston.

② Dorjahn, A. P. (1953), "Evidence by Torture in Ancient Athenian Courts", in *Studi Arangio-Ruiz* 3, 77 – 80.

③ Dorjahn, A. P. (1952), "On Slave-evidence in Greek Law", *CJ* 47, 188.

④ Dorjahn, A. P. (1941), "On the Athenian Anakrisis", *CPh* 36, 182 – 185.

⑤ Dorjahn, A. P. (1938), "Outside Influence on Athenian Courts", *Philological Quarterly* 17, 18 – 25.

⑥ Dorjahn, A. P. (1937), "Intimidation in Athenian Courts", *CPh* 32, 341 – 348.

⑦ Dorjahn, A. P. (1935), "Anticipation of Arguments in Athenian Courts", *TAPhA* 66, 274 – 295.

⑧ Dorjahn, A. P. (1930), "Extenuating Circumstances in Athenian Courts", *CPh* 25, 162 – 172.

⑨ Dorjahn, A. P. (1928), "Legal Precedent in Athenian Courts", *Philological Quarterly* 7, 375 – 389.

⑩ Dorjahn, A. P. (1927), "Poetry in Athenian Courts", *CPh* 22, 85 – 93.

⑪ Larsen, J. A. O. (1968), *Greek Federal States: Their Institutions and History*, Oxford.

⑫ Larsen, J. A. O. (1955), *Representative Government in Greek and Roman History*, Berkeley.

⑬ Larsen, J. A. O. (1967), "Epirote Grants of Citizenship to Women Again", *CPh* 62, 255 – 256.

⑭ Larsen, J. A. O. (1960), "A New Interpretation of the Thessalian Confederacy", *CPh* 55, 229 – 248.

⑮ Larsen, J. A. O. (1960), "Orchomenos and the Formation of the Beotian Confederacy in 447 B. C.", *CPh* 55, 9 – 18.

⑯ Larsen, J. A. O. (1934), *The Constitution of the Peloponnesian League.* Ⅱ, *Classical Philology*, Vol. 29, No. 1, pp. 1 – 19.

⑰ Larsen, J. A. O. (1932), *Sparta and the Ionian Revolt: A Study of Spartan Foreign Policy and the Genesis of the Peloponnesian League*, *Classical Philology*, Vol. 27, No. 2, pp. 136 – 150.

(八)欧文·巴坎(Irving Barkan)

巴坎曾任职于美国芝加哥大学,在古希腊法律史研究方面的代表作包括专著《古典雅典的死刑》①(在前述罗伯特·J.邦纳教授指导下完成),以及论文《古典雅典作为刑罚的监禁》②等。

(九)库尔特·冯·弗里茨(Kurt von Fritz,1900～1985年)③

弗里茨是欧美国家最知名的古希腊史学者之一,第二次世界大战期间移居美国,曾长期(1937～1954年)任教于美国哥伦比亚大学。弗里茨身后留下了超过260部令人印象深刻的作品,其中包括15本独著作品,他对希腊的哲学、科学、诗歌和历史学都有深入研究,并始终关注古希腊的公正政体问题研究。在《古典古代的混合政体理论》④一书中,弗里茨分析了混合政体理论的起源等问题,认为混合政体理论经过柏拉图—亚里士多德—波利比阿等人的努力后最终发展成为对权力制衡的理论。弗里茨在古希腊法律史研究方面的代表作品主要包括专著《古希腊罗马的宪法历史与宪法理论》⑤,以及论文《梭伦反"内乱中中立"的立法》⑥、《亚里士多德雅典宪法的组成和所谓的德拉古宪法》⑦、《"hektemoros"的意义》⑧、《再论"hektemoroi"》⑨等。

---

① Barkan,I. (1935),*Capital Punishment in Ancient Athens*,New York.

② Barkan,I. (1936),"Imprisonment as a Penalty in Ancient Athens",*CPh* 31,338－341.

③ 弗里茨1900年生于德国梅斯,先后在弗莱堡大学和慕尼黑大学学习古典文献学,1923年以论文《诺普人第欧根尼研究》获得博士学位。1933年弗里茨任罗斯托克大学副教授,1937年任教于美国哥伦比亚大学,1954年到德国任教于柏林自由大学,1958年任教于慕尼黑大学直到1968年退休。

④ Von Fritz,K.,*The Theory of the Mixed Constitution in Antiquity*,New York,1954.

⑤ Von Fritz, K., *Schriften zur griechischen und römischen Verfassungsgeschichte und Verfassungstheorie de Gruyter*,Berlin u. a. 1976.

⑥ Von Fritz, K. (1977),"Nochmals das solonische Gesetz gegen Neutralität im Bürgerzwist", *Historia* 26,245－247.

⑦ Von Fritz,K. (1954),"The Composition of Aristotele's Constitution of Athens and the So-called Draconian Constitution",*CPh* 49,73－93(=Fritz,Schriften,71－98).

⑧ Von Fritz,K. (1940),"The Meaning of Hektemoros",*AJPh* 61,54－61(=Fritz,Schriften,110－116).

⑨ Von Fritz,K. (1943),"Once More the Hektemoroi",*AJPh* 64,24－43(=Fritz,Schriften,117－134).

(十)汉斯·朱利叶斯·沃尔夫(Hans Julius Wolff,1902~1983年)[①]

沃尔夫是欧美国家最知名的古希腊法律史学者之一,第二次世界大战期间移居美国,曾长期(1939~1952年)担任美国多所大学古典学教授,在古希腊法律史研究方面的代表作有专著《古代世界的竞争法律制度问题》[②]、《雅典民主政治中的立法和违法(违宪)审查:以对"graphe paranomon"程序的研究为中心》[③]及去世后由汉斯-阿尔伯特·鲁普雷希特(Hans-Albert Rupprecht)教授整理出版的《托勒密王朝时期埃及纸莎草纸所记载的古希腊法律研究(卷1)》[④]等,以及论文《古希腊法中的法条竞合问题》[⑤]、《古希腊法律铭文合集》[⑥]、《古希腊法律概念的起源和发展》[⑦]、《古希腊法律史:它的功能和可能性》[⑧]、《古希腊法学:任务、问题和可能性》[⑨]、《作为古希腊遗产的重要组成部分之一的古希腊

---

① 沃尔夫1902年出生于一个德国犹太人家庭,曾在柏林大学和罗斯托克大学学习古代历史语言学和法律,1932年获得博士学位,之后短期担任过代理法官,纳粹上台后,他于1935年流亡巴拿马并在数个大学任教。1939年移居美国,先后任职于美国中西部的多个大学。1952年回到德国,在美因茨大学教授罗马法。1955年任弗莱堡大学教授,教授希腊法和罗马法,并创建了古希腊法律史研究中心。他的研究领域为古典雅典时期的法律以及托勒密埃及时期的纸莎草纸法律文献。1972年获雅典大学授予名誉博士学位。1974年至1975年成为普林斯顿大学高等研究院客座研究员。沃尔夫教授一生著作等身,为德国和欧洲古希腊法律史研究做出了杰出的贡献。

② Hans Julius Wolff(1979), *Das Problem der Konkurrenz von Rechtsordnungen in der Antike*, Heidelberg(Sitzungsberichte der Heidelberger Akademie der Wissenschaften, Philos. – Histor. Klasse 5).

③ Hans Julius Wolff(1970b), *Normenkontrolle und Gesetzesbegriff in der athenischen Demokratie. Untersuchungen zur graphe paranomon*, Heidelberg (Sitzungsberichte der Heidelberger Akademie der Wissenschaften, Philos. -Histor. Klasse 2).

④ Das recht der griechischen papyri ägyptens in der zeit der ptolemäer und des prinzipats Vol. Ⅰ, 2002.

⑤ Hans Julius Wolff (1983), "Zum Problem der dogmatischen Erfassung des altgriechischen Rechts", in Symposion 1979, 7–20.

⑥ Hans Julius Wolff(1982), "Sammlung griechischer Rechtsinschriften", *ZPE* 45, 123–126.

⑦ Hans Julius Wolff (1980), "Vorgeschichte und Entstehung des Rechtsbegriffs in fruhen Griechentum", in W. Fikentscher, H. Franke & O. Kohler (eds), Entstehung und Wandel rechtlicher Traditionen, 557–579, Freiburg (= "Preistoria ed origine del concetto di diritto nell'esperienza greca arcaica" Studi Sanfilippo Ⅱ, 759–780, Roma 1982).

⑧ Hans Julius Wolff (1975), "Greek Legal History-Its Functions and Potentialities", *Washington University Law Quarterly*, 395–408 [= Revista de Estudios Historico-Juridicos 1(1976) 136–148].

⑨ Hans Julius Wolff (1975), "Juristische Gräzistik-Aufgaben, Probleme, Möglichkeiten", in Symposion 1971, 1–22.

法》①、《古希腊法律史思想史研究的意义》②、《铭文学在希腊法律史研究中的重要性》③、《古雅典的违法审查：Die graphe paranomon》④、《雅典法院演讲词的法律史研究方法问题》⑤、《新的法律文件Ⅳ：古希腊法中的财产》⑥、《作为古典研究和法律关注的古希腊法律史》⑦、《作为顾问的德摩斯梯尼：古典雅典法律顾问的功能和方法》⑧、《法律史学家和私法学说》⑨、《雅典（法律）条款：古老诉讼形式的贡献》⑩、《比较法律史视野下的债务和损害赔偿之诉》⑪、《古希腊法中合同责任的结构》⑫、《古希腊的法学家》⑬、《雅典法中的索赔时效》⑭、《希腊法的成文法和习

---

① Hans Julius Wolff(1973),"Das Recht als Komponente des griechischen Erbes",in Gehrig,H.(ed),Der Lebenswert des Griechischen,29-41,Karlsruhe(Veröffentlichungen der Katholischen Akademie der Erzdioezese Freiburg 29)(=Opuscula,1-13).

② Hans Julius Wolff(1973),"Zur Bedeutung der altgriechischen Rechtsgeschichte für die Rechtswissenschaft",in Xenion Zeppos,757-763.

③ Hans Julius Wolff(1973),"Die Bedeutung der Epigraphik für die griechische Rechtsgeschichte",in Akten des 6. Internationalen Kongresses,131-144.

④ Hans Julius Wolff(1972),"Normenkontrolle im klassischen Athen:Die graphe paranomon",in Tomos aphieromenos eis ton omotimon kathegeten Pan. Perdika,127-139,Athenai.

⑤ Hans Julius Wolff(1971),"Methodische Grundsatzfragen der rechtsgeschichtlichen Verwendung attischer Gerichtsreden",in La critica del testo Ⅱ(Atti del Ⅱ Congresso Internazionale della Società Italiana di Storia del Diritto,Venezia,18-22 settembre 1967),1123-1135,Florence(=Opuscula 27-39).

⑥ Hans Julius Wolff(1971),"Neue juristische Urkunden,Ⅳ:Eigentumsbindung nach griechischen Recht",ZRG 88,329-339.

⑦ Hans Julius Wolff(1970),"Griechische Rechtsgeschichte als Anliegen der Altertumswissenschaft und der Rechtswissenschaft",Ellenike Anthropistike Hetaireia 20,152-162(=Opuscula 15-24).

⑧ Hans Julius Wolff(1968),Demosthenes als Advokat,Berlin.(Schriftenreihe der iuristischen Gesellschaft 30)(="O Demosthenes hos dikegoros" Ephemeris Ellenon Nomikon 36(1969)305-314,translated as"Demosthenes as advocate:The functions and methods of legal consultants in classical Athens" with an epilogue by G. Thür in The Attic Orators,91-115.)

⑨ Hans Julius Wolff(1967),"Der Rechtshistoriker und die Privatrechtsdogmatik",in Festschrift für Fritz von Hippel,Tübingen,687-710(=Opuscula,41-64).

⑩ Hans Julius Wolff(1966),Die attische Paragraphe:ein Beitrag zum Problem der Auflockerung archaischer Prozessformen,Weimar.

⑪ Hans Julius Wolff(1966),"Debt and assumpsit in the light of comparative legal history",The Irish Jurist 1,316-327(=Opuscula,123-134).

⑫ Hans Julius Wolff(1966a),"La structure de l'obligation contractuelle en droit grec",RHDFE 44,569-583.

⑬ Hans Julius Wolff(1964),"Rechtsexperten in der griechischen Antike",in Festschrift für den 45. deutschen Juristentag,1-22,Karlsruhe(=Opuscula,81-102).

⑭ Hans Julius Wolff(1963),"Verjährung von Ansprüchen nach attischem Recht",in Eranion Maridaki,87-109.

惯法》①、《古希腊合同法》②、《法制史视野下的法律程序和实体法》③、《雅典的"Apotimema"(雅典租赁及嫁妆契约中的术语)》④、《雅典被监护人财产的租赁权》⑤、《希腊婚姻法的基本原则》⑥、《阿喀琉斯之盾》⑦、《古代法律史科学》⑧、《希腊城邦间司法诉讼的起源》⑨、《古代雅典的婚姻法和家庭组织》⑩、《德摩斯梯尼演说词中的法律受害者》⑪等。

二、20世纪中后期至今美国的古希腊法律史学者及其研究成果

(一)马丁·奥斯特瓦尔德(Martin Ostwald,1922～2010年)

马丁·奥斯特瓦尔德是一位德裔美国古典学者,1922年出生于德国多特蒙德,是一位犹太律师的长子。第二次世界大战期间奥斯特瓦尔德迁居加拿大、美国,先后毕业于多伦多大学和芝加哥大学,并于1952年获芝加哥大学博士学位,指导老师为库尔特·冯·弗里茨。后任教于卫斯理大学(1952～1953年)、哥伦比亚大学(1953～1958年)、斯沃斯莫尔学院(1958～1992年)、宾夕法尼亚大学

---

① Hans Julius Wolff (1962), "Gewohnheitsrecht und Gesetzesrecht in der griechischen Rechtsauffassung", in Deutsche Landesreferate zum Ⅵ. Intern. Kongress für Rechtsvergleichung in Hamburg, 99-120, Berlin (=Zur griechischen Rechtsgeschichte, 99-120, and as "Ethimikon dikaion kai nomoi tethemenou dikaiou kata tas peri dikaiou antilepseis ton archaion Ellenon" Ephemeris Ellenon Nomikon 29(1962)649-678).

② Hans Julius Wolff(1957), "Die Grundlagen des griechischen Vertragsrechts", *ZRG* 74, 26-72(=Zur griechischen Rechtsgeschichte, 483-533).

③ Hans Julius Wolff(1954), "Prozessrechtliches und materiellrechtliches Denken in rechtsgeschichtlicher Beleuchtung", in Studi in memoria di Paolo Koschaker Ⅱ, 405-423, Mailand.

④ Hans Julius Wolff(1954), "Das attische Apotimema", in Festschrift Rabel Ⅱ, 293-333.

⑤ Hans Julius Wolff(1953), "Verpachtung von Mundelvermogen in Attika", in Festschrift Lewald, 201-208.

⑥ Hans Julius Wolff(1952), "Die Grundlagen des griechischen Eherechts", *RHDFE* 20, 1-29 and 157-181 (=Atti del Terzo Congresso di Diritto Comparato Ⅰ, 213-257, Rome 1953 and in Zur griechischen Rechtsgeschichte, 620-654).

⑦ Hans Julius Wolff(1950), "Nochmals zum Schild des Achilles", Iura 1, 272-275.

⑧ Hans Julius Wolff(1950), "The Science of Ancient Legal History", *Law Guild Review* 10, 47-51.

⑨ Hans Julius Wolff(1946), "The Origin of Judicial Litigation Among the Greeks", *Traditio* 4, 31-87(=Beiträge, 1-90).

⑩ Hans Julius Wolff(1944), "Marriage Law and Family Organisation in Ancient Athens", *Traditio* 2, 43-95(=Beiträge, 155-242).

⑪ Hans Julius Wolff(1943), "The Dike Blabes in Demosthenes, or 51", *AJPh* 64, 316-324(=Beiträge, 91-101).

（与斯沃斯莫尔学院两校同时兼任），[1]1987年担任美国语言学协会主席，1991年当选为美国艺术与科学学院院士，1995年被瑞士弗里堡大学授予荣誉博士学位，2001年被德国多特蒙德大学授予荣誉博士学位。奥斯特瓦尔德的主要研究领域是古希腊的政治结构，曾翻译出版了《亚里士多德〈尼各马科伦理学〉》[2]，在古希腊法律史研究方面的成果主要包括专著《"Oligarchia"：古希腊宪法形式的演变》[3]、《从人民主权到法律主权：伯里克利时代的法律、社会和政治》[4]、《法律和雅典民主的开端》[5]、《不成文法和古代雅典的宪法始祖》[6]等，以及论文《雅典和哈尔基斯：一个关于帝国控制的研究》[7]、《分享和权利："公民"希腊和美国模式》[8]、《〈雅典政制〉中的战神山议事会》[9]、《安提丰"Peri Aletheias"中的法律和自然》[10]、《柏拉图关于法和自然的论述》[11]、《古希腊是否存在一个"agraphos"法的概念？》[12]、

---

① 奥斯特瓦尔德先后指导的博士研究生包括 Michael F. Arnush, Susan F. Elwyn, Vanessa B. Gorman, Charles W. Hedrick, Jr., Karl Maurer, Ellen Greenstein Millender, Mark H. Munn, Rob S. Rice, Eric W. Robinson, Scott Rusch。

② Ostwald, M. (1962), *Aristotle: The Nicomachean Ethics. Translation with Introduction, Notes, and Glossary*, Indianapolis and New York.

③ Ostwald, M. (2000), *Oligarchia: The Development of a Constitutional form in Ancient Greece*, Stuttgart.

④ Ostwald, M. (1986), *From Popular Sovereignty to the Sovereignty of Law: Law, Society, and Politics in Fifth-century Athens*, Berkeley.

⑤ Ostwald, M. (1969), *Nomos and the Beginnings of the Athenian Democracy*, Oxford.

⑥ Ostwald, M. (1952), *The Unwritten Laws and the Ancestral Constitution of Ancient Athens*, Columbia.

⑦ Ostwald, M. (2002), "Athens and Chalkis: A Study in Imperial Control", *JHS* 122, 134 – 143.

⑧ Ostwald, M. (1996), "Shares and Rights: 'Citizenship' Greek and American Style", in Ober, J. & Ch. Hedrick (eds), *Demokratia. A Conversation on Democracies, Ancient and Modern*, 49 – 61, Princeton (= Ostwald, Language and history, 7 – 21).

⑨ Ostwald, M. (1993), "The Areopagus in the Athenaion Politeia", in *Aristote et Athenes*, 139 – 153 (= Ostwald, *Language and History*, 230 – 244).

⑩ Ostwald, M. (1990), "Nomos and Physis in Antiphon's Peri Aletheias", in Griffith, M. & D. J. Matronarde (eds), *Cabinet of the Muses: Essays on Classical and Comparative Literature in Honor of Th. G. Rosenmeyer*, 293 – 306, Atlanta (= Ostwald, Language and history, 158 – 174).

⑪ Ostwald, M. (1977), "Plato on Law and Nature", in North, H. F. (ed) *Interpretations of Plato. A Swarthmore Symposium*, 41 – 63, Leiden (Mnemosyne Suppl. 50).

⑫ Ostwald, M. (1973), "Was there a Concept Agraphos Nomos in Classical Greece?", in Mourelatos, P. D. & R. M. Rorty (eds), *Exegesis and Argument. Studies in Greek Philosophy presented to G. Vlastos*, 70 – 104, Assen (Phronesis Suppl 1) (= Ostwald, Language and history, 125 – 157).

《品达、法律和赫拉克勒斯》①、《雅典反对僭政和颠覆的法律》②、《Prytaneion 法令再审视》③等。

（二）拉斐尔·希利（Raphael Sealey，1927～2013 年）

拉斐尔·希利 1927 年出生于英国米德尔斯堡，早年就读于牛津大学，曾先后任教于英国北威尔士大学、玛丽女王学院、伦敦大学和美国纽约州立大学布法罗分校，1967～2000 年任职于美国加州大学伯克利分校，主要研究方向为古希腊法律史。希利退休后继续担任加州大学伯克利分校荣誉教授直至 2013 年去世。希利教授在古希腊法律史研究方面的成果主要包括专著《雅典共和国：民主抑或法治》④、《古希腊的妇女和法律》⑤、《古希腊人的正义》⑥、《古希腊城邦史》⑦、《德摩斯梯尼和他的时代》⑧等，以及论文《Ath. Pol 25.2 和 Lys. fr. 178：战神山议事会的附加功能》⑨、《雅典的合法纳妾》⑩、《雅典的凶杀法庭》⑪、《雅典公民和城邦如何开始发生联系》⑫、《雅典的法律概念》⑬、《埃菲阿尔特斯、检举和委员会》⑭、《梭伦立法的日期》⑮、《Probouleusis 和主权会议》⑯、《埃菲阿尔特斯》⑰、《惩罚战神山

① Ostwald, M. (1965), "Pindar, nomos and Herakles (Pindar, frg. 169 [Snell3] and POxy. No. 2450, frg. 1)", *HSCP* 69, 109-138 (= Ostwald, Language and history, 93-124).

② Ostwald, M. (1955), "The Athenian Legislation Against Tyranny and Subversion", *TAPhA* 86, 103-128.

③ "The Prytaneion Decree Re-examined", *American Journal of Philology* 72 (1951) 24-46.

④ Sealey, R. (1987), *The Athenian Republic: Democracy or the Rule of Law?*, London.

⑤ Sealey, R. (1990), *Women and Law in Classical Greece*, Princeton.

⑥ Sealey, R. (1994), *The Justice of the Greeks*, Ann Arbor.

⑦ Sealey, R. (1976), *A History of the Greek City States*, 700-338 *B. C.*, Oakland: University of California Press.

⑧ Sealey, R. (1993), *Demosthenes and His Time*, Oxford: Oxford University Press.

⑨ Sealey, R. (1991), "Ath. Pol 25.2 and Lys. fr. 178: Additional Functions of the Areopagite Council", *JHS* 111, 210.

⑩ Sealey, R. (1984), "On Lawful Concubinage in Athens", *ClAnt* 3, 111-133.

⑪ Sealey, R. (1983b), "The Athenian Courts for Homicide", *CPh* 78, 275-296.

⑫ Sealey, R. (1983a), "How Citizenship and the City began in Athens", *AJAH* 8, 97-129.

⑬ Sealey, R. (1982), "On the Athenian Concept of Law", *CJ* 77, 289-302.

⑭ Sealey, R. (1981), "Ephialtes, Eisangelia, and the Council", in G. S. Schrimpton & D. J. McGargar (eds) *Classical Contributions. Studies in Honour of Malcolm Francis MacGregor*, 125-134, New York.

⑮ Sealey, R. (1978), "Zum Datum der solonischen Gesetzgebung", *Historia* 28, 238-241.

⑯ Sealey, R. (1969), "Probouleusis and the Sovereign Assembly", *CSCA* 2, 247-269.

⑰ Sealey, R. (1964), "Ephialtes", *CPh* 59, 11-22.

议事会成员》①、《IG II2 1609 和第二雅典海上同盟的转型》②等。

(三)艾伦·林德利·伯格霍尔德(Alan Lindley Boegehold)

伯格霍尔德早年获哈佛大学博士学位,后一直任教于美国布朗大学古典系至退休,在古希腊法律史方面的研究成果主要包括专著《雅典法庭:位置、建筑物、设施、程序和证明》③、《亚里士多德和民众法庭》④,主编《雅典人身份和公民意识》⑤等,以及论文《Leogoros 在法庭上说了什么:基于"Andocides 1.41"》⑥、《雅典法律变革的阻力》⑦、《公元前 451/450 年伯利克里公民身份法》⑧、《三个法庭审判日》⑨、《安多喀德斯和 Patrokleides 法令》⑩、《雅典投票程序研究》⑪、《亚里士多德〈雅典政制〉(65.2):官方令牌》⑫等。

(四)莎莉·C.汉弗莱斯(Sally C. Humphreys)

汉弗莱斯 1957 年获牛津大学学士学位,1959 年获伦敦大学学院历史学硕士学位,自 1985 年以来一直担任美国密歇根大学历史学教授,在古希腊法律史方面的研究成果主要包括专著《人类学和古希腊人》⑬、主编《法律演说》⑭等,以及论

---

① Sealey, R. (1958), "On Penalizing Areopagites", *AJPh* 79, 71－73(＝R. Sealey, Essays in Greek politics, 183－185, New York 1967).

② Sealey, R. (1957), "IG II2 1609 and the Transformation of the Second Athenian Sea-league", *Phoenix* 11, 95－111.

③ Boegehold, A. L. (1995), *The Lawcourts at Athens: Sites, Buildings, Equipment, Procedure and Testimonia, Princeton*(The Athenian Agora 28).

④ Boegehold, A. L. (1958), *Aristotle and the Dikasteria*, diss. Har.

⑤ Alan L. Boegehold, Adele C. Scafuro eds. (2002), *Athenian Identity and Civic Ideology*, Johns Hopkins University Press; Revised ed.

⑥ Boegehold, A. L. (2009), "What is Leogoros Saying? Andocides 1.41", in Karamalengou, E. & Eug. Makriyanni (eds), *Antiphilesis. Studies on Classical, Byzantine and Modern Greek Literature and Culture in Honour of John-Theophanes A. Papademetriou*, 283－285, Stuttgart.

⑦ Boegehold, A. L. (1996), "Resistance to Change in the Law at Athens", in J. Ober & Ch. Hedrick jr(eds), *Demokratia. A Conversation on Democracies, Ancient and Modern*, 203－214, Princeton.

⑧ Boegehold, A. L. (1994), "Perikles' Citizenship Law of 451/0 BC", in *Athenian identity*, 57－66.

⑨ Boegehold, A. L. (1991), "Three Court Days", in Symposion 1990, 165－182.

⑩ Boegehold, A. L. (1990), "Andocides and the Decree of Patrokleides", *Historia* 39, 149－162.

⑪ Boegehold, A. L. (1963), "Towards a Study of Athenian Voting Procedure", *Hesperia* 32, 366－374.

⑫ Boegehold, A. L. (1960), "Aristotle's Athenaion Politeia 65.2: The 'official token'", *Hesperia* 29, 393－401.

⑬ Humphreys, S. C. *Anthropology and the Greeks*, Routledge; Reprint, 2005.

⑭ Humphreys, S. C. (1985 eds) *Discourse of Law*, Routledge.

文《梭伦对收养和遗嘱的论述》[①]、《法律、法院和程序》[②]、《古典雅典亲戚之间的婚姻》[③]、《认识德拉古凶杀法的一条历史路径》[④]、《古代和古典时期希腊的法律演讲》[⑤]、《希罗多德(著作中)的法律、习俗和文化》[⑥]、《雅典法庭中的亲属模式》[⑦]、《舞台上的社会关系:古典雅典的证人》[⑧]、《古代阿提卡法律程序的演变》[⑨]、《犬儒学派的私生子》[⑩]等。

(五)大卫·科恩(David Cohen)

大卫·科恩早年先后获得加州大学洛杉矶分校法学博士学位和剑桥大学古典学博士学位,1979～2012 年任教于加州大学伯克利分校,现为夏威夷大学威廉·理查森法学院法学教授、加州大学伯克利分校研究生院教授。科恩教授是伯克利战争罪行研究中心的创始董事,主要研究领域为人权、战争犯罪以及古典法律史,在古希腊法律史方面的研究成果主要包括专著《法律、性和社会:古典雅典道德规范的执行》[⑪]、《古典雅典的法律、暴力和社区》[⑫]、《雅典法中的盗窃》[⑬],以及论文《雅典的民主和个人权利》[⑭]、《惩罚理论》[⑮]、《古典雅典公共场合下的妇

---

① Humphreys, S. C. (2002), "Solon on Adoption and Wills", *ZRG* 119, 340 – 347.

② Humphreys, S. C. (1997), "Leggi, Tribunali, Processi", in I Greci 2, 541 – 566.

③ Humphreys, S. C. (1994), "Le mariage entre parents dans l'Athènes classique", in Bonte, P. (ed), Épouser au plus proche. Inceste, prohibition et stratégies matrimoniales autour de la Méditerranée, 31 – 58, Paris.

④ Humphreys, S. C. (1992), "A Historical Approach to Drakon's Law on Homicide", in Symposion 1990, 17 – 45.

⑤ Humphreys, S. C. (1988), "The Discourse of Law in Archaic and Classical Greece", *Law and History Review* 6, 465 – 493.

⑥ Humphreys, S. C. (1987), "Law, Custom and Culture in Herodotus", *Arethousa* 20, 211 – 220.

⑦ Humphreys, S. C. (1986), "Kinship Patterns in the Athenian Courts", *GRBS* 27, 57 – 92.

⑧ Humphreys, S. C. (1985), "Social Relations on Stage: Witnesses in Classical Athens", *History and Anthropology* 1, 313 – 369(= The Attic Orators, 140 – 213).

⑨ Humphreys, S. C. (1983), "The Evolution of Legal Process in Ancient Attica", in Gabba, E. (ed), Tria Corda. Studi in onore di Arnaldo Momigliano, 229 – 256, Como(Biblioteca di Athenaeum 1).

⑩ Humphreys, S. C. (1974), "The Nothoi of Kynosarges", *JHS* 94, 88 – 95. Hunt, P. (2010) War, Peace and Alliance in Demosthenes' Athens, Cambridge.

⑪ Cohen, D. (1991b), *Law, Sexuality and Society: The Enforcement of Morals in Classical Athens*, Cambridge.

⑫ Cohen, D. (1995b), *Law, Violence and Community in Classical Athens*, Cambridge.

⑬ Cohen, D. (1983), *Theft in Athenian Law*, München(MBPaR 74).

⑭ Cohen, D. (2006), "Democracy and Individual Rights in Athens", *Philosophical Inquiry* 27, 13 – 26.

⑮ Cohen, D. (2005c), "Theories of Punishment", in *The Cambridge Companion*, 170 – 182.

女：性别、公民权和社会地位》①、《古典雅典的犯罪、刑罚和法治》②、《雅典法庭中的书写、法律和法律实践》③、《正义的修辞：公元前403年雅典民主恢复时期和解和报复的策略》④、《德摩斯梯尼片段41和57中记载的雅典妇女、财产和身份》⑤、《雅典的民主和个人权利》⑥、《古典雅典的隔离、分离和妇女身份》⑦、《古典雅典的法治和民主意识形态》⑧、《古典雅典的同意和性关系》⑨、《古典雅典的修辞、道德和法治》⑩、《柏拉图〈法治篇〉中的法律、自治和政治共同体》⑪、《古典雅典的荣誉、仇恨和诉讼》⑫、《德摩斯梯尼"控告米迪亚斯"和雅典诉讼》⑬、《辩论（与Clifford Handley）：古典雅典的法律、社会和同性恋》⑭、《性欲、暴力和雅典的"hybris"法律》⑮、《雅典通奸的社会环境分析》⑯、《最新资料和希腊法律制度的

---

① Cohen, D. (2005), "Women in Public: Gender, Citizenship, and Social Status in Classical Athens", in Symposion 2001, 33 – 46 (with a reply by L. Foxhall, 47 – 50).

② Cohen, D. (2005), "Crime, Punishment, and the Rule of Law in Classical Athens", in *The Cambridge Companion*, 211 – 235.

③ Cohen, D. (2003), "Writing, Law, and Legal Practice in the Athenian Courts", in Yunis, H. (ed), *Written Texts and the Rise of Literate Culture in Ancient Greece*, 78 – 96, Cambridge.

④ Cohen, D. (2001), "The Rhetoric of Justice: Strategies of Reconciliation and Revenge in the Restoration of Athenian Democracy in 403 BC", *European Journal of Sociology* 42, 335 – 56.

⑤ Cohen, D. (1998), "Women, Property and Status in Demosthenes 41 and 57", Dike 1, 53 – 61.

⑥ Cohen, D. (1997), "Democracy and Individual Rights in Athens", *ZRG* 114, 27 – 44 (= Anagnostopoulos, Y. (ed), *Law and Rights in the Ancient Greek Tradition*, 13 – 26, Thessaloniki 2006).

⑦ Cohen, D. (1996), "Seclusion, Separation, and the Status of Women in Classical Athens", in McAuslan, I. & P. Walcot (eds), *Women in Antiquity*, 135 – 45, Cambridge.

⑧ Cohen, D. (1995), "The Rule of Law and Democratic Ideology in Classical Athens", in Die Athenische Demokratie, 227 – 248.

⑨ Cohen, D. (1993), "Consent and Sexual Relations in Classical Athens", in Laiou, A. E. (ed), *Consent and Coercion to Sex and Marriage in Ancient and Medieval Societies*, 5 – 16, Washington D. C.

⑩ Cohen, D. (1993), "Rhetoric, Morals, and the Rule of Law in Classical Athens", *ZRG* 110, 1ff.

⑪ Cohen, D. (1993), "Law, Autonomy and Political Community in Plato's Laws", *CPh* 88, 301 – 317.

⑫ Cohen, D. (1992), "Honor, Feud, and Litigation in Classical Athens", *ZRG* 109, 100 – 115.

⑬ Cohen, D. (1992), "Demosthenes' Against Meidias and Athenian Litigation", in Symposion 1990, 155 – 164.

⑭ Cohen, D. (1991), "Debate (with Cliford Handley): Law, Society and Homosexuality in Classical Athens", *P & P* 133, 167 – 194.

⑮ Cohen, D. (1991), "Sexuality, Violence and the Athenian Law of Hybris", *G & R* 38, 171 – 188.

⑯ Cohen, D. (1990), "The Social Context of Adultery at Athens", in *Nomos*, 147 – 166.

"重建"》①、《古希腊法研究的问题、方法和模式》②、《古希腊法中对不敬神罪的起诉》③、《古典雅典的法律、社会和同性恋》④、《柏拉图〈法律篇〉中妇女的法律地位和政治角色》⑤、《埃斯库罗斯的神义论:〈俄瑞斯忒亚〉中的正义和僭主》⑥、《阿里斯托芬和雅典涉及通奸惩罚的法律》⑦、《雅典涉及通奸的法律》⑧、《柏拉图〈法律篇〉记载的盗窃和雅典的法律实践》⑨、《伊利亚特中记载的"Horkia"和"horkos"》⑩等。

(六)罗伯特·W.华莱士(Robert W. Wallace,1950年至今)

华莱士早年获哈佛大学博士学位,现任美国西北大学温伯格艺术与科学学院教授,在古希腊法律史方面的研究成果主要包括专著《重建达蒙:伯利克里时代雅典的音乐、智慧教育和政治》⑪、《公元前307年的战神山议事会》,⑫以及论文《柏拉图笔下的苏格拉底对民主雅典法律的服从》⑬、《苏格拉底和民主制法律:柏拉图的(克利同篇)和(申辩篇)》⑭、《希腊民主城邦、罗马共和国和现代自由主义国

---

① Cohen, D. (1990), "Late Sources and the 'Reconstruction' of Greek Legal Institutions", in Symposion 1988, 283 – 293.

② Cohen, D. (1989), "Problems, Methods, and Models in the Study of Greek Law", *ZRG* 106, 81 – 105.

③ Cohen, D. (1988), "The Prosecution of Impiety in Athenian Law", *ZRG* 110, 695 – 701 (= Symposion 1985, 99 – 109).

④ Cohen, D. (1987), "Law, Society and Homosexuality in Classical Athens", *P &P* 117, 3 – 21 (= Osborne, R. (ed) (2004) Studies in ancient Greek and Roman society, 61 – 77, Cambridge).

⑤ Cohen, D. (1987), "The Legal Status and Political Role of Women in Plato's Laws", *RIDA* 34, 27 – 40.

⑥ Cohen, D. (1986), "The Theodicy of Aeschylus: Justice and Tyranny in the Oresteia", *G &R* 33, 129 – 141.

⑦ Cohen, D. (1985), "A Note on Aristophanes and the Punishment of Adultery in Athenian Law", *ZRG* 102, 385 – 387.

⑧ Cohen, D. (1984), "The Athenian Law of Adultery", *RIDA* 31, 147 – 165.

⑨ Cohen, D. (1982), "Theft in Plato's Laws and Athenian Legal Practice", *RIDA* 29, 121 – 143.

⑩ Cohen, D. (1980), "'Horkia' and 'Horkos' in the Iliad", *RIDA* 27, 49 – 68.

⑪ Wallace, R. W. (2015), *Reconstructing Damon. Music, Wisdom Teaching, and Politics in Perikles' Athens*, Oxford: Oxford University Press.

⑫ Wallace, R. W. (1989), *The Areopagus Council to* 307 *B. C.*, Baltimore-London.

⑬ Wallace, R. W. (2011), "Plato's Socrates on Obeying the Laws of Democratic Athens", *Philosophia* 41, 87 – 96.

⑭ Wallace, R. W. (2010), "Socrates and Democratic Law: Plato's Crito and Apology", in Thür, G. (ed) Symposion 2009. Vorträge zur griechischen und hellenistischen Rechtsgeschichte (Seggau, 25. – 30. August 2009), 109 – 116, Wien.

家下的个人自由》①、《法律抑或自然：反民主的背景分析》②、《在古典雅典法律的敌人》③、《古典雅典的自由、共同体和法律》④、《雅典关于法律行为的法律规定：关于自由的两个争论》⑤、《古典雅典自由起诉诉讼的撤回：基于“谄媚”和其法律特质的一个案例分析》⑥、《法律和修辞：雅典法庭的共同体正义》⑦、《在民主雅典的听从公理》⑧、《法律、阿提卡喜剧和喜剧演员演说的规定》⑨、《在古典雅典说话而不是听的权力》⑩、《雅典法律和法律程序中的揭示》⑪、《公元前 4 世纪晚期雅典的“Diamarturia”(抗议)：关于“奶酪罐”的研究》⑫、《战胜山议事会的调查和报告与德摩斯梯尼的战神山议事会法令》⑬、《亚里士多德(雅典政制)的结构》⑭、《古典雅典未确定或潜在的丧失公民权》⑮、《公元前 4 世纪雅典没有涉及性行为

---

① Wallace, R. W. (2009), "Personal Freedom in Greek Democracies, Republican Rome and Modern Liberal States", in *Greek and Roman Political Thought*, 164 – 177.

② Wallace, R. W. (2007), "Nomos/Phusis: The Antidemocratic Context", in Pierris, A. L. (ed), *Phusis and Nomos: Power, Justice and the Agonistical Ideal of Life in High Classicism*, 23 – 44, Patras.

③ Wallace, R. W. (2007), "Law's Enemies in Ancient Athens", in Symposion 2005, 183 – 196.

④ Wallace, R. W. (2006), "Freedom, Community, and Law in Classical Athens", in Anagnostopoulos, Y. (ed), *Law and Rights in the Ancient Greek Tradition*, 57 – 78, Thessaloniki.

⑤ Wallace, R. W. (2006), "The Legal Regulation of Conduct at Athens: Two Controversies on Freedom", Dike 9, 107 – 128 (= Etica e Politica 9 (2007) 155 – 171).

⑥ Wallace, R. W. (2006), "Withdrawing Graphai in Ancient Athens-A Case Study in 'Sycophancy' and Legal Idiosyncrasies", in Symposion 2003, 57 – 72.

⑦ Wallace, R. W. (2006), "Law and Rhetoric: Community Justice in Athenian Courts", in Kinzl, K. H. (ed), *A Companion to the Classical Greek World*, 416 – 431, Oxford.

⑧ Wallace, R. W. (2005), "'Listening to' the Archai in Democratic Athens", in Symposion 2001, 147 – 157.

⑨ Wallace, R. W. (2005), "Law, Attic Comedy, and the Regulation of Comic Speech", in *The Cambridge Companion*, 357 – 373.

⑩ Wallace, R. W. (2004), "The Power to Speak-and not to Listen-in Ancient Athens", in *Free Speech*, 221 – 232.

⑪ Wallace, R. W. (2003), "Phainein in Athenian Laws and Legal Procedures", in Symposion 1999, 167 – 183.

⑫ Wallace, R. W. (2001), "Diamarturia in Late Fourth-century Athens: Notes on a 'Cheese Pot' (SEG XXXVI 296)", in Symposion 1997, 89 – 102.

⑬ Wallace, R. W. (2000), "Investigations and Reports 'by the Areopagos Council and Demosthenes' Areopagos Decree", in *Polis and Politics*, 581 – 596.

⑭ Wallace, R. W. (1999), "The Structure of Aristotle's Athenaion Politeia", in Mellor, M. & L. Tritle (eds), *Text and Tradition: Studies in Greek History and Historiography in Honor of M. Chambers*, 239 – 257, Claremont, Cal.

⑮ Wallace, R. W. (1998), "Unconvicted or Potential Atimoi in Ancient Athens", Dike 1, 63 – 78.

的立法活动》[①]、《民主雅典的法律、自由和公民权利的概念》[②]、《雅典涉及诽谤的法律》[③]、《民主正义 vs. 无律师》[④]、《古典雅典民主制下的个人行为和法律制裁》[⑤]、《〈雅典政制〉中的亚里士多德政治思想》[⑥]、《亚里士多德政体(思想)和雅典政制卷(4)》[⑦]、《伊索格拉底(战神山议事会辩)发布的时间》[⑧]、《梭伦改革的时间》[⑨]、《艾斐烈特(改革)和战神山议事会》[⑩]、《公元前5世纪早期厄立特里亚代理人法令》[⑪]、《所欠 Karystos 城的债务》[⑫]等。

(七)迈克尔·加加林(Michael Gagarin)

加加林曾任美国得克萨斯大学奥斯丁分校古代史教授、荣誉教授,在古希腊法律史方面的研究成果主要包括专著《德拉古和早期雅典杀人法》[⑬]、《早期希腊法》[⑭]、《雅典人安提丰:智者时代的演说、法律和正义》[⑮]、《谋杀赫罗德斯:安提丰

---

① Wallace, R. W. (1997), "On Not Legislating Sexual Conduct in Fourth-century Athens", in Symposion 1995, 151 - 166.

② Wallace, R. W. (1996), "Law, Freedom, and the Concept of Citizen's Rights in Democratic Athens", in Ober, J. & Ch. Hedrick jr (eds), *Demokratia: A Conversation on Democracies, Ancient and Modern*, 105 - 119, Princeton.

③ Wallace, R. W. (1994), "The Athenian Laws on Slander", in Symposion 1993, 109 - 124.

④ Wallace, R. W. (1994), "Democratic Justice-no Lawyers", in *A Challenge to Democracy*, 69 - 80, Washington D. C.

⑤ Wallace, R. W. (1993), "Personal Conduct and Legal Sanction in the Democracy of Classical Athens", in Zlinsky, J. (ed), Questions de responsabilité (XLVe Session de la Société Internationale "Ferdinand de Visscher" pour l'Histoire des Droits de l'Antiquité), 397 - 413, Miskolc-Eger.

⑥ Wallace, R. W. (1993), "La Politeia Aristotelica e l'Athenaion Politeia", in Cresci, L. R. & L. Piccirilli (eds), L'Athenaion Politeia di Aristotele, 25 - 52, Genova.

⑦ Wallace, R. W. (1992), "Aristotelian Politeiai and Athenaion Politeia 4", in *Nomodeiktes*, 269 - 286.

⑧ Wallace, R. W. (1986), "The Date of Isokrates' Areopagitikos", *HSCP* 90, 77 - 84.

⑨ Wallace, R. W. (1983), "The Date of Solon's Reforms", *AJAH* 8, 81 - 95.

⑩ Wallace, R. W. (1974), "Ephialtes and the Areopagus", *GRBS* 15, 259 - 269.

⑪ Wallace, W. (1936), "An Eretrian Proxeny Decree of the Early Fifth Century", *Hesperia* 4, 273 - 284.

⑫ Wallace, W. P. (1962), "Loans to Karystos", *Phoenix* 16, 15 - 28.

⑬ Gagarin, M. (1981), *Drakon and Early Athenian Homicide Law*.

⑭ Gagarin, M. (1986), *Early Greek Law*.

⑮ Gagarin, M. (2002), *Antiphon the Athenian: Oratory, Law and Justice in the Age of the Sophists*, University of Texas Press.

卷(5)研究》①、《写作古希腊法》②、《雅典法律演说词》③,与其他学者合作完成了《古代格尔蒂的法律》④、《剑桥古希腊法指南》⑤、《古希腊从荷马到智者时代的政治思想》⑥等书,此外还编译出版了《安提丰演说集》⑦等。

加加林教授在古希腊法律史研究方面的论文作品主要包括《格尔蒂的妇女和法律》⑧、《格尔蒂法》⑨、《古代和古典时期格尔蒂的书面神圣法》⑩、《格尔蒂的法律程序》⑪、《格尔蒂的农奴和奴隶》⑫、《格尔蒂的妇女和财产》⑬、《早期雅典演说术中的理性论争》⑭、《雅典法中当事人的宣誓》⑮、《从口头法到书面法:德拉古和它的荷马时期渊源》⑯、《在希腊和近东的法律订立》⑰、《梭伦法中的法律程序》⑱、

---

① Gagarin, M. (1989), *The Murder of Herodes: A Study of Antiphon*, Peter Lang GmbH.

② Gagarin, M. (2008), *Writing Greek Law.*

③ Gagarin, M. (2011), *Speeches from Athenian Law*, University of Texas Press.

④ Gagarin, M. (2016), Paula Perlman, *The Laws of Ancient Cretec.* 650 – 400 *BCE*, Oxford University Press.

⑤ Gagarin, M. (2005), David Cohen (ed), *The Cambridge Companion to Ancient Greek Law*, Cambridge.

⑥ Gagarin, M. (1995), Paul Woodruff, *Early Greek Political Thought from Homer to the Sophists*, Cambridge.

⑦ Gagarin, M. (1997), *Antiphon, the Speeches* (edition and commentary), Cambridge Greek and Latin Classics, Cambridge.

⑧ Gagarin, M. (2012), "Women and Law in Grotyn", *Index* 40, 57 – 67.

⑨ Gagarin, M. (2012), "The Laws of Crete", in Legras, B. (ed), Transferts culturels et droits dans le monde grec et hellénistique (Actes du colloque international, Reims, 14 – 17 mai 2008), 17 – 30, Paris.

⑩ Gagarin, M. (2011), "Writing Sacred Laws in Archaic and Classical Crete", in Lardinois, A. P. M. H., Blok, J. H. & M. G. M. van der Poel (eds), *Sacred Words: Orality, Literacy and Religion*, 113 – 42, Leiden (Orality and literacy in the ancient world 8) (Mnemosyne Suppl. 332).

⑪ Gagarin, M. (2010b), "Legal Procedure in Gortyn", in Thür, G. (ed), Symposion 2009. Vorträge zur griechischen und hellenistischen Rechtsgeschichte (Seggau, 25. – 30. August 2009), 127 – 46, Wien (with a response by G. Thür).

⑫ Gagarin, M. (2010), "Serfs and slaves at Gortyn", ZRG 127, 14 – 31.

⑬ Gagarin, M. (2008), "Women and Property at Gortyn", Dike 11, 8 – 26.

⑭ Gagarin, M. (2007), "Rational Argument in Early Athenian Oratory", in Powell, J. (ed), Logos. *Rational Argument in Classical Rhetoric*, 9 – 18, London (BICS Suppl. 96).

⑮ Gagarin, M. (2007), "Litigants' oaths in Athenian Law", in *Horkos*, 39 – 47.

⑯ Gagarin, M. (2007), "From Oral Law to Written Laws: Dracon's Law and its Homeric Roots", in Symposion 2005, 1 – 18.

⑰ Gagarin, M. (2006), "Inscribing Laws in Greece and the Near East", in Symposion 2003, 9 – 20.

⑱ Gagarin, M. (2006), "Legal Procedure in Solon's Laws", in *Solon of Athens*, 261 – 275.

《早期希腊法》①、《希腊法律的统一》②、《德拉古杀人法:为什么由其制定?》③、《书面雅典法》④、《格尔蒂的法治》⑤、《"kakourgoi"是哪些人? 雅典法律中的职业罪犯》⑥、《法律新建:古希腊法中的书面文本》⑦、《雅典法中的故事叙述》⑧、《苏格拉底和安提丰:在古典雅典受审的知识分子》⑨、《古希腊法的书面和口头形式》⑩、《格尔蒂法典和古希腊的法律程序》⑪、《阿提卡演说术中妇女的声音》⑫、《法勒鲁姆的德米特里(统治雅典10年至公元前307年)立法与雅典法律的转变》⑬、《柏拉图〈法律篇〉与古希腊法》⑭、《雅典凶杀法中的巴赛勒斯》⑮、《格尔蒂法中的修辞与反修辞》⑯、《古希腊演说术的口头性》⑰、《雅典法庭中的妇女》⑱、

① Gagarin, M. (2005), "Early Greek Law", in *The Cambridge Companion*, 82 - 95.

② Gagarin, M. (2005), "The Unity of Greek Law", in *The Cambridge Companion*, 29 - 40.

③ Gagarin, M. (2005), "Le loi de Dracon sur l'homicide: pourquoi était-elle écrite?", in Le législateur et la loi, 119 - 126.

④ Gagarin, M. (2004), "Writing Athenian Law", in *Law, Rhetoric, and Comedy*, 15 - 32.

⑤ Gagarin, M. (2004), "The Rule of Law in Gortyn", in *The Law and the Courts*, 173 - 184.

⑥ Gagarin, M. (2003), "Who were the Kakourgoi? Career Criminals in Athenian Law", in Symposion 1999, 183 - 192.

⑦ Gagarin, M. (2003), "Letters of the Law: Written Texts in Archaic Greek Law", in Yunis, H. (ed), *Written Texts and the Rise of Literate Culture in Ancient Greece*, 59 - 77, Cambridge.

⑧ Gagarin, M. (2003), "Telling Stories in Athenian Law", *TAPhA* 133, 197 - 207.

⑨ Gagarin, M. (2002), "Socrates and Antiphon: Intellectuals on Trial in Classical Athens", in *Mélanges Dimakis*, 397 - 404.

⑩ Gagarin, M. (2001), "Ecriture et oralité en droit grec", *RHDFE* 79, 447 - 462.

⑪ Gagarin, M. (2001), "The Gortyn Code and Greek Legal Procedure", in Symposion 1997, 41 - 52.

⑫ Gagarin, M. (2001), "Women's Voices in Attic Oratory", in Lardinois, A. & L. McClure (eds), *Making silence Speak: Women's Voices in Greek Literature and Society*, 161 - 176, Princeton.

⑬ Gagarin, M. (2000), "The Legislation of Demetrius of Phalerum and the Transformation of Athenian Law", in Fortenbaugh, W. W. & E. Schütrumpf (eds), Demetrius of Phalerum: Text, Translation and Discussion, 347 - 365, New Brunswick (Rutgers University Studies in Classical Humanities 9).

⑭ Gagarin, M. (2000), "Le code de Platon et le droit grec", in La codification, 215 - 227.

⑮ Gagarin, M. (2000), "The Basileus in Athenian Homicide Law", in *Polis and Politics*, 569 - 580.

⑯ Gagarin, M. (1999), "Rhetorique et Anti-rhetorique dans les Lois de Gortyne", in Dobias, C. (ed), Des dialectes grecs aux Lois de Gortyne, 65 - 74, Nancy (Etudes anciennes 21).

⑰ Gagarin, M. (1999), "The Orality of Greek Oratory", in MacKay, F. A. (ed), *Signs of Orality: The Oral Tradition and its Influence in the Greek and Roman World*, 163 - 180, Leiden (Mnemosyne Suppl. 188).

⑱ Gagarin, M. (1998), "Women in Athenian Courts", Dike 1, 39 - 52. Gagarin, M. (1997), "Oath and Oath-challenges in Greek Law", in Symposion 1995, 125 - 134.

《雅典法中奴隶的侵权》[①]、《格尔蒂法典的第一法律重新审视》[②]、《格尔蒂法典中妇女的经济地位:追溯和变化》[③]、《正义之诗:赫西奥德和古希腊法的起源》[④]、《在安提丰演说词中证据的性质》[⑤]、《雅典凶杀法中对事先筹划的考量》[⑥]、《在格尔蒂证据的功能》[⑦]、《格尔蒂法典的第一法律》[⑧]、《格尔蒂法典的组织结构》[⑨]、《格尔蒂法中的证人证词》[⑩]、《"mosthetai"和早期雅典僭主法》[⑪]、《雅典涉及hybris的法律》[⑫]、《雅典杀人罪的起诉》[⑬]、《雅典凶杀法中的自助行为》[⑭]、《安提丰〈Tetralogies〉中公正和不公正杀人行为的禁止》[⑮]、《苏格拉底的hybris和阿基比阿德的失败》[⑯]、《雅典娜的投票》[⑰]、《赫西奥德关笔下于珀耳塞斯的争议》[⑱]、《古代希腊思想中的法律》[⑲]、《(工作与时日)中的法律》[⑳]、《柏拉图写作(普罗泰

---

① Gagarin, M. (1996), "The Torture of Slaves in Athenian Law", *CPh* 91, 1 – 18. (= "La torture des esclaves dans le droit athénien", in Pierre Carlier, (ed), Le IVe siècle av. J.-C. Approches historiographiques, 273 – 279, Paris 1996).

② Gagarin, M. (1995), "The First Law of the Gortyn Code Revisited", *GRBS* 36, 7 – 15.

③ Gagarin, M. (1994), "The Economic Status of Women in the Gortyn Code: Retroactivity and Change", in Symposion 1993, 61 – 72.

④ Gagarin, M. (1992), "The Poetry of Justice: Hesiod and the Origins of Greek Law", *Ramus* 21, 61 – 78.

⑤ Gagarin, M. (1990), "The Nature of Proofs in Antiphon", *CPh* 85, 22 – 32 (= The Attic Orators, 214 – 228).

⑥ Gagarin, M. (1990), "Bouleusis in Athenian Homicide Law", in Symposion 1988, 81 – 99 (= Abstracts of American Philological Association 1988, 110).

⑦ Gagarin, M. (1989), "The Function of Witnesses at Gortyn", in Symposion 1985, 29 – 55.

⑧ Gagarin, M. (1988), "The First Law of the Gortyn Code", *GRBS* 28, 335 – 43.

⑨ Gagarin, M. (1982), "The Organization of the Gortyn Law-code", *GRBS* 23, 129 – 146.

⑩ Gagarin, M. (1984), "The Testimony of Witnesses in the Gortyn Laws", *GRBS* 25, 345 – 349.

⑪ Gagarin, M. (1981), "The Mosthetai and the Earliest Athenian Tyranny Law", *TAPhA* 111, 71 – 77.

⑫ Gagarin, M. (1979), "The Athenian Law Against Hybris", in Bowersock, G. W., Burkert, W. & M. C. J. Putnam (eds), Arktouros: *Hellenic Studies Presented to B. M. W. Knox*, 229 – 236, Berlin-NewYork.

⑬ Gagarin, M. (1979), "The Prosecution of Homicide in Athens", *GRBS* 20, 301 – 323.

⑭ Gagarin, M. (1978), "Self-defense in Athenian Homicide Law", *GRBS* 19, 111 – 120.

⑮ Gagarin, M. (1978), "The Prohibition of Just and Unjust Homicide in Antiphon's Tetralogies", *GRBS* 19, 291 – 306.

⑯ Gagarin, M. (1977), "Socrates 'Hybris and Alcibiades' Failure", *Phoenix* 31, 22 – 37.

⑰ Gagarin, M. (1975), "The Vote of Athena", *AJPh* 96, 121 – 127.

⑱ Gagarin, M. (1974), "Hesiod's Dispute with Perses", *TAPhA* 104, 103 – 111.

⑲ Gagarin, M. (1974), "Dike in Archaic Greek Thought", *CPh* 69, 186 – 197.

⑳ Gagarin, M. (1973), "Dike in the Works and Days", *CPh* 68, 81 – 94.

戈拉篇)的目的》①等。

(八)爱德华·E.科恩(Edward E. Cohen)

爱德华·E.科恩曾任美国宾夕法尼亚大学古代史教授,他在古希腊法律史方面的研究成果主要包括专著《古代雅典的海事法庭》②、《雅典的经济与社会:银行业为视角》③、《雅典国家》④、《金钱、劳动和土地:研究古希腊经济的途径》⑤,以及《雅典的奴隶力量:法律理论和经济现实》⑥、《雅典影响卖淫的法律》⑦、《雅典卖淫行为的定义》⑧、《雅典的诺成合同》⑨、《法律拟制:雅典的贸易法》⑩、《自由和非自由性工作:对雅典卖淫行为的一个解决分析》⑪、《商法》⑫、《意想不到的后果?雅典税法的经济效应》⑬、《职业道德和雅典卖淫行为的实践》⑭、《公元前4世纪雅典卖淫的书面合同》⑮、《"合同之下的性行为":公元前4世纪雅典卖淫行

---

① Gagarin, M. (1969), "The Purpose of Plato's Protagoras", *TAPA* 100, 133 - 164.

② Cohen, E. E. (1973), *Ancient Athenian Maritime Courts*, Princeton.

③ Cohen, E. E. (1992), *Athenian Economy and Society: A Banking Perspective*, Princeton.

④ Cohen, E. E. (2000), *The Athenian Nation*, Princeton.

⑤ Cohen, E. E. (2002), *Money, Labour and Land: Approaches to the Economies of Ancient Greece*, co-editor with Paul Cartledge and Lin Foxhall.

⑥ Cohen, E. E. (2007), "Slave Power at Athens: Juridical Theory and Economic Reality", in *Individus*, groupes et politique, 155 - 170.

⑦ Cohen, E. E. (2007), "Laws Affecting Prostitution at Athens", in Symposion 2005, 201 - 224.

⑧ Cohen, E. E. (2006), "La Definition de la Prostitution a Athenes", in Dlugosz, D. (ed), Grecs, Juifs, Polonais: A la recherche des racines de la civilisation européenne (Actes du colloque international tenu à Paris le 14 novembre 2003 dédié à Joseph Meleze-Modrzejewski), 117 - 122, Paris-Varsovie.

⑨ Cohen, E. E. (2006), "Consensual Contracts at Athens", in Symposion 2003, 73 - 92.

⑩ Cohen, E. E. (2006), "A Legal Fiction: The Athenian Law of Sale", in van Alfen, P. (ed), Agoranomia: Studies in Money and Exchange Presented to John H. Kroll, 87 - 98, New York.

⑪ Cohen, E. E. (2006), "Free and Unfree Sexual Work: An Economic Analysis of Athenian Prostitution", in *Prostitutes & Courtesans*, 95 - 124.

⑫ Cohen, E. E. (2005), "Commercial Law", in *The Cambridge Companion*, 290 - 302.

⑬ Cohen, E. E. (2005), "Unintended Consequences? The Economic Effect of Athenian Tax Laws", in Symposion 2001, 159 - 173.

⑭ Cohen, E. E. (2005), "Work Ethics and the Practice of Prostitution at Athens", *MedAnt* 8, 39 - 62.

⑮ Cohen, E. E. (2000), "Written Contracts of Prostitution in Fourth-century Athens", in *Timai Triantaphyllopoulou*, 109 - 122.

为的法律背景》[①]、《雅典的富有奴隶：法律权利与经济义务》[②]、《阿提卡的本地人：雅典的国籍和公民权》[③]、《银行作为家族企业：影响妻子和奴隶的法律改良》[④]、《雅典银行的商业贷款：计量错误和法庭（诉讼）方法》[⑤]、《一个反相研究：在雅典的"海运贷款"和"着陆贷款"》[⑥]等。

（九）埃德温·M. 卡拉万（Edwin M. Carawan）

埃德温·M. 卡拉万曾获北卡罗来纳大学博士学位，现为密苏里州立大学现代和经典语言系教授，研究专长为古希腊法律与修辞，在古希腊法律史方面的研究成果主要包括专著《修辞学与德拉古法》[⑦]，以及论文《控告"Nikomachos"》[⑧]、《伯利克里：年轻人和公民身份法》[⑨]、《记忆术（助记符）有什么作用》[⑩]、《"Arginusai"将军的审判与"司法审查"的曙光》[⑪]、《简介：演讲稿撰写人的艺术和想象的共同体》[⑫]、《宣誓与合同》[⑬]、《雅典的口头"协议"、书面合同和法律的界

---

① Cohen, E. E. (2000), "'Whoring under contract': The Legal Context of Prostitution in Fourth-Century Athens", in *Law and Social Status*, 113 – 147.

② Cohen, E. E. (1998), "The Wealthy Slaves of Athens: Legal Rights, Economic Obligations", in *Le monde Antique*, 105 – 129.

③ Cohen, E. E. (1997), "The Astoi of Attika: Nationality and Citizenship at Athens", in Symposion 1995, 57 – 95.

④ Cohen, E. E. (1991), "Banking as a Family Business: Legal Adaptations Affecting Wives and Slaves", in Symposion 1990, 239 – 263.

⑤ Cohen, E. E. (1990), "Commercial Lending by Athenian Banks: Cliometric Fallacies and Forensic Methodology", *CPh* 85, 177 – 190.

⑥ Cohen, E. E. (1990), "A Study in Contrast: 'Maritime Loans' and 'Landed Loans' at Athens", in Symposion 1988, 57 – 79.

⑦ Carawan, E. M. (1998), *Rhetoric and the Law of Draco*, Oxford.

⑧ Carawan, E. M. (2010), "The Case Against Nikomachos", *TAPhA* 140, 71 – 96.

⑨ Carawan, E. M. (2008), "Perikles the Younger and the Citizenship Law", *CJ* 103, 383 – 406.

⑩ Carawan, E. M. (2008), "What the Mnemones Know?", in Mackay, E. A. (ed), *Orality, literacy, Memory in the Ancient Greek and Roman World*, 163 – 184, Leiden (Orality and literacy in ancient Greece 7. Mnemosyne Suppl. 298).

⑪ Carawan, E. M. (2007), "The Trial of Arginusai Generals and the Dawn of 'Judicial Review'", Dike 10, 19 – 56.

⑫ Carawan, E. M. (2007), "Introduction: The Speechwriter's Art and the Imagined Community", in The Attic Orators, xi-xxiv.

⑬ Carawan, E. M. (2007), "Oath and Contract", in Horkos, 73 – 80.

限》①、《雅典合同法》②、《大赦和考虑到三十僭主的原因》③、《安多喀德斯的辩护和麦克道威尔的解决方案》④、《雅典大赦和法律监督》⑤、《法律预先判断什么：Paragraphe 和早期问题理论》⑥、《德伊阿尼拉的罪》⑦、《俄狄浦斯王的诏书》⑧、《四联剧和雅典凶杀案审判》⑨、《僭政和流放：AthPol 16.10》⑩、《"Ephetai"和演说家时代雅典凶杀案审理法庭》⑪、《斐瑞托法庭和流放杀人犯的审理》⑫、《修西得底斯和司提辛布罗都斯对地米斯托克利流放的记载》⑬、《"Eisangelia and Euthyna"：米太亚德、地米斯托克利和西蒙等人的审判》⑭、《"Apophasis and Eisangelia"：雅典政治审判中战神山议事会的角色》⑮、《"Akriton Apokteinai"：公元前4世纪雅典的无审判执行》⑯、《（爰）：公元前4世纪雅典法庭的拷问》⑰等。

---

① Carawan, E. M. (2007), "Oral 'Agreement', Written Contract, and the Bonds of Law at Athens", in *Politics of Orality*, 321 – 342.

② Carawan, E. M. (2006), "The Athenian Law of Agreement", *GRBS* 46, 339 – 374.

③ Carawan, E. M. (2006), "Amnesty and Accounting for the Thirty", *CQ* 56, 57 – 76.

④ Carawan, E. M. (2004), "Andocides' Defence and MacDowell's Solution", in *Law, Rhetoric, and Comedy*, 103 – 112.

⑤ Carawan, E. M. (2002), "The Athenian Amnesty and the 'Scrutiny of Laws'", *JHS* 122, 1 – 23.

⑥ Carawan, E. M. (2001), "What the Laws have Prejudged: Paragraphe and Early Issue Theory", in Wooten, C. W. (ed), *The orator in action and theory in Greece and Rome*, 17 – 51, Leyden (Mnemosyne Suppl. 225).

⑦ Carawan, E. M. (2000), "Deianira's Guilt", *TAPhA* 130, 189 – 237.

⑧ Carawan, E. M. (1999), "The Edict of Oedipus (Oedipus Tyrannus 223 – 251)", *AJPh* 120, 188 – 222.

⑨ Carawan, E. M. (1993b), "The Tetralogies and Athenian Homicide Trials", *AJPh* 114, 235 – 270.

⑩ Carawan, E. M. (1993a), "Tyranny and Outlawry: AthPol 16.10", in *Nomodeiktes*, 305 – 319.

⑪ Carawan, E. M. (1991), "Ephetai and Athenian Courts for Homicide in the Age of the Orators", *CPh* 86, 1 – 16.

⑫ Carawan, E. M. (1990b), "Trial of Exiled Homicides and the Court at Phreatto", *RIDA* 37, 47 – 67.

⑬ Carawan, E. M. (1989), "Thucydides and Stesimbrotus on the Exile of Themistocles", *Historia* 38, 144 – 161.

⑭ Arawan, E. M. (1987), "Eisangelia and Euthyna: The Trials of Miltiades, Themistokles, and Cimon", *GRBS* 28, 167 – 208.

⑮ Carawan, E. M. (1985), "Apophasis and Eisangelia: The Role of the Areopagus in Athenian Political Trials", *GRBS* 26, 115 – 140.

⑯ Carawan, E. M. (1984), "Akriton Apokteinai: Execution without Trial in Fourth-century Athens", *GRBS* 25, 111 – 121.

⑰ Carawan, E. M. (1983), "Erotesis: Interrogation in the Courts of Fourth-century Athens", *GRBS* 24, 9 – 226.

(十)乔赛亚·奥伯(Josiah Ober)

乔赛亚·奥伯1975年获明尼苏达大学历史学学士学位,1980年在密歇根大学历史系以论文《雅典对军事压力的反应和阿提卡的防御:公元前404~322年》(*Athenian Reactions to Mlilitary Pressure and the Defense of Attica,404-322 B. C.*)获博士学位,1980~1990年任蒙大拿州立大学古代历史学教授,1990~2006年任普林斯顿大学古典学和人类价值研究中心双聘教授,2006年至今任斯坦福大学古典学和政治学双聘教授。奥伯教授曾经多次获得美国国家人文中心(National Humanities Center)、希腊研究中心(Hellenic Studies Center)、行为科学高级研究中心(Center of Advanced Studies of Behavioral Science)、美国学术团体协会(American Council of Learned Societies)、古根海姆基金会(Guggenheim Foundations)等学术机构的研究基金。奥伯是美国著名古希腊历史学家切斯特·斯塔尔(Chester Starr)的学生,是古典学者马峻(John Ma)、古希腊历史学家艾米莉·麦基尔(Emily Mackil)和政治理论家瑞安·巴洛特(Ryan Balot)的老师。奥伯早期以研究雅典军事史见长如其代表作《阿提卡要塞》[①],后来以雅典民主政治为主要研究领域如其专著《民主雅典的大众与精英》[②]、《雅典革命》[③]、《民主雅典的不同政见》[④]、《雅典遗产》[⑤]、《民主与知识》[⑥]、《古希腊的崛起与衰落》[⑦]等。奥伯的早期作品被学者莫恩斯·赫尔曼·汉森(Mogens Herman Hansen)批评为过分强调雅典的思想层面而忽视了其制度层面,[⑧]P. J. 罗德斯(P. J. Rhodes)则指责奥伯为鼓吹雅典民主而放弃学术的公正性。[⑨] 不过奥伯的作品总体上受到好评,

---

① Ober, J. (1985), *Fortress Attica: Defense of the Athenian Land Frontier, 404-322 B. C.*, Leiden: E. J. Brill. 1985.

② Ober, J. (1989), *Mass and Elite in Democratic Athens: Rhetoric, Ideology, and the Power of the People*, Princeton: Princeton University Press.

③ Ober, J. (1996), *The Athenian Revolution: Essays on Ancient Greek Democracy and Political Theory*, Princeton: Princeton University Press.

④ Ober, J. (1998), *Political Dissent in Democratic Athens: Intellectual Critics of Popular Rule*, Princeton University Press.

⑤ Ober, J. (2005), *Athenian Legacies: Essays on the Politics of Going on Together*, Princeton University Press.

⑥ Ober, J. (2008), *Democracy and Knowledge: Innovation and Learning in Classical Athens*, Princeton University Press.

⑦ Ober, J. (2015), *The Rise and Fall of Classical Greece*, Princeton: Princeton University Press.

⑧ Mogens Herman Hansen (1999), *The Athenian Democracy in the Age of Demosthenes: Structure, Principles, and Ideology*, University of Oklahoma Press.

⑨ P. J. Rhodes, *Ancient Democracy and Modern Ideology*, Duckworth: London, 2003.

如保罗·卡特里奇就认为,其《民主雅典的大众与精英》一书是一项开拓性的工作。

奥伯教授在古希腊法律史方面的研究成果主要包括论文《苏格拉底和民主雅典》①、《准入、公平和交易成本:公元前375/374年雅典尼科丰银币法》②、《能力和教育:(雅典演说家)说服的力量》③、《梭伦和"界碑":古雅典的既成事实》④、《准权利:公民参与与消极自由》⑤、《法和政理论》⑥、《作为治疗"内讧"手段的僭主杀戮:一个基于图像和文本的政治辩论》⑦、《社会科学史、文化史和公元前402年的大赦》⑧、《作为法律的奴隶而自由生活:苏格拉底们为什么生活在雅典》⑨、《古希腊界碑:人造文本和内在意义的偶然性》⑩等。

(十一)理查德·加纳(Richard Garner)

加纳先后毕业于普林斯顿大学、哈佛大学,获得斯拉夫学学士、硕士学位,随后赴芝加哥大学研习古典学,此后又回到哈佛大学完成博士学位论文获得博士学位,1984~1994年任教于耶鲁大学,1994年起转任艾德菲大学教授、荣誉学院院长。加纳在古希腊法律史方面的研究成果主要包括专著《古典雅典的法律和社

---

① Ober, J. (2010), "Socrates and democratic Athens", in Morrison, D. R. (ed), *The Cambridge Companion to Socrates*, 138–178, Cambridge.

② Ober, J. (2009) "Access, Fairness and Transactions Costs: Nikophon's Law on Silver Coinage (Athens, 375/4 BC)", Princeton/Stanford Working Papers in Classics 5.

③ Ober, J. (2007), "Ability and Education: The Power of Persuasion", in *The Attic Orators*, 271–311 (= originally chapter 4 of Mass and elite in democratic Athens, Princeton 1989).

④ Ober, J. (2006), "Solon and the Horoi: Facts on the Ground in Archaic Athens", in *Solon of Athens*, 441–456.

⑤ Ober, J. (2005b), "Quasi-rights: Participatory Citizenship and Negative Liberties", *Social Philosophy and Policy* 17, 27–61 (= Athenian legacies. Essays on the politics of going on together, 92–127, Princeton).

⑥ Ober, J. (2005a), "Law and Political Theory", in *Ancient Greek Law*, 394–411.

⑦ Ober, J. (2003), "Tyrant Killing as Therapeutic Stasis: A Political Debate in Images and Texts", in *Popular Tyranny*, 215–250.

⑧ Ober, J. (2002), "Social Science History, Cultural History, and the Amnesty of 403", *TAPhA* 132, 127–138.

⑨ Ober, J. (2000), "Living Freely as a Slave of the Law: Notes on why Sokrates lives in Athens", in *Polis and Politics*, 541–552.

⑩ Ober, J. (1995), "Greek Horoi: Artifactual Texts and the Contigency of Meaning", in Small, D. B. (ed), *Methods in the Mediterranean: Historical and Archeological Views on Texts and Archaeology*, 91–123, Leiden.

会》[①]等。

（十二）萨拉·福迪克（Sara Forsdyke，1967 年至今）

福迪克现任美国密歇根大学人文学院古典系教授，在古希腊法律史研究方面的成果主要包括专著《流放、陶片放逐和民主：古希腊的驱逐政治》[②]等以及论文《僭政的用途和滥用》[③]、《古希腊的街头剧和流行正义》[④]、《流放、陶片放逐和雅典民主》[⑤]等。

（十三）大卫·Mirhady（David Mirhady，1960 年至今）

Mirhady 现任职于美国罗格斯大学，他在古希腊法律史研究方面的研究成果主要包括合著的《伊苏克拉底（一）译评》[⑥]一书，以及论文《德拉古的（司法）程序》[⑦]、《"exetasis"的出现和重现》[⑧]、《迪卡斯特里法院的宣誓和事实问题》[⑨]、《亚里士多德和法庭》[⑩]、《雅典的合同》[⑪]、《在欧里庇德斯〈希波吕托斯〉中的法医证据》[⑫]、《雅典的民主证人》[⑬]、《雅典人实行拷问的理由》[⑭]、《作为律师的德摩斯梯尼：私人演讲》[⑮]、《雅典陶片放逐的礼仪背景》[⑯]、《雅典的拷打和修辞》[⑰]、《亚里

---

① Richard Garner, R. (1987), *Law and Society in Classical Athens*, New York.

② Forsdyke, S. (2005), *Exile, Ostracism, and Democracy: The Politics of Expulsion in Ancient Greece*, Princeton.

③ Forsdyke, S. (2009), "The Uses and Abuses of Tyranny", in *Greek and Roman Political Thought*, 231 - 246.

④ Forsdyke, S. (2008), "Street Theater and Popular Justice in Ancient Greece", *P & P* 201, 3 - 50.

⑤ Forsdyke, S. (2000), "Exile, Ostracism, and Athenian Democracy", *ClAnt* 19, 232 - 263.

⑥ Mirhady, D. C. & Y. L. Too. (2000), *Isocrates* 1, *Austin*, *Texas* (The oratory of classical Greece 4).

⑦ Mirhady, D. C. (2008), "Drakonian Procedure", in *Epigraphy and the Greek Historian*, 15 - 30.

⑧ Mirhady, D. C. (2008), "The Disappearance and Reappearance of Exetasis", *Mouseion* 8, 395 - 408.

⑨ Mirhady, D. C. (2007), "The Dikasts' Oath and the Question of Fact", in *Horkos*, 48 - 59.

⑩ Mirhady, D. C. (2006), "Aristotle and the Law Courts", *Polis* 23, 302 - 318.

⑪ Mirhady, D. C. (2004b), "Contracts in Athens", in *Law, Rhetoric and Comedy*, 51 - 63.

⑫ Mirhady, D. C. (2004a), "Forensic Evidence in Euripides' Hippolytus", *Mouseion* 4, 17 - 34.

⑬ Mirhady, D. C. (2002), "Athens' Democratic Witnesses", *Phoenix* 56, 255 - 74.

⑭ Mirhady, D. C. (2000b), "The Athenian Rationale for Torture", in *Law and Social Status*, 53 - 74.

⑮ Mirhady, D. C. (2000a), "Demosthenes as Advocate: The Private Speeches", in Worthington, I. (ed), *Demosthenes: Statesman and Orator*, 181 - 204, London.

⑯ Mirhady, D. C. (1997), "The Ritual Background to Athenian Ostracism", *AHB* 11, 131 - 119.

⑰ Mirhady, D. C. (1996), "Torture and Rhetoric in Athens", *JHS* 116, 119 - 131 (= The Attic Orators, 247 - 270).

士多德和阿那克西米尼论述中的非技术性证据》①、《雅典的誓言挑战》②、《亚里士多德论法律修辞》③、《(古雅典迪卡斯特里法院的)审判官参与》④等。

(十四)弗吉尼亚·J. 亨特(Virginia J. Hunter)

亨特现任职于纽约大学历史系,在古希腊法律史方面的研究成果主要包括专著《监控雅典:阿提卡法律诉讼的社会控制》⑤等,以及论文《柏拉图〈法律篇〉中的犯罪和罪犯》⑥、《柏拉图的监狱》⑦、《是否雅典人有犯罪的用词》⑧、《Pittalacus 和 Eucles:雅典公共服务中的奴隶》⑨、《古典雅典的公共债务监管》⑩、《雅典法律中的身份区分简介》⑪、《雅典监狱:一个比较的方法》⑫、《雅典法律中的父系亲属和雅典的家庭实践:对妇女的影响》⑬、《构建公民的身体:古典雅典的体罚》⑭等。

(十五)丹妮尔·S. 艾伦(Danielle S. Allen)

艾伦现任芝加哥大学古典学和政治学教授、人文学院院长,主要研究方向为公元前5世纪晚期至公元前4世纪早期雅典的领导力问题,在古希腊法律史方面的研究成果主要包括专著《普罗米修斯的世界:民主雅典的惩罚政治》⑮,以及论文《古希腊戏剧和法律》⑯、《古典雅典的监禁》⑰等。

---

① Mirhady, D. C. (1991), "Non-technical Pisteis in Aristotle and Anaximenes", *AJPh* 112, 5 – 28.

② Mirhady, D. C. (1991), "The oath-challenge in Athens", *CQ* 41, 78 – 83.

③ Mirhady, D. C. (1990), "Aristotle on the Rhetoric of Law", *GRBS* 31, 393 – 410.

④ Mirhady, D. C. & C. Schwarz (2011), "Dicastic Participation", *CQ* 61, 744 – 748.

⑤ Hunter, V. J. (1994), *Policing Athens: Social control in the Attic lawsuits*, Princeton.

⑥ Hunter, V. J. (2009), "Crime and Criminals in Plato's Laws", *Mouseion* 9, 1 – 20.

⑦ Hunter, V. J. (2008), "Plato's Prison", *G &R* 55, 193 – 201.

⑧ Hunter, V. J. (2007), "Did the Athenians have a Word for Crime?", Dike 10, 5 – 18.

⑨ Hunter, V. J. (2006), "Pittalacus and Eucles: Slaves in the Public Service of Athens", *Mouseion* 6, 1 – 14.

⑩ Hunter, V. J. (2000), "Policing Public Debtors in Classical Athens", *Phoenix* 54, 21 – 38.

⑪ Hunter, V. J. (2000), "Introduction: Status Distinctions in Athenian Law", in *Law and Social Status*, 1 – 29.

⑫ Hunter, V. J. (1997), "The Prison of Athens: A Comparative Approach", *Phoenix* 51, 296 – 326.

⑬ Hunter, V. J. (1993), "Agnatic Kinship in Athenian Law and Athenian Family Practice: Its Implications for Women", in *Law, Politics and Society*, 100 – 121.

⑭ Hunter, V. J. (1992), "Constructing the Body of the Citizen: Corporal Punishment in Classical Athens", *EMC/CV* 36, 271 – 291.

⑮ Allen, D. S. (2000), *The world of Prometheus: The Politics of Punishing in Democratic Athens*, Princeton.

⑯ Allen, D. S. (2005), "Greek tragedy and law", in *The Cambridge Companion*, 374 – 393.

⑰ Allen, D. S. (1997), "Imprisonment in Classical Athens", *CQ* 47, 121 – 135.

(十六)哈维·尤尼斯(Harvey Yunis)

尤尼斯现任美国莱斯大学古典学教授,在古希腊法律史方面的研究成果主要包括译评《德摩斯梯尼:论王权》①、《德摩斯梯尼:演说词18~19卷》②,以及论文《柏拉图(苏格拉底的申诉)和伊索克拉底(易物)种的法律修辞》③、《公元前4世纪雅典的法律修辞》④、《公元前4世纪雅典的法律、政治和违法法令诉讼》⑤等。

(十七)辛西娅·B.帕特森(Cynthia B. Patterson)

辛西娅·B.帕特森现为亚特兰大埃默里大学历史学副教授,主要研究方向为古希腊家庭和社会史,在古希腊法律史研究方面的成果主要包括专著《古希腊历史上的家庭》⑥、《公元前451年至前450年伯利克里公民身份法》⑦等,以及论文《其他人的命运:伯利克里雅典时期的奴隶、外国人和妇女》⑧、《雅典公民身份法》⑨、《城邦和尸体:民主雅典的埋葬制度》⑩、《雅典司法的热情好客:法庭上的外邦人》⑪、《雅典法中的婚姻和已婚妇女》⑫、《那些雅典私生子们》⑬等。

(十八)瑞安·克里格·巴勒特(Ryan Krieger Balot)

巴勒特现任职于美国联合学院古典系,是前述乔赛亚·奥伯教授的学生,主

---

① Yunis, H. (2001), *Demosthenes: On the Crown*, Cambridge.

② Yunis, H. (2005), *Demosthenes: Speeches* 18 – 19, Austin, Tx (The oratory of classical Greece 9).

③ Yunis, H. (2010), "The Rhetoric of Law in Plato's Apology of Socrates and Isocrates' Antidosis", in Yunis, H. (2007), "Politics as Literature: Demosthenes and the Burden of the Athenian Past", in *The Attic Orators*, 372 – 390.

④ Yunis, H. (2005), "The Rhetoric of Law in Fourth-century Athens", in *The Cambridge Companion*, 191 – 208.

⑤ Yunis, H. (1988), "Law, Politics, and the Graphe Paranomon in Fourth-century Athens", *GRBS* 29, 361 – 82.

⑥ Patterson, C. B. (1998), *The Family in Greek History*, Cambridge, Mass.

⑦ Patterson, C. B. (1981), *Perikles' Citizenship Law of 451 – 50 B. C.*, New York.

⑧ Patterson, C. B. (2007), "Other Sorts: Slaves, Foreigners and Women in Periclean Athens", in Samons Ⅱ, L. J. (ed), *The Cambridge Companion to the Age of Pericles*, 153 – 178, Cambridge.

⑨ Patterson, C. B. (2005), "Athenian Citizenship Law", in *The Cambridge Companion*, 267 – 289.

⑩ Patterson, C. B. (2002), "The Polis and the Corpse: The Regulation of Burial in Democratic Athens", in *Demokratie, Recht und Soziale Kontrolle*, 93 – 108.

⑪ Patterson, C. B. (2000), "The Hospitality of Athenian Justice: The Metic in Court", in *Law and Social Status*, 93 – 112.

⑫ Patterson, C. B. (1991), "Marriage and the Married Woman in Athenian Law", in Pomeroy, S. B. (ed), *Women's History and Ancient History*, 48 – 72, Chapel Hill.

⑬ Patterson, C. B. (1990), "Those Athenian Bastards", *ClAnt* 9, 40 – 73.

要研究方向为古典社会的政治思想，曾主编出版《希腊罗马政治思想指南》①，在古希腊法律史研究方面的代表作包括专著《古典雅典的贪欲与不公正》②、《民主城邦的勇气：古典雅典的意识形态和批判》③等。

（十九）阿德里安·兰尼（Adriaan Lanni）

兰尼曾先后就读于耶鲁大学（1994 年获古典文明学士）、剑桥大学（1996 年获古典学硕士）、耶鲁大学（1999 年获法学博士）、密歇根大学（2003 年获历史学博士学位），2003 年开始任教于哈佛大学法学院，现任哈佛大学法学院 Touroff-Glueck 教授，在古希腊法律史方面的研究成果主要包括专著《古典时期雅典法院的法律和正义》④、《古典雅典的法律与秩序 》⑤等，以及论文《古典雅典的过渡期正义：一个案例研究》⑥、《雅典卖淫法的惊人效果》⑦、《古代雅典法庭的社会规范》⑧、《司法审查和雅典宪法》⑨、《古希腊的战争法》⑩、《雅典在合同案件中规范法律预见性的方法》⑪、《雅典法庭中的相关性》⑫、《最正确的判决：古典雅典正义的模式》⑬、《基于先例的争辩：雅典实践的现代观点》⑭、《凶杀法庭和陪审法庭：

---

① Balot, R. K. (2009), *A Companion to Greek and Roman Political Thought*, Wiley-Blackwell.

② Balot, R. K. (2001), *Greed and Injustice in Classical Athens*, Princeton.

③ Balot, R. K. (2014), *Courage in the Democratic Polis: Ideology and Critique in Classical Athens*, Oxford and New York: Oxford University Press.

④ Lanni, A. (2006), *Law and Justice in the Courts of Classical Athens*.

⑤ Lanni, A. (2016), *Law and Order in Ancient Athens*, Cambridge University Press.

⑥ Lanni, A. (2010b), "Transitional Justice in Ancient Athens: A Case Study", *University of Pennsylvania Journal of International Law* 32, 551ff.

⑦ Lanni, A. (2010a), "The Expressive Effect of the Athenian Prostitution Laws", *ClAnt* 29, 45 - 67.

⑧ Lanni, A. (2009b), "Social Norms in the Ancient Athenian Courts", *Journal of Legal Analysis* 1, 691 - 736.

⑨ Lanni, A. (2009a), "Judicial Review and the Athenian Constitution", in Hernandez, A.-Chr. (ed), Démocratie athénienne-démocratie moderne: Tradition et Influences, 235 - 263, Genève (Fondations Hardt 56).

⑩ Lanni, A. (2008), "The Laws of War in Ancient Greece", *Law and History Review* 26, 469ff.

⑪ Lanni, A. (2007), "Athenian Approaches to Legal Predictability in Contract Cases", in Symposion 2005, 225 - 236.

⑫ Lanni, A. (2005), "Relevance in Athenian Courts", in *The Cambridge Companion*, 112 - 128.

⑬ Lanni, A. (2004b), "'Verdict Most Just': The Modes of Classical Athenian Justice", *Yale Journal of Law & Humanities* 16, 277 - 321.

⑭ Lanni, A. (2004a), "Arguing from 'Precedent': Modern Perspectives on Athenian Practice", in *The Law and the Courts*, 159 - 172.

范例不被遵循》①、《古典雅典法庭的先例和法律推理：一种崇高的谎言？》②、《体育观众还是严肃政治？群众围观和雅典法庭》③等。

---

① Lanni, A. (2000), "The Homicide Courts and the Dikasteria: A Paradigm not Followed", *GRBS* 41, 311 – 330.

② Lanni, A. (1999), "Precedent and Legal Reasoning in Classical Athenian Courts: A Noble Lie?", *American Journal of Legal History* 43, 27 – 51.

③ Lanni, A. (1997), "Spectator Sports or Serious Politics? Hoi periestekotes and the Athenian Lawcourts", *JHS* 117, 183 – 189.

第四章　欧美国家古希腊法律史研究的专业刊物与资料汇编

雅典演说家的法庭演说词、石刻立法铭文、埃及出土的纸莎草纸文献是英美国家学者进行古希腊法律史研究的基础性资料，其中希腊化托勒密埃及时期保留下来的纸莎草纸文献包含了大量官方法律文献和私人合同交易记录，成为近年来学者对古希腊法进行实证研究的重点资料。以下从古希腊法律史研究的专业性角度对欧美国家古希腊法律史学者参与编辑的欧洲古希腊及希腊化法律史研究会集刊、Dike 杂志、原始资料汇编、研究文献索引等做一简要介绍。①

第一节　欧美国家古希腊法律史研究的专业刊物

一、欧洲古希腊及希腊化法律史研究会集刊

欧洲古希腊及希腊化法律史研究会由德国的沃尔夫教授、法国的 Modrzejewski 教授（波兰裔）和意大利的比斯卡第教授于 1971 年发起设立，学会成立的目的是想要将当时对古希腊法感兴趣的世界各地学者联合起来，并通过组织定期会议和出版相关的会议文集为深入系统的

---

① 一般性的古希腊历史研究资料如工具书、原始资料、主要期刊、网络资源等，参考了黄洋、晏绍祥的《希腊史研究入门》（北京大学出版社 2009 年版）附录部分。

学术交流奠定基础。1971 年欧洲古希腊及希腊化法律史研究会在德国 Rheda 城堡举办了第一届 Symposion 研讨会，此后又相继举办了 18 次会议（截至 2011 年）。在最近 30 年，这些会议成为古希腊法律史研究与发展的最主要工具。

欧洲古希腊及希腊化法律史研究会集刊的正式名称是“Symposion，Vorträge zur griechischen und hellenistischen Rechtsgeschichte”，[①]得名于柏拉图的名著 Symposion，一般习惯译为《会饮篇》，“欧洲古希腊及希腊化法研究会集刊”（Vorträge zur griechischen und hellenistischen Rechtsgeschichte）是该系列论文集刊的副标题。从 Symposion 1971 开始，先后出版有 Symposion 1974、Symposion 1977、Symposion 1982、Symposion 1985、Symposion 1988、Symposion 1990、Symposion 1993、Symposion 1995、Symposion 1997、Symposion 1999、Symposion 2001、Symposion 2005、Symposion 2007、Symposion 2009、Symposion 2011 等共 16 卷。

以 Symposion 1971 为例，其全称为“Symposion 1971：Vorträge zur griechischen und hellenistischen Rechtsgeschichte / in Gemeinschaft”，由沃尔夫教授、Josef Modrzejewski 博士、Dieter Norr 博士编辑，收录论文涵盖了德语、法语和意大利语。沃尔夫教授在前言中写道：“1971 年 9 月 1 日至 4 日，在（德国）比勒菲尔德大学跨学科研究中心的召集下，26 位法学家、语言学家和古代史学家齐聚比勒菲尔德附近的雷达城堡，讨论了古希腊和希腊化法律史问题。这次前所未有的会议出版的文集除了一个例外（艾利亚斯 · 拜克曼：《雅典的婚姻》，纽约），收录的都是会上所做的报告，以及一个（克林根贝格）碍于时间限制未能口述只能演示的内容。”Symposion 1971 体系目录如下：

前言Ⅶ

略缩语Ⅷ

汉斯 · 尤里乌斯 · 沃尔夫：《古希腊法学研究的任务、问题、可能性》

Johannes Triantaphyllopoulos：《古希腊的法哲学与实体法》

艾伯哈特 · 鲁申布什：《早期古希腊渊源研究情况概览，重点兼顾法律史学者的需求》

弗里茨 · 葛施尼策：《古希腊国际法的一个交易类型：以克里特岛 Praisos 地

---

① 此处德文的原意是“欧洲古希腊及希腊化法讲座”，意译为“欧洲古希腊及希腊化法研究会集刊”是为了理解上的方便。该套丛书笔者曾于英国伦敦古典学会图书馆影印大部分，较罕见的前期两卷由丛书的主编之一 Gerhard Thür 教授来华访问时借笔者复印获得，特致谢意。

区为例》

Georges Daux：帕加马（位于小亚细亚）国王阿塔罗斯与格尔蒂岛马拉城之间的条约

Giuseppe Ignazio Luzzatto：《罗马元首制时期附属于执政官的雅典城邦》

马里奥·塔拉曼卡：《雅典关于资格审查的审判制度》

迪特里希·贝伦德：《柏拉图法律篇手稿937段所记载的古希腊再审程序》

格尔哈特·提尔：《雅典诉讼程序剖析——以伊索克拉底（卷17）记载的Trapezitikos案为例》

哈拉德·迈尔－劳林：《希腊化时期埃及纸莎草纸文献中的katháper程序》

克劳德·莫斯：公元前4世纪至公元前3世纪雅典的外国人

Evanghelos Karabelias：古希腊喜剧中的女继承人制度与拉丁语中相关制度的起源

阿诺德克兰茨莱因：《雅典石刻铭文中关于雅典承诺制度的记载》

本亚明·纳达尔：《博斯普鲁斯王国的解放奴隶运动与中世纪"教会释奴"制度的起源》

约翰内斯·赫尔曼：《处分授权作为希腊不同交易类型的构建基础》

Louis R. F. Germain：界石——古希腊的不动产物权公示制度（设置于土地上的界石或雕刻于房屋墙上的告示）

艾伯哈特·克林根贝格：《柏拉图关于蜜群（饲养员）所有权的法律记载》

文献索引

名词索引

从以上目录可以看出，作为最早的一本古希腊法专业研究论文集，Symposion 1971对古希腊法律史研究的基本理论问题关注较多，其中较多关注的是古希腊的公法领域，尤以诉讼制度为着重点。纵观其中收录的论文都是史料翔实、论证充分的大家之作。在此后的几卷集刊中，还增加了评议人针对每篇论文的评议文章。

二、Dike杂志

"Dike"在古希腊语中是法律的同名词，该杂志是由意大利米兰比可卡大学Alberto Maffi教授主编的一本专门刊登古希腊法主题论文的年刊，每年12月出版，从1998年第1卷开始至2014年已出版17卷（所有收录文章都可以网络下载）。以1998年Dike杂志第1卷为例，其目录如下：

ARCADIA

G. Thür, IPArk 8:“神的审判”抑或“特赦令”？［IPArk 8:« Gottesurteil » oder « Amnestiedekret »?（Nochmals zu IG V 2,262）］

ATTICA

J. F. Nieto，萨摩斯赔偿制度中成本的计算［El cálculo de los gastos y la indemnización de Samos（IG I^3 363）］

M. Gagarin，雅典法庭中的妇女（Women in Athenian Courts）

D. Cohen，德摩斯梯尼片段 41 和 57 所反映出的雅典妇女、财产和地位（Women, Property and Status in Demosthenes 41 and 57）

R. W. Wallace，古代雅典未定罪的或潜在的剥夺公民权利（Unconvicted or Potential « Átimoi » in Ancient Athens）

C. Mossé，审判富基翁（Le procès de Phocion）

CRETA

R. Martini，格尔蒂土地制度（La terra a Gortina）

A. Magnelli，格尔蒂岛新出土发现的关于奴隶解放的铭文（Una nuova epigrafe gortinia in materia di manomissione）

J. -M. Bertrand, Magnètes 城所体现的柏拉图式的政治构想（Formes du discours politique dans la cité des Magnètes platoniciens）

EGITTO

J. M. Modrzejewski，“言有害”和“淫亵”：古希腊和希腊化法律中规定的谩骂（犯罪）行为（« Paroles néfastes » et « vers obscènes ». À propos de l'injure verbale en droit grec et hellénistique）

LETTURE

M. Faraguna，一项新的研究：« Rationes Centesimarum »（Un nuovo studio sulle « Rationes Centesimarum »）

A. Maffi，怀念 Biscardi Arnaldo 教授（Biscardi Arnaldo: in memoriam）

从上目录可以看出该杂志所涉及的古希腊法论文按地区分类，分别涉及古希腊的阿卡迪亚（ARCADIA，位于伯罗奔尼撒半岛）、雅典、格尔蒂岛（CRETA）及希腊化时期埃及（EGITTO）的法律制度。所涉及主题以古希腊的刑事案件、财产案件、女性地位为主。每篇论文的作者也都是该领域的权威学者，包括 G. Thür、D. Cohen、M. Gagarin、R. W. Wallace 等知名学者。

第二节　欧美国家古希腊法律史研究的原始资料汇编、研究文献索引和研究入门指南

一、原始法律资料汇编

关于古希腊法律的原始资料汇编主要包括三类：

（一）法律法令的汇编

1.《希腊城邦的法律》（*The Decrees of the Greek States*, Rhodes, P. J. & D. M. Lewis., Oxford, 1997）；

2.《公元前352年/351年~公元前322年/321年雅典碑铭法律法令汇编》（*Inscribed Athenian Laws and Decrees* 352/351 – 322/321 *B. C.*, Lambert, S. D., Leiden, 2012）；

3.《希腊罗马时期埃及的纸莎草纸法律（公元前332年~公元640年）》（*The Law of Greco-Roman Egypt in the Light of the Papyri*, 332 *B. C.*– 640 *A. D*, Raphael Taubenschlag, 1944）；

4.《亚历山大时期的雅典：公元前338年~公元前322年雅典的过时法律法令》（*Athens in the Age of Alexander*: *The Dated Laws and Decrees of the Lykourgan Era* 338 – 322 *B. C.*, Cynthia Jane Schwenk, 1985）。

（二）涉及雅典法律的演说词汇编

1.《雅典法律演说词》（*Speeches from Athenian Law*）①；

2.《民主雅典的法律演说》（*Legal Speeches of Democratic Athens*）②；

3.《德摩斯梯尼演说词节选》（*Demosthenes. Selected Private Speeches*）③。

（三）涉及古希腊法律的文献汇编

1.《公元前5世纪希腊历史文献》（*Greek Historical Documents*: *The Fifth Century B. C.*）④；

2.《希腊化时期希腊历史文献》（*Greek Historical Documents*: *The Hellenstic*

---

① Gagarin, M. (2011), *Speeches from Athenian Law*, University of Texas Press.

② Wolpert, A. & K. Kapparis (eds.) (2011), *Legal Speeches of Democratic Athens. Sources for Athenian History*, Indianapolis.

③ Carey, C. & R. A. Reid (1985), *Demosthenes. Selected Private Speeches*, Cambridge.

④ Lewis Naphtali (1971) eds., *Greek Historical Documents*: *The Fifth Century B. C.*, Toronto: Hakkert.

Period)①；

3.《公元前 359 年～公元前 323 年希腊历史铭刻》(*Greek Historical Inscriptions* 359－323 *B. C.*)②；

4.《公元前 404 年～公元前 323 年希腊历史铭刻》(*Greek Historical Inscriptions* 404－323 *B. C.*)③。

二、研究文献索引

关于古希腊法律史研究成果的研究文献索引以詹姆斯等编《古希腊法书目参考》(*A Working Bibliography of Greek Law*,1927)、桑达等编《新古希腊法书目参考》[*A New Working Bibliography of Ancient Greek Law*(7th－4th centuries B. C.),2011]最为典型,尤以后者最为完善,不仅按照作者姓名做出索引,而且依据法学理论区分不同进行归类整理。就古希腊史整体研究而言,最为权威的研究文献索引是法国学者编著的《古典学年鉴》(L'année philologique:bibliographie critique et analytique de l'antiquité gréco-latine),该刊从 1928 年开始出版,每年出版一卷,按门类和专题收录本年度出版和发表的所有相关研究成果,范围涵盖欧洲所有主要语言。

三、研究入门指南

关于古希腊法律史研究的入门类参考书以加加林教授和科恩教授主编的《剑桥古希腊法律指南》④为代表,该书全面介绍了过去 30 年与古代希腊法律相关的主题,涉及古代雅典的法律程序和实体法、古代希腊化时期的法律实施等领域,为读者提供了古希腊克里特岛和希腊化时期埃及托勒密王朝法律实施的真实证据,以及古希腊法律和宗教、哲学、政治理论、修辞以及戏剧之间的相互融合、相互影响,无论是古希腊法的专业研究者还是普通读者,都能从本书提供的新视角中获益。该书收录

---

① Roger S. Bagnall & Peter Derow(1981)eds. ,*Greek Historical Documents*:*The Hellenistic Period*, Chico(California).

② P. J. Rhodes(1971)eds. ,*Greek Historical Inscriptions* 359－323*B. C.* ,London Association of Classical Teachers.

③ P. J. Rhodes & R. Osborne(2007)eds. ,*Greek Historical Inscriptions* 404－323 *B. C.* ,Oxford University Press.

④ 笔者曾与《剑桥古希腊法律指南》主编之一加加林教授有过一面之缘,并蒙加加林教授不弃获赠该书,每每捧读,都获益匪浅。在本书的校稿过程中,获悉《剑桥古希腊法律指南》一书已由邹丽、叶友珍两位青年才俊翻译,并由华东师范大学出版社 2017 年出版,作为古希腊法律史的一名初学者不禁与有荣焉。

来自不同国家和不同思想流派的作者撰写而成的22篇研究论文,基本涵盖了古代希腊法律所有的研究领域,全面概述了古代希腊法律的两大主题:古典雅典的程序法和实体法,同时也大量涉及希腊化时代的具体法律实践。该书的具体目录如下:

附　录

附录一：古希腊语法律术语（古希腊语、英语对照）[1]

1. agoranomos（Greek：ἀγορανόμος，ἀγορανόμοι）

agoranomos，agoranomoi · Lit. “agora-regulator（s）”：public officials attested in a large number of Greek poleis；their duties consisted of supervising the commercial aspects of the agora.

2. aidesis（Greek：αἴδεσις）

aidesis · Because homicide in Athenian law was a matter for private prosecution，the relatives of the dead man，as prosecutors，were under certain circumstances permitted or expected to grant pardon（aidesis）to his killer. Once this had been done，the killer was immune from further prosecution.（The derivation of the term is unclear：it is certainly connected with the verb aideomai “to feel shame，awe or

① This glossary consists of excerpts from S. C. Todd，“Glossary”，in P. A. Cartledge et al.，*Nomos：Essays Athenian Law，Politics and Society*（Cambridge，1990），selected by Michael de Brauw（University of Texas at Austin）. Todd's complete glossary（with some changes）also appears in The Shape of Athenian Law（Oxford，1993）. This excerpted selection was first published electronically as part of the online discussion series “Athenian Law in its Democratic Context”，organized by Adriaan Lanni and sponsored by Harvard University's Center for Hellenic Studies.

respect”; LSJ notes that the verb can be used to mean “to respect another's misfortune” and thus “to be reconciled to him”; but unlike English “reconciliation”, aidesis is only used to denote the action of the wronged party.)

3. anakrisis(Greek: ἀνάκρισις)

anakrisis · A preliminary hearing before the public official within whose court a case will later be heard(for the role of the presiding official within a lawcourt, see sv. arkhon). Lit., “examination”, but it should not be equated with the inquisitorial instruction of civil-law systems: an Athenian public official had very restricted discretion; and unlike an arbitrator(see sv. diaitetes), his function was not to settle the case.

4. antidosis(Greek: ἀντίδοσις)

antidosis · Lit. “a giving in exchange”. A man who was nominated to perform a liturgy could avoid this duty if he could name another citizen who was richer and better qualified to perform the task. If the man challenged agreed that he was richer, he had to take over the liturgy; if he claimed to be poorer, then the challenger could insist on an exchange of all their property to test the claim—in which case the challenger would himself perform the liturgy as the new owner of the(putatively) greater estate. This process of exchange was called antidosis. The advantage of the system from the viewpoint of the democracy was that it encouraged the rich to be suspicious of each other, instead of being hostile towards the state; but although we know of several challenges, there is no attested case in which the exchange was completed.

5. apagoge(Greek: ἀπαγωγή)

apagoge, pl. apagogai · Lit. “dragging away”, i. e., to the appropriate magistrate. Summary arrestwas permitted against certain categories of criminal, such as thieves and highwaymen, if they were caught ep'autophori—red handed. If the accused admitted his guilt before the magistrate he was promptly executed; only if he claimed to be innocent was he put on trial. See also sv. ephegesis.

6. apographe(Greek: ἀπογραφή)

apographe · Lit. “a(written) list”: a catalogue of some or all of the property of a man in debt to the state. The state took no initiative in the confiscation of property: this was left either to private individuals or else, it appears, to local deme's officials.

The term apographe is used to describe the list itself, the process of denunciation, and any judicial hearing arising out of the case. See also sv. phasis.

7. apophasis (Greek: ἀπόφασις)

apophasis · Lit. "a showing forth, declaration". A procedure newly instituted around the middle of the fourth century: either on the invitation of the ekklesia or on its own initiative, the Areiopagos could investigate any matter involving public security and present a report (apophasis) to the ekklesia, recommending particular action, for instance the prosecution of a named individual. (Apophasis is the subject of a Demos article.)

8. apragmon (Greek: ἀπράγμων, ἀπράγμονες; ἀπραγμοσύνη)

apragmon, pl. apragmones (adj.); apragmosune (abstract noun) · Lit. "one who does not conduct business": a person who refrains from taking part in public affairs. It can be either a positive or a negative characteristic, depending on the attitude of the speaker ("philosophical contemplation" or "political irresponsibility"). For the opposite characteristic, see sv. polupragmon.

9. Areiopagos (Greek: Ἄρειος πάγος; Ἄρεος πάγος)

Athens.

Areiopagos · The ancient and originally aristocratic council of Athens; its membership comprised those who had completed a term as one of the nine archons. Its powers had been severely restricted by the democratic reforms of Ephialtes in the 460s BCE, which left it as little more than the main court for cases of homicide; in the fourth century however other powers were added, most notably apophasis.

10. arkhon (Greek: ἄρχων, ἄρχοντες)

Athens.

arkhon, pl. arkhontes (participle acting as a noun), Eng. archon or arkhon · Lit. "one who is in authority". Used in three senses: loosely, to refer to any Athenian public official; more strictly (usually a collective plural) to describe the "nine arkhons"; specifically, as the title of the senior of the nine arkhonships. These were still the titular chief magistrates of Athens, but their real authority had been severely restricted ever since they began to be appointed by lot, apparently in the 480s. They retained however an honorific position, particularly in the administration of justice: or instance, former arkhons became members of the Areiopagos for life; and during their year of office they processed the litigation presented to the most important of the dikasteria, and presided over trials held there, although in this capacity they were by now little more thannon-voting (and non-speaking) chairmen. The three senior arkhons each had a specific title and competence: the arkhon (the eponymous official of Athens who gave his name to the civil year) heard cases involving family and inheritance matters of citizens; the arkhon basileus (lit. "king arkhon") presided over religious matters, including sacrilege and homicide; the polemarkhos (lit. "war arkhon", but by now all his military functions had been handed over to the strategoi) dealt with family and inheritance cases involving metics and apparently cases involving certain other privileged foreigners also. The other six arkhons were called thesmothetai (sing. thesmothetes: originally perhaps "establisher of judgements" rather than "maker of laws"); they heard those public cases, and perhaps also some private ones, which did not fall within the competence of the three senior arkhons or of other named officials.

11. astunomos (Greek: ἀστυνόμος, ἀστυνόμοι)

Athens.

astunomos, pl. astunomoi · Lit. "one who regulates (affairs within) the astu (the built-up area of Athens)". A board of public officials charged with the general supervisory duties which we associate with the police. Unlike the police, however, they did not undertake the investigation of crime. Nor were they much concerned with the arrest or punishment of accused or convicted criminals: this role was played by the Eleven.

12. atimia (Greek: ἀτιμία (loss of τιμή))

Athens.

atimia (abstract noun) · Lit. "loss of time, honour". In early archaic Athens, atimia seems to have meant outlawry, the total deprivation of all rights, such that a citizen could kill an atimos (pl. atimoi: person suffering from atimia) without committing an offence or apparently incurring blood-guilt. Well before the classical period, however, atimia had already been restricted in its scope to mean the loss of some or all of a man's active rights as a citizen. Such atimia could be partial or total; it could be imposed permanently by a court, or it could be the (theoretically) temporary result of an unpaid debt to the state, a condition which would automatically terminate if the debt were ever paid off. A man subject to total atimia could not appear in certain public places, could not take part in public life, and could not appear in court. If he broke any of these bans, he was liable to apagoge and death. But he did retain his private rights as a citizen: to kill him would be murder; he was not formally exiled; and he continued to own his property—though his lack of the capacity to sue may have made it difficult procedurally to defend these rights, and many may have found life under such restrictions so intolerable that voluntary exile seemed preferable. A man subject to partial atimia lost either a particular right or rights, or else the power to exercise his rights in a particular situation: for instance, the ability to bring certain types of prosecution.

13. basileus(Greek: βασιλεύς)

basileus See sv. arkhon.

14. boule(Greek: βουλή)

boule · Lit. "council". The democratic council of 500 men, appointed annually by lot from among citizens aged at least thirty, and with severe restrictions on repeated membership. Its chieffunction was to prepare the agenda for meetings of the ekklesia, and to undertake certain routine administrative duties, in particular that of co-ordinating the activities of numerous boards of minor officials; but it had also certain independent judicial powers, mainly but not only in cases of limited importance: in some cases of eisangelia, the boule could decide whether to refer the trial to the ekklesia or to a dikasterion.

15(ho) boulomenos(Greek: ὁβουλόμενος)

(ho)boulomenos · Lit. "anyone who wishes". Whereas prosecution in a dike could only be brought by the aggrieved party, in a graphe or other public case it could be brought by any qualified person(which normally meant any Athenian citizen who was not himself atimos).

16. diadikasia(Greek: διαδικασία)

diadikasia · Lit. "judgement(contested) between": a dispute between two people who each claim the same thing, in particular a contested inheritance.

17. diaitetes(Greek: διαιτητής, διαιτηταί)

diaitetes, pl. diaitetai · An arbitrator. Throughout the history of Athenian law, it had always been open for litigants to arrange arbitration(diaita) on a private basis: in theory, the decision of a private arbitrator was binding, presumably because the litigants had voluntarily contracted to accept it. There was also, however, a system of public arbitration, introduced c. 400 BCE: every hoplite (or possibly every citizen), in the year that he ceased to be eligible for military service at the age of 59, had to serve as public arbitrator; and every dike (private dispute) was allocated by lot to one of them for an attempt at preliminary resolution. In such cases arbitration was compulsory (litigants were obliged to attend) but it was not binding (a dissatisfied litigant could refuse to accept the verdict: see sv. ephesis). According to Aristotle, the job of the arbitrator (private or public) is unlike that of the dikastes in several respects: he should try to reconcile the parties before imposing a solution; he has the discretion to bring in a decision mid-way between the demands of the litigants; and in his judgement he should look to epieikeia ("equity", but see further sv. epieikeia) rather than to dike ("justice").

18. diamarturia (Greek: διαμαρτυρία)

diamarturia · A formal presentation of a witness (martus) whose evidence serves to compel the public official before whom it is presented either to act in a certain way, or (more commonly) to desist from so acting. As a result of the introduction of paragraphe around 400 BCE, the scope of diamarturia was soon rapidly restricted: after 380 BCE, its only attested use is in inheritance cases, where a legitimate son could have a claim by a more remote relative quashed on the grounds that the case was not actionable; to re-open the case, the rival claimant would have successfully to prosecute the witness by dike pseudomarturion.

19. dike (Greek: δίκη, δίκαι)

dike, pl. dikai · A concept of wide scope: "justice", "good order", "judgement". But it can also refer to the process by which a just settlement is determined, thus "a lawsuit", "a trial", and even "the case which one pleads" or "the penalty which one has to pay". In the sence of "lawsuit", dike can be used either generically, to refer to any type of indictment, or else (more commonly) in asemi-technical sense, to denote the older "private suit" (which only the aggrieved party or his immediate or his immediate personal representatives could bring) as opposed to the newer "public suit" (graphe), which could be brought by any citizen in good standing; it should however be noted that the category of public procedure was broader than that of graphe, and included a number of extraordinary procedures which were not themselves graphai, see for instance svv. apagoge, apophasis, eisangelia, euthunai, phasis.

Note: It seems that these indictments in Athenian law were only allowed if use of the dike or graphe procedure against a particular offence was authorised by statute; whether the defendant's alleged behavior fell within the terms of this offence could of course be a matter for debate. An indictment was normally described as a dike (or graphe, as appropriate), qualified by the name of the offence, usually in the genitive case: thus graphe hubreos, a public indictment for hubris.

20. diomosia (Greek: διωμοσία)

diomosia · A special oath taken in cases of homicide: in all other cases the litigants alone swore the antimosia (lit. "oath [of two people] against each other"); in homicide cases all the witnesses had to join in the oath of their principals, which was for this reason known as the diomosia (lit. "oath between [more than two people]").

21. dokimasia (Greek: δοκιμασία, δοκιμασίαι)

dokimasia, pl. dokimasiai · An investigation held either by the boule or in a court, to test whether a man was formally qualified either to hold the public office to which he had been appointed or else to exercise a privilege to which he was laying claim. Dokimasiai were of various types, and were for the most part held in advance: no public official, whether elected or appointed by lot, could hold office without having passed his dokimasia; and newly enrolled citizens, whether by birth or by naturalisation (uncommon), were among those similarly tested. In these cases a man who was rejected suffered disqualification but no further penalty; a public speaker however (see sv. rhetor) could be challenged to undergo a retroactive dokimasia before a court, and this had more of the nature of a regular trial, in that if convicted he would apparently be punished.

22. eisangelia (Greek: εἰσαγγελία, εἰσαγγελίαι)

eisangelia, pl. eisangeliai · Lit. "public announcement, laying of information": a form of public indictment broadly corresponding to impeachment in the USA. It was available for use against any public official during or after his term of office (he would normally be suspended from office for the duration of the trial) or against any political leader who had made a public proposal. It seems that the case could be brought either directly to the ekklesia or else to the boule, and that the final hearing would take place either before the ekklesia or (more commonly, and in every known case after 360 B. C.) before a dikasterion.

23. ekdosis (Greek: ἔκδοσις)

ekdosis · Lit. "giving forth": the ceremony at which the kurios of a betrothed bride gave her into the hand of her new husband. Marriage in Athenian law took one of two forms, either by engue and ekdosis or else (if a man died leaving his daughter with no kurios to give her away, and no heir to his property) by the epidikasia of the epikleros.

24. ekklesia (Greek: ἐκκλησία)

Athens.

ekklesia · The public assembly of Athens, held usually on the Pnyx, at which all adult male citizens were formally entitled to attend, vote, and speak.

25. (the) Eleven (Greek: οἱ Ἕνδεκα)

Athens.

(the) Eleven; Gk. hoi hendeka · A board of public officials responsible for the state prison of Athens. The majority of apagogai were brought before them, and they were in charge of all executions.

26. emporike (Greek: ἐμπορικὴ δίκη, ἐμπορικαὶ δίκαι)

Attica.

emporike dike., pl. emporikai dikai · A case involving emporoi, traders who import goods (especially the extra grain which was needed to feed the population of Attica). Because of the urgency of the trade, such cases had rapid and privileged access to the courts; but it is not clear whether the term emmenos, commonly used to describe them, should be interpreted to mean that the case must be completed within a month (the traditional view), or (as has recently been argued) that there was an opportunity every month to initiate such cases; it is uncertain also whether such litigation could take place only during the summer months or only during the winter months. It is possible that other special rules may have applied in these cases.

27. endeixis (Greek: ἔνδειξις, ἐνδείξεις)

endeixis, pl. endeixeis · A procedure closely related to apagoge. The precise significance of the term is disputed: traditionally it was thought to be a denunciation made before a public official who would then himself arrest the culprit; but it may instead have been used by the plaintiff in some cases as a voluntary preliminary to apagoge.

28. engue(Greek:ἐγγύη,ἐγγύαι; ἐγγυητής)

engue,pl. enguai; enguetes · A surety:the engue is the thing which is pledged as security,and the enguetes the person who pledges or commits himself as a pledge. Such sureties were used in a range of legal contexts:to guarantee the payment of a fine or the appearance of a defendant(particularly a foreigner) in court; and as a deposit payable to those who contracted from the state the right to collect taxes or to operate mining concessions. But the most notable use of engue was as the necessary prelude to ekdosis in the regular Athenian form of marriage,corresponding to(but much stronger than) the modern engagement.

29. ephesis(Greek:ἔφεσις)

ephesis · Refusal to accept the decision of an official or a court of first instance, combined with a demand for the dispute to be resolved by a higher authority. For instance,Solon in the 590s is said to have introduced "ephesis to the dikasterion" as a curb on the summary jurisdiction of public officials; and from their introduction in c. 400 B. C. ,the decisions of public arbitrators were similarly subject to ephesis. Ephesis is traditionally translated " appeal", but this can havemisleading connotations. An appeal in English law is brought on the initiative of a dissatisfied litigant(in criminal cases,a convicted defendant) after the court of first instance has decided against him/her; it is his/her duty to persuade the appellate court to reverse the decision,and he/she becomes in a sense the plaintiff in the process. In Athens,there were at least some situations in which ephesis could take place before the lower authority had reached a decision; it was the duty of the original plaintiff, not of the dissatisfied litigant, to persuade the court to act(that it,the court was retrying the case from scratch and not reviewing a decision already made); and it is possible that in the case of Solonian ephesis,this referral was automatic and did not depend on an initiative taken by one of the two litigants.

30. epieikeia(Greek:ἐπιείκεια)

epieikeia · Aristotle says that it is the function of the dikastes(juror/judge) to judge according to dike("justice"),but that the diaitetes(arbitrator) should make his decision according to epieikeia. It is conventional therefore to translate epieikeia as "equity", since this is a standard and convenient way to describe "fairness" or "natural justice" as opposed to the strict application of legal rules. There are however certain problems here. "Equity" in English law can mean simply "fairness", but it is also the name given to the system of law developed originally by the Court of Chancery (the Lord Chancellor's court), to provide relief in cases where to apply the rules of the common law would have seemed manifestly unfair. "Equity" in this sense is itself a body of rules; it is found only in countries which base their legal system on the common law; and it is clearly not what Aristotle is talking about. It should indeed be noted that Aristotle's statement of theory receives little acknowledgment in Athenian practice: when a litigant in an extant speech pleads for the application of natural justice in his favour, he characteristically describes this as dike and not as epieikeia.

31. epikleros (Greek: ἐπίκληρος, ἐπιλκηρώτη)

epikleros (fem. adj. acting as noun), epiklerote (abstract noun) · An epikleros was the daughter of a man who died leaving no male heir; she was not his heiress, but possession of his estate went together with her hand in marriage. This system of inheritance is described as the epiklerate: for further details, see sv. inheritance; and for comparison, see sv. engue and sv. ekdosis. (The etymology of epikleros is unclear: it may possibly mean "one to whom the property pertains", but more likely is "one who pertains to the property".)

32. euthune (Greek: εὐθύνη, εὔθυναι)

euthune, normally pl. euthunai · Lit. "the action of setting straight". Every public official at Athens had to undergo at the end of his term an examination of his conduct in office. If he had handled public money, he had to present his accounts (logoi, pl.); in all cases he had to seek approval of the way he had used his powers (euthunai properly so called, but the term euthunai came also to be applied to the whole process of audit, logoi included). The examination was conducted by boards of logistai (pl.) and euthunoi (pl.), as appropriate; but any private citizen could bring a charge at any stage during the proceedings.

33. exegetes (Greek: ἐξηγητής, ἐξηγηταί)

exegetes, pl. exegetai · Lit. "interpreter". A group of officials who expound the proper procedurein situations which raise unusual questions of religious law. Their activity is attested in several cases, all of homicide; and in each case they are responding to an inquiry by an individual by an individual rather than as expert witnesses before a court. In one case they offer also to advise a litigant, implying that this was something more than their regular function of interpreting the law.

34. graphe(Greek: γραφή, γραφαί)

graphe, pl. graphai · Lit. "a writing"; hence, "a written indictment", cf. Eng. "writ". This was the name given to the new "public" form of ordinary prosecution introduced apparently by Solon in the 590s. Its characteristic was that the indictment could be brought by any qualified citizen (ho boulomenos), whereas the older dike procedure could be brought only by the injured party. Graphai and other public procedures appear to have given rise to higher penalties, and thus to have rewarded a successful plaintiff much more heavily than did dikai; but they were also considerably more risky: a plaintiff in a public suit who failed to obtain 20 per cent of the votes of the jury could expect to suffer a heavy fine and possibly also other penalties (e. g. at least partial atimia).

35. klepsudra(Greek: κλεψύδρα)

klepsudra · Lt. "water-stealer". A water-clock, used to regulate the length of the proceedings in legal cases. It consisted of a bowl of water with a small hole near the base, such that the hole could be stopped or opened as desired: normally two such bowls were used, the one being allowed to empty its contents into the other, and then vice versa, to measure the passage of time. In any category of case, a set number of bowls-full was allocated to each speaker, but the flow of water was stopped for the reading of laws and the testimony of witness.

36. kurios(Greek: κύριος)

kurios · Lit. "master", "lord", or in certain contexts "sovereign". An Athenian woman had to be represented in legal transactions by a male relative, who was described as her kurios: in the case of an unmarried girl or widow who had returned to the house of her family, this would normally be her father or (failing him) her brother or paternal uncle, but it could even be her adult son. A married woman was represented by her husband, but it appears that her agnatic kurios did retain certain rights: for instance, the reversion of her dowry. Confusingly, the term kurios was also used to denote the owner of property or the master of a household, and there are contexts in which the two uses might conflict: a married son, for instance, would be kurios of his wife; but his father may still be kurios of his household.

37. logographos(Greek: λογογράφος, λογογράφοι)

logographos, pl. logographoi · Lit. "speech-writer": specifically, a professional writer of speeches for litigants to deliver in court. It has recently been argued that the logographos did not normally write the speech so much as help the litigant to prepare it, but this view is contested.

38. nomos(Greek: νόμος, νόμοι)

nomos, pl. nomoi · Lit. a "norm", in the sense both of "custom" and of "law". Nomos is often contrasted, especially in fifth-century Greek thought, with phusis(lit. "nature"); the latterrepresents underlying reality, and the former denotes the patterns by which men try to shape this. In this sense nomos is normally translated "convention".

39. nomothesia(Greek: νομοθεσία; νομοθέτης, νομοθέται)

nomothesia, nomothetes, pl. nomothetai · Nomothesia is the process of enacting laws(of general and/or permanent validity). After 403 BCE, this was taken out of the hands of the ekklesia and given to the nomothetai, in order to provide a check on the passage of reckless legislation. The precise arrangements for the process seem to have been revised several times during the fourth century; but it is notable that the nomothetai were a body selected by lot from among the panel of eligible dikastai. Their function was to hear in detail(but not apparently to discuss) the arguments for and against any proposed legislative change, and to make a final and authoritative decision. They could however only act when requested to do so on the initiative of the ekklesia.

40. nothos(Greek: νόθος, νόθοι)

nothos, pl. nothoi · Lit. "a bastard". In the classical period, Athenian citizenship was confined to those born of citizen parents on both sides. The child of an unmarried union between citizen and non-citizen was clearly illegitimate, and had rights neither of inheritance nor of citizenship. The status of the child of unmarried citizen parents is less clear: such a person was clearly a nothos without rights of inheritance, but it is disputed whether s/he was or was not a citizen. It is possible, though less certain, that the word nothos was used to describe the child of a mixed marriage even in those contexts(e. g. before 450 BCE) where such a marriage was legally permissible, even though such a child might have full rights to inheritance as well as to citizenship.

41. oikos(Greek: οἶκος)

oikos · A household: the word can be used to describe people or family property or a building, or all three together. The term is rarely used in the formulation of Athenian statutes, but the concept seems to play an important rôle not only in family but in citizenship law: see svv. kurios, nothos.

42. paragraphe(Greek: παραγραφή)

paragraphe · A counter-indictment, in which the defendant charges the plaintiff with bringing an illegal prosecution. The procedure was invented (or possibly re-organised) around 400, to help those threatened with charges which broke the Amnesty: the latter had been imposed under Spartan supervision to protect former supporters of the Thirty Tyrants, the oligarchic junta of 404/3 which had been overthrown by the democratic restoration of 403/2. Paragraphe, however rapidly extended its scope: for the defendant, it seems to have had the advantage that it was itself a prosecution; whereas the older procedure of diamarturia simply served to block a particular claim by the plaintiff, paragraphe enabled the defendant to turn the tables, becoming himself the prosecutor and (if successful) imposing a penalty on his opponent.

43. (graphe) paranomon(Greek: γραφὴ παρανόνων)

(graphe) paranomon · A public indictment against the proposer of a new psephisma(decree), charging that his proposal is unconstitutional (lit. "against the law"): One of the most extensivelydocumented of all Athenian legal procedures, and one of the most overtly political: the prosecutor might claim for instance that the bill had been proposed without the necessary formalities; but many of the extant graphai paranomon are directed against honorary decrees, and in these the prosecutor regularly bases his case on the claim that the honour is itself undeserved. The procedure could be employed against proposals both before and after they had been voted on by the ekklesia. Until 403 B. C., it was apparently used without discrimination against both nomoi(laws) and psephismata; but in that year a formal distinction was for the first time drawn between the two types of statute (see sv. nomos, Legislation). The old procedure of graphi paranomon was retained for use against psephismata; but a new parallel procedure, the graphi nomon me epitedeion theinai, was felt to be required for use against unconstitutional (lit. "inexpedient") nomoi.

44. phasis (Greek: φάσις)

phasis · Lit. "a showing forth, declaration": denunciation of a man who is illegally withholding property which belongs to the state. Unlike the related (and much better attested) procedure of apographe, phasis was apparently directed against the person rather than the property.

45. polupragmon (Greek: πολυπράγμων, πολυπράγμονες)

polupragmon, pl. polupragmones (adj.); polupragmosune (abstract noun) · Lit. "one who conducts much business", i. e. "too much". Usually pejorative in the eyes of the speaker. The fifth-century Athenian empire was according to its opponents the product of cooperative Athenian polupragmosune; on an individual level, the term has overtones of "officious" and "busybody."

46. probole (Greek: προβολή, προβολαί)

probole, pl. probolai · Lit. "a throwing forward". A preliminary accusation, which an intending plaintiff could bring before the ekklesia (Assembly) rather than directly to a dikasterion (court). This vote of the ekklesia had no formal effect: it did not bind a successful plaintiff to continue his action in court, nor apparently did it prevent him from doing so if unsuccessful; it imposed no penalty either on plaintiff or on defendant. It did however strengthen the hand of the successful plaintiff: after the manner of a straw poll, it showed which way the wind was blowing. We hear of probole being used in disputes which arise at festivals, and also against sycophants and against political leaders (presumably) who have allegedly deceived the people with false promises.

47. (dike) pseudomarturion (Greek: δίκη ψευδομαρτυριῶν)

(dike) pseudomarturion · Lit. "(prosecution concerning) false witness": a private indictment against a martus ("witness"). This is by its nature a secondary action, brought against a man who has been a witness in previous legal proceedings, and charging him with having given a false or illegal testimony.

48. sukophantes(Greek:συκοφάντης,συκοφάνται; συκοφαντεῖν)

sukophantes,pl. sukophantai(noun); sukophantein(verb) · A term of disputed etymology and disputed meaning,used pejoratively to describe an officious litigant. Conventionally transliterated as "sycophant" or "sykophant", but the English adjective "sycophantic" derivesfrom a later, post-classical development in the meaning of the word.

49. sunegoros(Greek:συν ήγορος,συν ήγοροι)

sunegoros,pl. sunegoroi · Most commonly,a person who appears in court to speak on behalf of a litigant. Lit "speaker together with", thus at least in theory preserving the rule that litigants could not be represented by advocates:The sunegoros was officially the supporting speaker. The word is also used to describe a speaker appointed to represent the state, normally as prosecutor; but the overwhelming majority even of public prosecutions were brought by private individuals.

附录二:古希腊法律史研究外文参考书目

A

Adcock,F. E. (1953),"Greek and Macedonian Kingship",*Proceedings of the British Academy* 39,163 – 180.

Adcock,F. E. (1927),"Literary Tradition and Early Greek Codemakers", *Cambridge Historical Journal* 2,95 – 109.

Adcock,F. E. (1916),"Constitutions",in Whibley,L. (ed),*A Companion to Greek Studies* 3,429 – 463,Cambridge.

Adeleye,G. (1983),"The Purpose of the Dokimasia",*GRBS* 24,295 – 306.

Adeleye,G. (1977 – 1978),"The Arginusai Affair and Theramenes' Rejection at the Dokimasia of 405/4 B. C.",*Museum Africum* 6,94 – 99.

Adkins,A. W. H. (1960),"Honour and Punishment in the Homeric Poems", *BICS* 8,23ff.

Ager, S. (1996), Interstate Arbitrations in the Greek World, 337 – 90BC, Berkeley. (Hellenistic culture and society 18)

Aleshire,S. (1994),"The Demos and the Priests: The Selection of Sacred

Officials at Athens from Cleisthenes to Augustus", in *Ritual, Finance, Politics*, 326 – 337.

van Alfen, P. (2010), "Social Controls, Institutions, and the Regulation of Commodities in Classical Aegean Markets", *MBAH* 28, 197 – 229.

Allen, J. T. (1904), "On Secrecy in Voting in the Athenian Lawcourts in the Fifth Century B. C.", *CR* 18, 456 – 458.

Allen, R. E. (1996), "The Trial of Socrates: A Study in the Morality of the Criminal Process", in Prior, W. J. (ed), *Socrates: Critical Assessments Vol. II: Issues Arising from the Trial of Socrates*, 1 – 14, London.

Allen, R. E. (1972), "Law and Justice in Plato's Crito", *Journal of Philosophy* 69, 557 – 567.

Alonso, V. (2007), "War, Peace and International Law in Ancient Greece", in Raaflaub, K. (ed) (2007), *War and Peace in the Ancient World*, 206 – 225, Oxford.

d'Amico, D. J. (2010), "The Prison in Economics: Private and Public Incarceration in Ancient Greece", *Public Choice* 145, 461 – 482.

Amit, M. (1970), "The Constitution of Mantineia", in Rozelaar, M. & B. Shimron (eds), *Commentationes ad Antiquitatem Classicam Pertinentes in Memoriam B. Katz*, 118 – 123, Tel Aviv.

Amundsen, D. W. (1977), "The Liability of the Physician in Classical Greek Legal Theory and Practice", *JHM* 32, 172 – 203.

Amundsen, D. W. & G. B. Ferngren. (1977), "The Physician as an Expert Witness in Athenian Law", *BHM* 51, 202 – 213.

Amundsen, L. (1957), "The Classical Greek Background of Ptolemaic Law and Administration of Justice", in Hoeg, C., Krarup, P., Rils, J. P. & I. Magnussen (eds), *Acta Congressus Madvigiani* (Proceedings of the second international congress of classical studies), I, 251 – 265, Copenhagen.

Anderson, G. (2009), "The Personality of the Greek State", *JHS* 129, 1 – 22.

Anderson, G. (2003), The Athenian Experiment: Building an Imagined Political Community in Ancient Attica, 508 – 490 B. C., Ann Arbor, Mich.

Andrews, J. A. (2004), "Pericles on the Athenian Constitution (Thuc. 2. 37)", *AJPh* 125, 539 – 561.

Andrewes, A. (1966), "The Government of Classical Sparta", in *Ancient Society and Institutions*, 1 – 20.

Andrewes, A. (1963), The Greek Tyrants, New York.

Andrewes, A. (1954), Probouleusis. Sparta's Contribution to the Technique of Government, Oxford.

Andriolo, N. (2008), "Caronda e la dike pseudomartyrion" RSA 38, 9 – 16.

Andriolo, N. (2006 – 2007), "Neera: un processo pubblico ad Atene per usurpazione della cittadinanza", Atti e memorie dell'Ateneo di Treviso 24, 337 – 344.

Andriolo, N. (2006), La democrazia rinnovata: Atene agli inizi del IV sec. a. C., Padova.

Andriolo, N. (2005 – 2006), "L' 'eisanghelia' contro Licofrone", Atti e memorie dell'Ateneo di Treviso 23, 49 – 54.

Andriolo, N. (2004), Magistrature ad Atene dal 413 al 401 a. C., Padova.

Andriolo, N. (2003), "I syngrapheis del 411 a. C. ad Atene", in Miscellanea Sartori, 49 – 60.

Andriolo, N. (2002), "Il procedimento penale contro Leocrate", *Patavium* 10 (20), 57 – 67.

Andriolo, N. (2002), "Syndikoi", *DHA* 28, 11 – 18.

Andriolo, N. (2001), "La costituzione dei Cinquemila", *Patavium* 9 (18), 13 – 31.

Andriolo, N. (2001), "Hai dialyseis del 403 a. C. in Atene", *Patavium* 9 (17), 19 – 36.

Andriolo, N. (2000 – 2001), "I dieci ad Atene", Atti dell'istituto Veneto di Scienzi, Lettere ed Arti (Classe di scienze morali) 159, 767 – 781.

Andriolo, N. (2000), "La concessione della cittadinanza ateniese ai Sami nel 405/403 – 2 a. C.", Patavium 15, 37 – 51.

Andriolo, N. (1999), "Dieteti", in Atti del XI Congresso Internazionale di Epigrafia Greca e Latina I, (Roma, 18 – 24 settembre 1997), 167 – 176, Roma.

Andriolo, N. (1995 – 1996), "Eisangelia", Atti dell'Istituto Veneto di Scienze, Lettere ed Arti (Classe di scienze morali) 154, 173 – 195. Anton, J. P. (1988) "Revolutions, Reforms and Educational Philosophy in Aristotle's Theory of Constitutional Law", in *Philosophy of Law*, 58 – 62.

Aperghis, G. C. (1997 – 1998), "A Reassessment of the Laurion Mining Lease

Records" ,*BICS* 42,1 -20.

Arnaoutoglou,I. (2010), "Onomastics and Law. Dike and-dike Names", in Catling,R. W. V. & F. Marchand (eds), *Onomatologos. Studies in Greek Personal Names Presented to Elaine Matthews*,582 -600,Oxford.

Arnaoutoglou,I. (2008), "The Trial of Phokion, Athens 318 BC", *EHHD* 41, 21 -39. (in Greek)

Arnaoutoglou,I. (2007), "Fear of Slaves in Ancient Greek Legal Texts", in *Fear of Slaves*,133 -144.

Arnaoutoglou,I. (2004), "Aspects of Oral Law in Archaic Greece", in *Law, Rhetoric,and Comedy*,1 -14.

Arnaoutoglou,I. (2003), "Ancient Greek Laws in the World Wide Web", *Imeros* 3,181 -188.

Arnaoutoglou, I. (1998), "Between Koinon and Idion: Legal and Social Dimensions of Religious Associations in Ancient Athens" ,in *Kosmos*,68 -83.

Arnaoutoglou,I. (1998),Ancient Greek Laws. A Sourcebook,London.

Arnaoutoglou,I. (1993),"Pollution in the Athenian Homicide Law",*RIDA* 40, 109 -37.

Arnold,Th. (1874), "On the Spartan Constitution", in Thucydides. De bello Peloponnesiaco 8,1,app. ii,525 -532,Oxford.

Asano, K. (1974), "Some Problems of the Athenian Law of Property", *Hitotsubashi Ronso*(*Hitotsubashi Review*)72,15 -33.

Asano, K. (1972), "A Study of Property Rights in Ancient Greece", *Hitotsubashi Ronso*(*Hitotsubashi Review*)67,77 -95.

Asper,M. (2004), "Law and Logic: Towards an Archaeology of Abstract Reason",*AION* 26,73 -94.

Atkinson,J. (2003), "Athenian Law and the will of the People in the Fourth Century B. C. ",*AClass* 46,21 -48.

Atkinson,K. M. T. (1939), "Athenian Legislative Procedure and Revision of Laws",*Bulletin of the John Rylands Library*(Manchester)23,107 -150.

Austin, C. (2008), "Marriage on the Rocks: Pamphile in Menander's Epitrepontes",*AAntHung* 48,19 -28.

Avramovic,S. (2010),"Katoikodomeo in Isaeus, Ⅷ 41. Imprisonment,Hybris and Atimia in Athenian Law" ,*ZRG* 127,261 – 274.

Avramovic, S. (2010), "From General Legal History Towards Comparative Legal Traditions", *Belgrade Law Review* 58. (http://papers.ssrn.com/sol3/papers.cfm? abstract_id = 1626756) Avramovic, S. (2008), "Hybris in Ancient Athens: Legal Aspects and Modern Challenges", Zbornik Matice srpske za klasicne studije 10, 203 – 222. (in Serbian)

Avramovic, S. (2005), "The Rhetra of Epitadaeus and Testament in Spartan Law", in Symposion 2001, 175 – 186. (= Zbornik Pravnog Fakulteta Sveucilista u Rijeci, Suppl. 1, 2001, 61 – 74 (in Serbian)) (with a reply by Todd, S. C., 187 – 195)

Avramovic, S. (1998), "Elements of Legal State and Individual Rights in Athens", in Pravna drzava u antici-pro et contra, 7 – 41, Belgrade. (in Serbian)

Avramovic, S. (1997), "Traces of Legal State in Athenian Democracy", Pravni Zivot 12, 1343 – 1363. (in Serbian)

Avramovic, S. (1991), "Prison in Athenian Law and 'katoikodomein' of Isaeus", *Annals of the Faculty of Law*, Belgrade University, 10 – 18.

Avramovic, S. (1987), "Agrarian Property Relations in the Code of Gortyn", Zbornik Pravnog Fakulteta u Rijeci 8, 21 – 31. (in Serbian)

Avramovic, S. (1987), "Differences in Legal Nature among Testament in Roman Law and Ancient Greek Legatentestament", *Annals of the Faculty of Law*, Belgrade University, 9 – 18. (in Serbian)

Avramovic, S. (1986), "Differences in Legal Nature among Testament in Roman Law and Ancient Greek Testamentary Adoption", *Annals of the Faculty of Law*, Belgrade University, 3 – 13. (in Serbian)

Avramovic, S. (1985), "Specific Features of Legal Procedure in Ancient Athens", *Advokatura* 41, 65 – 71. (in Serbian)

Avramovic, S. (1982), "Remarks about the So-called Law of Epitadeus", *Advokatura* 4, 56 – 68. (in Serbian)

Avramovic, S. (1982), "Division on Public and Private Law in Greek-city States", *Annals of the Faculty of Law*, Belgrade University, 821 – 826. (in Serbian)

Avramovic, S. (1979), "Epikleros, Kadestai and Epiballontes in Ancient Greek Law", *Annals of the Faculty of Law*, Belgrade University, 475 – 490. (in Serbian)

B

Baba, K. (1984), "On Kerameikos inv. I 388 (SEG XXII 79). A Note on the Formation of the Athenian Metic Status", *ABSA* 79, 1 – 5.

Baba, K. (1965), "The Ability of Metics to bring a Legal Suit in Athens", *Journal of Aoyama Gakuin Woman's Junior College* 19, 1 – 18.

Baba, K. (1963), "Athenian Citizen and Metics", in *Essays on Ancient History*, 7, 48 – 79, Tokyo.

Baba, K. (1962), "Non-citizen's Ownership of Real Property in Attica", *Shigaku Zasshi* 71(8), 1 – 34.

Bakewell, G. (2008 – 2009), "Forbidding Marriage: Neaira 16 and Metic Spouses at Athens", *CJ* 104, 97 – 109.

Bakewell, G. W. (1999 – 2000), "Lysias 12 and Lysias 31: Metics and Athenian Citizenship in the Aftermath of the Thirty", *GRBS* 40, 5 – 22; 41, 5 – 22.

Bakewell, G. W. (1997), "Metoikia in the Supplices of Aeschylus", *ClAnt* 16, 209 – 228.

Balcer, J. M. (1978), The Athenian Regulations for Chalkis: Studies in the Athenian Imperial Law, Wiesbaden. (Historia Einzelschrift 33)

Balogh, E. (1953), "Adaptation of Law to Economic Conditions in Ancient Greece", in *Studi Arangio-Ruiz* 3, 189 – 198.

Balogh, E. (1953), "Some Notes on Adultery and the Epikleros According to Ancient Athenian Law", in Studi in memoria di E. Albertario II, 683 – 719, Milano.

Balogh, E. (1949), "Cicero and the Greek Law", in *Scritti Ferrini* 3, 1 – 27.

Balot, R. K. (2001), Greed and Injustice in Classical Athens, Princeton.

Barber, B. R. (1996), "Misreading Democracy: Peter Euben and the Gorgias", in Ober, J. & Ch. Hedrick jr (eds), *Demokratia. A Conversation on Democracies, Ancient and Modern*, 361 – 375, Princeton.

Barkan, I. (1936), "Imprisonment as a Penalty in Ancient Athens", *CPh* 31, 338 – 341.

Barkan, I. (1935), Capital Punishment in Ancient Athens, NewYork.

Barker, E. (1918), Greek Political Theory. Plato and His Predecessors, London.

Barnett, L. D. (1897), "Some Conjectures on the Drakonian and Solonian

Constitutions", *PCPS* 46 –48, 3 –5.

Baron, Chr. A. (2006), "The Aristoteles Decree and the Expansion of the Second Athenian League", *Hesperia* 75, 379 –96.

Bateman, J. J. (1962), "Some Aspects of Lysias' Argumentation", *Phoenix* 16, 157 –177.

Bateman, J. J. (1958), "Lysias and the Law", *TAPhA* 89, 276 –285.

Bates jr, C. A. (2002), Aristotle's "best regime". Kingship, Democracy and the Rule of Law, Baton Rouge, LA.

Battaglini, M. (1957), Contributo alla storia del controlo di costituzionalità delle leggi, Milano.

Baulslaugh, R. A. (1991), The Concept of Neutrality in Classical Greece, Berkeley.

Bauman, R. A. (1996), "The Interface of Greek and Roman Law", *RIDA* 43, 39 –62.

Bauman, R. A. (1990), Political Trials in Ancient Greece, London.

Bayonas, A. M. (1966), The Idea of Legislation in the Earlier Platonic Dialogues, Athens.

Bayonas, A. M. (1964), "Paratirisseis epi tou noematos tes nomothessias eis to Symposion tou Platonos", in Charis Konstantino I. Vourveri, 251 –71, Athenai.

Bearzot Cinzia (2009), "La sovversione dell'ordine costituito nei discorsi degli oligarchici ateniesi", in Urso, G. (ed), Ordine e sovversione nel mondo greco e romano (Atti del convegno internazionale, Cividale del Friuli, 25 –27 settembre 2008), 69 –86, Pisa.

Bearzot Cinzia (2009), "'Partis politiques', cités, états fédéraux: Le témoignage de l'historien d'Oxyrhynchos", Mouseion 9, 239 –256.

Bearzot Cinzia (2008), La giustizia nella Grecia antica, Roma.

Bearzot Cinzia (2007), "I nomophylakes in due lemmi di Polluce (Ⅷ 94 nomophylakes e Ⅷ 102 hoi endeka)", in L'Onomasticon, 43 –68.

Bearzot Cinzia (2007), "Political Murder in Classical Greece", AncSoc 37, 37 –62.

Bearzot Cinzia (2006), "Diritto e retorica nella polis democratica ateniese", Dike 9, 129 –155.

Bearzot Cinzia (2005), "Né cittadini, né stranieri: apeleutheroi e nothoi in Atene", in Il cittadino, lo straniero, 77 - 92.

Bearzot Cinzia (2005), "I douloi/perioikoi di Argo. Per una riconsiderazione della tradizione letteraria", Incid Antico 3, 61 - 82.

Bearzot Cinzia (2004), "Politeia cittadina e politeia federale in Senofonte", in Poleis e politeiai, 229 - 258.

Bearzot Cinzia (2004), Federalismo e autonomia nelle Elleniche di Senofonte, Milano.

Bearzot Cinzia (2003), "Isocrate e la seconda lega ateniese", in Orth, W. (ed), Isokrates-Neue Ansätze zur Bewertung eines politischen Schriftstellers, 62 - 77, Trier. (Wuppertaler Beiträge zur Geisteswissenschaft 2)

Bearzot Cinzia (2001), "La sesta orazione pseudolisiana e il suo contributo al dibattito sull'amnistia", in Poikilma, I, 89 - 110.

Bearzot Cinzia (2001), "Guerra e costituzione in Isocrate (Panath. 114 - 118)", in Sordi, M. (ed) Il pensiero sull guerra nel mondo antico, 69 - 85, Milano.

Bearzot Cinzia (2001), "Apragmosyne, identità del meteco e valori democratici in Lisia", in Identità e valori fattori di aggregazione e fattori di crisi nell'esperienza politica antica (Atti del convegno, Bergamo-Brescia, 16 - 18 dicembre 1998), 63 - 80, Roma. (= Vivere da democratici, 121 - 140)

Bearzot Cinzia (2001), "Stasis e polemos nel 404", in Il pensiero sulla guerra nel mondo antico, 19 - 36, Milano. (CISA 27) (= Vivere da democratici, 101 - 119)

Bearzot Cinzia (2000), "La XX orazione pseudolisiana e la 'prima restaurazione', della democrazia nel 410" in Studium atque urbanitas. Miscellanea Daris, 85 - 99, Galatina. (Papyrologica Lupiensia 9) (= Vivere da democratici, 141 - 156)

Bearzot Cinzia (1999), "Gruppi di opposizione organizzata e manipolazione del voto nell'Atene democratica", in Sordi, M. (ed), Fazioni e congiurie nondo antico, 265 - 307, Milano. (CISA 25)

Bearzot Cinzia (1998), "Criteri alternativi di applicazione dell'amnistia in Lisia", in Sordi, M. (ed), Responsabilità, perdono e vendetta nel mondo antico, 111 - 144, Milano. (CISA 24)

Bearzot Cinzia (1997), "Perdonare il traditore? La tematica amnistiale nel dibattito sul richiamo di Alcibiade", in Amnistia, perdono, 29 – 52.

Bearzot Cinzia (1997), "Ancora sui Plateesi e la fratrie di Atene", Simblos 2, 43 – 60.

Bearzot Cinzia (1997), "Lisia e l'amnistia: l'orazione XXV e il suo sfondo politico", in Amnistia, perdono, 59 – 75.

Bearzot Cinzia (1997), Lisia e la tradizione su Teramene. Commento storico alle orazioni XII e XIII del corpus Lysiacum, Milano.

Bearzot Cinzia (1996), "Anomalie procedurali ed elusione del 'nomos' nei processi per tradimento: 'eisanghelia' e 'asebeia'", in Processi e politica, 71 – 92.

Bearzot Cinzia (1994), "Esilii, deportazioni, emigrazioni forzate in Atene", in Sordi, M. (ed), Emigrazione, e immigrazione nel mondo antico, 141 – 167, Milano.

Bearzot Cinzia (1991), "Per una nuova imagine di Teramene. P. Mich. inv. 5982 e il processo di Eratostene", in L'immagine dell'uomo politico: vitta pubblica e morale nell'antichità, 65 – 87, Milano. (CISA 17) (= Vivere da democratici, 15 – 36).

Bearzot Cinzia (1990), "Sul significato del devieto di exo tou pragmatos legein in sede areopagitica", Aevum 64, 47 – 55.

Bechtle, G. (1996), "A Note on Pseudo-Xenophon, the Constitution of the Athenians 1, 11", CQ 46, 564 – 566.

Beck, H. (2003), "Freiheit und Herrschaft in der athenischen Demokratie: Aristoteles, Niklas Luhmann und die 'archai' der Polis", in Brodka, D., Janik, J. & S. Sprawski (eds), Freedom and its limits in the ancient world (Proceedings of a colloquium held at the Jagellonian University, Krakow, September 2003), 37 – 53, Krakow.

Beck, H. (2001), "'The Laws of the Fathers' Versus 'the Laws of the League': Xenophon on federalism", *CPh* 96, 355 – 375.

Beck, H. (2000), "Thebes, the Boiotian League, and the 'Rise of Federalism' in Fourth Century Greece", in Angeli Bernardini, P. (ed), Presenza e funzione della città di Tebe nella cultura greca (Atti del convegno internazionale, Urbino, 7 – 9 luglio 1997), 331 – 344, Pisa.

Beck, H. (1999), "Ostlokris und die 'Tausend Opuntier'. Neue Überlegungen zum Siedlergesetz für Naupaktos", ZPE 124, 53 – 62.

Beck, H. (1997), Polis und Koinon. Untersuchungen zur Geschichte und Struktur der griechischen Bundesstaaten im 4. Jahrhundert v. Chr., Stuttgart. (Historia Einzelschriften 114) Bederman, D. J. (2001) International law in antiquity, Cambridge. (Cambridge studies in international and comparative law 16)

Bederman, D. J. (1996), "Reception of the Classical Tradition in International Law: Grotius' De Jure Belli Ac Pacis", *Emory International Law Review* 10, 1 – 53.

Beiner, R. (1990), "Symposium on Classical Philosophy and the American Constitutional Order: The Liberal Regime", *Chicago-Kent Law Review* 66, 73 – 92.

Bel'ajev, S. A. (1979), "La colonisation grecque antique du point de vue du droit grec", in Lordkipanidze, O. (ed), Problèmes de la colonisation grecque de la region pontique du Nord et de l'Est, 47, Tbilisi.

Berent, M. (2000), "Sovereignty: Ancient and Modern", *Polis* 17, 2 – 34.

Berent, M. (1998), "Stasis, or the Greek Invention of Politics", *HPTh* 19, 331 – 362.

Beringer, W. (1984), "Freedom, Family and Citizenship in Early Greece", in Eadie, J. L. & J. Ober (eds), *The Craft of the Ancient Historian. Essays in Honor of Chester Starr*, 41 – 56, Washington D. C.

Beringer, W. (1964), "Der Standort des oikeus in der Gesellschaft des homerischen Epos", Historia 13, 1 – 20.

Berman, P. S. (1994), "Rats, Pigs, and Statues on Trial: The Creation of Cultural Narratives in the Prosecution of Animals and Inanimate Objects", *New York University Law Review* 69, 288 – 326.

Bernard, Ph. (1825), De archontibus reipublicae Atheniensium, Louvain.

Bers, V. (2003), Demosthenes, Speeches 50 – 59, Austin, Tx. (The oratory of classical Greece 6)

Berneker, E. (1974), "Magie im alten griechischen Recht", in Studi in onore di Giuseppe Grosso 6, Torino, 77 – 143.

Berneker, E. (1971), "Der Felssturz im alten griechischen Recht", in Studi Volterra I, 87 – 97, Milano.

Berneker, E. (1966), "Die Strafe des Felsturzes im alten griechischen Recht", in Studien zur Strafrechtswissenschaft. Festschrift für Ulrich Stock zum 70. Geburtstag, 15 – 26, Würzburg.

Berneker, E. (1964), "Der Ursprung des doppelten Parteieneides im altgriechischen Verfahrensrecht", in Synteleia Arangio-Ruiz, 743 - 749.

Berneker, E. (1956), "Hochverrat und Landesverrat im griechischen Recht", Eos 48, 105 - 137.

Berneker, E. (1954), "Der Versuch im griechischen Recht", in Festschrift Rabel II, 33 - 77.

Berneker, E. (1950), "Das wiederholte Prozessieren in den antiken Rechten", JJP 4, 253 - 264.

Bers, V. (2002), "What to Believe in Demosthenes 57, Against Eubulides", *Hyperboreus* 8, 232 - 239.

Bers, V. (2000), "Just Rituals. Why the Rigmarole of Fourth-century Athenian lawcourts?", in *Polis and Politics*, 553 - 562.

Bers, V. (1975), "Solon's Law Forbidding Neutrality and Lysias 31", *Historia* 24, 493 - 498.

Bertrand, J. -M. (2009), "A propos de la Rhétorique d'Aristote (I, 1373b 1 - 1374b 23). Analyse du processus judiciaire. IV. Épieikeia", Cahiers Glotz 20, 7 - 27.

Bertrand Jean-Marie (2008), "Réflexions sur la doctrine d'Antiphon, la révolution des Quatre Cents et la tyrannie des Trente", Philosophie Antique 8, 7 - 22.

Bertrand Jean-Marie (2007), "A propos de la Rhétorique d'Aristote (I, 1373b1 - 1374b23), analyse du processus judiciaire", in Symposion 2005, 237 - 253.

Bertrand Jean-Marie (2006), "Quelques réflexions sur la façon dont Platon fait parler le lois", Dike 9, 93 - 105.

Bertrand Jean-Marie (2006), "À propos de la Rhétorique d'Aristote (I, 1373b1 - 1374b23), analyse du processus judiciaire II. anakrisis/erôtèsis", in Symposion 2003, 191 - 202.

Bertrand Jean-Marie (2005), "Rhétorique judiciaire et rétroactivité de la loi en Grèce ancienne", in Le législateur et la loi, 77 - 89.

Bertrand Jean-Marie (2005), "La cité des Magnètes dans les Lois de Platon", in Hansen, M. H. (ed), *The Imaginary polis*, 152 - 163, Copenhagen. (Acts of the Copenhagen Polis Center 7)

Bertrand Jean-Marie (2003), "De la fiction en droit grec. Quelques réflexions", in Symposion 1999, 387 - 412.

Bertrand Jean-Marie(2002), " A propos de la ' Rhetorique ' d'Aristote (I 1373b1 - 1374b23), analyse du processus judiciaire: (to epigramma-to enklema)",Dike 5,161 - 185.

Bertrand Jean-Marie(2001), " Sur le statut des esclaves dans la cité des Magnètes,fictions juridiques et pouvoir politique",in Lisi,F. (ed),Plato's Laws and its Historical Significance(Selected papers of the I international congress on ancient thought,Salamanca 1998),193 - 202,Sankt Augustin.

Bertrand Jean-Marie (2001a), "Platon et les lois sur la discipline militaire", Quaderni del Dipartimento di Filologia, linguistica e tradizione classica Augusto Rostagni,9 - 27,Bologna.

Bertrand Jean-Marie(2000),"Le citoyen des cités platoniciennes",Cahiers Glotz 11,37 - 55.

Bertrand Jean-Marie(2000),"La fiction en droit grec. La loi sur l'homicide dans une inscription de Locride",*RHDFE* 78,219 - 231.

Bertrand Jean-Marie(1999),"De la stasis dans les cités platoniciennes",Cahiers Glotz 10,209 - 224.

Bertrand Jean-Marie (1999), De l'écriture à l'oralité. Lectures des "Lois" de Platon,Paris.

Bertrand Jean-Marie(1998),"Du nid au pilori. Le clair et l'obscur dans la cité des Magnètes platoniciens",Ktema 23,423 430

Bertrand Jean-Marie (1997), " De l'usage de l'epigraphie dans la cité des Magnètes platoniciens",in Symposion 1995,27 - 47.

Bertrand Jean-Marie(1996), "Langage juridique et discours politique dans les cités grecques de l'Antiquité. Réfléxions sur les Lois de Platon",Langage et société 77,55 - 81.

Bertrand Jean-Marie (1992), Cités et royaumes du monde grec: éspace et politique,Paris.

Best,J. (1979), "What is Law? The Minos Reconsidered", *Interpretation* 8, 102 - 113.

Beys,K. (2010),"The Legal,Political,Philosophical and Religious Dimensions of Socrates' Trial and Execution",*Peitho* 1,45 - 55. (Translation into Polish of Beys (2003))

Beys,K. (1994),"The Democratic Principle in the System of Judicial Protection of the Athenian City",Dike(International)1,10 - 17.

Bile,M. (2009),"Epigraphie,dialectologie et lexique",in Estudios de epigrafia griega,119 - 127.

Bile,M. (2002),"Quelques aperçus de la société gortynienne d'après les lois de Gortyne VI 56 - VII 10",in Mélanges Dimakis,115 - 132.

Bile,M. (2000),"IC IV 41 et le sens de epidiomai",in La codification,161 - 174.

Bile, M. (1995), "Les lois de Gortyne: necessité d'une approche pluridisciplinaire?",in Brixhe,Cl. (ed),Hellenika Symmikta. Histoire,Linguistique, Epigraphie,7 - 22,Nancy-Paris. (Études d'archéologie classique 8)

Bile, M. (1994), "L'organisation materielle du texte des lois de Gortyn", Verbum 17,203 - 217.

Bile,M. (1993),"Une relecture des Lois de Gortyne d'après M. Mauss et Cl. Levi-Strauss",in Crespo,E. ,Garcia-Ramon,J. L. & Ar. Strinao(eds),Dialectologia Graeca(Actas del II Coloquio Internacional de Dialectologia Griega,Miraflores de la Sierra Madrid,19 - 21 de junio de 1991),23 - 28,Madrid.

Bile, M. (1981), "Le vocabulaire des structures sociales dans les Lois de Gortyne",Verbum 4,11 - 45.

Bile,M. (1980),"Systeme de parenté et systèmes matrimoniaux ὰ Gortyne", Verbum 3,1 - 21.

Bile, M. & J. Lallot (2008), "Les oppositions aspectuelles dans la 'loi de Gortyne'",in Hodot,R. & G. Vottero(eds),Dialectes grecs et aspect verbal(Actes de la table ronde de Saint-Etienne,17 - 18 juin 2004),7 - 27,Nancy. Bickford,S. (2009), "'This way of life, this contest': rethinking Socratic citizenship", in Salkever,S. (ed)The Cambridge companion to ancient Greek political thought,126 - 155,Cambridge.

Bicknell,J. (1979),"Plato,Laws 755d and the Athenian Strategia",*Historia* 28,111 - 112.

Biscardi Arnaldo(1997),"On 'aequitas' and 'epieikeia'", in *Aequitas and Equity:Equity in Civil Law and Mixed Jurisdictions*(Second international conference on Aequitas and equity, Jerusalem May 1993),1 - 11,Jerusalem. (= Biscardi,

Scritti,287ff.)

Biscardi. A. (1990), "Sulla cosiddetta consensualità del contratto dotale in diritto attico", in Symposion 1988,3 - 13. (= Biscardi, Scritti,275 - 286)

Biscardi Arnaldo(1989), "Contratto di lavoro e 'misthosis' nella civiltà greca del diritto", RIDA 36,75 - 98. (= Biscardi, Scritti,257 - 274)

Biscardi Arnaldo(1988), "Mariage d'amour et mariage sans amour en Grèce, à Rome et dans les Evangiles", in Eros et droit, 3 - 11. (= AFGG 20 (1984 - 85) 205 - 213 and in Biscardi, Scritti,239 - 248)

Biscardi Arnaldo (1986), "La successione legitima degli ascedenti nel diritto ereditario panellenico: uno spunto epigrafico del VI o V secolo a. C.", SDHI 51, 276 - 282. (= Symposion 1985,7 - 13 and Biscardi, Scritti,249 - 256)

Biscardi Arnaldo (1984), "Polis, politeia, politeuma", in Atti del XVII congresso internazionale di Papirologia,201 - 215, Napoli. (= Biscardi, Scritti,221 - 238)

Biscardi Arnaldo(1984), "Nota minima sugli 'ectemoroi'", in Aux origines de l'Hellénisme. La Crète et la Grèce. Hommage à H. van Effenterre, 193 - 197, Paris. (Publications de la Sorbonne. Histoire ancienne et médiévale 15) (= Biscardi, Scritti, 215 - 220)

Biscardi Arnaldo(1983), "Le régime de la pluralité hypothécaire en droit grec et romain", JJP 19,41 - 59. (= Biscardi, Scritti, 173 - 198)

Biscardi Arnaldo(1983), "La città antica come fatto di cultura nei suoi aspetti giuridici: introduzione", in La città antica come fatto di cultura, Como, 177 - 184.

Biscardi Arnaldo (1982), "Introduction à l'étude des pratiques commerciales dans l'histoire des droits de l'antiquité", RIDA 29,21 - 44.

Biscardi Arnaldo(1982), Diritto greco antico, Milano.

Biscardi Arnaldo (1981), "Osservazioni critiche sulla terminologia diatheke, diatithesthai", in Symposion 1979,21 - 35. (= Biscardi, Scritti, 199 - 214)

Biscardi Arnaldo (1979), "Diritto greco e scienza del diritto", in Symposion 1974,1 - 23. (= Biscardi, Scritti, 133 - 156)

Biscardi Arnaldo (1971), "Prassi e teoria della 'misthosis' nel diritto contrattuale attico", SDHI 37,350 - 361. (= Biscardi, Scritti, 103 - 118)

Biscardi Arnaldo (1970), "La 'gnome dikaiotate' et l'interpretation des lois dans la Grece ancienne",RIDA 17,219 -232. (=Biscardi,Scritti,89 -102)

Biscardi Arnaldo(1969),"Die mehrfache Verpfändung einer Sache von attischen bis zum spätrömischen Recht",ZRG 86,146 -168.

Biscardi Arnaldo(1966),"Il cosidetto 'testamento' di Knemone",SDHI 32, 173 -184. (=Biscardi,Scritti,75 -88)

Biscardi Arnaldo(1958),"Idées maitresses du régime de l'indivision en droit grec",RHDFE 36,321 -348.

Biscardi Arnaldo(1955),"La genesi della nozione di comproprietà",Labeo 1, 154ff.

Biscardi Arnaldo(1955),"Sul regime della comproprietà in diritto attico", in Studi Paoli,105 -144. (=Biscardi,Scritti,23 -74)

Biscardi Arnaldo(1934),"I rapporti tra proix ed engyesis nel diritto matrimoniale attico",SIFC 11,57 -80. (=Biscardi,Scritti di diritto greco,1 -22)

Bissa,E. M. A. (2009),Governmental intervention in foreign trade in archaic and classical Greece,Leiden. (Mnemosyne Suppl. 312)

Bissa,E. M. A. (2008),"Investment patterns in the Laureion mining industry in the fourth century BCE",Historia 57,263 -274.

Blanshard, A. J. L. (2010), "War in the Law-court: Some Athenian Discussions", in Pritchard, D. M. (ed), *War, Democracy and Culture in Classical Athens*,203 -224,Cambri dge.

Blanshard,A. J. L. (2004),"Depicting Democracy: An Exploration of Art and Text in the Law of Eukrates",JHS 124,1 -15.

Blanshard,A. J. L. (2004),"What Counts as the Demos? Some Notes on the Relationship between the Jury and the 'people' in Classical Athens",*Phoenix* 58, 28 -48.

Blickman, D. (1986), "The Myth of Ixion and Pollution for Homicide in Archaic Greece",*CJ* 81,193 -208.

Bloch, A. (1975), "Litterarische und inschriftliche Gesetzprosa im griechischen",MH 32,135 -154.

Bloch,H. (1953),"The Exegetes of Athens and the Prytaneion Decree",*AJPh* 74,407 -418

Blok,J. H. (2009),"Perikles' Citizenship Law: A New Perspective",*Historia*

58,141 – 170.

Blok, J. H. (2006), "Solon's Funerary Laws: Questions of Authenticity and Functions", in *Solon of Athens*, 197 – 247.

Blok, J. H. (2005), "Becoming Citizens. Some Notes on the Semantics of 'citizen' in Archaic Greece and Classical Athens", *Klio* 87, 7 – 40.

Blyth, D. (2000), "Socrates' Trial and Conviction of the Jurors in Plato's Apology", *Philosophy & Rhetoric* 33, 1 – 22.

Bodéüs, R. (1991), "Law and Regime in Aristotle", in Lord Carnes & D. K. O'Connor (eds), *Essays on the Foundation of Aristotelian Political Science*, 234 – 248, Berkeley.

Boegehold, A. L. (2009), "What is Leogoros saying? Andocides 1. 41", in Karamalengou, E. & Eug. Makriyanni (eds), *Antiphilesis. Studies on Classical, Byzantine and Modern Greek Literature and Culture in Honour of John-Theophanes A. Papademetriou*, 283 – 285, Stuttgart.

Boegehold, A. L. (2000), "At Home. Lysias 1. 23", in *Polis and Politics*, 597 – 600.

Boegehold, A. L. (1999), When a Gesture was Expected: A Selection of Examples from Archaic and Classical Greek Literature, Princeton.

Boegehold, A. L. (1996), "Resistance to Change in the Law at Athens", in J. Ober & Ch. Hedrick jr (eds), *Demokratia. A Conversation on Democracies, Ancient and Modern*, 203 – 214, Princeton.

Boegehold, A. L. (1995), The Lawcourts at Athens: Sites, Buildings, Equipment, Procedure and Testimonia, Princeton. (The Athenian Agora 28)

Boegehold, A. L. (1994), "Perikles' Citizenship Law of 451/0 BC", in *Athenian Identity*, 57 – 66.

Boegehold, A. L. (1991), "Three Court Days", in Symposion 1990, 165 – 182.

Boegehold, A. L. (1990), "Andocides and the Decree of Patrokleides", *Historia* 39, 149 – 162.

Boegehold, A. (1985), "Lykurgos 1. 149", *CPh* 80, 132 – 135.

Boegehold, A. L. (1982), "A Lid with Dipinto", in *Studies Vanderpool*, 1 – 7.

Boegehold, A. L. (1976), "Ten Distinctive Ballots. The Law Court in Zea", *CSCA* 9, 8 – 17.

Boegehold, A. L. (1972), "The Establishment of a Central Archive at Athens", *AJA* 76, 23 - 30.

Boegehold, A. L. (1963), "Towards a Study of Athenian Voting Procedure", Hesperia 32, 366 - 374.

Boegehold, A. L. (1960), "Aristotle's Athenaion Politeia 65. 2: The 'official token'", *Hesperia* 29, 393 - 401.

Boegehold, A. L. (1958), Aristotle and the Dikasteria, diss. Harvard.

den Boer, W. (1973), "Aspects of Religion in Classical Greece", *HSCP* 77, 1 - 21.

Boeckh, Aug. (1886), Die Staatshaushaltung der Athener, 3 vols, Berlin.

Boeckh, Aug. (1840), Urkunden über das Seewesen des attischen Staates-gestellt erläutert, Berlin.

Boeckh, Aug. (1826), De Areopago: Dissertatio prior, Berlin.

Boeckh, Aug. (1826), De Sophoclis Oedipi Colonei tempore; dissertatio altera, Berlin. (= Boeckh, Kleine Schriften, 4, 228 - 234)

Boeckh, Aug. (1825 - 1826), De Sophoclis Oedipi Colonei tempore; dissertatio prior, Berlin. (= Boeckh, Kleine Schriften, 4, 120 - 124)

Boeckh, Aug. (1821), De orois atticis, Berlin.

Boeckh, Aug. (1819 - 1820), De ephebia attica; dissertatio ii. De militaribus epheborum tirocensis, Berlin. (= Boeckh, Kleine Schriften, 4, 137 - 148)

Boeckh, Aug. (1819), De ephebia attica; dissertatio prior, Berlin. (= Boeckh, Kleine Schriften, 4, 137 - 148)

Boeckh, Aug. (1818), "Von den Zeitverhältnissen in Demosthenes' Rede gegen Meidias", APA, 60 - 100. (= Boeckh, Kleine Schriften, 5, 153 - 204).

Boeckh, Aug. (1817 - 1818), De pseudomarturiôn et pseudokletias actione, Berlin. (= Boeckh, Kleine Schriften, 4, 149 - 156)

Boeckh, Aug. (1815), "Über die laurischen Silberbergwerke in Attika", APA, 85 - 140. (= Boeckh, Kleine Schriften, 5, 1 - 64)

Boegehold, A. L. (2009), "What is Leogoros saying? Andocides 1. 41," in Karamalengou, E. & Eug. Makriyanni (eds), Antiphilesis. Studies on Classical, byzantine and Modern Greek literature and Culture in Honour of John-Theophanes A. Papademetriou, 283 - 285, Stuttgart.

Boegehold, A. L. (2000), "At Home. Lysias 1. 23", in *Polis and Politics*, 597 – 600.

Boegehold, A. L. (1999), When a Gesture was Expected: A Selection of Examples from Archaic and Classical Greek Literature, Princeton.

Boegehold, A. L. (1996), "Resistance to change in the law at Athens", in J. Ober & Ch. Hedrick jr. (eds), Demokratia. A Conversation on Democracies, Ancient and Modern, 203 – 214, Princeton.

Boegehold, A. L. (1995), The Lawcourts at Athens: Sites, Buildings, Equipment, Procedure and Testimonia, Princeton. (The Athenian Agora 28)

Boegehold, A. L. (1994), "Perikles' Citizenship Law of 451/0 BC", in *Athenian Identity*, 57 – 66.

Boegehold, A. L. (1991), "Three Court Days", in Symposion 1990, 165 – 182.

Boegehold, A. L. (1990), "Andocides and the Decree of Patrokleides", *Historia* 39, 149 – 162.

Boegehold, A. (1985), "Lykurgos 1. 149", *CPh* 80, 132 – 135.

Boegehold, A. L. (1982), "A lid with dipinto", in *Studies Vanderpool*, 1 – 7.

Boegehold, A. L. (1976), "Ten Distinctive Ballots. The Law Court in Zea", *CSCA* 9, 8 – 17.

Boegehold, A. L. (1972), "The Establishment of a Central Archive at Athens", *AJA* 76, 23 – 30.

Boegehold, A. L. (1963), "Towards a Study of Athenian Voting Procedure", *Hesperia* 32, 366 – 374.

Boegehold, A. L. (1960), "Aristotle's Athenaion Politeia 65. 2: The 'Official Token'", *Hesperia* 29, 393 – 401.

Boegehold, A. L. (1958), Aristotle and the Dikasteria, diss. Har.

Bohacek, M. (1952), "Arbitration and State-organized Tribunal in the Ancient Procedure of the Greeks and Romans", *Iura* 3, 191 – 215.

du Bois, P. (1988), "Inscription, the Law, and the Comic Body", *Metis* 3, 69 – 84.

Bolmarcich, S. (2010), "Communal Values in Ancient Diplomacy", in Rosen, R. M. & I. Sluiter (eds), Valuing others in Classical Antiquity, 113 – 136, Leiden. (Mnemosyne Suppl. 323)

Bolmarcich, S. (2009), "The Athenian Regulations for Samos (IG I3 48) Again", *Chiron* 39, 45 – 64.

Bolmarcich, S. (2007), "The Afterlife of a Treaty", *CQ* 57, 477 – 489.

Bolmarcich, S. (2007), "Oaths in Greek International Relations", in *Horkos*, 26 – 38.

Bolmarcich, S. (2005), "Thucydides 1. 19. 1 and the Peloponnesian League", *GRBS* 45, 5 – 34.

Bolonyai, G. (2008), "A Numbers Game: An Interpretation of Lysias 17", *CQ* 58, 491 – 499.

Bonner, R. J. (1940), "The Use of Hemlock for Capital Punishment", in Athenian Studies Presented to W. S. Ferguson, 299 – 302, Cambridge, Mass. (HSCP Suppl. 1)

Bonner, R. J. (1927), Lawyers and Litigants in Ancient Athens: The Genesis of the Legal Profession, Chicago.

Bonner, R. J. (1924), "Administration of Justice under Pisistratus", *CPh* 19, 359 – 361.

Bonner, R. J. (1922), "Wit and Humor in Athenian Courts", *CPh* 17, 97 – 103.

Bonner, R. J. (1921), "The Megarian Decrees", *CPh* 16, 238 – 245.

Bonner, R. J. (1920), "The Legal Setting of Isocrates' Antidosis", *CPh* 15, 193 – 197.

Bonner, R. J. (1919), "Apollodorus vs. Phormio; Criminal Assault", *CPh* 14, 83 – 84.

Bonner, R. J. (1916), "The Institution of Athenian Arbitrators", *CPh* 11, 191 – 195.

Bonner, R. J. (1913), "The Minimum Vote in Ostracism", *CPh* 8, 223 – 225.

Bonner, R. J. (1912), "Evidence in the Areopagus", *CPh* 7, 450 – 456.

Bonner, R. J. (1912), "Administration of Justice in the Age of Hesiod", *CPh* 7, 17 – 23.

Bonner, R. J. (1911), "Administration of Justice in the Age of Homer", *CPh* 6, 12 – 36.

Bonner, R. J. (1910), "The Boeotian Federal Constitution", *CPh* 5, 405 – 417.

Bonner, R. J. (1908), "The Legal Setting of Plato's Apology", *CPh* 3, 169 –

177.

Bonner, R. J. (1908), "The Use and Effect of Attic Seals", *CPh* 3, 399 - 407.

Bonner, R. J. (1907), "The Jurisdiction of Athenian Arbitrators", *CPh* 2, 407 - 418.

Bonner, R. J. (1906), "Did Women Testify in Homicide Cases at Athens?", *CPh* 1, 127 - 132.

Bonner, R. J. (1905), Evidence in Athenian Courts, Chicago.

Bonner, R. J. & G. Smith (1945), "The Administration of Justice in Boeotia", *CPh* 40, 11 - 23.

Bonner, R. J. & G. Smith (1943), "Administration of Justice in the Delphic Amphictiony", *CPh* 38, 1 - 12.

Bonner, R. J. & G. Smith (1942), "Administration of Justice in Sparta", *CPh* 37, 113 - 129.

Bonner, R. J. & G. Smith (1930 - 1938), The Administration of Justice from Homer to Aristotle, 2 vols, Chicago.

Borthwick, E. K. (2000), "Aristophanes and the Trial of Thucydides Son of Melesias (Acharnians 717)", *Phoenix* 54, 203 - 211.

Bosanquet, B. (1877), "Grote on the Athenian Constitution", *The Academy* 12, 220 - 221.

Botsford, G. W. (1910), "The Constitution and Politics of the Boeotian League from its Origin to the Year 387 B. C.", *Political Science Quarterly* 25, 271 - 296.

Botsford, G. W. (1893), The Athenian Constitution, New York. (Cornell Studies in Classical Philology 4)

Bourke, G. F. (2011), "The Eleian Asylia: A Defence of the Ancient Texts", Hermes 139, 413 - 430.

Bowden, H. (2003), "The Functions of the Delphic Amphictyony before 346 BCE", *SCI* 22, 43 - 66.

Bradley, K. & P. Cartledge (eds) (2011), *The Cambridge World History of Slavery, Vol. 1: The Ancient Mediterranean World*, Cambridge.

Braithwaite, W. T. (1994), "An Introduction for Judges and Lawyers to Plato's Apology of Socrates", *Loyola University of Chicago Law Journal* 25, 507 - 533.

Brancacci, A. (1989), "Justice, War and Civil War in Plato's Laws 624a -

630a", in Boudouris, K. (ed), On Justice. Plato's and Aristotle's Conception of Justice in Relation to Modern and Contemporary Theories of Justice (Proceedings of the third international philosophy symposium, Athens, May 1987), 89 – 94, Athens

Braund, D. (2002), "Friends and Foes: Monarchs and Monarchy in Fifth-century Athenian Democracy", in *Alternatives to Athens*, 103 – 118.

de Brauw, M. (2002), "'Listen to the Laws Themselves' Citations of Laws and Portrayal of Character in Attic Oratory", *CJ* 97, 161 – 76.

de Brauw, M. & J. Miner (2004), "Androtion's Alleged Prostitution Contract: Aes. 1.165 and Dem. 22.23 in light of P. Oxy. VII 1012", *ZRG* 121, 301 – 311.

Bremmer, J. N. (2000), "Fosterage, Kinship, and the Circulation of Children in Ancient Greece", *Dialogos* 6, 1 – 20.

Bremmer, J. (1983), "The Importance of the Maternal Uncle and Grandfather in Archaic and Classical Greece and Early Byzantium", *ZPE* 50, 173 – 186.

Brickhouse, Th. C. & N. D. Smith (2002), The Trial and Execution of Socrates, Sources and Controversies, New York.

Bridges, A. P. (1980), "The Athenian Treaty with Samos, ML 56", *JHS* 100, 185 – 188.

Brock, R. (2010), "Citizens and Non-citizens in Athenian Tragedy", in *Law and Drama in Ancient Greece*, 94 – 107.

Brock, R. (1988), "The Courts in 411", *LCM* 13, 133 – 136.

Brooks, R. (2006), "The Emergence of the Hellenic Deliberative Ideal: The Classical Humanist Conception of Comparative Law", *Hastings International & Comparative Law Review* 30, 43 – 77.

Brown, E. (2009), "The Emergence of Natural Law and the Cosmopolis", in Salkever, St. (ed), The Cambridge Companion to Ancient Greek Political Thought, 331 – 364, Cambridge.

Brown, L. (2004), "Did Socrates Agree to Obey the Laws of Athens?", in Karasmanis, V. (ed), Socrates: 2400 Years since his Death (399 B. C. – 2001 A. D.) (International Symposium Proceedings, 13 – 21 July 2001), 157 – 168, Athens. (with a reply by Chloe Balla, 169 – 172)

Brown, L. (2002), "Did Socrates Agree to Obey the Laws of Athens?", in Clark, G. & T. Rajak (eds), Philosophy and Power in the Graeco-Roman World.

Essays in Honour of Miriam Griffin, 13 – 30, Oxford. (= Judson, L. & V. Karasmanis (eds) (2006), Remembering Socrates: Philosophical Essays, 72 – 87, Oxford.)

Brown, P. G. M. (1991), "Athenian Attitudes to Rape and Seduction: The Evidence of Menander's 'Dyskolos'", *CQ* 41, 533 – 534.

Brown, P. G. M. (1983), "Menander's Dramatic Technique and the Law of Athens", *CQ* 33, 412 – 420.

Browers, M. L. (1995), "Piecemeal Reform in Plato's Laws", *Political Studies* 43, 117 – 74.

Bruun, Chr. (2000), "Water Legislation in the Ancient World (c. 2200 BC-c. A. D. 500): The Greek world", in Wikander, O. (ed), Handbook of Ancient Water Technology, 557 – 573, Leiden. (Technology and change in History 2)

Bruun, Chr. (2000), "Water Legislation in the Ancient World (c. 2200 BC-c. A. D. 500): The Roman World", in Wikander, O. (ed), Handbook of Ancient Water Technology, 575 – 604, Leiden. (Technology and change in History 2)

Buck, R. J. (1985), "Boiotian Oligarchies and Greek Oligarchic Theory", in Fossey, J. & H. Giroux (eds), Proceedings of the third international conference on Boiotian antiquities (Montreal-Quebec, 31. x. 1979 – 4. xi. 1979), 25 – 32, Amsterdam.

Buck, R. J. (1972), "The Formation of the Boeotian League", *CPh* 67, 94 – 101.

Buck, R. J. (1965), "The Reforms of 487 B. C. in the Selection of Archons", *CPh* 60, 96 – 101.

Buckler, J. (1971), "Theban Treaty Obligations in IG II2 40. A Postscript", *Historia* 20, 506 – 508.

Buddensiek, Fr. (2000), "Why Socrates was Sentenced to Death: Some thoughts on Double Standards Behaviour", in Pollman, K. (ed), Double Standards in the Ancient and Medieval World, 95 – 106, Göttingen.

Buis, E. J. (2008), "Les (en) jeux d'un 'affranchissement' dramatique: la subjectivité légale de Xanthias dans les Grenouilles d'Aristophane", in Hommage à J. Annequin, 419 – 435.

Buis, E. (2008), "Del derecho griego (Solón, F60a [R]) a las XII Tablas: un caso de intertextualidadjurídica", Florentia Iliberritana 19, 39 – 70.

Buis, E. J. (2007), "¿La marca de la bestia? Homicidio y responsabilidad criminal de los animales en el derecho ateniense", in Barrancos, D., E. Caballero del Sastre et al. (eds) Monstruos y Monstruosidades. Perspectivas disciplinarias Ⅱ, (Actas de las Ⅲ Jornadas de Reflexión "Monstruos y Monstruosidades"), 464 – 477, Buenos Aires.

Buis, E. (2007), "¿ Acreedores razonables o usureros malintencionados? Estrepsíades y la caracterización cómica de los prestamistas en Ar. Nu. 1214 – 1300" Anales de Filología Clásica 20, 59 – 91.

Buis, E. (2007), "Prostatai y proxenoi cómicos: la hospitalidad subvertida y la desprotección de extranjeras y marginales en dos pasajes aristofánicos (Ra. 550 – 578, Th. 574 – 628)", Limes 19, 61 – 83.

Buis, E. (2007), "From Inscriptions to the Dramatic Text: Literary Reminders of Lawmaking in Athenian Law and Comedy", in Brupbacher, O. et al. (eds), Erinnern und Vergessen (Jahrbuch juge Rechtsgeschichte 2), 40 – 64, München.

Buis, E. (2007), "Del lecho al juzgado, del sexo al derecho: un juego de palabras significativo en Asambleistas de Aristófanes", Dike 10, 85 – 110.

Buis, E. (2006), "Sofística, interpretación jurídica y comedia: la ley contra la goneon kakosis y la convencionalidad del derecho ateniense en Aristófanes", in Gastaldi, V. & L. Gambon (ed), Sofística y teatro griego. Retorica, Derecho y Sociedad, 103 – 136, Bahía Blanca.

Buis, E. J. (2005), "Un 'crimen ferpecto': el denotero del heroe comico frente a las leyes atenienses en Aves de Aristofanes", in Ut par delicto, 109 – 126.

Buis, E. J. (2005), "Como plagiar la litigiosidad del enemigom y no perder en el intento: la estrategia desvergonzada de la mimesis juridica como clave de lectura en Caballeros", Eirene 41, 140 – 160.

Buis, E. J. (2005), "El caso de la viuda de Diodoto o una poetica de la ausencia: retórica judicial y enunciación femenina en Lys. 32. 12 – 17", LEC 73, 193 – 215.

Buis, E. J. (2004), "How to Play Justice and Drama in Antiquity: Law and Theater in Athens as Performative Rituals", *Florida Journal of International Law* 16, 697 – 725.

Buis, E. J. (2003), "La ceguera de los justos. Trasgresión, condena y compensación en la mythopoesis tiresiana", Göttinger Forum für Altertumswissenschaft 6, 151 - 196.

Buis, E. J. (2003), "La defensa de los ancianos en corte y el 'juicio justo' (Ar. Ach. 676 - 718): una propuesta legislativa en la comedia ateniense", in Garcia Negroni, M. M. (ed), La Argumentación (Actas del Congreso Internacional), 309 - 319, Buenos Aires.

Buis, E. J. (2003), "Los limites de la graphe ambloseos: la(i)licitud del aborto en el derecho ateniese", Argos 27, 41 - 62.

Buis, E. J. (2003), "Arrojar luz al texto cómico: juego léxico y denuncias por phasis en 'Acarnienses', de Aristófanes", Circe 8, 91 - 109.

Buis, E. J. (2003), "En busca del equilibrio perdido: la penalización de la violencia como espectáculo en Aves de Aristófanes", in Frenkel, D., Buzón, R., Cavallero, P. & A. Nocito (eds), Koronís. Homenaje a Carlos Ronchi March, 113 - 142, Buenos Aires.

Buis, E. J. (2003), "Matrimonios en crisis y respuestas legales: el divorcio unilateral o de comun acuerdo en el derecho ateniese", Faventia 25, 9 - 29.

Buis, E. (2002), "La acusación de Myrtia contra Filocleón (Avispas, vv. 1388 - 1412): ¿un ejemplo de la legitimación activa de la mujer en los litigios mercantiles?", in La cultura grecolatina enAmérica Latina (Actas XI Jornadas de Estudios Clásicos 28 - 29 de junio de 2001), 50 - 59, Buenos Aires.

Buis, E. J. (2002), "El hombre y el castigo de su hybris en Aves de Aristófanes: justicia de Zeus o ley ateniense?", in Grammatico, G. & Ant. Arbea (eds.) El hombre, todo el hombre, 159 - 169, Santiago, Chile.

Buis, E. J. (2002), "El derecho griego y la muerte burlada en Aves de Aristófanes", in M. E. Steinberg, R. Buzón, Cavallero, P. A. & A. Romano (eds), Los estudios clásicos ante el cambio de milenio: vida, muerte, cultura I, 143 - 156, Buenos Aires.

Buis, E. J. (2002), "Labores propias, ¿litigios ajenos?: la mujer frente a las controversias mercantiles en la comedia aristofanica", QUCC 72, 41 - 62.

Buis, E. (2001), "¿Una cuestión moderna? Divorcio remedio y divorcio sanción en el derecho griego antiguo: los casos de Atenas y Gortina", in Ponencias del VIII Congreso Nacional y VII Latinoamericano de Derecho Privado, en homenaje al Prof.

Roberto López Cabana, 139 – 143, Buenos Aires.

Buis, E. J. (2001), "Persuadir, legislar y juzgar en Aves. Aristofanes y los alcances juridico-politicos del uso de hipstesis eventuales", Argos 24, 7 – 22.

Buis, E. J. (2001), "Ciudadanos y extranjeros en Aves de Aristofanes: los tirminos de una ley impuesta", Nova Tellus 19, 55 – 73.

Buis, E. J. (2000), "Pisetero y la funcionalidad del derecho sucesorio atico en Aves de Aristofanes", in Actas X Jornadas de Estudios Clasicos "La cultura grecolatina en Africa", 13 – 19, Buenos Aires.

Buis, E. (1999), "Las garantías del ciudadano y la naturalización de extranjeros en la antigua Atenas: una lectura de ciertos testimonios de la oratoria griega a la luz del art. 20 de nuestra Constitución Nacional", in Ponencias del IIo Congreso de Derecho Público, 133 – 137, Buenos Aires.

Buis, E. & A. Mederos (2006), "Derecho patrimonial y bases jurídicas generales en materia de intereses en el bloque normativo grecorromano", in Carvajal, P. I. (ed), Estudios de Derecho Romano en Homenaje al Profesor Dr. D. Francisco Samper, 179 – 201, Santiago, Chile.

Buis, E. & A. S. Mederos (2005), "Del tókos a las usurae: la regulación de los intereses en la Antigua Grecia y en el derecho romano", in Homenaje al Dr. Luis Rodolfo Argüello (Trabajos Presentados – XVII Encuentro Nacional de Profesores de Derecho Romano de la República Argentina), 345 – 359, General Roca.

Bujuklic, Z. (1999), "Ancient and Modern Concepts of Lawfulness", *RIDA* 46, 123 – 163.

Burchfiel, K. J. (1994), "The Myth of 'Prelaw' in Early Greece", in Symposion 1993, 79 – 104.

Burckhardt, J. (1899), "Sklaverei in Griechenland", Die Zukunft 25, 17 – 31.

Burford, A. (1969), The Greek Temple Builders at Epidauros: A Social and Economic Study of Building in the Asklepian Sanctuary, During the Fourth and Third Centuries B. C., Liverpool.

Burgess, S. (2005), "The Athenian Eleven: Why Eleven?", *Hermes* 133, 328 – 336.

Burnett, A. (1976), "Tribe and City, Custom and Decree in Children of Heracles", *CPh* 71, 4 – 26.

Burns, T. (2011), Aristotle and Natural Law, London.

Burns, T. (1998), "Aristotle and Natural Law", *HPTh* 19, 142 – 166.

Burnyeat, M. F. (1997), "The Impiety of Socrates", *AncPh* 17, 1 – 12.

Burnyeat, M. F. (1994), "Did the Ancient Greeks have the Concept of Human Rights?", *Polis* 13, 1 – 11. (= Hyperboreus 1(1994)19 – 28 in Russian)

Bushala, E. W. (1968), "Torture of Non-citizens in Homicide Investigations", *GRBS* 9, 61 – 68.

Butkevych, O. (2003), "History of Ancient International Law: Challenges and Prospects", *Journal ofthe History of International Law* 5, 189 – 235.

Butler, D. (1962), "Competence of the Demos in the Spartan Rhetra", *Historia* 11, 385 – 396.

Buttrey, T. V. (1981), "More on the Athenian Coinage Law of 375/4 B. C.", Numismatica e Antichità Classiche 10, 71 – 94.

Buttrey, T. V. (1979), "The Athenian Currency Law of 375/4 B. C.", in Mørkholm, O. & N. M. Waggoner(eds), Greek numismatics and archaeology. Essays in honour of Margaret Thompson, 33 – 45, Wetteren.

Butz, P. A. (1996), "Prohibitionary Inscriptions, Xenoi and the Influence of the Early Greek Polis", in Hägg, R. (ed), The Role of Religion in the Early Greek Polis (Proceedings of the third international seminar on ancient Greek cult, organized by the Swedish Institute at Athens, 16 – 18 October 1992), 75 – 95, Stockholm.

C

Cabanes, P. (2010), "La structure familiale dans le cadre social et économique de l'Epire antique", in Antonetti, Cl. (ed), Lo spazio ionico e le comunità della Grecia nord-occidentale: territorio, società e istituzioni (Atti del convegno internazionale, Venezia, 7 – 9 gennaio 2010), 327 – 40, Pisa.

Cabanes, P. (2002), "Les affranchissements à Bouthrotos(Albanie) – de 230 a 44 avant J.-C.", Orbis Terrarum 8, 59 – 74.

Cabanes, P. (1999), "États fédéraux et koina en Grèce du Nord et en Illyrie méridionale", in Cabanes, P. (ed) L'Illyrie méridionale dans l'Antiquité Ⅲ (Actes du IIIe Colloque international de Chantilly, 16 – 19 octobre 1996), 373 – 382, Paris.

Cabanes, P. (1998), "Épigraphie et affranchis du monde grec: acquis et problèmes", in LeBohec, Y. & Y. Roman (eds), Épigraphie et histoire: acquis et problèmes, 53 – 60, Lyon.

Cabanes, P. (1989), "Le koinon des Prasaiboi: institutions et société d'après les inscriptions de Bouthrotos", in Symposion 1982, 147 – 184.

Cabanes, P. (1982), "Les états fédéraux de Grèce du nord-ouest: pouvoirs locaux et pouvoir fédéral", in Symposion 1979, 97 – 112.

Cabanes, P. (1982), "La loi des ateknoi dans les affranchissements d'Epire", in Symposion 1977, 215 – 222.

Cabanes, P. (1980), "Société et institutions dans les monarchies de la Grèce septentrionale au IVe siècle", REG 93, 324 – 351.

Cabanes, P. (1976), "Recherches sur les Etats fédéraux en Grèce", Cahiers d'histoire 21, 391 – 407.

Cabanes, P. & J. Andreou (1985), "Le reglement frontalier entre les cités d'Ambracie et de Charadros", BCH 109, 499 – 544.

Cairns, D. L. (2011), "Ransom and Revenge in the Iliad", in Lambert, St. (ed), Sociable Man: Essays on Ancient Greek Social Behaviour in Honour of N. Fisher, 87 – 116, Swansea.

Cairns, D. L. (1993), Aidos: The Psychology and Ethics of Honour and Shame in Ancient Greek Literature, Oxford.

Cairns, F. (2002), "The Civic Status of Theodotos in Lysias 3", *Emerita* 70, 197 – 204.

Cairns, F. (1996), "Hybris, Dishonour and Thinking big", *JHS* 116, 1 – 32.

Cairns, F. (1991), "The Laws of Eretria (IG XII. 9 1273 and 1274): Epigraphic, Legal, Historical, and Political Aspects", *Phoenix* 45, 297 – 313.

Cairns, H. (1958), "Plato as jurist", in Friedländer, P. (ed), Plato. An Introduction, 286 – 290, Princeton, NJ.

Caldwell, W. E. (1919), Hellenic Conceptions of Peace, diss. New York.

Calero Secall, I. (2011), "Alianzas matrimoniales, familia y parentesco en las tragedias de Euripides", in de Martino, F. & C. Morenilla (eds), Teatro y sociedad en la antigüedad clasica. La mirada de las mujeres, 129 – 145, Bari.

Calero Secall, I. (2010), "El uso del proverbioἀπὸ para precisar el vocabulario juridico en las Leyes de Gortina", Myrtia 25, 9 – 23.

Calero Secall, I. (2010), "Terminologia juridica cretense en materia de familia y propiedad: del uso en la lengua comun a tecnicismo", in Cortes Gabaudan, F. & J. V. Mendez Dosuna (eds), Dic mihi, Musa, virum. Homenaje al profesor A. Lopez Eire, 77 – 86, Salamanca.

Calero Secall, I. (2009), "Las rentas de una propriedad: Epikarpia frente a karpos en el codigo de Gortina", in Estudios de epigrafia griega, 129 – 136.

Calero Secall, I. (2008), "Euripides ante la represión social y legal de las transgresiones sexuales femeninas", in Banuls, J. V., de Martino, Fr. & C. Morenilla (eds), Teatro y sociedad en la Antigüedad clásica: las relaciones de poder en época de crisis, 95 – 118, Bari.

Calero Secall, I. (2007), "Dones, lleis i l'opinio dels ciutadans en l'Atenes clasica: Euripides i Plato", in Zaragoza Gras, J. (ed), Invisibilitat i poder: cares del femen a la Grecia antiga, 19 – 51, Tarragona.

Calero Secall, I. (2006), "Aristeneto y la realidad juridica en torno a cuestiones matrimoniales", in Rodriguez Pantoja, M. (ed), Las raices clasicas de Andalucia: actas del Ⅳ congreso andaluz de estudios clasicos 1, 189 – 195, Cordoba.

Calero Secall, I. (2006), "Los delitos de adulterio y rapto en la ficción de la novela griega", Minerva 19, 63 – 83.

Calero Secall, I. (2004), "El privilegio de masculinidad y los derechos femeninos en las transmisiones patrimoniales de la Grecia clasica", in Nomos. Direito e sociedade, 153 – 174.

Calero Secall, I. (2003), "Los órdenes sucesorios en derecho griego. Un testimonio etolio (IG IX I2 2)", in Symposion 1999, 257 – 272.

Calero Secall, I. (2002), "Mujer y ley: aspectos de derecho matrimonial en la Grecia clásica", in Alfaro Giner, A., Garcia Sanchez, M. & M. Alamar Laparra (eds), Actas del tercer y cuarto seminarios de estudios sobre la mujer en la Antigüedad (Valencia, 28 – 30 abril 1999 y 12 – 14 abril 2000), 151, Valencia.

Calero Secall, I. (1997), Leyes de Gortina, Madrid.

Calero Secall, I. (1994 – 1995), "La mujer y el matrimonio en las sociedades griegas de Atenas y Gortyna y en el mundo islamico: un estudio comparativo", Florentia Iliberritana 4 – 5, 89 – 107.

Calhoun, G. M. (1944), Introduction to Greek Legal Science, Oxford.

Calhoun, G. M. (1930), "Risk in Sea Loans in Ancient Athens", *Journal of Economic and Business History* 2, 561 – 584.

Calhoun, G. M. (1927), The Growth of Criminal Law in Ancient Greece, Berkeley.

Calhoun, G. M. (1924), "The Jurisprudence of the Greek City", Columbia Law Review 94, 154 – 171.

Calhoun, G. M. (1924), "The Materials for a Study of Greek Law", *California Law Review* 12, 463 – 480.

Calhoun, G. M. (1923), "Greek Law and Modern Jurisprudence", *California Law Review* 11, 295 – 312.

Calhoun, G. M. (1921), "The Early History of Crime and Criminal Law in Greece", *Proceedings of the Classical Association of England* 18, 86 – 104.

Calhoun, G. M. (1921), "Demosthenes Against Boeotus xxxix, 37, 38", *CPh* 16, 287 – 288.

Calhoun, G. M. (1919), "Oral and Written Pleading in Athenian Courts", *TAPhA* 50, 177 – 193.

Calhoun, G. M. (1919), "Athenian Magistrates and Special Pleas", *CPh* 14, 338 – 350.

Calhoun, G. M. (1918), "The Status of Callistratus in the Litigation over the Estate of Conon. Demosthenes xlviii, 31, 43 ff", *CPh* 13, 410 – 412.

Calhoun, G. M. (1915), "Perjury before Athenian Arbitrators", *CPh* 10, 1 – 7.

Calhoun, G. M. (1915), "The will of Pasion and its seals. Demosthenes, xlv, 17", *CPh* 10, 75 – 76.

Calhoun, G. M. (1914), "Documentary Frauds in Litigation at Athens", *CPh* 9, 134 – 144.

Calhoun, G. M. (1913), Athenian Clubs in Politics and Litigation, Austin, Texas. (University of Texas bulletin, No. 262; Humanistic series, No. 14)

Calhoun, G. M. & C. Delamere (1927), A Working Bibliography of Greek Law, Cambridge, Mass.

Callaway, C. (1998), "Odysseus' three Unsworn Oaths", *AJPh* 119, 159 – 170.

Callaway, C. (1993), "Perjury and the Unsworn Oath", *TAPhA* 123, 15 – 26.

Calvert, Br. (1997), "The Death Penalty in Plato's Laws", in *Justice v. Law*,

243 – 262.

Calvert, Br. (1987), "Slavery in Plato's Republic", *CQ* 37, 367 – 372.

Camassa, G. (2011), "Les (nouvelles) lois de Clisthène et leur histoire", in Azoulay, V. & P. Ismard (eds), Clisthène et Lycurgue d'Athènes. Autour du politique dans la cité classique, 43 – 58, Paris.

Camassa, G. (2011), Scrittura e mutamento delle leggi nel mondo antico: dal Vicino Oriente alla Grecia di età arcaica e classica, Roma.

Camassa, G. (2007), "La legislazione ateniese del V e del IV secolo a. C.", Il pensiero politico 40, 211 – 221.

Camassa, G. (2005), "Du changement des lois", in Le législateur et la loi, 29 – 36.

Camassa, G. (2000), "Cronaca degli anni fecondi: Clistene, il demos e le eterie", QS 51, 41 – 56.

Camassa, G. (1999), "La lex sacra di Selinunte", in Gulletta, M. I. (ed), Sicilia epigrafica (Atti del convegno intternazionale, Erice 15 – 18 ottobre 1998), I, 141 – 148, Pisa. (ASNP Serie IV, Quaderni 1)

Camassa, G. (1996), "Leggi orali e leggi scritte. I legislatori", in I Greci 2, 561 – 576.

Camassa, G. (1994), "Verschriftung und Veränderung der Gesetze", in Rechtskodifizierung, 97 – 112.

Camassa, G. (1988), "Aux origines de la codification écrite des lois en Grèce", in Detienne, M. (ed), Les savoirs de l'écriture en Grèce ancienne, 130 – 155, Lille. (Cahiers de Philologie 14)

Camassa, G. (1987), "La codificazione delle leggi e le istituzioni politiche delle città greche della Calabria in età arcaica e classica", in Settis, S. (ed), Storia della Calabria. I La Calabria antica I, 619 – 56, Roma.

Camassa, G. (1986), "Il 'pastorato' di Zaleuco", Athenaeum 64, 139 – 146.

Canevaro, M. & E. M. Harris (2012), "The documents in Andocides' On the Mysteries", CQ 62, 98 – 129.

Cantarella, Eva (2011), "Greek Law and the Family", in Rawson, B. (ed), A Companion to Families in the Greek and Roman Worlds, 331 – 345, London. (= Cantarella, Diritto e società, 447 – 464)

Cantarella, Eva (2010), "Fathers and Sons in Athenian Law and Society", in Thür, G. (ed), Symposion.

Cantarella, Eva (2005), "Gender, Sexuality, and Law", in The Cambridge Companion, 236 - 253. (= Cantarella, Diritto e società, 401 - 420)

Cantarella, Eva (2002), "Dispute Settlement in Homer: Once Again on the Shield of Achilles", in Mélanges Dimakis, 147 - 166. (= Cantarella, Diritto e società, 171 - 192)

Cantarella, Eva (2001), "Private Revenge and Public Justice: The Settlement of Disputes in Homer's Iliad", *Punishment & Society* 3, 473 - 483. (= Cantarella, Diritto e società, 137 - 150)

Carawan, E. M. (2010), "The Case Against Nikomachos", *TAPhA* 140, 71 - 96.

Carawan, E. M. (2008), "Perikles the Younger and the Citizenship Law", *CJ* 103, 383 - 406.

Carawan, E. M. (2008), "What the Mnemones Know?", in Mackay, E. A. (ed), Orality, Literacy, Memory in the Ancient Greek and Roman World, 163 - 184, Leiden. (Orality and literacy in ancient Greece 7. Mnemosyne Suppl. 298)

Carawan, E. M. (2007), "The Trial of Arginusai Generals and the Dawn of 'Judicial Review'", Dike 10, 19 - 56.

Carawan, E. M. (2007), "Introduction: The Speechwriter's Art and the Imagined Community", in *The Attic Orators*, xi - xxiv.

Carawan, E. M. (2007), "Oath and Contract", in Horkos, 73 - 80.

Carawan, E. M. (2007), "Oral 'Agreement', Written Contract, and the Bonds of Law at Athens", in *Politics of Orality*, 321 - 342.

Carawan, E. M. (2006), "The Athenian Law of Agreement", *GRBS* 46, 339 - 374.

Carawan, E. M. (2006), "Amnesty and Accounting for the Thirty", *CQ* 56, 57 - 76.

Carawan, E. M. (2004), "Andocides' Defence and MacDowell's Solution", in *Law, Rhetoric, and Comedy*, 103 - 112.

Carawan, E. M. (2002), "The Athenian Amnesty and the 'Scrutiny of Laws'", *JHS* 122, 1 - 23.

Carawan, E. M. (2001), "What the Laws have Prejudged: Paragraphe and Early

Issue Theory",in Wooten,C. W. (ed),The Orator in Action and Theory in Greece and Rome,17 –51,Leyden. (Mnemosyne Suppl. 225)

Carawan,E. M. (2000),"Deianira's Guilt",TAPhA 130,189 –237.

Carawan,E. M. (1999),"The Edict of Oedipus (Oedipus Tyrannus 223 –251)",*AJPh* 120,188 –222.

Carawan,E. M. (1998),Rhetoric and the Law of Draco,Oxford.

Carawan,E. M. (1993),"The Tetralogies and Athenian Homicide Trials",*AJPh* 114,235 –270.

Carawan,E. M. (1993),"Tyranny and Outlawry: AthPol 16. 10",in *Nomodeiktes*,305 –319.

Carawan,E. M. (1991),"Ephetai and Athenian Courts for Homicide in the Age of the Orators",*CPh* 86,1 –16.

Carawan,E. M. (1990),"Trial of Exiled Homicides and the Court at Phreatto",*RIDA* 37,47 –67.

Carawan,E. M. (1990),"Five Talents Cleon Coughed up: Schol. Ach. 6",*CQ* 40,136 –147.

Carawan,E. M. (1989),"Thucydides and Stesimbrotus on the Exile of Themistocles",*Historia* 38,144 –161.

Carawan,E. M. (1987),"Eisangelia and Euthyna: The trials of Miltiades, Themistokles,and Cimon",*GRBS* 28,167 –208.

Carawan,E. M. (1985),"Apophasis and Eisangelia: The role of the Areopagus in Athenian Political Trials",*GRBS* 26,115 –140.

Carawan,E. M. (1984),"Akriton Apokteinai: Execution without Trial in Fourth-century Athens",*GRBS* 25,111 –121.

Carawan,E. M. (1983),"Erotesis: Interrogation in the courts of Fourth-century Athens",*GRBS* 24,209 –226.

Carey,C. (2007),"Tragic Law",*Dioniso* 6,22 –33.

Carey,C. (2005),"An Overlooked Papyrus of Isaios",*BICS* 48,15 –26.

Carey,C. (2004),"Antiphon's Daughter",in *Law,Rhetoric,and Comedy*,1 –14.

Carey,C. (2004),"Offence and Procedure in Athenian Law",in *The Law and the Courts*,111 –136.

Carey, C. (2000), "Comic Law", Annali dell'Universitð di Ferrara, Sez. Lettere 1, 65 - 86.

Carey, C. (2000), Aeschines, Austin, Tx. (The oratory of classical Greece 3)

Carey, C. (1998), "The Shape of Athenian Laws", *CQ* 48, 93 - 109.

Carey, C. (1997), Trials from Classical Athens, London.

Carey, C. (1996), "Nomos in Attic Rhetoric and Oratory", *JHS* 116, 33 - 46.

Carey, C. (1995), "Rape and Adultery in Athenian Law", *CQ* 45, 407 - 417.

Carey, C. (1995), "The Witness's Exomosia in the Athenian Courts", *CQ* 45, 114 - 119.

Carey, C. (1994), "'Artless' Proofs in Aristotle and the Orators", *BICS* 39, 95 - 106. (= The Attic Orators, 229 - 246)

Carey, C. (1994), "Rhetorical Means of Persuasion", in Worthington, I. (ed), Persuasion: Greek Rhetoric in Action, 26 - 45, London.

Carey, C. (1993), "Return of the Radish or Just When You Thought it was Safe to go Back into the Kitchen", *LCM* 18, 53 - 55.

Carey, C. (1992), Apollodorus Against Neaira, Warminster.

Carey, C. (1991), "Apollodoros' Mother: The Wives of Enfranchised Aliens in Athens", *CQ* 41, 84 - 89.

Carey, C. (1989), Lysias: Selected speeches, Cambridge.

Carey, C. (1988), "A Note on Torture in Athenian Homicide Cases", *Historia* 37, 241 - 245.

Carey, C. & R. A. Reid (1985), Demosthenes: Selected Private Speeches, Cambridge.

Carey, C. et al. (2008), "Fragments of Hypereides' Against Diondas from the Archimedes Palimpsest", *ZPE* 165, 1 - 19.

Cargill, J. (1981), The Second Athenian League: Empire or Free Alliance?, Berkeley.

Carlier, P. (2007), "Are the Homeric Basileis 'Big Men'", in Morris, S. P. & R. Laffineur (eds), Epos. Reconsidering Greek epic and Aegean bronze archaeology (Proceedings of the 11th international conference, Los Angeles, UCLA-The J. Paul Getty Villa, 20 - 23 April 2006), 121 - 128, Liege-Austin, Tx. (Aegaeum 28)

Carlier, P. (2006), "Anax and Basileus in the Homeric Poems", in Deger-

Jalkotzy, S. & I. S. Lemos (eds), Ancient Greece. From the Mycenaean palaces to the age of Homer, 101 – 109, Edinburgh.

Carnes, J. (2006), "Plato in the Courtrooms: The Surprising Influence of the Symposium", in Lesher, J., Nails, D. & F. C. C. Sheffield (eds), Plato's Symposium. Issues in interpretation and reception (Conference held at the Centre for Hellenic Studies in Washington D. C. in August 2005), 272 – 291, Washington D. C.

Carney, E. (2010), "Putting Women in their Place: Women in Public under Philip Ⅱ and Alexander Ⅲ and the Last Argeads", in Carney, E. & D. Ogden (eds), Philip Ⅱ and Alexander the Great. Father and son, lives and afterlives, 43 – 54, Oxford.

Carter, D. M. (2007), "Could a Greek Oath Guarantee a Claim Right?", in *Horkos*, 60 – 72.

Carter, D. M. (2004), "Citizen Attribute, Negative Right: A Conceptual Difference between Ancient and Modern Ideas of Freedom of Speech", in *Free Speech*, 197 – 220.

Carter, L. B. (1986), The Quiet Athenian, Oxford.

Cartledge, P. (2009), "'Rights', Individuals and Communities in Ancient Greece", in *Greek and Roman Political Thought*, 149 – 163.

Cartledge, P. (2000), "Spartan justice? or 'the State of the Ephors'?", Dike 3, 5 – 26.

Cartledge, P. (1998), "Laying down Polis Law", *CR* 49, 465 – 469.

Cartledge, P. (1993), "Like a Worm i' the Bud?: A Heterology of Classical Greek Slavery", *G & R* 40, 163 – 180.

Cartledge, P. (1990), "Fowl Play: A Curious Lawsuit in Classical Athens", in *Nomos*, 41 – 62.

Cartledge, P. (1976), "A New 5th-century Spartan Treaty", *LCM* 1, 87 – 92.

Casson, L. (1990), "New Light on Maritime Loans: PVindob. G 40882", *ZPE* 84, 195 – 206.

Casson, L. (1957), "New Light on Maritime Loans", *Eos* 48, 89 – 93.

Cataldi, S. (2007), "Atene e l'Occidente: Trattati e alleanze dal 433 al 424", in Greco, E. & M. Lombardo (eds), Atene e l'Occidente. I grandi temi: Le premesse, I protagonisti, le forme della communicazione e dell'interazione, I modi dell'intervento ateniese in Occidente(Atti del convegno internazionale, Atene 25 – 27 maggio 2006), 421 – 470, Atene.

Cataldi, S. (2003), "La costituzione ateniese e gli alleati nel V secolo a. C.", in Da Omero alla costituzione europea, 97 – 132.

Cataldi, S. (2002), "Democrazia e facoltà di parola nel 'Vecchio Oligarca'", Ktema 27, 173 – 181.

Cataldi, S. (2000), "Akolasia e isegoria di meteci e schiavi nell'Atene dello Pseudo-Senofonte: una riflessione socio-economica", in Sordi, M. (ed), L'opposizione nel mondo antico, 75 – 101, Milano.

Cataldi, S. (1996), "I processi agli strateghi della prima spedizione in Sicilia e la politica cleoniana", in Processi e politica, 37 – 63.

Cataldi, S. (1992), "Statuto e capacità giuridica dello straniero nella stele di Stinfalo", in L'étranger, 127 – 146.

Cataldi, S. (1983), Symbolai e relazioni tra le città greche nel V sec. a. C., Pisa.

Cataldi, S. (1982), "Contributo alla storia del diritto creditizio. Symbolaia e synallagmata in Aristotele", Apollinaris 55, 194 – 213.

Cataldi, S. (1982), "La struttura del rapporto creditizio e il diritto reale del creditore nell'orazione demostenica 'contro Panteneto'", in Studi Biscardi 3, 423 – 444.

Cataldi, S. (1981), "Note di lessico tecnico giuridico: Symbolaion in Platone", Vichiana 10, 157 – 62.

Cataldi, S. (1979), "Atene polis ekkletos. Ephesimoi ed ekkletoi dikai", ASNP 9, 1 – 37.

Cataldi, S. (1977), "Commento storico-giuridico al trattato di assistenza giudiziaria tra Delfi e Pellana", ASNP 7, 459 – 573.

Cataldi, S. (1976), "La restituzione della terra ai Mitilinesi e le rinnovate xymbolai tra Atene e Mitilene", ASNP 6(1), 15 – 34.

Cataldi, S. (1976), "A proposito del proxenos di IG ix I2, 717", ASNP 6(2), 401 – 410.

Cavanaugh, M. B. (2001), "Order in Multiplicity: Aristotle on Text, Context, and the Rule of Law", *North Carolina Law Review* 79, 577 – 661.

Cawkwell, G. L. (1995), "Early Greek Tyranny and the People", *CQ* 45, 73 - 86. (= Cyrene to Chaeronea. Selected essays on ancient Greek history, 33 - 53, Oxford 2011)

Cawkwell, G. L. (1973), "The Foundation of the Second Athenian Confederacy", *CQ* 23, 47 - 60. (= Cyrene to Chaeronea. Selected essays on ancient Greek history, 192 - 211, Oxford 2011)

Cawkwell, G. L. (1969), "The Crowning of Demosthenes", *CQ* 19, 163 - 180.

Chacon, R. J. (1958), Plato's Theory of Punishment, diss. Harvard.

Champion, Gr. (2009), "Imperial Ideologies, Citizenship Myths, and Legal Disputes in Classical Athens and Republican Rome", in *Greek and Roman Political Thought*, 85 - 99.

Chaniotis, A. (2009), "The Dynamics of Ritual Norms in Greek Cult", in La norme, 91 - 105.

Chaniotis, A. (2007), "Die Entwicklung der griechischen Asylie. Ritualdynamik und die Grenzen des Rechtsvergleichs", in Gesetzgebung in antiken Gesellschaften, 233 - 246.

Chaniotis, A. (2005), "The Great Inscription, its Political and Social Institutions and the Common Institutions of the Cretans", in La Grande Iscrizione, 175 - 194.

Chaniotis, A. (2004), "Justifying Territorial Claims in Classical and Hellenistic Greece: The Beginnings of International Law", in *The Law and the Courts*, 185 - 228.

Chaniotis, A. (2002), "Some Cretan Bastards", *Cretan Studies* 7, 51 - 57.

Chaniotis, A. (1997), "Reinheit des Körpers-Reinheit des Sinnes in den griechischen Kultgesetzen", in Assman, J. & T. Sundermeier (eds), Schuld, Gewissen und Person. Studien zur Geschichte des inneren Menschen, 142 - 179, Gütersloh.

Chaniotis, A. (1996), "Conflicting Authorities: Asylia between Secular and Divine Law in the Classical and Hellenistic Poleis", Kernos 9, 65 - 86.

Chaniotis, A. (1994), "Die sylan Klausel im Vertrag zwischen Lyttos und Malla (Staatsvertrage Ⅲ 511)", ZRG 111, 421 - 424.

Chaniotis, A. (1992), "Watching a Lawsuit: A New Curse Tablet from Southern Russia", *GRBS* 33, 69ff.

Chaniotis, A. (1988), "Habgierige Götter, habgierige Städte. Heiligtumsbesitz und Gebietsanspruch in den kretischen Staatsverträgen", Ktema 13, 21 - 39.

Chase, A. H. (1933), "The Influence of Athenian Institutions on the Laws of Plato", *HSPS* 44, 131 – 192.

Chowdharay-Best, G. (1976), "Ancient Maritime Law", *Mariner's Mirror* 62, 81 – 91.

Christ, J. K. F. (1879), De publicis populi Atheniensis rationibus saeculo a. Ch. quinto et quarto, Greifswald.

Christ, M. R. (2010), "Helping and Community in the Athenian Lawcourts", in Rosen, R. M. & I. Sluiter (eds), Valuing others in Classical Antiquity, 205 – 232, Leiden. (Mnemosyne Suppl. 323)

Christ, M. R. (2008), "Imagining Bad Citizenship in Classical Athens: Aristophanes' Ecclesiazusae 730 – 876", in Sluiter, I. & R. M. Rosen (eds), Kakos. Badness and Anti-value in Classical Antiquity, 169 – 184, Leiden. (Mnemosyne Suppl. 307)

Christ, M. R. (2007), "The Evolution of the Eisphora in Classical Athens", *CQ* 57, 53 – 69.

Christ, M. R. (2006), The Bad Citizen in Classical Athens, Cambridge.

Christ, M. R. (2004), "Draft Evasion Onstage and Offstage in Classical Athens", *CQ* 54, 33 – 57.

Christ, M. R. (1998), "Legal Self-help on Private Property in Classical Athens", *AJPh* 119, 521 – 545.

Christ, M. R. (1998), The Litigious Athenian, Baltimore.

Christ, M. R. (1992), "Ostracism, Sykophancy, and Deception of the Demos: [Arist.] Ath. Pol. 43. 5", *CQ* 42, 336 – 346.

Christ, M. R. (1990), "Liturgical Avoidance and Antidosis in Classical Athens", *TAPhA* 120, 147 – 169.

Christophilopoulos, A. P. (1986), "Sumpraxe suggenon se dikaiopraxies. Ho ton ateknon nomos", in Kremmydas, V., Maltezou, Chr. & N. Panayotakes (eds), Aphieroma ston N. Svorono I, 358 – 361, Rethymno.

Christophilopoulos, A. P. (1979), "Oikogeneiakai kai kleronomikai schesseis eis hellenikas epigraphas", in Christophilopoulos, A. P. Nomika Epigraphika. Seira deutera, 70 – 85, Athenai.

Christophilopoulos, A. P. (1979), "He katachoresis dikaiopraktikon engraphon eis ta demosia archeia", in Christophilopoulos, A. P. Nomika Epigraphika. Seira deutera, 9 – 69, Athenai.

Christophilopoulos, A. P. (1977), "Epitropeia eis to ektos Athenon hellenikon dikaion", in Christophilopoulos, A. P. Nomika Epigraphika, 62 – 68, Athenai.

Christophilopoulos, A. P. (1977), "Orphanika eis epigraphen ek Pergamou", in Christophilopoulos, A. P. Nomika Epigraphika, 69 – 70, Athenai.

Christophilopoulos, A. P. (1977), "Epitaphioi epigraphai me chrematikas poinas", in Christophilopoulos, A. P. Nomika Epigraphica, 9 – 49, Athenai.

Christophilopoulos, A. P. (1977), "Diorthotika kai hermeneutika eis nomikas epigraphas", in Christophilopoulos, A. P. Nomika Epigraphica, 71 – 73, Athenai.

Christophilopoulos, A. P. (1977), "Enktesis eis to ektos Athenon hellenikon dikaion", in Christophilopoulos, A. P. Nomika Epigraphika, 50 – 55, Athenai.

Christophilopoulos, A. P. (1977), "Thneta kai athanata eis to hellenikon dikaion", in Christophilopoulos, A. P. Nomika Epigraphika, 56 – 61, Athenai.

Christophilopoulos, A. P. (1973), "Kleine Beiträge zur griechischen Rechtsgeschichte", in Xenion Zeppos I, 439 – 445.

Christophilopoulos, A. P. (1968), "Nomophylakes kai thesmophylakes", Platon 20, 134 – 143. (= Dikaion kai Istoria, 33 – 43).

Christophilopoulos, A. P. (1967), "He nomothetike leitourgia eis tas hellenikas poleis", Athena 69, 17ff. (= Dikaion kai Istoria, 1 – 32).

Christophilopoulos, A. P. (1965), "Pragmatikai douleiai en attikais epigraphais", Athena 68, 257 – 261. (= Dikaion kai Istoria, 55 – 59).

Christophilopoulos, A. P. (1964), "Ges kai oikias enktesis kata to attikon dikaion", in Charisterion Orlandos I, 250 – 260. (= Dikaion kai Historia, 44 – 54).

Christophilopoulos, A. P. (1951), O met'allodapes gamos kata to archaion hellenikon kai to hellenistikon dikaion, Athenai. (Pragmateiai Akademias Athenon 17) (= Dikaion kai Istoria, 68 – 85)

Christophilopoulos, A. P. (1950), "Athanatos en droit grec", RIDA 4, 297 – 301. (= Dikaion kai Historia, 86 – 89). Chroust, A. -H. (1969 – 70), "Estate planning in Hellenic antiquity. Aristotle's last will and testament", Notre Dame Law 45, 629ff.

Chroust, A. -H. (1967), "Aristotle's Last will and Testament", *WS* 80, 90 – 114.

Chroust, A. -H. (1959), "Treason and Patriotism in Ancient Greece", *Journal of the History of Ideas* 15,280 – 288.

Chroust, A. -H. (1954), "The Legal Profession in Athens", *Notre Dame Lawyer* 29,339 – 389.

Chroust, A. -H. (1954), "International Treaties in Antiquity", *Class Med* 15, 60 – 107.

Ciccia, C. (2001), "Priscus Legislator Charondas", *Latinitas* 49,151 – 160.

Citti, V. (1988), "The Ideology of Metics in Attic Tragedy", in Yuge, T. & M. Doi(eds), Forms of Control and Subordination in Antiquity, 455 – 464, Leiden.

Clark, R. B. (2000), "Platonic Love in a Colorado Courtroom: Martha Nussbaum, John Finnis, and Plato's Laws in Evans v. Romer", *Yale Journal of Law and Humanities* 12(1), 1 – 38.

Classen, C. J. (1991), "The Speeches in the Courts of Law: A Three-cornered Dialogue", *Rhetorica* 9,195 – 207.

Clinton, K. (1982), "The Hature of the Late Fifth-century Revision of the Athenian Law Code", in *Studies Vanderpool*, 27 – 37.

Clinton, K. (1980), "A Law in the City Eleusinion Concerning the Mysteries", *Hesperia* 49,258 – 288.

Cohen, D. (2006), "Democracy and Individual Rights in Athens", *Philosophical Inquiry* 27,13 – 26.

Cohen, D. (2005), "Theories of Punishment", in *The Cambridge Companion*, 170 – 182.

Cohen, D. (2005), "Women in Public: Gender, Citizenship, and Social Status in Classical Athens", in Symposion 2001, 33 – 46. (with a reply by L. Foxhall, 47 – 50)

Cohen, D. (2005), "Crime, Punishment, and the Rule of Law in Classical Athens", in *The Cambridge Companion*, 211 – 235.

Cohen, D. (2003), "Writing, Law, and Legal Practice in the Athenian Courts", in Yunis, H. (ed), Writtentexts and the rise of literate culture in ancient Greece, 78 – 96, Cambridge.

Cohen, D. (2001), "The Rhetoric of Justice: Strategies of Reconciliation and Revenge in the Restoration of Athenian Democracy in 403 BC", *European Journal of Sociology* 42,335 – 56.

Cohen, D. (1998), "Women, Property and Status in Demosthenes 41 and 57",

Dike 1,53 – 61.

Cohen,D. (1997),"Democracy and Individual Rights in Athens",*ZRG* 114, 27 – 44. (= Anagnostopoulos,Y. (ed),Law and rights in the ancient Greek tradition, 13 – 26,Thessaloniki 2006)

Cohen,D. (1996),"Seclusion,Separation,and the Status of Women in Classical Athens", in McAuslan, I. & P. Walcot (eds), Women in Antiquity, 135 – 145, Cambridge.

Cohen, D. (1995), Law, Violence and Community in Classical Athens, Cambridge.

Cohen,D. (1995),"The Rule of Law and Democratic Ideology in Classical Athens",in Die athenische Demokratie,227 – 248.

Cohen,D. (1993),"Consent and Sexual Relations in Classical Athens", in Laiou,A. E. (ed), Consent and Coercion to Sex and Marriage in Ancient and Medieval Societies,5 – 16,Washington D. C.

Cohen, D. (1993), "Rhetoric, Morals, and the Rule of Law in Classical Athens",ZRG 110,1ff.

Cohen,D. (1993),"Law,Autonomy and Political Community in Plato's Laws", *CPh* 88,301 – 317.

Cohen,D. (1992),"Honor,Feud,and Litigation in Classical Athens",*ZRG* 109, 100 – 115.

Cohen,D. (1992),"Demosthenes' Against Meidias and Athenian Litigation",in Symposion 1990,155 – 164.

Cohen, D. (1991), "Debate (with Cliford Handley): Law, Society and Homosexuality in Classical Athens",*P &P* 133,167 – 194.

Cohen,D. (1991),Law,Sexuality and Society:The Enforcement of Morals in Classical Athens,Cambridge.

Cohen,D. (1991),"Sexuality,Violence and the Athenian Law of Hybris",*G&R* 38,171 – 188.

Cohen,D. (1990),"The Social Context of Adultery at Athens", in *Nomos*, 147 – 166.

Cohen,D. (1990),"Late Sources and the 'Reconstruction' of Greek Legal Institutions",in Symposion 1988,283 – 293.

Cohen, D. (1989), "Problems, Methods, and Models in the Study of Greek Law", *ZRG* 106, 81 – 105.

Cohen, D. (1988), "The Prosecution of Impiety in Athenian Law", *ZRG* 110, 695 – 701 (= Symposion 1985, 99 – 109).

Cohen, D. (1987), "Law, Society and Homosexuality in Classical Athens", *P&P* 117, 3 – 21. (= Osborne, R. (ed) (2004), Studies in ancient Greek and Roman society, 61 – 77, Cambridge)

Cohen, D. (1987), "The Legal Status and Political Role of Women in Plato's Laws", *RIDA* 34, 27 – 40.

Cohen, D. (1986), "The Theodicy of Aeschylus: Justice and Tyranny in the Oresteia", *G&R* 33, 129 – 141.

Cohen, D. (1985), "A Note on Aristophanes and the Punishment of Adultery in Athenian Law", *ZRG* 102, 385 – 387.

Cohen, D. (1984), "The Athenian Law of Adultery", *RIDA* 31, 147 – 165.

Cohen, D. (1983), Theft in Athenian Law, München. (MBPaR 74)

Cohen, D. (1982), "Theft in Plato's Laws and Athenian Legal Practice", *RIDA* 29, 121 – 143.

Cohen, D. (1980), "'Horkia' and 'horkos' in the Iliad", *RIDA* 27, 49 – 68.

Cohen, E. E. (2007), "Slave Power at Athens: Juridical Theory and Economic Reality", in *Individus, Groupes et Politique*, 155 – 170.

Cohen, E. E. (2007), "Laws Affecting Prostitution at Athens", in Symposion 2005, 201 – 224.

Cohen, E. E. (2006), "La definition de la prostitution a Athenes", in Dlugosz, D. (ed), Grecs, Juifs, Polonais. A la recherche des racines de la civilisation européenne (Actes du colloque international tenu à Paris le 14 novembre 2003 dédié à Joseph Meleze-Modrzejewski), 117 – 122, Paris-Varsovie.

Cohen, E. E. (2006), "Consensual Contracts at Athens", in Symposion 2003, 73 – 92.

Cohen, E. E. (2006), "A legal Fiction: The Athenian Law of Sale", in van Alfen, P. (ed), Agoranomia: Studies in money and exchange presented to John H. Kroll, 87 – 98, New York.

Cohen, E. E. (2006), "Free and Unfree Sexual Work: An Economic Analysis of

Athenian Prostitution", in *Prostitutes & courtesans*, 95 – 124.

Cohen, E. E. (2005), "Commercial Law", in *The Cambridge Companion*, 290 – 302.

Cohen, E. E. (2005), "Unintended Consequences? The Economic Effect of Athenian Tax Laws", in Symposion 2001, 159 – 173.

Cohen, E. E. (2005), "Work Ethics and the Practice of Prostitution at Athens", *MedAnt* 8, 39 – 62.

Cohen, E. E. (2000), "Written Contracts of Prostitution in Fourth-century Athens", in *Timai Triantaphyllopoulou*, 109 – 122.

Cohen, E. E. (2000), "'Whoring under Contract': The Legal Context of Prostitution in Fourth-century Athens", in *Law and Social Status*, 113 – 147.

Cohen, E. E. (2000), The Athenian Nation, Princeton.

Cohen, E. E. (1998), "The Wealthy Slaves of Athens: Legal Rights, Economic Obligations", in Le monde antique, 105 – 129.

Cohen, E. E. (1997), "The astoi of Attika: Nationality and Citizenship at Athens", in Symposion 1995, 57 – 95.

Cohen, E. E. (1994), "Trapezes kai trapezikes ergassies sten klassike Athina-He nomike thessi ton gunaikon kai doulon", in Symboles Ⅱ, 149 – 176.

Cohen, E. E. (1992), Athenian Economy and Society: A Banking Perspective, Princeton.

Cohen, E. E. (1991), "Banking as a Family Business: Legal Adaptations Affecting Wives and Slaves", in Symposion 1990, 239 – 263.

Cohen, E. E. (1990), "Commercial Lending by Athenian Banks: Cliometric Fallacies and Forensic Methodology", *CPh* 85, 177 – 90.

Cohen, E. E. (1990), "A Study in Contrast: 'Maritime Loans' and 'Landed Loans' at Athens", in Symposion 1988, 57 – 79.

Cohen, E. E. (1973), Ancient Athenian Maritime Courts, Princeton.

Cohn-Haft, L. (1995), "Divorce in Classical Athens", *JHS* 115, 1 – 14.

Collins, S. D. (2006), Aristotle and the Rediscovery of Citizenship, Cambridge.

Collins Reilly, L. (1978), Slaves in Ancient Greece. Slaves from Greek Manumission Inscriptions, Chicago.

Colson, D. D. (1985), "On Appealing to Athenian Law to Justify Socrates'

Disobedience", Apeiron 19, 133 – 151.

Connor, W. R. (1993), "The Histor in History", in Nomodeiktes, 3 – 15.

Connor, W. R. (1991), "The other 399: Religion and the Trial of Socrates", in M. A. Flower & M. Toher (eds), Georgica. Greek Studies in Honour of George Cawkwell, 49 – 56, London. (BICS Suppl. 58)

Connor, W. R. (1985), "The Razing of the House in Greek Society", *TAPhA* 115, 79 – 102.

Cooper, C. (2008), "Hypereides, Aristophon, and the Settlement of Keos", in *Epigraphy and the Greek Historian*, 31 – 56.

Cooper, G. (2007), "Forensic oratory", in Worthington, I. (ed), A Companion to Greek Rhetoric, 203 – 214, Oxford.

Cooper, J. M. (1996), "Justice and Rights in Aristotle's Politics", *Review of Metaphysics* 49, 859 – 72.

Corbett, R. J. (2009), "The Question of Natural Law in Aristotle", *History of Political Thought* 30, 229 – 50.

Corcoran, M. G. (1992), "Aristotle's Poetic Justice: The Nicomachean Ethics and Oedipus the King", *Iowa Law Review* 77, 837ff.

Corcoran, M. G. (1989), "The Last Judgment of Plato's Gorgias: Mythos to you, Logos to Me", *Iowa Law Review* 74, 755 – 835.

Corwin, E. E. (1913 – 1914), "American and Greek Jurisprudence Compared", Case and Comment 20, 117 – 119.

Corwin, E. E. (1912 – 1913), "American and Greek Jurisprudence Compared", *Ohio Law Reporter* 10, 57 – 68.

Cover, R. M. (1986), "Violence and the Word", *Yale Law Journal* 95, 1601 – 1629.

Cox, Ch. (2011), "Marriage in ancient Athens", in Rawson, B. (ed), A Companion to Families in the Greek and Roman Worlds, 231 – 244, London.

Craig, A. (1991), "Gender, Difference, and Postmodernism: Women and Law in Classical Greece", *Michigan Law Review* 89, 1610 – 1617.

Craik, E. M. (1993), "Unwritten laws", LCM 18, 123 – 125.

Craik, E. M. (1984), "Marriage in Ancient Greece", in Craik, E. M. (ed), Marriage and Property, 8 – 29, Aberdeen.

Crawford, M. (1997), "Greek and Roman Juridical Epigraphy", in Christol, M & O. Mason (eds), Actes.

Croix, G. E. M. (1974), "Ancient Greek and Roman Maritime Loans", in W. H. Edey & B. Yamey (eds), Debits, Credits, Finance and Profits: Essays in Honour of W. T. Baxter, 41 - 59, London.

Croix, G. E. M. (1970), "Some Observations on the Property Rights of Athenian Women", CR 20, 273 - 278.

Croix, G. E. M. (1961), "Notes on Jurisdiction in the Athenian Empire", CQ 11, 94 - 112; 268 - 280.

Croix, G. E. M. (1956), "The Constitution of the Five Thousand", *Historia* 5, 1 - 23.

Croix, G. E. M. (1954), "The Character of the Athenian Empire", *Historia* 3, 1 - 41.

Cronin, J. F. (1939), "The Athenian Juror and Emotional Pleas", *CJ* 34, 471 - 479.

Cronin, J. F. (1936), The Athenian Juror and his Oath, diss. Chicago.

Crook, J. A. (1996), "Legal History and General History", *BICS* 41, 31 - 36.

Crosby, M. (1957), "More Fragments of Mining Leases from the Athenian Agora", *Hesperia* 26, 1 - 23.

Crosby, M. (1950), "Excavations in the Athenian Agora: The Leases of the Laureion Mines", *Hesperia* 19, 189 - 312.

Cudjoe, R. V. (2010), The Social and Legal Position of Widows and Orphans in Classical Athens, Athens (Symboles. Contributions to the research of ancient Greek and Hellenistic law 3).

Cudjoe, R. V. (2005), "The Purpose of the Epidikasia for an Epikleros in Classical Athens", Dike 8, 55 - 88.

Cudjoe, R. V. & S. Adam-Magnissali (2010), "Family Law in [Demosthenes] 43 Against Macartatus, 75", *EHHD* 42, 67 - 73.

Cusher, B. E. (2011), "From Natural Catastrophe to the Human Catastrophe: Plato on the Origin of Written Law", Law, Culture and the Humanities, http://lch.sagepub.com/content/early/recent.

Czerwinska, J. (1988), "The State and the Law in the Light of Sophistic

Doctrine and Historical Worksof Thucydides", Symbolae Philologorum Posnanesium Graecae et Latinae 7,37 - 49.

D

D'Amato, A. (1976), "Obligation to Obey the Law: A Study of the Death of Socrates", *Southern California Law Review* 49, 1079 - 1108.

Damaska, M. R. (1986), The Faces of Justice and State Authority: A Comparative Approach to the Legal Process, New Haven.

Danzig, G. (2003), "Apologizing for Socrates: Plato and Xenophon on Socrates' Behaviour in Court", *TAPhA* 133, 281 - 321.

Dareste Rodolphe (1908), "Notes sur l'hypothèque en droit grec", NRHD 32, 639 - 649.

Dareste Rodolphe (1906), "La dike exoúles en droit attique", Revue 30, 101 - 104.

Dareste Rodolphe (1906), "Le droit criminel en Grèce", in Nouvelles études d'histoire du droit, 41 - 52, Paris.

Dareste Rodolphe (1895), "Une pretendue loi de Solon", REG 8, 1 - 6.

Dareste Rodolphe (1893), La science du droit en Grèce; Plato, Aristote, Théophraste, Paris.

Dareste Rodolphe (1891), "Un nouveau fragment des lois de Solon", Revue 15, 97.

Dareste Rodolphe (1889), "Du droit des représailles principalement chez les anciens Grecs", REG 2, 305 - 321.

Dareste Rodolphe (1886), "La loi de Gortyne", NRHD 10, 241 - 275.

Dareste Rodolphe (1885), "Les inscriptions hypothécaires en Grèce", NRHD 9, 1 - 14.

Dareste Rodolphe (1884), "La transcription des ventes, en droit hellénique, d'après les monuments épigraphiques récemment découverts", NRHD 8, 373 - 394.

Dareste Rodolphe (1884), "Sur la suggraphé en droit grec et en droit romain", BCH 8, 362 - 376.

Dareste Rodolphe (1882), "Les testaments des philosophes grecs", AEG 16, 1 - 21.

Dareste Rodolphe (1879), "La législation criminelle des Athéniens", ASMP 111,279 - 297.

Dareste Rodolphe(1879),Plaidoyers politiques Démosthène,Paris.

Dareste Rodolphe(1878),"Le droit criminel athénien",AEG 12,29 - 47.

Dareste Rodolphe(1878),"Esquisse du droit criminel athénien",JS,625 - 639.

Dareste Rodolphe (1878), " Explication d'une inscription hypothécaire-découverte à Spata",BCH 2,485 - 489.

Dareste Rodolphe(1877),"Mémoire sur les entreprises de travaux publics chez les Grecs",AEG 11,107 - 117.

Dareste Rodolphe(1877),"Mémoire sur une ancienne loi éphésienne", ASMP 108,703 - 718.

Dareste Rodolphe(1875),Plaidoyers civils de Démosthène,Paris.

Dareste Rodolphe(1870 - 1871),"Études sur le traité des lois de Théophraste", RLAM,262 - 294.

Dareste Rodolphe(1867),Du prêt à la grosse chez les Athéniens,études sur les quatre plaidoyers attribués à Démosthène contre Zénothémis, Phormion, Lacrite et Dionysodore,Paris.

Dareste,R, Haussoullier, B. & Th. Reinach (eds) (1895 - 1904), Recueil des inscriptions juridiques grecques,2 vols,Paris. Dargan,M. F. (1970),The interplay of ethos and legal issues in certain private orations of Demosthenes, diss. Ohio State University.

David Asheri (1982), " Formes et procedures de reconciliation dans les cités grecques:le décret de Nacone",in Symposion 1977,135 - 146.

David Asheri (1980), " Rimpatrio di esuli e ridistribuzioni di terre nelle citta siceliote,ca. 466 - 461 a. C. ",in Studi Manni,143 - 158.

David Asheri(1979),"Rimpatrio di esuli a Selinunte",*ASNP* 7,479 - 497.

David Asheri (1977), " Tyrannie et mariage forcé. Essai d'histoire sociale grecque",Annales ESC 32,21 - 48.

David Asheri(1969),Leggi greche sul problema dei debiti,Pisa.

David Asheri(1967),"Il 'rincalzo misto' a Naupatto(ante 456 a. C.)",PdP 22,343 - 358.

David Asheri(1966),Distribuzioni di terre nelle antica Grecia,Torino.

David Asheri(1965),"Distribuzione di terre e legislazione agraria nella Locride Occidentale",JJP 15,313 -328.

David Asheri(1964),"Gli impegni politici nel giuramento degli eliasti ateniesi" Rendiconti dell' Accademia Nazionale dei Lincei, 281 - 293. (Classe di scienze morali,storiche e filol. Ser. 8,19(7 -12))

David Asheri(1963),"Laws of Inheritance, Distributions of Land and Political Constitutions in Ancient Greece",*Historia* 12,1 -21.

David Asheri(1961),"Sulla legge di Epitadeo",Athenaeum 39,45 -68.

David Asheri(1960),"L'oikos eremos nel diritto successorio attico",AG 159, 7 -24. Ashmonti, L. A. (2006), "The Arginusae Trial, the Changing Role of Strategoi,and the Relationship between Demos and Military Leadership in Late-fifth Century Athens",BICS 49,1 -21.

David,E. (1985),"The trial of Spartan kings",*RIDA* 32,131 -140.

David,E. (1978),"The Spartan sussitia and Plato's Laws",*ADPh* 99,486 -95.

Davies,J. K. (2005), "The Gortyn laws", in *The Cambridge Companion*, 305 -327.

Davies,J. K. (2004),"The Concept of the 'Citizen'", in *Poleis e politeiai*, 19 -30.

Davies,J. K. (2002),"A Wholly Non-Aristotelian Universe: The Molossians as Ethnos, State and Monarchy",in *Alternatives to Athens*,234 -258.

Davies,J. K. (1998),"Deconstructing Gortyn: When is a Code a Code?", in *Law in its Political Setting*,33 -56.

Davies,J. K. (1994),"On the Non-usability of the Concept of 'Sovereignty' in an Ancient Greek Context",in Federazioni e federalismo,51 -65.

Davies,J. K. (1977 -78),"Athenian Citizenship: The Descent Group and the Alternatives",*CJ* 73,105 -121. (=Rhodes,P. J. (ed)(2004),Athenian democracy, 18 -39,Edinburgh)

Davies,J. K. (1967),"Demosthenes on Liturgies: A Note",*JHS* 87,33 -40.

Davis,G. (2011),"Axones and Kyrbeis: A New Solution to an Old Problem", *Historia* 60,1 -35.

Davis,M. (1999 - 2000), "The Tragedy of Law: Gyges in Herodotus and Plato",*The Review of Metaphysics* 53,635 -655.

Davis, M. (1969), "Monetary Fines and Limitations in Plato's Magnesia", *CPh* 64, 98 - 101.

Davis, M. (1960), "The Place of Law in Projected Platonic Cities", *SO* 36, 72 - 85.

Davis, Ph. D. (1936), "An Eleusinian Building Contract IG II2 1681(341 - 390 B. C.)", in Classical Studies Presented to E. Capps on his seventieth birthday, 86 - 89, Princeton.

Davison, J. A. (1951), "Court Trials of the Philosophers", Proceedings of the Classical Association(London) 48, 33.

Deene, M. (2011), "Naturalized Citizens and Social Mobility in Classical Athens: The case of Apollodorus", *Greece & Rome* 58, 159 - 175.

Deiters, P. K. E. (1904), De Cretensium Titulis Publicis Quaestiones Epigraphicae, Jena.

Demont, P. (2011), "Les nouveaux fragments d'Hypéride", REG 124, 21 - 45.

Demont, P. (2006), "Hybris, 'outrage', 'anomia' et 'demesure' de Gernet a Fischer: quelques remarques", in Mélanges Casevitz, 347 - 360.

Demont, P. (2003), "Le kleroterion('machine a tirer au sort') et la democratie athenienne", Bulletin de l'Association G. Bude, 26 - 52.

Demont, P. (2001), "Le tirage au sort des magistrates ὰ Athènes: un problème historique et historiographique", in Sorteggio pubblico, 63 - 81. Dent, N. J. H. (1983) „Common, civic and Platonic justice in the Republic" Polis 5, 1 - 33.

Develin, R. (1985), "Philochoros on Ostracism", CivClCh 6, 25 - 31.

Develin, R. (1985), "Age Qualifications for Athenian Magistrates", *ZPE* 61, 149 - 159.

Develin, R. (1977), "Solon's Law on Stasis", *Historia* 26, 507 - 508.

Develin, R. (1973), "The Good Man and the Good Citizen in Aristotle's Politics", *Phronesis* 18, 71 - 79.

Dewald, C. (2003), "Form and Content: The Question of Tyranny in Herodotus", in *Popular Tyranny*, 25 - 58.

Dignas, B. (2000), "The Leases of Sacred Property at Mylasa: An Alimentary Scheme for the Gods", Kernos 13, 117 - 126.

Dihle, A. (2006), "Gesetz, Gerechtigkeit und Billigkeit bei Aristoteles", in

Gesetz und Gesetzlichkeit,23 - 37.

Diller,A. (1935), "Scrutiny and Appeal in Athenian Citizenship", *CPh* 30, 302 - 311.

Diller,A. (1932), "The Decree of Demophilus,346 - 345 B. C.", *TAPhA* 63, 193 - 205.

Dillon,J. M. (2004),Salt and Olives: Morality and Custom in Ancient Greece, Edinburgh.

Dillon,M. P. J. (1996), "The Importance of the Water Supply at Athens: The Role of the Epimeletes ton Krenon", *Hermes* 124,192 - 204.

Dillon,M. P. J. (1995), "By Gods, Tongues, and Dogs; the use of Oath in Aristophanic Comedy", *G &R* 42,135 - 151.

Dimakis,P. D. (2001), "To dikaiiko lexilogio", in Chrestides, A. Ph. (ed), Historia tes hellenikes glossas,55ff. ,Thessaloniki.

Dimakis,P. D. (1998), "He klese tou patera stin kleronomia tou proapobiosanta giou tou",in Dosis agathe. Timetikos tomos Dem. Korsou,113ff. ,Athina.

Dimakis, P. D. (1998), "Indices du pouvoir des femmes dans l'Athènes classique",in Le monde antique,147 - 154.

Dimakis,P. D. (1997b), "Threskeia kai anexithreskeia sten archaia Ellada", in He threskeutike eleutheria,51 - 62,Athina. (Dikanikoi dialogoi 4)

Dimakis,P. D. (1997), "Les ambassadeurs dans la Grèce antique", BIDR 39, 87 - 91.

Dimakis,P. D. (1996),Attiko Dikaio I: To oikogeneiako dikaio tes Athinas kata tous klassikous chronous 2,Athina.

Dimakis,P. D. (1995), "Presbeis kai proxenoi sten archaia Ellada",in Mélanges G. C. Vlachos,163 - 188,Athina.

Dimakis,P. D. (1995), "Ekdiloseis dimokratikou pneumatos stous thesmous tou Attikou idiotikou dikaiou",in He Athenaike demokratia. Meletes gia to politeuma kai tin ideologia ton Athenaion,115 - 149,Athina.

Dimakis,P. D. (1994), "He meionektike thessi ton gynaikon sten klassike Sparte",in Prosopa kai thesmoi,35 - 51.

Dimakis,P. D. (1994), "Note al testamento di Epicuro", in Studi Biscardi 6, 471 - 492. (= "Scholia ste diatheke tou Epikourou" in Prosopa kai thesmoi,226 -

243.)

Dimakis, P. D. (1994), "He dike tes Neairas", in Prosopa kai thesmoi, 102 - 135.

Dimakis, P. D. (1994), "He dike tou Sokrate", in Prosopa kai thesmoi, 244 - 270.

Dimakis, P. D. (1994), Isaiou logoi, vol. A', Athina.

Dimakis, P. D. (1992), "Dikasteria kai dikazomenoi sten klassike Sparte", Lakonikai Spoudai 11, 32 - 57. (= Prosopa kai thesmoi, 178 - 201)

Dimakis, P. D. (1992), "Liga logia gia to archaio elleniko kai to Attiko dikaio", in Symboles I, 159 - 193.

Dimakis, P. D. (1991), "Mia arketa perierge sumvasse ergasias sten Athena ton klassikon chronon", in Prosopa kai thesmoi, 157 - 166.

Dimakis, P. D. (1991), "Scholia pano sti diatheke tou Aristotele", in Archaio Elleniko Dikaio, 45 - 61.

Dimakis, P. D. (1990), "La posizione inferiore delle donne nella Sparta classica", in Symposion 1988, 201 - 212.

Dimakis, P. D. (1989), "Anchisteia. H me anamenomeni exelixe tes ennoias enos orou tou klasikou mas dikaiou", in Charisterion. Summeikta pros timen Georgiou M. Papachatze, 449 - 467, Athina.

Dimakis, P. D. (1989), "Quelques rémarques à propos de la position juridique des Athéniennes (Atthides) à l'époque classique (Tentative en vue de l'effondrement d'un myth)", in Symposion 1985, 221 - 233.

Dimakis, P. D. (1987), "He thessi ton gynaikon sten Athena tes klassikes epoches", in Prosphora ston G. Michaelide-Nouaro I, 367 - 391, Athena. (= Prosopa kai thesmoi, 17 - 34)

Dimakis, P. D. (1983), Stoicheia attikou dikaiou I. To oikogeneiakon dikaion ton Athenon kata tous klassikous chronous, Athinai.

Dimakis, P. D. (1979), "L'omicidio secondo i Greci ed i Romani", Labeo 25, 209 - 212.

Dimakis, P. D. (1978), "A propos du droit de propriété de la femme mariée sur les biens dotaux d'après le droit grec ancien", in Symposion 1974, 227 - 243. (= "Eichan kurioteta oi gynaikes pano sta proikoa tous pragmata kata to archaio helleniko dikaio",in Prosopa kai thesmoi,52 – 63)

Dimakis,P. D. (1972),"Archaio helleniko dikaio",in Historia tou Hellenikou Ethnous 3,536 – 547,Athina.

Dimakis,P. D. (1969),"Scholia tina eis ten diatheken tou Platonos", in Aphieroma eis Charalampon N. Frangistan epi tei sumplerossei triakontapentaetous kathegesias,5,287 – 307,Thessaloniki. (= Prosopa kai thesmoi,209 – 226)

Dimakis,P. D. (1969),"He meionektike thesis tes gunaikos eis to kleronomikon dikaion tes Gortynos", in Eis mnemen Konstantinou N. Karaba, 127 – 145, Thessaloniki. (EESNOE 10)

Dimakis, P. D. (1963), "Stoicheia attikou dikaiou eis ten komodian tou Menandrou Dyskolos",in Eranion Maridaki I,9 – 42. (= "Elements de droit attique dans la comédie Dyscolos de Ménandre" Nea Hestia 1965,922 – 923)

Dimakis, P. D. (1959), O thesmos tes proikos kata to archaion ellenikon dikaion,Athina.

Dodds,E. R. (1951),The Greeks and the irrational,Berkeley.

Dönges,N. A. (1996),"Ostracism and the boulai of Kleisthenes",Historia 45, 387 – 404.

Dörmer, W. (1883), "De Graecorum sacrificulis qui ieropoioi dicuntur", Dissertationes philologicae Argentoratenses 8,1 – 75.

Domanski, A. (1999), "Why ought we to obey the law? Plato's startling answer",Akroterion 44,24 – 37.

Dorjahn,A. P. (1978),"On Lysias 5.4",CB 55,44.

Dorjahn,A. P. (1971),"On Slave-evidence in the Athenian Courts",CB 47, 45 – 46.

Dorjahn,A. P. (1953),"Evidence by Torture in Ancient Athenian Courts",in Studi Arangio-Ruiz 3,77 – 80.

Dorjahn,A. P. (1952),"On Slave-evidence in Greek Law",*CJ* 47,188.

Dorjahn,A. P. (1946),Political Forgiveness in Old Athens:The Amnesty of 403 B. C.,Evanston.

Dorjahn,A. P. (1941),"On the Athenian Anakrisis",*CPh* 36,182 – 185.

Dorjahn,A. P. (1938),"Outside Influence on Athenian Courts",*Philological Quarterly* 17,18 – 25.

Dorjahn, A. P. (1937), "Intimidation in Athenian Courts", *CPh* 32, 341 - 348.

Dorjahn, A. P. (1935), "Anticipation of Arguments in Athenian Courts", *TAPhA* 66, 274 - 295.

Dorjahn, A. P. (1930), "Extenuating Circumstances in Athenian Courts", *CPh* 25, 162 - 172.

Dorjahn, A. P. (1928), "Legal Precedent in Athenian Courts", *Philological Quarterly* 7, 375 - 389.

Dorjahn, A. P. (1927), "Poetry in Athenian Courts", *CPh* 22, 85 - 93.

Dorjahn, A. P. & J. F. Cronin (1938), "Outside influences on Athenian Courts", *PhQ* 17, 18 - 25.

von Dornum, D. D. (1997), "The Straight and the Crooked: Legal Accountability in Ancient Greece", *Columbia Law Review* 97, 1483 - 1518.

Dover, K. J. (1978), Greek Homosexuality, London.

Dover, K. J. (1974), Greek Popular Morality in the Time of Plato and Aristotle, Berkeley.

Dover, K. J. (1968), Lysias and the Corpus Lysiacum, Berkeley.

Dover, K. J. (1964), "Eros and Nomos", *BICS* 11, 31 - 42.

Dover, K. J. (1963), "Androtion on Ostracism", *CR* 13, 256 - 257. (= The Greeks and their legacy Ⅱ, 83 - 85)

Dover, K. J. (1955), "Anapsephisis in Fifth-century Athens", *JHS* 75, 17 - 20. (= The Greeks and their legacy Ⅱ, 187 - 193)

Dow, St. (1963a), "The Athenian Anagrapheis", *HSCP* 67, 37 - 54.

Dow, St. (1961), "The Walls Inscribed with Nikomakhos' Law Code", *Hesperia* 30, 58 - 73.

Dow, St. (1959), "The Lawcodes of Athens", *Proceedings of the Massachusetts Historical Society* 71, 3 - 36.

Dow, St. (1941), "Greek Inscriptions: The Athenian Law Code of 411 - 401 BC", *Hesperia* 10, 31 - 37.

Dow, St. (1939), "Aristotle, the Kleroteria and the Courts", *HSCP* 50, 1 - 34. (= Rhodes, P. J. (ed) (2004), Athenian democracy, 62 - 94, Edinburgh)

Drapkin, I. (1989), Crime and Punishment in the Ancient World, Lexington, Mass.

Dreher, M. (2012), "Die Rechtskultur der Westgriechen", in Legras, B. (ed), Transferts culturels et droits dans le monde grec et hellénistique (Actes du colloque international, Reims, 14 – 17 mai 2008), 63 – 78, Paris.

Dreher, M. (2007), "Das Bürgerrecht im griechischen Sizilien zwischen Recht und Politik", in Symposion 2005, 57 – 78.

Dreher, M. (2006), "Die Primitivität der frühen spartanischen Verfassung", in Luther, A., Meier, M. & L. Thommen (eds), Das frühe Sparta, 43 – 62, Stuttgart.

Dreher, M. (2005), "Die fremden Hiketai und die verfremdete Asylie in den Hiketiden des Aischylos", in Riemer, U & P. Riemer (eds), Xenophobie-Philoxenie. Vom Umgang mit Fremden in der Antike, 65 – 88, Stuttgart.

Dreher, M. (2003), "Der Prozeß gegen Xenophon", in Symposion 1999, 209 – 228. (= Tuplin, Chr. (ed), Xenophon and his world (Papers from a conference held in Liverpool in July 1999), 55 – 70, Stuttgart 2004. (Historia Einzelschriften 172))

Dreher, M. (2003), "Hikesie und Asylie in den Hiketiden des Aischylos", in Das antike Asyl, 59 – 84.

Dreher, M. (2003), "Symmachia und Sympoliteia in den griechischen Welt bis 323 v. Chr.", in Buraselis, K. & Kl. Zoumboulakis (eds), The Idea of European Community in History Vol. Ⅱ. Aspects of Connecting Poleis and Ethne in Ancient Greece, 27 – 39, Athens.

Dreher, M. (2000), "Verbannung ohne Vergehen. Der Ostrakismos (das Scherbengericht)", in Große Prozesse, 66 – 80.

Dreher, M. (1995), Hegemon und Symmachoi. Untersuchungen zum zweiten athenischen Seebund, Berlin.

Dreher, M. (1995), "Poleis und nicht-Poleis im zweiten athenischen Seebund", in Hansen, Sources, 171 – 200.

Dreher, M. (1990), "Ein athenischer Synedros im zweiten athenischen Seebund. Klope in Dem. 24. 127", in Symposion 1988, 149 – 172.

Dreher, M. (1989), "Zu IG II2 404, dem attischen Volksbeschluss über die Eigenstaatlichkeit der keischen Poleis", in Symposion 1985, 263 – 283.

Dreizehnter, A. (1978), "The legislation of Demetrius of Phalerum and the trasformation of Athenian law", in Fortenbaugh, W. W. & E. Schutrumpf (eds), Demetrius of Phalerum. Text, translation and discussion, New Brunswick, 347 – 365.

(Rutgers University Studies in classical Humanities 9)

Drews, R. (1983), Basileus. The evidence for kingship in geometric Greece, New Haven. (Yale classical monographs 4)

Due, B. (1980), Antiphon. A study in argumentation, Copenhagen. (Opuscula Graecolatina 17)

Dusanic, S. (2010), "Plato's Projects for a Confederate Sicily and the Constitutional Patterns in the Third Book of the Laws", *Aevum* 84, 61 – 68.

Dusanic, S. (2002), "Plato on Legislation: Two Historical Aspects of the Problem", *ZAnt* 52, 47 – 54.

Dusanic, S. (2002), "Les Lois et les programmes athéniens de reforme constitutionnelle au milieu du IVe siècle", *RFHIP* 16, 341 – 350.

Dusanic, S. (1994), "Plato and the two maritime confederacies of Athens", in Federazioni e federalismo, 87 – 106.

Dusanic, S. (1978), "The horkion ton oikisteron and fourth-century Cyrene", Chiron 8, 541 – 560.

Dusanic, S. (1978), "Notes épigraphiques sur l'histoire arcadienne du IVe siècle", BCH 102, 333 – 358.

Dusanic, S. (1972), "Synoecisme entre les Orchomeniens et les Euaimniens (Staatverträge 297)", in Akten des 6. Internationalen Kongresses, 554 – 556.

Dusanic, S. (1970), Arkadski savez IV veka, Beograd.

Duxbury, N. (1989), "Foundations of Legal Tradition: The Case of Ancient Greece", *Legal Studies* 9, 241 – 260.

Dyovouniotes, G. (1901), "Hermeneia nomikes epigraphes ek tes en Krete Gortynos", Epeteris Philologikou Syllogou Parnassou 5, 146 – 150.

E

Easterling, P. (2008), "Fata Libellorum: Hyperides and the Transmission of Attic Orators", *AAntHung* 48, 11 – 18.

Ebbott, M. (2003), Imagining Illegitimacy in Classical Greek Literature, Oxford.

Eberz, J. O. (1911), "Platons Gesetze und die sicilische Reform", AGPh 25, 162 – 174.

Eck, B. (2012), La mort rouge: homicide, guerre et souillure en Grèce ancienne,

Paris.

Eder, W. (1986), "The Political Significance of the Codification of Law in Archaic Societies: An Unconventional Hypothesis", in Raaflaub, K. (ed), Social Struggles in Archaic Rome, 262 – 300, Berkeley.

Edwards, M. J. (2010), "Rhetoric and the Law in Classical Athens: The Case(s) of Isaeus", in Cortes Edwards, M. J. (2009), "Isaeus and the Athenian Inheritance Laws", in Symposion 2007, 41 – 54.

Edwards, M. J. (2008), "Some thoughts on the Text of Isaios", *AAHung* 48, 115 – 120.

Edwards, M. J. (2007), Isaeus, Austin, Texas. (The oratory of classical Greece 11)

Edwards, M. J. (2002), "A Note on Isaeus 4.7", *Mnemosyne* 55, 87 – 88.

Edwards, M. J. (1995), Greek orators Ⅳ: Andocides, Warminster.

Edwards, M. J. & S. Usher (1985), Greek orators I: Antiphon and Lysias, Warminster.

Effenterre, H. V (2003), "Un mort parle toujours", in Symposion 1999, 21 – 26.

Effenterre, H. V (2000), "Sanction contre un juge", in Timai Triantaphyllopoulou, 69 – 76.

Effenterre, H. V (1993), "Modernité du droit grec: un patrimoine", in Cahiers Glotz 4, 1 – 11.

Effenterre, H. V (1991), "Criminal Law in Archaic Crete", in Symposion 1990, 83 – 6.

Effenterre, H. V (1989), "Les degrés de la liberté dans les cités grecques", Recueils de la société Jean Bodin 46 (L'individu face au pouvoir) I, 97 – 104.

Effenterre, H. V (1989), "Droit et prédroit en Grèce depuis le dechiffrement du Linéaire B", in Symposion 1985, 3 – 7.

Effenterre, H. V (1989), "Préliminaires épigraphiques aux études d'histoire du droit grec", in Symposion 1982, 1 – 8. (= Cretica selecta, 819 – 826)

Effenterre, H. V (1985), "Damos, damioi et damiorgoi", in Pepragmena tou 9ou Diethnous Kretologikou Synedriou, I, 385 – 396, Herakleio.

Effenterre, H. V (1984), "Problèmes d'épigraphie juridique grecque", RHDFE 62, 47 – 52.

Effenterre, H. V(1982), "Les epiballontes", in Studi Biscardi 3, 459 – 62.

Effenterre, H. V(1982), "Le droit et la langue. A propos du code de Gortyne", in Symposion 1979, 113 – 128. (= Epeteris Panteiou Panepistemiou 1981, 115 – 128 and Cretica selecta, 663 – 676)

Effenterre, H. V (1982), "Andichazo dans le traité Oiantheion-Chaleion", in Symposion 1977, 85 – 97.

Effenterre, H. V(1980), "La fondation de Paestum", PdP 35, 161 – 175.

Effenterre, H. V(1974), "Thémistodikè", in Mélanges Seston, 481 – 488.

Effenterre, H. V(1973), "Le contrat de travail du scribe Spensithios", BCH 97, 31 – 46. (= Cretica selecta, 619 – 634)

Effenterre, H. V, & M. (2001), "Le vocabulaire de l'appartenance dans la loi de Gortyne", in Symposion 1997, 21 – 31.

Effenterre, H. V, & M. (2000), "La codification gortynienne, mythe ou realité?", in La codification, 175 – 184.

Effenterre, H. V, & M. (1997), "Du nouveau sur le Code de Gortyne", in Symposion 1995, 11 – 15.

Effenterre, H. V, & M. (1994), "Écrire sur les murs", in Rechtskodifizierung, 87 – 96.

Effenterre, H. V, & M. (1993), "Arbitrages homériques", in Symposion 1993, 3 – 10.

Effenterre, H. V, & M. (1990), "Le contrôle des etrangers dans la cité grecque", in Symposion 1988, 251 – 259.

Effenterre, H. V, & M. (1988), "L'acte de fraternisation de Nakone", MEFRA 100, 687 – 700.

Effenterre, H. V, & M. (1985), "Nouvelles lois archaiques de Lyttos", BCH 109, 157 – 188. (= Cretica selecta, 725 – 756) Ehrenberg, V. (1943), "An early source of polis-constitution", CQ 37, 14 – 18.

Eichhoff, K. (1879), Über die Blutrache bei den Griechen, Duisburg.

Eidinow, E. (2011), "Sex, Religion, and the Law", in Golden, M. & P. Toohey (eds), A Cultural History of Sexuality. I. A Cultural History of Sexuality in the Classical World, 91 – 101, New York.

Eidinow, E. (2010), "Patterns of Persecution: 'Witchcraft' Trials in Classical

Athens", *P &P* 208,9 - 35.

Eilers, C. (2008), "Forgery, Dishonesty and Incompetence in Josephus' Acta: The Decrees of Athens (AJ 14,149 - 155)", *ZPE* 166,211 - 217.

Ekatomati, G. (2009), "Contrats d'entreprise dans le milieu médical et responsabilité contractuelle", RIDA 56, 13 - 26.

El Khouly, H. (2011), "The Spartan Citizen According to Plato's Laws", in Moutsopoulos, E. & M. Protopappas - Marnelli (eds), The Notion of Citizenship in Greek Philosophy (Proceedings of the 2nd international conference of philosophy, Alexandria, 4 - 6 March 2010), 92 - 99, Athens.

Elden, S. (2003), "Another Sense of Demos: Kleisthenes and the Greek Division of the Polis", Democratization 10, 135 - 156.

Engen, D. T. (2005), "'Ancient Greenbacks': Athenian Owls, the Law of Nikophon, and the Greek Economy", *Historia* 54,359 - 381.

Engle, E. (2008), "Aristotle, Law and Justice: The Tragic Hero", *Northern Kentucky Law Review* 35, 1 - 18.

Epstein, S. (2011), "Direct Democracy and Minority Rule: The Athenian Assembly in its Relation to the Demos", in Herman, G. (ed), Stability and Crisis in the Athenian Democracy, 87 - 102, Stuttgart. (Historia Einzelschriften 220)

Epstein, S. (2010), "Attic Public Construction: Who were the Builders?", *AncSoc* 40, 1 - 14.

Errington, R. M. (1978), "The Nature of the Macedonian State under the Monarchy", *Chiron* 8, 77 - 133.

van den Es, A. H. G. P. (1864), De iure familiarum apud Athenienses libros tres, Leyden.

Evjen, H. D. (1970), "Apagoge and Athenian Homicide Procedures", *TR* 38, 403 - 415.

Evjen, H. D. (1962), An Institutional Study of the Athenian Law of Homicide During the Fourth Century B. C., diss. University of Wisconsin.

F

Fabiani, R. (2010), "Magistrates and Phylai in Late Classical and Early Hellenistic Iasos", in van Bremen, R. & J.-M. Carbon (eds), Hellenistic Karia

(Proceedings of the first international conference on Hellenistic Karia, Oxford 29 June – 2 July 2006), 467 – 482, Bordeaux.

Fantham, E. (1975), "Sex, Status and Survival in Hellenistic Athens: A Study of Women in New Comedy", *Phoenix* 26, 44 – 74.

Faraguna, M. (2012), "Diritto, economia, società: riflessioni su eranos tra età omerica e mondo ellenistico", in Legras, B. (ed.) Transferts culturels et droits dans le monde grec et hellénistique (Actes du colloque international, Reims, 14 – 17 mai 2008), 129 – 154, Paris.

Faraguna, M. (2011), "Legislazione e scrittura nella Grecia arcaica e classica", ZPE 177, 1 – 20.

Faraguna, M. (2010), "Tassazione diretta e tassazione indiretta: la legge granaria ateniese del 374/3 a. C.", in Cataudella, M. R., Greco, A. & G. Mariotta (eds), Strumenti e techniche della riscossione die tributi nel mondo antico (Atti del convegno nazionale, Firenze 6 – 7 dicembre 2007), 13 – 34, Padova.

Faraguna, M. (2010), "Il sistema degli appalti pubblici ad Atene nel IV sec. a. C. e la legge di Agirrio", in Magnetto, A., Erdas, D. & Chr. Carusi (eds), Nuove ricerche sulla legge granaria ateniese del 374/3 a. C., 129 – 48, Pisa.

Faraguna, M. (2009), "Oralità e scrittura nella prassi giudiziaria ateniese tra V e IV sec. a. C.", in Symposion 2007, 63 – 82.

Faraguna, M. (2008), "Calcolo economico, archivi finanziari e credito nel mondo greco tra VI e IV sec. a. C.", in Verboven, K., Vandorpe, K. & V. Chankowski (eds), Pistoi dia ten technen. Bankers, loans and archives in the ancient world. Studies in honour of R. Bogaert, 33 – 58, Leuven. (Studia Hellenistica 44)

Faraguna, M. (2007), "Tra oralità e scrittura: diritto e forme della comunicazione dai poemi omerici a Teofrasto", Etica e politica/Ethics and Politics 9, 75 – 111. (= Dike 9 (2006) 65 – 91)

Faraguna, M. (2006), "Gli archivi e la polis (problemi nuovi e vecchi alla luce di alcuni recenti documenti)", in La circulation de l'information dans les états antiques (Actes de la table ronde La circulation de l'information dans structures de pouvoirs dans l'antiquité Bordeaux 19 – 20 janvier 2002), 53ff., Bordeaux.

Faraguna, M. (2006), "Alcibiade, Cratero e gli archivi giudiziari ad Atene", in Faraguna, M. & V. Vedaldi Iasbez (eds), Dynasthai didaskein: studi in onore di F.

Cassola per il suo ottantessimo compleanno, 197 - 207, Trieste.

Faraguna, M. (2006), "La città di Atene e l'amministrazione delle miniere del Laurion", in Symposion 2003, 141 - 166.

Faraguna, M. (2005), "La figura dell'aisymnetes tra realtà storica e teoria politica", in Symposion 2001, 321 - 338.

Faraguna, M. (2005), "Scrittura e amministrazione nella città greche: gli archivi pubblici", QUCC 80, 61 - 86.

Faraguna, M. (2005), "Terra pubblica e vendite di immobili confiscati a Chio nel V sec. a. C.: per un'interpretazione di SGDI 5653 (DGE3 688)", in Crevatin, F. (ed), Scrivere leggere interpretare. Studi di antichità in onore di S. Daris, Trieste. (= http://www. sslmit. units. it/Crevatin/Documenti/Daris/Faraguna. pdf, Dike 8 (2005) 89 - 100)

Faraguna, M. (2003), "Vendite di immobili e registrazione pubblica nelle città greche", in Symposion 1999, 97 - 122.

Faraguna, M. (2002), "Commercio, scriturra, pratiche giuridiche: recenti studi sull'emporia greca", Dike 5, 109 - 135.

Faraguna, M. (2000), "A proposito degli archivi nel mondo greco", Chiron 30, 65 - 115.

Faraguna, M. (1999), "Intorno alla nuova legge ateniese sulla tassazione del grano", Dike 2, 63 - 97.

Faraguna, M. (1999), "Aspetti della schiavitù domestica femminile in Attica tra oratoria ed epigrafia", in Femmes-esclaves, 57 - 79.

Faraguna, M. (1998), "Un nuovo studio sulle rationes centesimarum", Dike 1, 171 - 180.

Faraguna, M. (1997), "Registrazioni catastali nel mondo greco: il caso di Atene", Athenaeum 85, 7 - 33.

Faraguna, M. (1996), "Aspetti de la schiavitu domestica femminile in Attica tra oratoria edepigrafia", in Donne schiave: modelli d'interpretazione anthropologica, economica e giuridica (Atti del XXI Colloquio Internazionale GIREA), 1 - 23; Napoli. Faraone, Chr. A. (2002), "Curses and social control in the lawcourts of classical Athens", in Demokratie, Recht und soziale Kontrolle, 77 - 92. (= Dike 2 (1999) 99 - 122)

Faraone, Chr. A. (1989), "An Accusation of Magic in Classical Athens (Ar. Wasps 946 - 948)", *TAPhA* 109, 149 - 160.

Faraone, Chr. A. (1985), "Aeschylus (Eum. 306) and Attic Judicial Curse Tablets", *JHS* 105, 150 - 154.

Farenga, V. (2006), Citizen and Self in Ancient Greece: Individuals Performing Justice and the Law, Cambridge.

Ferguson, R. A. (1996), "Untold Stories in the Law", in Brooks, P. & P. Gewirtz (eds), *Law's Stories: Narrative and Rhetoric in the Law*, 84 - 98, New Haven.

Ferguson, W. S. (1949), "Orgeonika", in Commemorative Studies in Honor of Theodore Leslie Shear, 130 - 163, Princeton. (Hesperia Suppl. 8)

Ferguson, W. S. (1944), "The Attic Orgeones", *HThR* 37, 61 - 140.

Ferguson, W. S. (1936), "The Athenian Lawcode and Old Attic Trittyes", in Classical Studies Presented to E. Capps, 144 - 158, Princeton.

Ferguson, W. S. (1911), "The Laws of Demetrius of Phalerum and their Guardians", Klio 11, 265 - 276.

Ferguson, W. S. (1910), "The Athenian Phratries", *CPh* 5, 257 - 284.

Ferguson, W. S. (1907 - 1909), "Researches in Athenian and Delian Documents", Klio 7, 213 - 240; 8, 338 - 355; 9, 304 - 340.

Fernάndez Nieto, F. J. (2006), "Titularidad y cesión de los derechos de la pesca marítima en la antigua Grecia", in Symposion 2003, 207 - 232.

Fernandez Nieto, F. J. (2003), "El derecho privado sobre el botín de guerra en el άmbito dorio (s. V - II a. C.)", in Symposion 1999, 355 - 370.

Fernandez Nieto, F. J. (1997), "Los reglamentos militares griegos y la justicia castrense en epoca hellenistica", in Symposion 1995, 221 - 244.

Fernandez Nieto, F. J. (1990), "La competencia penal de los estrategos", in Symposion 1988, 111 - 121.

Fernandez Nieto, F. J. (1989), "Die Freilassung von Sklaven in homerischer Zeit", in Symposion 1982, 21 - 30.

Fernandez Nieto, F. J. (1982), "Die Abänderungsklausel in den griechischen Staatsverträgen der klassischen Zeit", in Symposion 1979, 273 - 286. Fernάndez Nieto, F. J. (2006), "Titularidad y cesión de los derechos de la pesca marítima en la antigua Grecia", in Symposion 2003, 207 - 232.

Ferrante, D. (1972), Antifonte. Peri tou Heroidou phonou, Napoli.

Ferril, A. (1978), "Herodotus on Tyranny", *Historia* 27, 385 - 398.

Figueira, T. J. (2006), "Reconsidering the Athenian coinage decree", Annali dell'Istituto Italiano di Numismatica 52, 9 - 44.

Figueira, T. J. (2004), "The Nature of the Spartan kleros", in Figueira, Th. J. (ed), Spartan society, 47 - 76, Swansea.

Figueira, T. J. (2003), "Xenelasia and Social Control in Classical Sparta", *CQ* 53, 44 - 74.

Figueira, T. J. (1998), The Power of Money: Coinage and Politics in the Athenian empire, Philadelphia.

Figueira, T. J. (1987), "Residential Restrictions on the Athenian Ostracized", *GRBS* 28, 281 - 305.

Figueira, T. J. (1986), "Sitopolai and Sitophylakes in Lysias' 'Against the Graindealers': Governmental Intervention in the Athenian Economy", *Phoenix* 40, 149 - 171.

Filippi, F. (2009), "The Conception of Citizenship in Greek Antiquity as Civic Philia Among Equals", in *The Notion of Citizenship*, 203 - 221.

Filomusi-Guelfi, Fr. (1873), La dottrina dello stato nell'antichità Greca nei suoi rapporti con l'etica, Naples.

Fingarette, A. (1971), "A New Look at the Wall of Nikomakhos", *Hesperia* 40, 330 - 355.

Finkelberg, M. (2008), "Plato, Apology 28d 6 - 29a 1 and the ephebic oath", SCI 27, 9 - 15.

Finley, M. I. (1980), Ancient Slavery and Modern Ideology, London.

Finley, M. I. (1973), The Ancient Economy, Berkely.

Finley, M. I. (1968), "The Alienability of Land in Ancient Greece", *Eirene* 7, 25 - 32. (= Annales ESC 25(1970)1271 - 1277 and Finley, The use, 153 - 160)

Finley, M. I. (1966), "The Problem of the Unity of Greek Law", in La storia del diritto nel quadro delle scienze storiche (Atti del primo Congresso Internazionale della Società Italiana di Storia del Diritto, Rome, December 1963), 129 - 142, Firenze. (= Finley, The use, 134 - 152)

Finley, M. I. (1965), "La servitude pour dettes", *RHDFE* 43, 159 - 184.

Finley, M. I. (1960), "The Servile Statuses of Ancient Greece", *RIDA* 7, 165 - 189. (= Finley, Economy, 133 - 149)

Finley, M. I. (1957), "Homer and Mycenae: Property and Tenure", *Historia* 6, 133 - 159.

Finley, M. I. (1954), "Marriage, Sale and Gift in the Homeric World", *Seminar* 12, 121 - 33. (= RIDA 2(1955) 167 - 194 and Finley, Economy, 233 - 248)

Finley, M. I. (1953), "Multiple Charges of Real Property in Athenian Law. New Evidence from an Agora Inscription", in Studi Arangio-Ruiz 3, 473 - 491. (= "Mehrfache Belastung von Grundstückseigentum im attischen Recht. Neues Beweismaterial aus einer auf der Agora gefundenen Inschrift" in Zur griechischen Rechtsgeschichte, 534 - 558)

Finley, M. I. (1953), "Land, Debt and the Man of Property in Classical Athens", *Political Science Quarterly Review* 68, 149 - 168. (= Finley, Economy, 62 - 76)

Finley, M. I. (1952), Studies in Land and Credit in Ancient Athens. 500 - 200 B. C. The horoi inscriptions, New Brunswick, Princeton.

Finley, M. I. (1951), "Some Problems of Greek Law: A Consideration of Pringsheim on Sale", *Seminar* 9, 72 - 91.

Finley, M. I. (1935), "Emporos, Naukleros and Kapelos", *CPh* 30, 320 - 336.

Finzi, C. (1984), "Politica e diritto nel pensiero ellenico", in Negri, A. (ed), Grande antologia filosofica 32: Aggiornamento bibliografico, 355 - 364, Milano.

Fireman, P. (1957), Justice in Plato's Republic, New York.

Fischer, J. (2012), "Behinderung und Gesellschaft im klassischen Athen. Bemerkungen zur 24. Rede des Lysias", in Breitwieser, R. (ed), Behinderungen und Beeinträchtigungen (Disability and impairment in antiquity), 41 - 45, Oxford.

Fischer, R. (1881), Quaestionum de praetoribus atticis saeculi quinti et quarti a Ch. n. specimen, Königsberg.

Fisher, N. R. E. (2006), "Citizens, Foreigners and Slaves in Greek Society", in Kinzl, K. H. (ed), *A Companion to the Classical Greek World*, 327 - 349, Oxford.

Fisher, N. R. E. (2005), "Body-abuse: The Rhetoric of Hybris in Aeschines' Against Timarchos", in La violence, 67 - 89.

Fisher, N. R. E. (2001), Aeschines: Against Timarchos, Oxford.

Fisher,N. R. E. (2000),"Hybris,revenge and stasis in the Greek city-states",in van Wees,H. (ed),War and violence in ancient Greece,83 – 123,London.

Fisher,N. R. E. (1999), "Violence, Masculinity and the Law in Classical Athens",in Foxhall,L. & J. Salmon(eds),When Men were Men:Masculinity,Power and Identity in classical Antiquity,68 – 97,London.

Fisher,N. R. E. (1999), "Workshops of Villains: Was there much Organised Crime in Classical Athens?", in Hopwood, K. (ed), Organised Crime in Antiquity, 53 – 96, London.

Fisher,N. R. E. (1992),Hybris:A study in the Values of Honour and Shame in Ancient Greece,Warminster.

Fisher, N. R. E. (1989), "Drink, Hybris and the Promotion of Harmony in Sparta", in Powell, A. (ed), Classical Sparta. The Techniques behind her success, 26 – 50, London.

Fisher,N. R. E. (1987), "La legge sulla hybris ad Atene", AION(archeol)9, 99 – 115. (= "The law of hybris in Athens" in Nomos,123 – 138)

Fisher,N. R. E. (1976 – 1979),"Hybris and Dishonour",*G &R* 23,177 – 93 & 26,32 – 47.

Fitzgerald, J. T. (2006), "Perjury in Ancient Religion and Modern Law: A Comparative Analysis of Perjury in Homer and United States Law",in Foropoulos,J. (ed), The New Testament and Early Christian literature in Greco-Roman context. Studies in honor of D. E. Aune, 183 – 202, Leiden. (Supplements to Novum Testamentum 122)

Fleck,R. K. & F. A. Hanssen(2009),"'Rulers Ruled by Women' an Economic Analysis of the Rise and fall of Women's Rights in Ancient Sparta", *Economics of Governance* 10,221 – 245.

Fleck,R. K. & F. A. Hannsen(2006),"The Origins of Democracy:A Model with Application to Ancient Greece",*Journal of Law & Economics* 49,115 – 146.

Fleischanderl,Br. (1888),Die spartanische Verfassung bei Xenophon,Leipzig.

Fletcher,J. (2012),Performing oaths in classical Greek drama,Cambridge.

Fletcher,J. (2012),"Law and spectacle in Euripides' Hecuba", in Rosenbloom, D. & J. Davidson(eds), Greek drama IV. Texts, contexts, performance, 225 – 243, Oxford.

Fletcher, J. (2008), "Citing the Law in Sophocles' Antigone", *Mosaic* 41, 66 - 87.

Fletcher, J. (2008), "The trickster's oath in the Homeric Hymn to Hermes", AJPh 129, 23 - 46.

Fletcher, J. (2007), "Horkos in the Oresteia", in *Horkos*, 102 - 112.

Fletcher, J. (2005), "Perjury and the Perversion of Language in Euripides' Cyclops", in Harrison, G. W. M. (ed.) Satyr Drama: Tragedy at Play, 53 - 66, Swansea.

Fletcher, J. (2003), "Women and Oaths in Euripides", *Theatre Journal* 55, 29 - 44.

Floros, A. (1968), "To attikon kleronomikon dikaion kata tous logous tou Isaiou", Platon 39 - 40, 173 - 193.

Floyd, E. D. (1990), "The sources of Greek histor, 'judge, witness'", Glotta 68, 157 - 166.

Förster, P. E. P. (1847), De asylis Graecorum, Breslau.

Förster, R. (1875), "Antiquarisches. Kleroun und pleroun ta dikasteria", RhM 30, 284 - 988.

Forbes, C. A. (1953), Neoi. A Contribution to the Study of Greek Associations, Middletown, Conn.

Forbes, P. B. R. (1948), "Law and Politics in the Oresteia", *CR* 62, 99 - 104.

Ford, A. (1999), "Reading Homer from the Rostrum: Poems and Laws in Aeschines' Against Timarchus", in Goldhill, S. & R. Osborne (eds), Performance culture and Athenian democracy, 231 - 256, Cambridge.

Fornara, C. W. (1979), "The Phaselis Decree", *CQ* 29, 49 - 52.

Fornara, C. W. (1971), The Athenian Board of Generals from 501 to 404, Wiesbaden. (HistoriaEinzelschrift 16)

Fornara, C. W. (1970), "The Diapsephismos of Ath. Pol. 13. 5", *CPh* 65, 243 - 246.

Forrest, W. G. (1967), "Legislation in Sparta", *Phoenix* 21, 11 - 19.

Forrest, W. G. (1963), "The Date of the Lykourgan Reforms in Sparta", *Phoenix* 17, 157 - 179.

Forsdyke, S. (2009), "The Uses and Abuses of Tyranny", in *Greek and Roman*

Political Thought, 231 – 246.

Forsdyke, S. (2008), "Street Theater and Popular Justice in Ancient Greece", *P & P* 201, 3 – 50.

Forsdyke, S. (2005), Exile, Ostracism, and Democracy: The Politics of Expulsion in Ancient Greece, Princeton.

Forsdyke, S. (2000), "Exile, Ostracism, and Athenian Democracy", *ClAnt* 19, 232 – 263.

Forster, E. S. (1943), "Guilty or not Guilty? Four Athenian Trials", *G & R* 12, 21 – 27.

Fortenbaugh, W. W. (1993), "Theophrastus on Law, Virtue and the Particular Situation", in *Nomodeiktes*, 447 – 455.

Fortenbaugh, W. W. (1976), "Aristotle on Prior and Posterior, Correct and Mistaken Constitutions", *TAPhA* 106, 125 – 137.

Foucart, P. (1922), "Un décret athénien relatif aux combattants de Phylé", AIB 42, 323 – 355.

Foucart, P. (1902), "L'accusation contre Phryné", Revue 26, 216 – 218.

Foucart, P. (1902), "Une loi athénienne du iv siècle", JS, 177 – 193; 233 – 245.

Foucart, P. (1898), "Traité d'alliance de l'année 362", RA 33, 313 – 327.

Foucart, P. (1889), "Décret athénien de l'année 352, trouvé á Éleusis", BCH 13, 433 – 467.

Foucart, P. (1882), "L'arsenal de Philon. Contrat pour la construction de la sceuothèque à Zea", BCH 6, 540 – 555.

Foucart, P. (1879), "Consécration de deux esclaves à Poseidon", BCH 3, 96 – 99.

Foucart, P. (1878), "Mémoire sur les colonies athéniennes au v. et au iv. siècles", AIBS 9, 323 – 413.

Foucart, P. (1877), "Sur l'authenticité de la loi d'Évégoros", Revue 1, 168 – 181.

Foucart, P. (1874), "Mémoire sur un décret inédit de la ligue arcadienne en l'honneur de l'Athenien Phylarchos", AIBS 8, 93 – 119.

Foucart, P. (1873), De collegiis scenicorum artificum apud Graecos, diss. Paris.

Foucart, P. (1873), Des associations religieuses chez les Grecs. Thiases, eranes, orgeons, Paris.

Foucart, P. (1867), Mémoire sur l'affranchissement des esclaves, par forme de vente à divinité, d'après les inscriptions de Delphes, Paris. Foxhall, L. (1998), "The law and the lady: Women and legal proceedings in classical Athens", in Law in its political setting, 133 – 152.

Foxhall, L. (1990), "The Dependant Tenant: Land Leasing and Labour in Italy and Greece", *JRS* 80, 97 – 114.

Foxhall, L. (1989), "Household, Gender, and Property in Classical Athens", *CQ* 39, 22 – 44.

Francken, C. M. (1865), Commentationes Lysiacae, Utrecht.

Francotte, H. (1913), "Études sur Démosthène", MB 17, 69 – 90; 237 – 288.

Francotte, H. (1907), "Étude sur le système des impôts dans les citès et les royaumes grecs. Phoros, eisphora, syntaxis", MB 11, 53 – 81.

Francotte, H. (1906), "Le conseil et l'assemblée générale chez les Achéens", MB 10, 4 – 20.

Francotte, H. (1906), "L'organisation des cités à Rhodes et en Carie", MB 10, 127 – 159.

Francotte, H. (1904), "Loi et décret dans le droit public des Grecs", MB 8, 329 – 338. (= Francotte, Mélanges, 3 – 40)

Francotte, H. (1903), "De la condition des étrangers dans les cités grecques (Proxenes, évergètes, métèques, isoteles, étrangers résidents, epidames)", MB 7, 350 – 388. (= Francotte, Mélanges, 169 – 220)

Francotte, H. (1903), L'administration financière des cités grecques, Bruxelles. (MAB 63)

Francotte, H. (1901), "Formation des villes, des états, des confédérations et des ligues dans la Grèce ancienne", Bulletin de l'Académie royale des sciences, des lettres, et des beaux-arts de Belgique (Classe des lettres et des sciences morales et politiques), 949 – 1012.

Francotte, H. (1900 – 1901), L'industrie dans la Grèce ancienne, 2 vols, Bruxelles. (Bibliothèque de la Faculté de Philosophie et Lettres de l'Université de Liège 7 – 8)

Francotte, H. (1899 – 1900), "De la législation athénienne sur les distinctions honorifiques et spécialement des décrets des clérouchies athéniennes relatifs à cet objet" MB 3,246 - 281; 4,55 - 75; 105 - 123(= Francotte, Mélanges, 73 - 162)

Francotte, H. (1895), L'antidosis en droit athénien, Bruxelles. (MAB 51)

Francotte, H. (1892), L'organisation de la cité athénienne et la réforme de Clisthènes, Bruxelles. (MAB 48)

Francotte, H., Roersch, A. & J. Sencie (1900), "Bulletin d'épigraphie et d'institutions grecques, 1897 - 98", MB 4,126 - 146.

Francotte, H., Roersch, A. & J. Sencie (1899), "Bulletin d'épigraphie et d'institutions grecques, 1897 - 1998", MB 3,166 - 176; 304 - 326Frank, T. (1918 - 1919) "Representative government in the ancient polities" CJ 14,533 - 549.

Franke, Fr. (1860), "Lectiones Aeschineae", Philologus 1,427 - 476.

Franklin, S. B. (1901), "Public Appropriations for Individual Offerings and Sacrifices in Greece", *TAPhA* 32,72 - 82.

Fraser, P. M. (1995), "Citizen, Demesmen and Metics in Athens and Elsewhere", in Hansen, Sources, 64 - 90.

Fraser, P. M. (1972), "Notes on Two Rhodian Institutions: I. The Rhodian Public Bank, II. The Rhodian Jury System", *BSA* 67,113 - 124.

Fraser, P. M. (1952), "Alexander and the Rhodian Constitution", *PdP* 7,192 - 206.

Frede, D. (2005), "Citizenship in Aristotle's Politics", in Kraut, R. & St. Skulery (eds), Aristotle's Politics: Critical Essays, 167 - 184, Lanham, MD.

Freeman, K. (1952), "The Mystery of the Choreutes", in White, M. E. (ed), Studies in Honour of G. Norwood, 85 - 94, Toronto.

Freeman, K. (1946), The Murder of Herodes and Other Trials from the Athenian Law Courts, London.

French, A. (1994), "Pericles' Citizenship Law", *AHB* 8,71 - 75.

French, A. (1963), "Land Tenure and the Solon Problem", *Historia* 12,242 - 247.

Frisch, H. (1949), Might and Right in Antiquity. "Dike" from Homer to the Persian Wars, Copenhagen.

Frisch, H. (1942), The Constitution of the Athenians, Copenhagen.

Frisone, F. (2011), "Construction of Consensus. Norms and Change in Greek

Funerary Rituals", in Chaniotis, A. (ed), Ritual Dynamics in the Ancient Mediterranean: Agency, Emotion, Gender, Reception, 179 – 201, Stuttgart.

Frisone, F. (2000), Leggi e regolamenti funerari nel mondo Greco. I. Le fonti epigrafiche, Lecce.

Frisone, F. (1995), "Una legislazione funeraria a Gortina?", StAnt 8, 55 – 68.

Frisone, F. (1994), "Tra linguaggio rituale e vita materiale: le leggi sul rituale funerario nel mondo greco", in Historie, 183 – 210.

von Fritz, K. (1977), "Nochmals das solonische Gesetz gegen Neutralität im Bürgerzwist", Historia 26, 245 – 247.

von Fritz, K. (1954), "The Composition of Aristotele's Constitution of Athens and the So-called Draconian Constitution", *CPh* 49, 73 – 93. (= Fritz, Schriften, 71 – 98)

von Fritz, K. (1954), The Theory of the Mixed Constitution in Antiquity, New York.

von Fritz, K. (1943), "Once More the Hektemoroi", *AJPh* 64, 24 – 43. (= Fritz, Schriften, 117 – 134)

von Fritz, K. (1940), "The Meaning of Hektemoros", *AJPh* 61, 54 – 61. (= Fritz, Schriften, 110 – 116)

Frost, F. (2002), "Solon Pornoboskos and Aphrodite Pandemos", *Syllecta Classica* 13, 34 – 46.

Frost, M. (2005), Introduction to Classical Legal Rhetoric: A Lost Heritage, Aldershot.

Fuchs, E. (1998), "Vorteil und Recht in den Reden bei Thukydides", Lexis 16, 87 – 112.

Fuhr, K. (1877), Animadversiones in Oratores Atticos, Bonn.

Funke, P. (2011), "Drakon, Solon und der albanische Kanun. Einige Überlegungen zu einem Versuch in vergleichender Rechtsgeschichte", in Kämmerer, Th. R. (ed), Identities and societies in the ancient East-Mediterranean regions. Comparative approaches, 59 – 72, Münster.

Furukawa, K. (1983), "A Legal Relationship between Athens and the Allies in the Athenian Empire: A Remark on Jurisdiction", Rekishi Hyoron (*Historical Sciences Review*) 400, 36 – 59.

Furukawa, K. (1981), "Athenian Citizens' Estates and Slavery in the Speeches of Isaeus", *Dokkyo University Bulletin of Liberal Arts* 16, 25 – 56.

Furuyama, Y. (2000), "State Control over the Wine-trade of Thasos in the 5th Century B. C.", Seiyo Kotengaku Kenkyu (*Journal of Classical Studies*) 48, 31 – 41.

Fusai, S. (2006), Il processo omerico. Dall'histōr omerico all'historiē erodotea, Padova.

G

Gabrielsen, V. (1994), Financing the Athenian Fleet: Public Taxation and Social Relations, Baltimore.

Gabrielsen, V. (1981), Remuneration of State Officials in Fourth-century BC Athens, Odense. (Odense university classical studies 11)

Gagarin, M. (2012), "Women and law in Grotyn", Index 40, 57 – 67.

Gagarin, M. (2012), "The laws of Crete" in Legras, B. (ed), Transferts culturels et droits dans le monde grec et hellénistique (Actes du colloque international, Reims, 14 – 17 mai 2008), 17 – 30, Paris.

Gagarin, M. (2011), "Writing Sacred Laws in Archaic and Classical Crete", in Lardinois, A. P. M. H., Blok, J. H. & M. G. M. van der Poel (eds), Sacred words: Orality, literacy and religion, 113 – 42, Leiden. (Orality and literacy in the ancient world 8) (Mnemosyne Suppl. 332)

Gagarin, M. (2010), "Legal procedure in Gortyn", in Thür, G. (ed), Symposion 2009. Vorträge zur griechischen und hellenistischen Rechtsgeschichte (Seggau, 25. – 30. August 2009), 127 – 146, Wien. (with a response by G. Thür)

Gagarin, M. (2010), "Serfs and slaves at Gortyn", ZRG 127, 14 – 31.

Gagarin, M. (2008), "Women and Property at Gortyn", Dike 11, 8 – 26.

Gagarin, M. (2008), Writing Greek Law, Cambridge.

Gagarin, M. (2007), "Rational Argument in Early Athenian Oratory", in Powell, J. (ed), Logos. Rational Argument in Classical Rhetoric, 9 – 18, London. (BICS Suppl. 96)

Gagarin, M. (2007), "Litigants' Oaths in Athenian Law", in *Horkos*, 39 – 47.

Gagarin, M. (2007), "From Oral Law to Written Laws: Dracon's Law and its Homeric Roots", in Symposion 2005, 1 – 18.

Gagarin, M. (2006), "Inscribing Laws in Greece and the Near East", in Symposion 2003, 9 - 20.

Gagarin, M. (2006), "Legal Procedure in Solon's Laws", in Solon of Athens, 261 - 275.

Gagarin, M. (2005), "Early Greek Law", in The Cambridge Companion, 82 - 95.

Gagarin, M. (2005), "The Unity of Greek Law", in The Cambridge Companion, 29 - 40.

Gagarin, M. (2005), "La violence dans les plaidoyers attiques", in La violence, 365 - 376.

Gagarin, M. (2005), "Le loi de Dracon sur l'homicide: pourquoi était-elle écrite?", in Le législateur et la loi, 119 - 126.

Gagarin, M. (2004), "Writing Athenian Law", in *Law, Rhetoric, and Comedy*, 15 - 32.

Gagarin, M. (2004), "The Rule of Law in Gortyn", in *The Law and the Courts*, 173 - 184.

Gagarin, M. (2003), "Who were the Kakourgoi? Career Criminals in Athenian Law", in Symposion 1999, 183 - 192.

Gagarin, M. (2003), "Letters of the Law: Written Texts in Archaic Greek Law", in Yunis, H. (ed), Written texts and the rise of literate culture in ancient Greece, 59 - 77, Cambridge.

Gagarin, M. (2003), "Telling Stories in Athenian Law", *TAPhA* 133, 197 - 207.

Gagarin, M. (2002), "Socrates and Antiphon: Intellectuals on Trial in Classical Athens", in Mélanges Dimakis, 397 - 404.

Gagarin, M. (2002), Antiphon the Athenian. Oratory, Law, and Justice in the Age of the Sophists, Austin, Texas.

Gagarin, M. (2001), "Ecriture et oralité en droit grec", RHDFE 79, 447 - 462.

Gagarin, M. (2001), "The Gortyn Code and Greek Legal Procedure", in Symposion 1997, 41 - 52.

Gagarin, M. (2001), "Women's Voices in Attic Oratory", in Lardinois, A. & L. McClure (eds), Making Silence Speak: Women's Voices in Greek Literature and Society, 161 - 176, Princeton.

Gagarin, M. (2000), "The Legislation of Demetrius of Phalerum and the Transformation of Athenian Law", in Fortenbaugh, W. W. & E. Schütrumpf (eds), Demetrius of Phalerum. Text, Translation and Discussion, 347 - 365, New Brunswick. (Rutgers University Studies in Classical Humanities 9)

Gagarin, M. (2000), "Le code de Platon et le droit grec", in La codification, 215 - 227.

Gagarin, M. (2000), "The Basileus in Athenian Homicide Law", in *Polis and Politics*, 569 - 580.

Gagarin, M. (1999), "Rhetorique et anti-rhetorique dans les Lois de Gortyne", in Dobias, C. (ed), Des dialectes grecs aux Lois de Gortyne, 65 - 74, Nancy. (Etudes anciennes 21)

Gagarin, M. (1999), "The Orality of Greek Oratory", in MacKay, F. A. (ed), Signs of Orality. The Oral Tradition and its Influence in the Greek and Roman World, 163 - 180, Leiden. (Mnemosyne Suppl. 188)

Gagarin, M. (1998), "Women in Athenian Courts", Dike 1, 39 - 52.

Gagarin, M. (1997), Antiphon: The Speeches, Cambridge.

Gagarin, M. (1997), "Oath and Oath-challenges in Greek Law", in Symposion 1995, 125 - 134.

Gagarin, M. (1996), "The Torture of Slaves in Athenian Law", *CPh* 91, 1 - 18. (= "La torture des esclaves dans le droit athénien", in Pierre Carlier, (ed), Le IVe siècle av. J. -C. Approches historiographiques, 273 - 279, Paris 1996)

Gagarin, M. (1995), "The First Law of the Gortyn Code Revisited", *GRBS* 36, 7 - 15.

Gagarin, M. (1994), "The Economic Status of Women in the Gortyn Code: Retroactivity and Change", in Symposion 1993, 61 - 72.

Gagarin, M. (1992), "The Poetry of Justice: Hesiod and the Origins of Greek Law", *Ramus* 21, 61 - 78.

Gagarin, M. (1990), "The Nature of Proofs in Antiphon", *CPh* 85, 22 - 32. (= The Attic Orators, 214 - 228)

Gagarin, M. (1990), "Bouleusis in Athenian Homicide Law", in Symposion 1988, 81 - 99. (= Abstracts of American Philological Association 1988, 110)

Gagarin, M. (1989), The Murder of Herodes: A Study of Antiphon 5, New

York.

Gagarin, M. (1989), "The Function of Witnesses at Gortyn", in Symposion 1985, 29 - 55.

Gagarin, M. (1988), "The First Law of the Gortyn Code", *GRBS* 28, 335 - 43.

Gagarin, M. (1986), Early Greek law, Berkeley-London.

Gagarin, M. (1984), "The Testimony of Witnesses in the Gortyn Laws", *GRBS* 25, 345 - 349.

Gagarin, M. (1982), "The Organization of the Gortyn Law-code", *GRBS* 23, 129 - 146.

Gagarin, M. (1981), Drakon and Early Athenian Homicide Law, New Haven.

Gagarin, M. (1981), "The Themosthetai and the Earliest Athenian Tyranny Law", *TAPhA* 111, 71 - 77.

Gagarin, M. (1979), "The Athenian Law Against Hubris", in Bowersock, G. W., Burkert, W. & M. C. J. Putnam (eds), Arktouros. Hellenic Studies Presented to B. M. W. Knox, 229 - 236, Berlin-NewYork.

Gagarin, M. (1979), "The Prosecution of Homicide in Athens", *GRBS* 20, 301 - 323.

Gagarin, M. (1978), "Self-defense in Athenian Homicide Law", *GRBS* 19, 111 - 120.

Gagarin, M. (1978), "The Prohibition of Just and Unjust Homicide in Antiphon's Tetralogies", *GRBS* 19, 291 - 306.

Gagarin, M. (1975), "The Vote of Athena", *AJPh* 96, 121 - 127.

Gagarin, M. (1974), "Hesiod's Dispute with Perses", *TAPhA* 104, 103 - 111.

Gagarin, M. (1974), "Dike in Archaic Greek Thought", *CPh* 69, 186 - 197.

Gagarin, M. (1973), "Dike in the Works and Days", *CPh* 68, 81 - 94.

Gagarin, M. & D. M. MacDowell (1998), Antiphon and Andocides, Austin, Tx. (The oratory of classical Greece 1)

Gagarin, M. & P. Woodruff (2007), "Early Greek legal thought", in Miller jr., F. D., Stein, P. G. & A. Padovani (eds), A Treatise of Legal Philosophy and General Jurisprudence. Vol. 6: A history of the philosophy of law from the ancient Greeks to the Scholastics, 7 - 34, Berlin.

Gallo, Laura (2010), "Il nomos di Agirrio e una testimonianza di Demostene", in

Magnetto, A. , Erdas, D. & Chr. Carusi (eds), Nuove ricerche sulla legge granaria ateniese del 374/3 a. C. ,149 – 57, Pisa.

Gallo, Laura(2009), "L'isomoiria: realtà o mito", in Antonetti, Cl. & St. de Vido (eds) Temi Selinuntini, 129 – 136, Pisa.

Gallo, Laura (2005), " La tassazione della terra nelle poleis greche: alcune considerazioni sul caso di Atene", MedAnt 8, 171 – 184.

Gallo, Laura(2004), " I cittadini ' passive ' nelle poleis greche", in Poleis e Politeiai, 217 – 227.

Gallo, Laura(2000), "Le imposte dirette nelle poleis greche: un istituto tirannico?", MEP 3(4), 17 – 37.

Gallo, Laura(1999), "Solone, gli hektemoroi e gli horoi", AION(arch) 6, 59 – 71.

Gallo, Laura(1996), "Demetreo Falereo e il nomos arghias", AION 3, 107 – 114.

Gallo, Laura(1994), "Un'ipotesi sul nomos arghias", in Historie, 211 – 224.

Gallo, Laura (1993), " Le leggi suntuarie greche e l'alimentazione", AION (arch) 15, 173 – 203.

Gallo, Laura(1984), "La donna greca e la marginalità", QUCC 18, 7 – 51.

Gallo, Laura(1984), " La democrazia ateniese del IVe sec. a. C. e la paga dei funzionari publici", ASNP 14, 395 – 440.

Gallop, D. (1998), " Socrates, Injustice, and the Law: A Response to Plato's Critias", *AncPh* 18, 251 – 265.

Gardikas, K. G. (1971), " Symbole eis to phonikon dikaion ton archaion Ellenon", Platon 23, 132 – 166.

Gardikas, K. G. (1923), Quelques considerations sur le droit penal attique et les oeuvres des tragiques grecs, Bruxelles.

Gardikas, K. G. (1919), " To poinikon kai idia to phonikon dikaion par' Homero", Athena 30, 209 – 342.

Gardikas, K. G. (1919), Platon et Aristote: les pères de notre philosophie pénale. Contribution à l'étude de la philosophie pénale, Salonique.

Gardikas, K. G. (1918), L'homicide chez les anciens Hellènes et notamment chez les Attiques, Geneva.

Gardikas, K. G. (1918), To para tois archaiois Ellesi kai malista tois Attikois poinikon kai idia to phonikon dikaion, Athens.

Gardikas, K. G. (1903), "He gyne en to Elleniko politismo. A. He Ellenis en te Homerike epoche", Athena 14, 387 – 492.

Gardner, P. (1920), "The Financial History of Ancient Chios", *JHS* 40, 160 – 173.

Garland, R. (1989), "The Well-ordered Corpse: An Investigation into the Motives Behind the Greek Funerary Legislation", *BICS* 36, 1 – 15.

Garner, R. (1987), Law and Society in Classical Athens, New York.

Garnsey, P. (2007), Thinking about Property from Antiquity to the Age of Revolution, Cambridge.

Garnsey, P. (1998), "Grain for Athens", in Scheidel, W. (ed), Cities, Peasants and Food in Classical Antiquity, 183 – 200, Cambridge.

Garnsey, P. (1996), Ideas of Slavery from Aristotle to Augustine, Cambridge.

Gaudemet, Jean (1998), "Le monde antique et les droits de l'homme. Quelques observations", in Le monde antique, 175 – 183.

Gaudemet, Jean (1997), Les naissances du droit. Le temps, le pouvoir, et la science au service du droit, Paris.

Gaudemet, Jean (1996), "L'arbitrage dans les conflits territoriaux entre cités dans l'antiquité grèco-romaine. Le principe du status quo et l'uti possidetis", Recueils de la société Jean Bodin 63 (L'assistance dans la resolution des conflits), 37 – 46.

Gaudemet, Jean (1995), "Droits de l'homme' dans l'antiquité", in Collatio Iuris Romani, 105 – 115.

Gaudemet, Jean (1994), "'Antike Rechtsgeschichte' ou 'antike Rechte'?", RHDFE 72, 569 – 574.

Gaudemet, Jean (1970), "L'interpretation des lois et des actes juridiques dans le monde antique", RIDA 17, 235 – 249.

Gaudemet, Jean (1963), Les communautés familiales, Paris.

Gaudemet, Jean (1961), "Le problème de la responsabilité pénale dans l'antiquité", in Léauté, J. (ed.), La responsabilité pénale (Travaux du colloque de philosophie pénale, 12 au 21 janvier 1959), 49 – 80, Paris. (= Studi Betti II, 483 – 508 and in Études de droit romain III. Vie familiale et vie sociale, 457 – 484, Napoli

1979)

Gauthier, Philippe(1993), "Sur l'institution du misthos de l'assemblée d'Athènes (Ath. Pol. 41.3)", in Aristote et Athènes, 231 - 250. (= Rousset, D. (ed.) (2011) Philippe Gauthier. Études d'histoire et d'institutions grecques. Choix des ecrits, 493 - 516, Genève)

Gauthier, Philippe (1988), "Métèques, périèques et paroikoi: bilan et points d'interrogation", in Lonis, R. (ed), L'étranger dans le monde grec, 23 - 46, Nancy. (= Rousset, D. (ed) (2011), Philippe Gauthier. Études d'histoire et d'institutions grecques. Choix des ecrits, 55 - 80, Genève)

Gauthier, Philippe(1986), "L'octroi du droit de cité ɑ Athènes", REG 99, 119 - 133. (= Rousset, D. (ed) (2011), Philippe Gauthier. Études d'histoire et d'institutions grecques. Choix des ecrits, 35 - 54, Genève)

Gauthier, Philippe(1982), "Les saisies licites aux depens des étrangers dans les cités grecques", RHDFE 60, 553 - 576. (= Rousset, D. (ed) (2011), Philippe Gauthier. Études d'histoire et d'institutions grecques. Choix des ecrits, 81 - 112, Genève)

Gauthier, Philippe(1981), "La citoyenneté en Grèce et ɑ Rome: participation et intégration", Ktema 6, 167 - 179. (= Rousset, D. (ed) (2011), Philippe Gauthier. Études d'histoire et d'institutions grecques. Choix des ecrits, 13 - 34, Genève)

Gauthier, Philippe(1981), "De Lysias ɑ Aristote(Ath. Pol. 51.4): le commerce de grain ɑ Athènes et les fonctions des sitophylaques", RHDFE 59, 5 - 28. (= Rousset, D. (ed) (2011), Philippe Gauthier. Études d'histoire et d'institutions grecques. Choix des ecrits, 193 - 220, Genève)

Gauthier, Philippe(1978), "Sur une clause pénale de la loi athénienne relative ɑ la monnaie d'argent", RPh 52, 32 - 36.

Gauthier, Philippe(1977), "Les ventes publiques de bois et de charbon: ɑ propos d'une inscription de Délos", BCH 101, 103 - 108.

Gauthier, Philippe (1974), "'Generosité' romaine et 'avarice' grecque: sur l'octroi du droit de cité", in Mélanges Seston, 207 - 215. (= Rousset, D. (ed) (2011), Philippe Gauthier. Études d'histoire et d'institutions grecques. Choix des ecrits, 3 - 12, Genève)

Gauthier, Philippe (1973), "Notes sur l'étranger et l'hospitalité en Grèce et ɑ

Rome", AncSoc 4, 1 – 23.

Gauthier, Philippe (1972), Symbola. Les étrangers et la justice dans les cités grecques, Nancy. (Annales de l'Est publiées par l'Université de Nancy II 42)

Gauthier, Philippe (1971), "Les xenoi dans les textes athéniens de la seconde moitié du Ve siècle av. J. -C.", REG 84, 44 – 79.

Gauthier, Philippe (1968), "Les tyrans dans le monde grec antique", REG 81, 555 – 561.

Gauthier, Philippe & M. Hatzopoulos (1993), La loi gymnasiarchique de Beroia, Athènes. (Meletemata 16)

Gehrke, H. -J. (2006), "The Figure of Solon in the Athenaion Politeia", in Solon of Athens, 276 – 289.

Gehrke, H. -J. (2000), "Verschriftung und Verschriftlichung sozialer Normen im archaischen und klassischen Griechenland", in La codification, 141 – 159.

Gehrke, H. -J. (1998), "Verschriftung und Verschriftlichung im sozialen und politischen Kontext. Das archaische und klassische Griechenland", in Ehler, Chr. & U. Schäfer (eds), Verschriftung und Verschriftlichung. Aspekte des Medienwechsels in verschiedenen Kulturen und Epochen, 40 – 56, Tübingen.

Gehrke, H. -J. (1997), "Gewalt und Gesetz. Die soziale und politische Ordnung Kretas in der archäischen und klassischen Zeit", Klio 79, 23 – 68.

Gehrke, H. -J. (1997), "La stasis", in I Greci 2. ii, 453 – 480.

Gehrke, H. -J. (1993), "Konflikt und Gesetz. Überlegungen zur frühen Polis", in Bleicken, J. (ed), Colloquium aus Anlass des 80. Geburtstages von Alfred Heuss, 49 – 67, Kallmunz.

Gehrke, H. J. (1985), Stasis. Untersuchungen zu den inneren Kriegen in den griechischen Staaten des 5. und 4. Jahrhunderts v. Chr., München. (Vestigia 35) Louis Gernet (2000), "Le droit" (edited by A. Taddei) Dike 3, 177 – 286.

Gernet, Louis (1984), "Le droit pénal de la Grèce ancienne", in Du châtiment dans la cité, 9 – 35.

Gernet, Louis (1984), "Observations sur le mariage en Grèce", AION 6, 197 – 210.

Gernet, Louis (1984), "La famille dans l'antiquité grecque", AION 6, 173 – 196.

Gernet, Louis (1984), "Quelques désignations homériques de la parenté", AION

6,153 – 172.

Gernet, Louis (1981), "Capital punishment", in Louis Gernet, (ed), The anthropology of ancient Greece,252 – 276,Baltimore. (= Rhodes,P. J. (ed) (2004), Athenian democracy,132 – 160,Edinburgh)

Gernet,Louis (1979), "Aspetti del diritto servile ateniese", in Sichirollo, L. (ed),Schiavitù antica e moderna. Problemi,storia,istituzioni,65 – 94,Napoli.

Gernet,Louis (1959), "Note sur la notion de délit privé en droit grec", in Mélanges Lévy-Bruhl,393 – 405.

Gernet,Louis(1957),"Droit et ville dans l'Antiquité grecque",Recueils de la société J. Bodin 8 (La Ville),45 – 57. (= Droit et institutions,265 – 278 and in Gernet,Anthropologie,371 – 380)

Gernet, Louis (1956), "Le droit penal public à Athènes", Annuaire EPHE 1956 – 57,69 – 70. (= Gernet,Les Grecs,293 – 294)

Gernet,Louis(1956),"Horoi",in Studi Paoli,345 – 353. (= Gernet,Droit et institutions,251 – 264 and in Gernet,Anthropologie,360 – 370)

Gernet,Louis(1956),"Choses visibles et choses invisibles",RPhilos 46,79 – 86. (= Gernet,Anthropologie,405 – 414)

Gernet,Louis(1955),"Jeux et droit. Remarques sur le XXIII chant de l'Iliade", in Droit et société,9 – 18.

Gernet,Louis(1954 – 1957),Démosthène Plaidoyers civils I,II,Paris.

Gernet,Louis(1953),"Sur l'obligation contractuelle dans la vente hellénique", AHDO-RIDA 2,229 – 247. (= Gernet,Droit et Société,225 – 236)

Gernet,Louis(1951c),"Droit commercial et droit civil en Grèce",RHDFE 29, 457.

Gernet,Louis(1951),"Le droit de la vente et la notion du contrat en Grèce d'après M. Pringsheim",RHDFE 29,560 – 584.

Gernet, Louis (1951), "Droit et predroit en Grèce ancienne", L'Année Sociologique 1948 – 49,21 – 119. (= Gernet,Droit et institutions,7 – 119 and in Gernet,Anthropologie,175 – 280)

Gernet,Louis (1950), "Aspects du droit athènien de l'esclavage", AHDO 1, 159 – 187. (= Gernet,Droit et Société,151 – 172)

Gernet,Louis(1950),"Le droit grec ancien. Notions générales",in Conferences faites à l'Institut de droit romain en 1947,41 –54,Paris.

Gernet,Louis(1948),"La notion de democratie chez les Grecs",Revue de la Méditerranée 6,385 –393.(=Gernet,Les Grecs,272 –279)

Gernet,Louis(1939),"L'institution des arbitres publics à Athènes",REG 52,389 –414.(=Gernet,Droit et Société,103 –119)

Gernet,Louis(1938),"Sur les actions commerciales en droit athénien",REG 51,1 –44.(=Gernet,Droit et Société,173 –200)

Gernet,Louis(1938),"Introduction à l'étude du droit grec ancien",AHDO 2,261 –292.(=Zur griechischen Rechtsgesichte,4 –38,Darmstadt)

Gernet,Louis(1937),"Sur la notion de jugement en droit grec",AHDO 1,111 –114.(=Gernet,Droit et Société,61 –81)

Gernet,Louis(1937),"Notes de lexicologie juridique",in Mélanges Emile Boisacq,391 –398,Bruxelles.

Gernet,Louis(1936),"Quelques rapports entre la penalité et la religion dans la Grèce ancienne",AC 5,325 –339.(=Gernet,Anthropologie,288 –301)

Gernet,Louis(1936),"Vieilles legendes de Grèce",Ann. Univ. Algerie 2,14 –29.(=Gernet,Les Grecs,258 –271)

Gernet,Louis(1928),"Frairies antiques",REG 41,313 –359.

Gernet,Louis(1927),"La diamartyrie,procédure archaique du droit athénien",TR 6,5 –24.(=Gernet,Droit et Société,83 –102)

Gernet,Louis(1921),"Sur l'épiclérat",REG 34,337 –379.

Gernet,Louis(1920),"La création du testament",REG 33,123 –168 &249 –290.(="La loi de Solon sur le testament",in Gernet,Droit et société,121 –149)

Gernet,Louis(1918),"Note sur les parents de Démosthène",REG 31,185 –196.

Gernet,Louis(1917),"Hypothèses sur le contrat primitif on Grèce",REG 30,249 –293,363 –383.

Gernet,Louis(1917),Recherches sur le développement de la pensée juridique et morale en Grèce. Étude sémantique,Paris.

Gernet,Louis(1917),Platon Lois,livre ix,traduction et commentaire,Paris.

Gernet,Louis(1916),"Observations sur la loi de Gortyne",REG 29,383 –403.

Gernet,Louis(1910),"Une étude sur le mot engye dans Homère",REG 23,

375ff.

Gernet, Louis (1909), "Sur la designation du meurtrier", REG 22, 13ff. (= Gernet, Droit et société, 29 - 50)

Gernet, Louis (1909), "L'approvisionnement d'Athènes en blé au v. et iv. siècles", Bibliothèque de la Faculté des Lettres de l'Université de Paris 25, 268 - 391.

Gernet, Louis & M. Bizos (1924), Lysias Discours, 2 vols, Paris.

Geretz, T. R. (1976), The Sway of Knowing. Ethics, Politics and Law in Plato's Gorgias, diss. Yale University.

Gewirtz, P. (1988), "Aeschylus' Law", *Harvard Law Review* 101, 1043 - 1055.

Glazebrook, A. (2006), "The Bad Girls of Athens: The Image and Function of Hetairai in Judicial Oratory", in *Prostitutes & Courtesans*, 125 - 138.

Glazebrook, A. (2005), "Prostituting Female Kin (Plut. Sol. 23. 1 - 2)", Dike 8, 33 - 54.

Gofas, D. C. (1994), Thalassa kai sunallages sten archaia Ellada, Athina-Komotini. (= Meletes historias tou hellenikou dikaiou ton synallagon, 197 - 234)

Gofas, D. C. (1992), "To emporiko dikaio tes Athenaikes agoras kata ton 4 aiona p. Ch.", in Symboles I, 79 - 126. (= Meletes historias tou hellenikou dikaiou ton synallagon, 167 - 195)

Gofas, D. C. (1989), "Epiplous: une institution du droit maritime grec, antique, hellénistique, byzantin et postbyzantin", in Symposion 1985, 425 - 445. (= Meletes historias tou hellenikou dikaiou ton synallagon, 87 - 101)

Gofas, D. C. (1982), "La vente sur echantillon à Athènes d'après un texte d'Hypéride", in Symposion 1977, 121 - 130. (= Meletes historias tou hellenikou dikaiou ton synallagon, 79 - 85)

Gofas, D. C. (1979), "Les 'emmenoi dikai' à Thasos", in Symposion 1974, 175 - 186. (= Meletes historias tou hellenikou dikaiou ton synallagon, 71 - 77)

Gofas, D. C. (1971), "L' 'orkos neidies' à Thasos", BCH 95, 245 - 257. (= Meletes historias tou hellenikou dikaiou ton synallagon, 29 - 39)

Gofas, D. C. (1969), "Les carpologues de Thasos", BCH 93, 337 - 370. (= Meletes historias tou hellenikou dikaiou ton synallagon, 41 - 69)

Golden, M. (1984), "Slavery and homosexuality at Athens", Phoenix 38, 308 - 324.

Goldstein, J. A. (1972), "Solon's Law for an Activist Citizenry", *Historia* 21, 538 - 545.

Goligher, W. A. (1935), "Articles for an Attic law Lexicon", *Hermathena* 24 (49), 78 - 87.

Goligher, W. A. (1912 - 1913), "Athenian Clubs", *Hermathena* 17, 295 - 311.

Goligher, W. A. (1908), "The Boeotian Constitution", *CR* 22, 80 - 82.

Goligher, W. A. (1906 - 1907), "Studies in Attic law. I. Isaeus and Attic law. II. The Antidosis", Hermathena 14, 183 - 204; 481 - 515.

Gomme, A. W. (1950), "Pericles monarchos" JHS 70, 77. (= Perikles und seine Zeit, 143, Darmstadt 1979 (Wege der Forschung 412)).

Gomme, A. W. (1934), "Two Problems on Athenian Citizenship Law", *CPh* 29, 123 - 140. (= Essays in Greek History and Literature, 67 - 86, Oxford 1937)

Goodell, T. D. (1891), "Aristotle on the Public Arbitrators", *AJPh* 12, 319 - 326.

Goodwin, W. W. (1894), "The Athenian Graphe Paranomon and the American Doctrine of Constitutional Law", *TAPhA* 26, lx - lxi.

Gorlin, C. E. (1988), "The Spensithios Decree and Archaic Cretan Civil Status", *ZPE* 74, 159 - 165.

Gorman, V. B. (2002), "Milesian Decrees of Isopoliteia and the Refoundation of the City, 479 BCE", in Gorman, V. B. & E. W. Robinson (eds), Oikistes. Studies in constitutions, colonies, and military power in the ancient world offered in honor of A. J. Graham, 181 - 194, Leiden. (Mnemosyne Suppl. 234)

Gorman, R. J. & V. B. Gorman (2000), "The Tyrants Around Thoas and Damasenor (Plut. Q. G. 32. 298c - d)", *CQ* 50, 526 - 530.

Gottesman, A. (2010), "The beggar and the clod: the mythic notion of property in ancient Greece", TAPhA 140, 287 - 322.

Gottlieb, G. (1967), Timuchen. Ein Beitrag zum griechischen Staatsrecht, Heidelberg.

Gottschalk, H. B. (1972), "Notes on the Wills of the Peripatetic Scholars", *Hermes* 100, 314 - 328.

Gould, J. P. (1980), "Law, Custom and Myth: Aspects of the Social Position of Women in Classical Athens", *JHS* 100, 38 - 59.

Gowder, P., "Equality and the Rule of Law in Classical Athens" (May 9, 2012). Available at SSRN: http://ssrn.com/abstract = 2055435 or http://dx.doi.org/10.2139/ssrn.2055435.

Grace, E. (1992), "The 'Altogether' Xenos Killer in Attic Law", *VDI* 203, 28ff.

Grace, E. (1977), "Status Distinctions in Plato's Homicide Law", *VDI* 139, 71 – 81.

Grace, E. (1975), "Note on Dem. XLVII 72: 'Touton tas episkepseis einai'", Eirene 13, 5 – 18.

Grace, E. (1974), "The Legal Position of Slaves in Homicide Cases", *VDI* 128, 34 – 56.

Grace, E. (1973), "Status Distinctions in the Draconian Law", *Eirene* 11, 5 – 30.

Graham, A. J. (1971), Colony and Mother City in Ancient Greece, Manchester.

Grandjean, Y. (2010), "Tessères de juge thasiennes", in Philathenaios, 65 – 80.

Grandjean, Y. & Fr. Salviat (2006), "Règlements du Délion de Thasos", BCH 130, 293 – 327.

Grandjean, Y. & Fr. Salviat (1988), "Décret d'Athènes restaurant la démocratie a Thasos en 407 av. J.-C. IG XII. 8, 262 complété", BCH 112, 249 – 278.

Gray, V. J. (2004), "A Short Response to D. M. Johnson 'Xenophon's Socrates on Law and Justice'", *AncPh* 24, 442 – 446.

Greco, A. (2011), "'Having one's own' and distributive justice in Plato's Republic", *History of Political Thought* 32, 185 – 214.

Green, W. M. (1929), "Greek and Roman Law in the Trinummus of Palutus", *CPh* 24, 183 – 192.

Greenidge, A. H. J. (1914), A Handbook of Greek Constitutional History, London.

Greenstein Millender, E. (2002), "Nomos Despotes: Spartan Obedience and Athenian Lawfulness in Fifth-century Thought", in Gorman, V. B. & E. W. Robinson (eds), Oikistes. Studies in Constitutions, Colonies, and Military Power in the Ancient World Offered in Honor of A. J. Graham, 33 – 60, Leiden. (Mnemosyne Suppl. 234)

Grieve, L. C. C. (1902), "The Dead who are not Dead", *AJA* 6, 37 – 38.

Griffith, G. T. (1966), "Isegoria in the Assembly at Athens", in *Ancient Society and Institutions*, 115 – 138.

Griffith-Williams, B. (2012), "Oikos, family feuds and funerals: Argumentation and evidence in Athenian inheritance disputes", CQ 62, 145 – 162.

Griffith-Williams, B. (2011), "The Succession to the Spartan Kingship, 520 – 400 BC", BICS 54, 43 – 58.

Griffith-Williams, B. (2008), "'Those who Know the Facts': Witnesses and their Testimony in Isaios 9", *AAntHung* 48, 253 – 261.

Guschchin, V. (2009), "Athenian Ostracism and Ostraka: Some Historical and Statistical Observations", in *Greek History and Epigraphy*, 225 – 250.

Gwatkin, jr, W. E. (1957), "The Legal Arguments in Aeschine's 'Against Ctesiphon' and Demosthenes' 'On the Crown'", *Hesperia* 26, 129 – 141.

H

Hager, H. (1879), "How were the Bodies of Criminals at Athens Disposed of after Death?", *Journal of Philology* 8, 1 – 13.

Hahm, D. E. (2009), "The Mixed Constitution in Greek Thought", in *Greek and Roman Political Thought*, 178 – 198.

Hall, E. (1995), "Lawcourt Dramas: The Power of Performance in Greek Forensic Oratory", *BICS* 40, 39 – 58.

Hall, L. G. H. (1989), "Remarks on the Law of Ostracism", *Tyche* 4, 91 – 100.

Hall, R. W. (1989), "Plato and the Beginning of Natural Law", in Moors, K. (ed), Politikos: Selected Papers of the North American Chapter of the Society for Greek Political Thought, 78 – 92, Pittsburgh.

Hamburger, M. (1951), Morals and the Law. The Growth of Aristotle's Legal Theory, New Haven.

Hamel, D. (2003), Trying Neaira. The True Story of a Courtesan's Scandalous Life in Ancient Greece, New Haven.

Hamel, D. (1998), "Coming to Terms with Lipotaxion", *GRBS* 39, 361 – 405.

Hamel, D. (1998), Athenian Generals. Military Authority in the Classical Period, Leiden. (Mnemosyne Suppl. 182)

Hammer, D. (2005), "Plebiscitary Politics in Archaic Greece", *Historia* 54, 107 - 131.

Hammer, D. (1998), "Homer, Tyranny, and Democracy", *GRBS* 39, 331 - 360.

Hammond, B. E. (1895), The Political Institutions of the Ancient Greeks, London.

Hammond, N. G. L. (1999), "The Roles of the Epistates in Macedonian Context", *BSA* 94, 369 - 75.

Hammond, N. G. L. (1985), "The scene in Iliad 18.497 - 508 and the Albanian bloodfeud", BASP 22, 79 - 86.

Hammond, N. G. L. (1961), "Land Tenure in Athens and Solon's Seisachtheia", *JHS* 81, 76 - 98. (= Studies Hammond I, 104 - 144)

Hammond, N. G. L. (1952), "The Exegetai in Plato's Laws", *CQ* 2, 4 - 12. (= Studies Hammond I, 201 - 210)

Hammond, N. G. L. (1950), "The Lycurgean Reform at Sparta", *JHS* 70, 42 - 64. (= Studies Hammond I, 47 - 103)

Hammond, N. G. L. (1940), "The Seisachtheia and the Nomothesia of Solon", *JHS* 60, 71 - 83. (= Studies Hammond I, 145 - 169)

Hamza, G. (1991), Comparative Law and Antiquity, Budapest.

Hamza, G. (1989), "Quelques aspects de l'idée du contrat au domain des droits antiques en Méditerranée", in Symposion 1982, 9 - 20.

Hamza, G. (1987), "Comparative Law and the Graeco-Roman Antiquity", *ACD* 23, 71 - 84.

Handa, K. (1995), "Plato's Theory of Punishment in the Laws", Bulletin of Graduate Studies: Humanities, Social Sciences (Hosei University) 34, 1 - 16.

Hands, A. R. (1968), Charities and Social Aid in Greece and Rome, London.

Hands, A. R. (1959), "Ostraka and the Law of Ostracism: Some Possibilities and Assumptions", *JHS* 79, 69 - 79.

Hannick, J. -M. (1981), "Note sur la graphe paranomon", AC 50, 393 - 397.

Hannick, J. -M. (1976), "Droit de cité et mariages mixtes dans la Grèce classique", AC 45, 133.

Hansen, M. H. (2009), "A Note on Agyrrhios' Grain-tax Law of 374/3", in Greek History and Epigraphy, 145 - 154.

Hansen, M. H. (2007), "Ekklesia Synkletos in Classical Athens and the Ekklesiai Held in the Eighth Prytany of 347/6", *GRBS* 47, 271 – 306.

Hansen, M. H. (2003), "Lysias 14 and 15. A note on the graphe astrateias", in Gestures, 278 – 280.

Hansen, M. H. (1999), The Athenian Democracy in the Age of Demosthenes, London.

Hansen, M. H. (1997), "One Hundred and Sixty theses about Athenian Democracy", ClassMed 48, 205 – 265.

Hansen, M. H. (1995), The Trial of Socrates from the Athenian Point of View, Kopenhagen. (Det kongelige Danske Videnskabernes Selskab. Historisk. -filosofiske Meddel. 71)

Hansen, M. H. (1990), "The Political Power of the People's Court in Fourth-century Athens", in Murray, O. & S. Price (eds), The Greek City from Homer to Alexander, 207 – 226, Oxford.

Hansen, M. H. (1990), "Diokles' Law (Dem. xiv 42) and the Revision of the Athenian Corpus of Laws in the Archonship of Eukleides", ClassMed 41, 63 – 71.

Hansen, M. H. (1990), Aspects of the Athenian Law Code of 410/9 – 400/399 B. C., New York.

Hansen, M. H. (1989), "Demos, ekklesia and dikasterion. A Reply to M. Ostwald and J. Ober", ClassMed 40, 101 – 106. (= Hansen, Athenian ecclesia II, 213 – 218)

Hansen, M. H. (1987), "Graphe Paranomon Against Psephismata not Yet Passed by the ekklesia", ClassMed 38, 63 – 73. (= Hansen, Athenian ecclesia II, 271 – 281)

Hansen, M. H. (1987), The Athenian Assembly in the Age of Demosthenes, Oxford.

Hansen, M. H. (1986), "Klerosis ek Prokriton in Fourth-century Athens", *CPh* 81, 222 – 229.

Hansen, M. H. (1985), "Athenian Nomothesia", *GRBS* 26, 345 – 371.

Hansen, M. H. (1983), "Procheirotonia in the Athenian Ecclesia", in Hansen, Athenian ecclesia, 123 – 130.

Hansen, M. H. (1983), "Graphe or Dike Traumatos?", *GRBS* 24, 307 – 320.

Hansen, M. H. (1982), "Demographic Reflections on the Number of Athenian

Citizens 451 – 309 BC", *AJAH* 7, 172 – 189.

Hansen, M. H. (1982), "Atimia in Consequence of Private Debts", in Symposion 1977, 113 – 120.

Hansen, M. H. (1982), "Two Notes on the Athenian dikai emporikai", in Symposion 1979, 165 – 176.

Hansen, M. H. (1981 – 1982), "IG II2 412. A Fragment of Fourth-century Athenian Law", *ClassMed* 33, 119 – 123.

Hansen, M. H. (1981 – 1982), "The Athenian Heliaia from Solon to Aristotle", *ClassMed* 33, 9 – 47. (= Hansen, Athenian Ecclesia II, 219 – 257)

Hansen, M. H. (1981), "The Prosecution of Homicide in Athens", *GRBS* 22, 11 – 30.

Hansen, M. H. (1981) "Initiative and Decision: The Separation of Powers in Fourth Century Athens", *GRBS* 22, 345 – 370.

Hansen, M. H. (1980), "Perquisites for Magistrates in Fourth-century Athens", ClassMed 32, 105 – 125.

Hansen, M. H. (1980), "Eisangelia in Athens: A reply", *JHS* 100, 83 – 95.

Hansen, M. H. (1980), "Athenian Nomothesia in the Fourth Century BC and Demosthenes' Speech Against Leptines", *ClassMed* 32, 87 – 104.

Hansen, M. H. (1980), "Seven Hundred Archai in Classical Athens", *GRBS* 21, 315 – 330.

Hansen, M. H. (1979), "How often did the Athenian Dikasteria Meet?", *GRBS* 20, 27 – 53.

Hansen, M. H. (1979), "Did the Athenian Ecclesia Legislate after 403/2 B. C.?", *GRBS* 20, 27 – 53. (= Hansen, Athenian Ecclesia, 179 – 205)

Hansen, M. H. (1979), "Misthos for Magistrates in Classical Athens", *SO* 54, 5 – 22.

Hansen, M. H. (1978), "Demos, Ecclesia and Dicasterion in Classical Athens", *GRBS* 19, 127 – 146. (= Hansen, Athenian Ecclesia, 139 – 158)

Hansen, M. H. (1978), "Nomos and Psephisma in Fourth-century Athens", GRBS 19, 315 – 330. (= Hansen, Athenian Ecclesia, 161 – 176)

Hansen, M. H. (1976), Apagoge, Endeixis and Ephegesis Against Kakourgoi, Atimoi and Pheugontes: A Study in the Administration of Justice in the Fourth Century

B. C. ,Odense.

Hansen,M. H. (1976), "The Theoric Fund and the Graphe Paranomon Against Appolodorus", *GRBS* 17,235 – 246.

Hansen, M. H. (1975), Eisangelia: The Sovereignty of the People's Court in Athens in the Fourth Century B. C. and the Impeachment of the Generals and Politicians, Odense.

Hansen, M. H. (1974), The Sovereignty of the People's Court in Athens in Fourth Century B. C. and the Public Action Against Unconstitutional Proposals, Odense.

Hansen, M. H. (1973), Atimistraffen i Athen i klassisk tid, Odense.

Hansen, M. H. (1971), "Aspects of the Athenian Law Code of 410/409 – 400/399 BC", *HSCP* 75,199 – 201.

Hardcastle, M. (1980), "Some Non-legal Arguments in Athenian Inheritance Cases", Prudentia 12,11 – 22.

Harding, Ph. (1987), "Metics, Foreigners or Slaves? The Recipients of Honours in IG II2 10", *ZPE* 67,176 – 182.

Harding, Ph. (1974), "Androtion's View of Solon's Seisachtheia", *Phoenix* 28, 282 – 289.

Harrell, H. C. (1936), Public Arbitration in Athenian Law, Columbia. (The University of Missouri Studies 11,1)

Harris, E. M. (2012), "Hypotheca in Roman Law and Hypotheke in Greek Law", in Legras, B. (ed), Transferts culturels et droits dans le monde grec et hellénistique (Actes du colloque international, Reims, 14 – 17 mai 2008), 433 – 441, Paris.

Harris, E. M. (2010), "Is Oedipus Guilty? Sophocles and Athenian Homicide Law", in Law and drama in Ancient Greece, 122 – 146.

Harris, E. M. (2010), "The Rule of Law and Military Organization in the Greek Polis", in Thür, G. (ed), Symposion 2009. Vorträge zur griechischen und hellenistischen Rechtsgeschichte (Seggau, 25. – 30. August 2009), 405 – 18, Wien.

Harris, E. M. (2009 – 2010), "What are the Laws of Athens About? Substance and Procedure in Athenian Statutes?", Dike 12 – 13, 5 – 67.

Harris, E. M. (2008), Demosthenes Speeches 20 – 22, Austin, Texas. (The oratory of classical Greece 12)

Harris, E. M. (2007), "The Rule of Law in Athenian Democracy. Reflections on the Judicial Oath", in Etica e politica/Ethics and Politics 9, 55 – 74. (= Dike 9 (2006) 157 – 181)

Harris, E. M. (2007), "Did the Athenian Courts Attempt to Achieve Consistency? Oral Tradition and Written Records in the Athenian Administration of Justice", in *Politics of Orality*, 343 – 370.

Harris, E. M. (2007), "Who Enforced the Law in Classical Athens?", in Symposion 2005, 159 – 176.

Harris, E. M. (2006), "Law and Economy in Classical Athens: [Demosthenes] Against Dionysodorus", in Harris, Democracy and the rule of law, 143 – 162.

Harris, E. M. (2006), "Solon and the Spirit of the Laws in Archaic and Classical Greece", in Solon of Athens, 290 – 320. (= Harris, Democracy and the rule of law, 3 – 28)

Harris, E. M. (2005), "Feuding or the Rule of Law? The Nature of Litigation in Classical Athens. An Essay in Legal Sociology", in Symposion 2001, 125 – 141.

Harris, E. M. (2004), "More Thoughts on Open Texture in Athenian Law", in Nomos. Direito e sociedade, 241 – 262.

Harris, E. M. (2004), "Le rôle de l'epieikeia dans les tribunaux athéniens", RHDFE 82, 1 – 13.

Harris, E. M. (2004), "Antigone the Lawyer, or the Ambiguities of Nomos", in *The Law and the Courts*, 19 – 56. (= Harris, Democracy and the rule of law, 41 – 80)

Harris, E. M. (2004), "Did Rape Exist in Hellenistic Athens? Further Reflections on the Laws about Sexual Violence", Dike 7, 41 – 83. (= Harris, Democracy and the rule of law, 297 – 331)

Harris, E. M. (2002), "Did Solon Abolish Debt-bondage?", *CQ* 52, 415 – 430. (= Harris, Democracy and the rule of law, 249 – 270)

Harris, E. M. (2002), "Pheidippides the Legislator. A Note on Aristophanes' Clouds", *ZPE* 140, 3 – 5. (= Harris, Democracy and the rule of law, 425 – 430)

Harris, E. M. (2001), "How to kill in Attic Greek. The Semantics of the Verb (apo) Kteinein and their Implications for Athenian Homicide Law", in Symposion 1997, 75 – 88. (= Harris, Democracy and the rule of law, 391 – 404)

Harris, E. M. (2000), "Open Texture in Athenian Law", Dike 3, 29 – 79.

Harris, E. M. (1999), "The Penalty for Frivolous Prosecutions in Athenian Law", Dike 2, 123 – 142. (= Harris, Democracy and the rule of law, 405 – 422)

Harris, E. M. (1999), "Notes on the New Grain-tax Law", *ZPE* 128, 269 – 272.

Harris, E. M. (1997), "A New Solution to the Riddle of the Seisachtheia", in *The Development of the Polis*, 103 – 112.

Harris, E. M. (1997), "A Note on the Constitution of the Five Thousand", *ZPE* 116, 300.

Harris, E. M. (1997), "Lysias III and the Athenian Beliefs about Revenge", *CQ* 47, 363 – 366.

Harris, E. M. (1996), "A Note on Adoption and Deme Registration", *Tyche* 11, 123 – 127. (= Harris, Democracy and the rule of law, 365 – 370)

Harris, E. M. (1995), Aischines and Athenian Politics, New York.

Harris, E. M. (1994), "'In the Act' or 'Red-handed'? Apagoge to the Eleven and Furtum Manifestum", in Symposion 1993, 169 – 184. (= Harris, Democracy and the rule of law, 373 – 390)

Harris, E. M. (1993), "Apotimema: Athenian Terminology for Real Security in Leases and Dowry Agreement", *CQ* 43, 73 – 95. (= Harris, Democracy and the rule of law, 207 – 240)

Harris, E. M. (1993), "Law and Oratory", in Worthington, I. (ed), Persuasion: Greek Rhetoric in Action, 130 – 152, London.

Harris, E. M. (1992), "Women and Lending in Athenian Society. A Horos Re-examined", *Phoenix* 46, 309 – 321. (= Harris, Democracy and the rule of law, 333 – 346)

Harris, E. M. (1990), "Did the Athenians Regard Seduction as a Worse Crime than Rape?", *CQ* 40, 370 – 377. (= Harris, Democracy and the rule of law, 283 – 296)

Harris, E. M. (1990), "The Constitution of the Five Thousand", *HSCP* 93, 243 – 280.

Harris, E. M. (1989), "The Liability of Business Partners in Athenian Law: The Dispute between Lycon and Megacleides ([Dem.] 52. 20 – 1)", *CQ* 39, 339 – 343. (= Harris, Democracy and the rule of law, 241 – 248)

Harris, E. M. (1988), "When a Sale is not a Sale? The Riddle of Athenian Terminology for Real Security Revisited", *CQ* 38, 351 – 381. (= Harris, Democracy and the rule of law, 163 – 206)

Harris, E. M. (1988), "The Date of Apollodorus' Speech Against Timotheus and its Implications for Athenian History and Legal Procedure", *AJPh* 109, 44 – 52. (= Harris, Democracy and the rule of law, 355 – 364)

Harris, E. M. (1985), "The Date of the Trial of Timarchus", *Hermes* 113, 376 – 380.

Harrison, A. R. W. (1968 – 1971), The Law of Athens. Vol. Ⅰ: The Family and Property, Vol. Ⅱ: Procedure, Oxford.

Harrison, A. R. W. (1961), "Drakon's Protos Axon", *CQ* 11, 3 – 5.

Harrison, A. R. W. (1955), "Law-Making at Athens at the End of the Fifth Century B. C.", *JHS* 75, 26 – 35.

Harrison, A. R. W. (1947), "A Problem in the Rules of Intestate Succession at Athens", *CR* 61, 41 – 42.

Hartel, W. A. (1878 – 1879), "Studien über attisches Staatsrecht und Urkundenwesen", SAW 90, 543 – 624; 91, 101 – 194; 92, 87 – 196.

Harter-Uibopuu, K. (2001 – 2002), "The Asclepieia and Apolloneia of Epidauros. Malefactors at the Sacred Games", in Acts of the sixth international congress of Peloponnesian studies (Tripolis, 24 – 29 September 2000) II, 330 – 340, Athens. (Peloponnesiaka Suppl. 24)

Hartmann, E. (2007), Frauen in der Antike. Weibliche Lebenswelten von Sappho bis Theodora, Berlin.

Hartmann, E. (2007), "Geschlechterdefinition im attischen Recht: Bemerkungen zur sogenannten 'Kyrieia'", in Hartmann, E., Hartmann, U. & K. Pietzner (eds), Geschlechterdefinitionen und Geschlechtergrenzen in der Antike, 37 – 53, Stuttgart.

Hartmann, E. (2003), "Verlöbnis, Heirat, Hochzeitsopfer: der Zeugniswert der Hochzeitsrituale für den Nachweis des Bürgerrechts im demokratischen Athen", in Metzner-Nebelsick, C. et al. (eds), Rituale in der Vorgeschichte, Antike und Gegenwart, 165 – 170, Rahden, Westf.

Hartmann, E. (2002), Heirat, Hetaerentum und Konkubinat im klassischen Athen, Frankfurt.

Hartmann, E. (2000), "'Bastards' in classical Athens", in Pollmann, K. (ed), Double standards in theancient and medieval world, 43 – 53, Göttingen. Hasegawa, T. (1993) "The law of Epitadeus: The re-examination of classical Spartan society" Komazawa Shigaku (Journal of Historical Studies) 45, 66 – 100.

Hashiba, Y. (2006), "Athenian Bribery Reconsidered: Some Legal Aspects", *PCPS* 52, 62 – 80.

Hashiba, Y. (1998), "Dokimasia Reconsidered: What was its Purpose?", Kodai 8 – 9, 1 – 10.

Hashiba, Y. (1998), "Crime and Punishment in Athenian Democracy: From Virtue to Corruption", in *Iwanami World History* 2, 4, 191 – 209, Tokyo.

Hashiba, Y. (1996), "Bribery in the Athenian Democracy: Some Legal Aspects", *Cultura Antiqua* 48(7), 1 – 16.

Hashiba, Y. (1993), Impeachment in Athenian Democracy, Tokyo.

Hashiba, Y. (1992), "Crime and Law in Classical Athens", Rekishigaku Kenkyu (Journal of Historical Studies) 629, 1 – 14.

Hashiba, Y. (1990), "The Origin of Eisangelia and the Development of the Athenian Democracy", Shigaku Zasshi 99(10), 1 – 36.

Hashiba, Y. (1988), "On the eisangelia in Classical Athens", Hoseishi Kenkyu (Legal Historical Review) 37, 103 – 126.

Hashiba, Y. (1988), "Dokimasia (scrutiny) in Athens: The Purpose and its Significance for Democracy", Seiyo Kotengaku Kenkyu (Journal of Classical Studies) 36, 23 – 32.

Hashiba, Y. (1987), "Eisangelia in Classical Athens: The Procedure and its Significance for the Democracy", Shigaku Zasshi 96(7), 1 – 35.

Hatzfeld, J. (1940), "Socrate au procès des Arginuses", REA 42, 165 – 171.

Hatzis, A. H. (1947), "Archaioi Nomoi", Polemon 3, 91 – 93.

Hatzilambrou, R. (2010), "Isaeus' Art of Persuasion: The Case of his Third Speech", *WS* 123, 19 – 35.

Hatzopoulos, M. B. (2007), "Institution royale et communauté civique (Sparte, Épire, Macédoine)", in Simantoni-Bournia, E., Laimou, A. A., Mendoni, L. G. & N. Kourou (eds), Amymona erga. Timetikos tomos gia ton kathegete Vassili K. Lambrinoudaki, 474 – 485, Athena.

Hatzopoulos, M. B. (1999), "Formes d'État et régimes politiques en Grèce du Nord" in Cabanes, P. (ed), L'Illyrie méridionale dans l'Antiquité Ⅲ (Actes du IIIe Colloque international de Chantilly 16 – 19 Octobre 1996), 383 – 387, Paris.

Hatzopoulos, M. B. (1996), "Royaume de Macédoine et colonies grecques: langues et institutions", Cahiers Glotz 7, 25 – 38.

Havelock, E. A. (1978), The Greek Concept of Justice: From its Shadow in Homer to its Substance in Plato, Cambridge, Ma.

Havelock, E. A. (1969), "Dikaiosyne. An Essay in Greek Intellectual History", Phoenix 23, 49 – 70.

Havelock, E. A. (1952), "Why was Socrates Tried?", in White, M. E. (ed), Studies in Honour of G. Norwood, 95 – 109, Toronto.

Hawke, J. (2011), Writing Authority: Elite Competition and Written Law in Early Greece, Deklab, Ill.

Headlam, J. W. (1894), "In Answer to C. V. Thompson's Article on Slave Torture in Athens", *CR* 8, 136 – 137.

Headlam, J. W. (1893), "On the Proklesis eis Basanon in Attic Law", *CR* 7, 1 – 5.

Headlam, J. W. (1892 – 1893), "The Procedure of the Gortynian Inscription", *JHS* 13, 48 – 69.

Headlam, J. W. (1891), Election by lot at Athens, Cambridge. (Cambridge historical essays 4)

Healy, J. F. (1957), "Notes on the Monetary Union Between Mytilene and Phokaia", *JHS* 77, 267 – 268.

Heath, M. (1990), "Justice in Thucydides' Athenian Speeches", *Historia* 39, 385 – 400.

Hedrick jr, C. W. (2000), "For Anyone who Wishes to See", *AncW* 31, 127 – 135.

Hedrick jr, C. W. (1994), "The Zero Degree of Society: Aristotle and Athenian Citizen", in Euben, P. J. & J. R. Wallach (eds), Athenian political thought and the reconstitution of American democracy, 289 – 318, New York.

Hedrick jr., C. W. (1990), The Decrees of the Demotionidai, Atlanta. (American Classical Studies 22)

Hedrick jr, C. W. (1989), "The phratry fromm Paiania", *CQ* 39, 126 – 135.

Heftner, H. (2008), "Überlegungen zum athenischen Ostrakismos", Dike 11, 75 – 110.

Heftner, H. (2003), "Ende und 'Nachleben' des Ostrakismos in Athen", Historia 52, 23 – 38.

Heftner, H. (2003), "Bemerkungen zur Rolle der Probuloi während des oligarchischen Umsturzes in Athen 411 v. Chr.", Prometheus 29, 213 – 227.

Heftner, H. (2003), "Oligarchen, Mesoi, Autokraten: Bemerkungen zur antidemokratischen Bewegung des späten 5. Jh. v. Chr. in Athen", Chiron 33, 1 – 41.

Heftner, H. (2001), Der oligarchische Umsturz des Jahres 411 v. Chr. und die Helmis, A. (2010b), "Dikaio... me metro: emmetres diadromes sto archaio elleniko dikaio", in Timetikos tomos Mich. P. Stathopoulos Ⅱ, 3221 – 3230, Athina-Komotini.

Helmis, A. (2010), "Autoktonia kai dikaio sten ellenike archaioteta", in Pneumatos Dorema Georgio P. Nako, 505 – 520, Thessaloniki.

Helmis, A. (2007), "La privation de sépulture dans l'antiquité grecque", in Symposion 2005, 259 – 268.

Helmis, A. (2005), "Le 'degré zéro de l'écriture' du droit: ǎ propos des décrets de fondation des cités coloniales", in Le législateur et la loi, 127 – 138.

Helmis, A. (2005), "La mort de l'esclave et le droit dans l'Antiquite grecque", in Anastassiadis, V. I. & P. N. Doukellis (eds), Esclavage antique et discriminations socio-culturelles (Actes du XXVIIIe colloque international du GIREA, Mytilene, 5 – 7 decembre 2003), 91 – 106, Bern.

Helmis, A. (2001), "Sépultures et rituels juridiques en Grèce ancienne", in Hoffmann, G. & Adr. Lezzi-Hafter (eds), Les pierres de l'offrande. Autour de l'oeuvre de Christoph W. Clairmont, 175 – 183, Zürich.

Helmis, A. (1981), "La souillure du meurtre en Grece ancienne: le temoignage d'Antiphon", Cahiers du Centre de recherche de l'UER de sciences juridiques 2, 122 – 128.

Herrschaft der Vierhundert in Athen. Quellenkritische und historische Untersuchungen, Frankfurt.

Heftner, H. (2001), "Die pseudo-andokideische Rede 'Gegen Alkibiades'

([And.] 4) – ein autentischer Beitrag zu einer Ostrakophoriendebatte des Jahres 415 v. Chr.", Philologus 145, 39 – 56.

Heftner, H. (2000), "Der Ostrakismos des Hyperbolos: Plutarch, Pseudo-Andokides und die Ostraka", RhM 143, 32 – 59.

Heftner, H. (2000), "Zur Datierung der Ostrakisierung des Hyperbolos", RSA 30, 27 – 45.

Heftner, H. (1999), "Die Rede für Polystratos ([Lys.] 20) und die Katalogisierung der Fünftausend während des athenischen Verfassungsumsturzes von 411 v. Chr.", in Scherrer, P., Taeuber, H. & H. Thür (eds), Steine und Wege. Festschrift für D. Knibbe zum 65. Geburtstag, 221 – 226, Wien.

Heitsch, E. (2006), "Der Vertrag des Therimenes. Von den Schwierigkeiten einer Thukydides-interpretation", Hermes 134, 26 – 43.

Heitsch, E. (1989), "Der Archon Basileus und die attischen Gerichtshöfe für Tötungsdelikte", in Symposion 1985, 71 – 89. (= Heitsch, Gesammelte Schriften Ⅲ, 305ff)

Heitsch, E. (1984), Aidesis im attischen Strafrecht, Wiesbaden. (Akademie der Wissenschaften und der Literatur Mayence. Abhandlungen der Geistes-ind Sozialwissenschaftlichen Klasse 1) (= Heitsch, Gesammelte Schriften Ⅲ, 285 – 304)

Heitsch, E. (1984), Antiphon aus Rhamnous, Wiesbaden. (Akademie der Wissenschaften und der Literatur Mayence. Abhandlungen der Geistes-ind Sozialwissenschaftlichen Klasse 3)

Heitsch, E. (1980), Recht und Argumentation in Antiphons 6. Rede. Philologische Erläuterungen zu einem attischen Strafprozeß, Wiesbaden. (Akademie der Wissenschaftren und der Literatur Mayence. Abhandlungen der Geistes-und Sozialwissenschaftlichen Klasse 7) (= Heitsch, Gesammelte Schriften Ⅲ, 219 – 284)

Heitsch, E. (1961), "Recht und Taktik in der 7. Rede des Lysias. Ein Beitrag zur griechischen Rechtsgeschichte", MH 18, 204 – 219.

Henderson, M. M. (1977), "The decree of Themistokles", AClass 20, 85 – 104.

Herman, G. (2006), Morality and Behaviour in Democratic Athens: A Social History, Cambridge.

Herman, G. (1994), "How Violent was Athenian Society?", in *Ritual, Finance*, Politics, 99 – 117.

Herman, G. (1993), "Tribal and Civic Codes of Behaviour in Lysias I", *CQ* 43, 406－419.

Hermann, K. F. (1855), Über Grundsätze und Anwendung des Strafrechts im griechischen Alterthume, Berlin. (Abhandlungen der Gottinger Gesellschaft der Wissenschaften. Philologisch-Historische Klasse 6)

Hermann, K. F. (1853－1854), De syntelia in jure Graecorum publico. Index scholarum, Göttingen.

Hermann, K. F. (1849－1850), De Dracone legumlatore attico. Index scholarum, Göttingen.

Hermann, K. F. (1849), Über Gesetze und gesetzgebende Gewalt in Griechenland, Berlin. (Abhandlungen der Gottinger Gesellschaft der Wissenschaften. Philologisch-Historische Klasse 4)

Hermann, K. F. (1847), Symbolae ad doctrinam iuris attici de iniuriarum actionibus, Göttingen.

Hermann, K. F. (1847), Quaestiones de probole apud Atticos, Göttingen.

Hermann, K. F. (1846), De terminis eorumque religione apud Graecos, Göttingen.

Hermann, K. F. (1845－1846), Epicrisis de Demosthenis anno natali. Index scholarum, Göttingen.

Hermann, K. F. (1836), Juris domestici et familiaris apud Platonem in legibus cum veteris Graeciae inque primis Athenarum institutis comparatio, Marburg.

Hermann, K. F. (1835), Disputatio de equitibus atticis, Marburg.

Hermann, K. F. (1832), De condicione atque origine eorum qui homoei apud Lacedaemonios appellati sunt, Marburg. (＝Antiquitatum laconicarum libelli quatuor, 216ff., Marburg 1841)

Hermann, K. F. (1829), Quaestionum de jure et auctoritate magistratuum apud Athenienses capita duo, Heidelberg.

Herrmann, J. (1982), "Der Warenkauf in Platons 'Nomoi'", in Studi Biscardi II, 459－468. (＝Herrmann, Kleine Schriften, 84－93)

Herrmann, J. (1976), "Zum Eigentumserwerb beim Mobiliarkauf nach griechischem Recht", in Medicus, D. & H. H. Seiler (eds), Festschrift für Max Kaser zum 70. Geburtstag, 615－627, München. (＝Herrmann, Kleine Schriften, 71－83)

Herrmann, J. (1975), "Zum Rechtshilfevertrag zwischen Milet und Gortyn Milet I 3 Nr. 140 B = Inscr. Cret. IV S. 221 Nr. 161 = Die Staatsverträge des Altertums, Bd. 3 Nr. 482", ZPE 17, 127 - 139. (= Herrmann, Kleine Schriften, 46 - 58)

Herrmann, J. (1975), "Verfüngungsermächtigungen als Gestaltungselemente verschiedener griechischer Geschäftstypen", in Symposion 1971, 321 - 332. (= Herrmann, Kleine Schriften, 59 - 70)

Herrmann, J. (1974), "Die persönliche Sicherungen im griechischen Recht", Recueils de la société Jean Bodin 18 (Les surétés personnelles), 236 - 260. (= Herrmann, Kleine Schriften, 94 - 124)

Herrmann, J. (1967), "Nomos bei Herodot und Thukydides", in Conrad, H., Jahrreiß, H., Mikat, P., Mosler, H. & H. C. Nipperdey (eds), Gedächtnisschrift Hans Peters, 116 - 124, Berlin. (= Herrmann, Kleine Schriften, 3 - 11)

Herrmann, J. (1966), "Losentscheidung in Staat und Recht der Athener", in Seidl, E. (ed), Gedächtnisschrift für Rudolf Schmidt, 349 - 358, Berlin. (= Herrmann, Kleine Schriften, 37 - 45)

Herrmann, J. (1964), "Attische Redefreiheit", in Synteleia Arangio-Ruiz, 1142 - 1148. (= Herrmann, Kleine Schriften, 30 - 36)

Herrmann, K. (1878), Zur Echtheitsfrage von Lysias Rede x und xi, Hannover.

Herrmann, P. (1981), "Teos und Abdera im 5. Jahrhundert v. Chr. Ein neues Fragment der Teiorum Dirae", Chiron 11, 1 - 30.

Hergavault, M.-P. & M.-M. Mactoux (1974), "Esclaves et société d'après Démosthène", in Actes du colloque 1972 sur l esclavage, 57 - 103, Paris.

von Herzog, E. (1897), Zur Verwaltungsgeschichte des attischen Staats, Tübingen.

Hesk, J. (2007), "'Despisers of Commonplace': Meta-topoi and Para-topoi in Attic Oratory", Rhetorica 25, 361 - 384.

Hester, D. A. (1980), "Law and Piety in the Antigone. A Reply to J. Dalfen 'Gesetz ist nicht Gesetz...'", WS 14, 5 - 11.

Heuss, A. (1934), "Abschluss und Beurkundung des griechischen und römischen Staatsvertrages", Klio 27, 14 - 53; 218 - 257. (= Mélanges A. Heuss. Gesammelte Schriften I, 340 - 419, Stuttgart 1995)

Hewitt, A. (2008), "Universal Justice and Epieikeia in Aristotle", *Polis* 25, 115 - 130.

Hewitt, J. W. (1910), "The Necessity of Ritual Purification after Justifiable Homicide", *TAPhA* 41, 99 - 113.

Heydemann, V. (1880), "De senatu Atheniensium quaestiones epigraphicae selectae", Dissertationes philologicae Argentoratenses 4, 147 - 202. Hesk, J. (2007), "'Despisers of commonplace': Meta-topoi and para-topoi in Attic oratory", Rhetorica 25, 361 - 384.

Hester, D. A. (1980), "Law and Piety in the Antigone. A Reply to J. Dalfen 'Gesetz ist nicht Gesetz...'", WS 14, 5 - 11.

Heuss, A. (1934), "Abschluss und Beurkundung des griechischen und römischen Staatsvertrages", Klio 27, 14 - 53; 218 - 257. (= Mélanges A. Heuss. Gesammelte Schriften I, 340 - 419, Stuttgart 1995)

Hewitt, A. (2008), "Universal Justice and Epieikeia in Aristotle", *Polis* 25, 115 - 130.

Hewitt, J. W. (1910), "The Necessity of Ritual Purification after Justifiable Homicide", TAPhA 41, 99 - 113.

Hicks, R. D. (1906), "A Supposed Qualification for Election to the Spartan Senate", *CR* 20, 23 - 27.

Highby, L. I. (1936), The Erythrae Decree. Contributions to the Early History of the Delian League and the Peloponnesian Confederacy, Leipzig. (Klio Beihefte 36)

Hignett, C. (1952), A History of the Athenian Constitution to the End of the Fifth Century B. C., Oxford.

Hilderbrandt, P. (1891), "De causa Polystrati, Lysias xx", in Commentationes philologicae Monacenses, 177 - 181, München.

Hirayama, K. (1998), "Pollution of Homicide in Ancient Greece", *Classical Studies*(Kyoto) 15, 37 - 71.

Hitch, S. (2011), "Embedded Speech in the Attic Leges Sacrae", in Lardinois, A. P. M. H., Blok, J. H. & M. G. M. van der Poel (eds), Sacred words: Orality, literacy and religion, 101 - 112, Leiden. (Orality and literacy in the ancient world 8) (Mnemosyne Suppl. 332)

Hitz, Z. (2009), "Plato on the Sovereignty of Law", in *Greek and Roman*

Political Thought, 367 – 381.

Hodkinson, St. (2004), "Female Property Ownership and Empowerment in Classical and Hellenistic Sparta", in Figueira, Th. J. (ed), Spartan Society, 103 – 136, Swansea.

Hodkinson, St. (2000), Property and Wealth in Classical Sparta, London.

Hölkeskamp, K.-J. (2005), "What's in a Code? Solon's Laws between Complexity, Compilation and Contigency", *Hermes* 133, 280 – 293.

Hölkeskamp, K.-J. (2002), "Nomos, Thesmos und Verwandtes. Vergleichende Überlegungen zur Konzeptualizierung geschriebenen Rechts im klassischen Griechenland", in Demokratie, Recht und soziale Kontrolle, 109 – 114.

Hölkeskamp, K.-J. (2000), "(In –) Schriften und Monument. Zum Begriff des Gesetzes im archaischen und klassischen Griechenland", ZPE 132, 73 – 96.

Hölkeskamp, K.-J. (2000), "Agon und Argumentation. Rede und Redner in der archaischen Polis", in Raeck, W. & C. Neumeister (eds), Rede und Redner. Bewertung und Darstellung in den antiken Kulturen, 17 – 43, Möhnsee.

Hölkeskamp, K.-J. (1999), Schiedsrichter, Gesetzgeber und Gesetzgebung im archaischen Griechenland, Stuttgart. (Historia Einzelschriften 131)

Hölkeskamp, K.-J. (1995), "Arbitrators, Lawgivers, and the 'Codification of Law' in Archaic Greece: Problems and Perspectives", *Metis* 7, 49 – 81.

Hölkeskamp, K.-J. (1994), "Tempel, Agora und Alphabet. Die Entstehungsbedingungen von Gesetzgebung in der archaischen Polis", in Rechtskodifizierung, 135 – 164.

Hölkeskamp, K.-J. (1993), "Demonax und die Neuordnung der Bürgerschaft von Kyrene", Hermes 121, 404 – 421.

Hölkeskamp, K.-J. (1992), "Written Law in Archaic Greece", *PCPS* 38, 87 – 117. Hooker, J. T. (1988), "The Life and Times of Lycurgus the Lawgiver", *Klio* 70, 340 – 345.

Hooker, J. T. (1975), "The Original Meaning of Hybris", Archiv für Begriffsgeschichte 19, 125 – 137.

Hopper, R. J. (1943), "Interstate Juridical Agreements in the Athenian Empire", *JHS* 63, 35 – 51.

Horii, K. (1997), "Cleitophon's Amendment and the Patrios Politeia in Classical

Athens", *Cultura Antiqua* 49(5), 16 - 28.

Horii, K. (1993), "The So-called Nikomachos' Codification of Laws in his Second Term of 403 - 399 B. C. at Athens", *Review of Historical Studies* 20, 25 - 40.

Horii, K. (1992), "The Nikomachos' Earlier Law Code in Athens, 410 - 404 B. C.", Seiyo Kotengaku Kenkyu(*Journal of Classical Studies*) 40, 12 - 21.

Horii, K. (1989), "[Lysias] XX For Polystratos Reexamined", Kenkyu Kiyo (Bulletin of Radio Technical College) 17, 39 - 51.

Horii, K. (1987), "The Constitution of Theramenes", *Review of Historical Studies* 177, 27 - 44.

Horii, K. (1985), "On the Syngrapheis of Athens in 411 B. C.", Seiyoshi Gakuho(Review of Western History, Hiroshima University) 11, 1 - 15.

Horsley, G. A. R. (1982), "The Second Athenian Confederacy", in Hellenika: Essays, 131 - 150.

Horvath, L. (2008), "Note to Hyperides in Timandrum", AAntHung 48, 121 - 123.

Horvath, L. (2008), "Dating Hyperides' Against Diondas", ZPE 166, 27 - 36.

Horvath, L. (2007), "Hypereides' Rede gegen Athenogenes und die zeitgenössische Komödie", WS 120, 25 - 34.

Howenstein, M. S. (2009), "Socrates and the moral limits of legal obligation", Law, culture and the Humanities 5, 55 - 76.

Howenstein, M. S. (2000), "The Tragedy of Law and the Law of Tragedy in Sophocles' Antigone", *Legal Studies Forum* 24, 493 - 525.

Humphreys, S. C. (2002), "Solon on Adoption and Wills", *ZRG* 119, 340 - 347.

Humphreys, S. C. (1997), "Leggi, Tribunali, Processi", in I Greci 2, 541 - 566.

Humphreys, S. C. (1994), "Le mariage entre parents dans l'Athènes classique", in Bonte, P. (ed), Épouser au plus proche. Inceste, prohibition et stratégies matrimoniales autour de la Méditerranée, 31 - 58, Paris.

Humphreys, S. C. (1992), "A Historical Approach to Drakon's Law on Homicide", in Symposion 1990, 17 - 45.

Humphreys, S. C. (1988), "The Discourse of Law in Archaic and Classical Greece", *Law and History Review* 6, 465 - 493.

Humphreys, S. C. (1987), "Law, Custom and Culture in Herodotus", *Arethousa* 20, 211 – 220.

Humphreys, S. C. (1986), "Kinship Patterns in the Athenian Courts", *GRBS* 27, 57 – 92.

Humphreys, S. C. (1985), "Social Relations on Stage: Witnesses in Classical Athens", *History and Anthropology* 1, 313 – 369. (= The Attic Orators, 140 – 213)

Humphreys, S. C. (1983), "The Evolution of Legal Process in Ancient Attica", in Gabba, E. (ed), Tria Corda. Studi in onore di Arnaldo Momigliano, 229 – 256, Como. (Biblioteca di Athenaeum 1)

Humphreys, S. C. (1974), "The nothoi of Kynosarges", *JHS* 94, 88 – 95. Hunt, P. (2010) War, peace and alliance in Demosthenes' Athens, Cambridge.

Hunt, P. (2001), "The Slaves and the Generals of Arginusae", *AJPh* 122, 359 – 380.

Hunter, V. J. (2009), "Crime and Criminals in Plato's Laws", *Mouseion* 9, 1 – 20.

Hunter, V. J. (2008), "Plato's Prison", *G & R* 55, 193 – 201.

Hunter, V. J. (2007), "Did the Athenians have a Word for Crime?", Dike 10, 5 – 18.

Hunter, V. J. (2006), "Pittalacus and Eucles: Slaves in the Public Service of Athens", *Mouseion* 6, 1 – 14.

Hunter, V. J. (2000), "Policing Public Debtors in Classical Athens", *Phoenix* 54, 21 – 38.

Hunter, V. J. (2000), "Introduction: Status Distinctions in Athenian Law", in *Law and Social Status*, 1 – 29.

Hunter, V. J. (1997), "The Prison of Athens: A Comparative Approach", *Phoenix* 51, 296 – 326.

Hunter, V. J. (1994), Policing Athens: Social Control in the Attic Lawsuits, Princeton.

Hunter, V. J. (1993), "Agnatic Kinship in Athenian Law and Athenian Family Practice: Ist Implications for Women", in *Law, Politics and Society*, 100 – 121.

Hunter, V. J. (1992), "Constructing the Body of the Citizen: Corporal Punishment in Classical Athens", *EMC/CV* 36, 271 – 291.

Hutton, N. (2003 - 2004), "The Origin, Development and Future of Maritime Liens and the Action in Rem", *Tulane Maritime Law Journal* 28, 81 - 110.

Hyde, W. W. (1917 - 1918), "Homicide Courts of Ancient Athens", *Pennsylvania Law Review* 66, 319 - 362.

I

Ibbetson, D. (2004), "Wrongs and Responsibility in Pre-Roman Law", *The Journal of Legal History* 25, 99 - 127.

Ichiyanagi, T. (1990), Studies in the History of Legal thought in Ancient Greece, Tokyo.

Ichiyanagi, T. (1978 - 1980), "The Legal Position of Slaves in Homicide Cases: On Aspect of Ancient Greek Legal History in the V - IV Century B. C.", Bulletin of the Faculty of Education (Utsunomiya University) 28, 105 - 118; 29, 77 - 90; 30, 91 - 104.

Ikeda, T. (1988), "The King's Peace and the Formation of the Second Athenian Confederacy", *Review of Historical Studies* 179, 72 - 91.

Immerwahr, H. R. (1985), "The Date of the Construction of Solon's Axones", *Bulletin of the American Society of Papyrologists* 22, 117 - 121.

Ingalls, W. (2002), "Demography and Dowries: Perspectives on Female Infanticide in Classical Greece", *Phoenix* 56, 246 - 54.

Ingle, N. L. (1911), "The Original Function of the Boule at Athens", *CR* 25, 236 - 238.

Isager, S. (1981), "The Marriage Pattern in Classical Athens. Men and Women in Isaios", *ClassMed* 33, 81 - 96.

Isager, S. (1992), "Sacred and Profane Ownership of Land", in Wells, B. (ed), Agriculture in Ancient Greece, (Proceedings of the 7th International Symposium at the Swedish Institute at Athens 16 - 17 May 1990), 119 - 122, Stockholm. (Acta Instituti Atheniensi regni Sueciae ser. 4, 42)

Isager, S. & M. H. Hansen (1975), Aspects of Athenian Society in the Fourth Century BC: A Historical Introduction to and Commentary on the Paragraphe Speeches and the Speech Against Dionysodorus in the Corpus Demosthenicum, Odense.

Ita, T. (2000), "A Basic Study of Hekatostai Inscription. New Readings of

Texts", Seiyoshigaku Ronshi (Journal of Western History) 38, 158 – 179.

Ito, S. (1992), "The Legal Status of Athenian Bastards: A Critical Note", Shigaku Zasshi 101, 70 – 98.

Ito, S. (1988), "An Interpretation of the So-called Demotionid Inscription", Shirin (*Journal of History, Kyoto University*) 71, 1 – 37.

Ito, S. (1986), "Phaidippos an Athenian miner. A note on the poletai-inscriptions", in Festschrift Lauffer Ⅱ, 453 – 462.

Ito, S. (1983), "Phrateres as Athenian Citizens", Seiyo Kotengaku Kenkyu (*Journal of Classical Studies*) 33, 1 – 18.

Ito, S. (1981), "The Phratries in Classical Athens", Hoseishi Kenkyu (*Legal History Review*) 31, 35 – 60.

Ito. S. (1975), "The Historical Background of Dem. LIX", Seiyo Kotengaku Kenkyu (*Journal of Classical Studies*) 23, 1 – 17.

Ito, S. (1973), "Law and Society in Ancient Greece: Ancient Succession Practices", in Ho-shakaiguku Koza, 9, 131 – 150.

Ito, S. (1969), "Female Succession in Classical Crete", in Hidemura, K., Miura, I. & H. Ota (eds), Society and thought in Classical Antiquity, 169 – 194, Tokyo.

Ito, S. (1967), "The Changes of the Succession of Property in Classical Greece", Shigaku Zasshi 76(12), 1 – 43.

Ito, S. (1959), "The Ownership of the Laurion Mines: A Study of the Poletai-Inscriptions", Shigaku Zasshi 68(8), 1 – 28.

Ito, T. (2007), "What is the 'seisachtheia'?", *JCS* 55, 101 – 13. (in Japanese)

Ito, T. (1994), "The Hekatostai Inscriptions Reconsidered: Sale or Lease?", Shigaku Zasshi 103(7), 35 – 57.

Ito, T. (1993), "Leases of Public Land in Classical Athens: On their Social Status", in Ito, T., Katsura, M. & S. Yasunaga (eds), The ancient Mediterranean world: Greek and Roman studies presented to Ichiro Miura on his 80th birthday, 111 – 144, Tokyo.

Ito, T. (1986), "Solon, Land and Public Confiscation: A Study of Solon's Poems", Shigaku Zasshi 95(10), 1 – 36.

Ito, T. (1983), "Public Restrictions on the Kleros", SeiyoShigaku (*Studies in Western History*) 128, 33 – 49.

Iwata, T. (1974), "Some Questions on the Interpretations of Dem. XXXVI 3: An Aspect of the History of 'bank' in Ancient Greece", *Annual Report on Cultural Science* (The Faculty of Letters, Hokkaido University) 22, 1 – 119.

J

Jackson, A. H. (1969), "The Original Purpose of the Delian League", *Historia* 18, 12 – 16.

Jackson, C. N. (1919), "The Decree-seller in the Birds and the Professional Politicians at Athens", *HSCP* 30, 89 – 109.

Jackson, D. F. (2006), The Constitution of the Lacedaimonians by Xenophon of Athens, Lampeter.

Jackson, P. (1999), The Construction of Justice in Aiskhylos' Oresteia and Plato's Republic, diss. The State University of New Jersey.

Jacqmin, Cl. (2005 – 2008), "Woman between the Tyrant and the Polis. The Role of Women in Tyrannical Regimes", Kodai 15, 1 – 24.

Jameson, M. H. (1997), "Women and Democracy in Fourth-century Athens", in Hommage Garlan, 95 – 108.

Jameson, M. H. (1982), "The Leasing of Land in Rhamnous", in Studies Vanderpool, 66 – 74.

Jameson, M. H. (1955), "Seniority in the Strategia", *TAPhA* 86, 63 – 87.

Janda, J. (2009), "The concept of justice in Plato's Republic and in Aristotle's Nicomachean Ethics", Filozoficky Casopis 35, 3 – 23. (in Czeckh with English summary)

Janik, J. (2003), Terms of the Semantic Sphere of Dike and Themis in the Early Greek epic, Krakow. (Studies of the commission on classical philology 30)

Janik, J. (2002), "The meaning of justice in the poetry of Hesiod and its continuation in the lyric of Solon", Eos 89, 203 – 227.

Janik, J. (2000), "Dike and Themis in the Works of Homer", *Eos* 87, 5 – 31.

Janko, R. (2009), "Some Notes on the New Hyperides (Against Diondas)", *ZPE* 170, 16.

Jannelli, M. (1976), "I rapporti giuridici di Alessandro Magno con i Chii", in Studi Manni, 153 – 175.

Jannet, Cl. (1880), Les institutions sociales et le droit civil a Sparte 2, Paris.

Jay-Robert, G. (2009), Le sacré et la loi. Essai sur la notion d'hosion d'Homère à Aristote, Paris.

Jeffery, L. H. (1956), "The Courts of Justice in Archaic Chios", *BSA* 51, 157 - 167.

Jevons, F. B. (1895), "Work and Wages in Athens", *JHS* 15, 239 - 247.

Jevons, F. B. (1895), "Greek Law and Folklore", *CR* 9, 247 - 250.

Johansson, M. (2004), "Plutarch, Aelius Aristides and the Inscription from Troizen", *RhM* 147, 343 - 354.

Johansson, M. (2001), "The Inscription from Troizen: A Decree of Themistokles?", *ZPE* 137, 69 - 92.

Johnson, Van (1938), "Aristotle on nomos", CJ 33, 351 - 356.

Johnson, C. (1984), "Who is Aristotle's Citizen?", *Phronesis* 29, 73 - 90.

Johnson, D. M. (2003), "Xenophon's Socrates on Law and Justice", *AncPh* 23, 255 - 282.

Johnstone, S. (2003), "Women, Property, and Surveillance in Classical Athens", *ClAnt* 22, 247 - 274.

Johnstone, S. (2002), "Apology for the Manuscript of Demosthenes 59. 67", *AJPh* 123, 229 - 256.

Johnstone, S. (1999), Disputes and Democracy, The Consequences of Litigation in Ancient Athens, Austin, Texas.

Johnstone, S. (1998), "Cracking the Code of Silence: Athenian Legal Oratory and the History of Slaves and Women", in Joshel, S. R. & S. Murnaghan (eds), Women and slaves in Greco-Roman culture: Differential equations, 221 - 235, London.

Jolowicz, H. F. (1939), "Precedent in Greek and Roman Law", *BIDR* 46, 394 - 405.

Jones, A. H. M. (1966), "The Lykurgan Rhetra", in *Ancient society and Institutions*, 165 - 176.

Jones, A. H. M. (1957), Athenian Democracy, Oxford.

Jones, C. P. (2008), "Hyperides and the Sale of Slave Families", *ZPE* 164, 19 - 20.

Jones, C. P. (1999), Kinship Diplomacy in the Ancient World, Cambridge,

Mass.

Jones, J. W. (1956), The Law and Legal Theory of the Greeks, Oxford.

Jones, N. F. (1999), The Associations of Classical Athens. A Response to Democracy, New York.

Jones, N. F. (1991), "Enrollment Clauses in Greek Citizenship Decrees", *ZPE* 87, 79 – 102.

Jones, N. F. (1987), Public Organization in Ancient Greece. A Documentary Study, Philadelphia. (Memoirs of the American Philosophical Society 176)

Jones, W. (1779), Isaeus. Speeches of Isaeus, in Causes Concerning the Law of Succession to Property at Athens, London.

Jordan, B. (2004), "Supreme Command in the Athenian Board of Generals", *AHB* 18, 25 – 47.

Jordan, B. (2001), "Metic Trierach", *AHB* 15, 131 – 134.

Jordan, B. (1970), "A Note on the Athenian Strategia", *TAPhA* 101, 229 – 239.

Jordan, D. (2003), "A Letter from the Banker Pasion", in Jordan, D. & J. Traill (eds), Lettered Attica. A day of Attic epigraphy (Proceedings of the Athens Symposium, 8 March 2000), 23 – 39, Athens. (Publications of the Canadian Arcaeological Institute at Athens 3)

Jordan, D. (2000), "New Greek Curse Tablets (1985 – 2000)", *GRBS* 41, 5 – 46.

Jordovic, Iv. (2011), "Aristotle on Extreme Tyranny and Extreme Democracy", *Historia* 60, 36 – 64.

Joyce, C. J. (2008), "The Athenian Amnesty and Scrutiny of 403", *CQ* 58, 507 – 518.

Just, R. (1989), Women in Athenian Law and Life, London.

K

Kagan, D. (1963), "The Enfranchisement of Aliens by Cleisthenes", *Historia* 12, 41 – 46.

Kagan, D. (1961), "The Origin and Purpose of Ostracism", *Hesperia* 30, 393 – 401.

Kahane, Alt. (2010), "Antigone, Antigone: Lacan and the Structure of Law", in

Wilmer, S. E. & Au. Zukauskaite (eds), Interrogating Antigone in Postmodern Philosophy and Criticism, 147 – 167, Oxford.

Kahn, Ch. H. (1988), "Socrates and the Rule of Law", in *Philosophy of Law*, 11 – 16.

Kalimtzis, K. (2000), Aristotle on Political Enmity and Disease. An Inquiry into Stasis, Albany, N. Y.

Kahrstedt, U. (1938), "Untersuchungen zu athenischen Behörden II. Die Nomotheten und die Legislative in Athen", Klio 31, 1 – 32.

Kahrstedt, U. (1936), Studien zum öffentlichen Recht Athens Tl. 2: Untersuchungen zur Magistratur in Athen, Stuttgart.

Kahrstedt, U. (1936), Untersüchungen zur Magistratur in Athen, Stuttgart.

Kahrstedt, U. (1934), Studien zum öffentlichen Recht Athens Tl. 1: Staatgebiet und Staatangehörige in Athen, Stuttgart. (Göttinger Forschungen 4)

Kahrstedt, U. (1922), Griechisches Staatsrecht. I. Sparta und seine Symmachie, Götingen.

Kahrstedt, U. (1914), "Staatsrechtliches zum Putsch von 411", Hermes 49, 47 – 69.

Kamps, W. (1938), "L'emphytéose en droit grec et sa réception en droit romain", in Recueils de la société Jean Bodin 3 (La tenure), 67 – 121.

Kamps, W. (1938), "Une affaire de fraude successorale à Athènes", Annuaire de l'Institut de philologie et d'histoire orientale et slave 6, 15 – 27.

Kamps, W. (1937), "Les origines de la fondation cultuelle dans la Grèce ancienne", AHDO 1, 145 – 179.

Kamps, W. (1936), "La fiducie dans le droit de Grande Grèce et l'origine de la mancipatio familiae", TR 16, 142 – 155.

Kamps, W. (1935), "Testament grec et testament romain", RHDFE 14, 404 – 405.

Kamps, W. (1935), "Les différents aspects religieux et juridiques du culte des ancêstres", Revue de l'Institut de Sociologie 15, 118ff. Kapparis, K. (2011), "The terminology of prostitution in the ancient Greek world", in Glazebrook, A. & M. M. Henry (eds), Greek prostitutes in the ancient Mediterranean, 800 BCE – 200 CE, 222 – 255, Madison, Wisc.

Kapparis, K. (2005), "Immigration and Citizenship Procedures in Athenian Law", *RIDA* 52, 71 – 113.

Kapparis, K. (2001), Abortion in the Ancient World, London.

Kapparis, K. (1999) [D.] 59 Against Neaira, Berlin.

Kapparis, K. (1998), "Assessors of Magistrates (paredroi) in Classical Athens", *Historia* 47, 383 – 393.

Kapparis, K. (1998), "The Law on the Age of the Speakers in the Athenian Assembly", *RhM* 141, 255 – 259.

Kapparis, K. (1996), "Humiliating the Adulterer: The Law and the Practice in Classical Athens", *RIDA* 43, 63 – 77.

Kapparis, K. (1995), "When were the Athenian Adultery Laws Introduced?", *RIDA* 42, 97 – 122.

Kapparis, K. (1995), "The Athenian Decree for the Naturalisation of the Plataeans", *GRBS* 36, 359 – 378.

Karabelias, E. (2004), Recherches sur la condition juridique et sociale de la fille unique dans le monde grec ancien excepté Athènes, Athènes. (EHHD Par. 5)

Karabelias, E. (2002), L'épiclérat attique, Athenes. (EHHD Par. 3)

Karabelias, E. (1999), "L'expropriation en droit grec ancien", in Recueils de la société Jean Bodin 66 (L'expropriation), 21 – 54. (= Karabelias, Études, 191 – 227)

Karabelias, E. (1997), "L'arbitrage privé dans l'Athènes classique", in Symposion 1995, 135 – 149. (= Recueils de la société Jean Bodin 63 (L'assistance dans la resolution des conflits), 9 – 35 and in Karabelias, Études, 299 – 332)

Karabelias, E. (1992), "L'acte ὰ cause de mort (diathèke) dans le droit attique", Recueils de la société Jean Bodin 59 (Actes ὰ cause de mort), 47 – 121. (= Karabelias, Études, 103 – 190)

Karabelias, E. (1991), "La peine dans Athènes classique", Recueils de la société Jean Bodin 63 (La peine), 77 – 132. (= Karabelias, Études, 231 – 298)

Karabelias, E. (1990), "La succession ab intestat en droit attique", *JJP* 20, 55 – 74. (= Symposion 1982, 41 – 63)

Karabelias, E. (1990), "Le roman de Chariton d'Aphrodisias et le droit. Renversements de situation et exploitation des ambiguites juridiques", in Symposion 1988, 369 – 396. (= Karabelias, Études, 49 – 82)

Karabelias, E. (1989), "Inceste, mariage et strategies matrimoniales dans l'Athènes classique", in Symposion 1985, 233 - 253. (= Karabelias, Études, 83 - 102)

Karabelias, E. (1986), "Modalités successorales ab intestato à Gortyne", in Festschrift Kränzlein, 29 - 41.

Karabelias, E. (1984), "Le contenu de l'oikos en droit grec ancien", in Mneme Petropoulou I, 443 - 454.

Karabelias, E. (1983), "Homère, Platon et survivances littéraires de l'épiclérat", in Symposion 1979, 177 - 196.

Karabelias, E. (1982), "L'épiclérat à Sparte", in Studi Biscardi 2, 469 - 480.

Karabelias, E. (1979), "Contribution à l'étude de l'epidikasie attique", in Symposion 1974, 201 - 223.

Karabelias, E. (1970), "Une nouvelle source pour l'étude du droit attique: le 'Bouclier' de Menandre (P. Bodmer XXVI)", RHDFE 48, 357 - 389. (= Karabelias, Études, 17 - 48)

Karavites, P. (1992), Promise-giving and Treaty-making: Homer and the Near East, Leiden. (Mnemosyne Suppl. 119)

Karavites, P. (1987), "Diplomatic Envoys in the Homeric World", RIDA 34, 41 - 100.

Karavites, P. (1986), "Homer: Horkia, Horkos", *AncW* 14, 115 - 128.

Karavites, P. (1984), "The Political use of Eleutheria and Autonomia in the 4th Century among the Greek City-states", *RIDA* 31, 167 - 192.

Karavites, P. (1982), "'Eleutheria' and 'Autonomia' in Fifth Century Interstate Relations", *RIDA* 29, 145 - 162.

Karavites, P. (1982), Capitulations and Greek Interstate Relations. The Reflection of Humanistic Ideals in Political Events, Göttingen. (Hypomnemata 71)

Karavites, P. (1980), "'Euergesia' in Herodotus and Thucydides as a Factor in Interstate Relations", *RIDA* 27, 69 - 79.

Karayannis, A. D. (1992), "Entrepreneurship in Classical Greek Literature", *The South African Journal of Economics* 60, 67 - 93.

Karayannis, A. D. & A. N. Hatzis (2012), "Morality, Social Norms and the Rule of Law as Transaction Cost-saving Devices: The Case of Ancient Athens", *European*

Journal of Law and Economics 33(2012),621 –643.

Karnezis,I. E. (1978 – 1979), "The Non-aphairesis of the Epikleros and the Testamentary Engyete Woman in Classical Athens",*Athena* 77,145 –171.

Karnezis,I. E. (1977),"Misrepresentation of Attic Laws in Menander's Aspis", *Platon* 29,152 –155.

Karnezis,I. E. (1976 – 1977), "Parapoiessis attikon thesmon eis ton Dyskolon tou Menandrou",Athena 76,155 –165.

Karnezis,I. E. (1976),"A Roman Guardianship Law Incorrectly Related to Attic Law",*CB* 52,55 –56.

Karnezis,I. E. (1976),"The Law of Engye in Demosthenes XLVI 18,20,22", *Apollinaris* 49,278 –285.

Karnezis,I. E. (1976),Solonian Guardianship Laws of Classical Athens and the Senatus Consultum(Dig. 23. 2. 59). A Contribution to the Interpretation of the Attic Orators and to the Comparative Study of the Private Life of Classical Athens and Rome,Athens.

Kennedy,G. A. (1958),"The Oratory of Andocides",*AJPh* 89,37 –43.

Kennedy,R. F. (2009),Athen's Justice. Athena,Athens and the Concept of Justice in Greek Tragedy,New York.

Kennedy,R. F. (2006), "Justice,Geography and Empire in Aeschylus' Eumenides",*ClAnt* 25,35 –72.

Kenyon,F. G. (1904), "The Athenaion Politeia and the Hemera Diamemetremene",*CR* 18,337 –339.

Kerferd,G. B. (1953), "Protagoras' Doctrine of Justice and Virtue in the Protagoras of Plato",*JHS* 73,42 –45.

Keyt,D. (2011),"Plato on Justice",in Anagnostopoulos,G. (ed),Socratic, Platonic and Aristotelian Studies:Essays in Honor of G. Santas,255 –570,New York.

Keyt,D. (1991),"Aristotle's Theory of Distributive Justice",in Keyt,D. & F. Miller(eds),A Companion to Aristotle's Politics,238 –278,Oxford.

Keyt,D. (1991),"Aristotle on Natural Law and Justice",in Keyt,D. &F. Miller (eds),A Companion to Aristotle's Politics,279 –306,Oxford.

Khan,C. -A. B. (2005),"Aristotle,Citizenship,and the Common Advantage", *Polis* 22,1 –23.

Kidd, I. (1990), "The Case of Homicide in Plato's Euthyphro", in Craik, E. M. (ed), Owls to Athens. Essays on Classical Subjects Presented to sir Kenneth Dover, 213 – 222, Oxford.

Kindstrand, J. F. (1985), "The Length of the Speeches on the Assessment of the Penalty in Athenain Courts", *CQ* 35, 525 – 529.

King, H. T. & M. A. LeForestier (1994), "Arbitration in Ancient Greece", *Dispute Resolution Journal* 49, 38ff.

Kinz, S. E. (1997), "Love's Litigation: Plato's Phaedrus as Trial by Jury", *Duke Law Journal* 46, 815 – 864.

Kiyonaga, S. (1980), "The Tyrants and the Mediator in Archaic Mytilene", Gakushuin Shigaku (*Gakushuin Historical Review*) 16, 3 – 25.

Kiyonaga, S. (1964), "Periander's Prohibition from Getting Slaves", Rekishigaku Kenkyu (*Journal of Historical Studies*) 294, 1 – 13.

Kiyonaga, S. (1959), "A Study of Timema in the Solonian Constitution", Shigaku Zasshi 68, 1 – 33.

Klemm, D. E. (1989), "Gorgias, Law, and Rhetoric", *Iowa Law Review* 74, 819 – 826.

Klimchuk, D. (2003), "Aristotle on Intoxication and Liability", *History of Philosophy Quarterly* 20, 225 – 243.

Klingenberg, E. (1990), "Eigentumserwerb durch Fund", in Symposion 1988, 101 – 110.

Klingenberg, E. (1989), "Diakolyein antagonisten. Eine platonische Bestimmung des griechischen Wettkampfrechts: Pl. Leg. 955 a2 – b4", in Symposion 1982, 205 – 240. (= Studi Biscardi 6, 435 – 470)

Klingenberg, E. (1986), "Der Ring des Polykrates. Kannte das griechische Recht eine Dereliktion?", in Festschrift Kränzlein, 43 – 52.

Klingenberg, E. (1986), "I dina ba'eto i peschara ba'eto. Urteil, Schiedspruch und Vergleich im römischen, griechischen und judischen Recht", in Ehrlich, E. L., Klappert, B. & U. Ast (eds), "Wie gut sind deine Zelte, Jaakow. . . ", Festschrift zum 60 Geburtstag von R. Mayer, 63 – 75, Gerlingen.

Klingenberg, E. (1984), "Zum attischen Fundrecht in Menanders Epitrepontes", in Nörr, D. & D. Simon (eds), Gedachtnisschrift für W. Kunkel, 179 – 184, Frankfurt.

Klingenberg, E. (1983), "Die Aufgaben der städtischen Verwaltungbeamten in Griechenland", in Symposion 1979, 217 – 236.

Klingenberg, E. (1983), "Sull'interdipendenza tra l'agglomerato urbano e il diritto greco", in La cittὰ antica come fatto di cultura, 195 – 213, Como.

Klingenberg, E. (1982), "Das Zinsrecht in Platons 'Nomoi'", in Symposion 1977, 99 – 112.

Klingenberg, E. (1979), "La legge platonica sulle fontane pubbliche", in Symposion 1974, 288 – 303.

Klingenberg, E. (1976), Platons Nomoi Georgikoi und das positive griechische Recht, Berlin. (Münchener Universitätsschriften. Juristische Fakultät. Abhandlungen zurRechtswissenschaftlichen Grundlagenforschung 17).

Klingenberg, E. (1975), "Bemerkungen zum platonischen Bienenrecht Lg. 843 d7 – e1", in Symposion 1971, 347 – 354.

Klöckner, A. (2010), "New problems in Athenian Religion: The 'Sacred Law' from Aixone", in Dijkstra, J. Kroessen, J. & Y. Kuiper (eds), Myths, martyrs, and modernity: studies in the history of religions in honour of Jan N. Bremmer, 193 – 208, Leiden. (Studies in the history of religion 127)

Kloppenborg, J. S. & S. G. Wilson (eds) (1996), Voluntary associations in the Graeco-Roman world, London.

Klosko, G. (1988), "The Nocturnal Council in Plato's Laws", *Political Studies* 36, 74 – 88.

Klutz, G. A. (1821), De foedere boeotico, Berlin.

Knox, A. D. (1929), "A Strange Law at Sparta", *CR* 43, 52 – 53.

Knoepfler, D. (2004), "'Pauvres et malheureux Érétriens': Démosthène et la nouvelle loi d'Érétrie contre la tyrannie", in Poleis e politeiai, 19 – 30.

Knoepfler, D. (2002), "Un proxène malmené (Xenophon, Hell. VII 2, 16): critique des textes et histoire des institutions", Ktema 27, 71 – 78.

Knoepfler, D. (2002), "Loi d'Éretrie contre la tyrannie et l'oligarchie (deuxième partie)", BCH 126, 149 – 204.

Knoepfler, D. (2001), Décrets érétriens de proxénie et de citoyenneté, Lausanne. (Eretria. Fouilles et recherches 11)

Knoepfler, D. (2001), "Loi d'Éretrie contre la tyrannie et l'oligarchie (première partie)",BCH 125,195 - 238.

Knoepfler,D. (2001),"Le contrat d'Éretrie en Eubée pour le drainage de l'étang de Ptéchai", in Irrigation et drainage dans l'Antiquité. Qanats et canalisation souterraine en Iran,en Égypte et en Grèce(Séminaire tenu au Collège de France sous la direction de Pierre Briant),41 - 80,Paris.

Knoepfler,D. (2000),"La loi de Daitôndas,les femmes de Thèbes et le collège des béotarques au IVe et au IIIe siècle avant J.-C.",in Angeli Bernardini,P. (ed), Presenza e funzione della città di Tebe nella cultura greca (Atti del convegno internazionale,Urbino,7 - 9 luglio 1997),345 - 366,Pisa.

Knoepfler,D. (1989),"Un legislateur thebain chez Ciceron('De Legibus',II 15,37)", in Piérart, M. & O. Curty (eds), Historia testis. Mélanges d'épigraphie, d'histoire ancienne et de philologie offerts à Tadeusz Zawadki,37 - 60,Fribourg.

Knoepfler,D. (1986),"La royauté grecque",REG 99,332 - 341.

Knoepfler, D. (1980), "Sur une clause du traité de 394 avant J.-C. entre Athènes et Éretrie",AJPh 101,462 - 469.

Knoepfler,D. (1978),"Proxénies béotiennes du IVe siècle",BCH 102,375 - 393. Kobayashi, N. (1995), "Exegetai in Classical Athens", *Journal of Classical Studies* 43,22 - 31.

Koch, Chr. (2006), "Fremde im Dienst der Wiederrichtung von Volksherrschaften in griechischen Stadtstaaten",in Hengstl,J. & U. Sick(eds),Recht gestern und heute: Festschrift zum 85. Geburtstag von Richard Haase, 97 - 108, Wiesbaden. (Philippika 13)

Koch,Chr. (1999),"The Athenian Syngrapheis in the Fifth Century B. C.: Ad Hoc Drafting Committees or Elements of an Integrative Approach?",*RIDA* 46,13 - 42.

Koch,Chr. (1998 - 1999),"Rechtsinstitute für die politische Restitution in der griechischen Poleis",BIDR 40 - 41,253 - 311.

Koch, Chr. (1996), "Die Wiederherstellung der Demokratie in Ilion. Zum Wandel der Gesetzgebung gegen die Tyrannis in der griechischen-makedonischen Welt",ZRG 113,32 - 63.

Koch, Chr. (1995 - 1996), "Der Bouleuten-Eid: ein Beitrag zur Verfassungsentwicklung in Athen",BIDR 37 - 38,277 - 302.

Koch, Chr. (1993), "Die Herrschaft Athens im ersten athenischen Seebund: Rechtsvereinheitlichung im Verwaltungsverfahren", RIDA 40, 139 – 182.

Koch, Chr. (1991), Volksbeschlüsse in Seebundangelegenheiten. Das Verfahrensrecht Athens im ersten attischen Seebund, Frankfurt. (Europäische Hochschulschriften 3. Geschichte und ihre Hilfswissenschaften 466) Koerner, R. (1993) Inschriftliche Gesetzestexte der frühen griechischen Polis, Köln. (Akten der Gesellschaft für griechische und hellenistische Rechtsgeschichte 9)

Koerner, R. (1987), "Beamtenvergehen und deren Bestrafung nach frühen griechischen Inscriften", Klio 69, 450 – 498.

Koerner, R. (1985), "Diebtstahl im attischen Recht", Klio 67, 597 – 601.

Koerner, R. (1981), "Vier frühe Verträge zwischen Gemeinnwesen und Privatleuten auf griechische Inschriften", Klio 63, 179 – 216.

Koerner, R. (1974), "Zu Recht und Verwaltung der griechischen Wasserversorgung nach den Inschriften", AfP 22 – 23, 155 – 202.

Koerner, R. (1974), "Die Entwicklung der attischen Demokratie nach dem Peloponnesischen Kriege in Verfassung, Verwaltung und Recht", in Welskopf, E. Ch. (ed), Hellenische Poleis, 132 – 146, Berlin. Konstan, D. (2000), "Pity and the law in Greek theory and practice", Dike 3, 125 – 145.

Konstan, D. (1987), "Between courtesan and wife: Menander's Perikeiromene", Phoenix 41, 122 – 139.

Kotsiris, L. (1988), "An Antitrust Case in Ancient Greek Law", *International Lawyer* 22, 451ff.

Koulakiotis, E. (2008), "Greek Lawgivers in Plutarch: A Comparison between the Biographical Lycurgus and the Rhetorical Alexander", in Nikolaidis, A. G. (ed), The unity of Plutarch's work. "Moralia" themes in the "Lives", features of the "Lives" in the "Moralia", 403 – 422, Berlin. (Millenium-Studien 19)

Kränzlein, A. (1997), "Zum attischen Apotimema", Orbis Iuris Romani 3, 31 – 39. (= Rainer, J. M. (ed) (2010), Arnold Kränzlein. Schriften, 265 – 274, Wien)

Kränzlein, A. (1997), "Überlegungen zu den Freilassungsinschriften von Bouthrotos", in Symposion 1995, 205 – 210.

Kränzlein, A. (1983), "Die Bedeutung der Aufzeichnungen im heiligen Bezirk für die juristische Erfassung des Rechtsinstitutes. Freilassung in Delphi", in Festschrift

Sutter, 301 - 308. (= Rainer, J. M. (ed) (2010), Arnold Kränzlein. Schriften, 151 - 160, Wien)

Kränzlein, A. (1982), "Fragen der Rechtsverfolgung in Delphi zur Zeit der Freilassungsinschriften", in Mneme Petropoulou II, 52 - 75. (= Symposion 1982, 185 - 186, also Rainer, J. M. (ed) (2010), Arnold Kränzlein. Schriften, 161 - 170, Wien)

Kränzlein, A. (1980), "Bemerkungen zu Form der delphischen Freilassungen", RIDA 27, 81 - 91. (= Rainer, J. M. (ed) (2010), Arnold Kränzlein. Schriften, 113 - 120, Wien)

Kränzlein, A. (1979), "Bemerkungen zu den griechischen Freilassungsinschriften", in Symposion 1982, 237 - 248. (= Rainer, J. M. (ed) (2010), Arnold Kränzlein. Schriften, 121 - 130, Wien)

Kränzlein, A. (1975), Rechtsvorstellungen im altgriechischen und gräko-ägyptischen Rechtskreis, Graz. (= Rainer, J. M. (ed) (2010), Arnold Kränzlein. Schriften, 63 - 72, Wien)

Kränzlein, A. (1975), "Die attischen Aufzeichnungen über die Einlieferung von phialai exeleutherikai", in Symposion 1971, 255 - 264. (= Rainer, J. M. (ed) (2010), Arnold Kränzlein. Schriften, 79 - 88, Wien)

Kränzlein, A. (1972), "Eine atypische prasis epi lusei", in Festgabe für Arnold Herdlitczka, 161 - 166, München-Salzburg. (= Rainer, J. M. (ed) (2010), Arnold Kränzlein. Schriften, 55 - 62, Wien)

Kränzlein, A. (1970), "Zum attischen Erbtochterrecht", in Kuchinke, K. (ed), Rechtsbewahrung und Rechtsentwicklung. Festschrift für Heinrich Lange zum 70. Geburtstag, 37 - 46, München. (= Rainer, J. M. (ed) (2010), Arnold Kränzlein. Schriften, 15 - 24, Wien)

Kränzlein, A. (1970), "Ein Fall von Grundkredit im alten Griechenland (SEG XXIV 583)", in Bekker, W. G. & L. Schnorr von Carolsfeld (eds), Sein und Werden im Recht. Festgabe für Ulrich von Lübtow zum 70. Geburtstag am 21. August 1970, 173 - 179, Berlin. (= Rainer, J. M. (ed) (2010), Arnold Kränzlein. Schriften, 25 - 32, Wien)

Kränzlein, A. (1963), Eigentum und Besitz im griechischen Recht des fünften und vierten Jahrhunderts v. Chr., Berlin. (Berliner Juristische Abhandlungen 8)

Kränzlein, A. (1957), "Sachherrschaft über das Vermögen des Erblassers während der Erbtochterehe im Recht Athens zur Zeit der Redner", Labeo 3, 415.

Krasovec, J. (1993), "Plato's and Plutarch's theories of punishment", ZAnt 43, 5 – 30.

Kremmydas, Chr. (2012), Commentary on Demosthenes Against Leptines, Oxford.

Kremmydas, Chr. (2007), "Logical Argumentation in Demosthenes, Against Leptines", in Powell, J. (ed), Logos. Rational argument in classical rhetoric, 19 – 34, London. (BICS Suppl. 96)

Krentz, P. (1986), "The Rewards for Thrasyboulos' Supporters", *ZPE* 62, 201 – 204.

Krentz, P. (1980), "Foreigners Against the Thirty: IG ii2 10 Again", *Phoenix* 34, 298 – 306.

Kristensen, K. R. (2008), "The 'Ritual' of Legislation: Some Preliminary Reflections on the Interaction of Law and Religion in Ancient Crete", in Rasmussen, A. H. & S. W. Rasmussen (eds), Religion and Society. Rituals, Resources and Identity in the Ancient Graeco-Roman World (The BOMOS-conferences 2002 – 2005), 107 – 115, Roma. (Analecta Romana Instituti Danici Suppl. 40)

Kristensen, K. R. (2007), "Inheritance, Property, and Management: Gortynian Family Law Revisited", in Symposion 2005, 89 – 100.

Kristensen, K. R. (2005), Gortynloven: den store Indskrift fra Gortyn pa Kreta, Kopenhagen.

Kristensen, K. R. (2004), "Codification, Tradition and Innovation in the Law Code of Gortyn", Dike 7, 135 – 168.

Kristensen, K. R. (2004), "Gortynian Debt Bondage-Some New Consdierations on IC IV 41 iv – VII, 47 and 72 I. 56 – II. 2, X. 25 – 32", *ZPE* 149, 73 – 79.

Kristensen, K. R. (2002), "On the Gortynian PYLA and STARTOS of the 5th Century B. C. ", *ClassMed* 53, 65 – 80.

Kristensen, K. R. (1994), "Men, Women and Property in Gortyn: The Karteros of the Law Code", *ClassMed* 45, 5 – 26.

Kudryavtseva, T. V. (2008), "The Litigants on the Beme: The Speeches and Behaviour of the Parties in the Athenian Court", *VDI* 264, 3 – 18. (in Russian)

Kudryavtseva, T. V. (2007), "Sycophants and the Athenian Democracy", *VDI* 261, 174 – 184 (in Russian).

Kuenen-Jansens, L. J. Th. (1941), "Some Notes upon the Competence of the Athenian Women to Conduct a Transaction", *Mnemosyne* 9, 199 – 241.

Kulesza, R. (2008), "Spartan Gamos in the Classical Period", *Palamedes* 3, 135 – 166.

Künen-Janssens, L. J. T. (1941), "Some Notes upon the Competence of Athenian Women to Conduct a Transaction", *Mnemosyne* 9, 199 – 214.

Kyriazis, N. C. & M. C. Zouboulakis (2004), "Democracy, Sea Power and Institutional Change. An Economic Analysis of the Athenian Naval Law", *European Journal of Law and Economics* 17, 117 – 132.

Kyrkos, B. A. (2009), "A Good and Excellent Citizen (Arist. Pol. Γ4, 1276b 16)", in *The Notion of Citizenship*, 161 – 178. (in Greek)

L

L'Homme-Wery, L-M. (2008), "Perdre sa liberté et la retrouver dans l'Athènes de Solon", in Hommage à J. Annequin, 395 – 408.

L'Homme-Wéry, L.-M. (2005), "Le rôle de la loi dans la pensée politique de Solon", in Le législateur et la loi, 169 – 186.

L'Homme-Wery, L.-M. (2004), "La législation de Solon: une solution à la crise agraire d'Athènes?", Pallas 64, 145 – 156.

L'Homme-Wery, L.-M. (2002), "De l'eunomie solonienne à l'isonomie clisthénienne: d'une conception religieuse de la cité à sa rationalisation partielle", Kernos 15, 211 – 223.

L'Homme-Wéry, L.-M. (1999), "Eleusis and Solon's seisachtheia", GRBS 40, 109 – 133.

Lacey, W. K. (1968), The Family in Classical Greece, London.

dal Lago, E. & C. Katsari (eds) (2008), Slave Systems, Ancient and Modern, Cambridge.

Lakin, K. (2005), "Legal Pluralism in Archaic Greece", Princeton/Stanford Working Papers in Classics http://www. princeton. com/ ~ pcwpc/pdfs/lakin/120517. pdf.

Laks, A. (2006), "Form und Inhalt des platonischen Gesetzes", in Gesetz und Gesetzlichkeit, 11 - 22.

Lambert, S. D. (2010), "Inscribed treaties ca 350 - 312. An epigraphical perspective on Athenian foreign policy", in Reger, G., Ryan, F. X. & T. F. Winters (eds), Studies in epigraphy and history in honor of Stephen V. Tracy, 153 - 160, Bordeaux. (= Lambert, S. D. (2012), Inscribed Athenian laws and decrees 352/1 - 322/1 BC. Epigraphical essays, 377 - 388, Leiden)

Lambert, S. D. (2010), "Athens, Sokles and the exploitation of an Attic resource (IG ii2 411)", in Sekunda, N. (ed), Ergasteria: works presented to J. Ellis on his 80th birthday, 115 - 125, Gdansk. (= Lambert, S. D. (2012), Inscribed Athenian laws and decrees 352/1 - 322/1 BC. Epigraphical essays, 363 - 376, Leiden)

Lambert, S. D. (2007), "Athenian State Laws and Decrees, 352/1 - 322/1. IV Treaties and Other Texts", *ZPE* 161, 67 - 100. (= Lambert, S. D. (2012), Inscribed Athenian laws and decrees 352/1 - 322/1 BC. Epigraphical essays, 184 - 220, Leiden)

Lambert, S. D. (2007), "Athenian State Laws and Decrees, 352/1 - 322/1: III. Decrees Honouring Foreigners B. Other Awards", *ZPE* 159, 101 - 154. (= Lambert, S. D. (2012), Inscribed Athenian laws and decrees 352/1 - 322/1 BC. Epigraphical essays, 138 - 183, Leiden)

Lambert, S. D. (2006), "Athenian State Laws and Decrees, 352/1 - 322/1: III. Decrees Honouring Foreigners A. Citizenship, Proxeny and Euergesy", *ZPE* 158, 115 - 158. (= Lambert, S. D. (2012), Inscribed Athenian laws and decrees 352/1 - 322/1 BC. Epigraphical essays, 93 - 137, Leiden)

Lambert, S. D. (2005), "Athenian State Laws and Decrees 362/1 - 322/1: II Religious Regulations", *ZPE* 154, 120 - 159. (= Lambert, S. D. (2012), Inscribed Athenian laws and decrees 352/1 - 322/1 BC. Epigraphical essays, 48 - 92, Leiden)

Lambert, S. D. (2004), "Athenian State Laws and Decrees 352/1 - 322/1: I. Decrees Honouring Athenians", *ZPE* 150, 85 - 120. (= Lambert, S. D. (2012), Inscribed Athenian laws and decrees 352/1 - 322/1 BC. Epigraphical essays, 3 - 47, Leiden)

Lambert, S. D. (2004), "A House of the Piraeans?", *ZPE* 146, 91 - 92.

Lambert, S. D. (1997), "The Attic Genos Salaminioi and the Island of

Salamis", *ZPE* 119, 85 – 106.

Lambert, S. D. (1996), "Notes on Two Attic Horoi and Some Corrigenda to the Phratries of Attica", *ZPE* 110, 77 – 83.

Lambert, S. D. (1993), The Phratries of Attica, Ann Arbor, Mich.

Lambert, S. D. & E. Jones (1999), "Two Security Horoi from an Ore-washery at Agrileza, Southern Attica", *ZPE* 125, 131 – 136.

Lambrechts, A. (1958), L'aspect et le texte des décrets de proxénie d'Athènes jusqu'à l'an 323 av. J. C., Bruxelles. (in Flemish)

Lämmli, F. (1938), Das attische Prozessverfahren in seiner Wirkung auf die Gerichtsrede, Paderborn.

Lampros, S. P. (1873), De conditorum coloniarum graecarum indole praemiisque et honoribus, Leipzig.

Lang, M. L. (2004), The Athenian Citizen: Democracy in the Athenian Agora, Athens.

Lang, M. L. (1994), Life, Death, and Litigation in the Athenian Agora, Princeton, NJ.

Lang, M. L. (1967), "Revolution of the 400: Chronology and Constitutions", *AJPh* 88, 176 – 187.

Langdon, M. (1994), "Public Auctions in Ancient Athens", in *Ritual, Finance, Politics*, 253 – 265.

Lange, A. (1862), Darstellungen des athenischen Handels vom Ende der Perserkriege zur Unterjochung Griechenlands durch die Römer, Chemnitz.

Lanni, A. (2010), "Transitional Justice in Ancient Athens: A Case Study", *University of Pennsylvania Journal of International Law* 32, 551ff.

Lanni, A. (2010), "The Expressive Effect of the Athenian Prostitution Laws", *ClAnt* 29, 45 – 67.

Lanni, A. (2009), "Social Norms in the Ancient Athenian Courts", *Journal of Legal Analysis* 1, 691 – 736.

Lanni, A. (2009), "Judicial Review and the Athenian Constitution", in Hernandez, A. -Chr. (ed), Démocratie athénienne-démocratie moderne: tradition et influences, 235 – 263, Genève. (Fondations Hardt 56)

Lanni, A. (2008), "The Laws of War in Ancient Greece", *Law and History*

Review 26,469ff.

Lanni, A. (2007), "Athenian Approaches to Legal Predictability in Contract Cases", in Symposion 2005,225 - 236.

Lanni, A. (2006), Law and Justice in the Courts of Classical Athens, Cambridge.

Lanni, A. (2005), "Relevance in Athenian Courts", in *The Cambridge Companion*,112 - 128.

Lanni, A. (2004), "'Verdict Most Just': The Modes of Classical Athenian Justice", *Yale Journal of Law & Humanities* 16,277 - 321.

Lanni, A. (2004), "Arguing from 'Precedent': Modern Perspectives on Athenian Practice", in *The Law and the Courts*,159 - 172.

Lanni, A. (2000), "The Homicide Courts and the Dikasteria: A Paradigm not Followed", *GRBS* 41,311 - 330.

Lanni, A. (1999), "Precedent and Legal Reasoning in Classical Athenian Courts: A Noble Lie?", *American Journal of Legal History* 43,27 - 51.

Lanni, A. (1997), "Spectator Sports or Serious Politics? Hoi Periestekotes and the Athenian Lawcourts", *JHS* 117,183 - 189.

Lape, S. (2010), "Before Race: Theorizing Athenian Citizen Identity", in Bassi, K. & J. P. Euben (eds), When Worlds Elide. Classics, Politics, Culture, 185 - 228, New York.

Lape, S. (2010), Race and Citizen Identity in the Classical Athenian Democracy, Cambridge.

Lape, S. (2006), "The Psychology of Prostitution in Aeschines' Speech Against Timarchus", in *Prostitutes & Courtesans*,139 - 160.

Lape, S. (2002 - 2003), "Solon and the Institution of the 'Democratic' Family Form", *CJ* 98,117 - 140.

Lapini, W. (1994), "Note testuali sulla Athenaion Politeia dello pseudo-Senofonte", RFIC 122,129 - 138.

Larsen, J. A. O. (1968), Greek Federal States: Their Institutions and History, Oxford.

Larsen, J. A. O. (1967), "Epirote Grants of Citizenship to Women Again", *CPh* 62,255 - 256.

Larsen, J. A. O. (1964), "Epirote Grants of Citizenship to Women Again", *CPh* 59, 106 - 107.

Larsen, J. A. O. (1960), "A New Interpretation of the Thessalian Confederacy", *CPh* 55, 229 - 248.

Larsen, J. A. O. (1960), "Orchomenos and the Formation of the Beotian Confederacy in 447 B. C.", *CPh* 55, 9 - 18.

Larsen, J. A. O. (1955), Representative Government in Greek and Roman History, Berkeley.

Larsen, J. A. O. (1950), "Aristotle on the Electors of Mantineia and Representative Government", *CPh* 45, 180 - 183.

Larsen, J. A. O. (1949), "The Origin and Significance of the Counting of Votes", *CPh* 44, 164 - 181.

Larsen, J. A. O. (1946), "The Acharnians and the Pay of the Taxiarchs", *CPh* 41, 91 - 99.

Larsen, J. A. O. (1940), "The Constitution and Original Purpose of the Delian League", *HSCP* 61, 175 - 213.

Latte, K. (1968), "Themis und Verwandtes", in Latte, Kleine Schriften, 141 - 151.

Latte, K. (1948), "Kollektivbesitz und Staatsschatz in Griechenland", Akademie der Wissenschaften in Göttingen aus den Jahren 1945/48, Phil. -hist. Klasse, 64 - 75. (= Latte, Kleine Schriften, 294 - 312)

Latte, K. (1946), "Der Rechtsgedanke im archaischen Griechentum", Antike & Abendland 2, 63 - 76.

Latte, K. (1931), "Beiträge zum griechischen Strafrecht", Hermes 66, 30 - 48; 129 - 158. (= Zur griechischen Rechtsgeschichte, 263 - 314, Darmstadt and in Latte, Kleine Schriften, 252 - 293)

Latte, K. (1920 - 1921), "Schuld und Sünde in der griechischen Religion", Archiv für Religionswissenschaft 20, 254 - 298.

Latte, K. (1920), Heiliges Recht. Untersuchungen zur Geschichte der Sakralen Rechtsformen in Griechenland, Tübingen. Laurence, P. M. (1915), "Law of War in Ancient Greece", *LT* 139, 507 - 508.

Laurence, P. M. (1879), "Judges and Litigants", *Journal of Philology* 8, 125 -

132.

Lavelle, B. M. (1988), "A Note on the First Three Victims of Ostracism (Athenaion Politeia 22.4)", *CPh* 83, 131 – 135.

Lavery, G. (1974), "Training, Trade and Trickery: Three Lawgivers in Plutarch", *CW* 67, 369 – 381.

Lawless, J. M. (1994), "A Note on Menander Aspis 174 – 180", *Hermes* 122, 364 – 365.

Lawless, J. M. (1991), Law, Argument and Equity in the Speeches of Isaeus, diss. Brown University.

Leach, A. (1900), "The Athenian Democracy in the Light of Greek Literature", *AJPh* 21, 361 – 377.

Leaf, W. (1887), "The Trial Scene in Iliad xviii", *JHS* 8, 122 – 132.

Leahy, D. M. (1954), "Aegina and the Peloponnesian League", *CPh* 47, 232 – 243.

Lecrivain, Ch. (1941), La neutralité dans le droit international de la Grèce classique, Toulouse. (MAT s. 13, 3)

Lecrivain, Ch. (1940), "Varia. I. Caractère de l'exil ordinaire dans le droit pénal d'Athènes", REA 42, 214 – 218.

Lecrivain, Ch. (1939), "L'atimie civique en Grèce", MAT 13, 1, 29 – 58.

Lecrivain, Ch. (1938), Les jurys populaires en Grèce, Toulouse. (MAT s. 12, 16)

Lecrivain, Ch. (1937), Le pouvoir judiciaire des assemblées du peuple grec, Toulouse. (MAT s. 12, 15)

Lecrivain, Ch. (1936), Trois formes speciales d'accusation dasn le droit penal grec: L'apagoge-l'ephegesis et l'endeixis, Toulouse. (MAT s. 12, 14)

Lecrivain, C. (1935), L'adultère et la séduction dans le droit grec classique, Toulouse. (MAT s. 12, 13)

Lecrivain, Ch. (1934), "La prison et la peine de l'emprisonnement chez les Grecs", MAT 12, 12, 177 – 192.

Lecrivain, Ch. (1934), Le caractère juridique de l'abandon des nouveaux-nés en Grèce, Toulouse. (MAT s. 12, 12)

Lecrivain, Ch. (1933), Le suicide dans l'antiquité grecque, Toulouse. (MAT s.

12,11)

Lecrivain, Ch. (1932), "Notes de droit pénal grec. I: La bouleusis, II: L'avortement", in Mèlanges Glotz II, 527 – 534.

Lecrivain, Ch. (1930), Le concept moral et le delit de l'hybris chez des Grecs. Comparaison avec l'injure romaine, Toulouse. (MAT s. 12, 8)

Lecrivain, Ch. (1919), "L'exil politique dans l'histoire grecque", MAT 11, 7, 317 – 371.

Lecrivain, Ch. (1917), "Les hétairies dans la Grèce classique", MAT 11, 5, 183 – 208.

Lecrivain, Ch. (1916), "L'institution des otages dans l'antiquité", MAT 11, 4, 115 – 139.

Lecrivain, Ch. (1915), "L'arbitrage international dans la Grèce classique", MAT 11, 3, 1 – 24.

Lecrivain, Ch. (1912), "Témoignage dans le droit grec", MAT 12, 258 – 259.

Lecrivain, Ch. (1910), Les fondations perpetuelles dans le droit grec, Toulouse. (MAT s. 10, 10)

Lecrivain, Ch. (1905), "L'action populaire et les primes aux dénonciateurs dans le droit grec", MAT 10, 5, 40 – 50.

Lecrivain, Ch. (1897), Le droit de se faire justice soi-même et les represailles dans les relations internationales de la Grèce, Toulouse. (MAT s. 9, 9)

Lecrivain, Ch. (1896), "Quelques points de droit grec dans les plaidoyers de Ciceron", MAT 9, 8, 270 – 291.

Lecrivain, Ch. (1895), "Peines et stipulations du double et de l'hemiolion dans le droit grec", MAT 9, 7, 302 – 315.

Lecrivain, Ch. (1894), "Le cautionnement dans le droit grec classique", MAT 9, 6, 200 – 225.

Lecrivain, Ch. (1889), "L'antidose dans la législation athénienne", RH 40, 276 – 285.

Lentz, T. M. (1983), "Spoken Versus Written Inartistic Proofs in Athenian Courts", Ph & Rh 16, 246 – 261.

Leduc, Cl. (2003), "La citoyenneté dans la démocratique Athènes", in Firscbach, F. & A. Jaulin (eds), Démocratie antique et démocratie moderne, 81 – 102, Toulouse.

Leduc, Cl. (2001), "En quoi cela concerne-t-il l'archonte? (A. P. LVI, 2 - 5)", Pallas 56, 15 - 44.

Leduc, Cl. (1998), "L'adoption dans la cité des Atheniens, VI - IVe siècle av. J. -C.", Pallas 48, 175 - 202. (= La femme, la parenté et le politique. Parcours sensible d'une historienne. Hommage a Cl. Leduc, 175 - 202, Toulouse 2011. (Pallas 85))

Leduc, Cl. (1997), "La dot. Anthropologie et histoire", Clio. HFS 7, 18 - 50. (= La femme, la parenté et le politique. Parcours sensible d'une historienne. Hommage a Cl. Leduc, 155 - 174, Toulouse 2011. (Pallas 85))

Leduc, Cl. (1994 - 1995), "Citoyenneté et parenté dans la cité des Athéniens. De Solon à Périclès", Métis 9 - 10, 51 - 68.

Leduc, Cl. (1991), "Comment la donner en mariage? La mariée en pays grec (IXe - IVe s. av. J. -C.)", in Schmitt-Pantel, P. (ed), Histoire des femmes en Occident, 1. L'Antiquité, 259 - 318, Paris.

Leduc, Cl. (1984), "La dot de la mariée", in Femmes, feminisme et recherche (Actes du colloque national Toulouse, 17 - 19 décembre 1982), 168 - 175, Toulouse.

Leduc, Cl. (1982), "Reflexions sur le système matrimonial athénien à l'époque de la cité-état (VIe-IVe s. av. J. -C.)", in La dot, la valeur des femmes, 7 - 29, Toulouse.

Leduc, Cl. (1976), La "Constitution d'Athènes" attribuée à Xenophon, Paris. (Annales litteraires de l'Université de Besançon 192; Centre de recherche d'histoire ancienne 22)

Lehmann, G. A. (2011), "Normenkontrolle und Verantwortung des Burgers in der attischen Demokratie-Der Ephebeneid", in Bleckmann, B. & B. Dreyer (eds), Forschungen zur alten Geschichte. Kleine Schriften I, 455 - 470, Stuttgart.

Lehmann, G. A. (2001), Ansätze zu einer Theorie des griechischen Bundesstaates bei Aristoteles und Polybios, Göttingen.

Lehmann, G. A. (1995), "Il dominio dell'oligarchia nell'Atene classica: (411 - 410, 404 - 3 e 322 - 07 a. C.)", Simblos 1, 19 - 31.

Lehmann, G. A. (1995), "Überlegungen zu den oligarchischen Machtergreifungen im Athen des 4. Jh. V. Chr.", in Eder, W. (ed), Die athenische Demokratie im 4. Jahrhunderts v. Chr., 139 - 150, Stuttgart. (= Bleckmann, B. & B. Dreyer (eds),

Forschungen zur alten Geschichte. Kleine Schriften I,431 – 442,Stuttgart).

Lehmann,G. A. (1981),"Der Ostrakismos-Entsheid in Athen: von Kleisthenes zur Ära des Themistokles", *ZPE* 41,85 – 99. (= Bleckmann,B. & B. Dreyer(eds) (2011),Forschungen zur alten Geschichte. Kleine Schriften I,369 – 382,Stuttgart)

Lehmann,G. A. (1968),"Bemerkungen zur Themistokles-Inschrift von Troizen", Historia 17,276 – 288. (= Bleckmann,B. & B. Dreyer(eds)(2011),Forschungen zur alten Geschichte. Kleine Schriften I,259 – 270,Stuttgart)

Levick,B. (2012),"Women and Law",in James,Sh. L. & Sh. Dillon(eds),A Companion to Women in the Ancient World,96 – 106,London.

Lévy,Ed. (2006),"Archè chez Hérodote",in Mélanges Casevitz,89 – 98.

Lévy,Ed. (2005),"Isonomia",in Democrazia e antidemocrazia,119 – 137.

Lévy,Ed. (2004),"Dèmos chez Hérodote",Ktema 29,81 – 94.

Lévy,Ed. (2000),"La cohèrence du code de Gortyn",in La codification,185 – 214.

Lévy,Ed. (1998),"Diké chez Homère: entre privé et public",Ktèma 23,71 – 79.

Lévy,Ed. (1997),"Libres et non-libres dans le Code de Gortyne",in Hommage Garlan,25 – 41.

Lévy,Ed. (1996),"La tyrannie et son vocabulaire chez Polybe",Ktema 21,3 – 54.

Lévy,Ed. (1990),"Politeia et politeuma chez Polybe",Ktema 15,15 – 26.

Lévy,Ed. (1988),"Métèques et droit de résidence", in Lonis, R. (ed), L'étranger dans le monde grec(Actes du colloque organisée par l'Institut d'Études Anciennes,Nancy,mai 1987),47 – 67,Nancy.

Lévy,Ed. (1987),"La monarchie macédonienne et le mythe d'une royauté démocratique",Ktema 3,201 – 225.

Lévy,Ed. (1983),"Les trois traités entre Sparte et le roi",BCH 107,221 – 241.

Lévy,Ed. (1983),"Autonomia et eleutheria au Ve siècle",RPh 57,249 – 270.

Lévy,Ed. (1977),"La Grande Rhetra",Ktema 2,85 – 103.

Lévy,Ed. (1975),"Réformes et date de Solon. Réponse a F. Cassola",PdP 28, 88 – 91.

Lewis,B. V. (2009),"'Reason Striving to Become Law'. Nature and Law in

Plato's Laws", *The American Journal of Jurisprudence* 54, 67 – 91.

Leão, D. F. (2011), "In Defense of Medea: A Legal Approach to Euripides", *EHHD* 43, 9 – 26.

Leão, D. F. (2010), "The Legal Horizon of the Oresteia: The Crime of Homicide and the Founding of Areopagus", in *Law and Drama in Ancient Greece*, 39 – 60.

Leão, D. F. (2010), "Sólon e a experiência da viagem e do exílio: motivações politicas, económicas e legais", in Cortés Gabaudan, Fr. & J. V. Mendez Dosana (eds), Dic mihi Musa virum. Homenaje al profesor A. López Eire, 379 – 387, Salamanca.

Leão, D. F. (2006), "Dikai emporikai. Processos relativos a comerciantes maritimos na Grecia antiga", in de Oliveira, Fr., Thiercy, P. & R. Vilaça (eds), Mar Greco-Latino, 127 – 138, Coimbra.

Leão, D. F. (2006), "Os desencantos de Medeia: uma xene privada de kyrios, de oikos e de polis", in Suarez de la Torre, E. & M. C. Fialho (eds), Bajo el signo de Medea, 67 – 82, Coimbra.

Leão, D. F. (2005), "Sólon e a legislação em matéria de direito familiar", Dike 8, 5 – 32.

Leão, D. F. (2005), "Esposas, amantes e outras mulheres: legalidade e penalização des relações dentro do oikos", in Ut par delicto, 55 – 66.

Leão, D. F. (2005), "O horizonte legal de Oresteia: o crime de homicido e a fundação do tribunal do Areópago", Humanitas (Coimbra) 57, 3 – 38.

Leão, D. F. (2004), "Materia religiosa: processos de impiedade (asebeia)", in Nomos. Direito e sociedade, 201 – 226.

Leão, D. F. (2003), "Los limites de la globalización ciudadanía y exclusión en el derecho ático", Logos 3, 161 – 166.

Leão, D. F. (2003), Aristoteles. Constituição dos Atenienses, Lisboa.

Leão, D. F. (2002), "Legislação relativa as mulheres na Vita Solonis de Plutarco", in Actas do Congresso "Plutarco educador da Europa", 81 – 91, Lisboa.

Leão, D. F. (2002), "Solon e a lei sobre a neutralidade em tempo de stasis", Agora 4, 25 – 37.

Leão, D. F. (2001), Sólon: ética e politica, Lisboa.

Leão, D. F. (2001), "Nomos arghias", Logos 1, 103 – 108.

Leão, D. F. (2001), "Matrimonio, amor e sexo na legislação de Sólon",

Humanitas(Coimbra)53,113 - 132.

Lewis,B. V. (2009),"Higher Law and the Rule of Law. The Platonic Origin of an Ideal",*Pepperdine Law Review* 36,631 - 660.

Lewis,D. M. (1962),"The Federal Constitution of Keos",*BSA* 57,1 - 4.

Lewis,D. M. (1959),"Attic Manumissions",*Hesperia* 28,238.

Lewis, J. D. (2011), "Constitution and Fundamental Law. The Lesson of Classical Athens",in Frankel Paul,E. ,Miller jr,F. D. & J. Paul(eds),*What Should Constitutions Do*?,25 - 49,Cambridge.

Lewis,J. D. (2007),Early Greek Lawgivers,London.

Lewis,J. D. (2004),"Slavery and Lawlessness in Solonian Athens",Dike 7, 19 - 40.

Lewis, J. D. (2001), "'Dike', 'Moira', 'Bios' and the Limits to Understanding in Solon,13(West)",Dike 4,113 - 136.

Lewis,N. (1982),"'Aphairesis' in Athenian Law and Custom",in Symposion 1977,161 - 178.

Lewis,N. (1941),"Solon's Agrarian Legislation",*AJPh* 62,144 - 156.

Lewis,S. (2011),"Women and Tyranny",in Lambert,St. (ed),Sociable Man: Essays on Ancient Greek Social Behaviour in Honour of N. Fisher, 215 - 230, Swansea.

Lewis,S. (2009)Greek tyranny,Exeter.

von Leyden,W. (1967),"Aristotle and the Concept of Law",*Philosophy* 42, 1 - 19.

Lindsay,H. (2011),"Adoption and Heirship in Greece and Rome",in Rawson, B. (ed),A Companion to Families in the Greek and Roman Worlds,346 - 360, London.

Linforth,I. M. (1919),Solon the Athenian,Berkeley. (Publications in classical philology 6)

Link,St. (2008),"Aristoteles,Ephoros und die 'Kretische Verfassung'", *Gymnasium* 115,469 - 480.

Link,St. (2004),"Zur frühgriechischen Kyrieia",*ZRG* 121,44 - 93.

Link,St. (2004),"Die Nötigung des Mündels in Gortyn(IC IV 72,col. 2,16 - 20)",Dike 7,169 - 178.

Link,St. (2004),"Wenn die einen teilen wollen,die anderen aber nicht... :zum Großen Gesetz von Gortyn,col. 5,28 – 54",Göttinger Forum für Altertumswissenschaft 7,59 – 66.

Link,St. (2003),"Kosmoi, startoi und Iterationsverbote. Zum Kampf um das Amt des Kosmos auf Kreta",Dike 6,151 – 160.

Link,St. (2003),"Eunomie im Schloss der Rhetra?:zum Verhältnis von Tyr. 14W und Plut. Lyk. 6,2 und 8",Göttinger Forum für Altertumswissenschaft 6,141 – 150.

Link,St. (2002),"100 Städte – 100 Verfassungen? Einheitlichkeit und Vielfalt in den griechischen Städten Kretas",Cretan Studies 7,149 – 75.

Link,St. (2001),"'Dolos' und 'woikeus' im Recht von Gortyn",Dike 4, 87 – 112.

Link, St. (2000), Das frühe Sparta. Untersuchungen zur spartanischen Staatsbildung im 7. und 6. Jahrhundert v. Chr., St. Katharinen. (Pharos. Studien zur griechisch-römischen Antike 13)

Link,St. (1999),"Spartas Untergang",Laverna 10,17 – 37.

Link,St. (1998),"Durch diese Tür geht kein Wort hinaus(Plut. Lyk. 12,8). Bürgergemeinschaft und Syssitien in Sparta",Laverna 9,82 – 112.

Link,St. (1995),"Beuteteilung und Herrschaftsform bei Homer",Laverna 6, 147 – 162.

Link, St. (1994), "Zur archaischen Gesetzgebung in Katane und im epizephyrischen Lokroi",in Rechtskodifizierung,165 – 177.

Link,St. (1992),"Die Gesetzgebung des Zaleukos im epizephyrischen Lokroi", Klio 74,11 – 24.

Link, St. (1991), Landverteilung und sozialer Frieden im archäischen Griechenland,Stuttgart. (Historia Einzelschriften 69)

Link,St. (1991),"Das Siedlungsgesetz aus Westlokris(Bronze Pappadakis; IG IX. 1 Fasc 3,Nr. 609 = Meiggs-Lewis 13)",ZPE 87,65 – 77.

Lipka, M. (2002), "Notes on the influence of the Spartan Great Rhetra on Tyrtaeus,Herodotus and Xenophon", in Powell, A. & St. Hodkinson (eds), Sparta. Beyond the mirage,219 – 226,Cardiff.

Lipka, M. (2002), Xenophon's Spartan Constitution, Berlin. (Texte und

Kommentar 24)

Lipsius, J. H. (1924), "Chronologisches Verzeichnis der Schriften von Justus Hermann Lipsius", Bu 202, 30 – 36.

Lipsius, J. H. (1919), "Lysias' rede gegen Hippotherses und das attische Metoikenrecht", BSGW 71, 9ff.

Lipsius, J. H. (1916), "Die attische Steuerverfassung und das attische Volksvermogen", RhM 71, 161 – 186.

Lipsius, J. H. (1909), "Zum Recht von Gortyns", ASGW 27, 391 – 410.

Lipsius, J. H. (1905 – 1915), Das attische Recht und Rechtsverfahren, mit Benutzung des attischen Prozesses von M. H. E. Meier und G. F. Schoemann dargestellt von J. H. Lipsius, Leipzig.

Lipsius, J. H. (1904), "Über Antiphons Tetralogien", BSGW 56, 191 – 204.

Lipsius, J. H. (1898), "Beiträge zur Geschichte griechischer Bundesverfassungen", BSGW 50, 145 – 176.

Lipsius, J. H. (1896), "Zu Hypereides Rede gegen Athenogenes", Philologus 55, 39 – 45.

Lipsius, J. H. (1895), "Procheirotonie und Epicheirotonie", LSt 17, 403 – 412.

Lipsius, J. H. (1894), "Die Phratrie der Demotionidai", LSt 16, 159 – 171.

Lipsius, J. H. (1893), Von der Bedeutung des griechischen Rechts, Leipzig.

Lipsius, J. H. (1891), "Über das neugefundene Buch des Aristoteles vom Staat der Athener", BSGW 43, 41 – 69.

Lipsius, J. H. (1888), "Zu Demosthenes", LSt 11, 351 – 367.

Lipsius, J. H. (1883), "Über die Unechtheit der ersten Rede gegen Aristogeiton", LSt 6, 317 – 331.

Lipsius, J. H. (1881), "Miscellen: 1. Die Archonten im Areopag; 4. Zum boiotischen Kalender", LSt 4, 151 – 153, 155 – 156.

Lipsius, J. H. (1878), "Die athenische Steuerreform im Jahr des Nausinikos", NJ 117, 289 – 299.

Lipsius, J. H. (1878), "Über den Zeitpunkt der Mündigsprechung im attischen Rechte", NJ 117, 299 – 303.

Lisi, F. L. (2010), "Violence and law in Plato's second best constitution", in Bosch-Veciana, A. & J. Montserrat-Molas (eds), Philosophy and dialogue. Studies on

Plato's dialogues II,157 – 169,Barcelona.

Lisi,F. L. (2001),"The concept of law in Aristotle's Politics",in Cleary,J. J. & G. M. Gurtler (eds), Proceedings of the Boston Area Colloquium in ancient philosophy,29 – 61,Leiden.

Littman,R. J. (1979),"Kinship in Athens",AncSoc 10,5 – 31.

Llewellyn-Jones,L. (2011),"Domestic Abuse and Violence Against Women in Ancient Greece",in Lambert,St. (ed),Sociable Man:Essays on Ancient Greek Social Behaviour in Honour of N. Fisher,231 – 266,Swansea.

Lloyd-Jones,H. (1971),The Justice of Zeus,Berkeley.

Lockwood,T. C. (2003),"Justice in Aristotle's household and city",Polis 20, 1 – 21.

Lögdberg,L. E. (1898),Animadversiones de actione paranomon,Upsala.

Lönen, D. (1948), Dikè, een historisch-semantische analyse van het gerechtigheidsbegrip,Amsterdam.

Löning,T. C. (1987),The reconciliation agreement of 403/2 BC in Athens:Its content and application,Stuttgart. (Hermes Einzelschrift 53)

Lofberg,J. O. (1921 – 1922),"Trial by Jury in Athens and America",*CJ* 17, 3 – 15.

Lofberg,J. O. (1920),"The Sycophant-parasite",*CPh* 15,61 – 72.

Lofberg,J. O. (1917),Sycophancy in Athens,Chicago.

Loomis, W. T. (2003), "Slander in Ancient Athens: A Common Law Perspective",in Gestures,287 – 300.

Loomis, W. T. (1972), "The Nature of Premeditation in Athenian Homicide Law",JHS 92,86 – 95.

Lord,G. D. (1899),"An Attic lease inscription",AJA 3,44 – 53.

Lotze,D. (1997),"Il cittadino e la partecipazione al governo della polis", in Settis,S. (ed),I Greci. Storia,cultura,arte,società 2. Una storia greca II. Definizioni, 369 – 398,Torino.

Lotze,D. (1993 – 1994),"Bürger zweiter Klasse:Spartas Periöken",Akademie gemeinnutziger Wissenschaften zu Erfurt. Sitzungsberichte der Geisteswissenschaftlichen Klasse 2,37 – 51. (= Lotze,Bürger und Unfreie,171 – 183)

Lotze, D. (1988), "Grundbesitz-und Schuldverhältnisse im vorsolonische

Attika", in Herrmann, J. & J. Köhn(eds), Familie, Staat und Gesellschaftsformation, 442 - 447, Berlin(= Lotze, Bürger und Unfreie, 49 - 56).

Lotze, D. (1985), "Die Teilhabe des Bürgers an Regierung und Rechtsprechnung in der Organen derdirekten Demokratie des klassischen Athen", in Kluwe, E. (ed), Kultur und Fortschrift in der Blütezeit der griechischen Polis, 52 - 76, Berlin (= Kinzl, K. H. (ed) (1995), Demokratia, 372 - 411, Darmstadt and in Lotze, Bürger und Unfreie, 239 - 271).

Lotze, D. (1981), "Zwischen Politen und Metöken. Passivbürger im klassischen Athen?", Klio 63, 159 - 178. (= Lotze, Bürger und Unfreie, 283 - 309)

Lotze, D. (1971), "Zur Verfassung von Argos nach der Schlacht bei Sepeia", Chiron 1, 95 - 109. (= Lotze, Bürger und Unfreie, 69 - 86)

Lotze, D. (1962), "Zu de Foikees von Gortyn", Klio 40, 32 - 43.

Lotze, D. (1959), Metaxy eleutheron kai doulon. Studien zur Rechtsstellung unfreier Landbevölkerung in Griechenland bis zum 4. Jahrhundert v. Chr., Berlin.

Lotze, D. (1958), "Ektemoroi und vorsolonisches Schuldrecht", Philologus 102, 1 - 12. (= Lotze, Bürger und Unfreie, 15 - 26)

Lougovaya, J. (2008), "Age of the Trierachs in the Decree of Themistokles", ZPE 166, 113 - 114.

Louis, P. (1982), "L'eau et sa legislation chez Platon et Aristote", in F. & J. Métral(eds), L'homme et l'eau en Méditerranéen et au Proche-Orient, 103 - 109, Lyon. (Travaux de la Maison de l'Orient 3)

Loukopoulou, L. (1999), "Sur le statut et l'importance de l'emporion de Pistiros", BCH 123, 359 - 371.

Luban, D. (1987), "Some Greek Trials: Order and Justice in Homer, Hesiod, Aeschylus and Plato", *Tennessee Law Review* 54, 280 - 325.

Lucas, B. J. (1988), "Palto's Crito as Contribution to Philosophy of Law", in *Philosophy of Law*, 27 - 31.

Lücke, St. (1999), Syngeneia. Epigraphish-historische Studien zu einem Phänomen der antiken griechischen Diplomatie, Frankfurt. (Frankfurter Althistorische Beitrage 5)

Lugebil, K. (1861), "Über das Wesen und die historische Bedeutung des Ostrakismos in Athen", NJ 4, 117 - 175.

Lupu, E. (2005), Greek sacred law. A collection of new documents (NGSL), Leyden. (Religions in Graeco-Roman world 152)

Lupu, E. (2003), "Sacrifice at the Amphiaraeion and a Fragmentary Sacred Law from Oropos", Hesperia 72, 321 – 340.

Lytle, E. (2012), "He Thalassa Koine: Fishermen, the Sea and the Limits of Ancient Greek Regulatory Reach", ClAnt 31, 1 – 55.

M

Mac Armstrong, A. (1950), "Trial by Combat among the Greeks", *G & R* 19, 73 – 79.

Macan, R. W. (1886 – 1887), "On the Significance of the Lot and the Date of its Introduction at Athens", *Transactions of the Oxford Philological Society*, 4 – 9.

MacDonell, Sir John (1918), "Part of Greece in Jurisprudence and Legal History", *LT* 145, 463 – 464.

MacDonell, Sir John (1913 – 1914), "Treaties in Greece and the Middle Ages", *LT* 136, 155.

MacDowell, D. M. (2010), "Aristophanes and Athenian Law", in *Law and Drama* in Ancient Greece, 147 – 157.

MacDowell, D. M. (2009), "The Athenian Penalty of Epobelia", in Symposion 2007, 87 – 94.

MacDowell, D. M. (2006), "Mining Cases in Athenian Law", in Symposion 2003, 121 – 140.

MacDowell, D. M. (2005), "The Athenian Procedure of Dokimasia of Orators", in Symposion 2001, 79 – 87. (with a reply by Gagliardi, L., 89 – 97)

MacDowell, D. M. (2004), "Epikerdes of Kyrene and the Athenian Privilege of Ateleia", *ZPE* 150, 127 – 133.

MacDowell, D. M. (2004), Demosthenes: Speeches 27 – 38, Austin, Tx. (The oratory of classical Greece 8)

MacDowell, D. M. (2000), "Athenian Laws about Homosexuality", *RIDA* 47, 13 – 27.

MacDowell, D. M. (2000), "The Length of Trials for Public Offences in Athens", in *Polis and Politics*, 563 – 568.

MacDowell, D. M. (2000), Demosthenes. On the false embassy (Oration 19), Oxford.

MacDowell, D. M. (1993), "Foreign Birth and Athenian Citizenship in Aristophanes", in Sommerstein, A. H., Halliwell, J., Henderson, J. & B. Zimmermann (eds), Tragedy, Comedy and the Polis, 359 – 371, London.

MacDowell, D. M. (1992), "O Aristophanes kai ta Atheniaka dikasteria", in Symboles I, 137 – 158.

MacDowell, D. M. (1991), "The Athenian Procedure of Phasis", in Symposion 1990, 187 – 198.

MacDowell, D. M. (1990), Demosthenes. Against Meidias (Oration 21), Oxford.

MacDowell, D. M. (1989), "The Oikos in Athenian Law", *CQ* 39, 10 – 21.

MacDowell, D. M. (1989), "The Authenticity of Demosthenes 29 (Against Aphobos III) as a Source of Information about Athenian Law", in Symposion 1985, 253 – 263.

MacDowell, D. M. (1989), "Athenian Laws about Choruses", in Symposion 1982, 65 – 78.

MacDowell, D. M. (1988), "Greek Law", in Grant, R. M. & R. Kitzinger (eds), Civilisations of the Ancient Mediterranean I, 589 – 605, New York.

MacDowell, D. M. (1986), "The Law of Periandros about Symmories", *CQ* 36, 438 – 449.

MacDowell, D. M. (1986), Spartan Law, Edinburgh. (Scottish Classical Studies 1)

MacDowell, D. M. (1983), "Athenian Laws about Bribery", *RIDA* 30, 57 – 78.

MacDowell, D. M. (1982), "Love Versus Law: An Essay on Menander's Aspis", *G &R* 29, 42 – 52.

MacDowell, D. M. (1978), The Law in Classical Athens, London.

MacDowell, D. M. (1976), "Hybris in Athens", *G &R* 23, 14 – 31.

MacDowell, D. M. (1976), "Bastards as Athenian Citizens", *CQ* 26, 88 – 91.

MacDowell, D. M. (1975), "Law-making at Athens in the Fourth Century B. C.", *JHS* 95, 62 – 74.

MacDowell, D. M. (1971), Aristophanes' Wasps, Oxford.

MacDowell, D. M. (1971), "The Chronology of Athenian Speeches and Legal

Innovations in 401 – 398 B. C. ", *RIDA* 18, 267 – 273.

MacDowell, D. M. (1968), "Unintentional Homicide in the Hippolytos", *RhM* 111, 156 – 158.

MacDowell, D. M. (1963), Athenian Homicide Law in the Age of the Orators, Manchester.

MacDowell, D. M. (1962), Andocides. On the Mysteries, Oxford.

Mack, W. (2011), "The Proxeny-lists of Karthaia", *REA* 113, 319 – 344.

MacKenzie, M. M. (1981), Plato on punishment, Berkeley.

Mackil, E. (2008), "A Boiotian Proxeny Decree and Relief in the Museum of Fine Arts, Boston and Boiotian-Lakonian Relations in the 360s", Chiron 38, 157 – 194.

MacLeod, L. (2001), Dolos und Dike in Sophokles' Electra: An Ethical Study, Leiden.

MacNeal, R. A. (1992), Law and rhetoric in the Crito, Frankfurt. (European University Studies ser. 15, 56)

Mactoux, M. -M. (2009), "Esclave, fouet, rituel", in Bodiou, L., Mehl, V., Oulhen, J., Prost, F. & J. Wilgaux (eds), Chemin faisant. Mythes, cultes et société en Grèce ancienne. Mélanges en l'honneur de P. Brulé, 59 – 70, Rennes.

Mactoux, M. -M. (2008), "Regards sur la proclamation de l'affranchissement au theâtre ὰ Athènes", in Hommage ὰ J. Annequin, 437 – 451.

Mactoux, M. -M. (1999), "Esclaves-femmes dans le corpus d'Aristophane", in Femmes-esclaves, 21 – 46.

Mactoux, M. -M. (1990), "La polis en quête de théologie", in Mélanges Levêque 4, 289 – 313.

Mactoux, M. -M. (1988), "Lois de Solon sur les esclaves et formation d'une société esclavagiste", in Yuge, T. & M. Doi (eds), Forms of control and subordination in antiquity, 331 – 354, Leiden.

Mactoux, M. -M. (1986), "Les pratiques discursives comme strategie de reconnaissance (Lysias × × ×, Contre Nicomachos)", in L'Aveu, 27 – 51.

Mactoux, M. -M. (1980), Douleia. Esclavage et pratiques discursives dans l'Athènes classique, Paris.

Madden, M. S. (2006), "The Graeco-Roman Antecedents of Modern Tort

Law", *Brandeis Law Journal* 44,865 - 914.

Maeno, H. (1996), "Citizenship of Athenian Colonists in the Fourth Century B. C.", Hiroshima Shigaku Kenkyukai (*Review of Historical Studies*) 212, 49 - 66.

Maeno, H. (1995), "Citizenship of Athenian Colonists in the Fifth Century B. C. Its Dual Aspects", *Journal of Classical Studies* 43, 162 - 163.

Maezawa, N. (1994), "Solon's Reform and the Administration of Justice in Archaic Athens", Jinbun Ronkyu (*Journal of Social Science and Humanities*) 248, 21 - 62.

Maezawa, N. (1986), "Drakon's Law on Homicide and the Athenian Citizen-body", Hoseishi Kenkyu (*Legal Historical Review*) 35, 1 - 47.

Maezawa, N. (1982), "The Trial Scene on the Shield of Achilleus", Seiyoshi Kenkyu (*Study of European and American History*) 11, 25 - 43.

Maezawa, N. (1977), "Overseas Trade and Maritime Loans in Classical Athens", in Yuge, T. & S. Ito (eds), *State and Society in Classical Antiquity*, 107 - 146, Tokyo.

Maffi, A. (2005), "Family and Property Law", in *The Cambridge Companion*, 254 - 266.

Maguire, J. P. (1947), "Plato's Theory of Natural Law", *YCS* 10, 151 - 178.

Malkin, I. (1993), "Land Ownership, Territorial Possession, Hero Cults and Scholarly Theory", in *Nomodeiktes*, 225 - 234.

Manville, P. B. (1994), "Toward a New Paradigm of Athenian Citizenship", in *Athenian Identity*, 21 - 33.

Manville, P. B. (1990), The Origins of Citizenship in Ancient Athens, Princeton.

Manville, P. B. (1980), "Solon's Law of Stasis and Atimia in Archaic Athens", *TAPhA* 110, 213 - 221.

Margetić, L. (1965), "The Judge-affixer in the Judicial Procedure of Athens", *RIDA* 12, 149 - 155.

Mari, M. (2004), "Macedonians and pro-Macedonians in early Hellenistic Athens: Reflections on Asebeia", in Palagia, O. & St. V. Tracy (eds) (2004), The Macedonians in Athens 322 - 229 B. C. (Proceedings of an international conference held at the University of Athens, May 24 - 26, 2001), 82 - 92, Oxford.

Markle, M. M. (1990), "Participation of Farmers in Athenian Juries and

Assemblies",*AncSoc* 21,149 - 165.

Marr,J. L. & P. J. Rhodes(eds)(2008),The Old Oligarch. The Constitution of the Athenians Attributed to Xenophon,Oxford.

Marr,J. L. & N. Worswick(1994),"The Institution of Ostracism at Athens", *Ostraka* 3,285 - 290.

Marrou,H. I. (1975),"Le droit à l'education dans l'antiquité greco-romaine", Recueils de la société Jean Bodin 39(L'enfant V. Le droit à l'education),79 - 93.

Martha,J. (1877),"Inscription de Spata; Contrat de vente à réméré",BCH 1, 235 - 239.

Martin,A. (1989),"L'ostracisme Athénien:un demi-siècle de découvertes et de recherches",REG 102,124 - 145.

Martin,G. (2008),"The Witness's Exomosia in Athens",*CQ* 58,56 - 68.

Martin,G. (2006),"Forms of Address in Athenian Courts",*MH* 63,75 - 88.

Martin, R. (1980), "Relations entre métropoles et colonies: aspects institutionnelles",in Studi Manni,1433 - 1445.

Martin,T. R. (1991),"Silver coins and public slaves in the Athenian law of 375/4 BC", in Metcalf, D. M. (ed), Mnemata. Papers in memory of Nancy M. Waggoner,21 - 47,New York.

Martin V. (1963),"Quelques remarques à l'occasion d'une nouvelle édition des 'Staatsverträge des Altertums'",MH 20,230 - 233.

Martini,R. (2010),"La costituzione di Cirene",Rivista di Diritto Ellenico 1 = www. ledonline. it/rivista-diritto-ellenico.

Martini,R. (2005),Diritti greci,Bologna.

Martini,R. (2003),"'Fides' e 'pistis' in materia contratualle",in Garofalo, L. (ed) Il ruolo della buona fede oggettiva nell'esperienza giuridica storica e contemporanea(Atti del convegno internazionale di studi in onore di A. Burdese, Padova-Venezia-Treviso,14 - 16 giugno 2001),II,439 - 449,Padova.

Martini,R. (2003),"Filologi,giuristi e studio del diritto greco",SDHI 69, 645 - 648.

Martini,R. (2003),"Testamento e adozione ad Atene(e Roma)",in Symposion 1999,273 - 296.

Martini,R. (2002),"Diritto romano e 'diritto greco'(Un'esperienza didattica e di ricerca: Bilancio provvisorio)", Ius Antiquum 9, 32 – 37.

Martini, R. (2002 – 2003), "Una riforma processuale nelle Leggi di Platone", in Processo civile, 86 – 92.

Martini, R. (2000), "Il decreto d'investitura dei nomoteti", Dike 3, 113 – 123.

Martini, R. (2000), "Diritto greco e common law", Index 28, 41 – 46.

Martini, R. (1999), "XII Tavole e diritto greco", Labeo 45, 20 – 37.

Martini, R. (1998), "Diritto romano e diritti stranieri", Index 26, 409 – 416.

Martini, R. (1997), "Sul contratto d'opera nell'Atene classica", in Symposion 1995, 49 – 55.

Martini, R. (1997), "Alcune considerazioni a proposito degli apeleutheroi", in Moggi, M. & G. Cordiano (eds), Schiavi e dipendenti neel'ambito dell' "oikos" e della "familia" (Atti del XXII colloquio GIREA, Pontignano (Siena), 19 – 20 novembre 1995), 11 – 18, Pisa.

Martini, R. (1991), "Il mito del consenso nella dottrina del contratto", Iura 42, 97 – 109.

Matthaiou, A. P. (2010), "A treaty of Athens with Siphnos revisited", in Philathenaios, 45 – 54.

Matthaiou, A. P. (2009), "Mia lanthanousa epigraphe tes Siphnou", in Praktika 3ou Diethnous Siphnaikou Symposiou I, 75 – 84, Athena.

Mattingly, H. B. (2002), "The Athenian Decree for Chalkis (IG I3 40)", *CQ* 52, 377 – 379.

Mattingly, H. B. (2000), "The Athenian Treaties with Troizen and Hermione", *Historia* 49, 131 – 140.

Mattingly, H. B. (1997), "The Date and Purpose of the Pseudo-Xenophon Constitution of Athens", *CQ* 47, 352 – 357.

Mattingly, H. B. (1961), "The Athenian coinage decree", Hesperia 10, 148 – 188.

McCannon, B. C. (2010), "Homicide Trials in Classical Athens", *International Review of Law and Economics* 30, 46 – 51.

McCannon, B. C., "The Trial of Socrates" (September 22, 2008). Available at SSRN: http://ssrn.com/abstract = 1272103.

McElwee, L. A. (1975), Adeia. Amnesty and immunity at Athens from Solon to Demosthenes, New York.

McGlew, J. F. (1999), "Politics on the Margins: The Athenian Hetaireiai in 415 B. C.", *Historia* 48, 1 - 22.

McHardy, F. (2008), Revenge in Athenian culture, London.

McKeown, N. (2007), The Invention of Ancient Slavery?, London.

McKiernan, J. (2005), "Socrates and the Smith Act: The Dennis Prosecution and the Trial of Socrates in 399 B. C.", *Temple University Political & Civil Rights Law Review* 15, 65 - 119.

McKinlay, A. P. (1951), "Wine and the Law in Ancient Times", in Mylonas, G. E. & D. I. Raymond (eds) Studies Presented to D. M. Robinson on his Seventieth Birthday II, 858 - 867, St. Louis.

McPherran, M. I. (2004), "Justice and pollution in the Euthyphro", Apeiron 35, 105 - 129. (= in Kamtekar, R. (ed), Plato's Euthyphro, Apology and Crito. Critical essays, 1 - 22, Lanham, MD)

McQuillin, E. (1922), "Cities of Ancient Greece", *St. Louis Law Review* 7, 200 - 208.

Medda, E. (2003), Lysiae in Hippothersem, in Theomnestum et fragmenta ex incertis orationibus (P. Oxy. *xiii* 1606), Firenze.

Mederle, K. (1902), De jurisjurandi in lite attica decem oratorum aetate usu, München.

Mehl, A. (1982), "Für eine neue Bewertung eines Justizskandals. Der Arginusenprozess und seine Überlieferung vor dem Hintergrund von Recht und Weltanschauung im Athen des ausgehenden 5. Jh. v. Chr.", *ZRG* 99, 32 - 80.

Meier, M. (2000), "Zwischen Königen und Damos. Überlegungen zur Funktion und Entwicklung des Ephorats in Sparta (7. - 4. Jh. v. Chr.)", *ZRG* 117, 43 - 102.

Meier, M. H. E. (1855), De epistatis Atheniensibus commentariolum, Halle.

Meier, M. H. E. (1854), Index atticorum archontum eponymorum qui post ol. cxxi, 2 eum magistratum obtinuerunt, Halle.

Meier, M. H. E. (1853 - 1855), Commentatio epigraphica, Halle.

Meier, M. H. E. (1847), Commentatio de vita Lycurgi quae Plutarcho adscribitur et de Lycurgi orationum reliquis, Halle.

Meier, M. H. E. (1846), Die Privatschiedsrichter und die öffentlichen Diäteten Athens, so wie die Austrägalgerichte in den griechischen Staaten des Alterthums,

Halle.

Meier, M. H. E. (1843), Commentatio de proxenia; sive, De publico Graecorum hospitio, Halle.

Meier, M. H. E. (1830), Quanta levitate Graeci jusiurandum violaverint, Halle.

Meier, M. H. E. (1828), "Von der Blutgerichtsbarkeit des areopagitischen Rathes", *RhM* 2, 265 - 279.

Meier, M. H. E. (1819), Historiae juris attici de bonis damnatorum et fiscalium debitorum libri duo, Berlin.

Meier, M. H. E. & G. Fr. Schömann (1824), Der Attische Process, Halle.

Meiggs, R. & D. Lewis (1988), *A Selection of Greek Historical Inscriptions*, Oxford.

Meinecke, J. (1971), "Gesetzesinterpretation und Gesetzesanwendung im attischen Zivilprozess", *RIDA* 18, 275 - 360.

Meinel, M. (1975), Die Rechtfertigung des Staates bei Aristoteles, diss. Mainz.

Meister, R. (1908), "Eideshelfer im griechischen Rechte", *RhM* 63, 559 - 586.

Meister, R. (1898), "Elisches Amnestiegesetz auf einer Bronzetafel aus Olympia", *BSGW* 50, 218 - 228.

Meister, R. (1895), "Über das Colonialrecht von Naupaktos", *BSGW* 47, 272 - 334.

Meister, R. (1892), "Der*ariston* in Argos", *BPh* 12, 258 - 259.

Mele, A. (2005), "Gli Eleati tra oligarchia e democrazia", in Breglia, L. & M. Lupi (eds), Da Elea a Samo: filosofi e politici di fronte all'impero ateniese (Atti del convegno di studi, Santa Maria Capua Vetere, 4 - 5 giugno 2003), 9 - 30, Napoli.

Mele, A. (2004), "Costituzioni archaiche ed Eunomia", in *Poleis e politeiai*, 55 - 69.

Mele, A. (2003), "Legislazioni arcaiche fra tradizione e innovazione", in Da Omero alla costituzione europea, 1 - 11.

Meletopoulos, I. A. (1949), "Prasis epi lysei", *Polemon* 4, 41 - 72.

Meletopoulos, I. A. (1947), Dikastika pinakia kai "chalkia", Athenai.

Meletopoulos, I. A. (1936), Anagnorisis "chalkion" kleroumenon archonton tes Athenaikes politeias, Athenai.

Mélèze-Modrzejewski, J. (2005), "Greek Law in the Hellenistic Period: Family and Marriage", in *The Cambridge Companion*, 343 – 354.

Méléze-Modrzejewski, J. (1995), "Jewish Law and Hellenistic Legal Practice in the Light of Greek Papyri from Egypt", in Collatio Iuris Romani, 299 – 315.

Méléze-Modrzejewski, J. (1991), "Le sanction de l'homicide en droit grec et hellénistique", in Symposion 1990, 3 – 16. (= Mélanges Levêque 7, 244 – 259)

Meleze-Modrzejewski, J. (1982), "La structure juridique du mariage grec", in Symposion 1979, 37 – 72. (= Scritti in onore di Orsolina Montevecchi, 231 – 268, Bologna 1981 and in Statut personnel)

Menzel, A. (1938), "Protagoras als Gesetzgeber von Thurii", in Menzel, A. (ed), Hellenika. Gesammelte kleine Schriften, 66 – 82, Baden bei Wien.

Menzel, A. (1922), Kallikles. Eine Studie zur Geschichte der Lehre vom Rechte des Stärkeren, Vienna.

Menzel, A. (1910), "Protagoras als Gesetzgeber von Thurii", BSGW 62, 191 – 929.

Menzel, A. (1910), "Protagoras als Kriminalist", Österreichische Zeitschrift für Strafrecht 1, 389 – 404.

Menzel, A. (1910), "Protagoras, der älteste Theoretiker der Demokratie", Zeitschrift für Politik 3, 205 – 238.

Menzel, A. (1903), "Untersuchungen zum Sokrates-Processe", SAW 145(2), 1ff.

Meremetis, A. (1940), Verbrecher und Verbrechen: Untersuchungen zum Strafrecht in Platons Gesetzen, Borna-Leipzig.

Merriam, A. C. (1885 – 1886), "The Law Code of the Kretan Gortyn", *AJA* 1, 324 – 350; 2, 24 – 45. Merriam, A. C. (1885 – 1886), "The Law Code of the Kretan Gortyn", *AJA* 1, 324 – 350; 2, 24 – 45.

Meritt, B. D. (1954), "Athenian Covenant with Mytilene", *AJPh* 75, 359 – 368.

Meritt, B. D. (1952), "The Law Against Tyranny", *Hesperia* 21, 355ff.

Meritt, B. D. (1946), "The Athenian Alliances with Region and Leontinoi", *CQ* 40, 85 – 91.

Meritt, B. D. (1941), "Athens and the Delian League", in The Greek Political Experience. Studies in Honor of W. K. Prentice, 50 – 60, Princeton.

Meyer, E. A. (2010), Metics and the Athenian Phialai-inscriptions. A Study in

Athenian Epigraphy and Law, Stuttgart. (Historia Einzelschriften 208)

Meyer, E. R. (2012), "Two Grants of Politeia and the Molossians at Dodona", *ZPE* 180, 205 - 216.

Meyer, H. D. (1960), "Abfall und Bestrafung von Bündnern im attisch-delischen Seebund", HZ 191, 497 - 509.

Migeotte, L. (2010), "Pratiques financières dans un dème attique a la période classique: L'inscription de Plôtheia IG I3, 258", in Thür, G. (ed), Symposion 2009. Vorträge zur griechischen und hellenistischen Rechtsgeschichte (Seggau, 25 - 30 August 2009), 53 - 66, Wien. (with a response by D. Whitehead)

Migeotte, L. (2006), "Temene demosia", in Mélanges Casevitz, 187 - 195.

Migeotte, L. (2006), "La gestion des biens sacrés dans les cités grecques", in Symposion 2003, 233 - 254.

Migeotte, L. (2005), "Les pouvoirs des agoranomes dans les cités grecques", in Symposion 2001, 287 - 301.

Migeotte, L. (2001), "Quelques aspects légaux et juridiques de l'affermage des taxes en Grèce ancienne", in Symposion 1997, 165 - 174. (= Migeotte, L. (2010) Économie et finances publiques des cités grecques. I. Choix d'articles publiés de 1976 ǎ 2001, 409 - 418, Lyon)

Migeotte, L. (1998), "Les ventes de grain public dans les cités grecques aux périodes classique et hellénistique", in Nicolet, Cl. (ed.) La mémoire perdue. Recherches sur l'administration romaine, 229 - 244, Roma. (Collection de l'EFR 243)

Migeotte, L. (1997), "Le contrôle des prix dans les cités grecques", in Andreau, J., Briant, P. & Descat, R. (eds) Economie antique. Prix et formation de prix dans les économies antiques, 33 - 52, Saint-Bertrand-de-Comminges. (EAHSBC 3)

Migeotte, L. (1992), "Citoyens, femmes et étrangers dans les souscriptions publiques des cités grecques", CV 11, 293 - 308.

Migeotte, L. (1984), L'emprunt public dans les cités grecques. Recueil des documents et analyse critique, Paris.

Migeotte, L. (1983), "Souscriptions athéniennes de la periode classique", Historia 32, 129 - 148.

Migeotte, L. (1980), "Note sur l'emploi de prodaneizein", Phoenix 34, 219 - 226. (= Migeotte, L. (2010) Économie et finances publiques des cités grecques. I.

Choix d'articles publiés de 1976 à 2001,41 – 48,Lyon)

Migeotte,L. (1980),"Engagements et saisies de biens publics dans les cités grecques",in Mélanges d'études anciennes offertes à Monsieur Lebel,161 – 181,Québec. (= Migeotte,L. (2010),Économie et finances publiques des cités grecques. I. Choix d'articles publiés de 1976 à 2001,49 – 60,Lyon)

Migeotte,L. (1977),"Sur une clause des contrats d'emprunt d'Amorgos",AC 46,128 – 139. (= Migeotte,L. (2010),Économie et finances publiques des cités grecques. I. Choix d'articles publiés de 1976 à 2001,31 – 40,Lyon)

Migeotte,L. (1976),"Emprunts publics a Karystos",Phoenix 30,26 – 41. (= Migeotte,L. (2010),Économie et finances publiques des cités grecques. I. Choix d'articles publiés de 1976 à 2001,15 – 30,Lyon)

Miles,J. C. (1952),"The case of Leochares(Dem. Or. 44)",Hermathena 80,48 – 57.

Miles,J. C. (1951),"Some observations on Demosthenes' speech against Pantaenetus",Hermathena 78,50 – 66.

Miles,J. C. (1950),"The Court in Phreatto",*RIDA* 1,219 – 224.

Miles,J. C. (1950),"The Attic Law of Intestate Succession",*Hermathena* 74,69 – 77. (= Zur griechischen Rechtsgeschichte,655 – 665).

Miles,J. C. (1945)„A note on Iliad xviii 497 – 508" Hermathena 65,92 – 93.

Miller jr.,F. D. (2010),"The Rule of Law in Ancient Greek Thought",in Sellers,M. & T. Tomaszewski(eds),The Rule of Law in Comparative Perspective,11 – 18,Heidelberg.

Miller jr.,F. D. (2009),"Aristotle on the Ideal Constitution",in Anagnostopoulos,G. (ed),A Companion to Aristotle,540 – 54,London.

Miller jr.,F. D. (2009),"Origins of Rights in Ancient Political Thought",in Salkever,St. (ed),The Cambridge Companion to Ancient Greek Political Thought,301 – 330,Cambridge.

Miller jr.,F. D. (2006),"Legal and Political Rights in Demosthenes and Aristotle",in Anagnostopoulos,Y. (ed),Law and Rights in the Ancient Greek Tradition,27 – 56,Thessaloniki.

Miller jr.,F. D. (2005),"Property Rights in Aristotle",in Kraut,R. & St. Skulery(eds),Aristotle's Politics:Critical Essays,121 – 144,Lanham,MD.

Miller jr. ,F. D. (1996) ,"Aristotle and the Origins of Natural Rights" ,*Review of Metaphysics* 49,873 -907.

Miller jr. , F. D. (1995) , Nature, Justice and Rights in Aristotle's Politics, Oxford.

Miller jr. ,F. D. & C. - A. Biondi(eds) (2007) ,A history of the Philosophy of Law from the Ancient Greeks to the Scholastics,Amsterdam.

Miller, M. (1969) , " The Accepted Date for Solon: Precise but Wrong?", *Arethusa* 2,62 -86.

Miller,M. (1953) ,"Greek Kinship Terminology" ,*JHS* 73,46 -52.

MMiller,M. C. J. (2007) ," A Note on the Boiotian Constitution and P. Oxy. 842" ,*AncW* 38,109 -117.

Miller, O. (1888) , " Die Procheirotonie der Athener", in Hertz, M. (ed), Philologische Abhandlungen,189 -196,Berlin.

Miller,O. (1885) ,De decretis atticis quaestiones epigraphicae,Breslau.

Miller,S. G. (1972) ,"Mortgage horoi from the Athenian agora" ,Hesperia 41, 274 -281.

Millett,P. (2005) , " The Trial of Socrates Revisited", *European Review of History* 12,23 -62.

Millett,P. (1991) ,Lending and Borrowing in Classical Athens,Cambridge.

Millett,P. (1990) ,"Sale,Credit and Exchange in Athenian Law and Society" ,in *Nomos*,167 -194.

Millett,P. (1983) , " Maritime Loans and the Structure of Credit in Fourth-century Athens", in Garnsey, P. D. A. , Hopkins, M. K. & C. R. Whittaker (eds), Trade in the Ancient Economy,36 -52,London.

Millett, P. (1982), " The Attic Horoi Revisited in the Light of Recent Discoveries" ,*Opus* 1,219 -249.

Millett,P. & St. Todd(1990) ,"Law,Society and Athens" ,in *Nomos*,1 -18.

Miner,J. (2003) ,"Courtesan,Concubine,Whore:Apollodorus' Deliberate use of Terms for Prostitutes" ,*AJPh* 124,19 -37.

Mirhady,D. C. (2009) ,"Is the Wasps Anger Democratic?" ,in Cousland,J. R. C. & J. R. Hume(eds) ,The Play of Texts and Fragments. Essays in Honour of Martin Cropp,371 -387,Leiden.

Mirhady, D. C. (2008), "Drakonian Procedure", in Epigraphy and the Greek Historian, 15 – 30.

Mirhady, D. C. (2008), "The disappearance and reappearance of exetasis", Mouseion 8, 395 – 408.

Mirhady, D. C. (2007), "The Dikasts' Oath and the Question of Fact", in *Horkos*, 48 – 59.

Mirhady, D. C. (2006), "Aristotle and the Law Courts", *Polis* 23, 302 – 318.

Mirhady, D. C. (2004), "Contracts in Athens", in *Law, Rhetoric and Comedy*, 51 – 63.

Mirhady, D. C. (2004), "Forensic Evidence in Euripides' Hippolytus", *Mouseion* 4, 17 – 34.

Mirhady, D. C. (2002), "Athens' Democratic Witnesses", *Phoenix* 56, 255 – 74.

Mirhady, D. C. (2000), "The Athenian Rationale for Torture", in *Law and Social Status*, 53 – 74.

Mirhady, D. C. (2000), "Demosthenes as Advocate: The Private Speeches", in Worthington, I. (ed) Demosthenes: Statesman and Orator, 181 – 204, London.

Mirhady, D. C. (1997), "The Ritual Background to Athenian Ostracism", *AHB* 11, 131 – 119.

Mirhady, D. C. (1996), "Torture and Rhetoric in Athens", *JHS* 116, 119 – 131. (= The Attic Orators, 247 – 270)

Mirhady, D. C. (1991), "Non-technical Pisteis in Aristotle and Anaximenes", *AJPh* 112, 5 – 28.

Mirhady, D. C. (1991), "The Oath-challenge in Athens", *CQ* 41, 78 – 83.

Mirhady, D. C. (1990), "Aristotle on the Rhetoric of Law", *GRBS* 31, 393 – 410.

Mirhady, D. C. & Y. L. Too. (2000), Isocrates 1, Austin, Texas. (The oratory of classical Greece 4)

Mirhady, D. C. & C. Schwarz (2011), "Dicastic Participation", *CQ* 61, 744 – 748.

Mirkovi, M. (2011), "Son-in-law, Mother's Brother, and Father in Lycian Inscriptions", ZRG 128, 352 – 365.

Missiou-Ladi, A. (1987), "Coercive Diplomacy in Greek Interstate Relations", *CQ* 37, 336 – 345.

Mitchell, L. G. (2000), "A New Look at the Election of Generals at Athens", *Klio* 82, 344 – 360.

Mitsui, T. (1991), "Conflits de lois dans l'antiquité classique", Tsukuba Hosei (Review of Law and Political Science) 14, 24 – 64.

Mittica, M. P. (2006), Raccontado il possible: Eschilo e le narrazioni giuridiche, Milano.

Miyazaki, M. (1996), "On Public Arbitration in Athens", Seiyo Kotengaku Kenkyu (*Journal of Classical Studies*) 44, 73 – 83.

Miyazaki, M. (1993), "Sykophantai in Classical Athens", Shigaku Zasshi 107, 1 – 37.

Monoson, S. (2011), "Aristotle's Empirical Stance on Slavery", in Alston, R., Hall, E. & L. Proffitt (eds), Reading Ancient Slavery, 133 – 151, London.

Moore, J. M. (1983), Aristotle and Xenophon on Democracy and Oligarchy, London.

Moore, P. (2005), "Entre Antigone et Créon: la médiation juridique", in Guilbert, M. (ed), Antigone et le dévoir de sépulture (Actes du colloque internationale de l'Université de Lausanne (mai 2005)), 99 – 118, Genève.

Moreau, A. (1994 – 1995), "Médée ou la ruine des structures familiales", Cahiers du GITA 8, 173 – 194.

Moreau-Christophe, L.-M. (1849), Du droit à l'oisiveté et de l'organisation du travail servile dans les republiques grecques et romaine, Paris.

Morel, P.-M. (2000), "Épicure, l'histoire et le droit", REA 102, 393 – 411.

Morelli, D. (1955), "Gli stranieri in Rodi", SCO 5, 126 – 190.

Moreno, A. (2007), Feeding the Democracy. The Athenian Grain Supply in the Fifth and Fourth Centuries BC, Oxford.

Moreno, A. (2003), "Athenian Bread-baskets: The Grain-Tax-law of 374/3 B. C. Re-interpreted", *ZPE* 145, 97 – 106.

Moretti, L. (1961), Richerche sulle leghe greche, Rome.

Mori, M. (1999), "Le procedure anfizioniche nel 346 a. C.", Rivista di Cultura Classica e Medioevale 41, 97 – 109.

Mori, S. (1991), "Causes of crime in Plato's Laws book 9", JCS 39, 48 – 59.

Mori, V. (2010), Diritto naturale, sapienza morale, teologia politica nelle Leggi di Platone, Roma.

Morimura, S. (1988), Greek Views of Punishment, Tokyo.

Moroo, A. (1999), "Archaic Tyranny: A New Approach", *Chiba University of Commerce Review* 37, 49 – 68.

Moroo, A. (1991), "Athenian Overseas Officials and the Administration of the Athenian Empire", SeiyoShigaku (*Studies in Western History*) 160, 34 – 49.

Morris, C. D. (1884), "The Jurisdiction of the Athenians over their Allies", *AJPh* 5, 298 – 317.

Morris, I. (1992 – 1993), "Law, Culture and Funerary Art in Athens: 600 – 300 B. C.", *Hephaistos* 11 – 12, 35 – 50.

Morris, I. (1989 – 1990), "The Gortyn Code and the Greek Kinship", *GRBS* 31, 233 – 254.

Morris, S. P. (2003), "Imaginary Kings: Alternatives to Monarchy in Early Greece", in *Popular Tyranny*, 1 – 24.

Morrison, D. (2004), "Tyrannie et royauté selon le Socrate de Xénophon", Les Études Philosophiques 2004, 177 – 192.

Morrison, D. (2001), "Justice et légalité selon le Socrate de Xénophon", in Gourinat, J. -B. (ed), Socrate et les Socratiques, 45 – 70, Paris.

Morrow, G. R. (1960), "The Nocturnal Council in Plato's Laws", *AGPh* 42, 229 – 246.

Morrow, G. R. (1951), "The Popular Courts in Plato's Laws", *Scientia* 86, 145 – 150.

Morrow, G. R. (1948), "Plato and the Law of Nature", in Konvitz, M. R. & A. E. Murphy (eds), Essays in Political Theory Presented to G. H. Sabine, 17 – 44, Ithaca.

Morrow, G. R. (1941), "Plato and the Rule of Law", *Philosophical Review* 50, 105 – 136.

Morrow, G. R. (1941), "On the Tribal Courts in Plato's Laws", *AJPh* 62, 314 – 321.

Morrow, G. R. (1941), "The Status of the Alien in Plato's Laws", *Scientia* 70, 38 – 43.

Morrow, G. R. (1939), "Plato and Greek Slavery", Mind 48, 196 – 201.

Morrow, G. R. (1939), Plato's Law of Slavery and Its Relation to Greek Law,

Urbana, Ill.

Morrow, G. R. (1937), "The Murder of Slave in Attic Law", *CPh* 32, 210 - 227.

Mosley, D. J. (1972), "Diplomacy in Classical Greece", *AncSoc* 3, 1 - 17.

Mosley, D. J. (1971), "Spartan Kings and Proxeny", *Athenaeum* 49, 433 - 435.

Mosley, D. J. (1962), "An Athenian Law on Ambassadors?", *Proceedings of the African Classical Association* 5, 26 - 27.

Mosley, D. J. (1961), "Who 'signed' Treaties in Ancient Greece?", *PCPS* 7, 59 - 63.

Mossé Claude, (2007), "Justice et politique à Athènes", in Athènes et le politique, 133 - 146.

Mossé Claude, (2004), "Les citations des lois dans les plaidoyers des orateurs attiques", in Darbo-Peschanski, C. (ed), La citation dans l' Antiquité (Actes du colloque du PARSA Lyon, 6 - 8 novembre 2002), 95 - 101, Grenoble.

Mossé Claude, (2002), "Les orateurs et le droit", in Mélanges Dimakis, 453 - 460.

Mossé Claude, (2000), "L'ostracisme d'Hyperbolos", Eirene 36, 63 - 67.

Mossé Claude, (1998), "Le procès de Phocion", Dike 1, 79 - 86.

Mosse, Cl. (1998), "Quelques reflections sur l'ostracisme athénien", in Greco, E. (ed), Venticinque secoli dopo l'invenzione della democrazia (Paestum, 12 - 14 ottobre 1994), 39 - 50, Paestum-Rome.

Mossé Claude, (1997), "L'amnistie de 403: une illusion politique?", in Amnistia, perdono, 53 - 58.

Mossé Claude, (1996), "Due miti politici: Licurgo e Solone", in Settis, S. (ed), I Greci. Storia, cultura, arte, società. 2. Una storia greca I Formazione, 1325 - 1338, Torino.

Mossé Claude, (1992), "La place de la pallakè dans la famille athénienne", in Symposion 1990, 273 - 279.

Mossé Claude, (1991), "Le serment des héliastes", in Le serment, 395 - 400.

Mossé Claude, (1989), "Le Contre Spoudias de Démosthène et les droits économiques des femmes d'Athènes au IVe siècle", in Symposion 1985, 215 - 221.

Mossé Claude, (1989), "Quelques remarques sur la famille à Athènes à la fin du IVe siècle: le témoignage du theatre du Ménandre", in Symposion 1982, 129 - 134.

Mossé Claude, (1987), Le procès de Socrate, Bruxelles.

Mossé Claude, (1985), "De l'inversion de la dot antique", in Piault, C. (ed), Familles et biens en Grèce et à Chypre, 187 - 196, Paris.

Mossé Claude, (1985), "De l'ostracisme aux procès politique: le fonctionnement de la vie politique à Athènes", AION 9, 9 - 19.

Mossé Claude, (1983), "La démocratie athénienne et la protection de la propriété", in Symposion 1979, 261 - 272.

Mossé Claude, (1982), "Tyrannie et legitimité dans la Grèce ancienne", in Duverger, M. (ed), Dictatures et legitimité, 50 - 68, Paris.

Mossé Claude, (1975), "Météques et étrangers à Athènes au IVe-IIIe siècles avant notre ere", in Symposion 1971, 205 - 214.

Mossé Claude, (1974), "Les procès politiques et la crise de la démocratie athénienne", DHA 1, 207 - 236. (= "Die politischen Prozesse und die Krise der athenischen Demokratie" in Welskopf, Ch. (ed) (1974), Hellenische Poleis I, 60ff, Darmstadt)

Mossé Claude, (1969), La tyrannie dans la Grèce antique, Paris.

Mossé Claude, (1967), "La conception du citoyen dans la Politique d'Aristote", Eirene 6, 17 - 21.

Müller, W. I. (2002), "Weak Legs: Misbehavior before the Enemy", in Demokratie, Recht und soziale Kontrolle, 15 - 36.

Mühl, M. (1971), "Relikte der Tier-und Sachstrafe bei Homer", REG 84, 1 - 17.

Mühl, M. (1956), "Diodor über die solonische Gesetzgebung", WS 69, 203 - 205.

Mühl, M. (1953), "Solons sogenannte chreon apokope im Lichte der antike Überlieferung", RhM 96, 214 - 223.

Mühl, M. (1944), "Ein griechisches Urheberschutzgesetz", Philologische Wochenschrift 64, 191 - 192.

Mühl, M. (1939), "Die hellenischen Gesetzgeber als Erzieher", Neue Jahrbücher für Antike und deutsche Bildung 2, 305 - 315.

Mühl, M. (1936), "Eine alte hellenische Gesetzesformel. Zur Gesichte der dike aikeias", Klio 31, 113 - 115.

Mühl, M. (1933), Untersuchungen zur altorientalischen und althellenischen Gesetzgebung, Leipzig. (Klio Beihefte 29)

Mühl, M. (1928 – 1929), "Die Gesetze des Zaleukos und Charondas", Klio 22, 105 – 124; 23, 432 – 463.

Münscher, K. (1919 – 20), "Isaios", ZVR 37, 32 – 328.

Munn, M. (2006), The Mother of the Gods, Athens, and the Tyranny of Asia. A Study of Sovereignty in Ancient Religion, Berkeley.

N

Nadareishvili, K. (2003), "Women in the Law of Democratic Athens", *Phasis. Greek and Roman Studies* 5 – 6, 173 – 184.

Nadel, B. (1968), "Manumission dans le Bosphore et le droit grec", LF 91, 252 – 278.

Nafissi, M. (2010), "The Great Rhetra (Plut. Lyc. 6): A Retrospective and Intentional Construct?", in Foxhall, L., Gehrke, H. -J. & N. Luraghi (eds), Intentional History. Spinning Time in Ancient Greece, 89 – 119, Stuttgart.

Nafissi, M. (2007), "Forme di controllo a Sparta", Il pensiero politico 40, 329 – 344.

Nagashima, T. (1975), "On Paragraphe: An Aspect of Judicial System in Ancient Athens", Rekishi (*Tohoku Historical Journal*) 47, 1 – 15.

Nagatsgawa, Y. (1998), Freedom and Justice in Ancient Greece, Tokyo.

Nagy, G. (1995), "Images of Justice in Early Greek Poetry", in Irani, K. D. & M. Silver (eds), Social Justice in the Ancient World, 61 – 100, London.

Naiden, F. S. (2010), "The Legal (and other) Trials of Orestes", in *Law and Drama in Ancient Greece*, 61 – 76.

Naiden, F. S. (2009), "Sanctions in Sacred Laws", in Symposion 2007, 125 – 138.

Naiden, F. S. (2006), Ancient Supplication, Oxford.

Naiden, F. S. (2004), "Supplication and the Law", in *The Law and the Courts*, 71 – 92.

Nails, D. (2009), "The trial and death of Socrates", in Greek and Roman political thought, 323 – 338.

Nakamura, J. (1983), "The Trial of Socrates", Seiyoshi Kenkyu (*Study of European and American History*) 12, 33 – 52.

Nakategawa, Y. (1995), "Athenian Democracy and the Concept of Justice in Pseudo-Xenophon's Athenaion Politeia", *Hermes* 123, 28 – 46.

Nakategawa, Y. (1994), "Forms of Interstate Justice in the Late Fifth Century", *Klio* 76, 135 – 154.

Nakos, G. P. (1990), "Politeiologika Aristotele", in Aphieroma ston D. Konstantopoulo 2, 861 – 883, Thessaloniki.

Nawotka, K. (2004), "Legislation in the Pontic Colonies of Miletus", Eos 91, 234 – 241.

Nawotka, K. (1999), Boule and Demos in Miletus and Its Pontic Colonies from Classical Age until Third Century A. D., Wrocław.

Nef, H. (1943), "Zum Staatsrecht der Polis", Études Suisses d'Histoire Générale 1, 254 – 267.

Nelson, S. (1996), "Justice and Farming in the Works and Days", in Louden, R. B. & P. Schollmeier (eds), The Greeks and Us. Essays in Honour of A. W. H. Adkins, 7 – 42, Chicago.

Nemeth, G. (2009), "The Island of Laws", *ACD* 45, 5 – 14.

Nemeth, G. (2006), "The Citizen, the Foreigner and the Prostitute", in Nemeth, G. & P. Forisek (eds), Epigraphica III. Politai et cives, 27 – 41, Debrecen. (Hungarian Polis Studies 13)

Nemeth, G. (2005), "On Solon's Land Reform", *AAntHung* 45, 321 – 328.

Nemeth, G. (2001), "Metics in Athens", *AAntHung* 41, 331 – 348.

Nemeth, G. (1984), "Der Arginusen-Prozess. Die Geschichte eines politischen Justizmordes", Klio 66, 51 – 57.

Nenci, G. (1990), "Klarographia e adelphothetia. Osservazioni sul decreto di Nacona", in Symposion 1988, 173 – 177.

Nenci, G. (1982), "Considerazioni sui decreti da Entella", ASNP 12, 1069 – 1086.

Nenci, G. (1964), "Una ignorata revisione delle liste dei cittadini ateniesi nel 424 – 23 a. C.", RFIC 92, 173 – 179.

Nenci, G. (1963), Il giudice nei poemi omerici. Giustizia e società, Piacenza.

Nenci, G. (1958), "Il martys nei poemi omerici", PdP 13, 221 - 241.

Nevett, L. C. (1999), House and society in the ancient Greek world, Cambridge.

Nialicet, P. (1923), Platon jurisconsulte, Paris.

Niarchos, K. (1993), "The Concept of Law in Plato and Aristotle: Some Comments by Michael of Ephesos", Platon 45, 141 - 152.

Nightingale, A. W. (1999), "Plato's Lawcode in Context: Rule by Written Law in Athens and Magnesia", *CQ* 49, 100 - 122.

Nikitsky, A. (1903), "Anepibasia", *Hermes* 38, 406 - 413.

Niku, M. (2007), The Official Status of the Foreign Residents in Athens 322 - 120 BC, Helsinki. (Papers and monographs of the Finnish Institute at Athens 12)

Niku, M. (2004), "When and Why did the Athenian Metoikia System Disappear? The Evidence of Inscriptions", *Arctos* 38, 75 - 93.

Nöthe, H. (1889), Der delische Bund, seine Einrichtung und Verfassung, Magdeburg.

Nonet, Ph. (2006), "Antigone's Law", *Law, Culture and the Humanities* 2, 314 - 335. (followed by J. Frank, "On Antigone's law" 336 - 40)

Norena, C. F. (1998), "Divorce in Classical Athenian Society: Law, Practice and Power", Past Imperfect 7, 3 - 34.

Norton, F. O. (1908), A Lexicographical and Historical Study of Diatheke, Chicago.

Notari, T. (2007), "The scales as the symbol of justice in the Iliad", in Notari, T. Studia iuridico-philologica I. Studies in classical and medieval philology and legal history, 9 - 20, Budapest.

Notari, T. (2007), "Hesiod und die Aufänge der Rechtsphilosophie", in Notari, T. Studia iuridico-philologica I. Studies in classical and medieval philology and legal history, 21 - 44, Budapest.

Nowak, M. (2010), "Defining Prostitution in Athenian Legal Rhetorics", *The Legal History Review* 78, 183 - 197.

Noy, D. (2009), "Neaera's Daughter: A Case of Athenian Identity Theft?", *CQ* 59, 398 - 410.

Nussbaum, M. C. (1998), "Whether from Reason or Prejudice: Taking Money for Bodily Services", *Journal of Legal Studies* 27, 693 - 724.

Nussbaum, M. C. (1994), "Platonic Love and Colorado Law: The Relevance of Ancient Greek Norms to Modern Sexual Controversies", *Virginia Law Review* 80, 1515–1651.

Nussbaum, M. C. (1990), "Symposium on Classical Philosophy and the American Constitutional Order: Comments", *Chicago-Kent Law Review* 66, 213–242.

O

O'Donnell, M. D. S. (1995), "Reading Pictorial Narrative: The Law Court Scene of the Shield of Achilles", in Carter, J. B. & S. P. Morris (eds), The Ages of Homer: A Tribute to E. Townsend Vermeule, 315–334, Austin, Texas.

O'Neil, J. L. (2001), "Was the Athenian Gnome Dikaiotate a Principle of Equity?", *Antichthon* 35, 20–29.

O'Neil, J. L. (2000), "Royal Authority and City Law under Alexander and His Successors", *CQ* 50, 424–431.

O'Neil, J. L. (1999), "Political Trials under Alexander the Great and His Successors", *Antichthon* 33, 28–47.

O'Neil, J. L. (1988), "The Fourth Century Revival of the Council of Areiopagos", *Classicum* 14, 3–7.

O'Neil, J. L. (1978–1979), "The Constitution of Chios in the Fifth Century", *Talanta* 10/11, 66–73.

O'Sullivan, L. (2009), "Macedonians, heroes and Athenian burial laws", in Wheatley, P. & R. Hannah (eds), Alexander & his successors: Essays from the Antipodes, 118–135, Claremont, CA.

O'Sullivan, L. (2009), The regime of Demetrius of Phalerum in Athens, 317–307 BCE: a philosopherin politics, Leiden. (Mnemosyne Suppl. 318)

O'Sullivan, L. (2002), "The Law of Sophocles and the Beginnings of Permanent Philosophical Schools in Athens", *RhM* 145, 252–262.

O'Sullivan, L. (2001), "Philochorus, Pollux and the Nomophylakes of Demetrius of Phalerum", *JHS* 121, 51–62.

O'Sullivan, L. (1997), "Athenian Impiety Trials in the Late Fourth Century BC", *CQ* 47, 136–152.

Ober,J. (2010), "Socrates and Democratic Athens", in Morrison, D. R. (ed), The Cambridge Companion to Socrates, 138 – 178, Cambridge.

Ober,J. (2010), "The Instrumental Value of others and Institutional Change: An Athenian Case Study", Princeton/Stanford Working Papers in Classics 6, http://www.princeton.com/~pcwpc/pdfs/ober/021001.pdf.

Ober,J. (2009), "Access, Fairness and Transactions Costs. Nikophon's Law on Silver Coinage (Athens, 375/4 BC)", Princeton/Stanford Working Papers in Classics 5, http://www.princeton.com/~pcwpc/pdfs/ober/070901.pdf.

Ober,J. (2007), "Ability and Education: The Power of Persuasion", in The Attic Orators, 271 – 311. (= originally chapter 4 of Mass and elite in democratic Athens, Princeton 1989)

Ober,J. (2006), "Solon and the Horoi: Facts on the Ground in Archaic Athens", in *Solon of Athens*, 441 – 456.

Ober, J. (2005), "Quasi-rights: Participatory Citizenship and Negative Liberties", *Social Philosophy and Policy* 17, 27 – 61. (= Athenian legacies. Essays on the politics of going on together, 92 – 127, Princeton)

Ober,J. (2005), "Law and Political Theory", in *The Cambridge Companion*, 394 – 411.

Ober,J. (2003), "Tyrant Killing as Therapeutic Stasis: A Political Debate in Images and Texts", in *Popular Tyranny*, 215 – 250.

Ober,J. (2002), "Social Science History, Cultural History, and the Amnesty of 403", *TAPhA* 132, 127 – 138.

Ober,J. (2000), "Living Freely as a Slave of the Law. Notes on Why Sokrates Lives in Athens", in *Polis and Politics*, 541 – 552.

Ober, J. (1995), "Greek Horoi: Artifactual Texts and the Contigency of Meaning", in Small, D. B. (ed), Methods in the Mediterranean. Historical and Archeological Views on Texts and Archaeology, 91 – 123, Leiden.

Oda,H. (1982), "A New Document Relating to the Peloponnesian League", Kodai Shigaku (Kagoshima University) 30, 1 – 15.

Oda,H. (1976), "The Jury System of Athens in the Classical Age", Cultural Science Reports of Kagoshima University 12, 35 – 57.

Oda,H. (1968), "Civil Actions Resulting from Homicide in Athens and Their

Relation to Public Prosecution", Cultural Science Reports of Kagoshima University 4, 131 - 152.

Ogden, D. (2009), "Bastardy and fatherlessness in ancient Greece", in Hübner, S. R. & D. M. Ratzan (eds), Growing up Fatherless in Antiquity, 105 - 119, Cambridge.

Ogden, D. (2002), "Controlling Women's Dress: Gynaikonomoi", in Llewellyn-Jones, L. (ed), *Women's Dress in the Ancient Greek World*, 203 - 225, London.

Ogden, D. (1997), "Rape, Adultery and the Protection of Bloodlines in Classical Athens", in *Rape in antiquity*, 25 - 41.

Ogden, D. (1997), The Crooked Kings of Ancient Greece, London.

Ogden, D. (1996), Greek Bastardy in the Classical and the Hellenistic Periods, Oxford.

Ogden, D. (1995), "Women and Bastardy in Ancient Greece and the Hellenistic World", in Powell, A. (ed), *The Greek world*, 219 - 244, London.

Ogden, D. (1994), "Crooked Speech: The Genesis of the Spartan Rhetra", *JHS* 114, 85 - 102.

Okell, E. R. (2011), "Inheritance and the Athenian Nature of Sophoclean Tragedy", in Carter, D. M. (ed), *Why Athens? A Reappraisal of Tragic Politics*, 209 - 237, Oxford.

Olding, G. (2007), "Myth and Writing in Aeschines' Against Timarchus", in *Politics of Orality*, 155 - 170.

Oliva, P. (2006), "Solon in der Aristotelischen Athenaion Politeia", *Graecolatina Pragensia* 21, 231 - 241.

Oliver, G. J. (2009), "Honours for a Public Slave at Athens (IG II2 502 + Ag. I 1947; 302/1 BC)", in Themos, A. A. & N. Papazarkadas (eds), Attika Epigraphika. Meletes pros timen tou Chr. Habicht, 111 - 124, Athenai.

Oliver, G. J. (2007), "Citizenship: Inscribed Honours for Individuals in Classical and Hellenistic Athens", in *Individus, Groupes et Politique*, 273 - 292.

Oliver, J. H. (1959), "Text of the So-called Constitution of Chios from the First Half of the Sixth Century B. C.", *AJPh* 80, 296 - 301.

Oliver, J. H. (1954), "Jacoby's treatment of the exegetes", *AJPh* 75, 160 - 174.

Oliver, J. H. (1950), The Athenian Expounders of the Sacred and Ancestral Law, Baltimore.

Olsen, Fr. (1984), "Socrates on Legal Obligation: Legitimation Theory and Civil Disobedience", *Georgia Law Review* 18, 929 – 966.

Omitowoju, R. (2002), Rape and the Politics of Consent in Classical Athens, Cambridge.

Omitowoju, R. (1997), "Regulating Rape: Soap Operas and Self-interest in the Athenian Courts", in *Rape in Antiquity*, 1 – 24.

Osborne, M. J. (1980), "A Ghost Law", *ZPE* 38, 99 – 101.

Osborne, M. J. (1978), "Athenian Grants of Citizenship after 229 B. C. Again", *AncSoc* 9, 75 – 83.

Osborne, M. J. (1976), "Athenian Grants of Citizenship after 229 B. C.", *AncSoc* 7, 107 – 127.

Osborne, M. J. (1972), "Attic Grants of Citizenship", in Akten des 6. Internationalen Kongresses, 433 – 435.

Osborne, R. (2008), "Law and Religion in Classical Athens: The Case of the Dead", in Langenfeld, C. & I. Schneider (eds), Recht und Religion in Europa. Zeitgenössische Konflikte und historische Perspektiven, 46 – 58, Göttingen.

Osborne, R. (2003), "Changing the Discourse", in *Popular Tyranny*, 251 – 272.

Osborne, R. (2000), "Religion, Empire and Freedom for Slaves", in *Law and Social Status*, 75 – 92.

Osborne, R. (1997), "Law, the Democratic Citizen and the Representation of Women in Classical Athens", *P & P* 155, 3 – 33. (= Studies in ancient Greek and Roman society, 38 – 60, Cambridge 2004)

Osborne, R. (1997), "Law and Laws. How do we Join up the Dots?", in *The Development of the Polis*, 74 – 82.

Osborne, R. (1990), "Vexatious Litigation in Classical Athens: Sykophancy and the Sykophant", in *Nomos*, 83 – 102.

Osborne, R. (1988), "Social and Economical Implications of the Leasing of Land and Property in Classical and Hellenistic Greece", *Chiron* 18, 279 – 323.

Osborne, R. (1985), Demos: The Discovery of Classical Attica, Cambridge.

Osborne, R. (1985), "Law in Action in Classical Athens", *JHS* 105, 40 – 58.

Ostwald, M. (2002), "Athens and Chalkis: A Study in Imperial Control", *JHS* 122, 134 – 143.

Ostwald, M. (2000), Oligarchia. The Development of a Constitutional form in Ancient Greece, Stuttgart.

Ostwald, M. (1996), "Shares and Rights: 'Citizenship' Greek and American style", in Ober, J. & Ch. Hedrick (eds), Demokratia. A conversation on Democracies, Ancient and Modern, 49 – 61, Princeton. (= Ostwald, Language and history, 7 – 21)

Ostwald, M. (1993), "The Areopagus in the Athenaion Politeia", in Aristote et Athenes, 139 – 153. (= Ostwald, Language and history, 230 – 244)

Ostwald, M. (1993), "Stasis and Autonomia in Samos: A Comment on an Ideological Fallacy", SCI 12, 51 – 66. (= Ostwald, Language and history, 52 – 68)

Ostwald, M. (1990), "Nomos and Physis in Antiphon's Peri Aletheias", in Griffith, M. & D. J. Matronarde (eds), Cabinet of the Muses: Essays on Classical and Comparative Literature in Honor of Th. G. Rosenmeyer, 293 – 306, Atlanta. (= Ostwald, Language and history, 158 – 174.)

Ostwald, M. (1986), From Popular Sovereignty to the Sovereignty of Law. Law, Society, and Politics in Fifth-century Athens, Berkeley.

Ostwald, M. (1977), "Plato on Law and Nature", in North, H. F. (ed), Interpretations of Plato. A Swarthmore Symposium, 41 – 63, Leiden. (Mnemosyne Suppl. 50)

Ostwald, M. (1973), "Was there a Concept Agraphos Nomos in Classical Greece?", in Mourelatos, P. D. & R. M. Rorty (eds), Exegesis and Argument. Studies in Greek Philosophy presented to G. Vlastos, 70 – 104, Assen. (Phronesis Suppl 1) (= Ostwald, Language and history, 125 – 157)

Ostwald, M. (1969), Nomos and the Beginnings of the Athenian Democracy, Oxford.

Ostwald, M. (1965), "Pindar, nomos and Herakles (Pindar, frg. 169 [Snell3] and POxy. No. 2450, frg. 1)", *HSCP* 69, 109 – 138. (= Ostwald, Language and history, 93 – 124)

Ostwald, M. (1955), "The Athenian Legislation Against Tyranny and Subversion", *TAPhA* 86, 103 – 128.

Ostwald, M. (1952), The Unwritten Laws and the Ancestral Constitution of Ancient Athens, Columbia.

Ota, H. (1977), "On the Greek Concept of Ownership", Jimbun Gakuho

(*Journal of Social Sciences and Humanities*, Tokyo Metropolitan University) 118, 1 - 15.

Ota, H. (1969), "The Draconian Constitution", in Hidemura, K., Miura, I. & H. Ota (eds), *Society and thought in Classical Antiquity*, 71 - 100, Tokyo.

Ottone, G. (1992), "Tre note sulle 'defixiones iudiciariae' greche di età arcaica e classica", Sandalion 15, 39 - 51.

P

Palao Herrero, J. (2008), "La experiencia del derecho la quita de Solon", RGDR 10, 1 - 7. (= Anuario de derecho concursal 13 (2008) 307 - 318)

Palao Herrero, J. (2007), "Sobre el carácter consensual del contrato de compraventa ático clásico", RGDR 8, 1 - 29.

Palao Herrero, J. (2007), El sistema juridico atico clasico, Madrid.

Palao Herrero, J. (2006), "Los esclavos àticos", RGDR 6, 1 - 6.

Palao Herrero, J. (2005), "La soberana en el sistema juridico ático clásico", RGDR 5, 1 - 14.

Panayotou, S. (1974), "Plato's Euthyphro and the Attic Code on Homicide", *Hermes* 102, 419 - 437.

Pangle, T. (1990), "Symposium on Classical Philosophy and the American Constitutional Order: Theclassical Challenge to the American Constitution", *Chicago-Kent Law Review* 66, 145 - 176.

Papade, D. (2009), "The Meaning of Citizen in Aristotle", in The Notion of Citizenship, 179 - 189. (in Greek)

Pao, Ugo Enrico (1976), "Le fonti del diritto attico", in Altri studi, 19 - 30.

Pao, Ugo Enrico (1976), "Cittadinanza e nazionalità nell'antica Grecia", in Altri Studi, 197 - 199.

Pao, Ugo Enrico (1968), "L'antico diritto di Gortina", in Antologia giuridica romanistica ed antiquaria I, 17 - 48, Milano. (= Altri studi, 481 - 507)

Pao, Ugo Enrico (1962), "Sull'esistenza di archivi giudiziari in Atene", in Studi Betti 3, 1 - 13. (= Altri studi, 233 - 242)

Pao, Ugo Enrico (1961), "Nota sul verso 41 del Dyskolos di Menandro", Iura 12, 194 - 197. (= Altri studi 555 - 558)

Pao, Ugo Enrico (1961), "Note giuridiche sul Dyskolos di Menandro", MH 18, 53 - 62. (= Altri studi, 559 - 570)

Pao, Ugo Enrico (1959), "Zum attischen Strafrecht und Strafprozessrecht", ZRG 76, 97 - 112. (= Altri studi, 309 - 322)

Pao, Ugo Enrico (1958), "Le fonti del diritto attico", Studi Senesi 70, 163ff. (= Altri studi, 19 - 30)

Pao, Ugo Enrico (1957), "Les pouvoirs du magistrat de police dans le droit attique", RIDA 4, 151 - 164. (= Altri studi, 221 - 232)

Pao, Ugo Enrico (1956), "La notion de prorrhesis en droit attique", RIDA 3, 135 - 142. (= Altri studi, 243 - 249)

Pao, Ugo Enrico (1956), "Lo Stichus di Plauto e l'aferesi paterna in diritto attico", in Studi P. de Francisci I, 233 - 247, Milano. (= Altri studi, 161 - 173)

Pao, Ugo Enrico (1956), "Messa a punto su Demostene c. Apat. § 23", Iura 7, 118 - 120. (= Altri studi, 541 - 543)

Pao, Ugo Enrico (1955), "La legislazione sull' adulterio nel diritto di Gortina", in Studi in onore di G. Funaioli, 306 - 316, Rome.

Pao, Ugo Enrico (1954), "Les pouvoirs du magistrat en droit attique", RHDFE 32, 463 - 465.

Pao, Ugo Enrico (1953), "Droit attique et droit romain dans les rhéteurs latins", RHDFE 31, 175 - 199.

Pao, Ugo Enrico (1953), "Les limites juridiques de l'aphérésis paternelle dans le droit attique", Recueil de l'Academie de Législation 2, 3 - 10. (= Altri studi, 385 - 391)

Pao, Ugo Enrico (1953), "La sauvegarde de la legalité dans la démocratie athénienne", in Festschrift Lewald, 133 - 141. (= Altri studi, 187 - 196)

Pao, Ugo Enrico (1952), "L'assentiment paternel au mariage du fils dans le droit attique", AHDO - RIDA 1, 267 - 275. (= Altri studi, 377 - 383)

Pao, Ugo Enrico (1950), "Il reato di adulterio (moicheia) in diritto attico", SDHI 16, 123 - 182. (= Altri studi, 251 - 307)

Pao, Ugo Enrico (1950), "La ephesis eis to dikasterion en droit attique", RIDA 5, 325 - 334. (= Altri studi, 211 - 220)

Pao, Ugo Enrico (1949), "La loi de Solon sur les distances", RHDFE 26, 505 -

517. (= Altri studi,571 - 583)

Pao, Ugo Enrico (1948), "Le développement de la polis athénienne et ses consequences dans le droit attique", RIDA 1,153 - 159. (= Altri studi,179 - 185)

Pao, Ugo Enrico(1946), "La legitima aferesi dell'epikleros in diritto attico", in Miscellanea G. Mercati 5,524 - 537, Città del Vaticano. (= Altri studi,363 - 376)

Pao, Ugo Enrico (1946), "Diritto attico e diritto greco", in Scritti di diritto romano C. Ferrini, 573 - 593, Milano. (= Altri studi, 1 - 18 and Greek translation, Astikon kai koinon hellenikon dikaion, Athenai 1959)

Pao, Ugo Enrico(1943), "L'epikleros attica nella 'palliata' romana", A & R 11,19 - 28. (= Altri studi, 103 - 112 and Greek translation in Ephemeris Ellenon Nomikon 42(1975)814 - 818)

Pao, Ugo Enrico(1937), "La difesa del possesso in diritto attico", in Studi A. Albertoni 2,311 - 335, Padova. (= Altri studi,435 - 459)

Pao, Ugo Enrico(1936), "L'anchisteia nel diritto successorio attico", SDHI 2, 77 - 119. (= Altri studi, 323 - 361) (Greek translation as Problemata archaiou hellenikou kleronomikou dikaiou, Athenai 1963)

Pao, Ugo Enrico(1935), "Sull' inscindibilità del processo nel diritto attico", Rivista di diritto processuale civile 12,253 - 261. (= Altri studi,201 - 209)

Pao, Ugo Enrico (1935), "L' autonomia del diritto commerciale nella Grecia classica", Rivista di diritto commerciale 33, 36 - 54. (= Altri studi, 461 - 479) (Greek translation as, "To emporikon nautikon dikaion hos autoteles klados tou dikaiou eis ten klassiken Hellada", AID 2(1935)1 - 25)

Pao, Ugo Enrico(1933), "Sul periodo di attività dei tribunali commerciali in Atene", in Studi sul processo attico, Padova.

Pao, Ugo Enrico(1933), "Legge e giurisdizione in diritto attico", in Studi sul processo attico, Padova.

Pao, Ugo Enrico(1933), "La datio in solutum nel diritto attico", SIFC 10,181 - 206. (= Altri studi,409 - 434)

Pao, Ugo Enrico(1932), "Il processo di Agorato", RFIC 10,289 - 308. (= Altri studi,121 - 142)

Pao, Ugo Enrico(1932), "Sul diritto pignoratizio attico", AG 108,161 - 178. (= Altri studi,393 - 407)

Pao, Ugo Enrico (1932), "Problemi di diritto pubblico nel Critone platonico", RIFD 12, 605 - 620. (= Studi sul processo attico, Padova 1933)

Pao, Ugo Enrico (1932), "La scienza del diritto attico e le sue possibilità", Civiltà Moderna 4, 210 - 227. (= Studi sul processo attico, Padova 1933)

Pao, Ugo Enrico (1930), "Lo stato di cittadinanza in Atene", in Studi di diritto attico, 195 - 339, Firenze.

Pao, Ugo Enrico (1930), "Ipoteca e apotimema nel diritto attico", in Studi di diritto attico, 141 - 194, Firenze.

Pao, Ugo Enrico (1930), "Il prestito maritimo nel diritto attico", in Studi di diritto attico, 1 - 140, Firenze.

Pao, Ugo Enrico (1929), "Zur Gerichtszeit der dikai emporikai im attischen Recht", ZRG 49, 473 - 476. (= Altri studi, 19 - 30)

Papadodima, E. (2011), "Forms and Conceptions of Dike in Euripides' Heracleidae, Suppliants and Phoenissae", *Philologus* 155, 14 - 38.

Papakonstantinou, Z. (2008), Lawmaking and Adjudication in Archaic Greece, London.

Papakonstantinou, Z. (2007), "Legal Procedure in the Homeric Hymn to Hermes", *RIDA* 54, 83 - 110.

Papakonstantinou, Z. (2004), "Justice of the Kakoi: Law and Social Crisis in Theognis", Dike 7, 5 - 17.

Papakonstantinou, Z. (2002), "Written Law, Literacy and Social Conflict in Archaic and Classical Crete", *AHB* 16, 135 - 150.

Papazarkadas, N. (2011), Sacred and Public Land in Ancient Athens, Oxford.

Papazarkadas, N. (2007), "Four Athenian Deme Documents Revisited", *ZPE* 159, 155 - 177.

Papazoglou, F. (1995), "Sur la Condition des Hilotes Affranchis", *Historia* 44, 370 - 375.

Papierkowski, Z. (1957), "Penal Procedure in Ancient Greece and Rome", in *Commentarii Philologiae Classicae*, 159 - 179, Lublin. (in Polish)

Papillon, T. L. (2004), Isocrates 2, Austin, Tx. (The oratory of classical Greece 7)

Pappoulias, D. P. (1929), "Symbole eis ten historian tes ex adiathetou kleronomikes diadoches en toi hellenikoi dikaioi" ,PAkAth 4,418 - 429.

Pappoulias, D. P. (1912), To hellenikon astikon dikaion en te historike autou exelixei, Athenai. (= Pappoulias, D. P. (1913), "Das griechische Privatrecht in seiner historische Entwicklung", Themis 74, 153 - 177)

Pappoulias, D. P. (1912), Griechisches Recht und griechische Rechtsgeschichte, Athenai.

Pappoulias, D. P. (1911), Historike exelixis tou arrabonos en to enochiko dikaio, Leipzig.

Pappoulias, D. P. (1909), He empragmatos asphaleia kata to hellenikon kai romaikon dikaion, Leipzig.

Pappoulias, D. P. (1906), "Über die Proklamation des Archon Eponymos nach Aristoteles Athenaion Politeia", ZRG 27, 360ff.

Parmeggiani, G. (2004), "Isotimia. Considerazioni sulla storia e sulla storiografia su Sparta in età arcaica e classica", RSA 34, 73 - 128.

Parmentier-Morin, E. (2004), "Recherches sur le vocabulaire politique d' Aristote: demos et plethos dans la Constitution d'Athènes et dans le livre III de la Politique", Ktema 29, 95 - 108.

Parodi Remon, A. (2004), "El derecho en Antigona, natural o positivo?", Dikaiosyne 12, 109 - 120.

Parsikov, A. J. (1974), "Juridical institutions in the Athenian arche", VDI 128, 57 - 68.

Partsch, J. (1909), Griechisches Bürgschaftsrecht. Tl. I. Das Recht des altgriechische Gemeindestaats, Leipzig.

Parush, A. (2001), "The Courtroom as Theater and the Theater as Courtroom in Ancient Athens", *Israel Law Review* 35, 118 - 137.

Pascual, J. (2007), "La sympoliteia griega en las épocas clásica y helenística", Gerion 25, 167 - 186.

Passias, I. (1932), Essai sur le droit maritime des anciens Hellenes, Wetteren.

Parke, H. (1945), "The Deposing of Spartan Kings", *CQ* 39, 106 - 112.

Parker, P. (2010), "Contracting caterers on Keos", in Dijkstra, J. Kroessen, J. & Y. Kuiper (eds), Myths, Martyrs, and Modernity: Studies in the History of Religions in Honour of Jan N. Bremmer, 209 - 218, Leiden. (Studies in the history of religion

127)

Parker, R. (2005), "Law and Religion", in *The Cambridge Companion*, 61 – 81.

Parker, R. (2004), "What are Sacred Laws?", in *The Law and the Courts*, 57 – 70.

Parker, R. (1983), Miasma. Pollution and Purification in Early Greek Religion, Oxford.

Parker, V. (2007), "Tyrants and Lawgivers", in Shapiro, H. A. (ed), The Cambridge Companion to Archaic Greece, 13 – 39, Cambridge.

Parker, V. (1998), "Tyrannos. The Semantics of a Political Concept from Archilochus to Aristotle", *Hermes* 126, 145 – 172.

Parush, A. (2001), "The Courtroom as Theater and the Theater as Courtroom in Ancient Athens", *Israel Law Review* 35, 118 – 137.

Patterson, C. B. (2007), "Other Sorts: Slaves, Foreigners and Women in Periclean Athens", in Samons II, L. J. (ed), The Cambridge Companion to the Age of Pericles, 153 – 178, Cambridge.

Patterson, C. B. (2005), "Athenian Citizenship Law", in The Cambridge Companion, 267 – 289.

Patterson, C. B. (2002), "The Polis and the Corpse: The Regulation of Burial in Democratic Athens", in Demokratie, Recht und soziale Kontrolle, 93 – 108.

Patterson, C. B. (2000), "The Hospitality of Athenian Justice: The Metic in Court", in *Law and Social Status*, 93 – 112.

Patterson, C. B. (1998), The Family in Greek History, Cambridge, Mass.

Patterson, C. B. (1991), "Marriage and the Married Woman in Athenian Law", in Pomeroy, S. B. (ed), Women's History and Ancient History, 48 – 72, Chapel Hill.

Patterson, C. B. (1990), "Those Athenian Bastards", *ClAnt* 9, 40 – 73.

Patterson, C. B. (1987), "'Hai Attikai'. The other Athenians", in Skinner, M. B. (ed), Rescuing Creusa: New Methodological Approaches to Women in Antiquity, 49 – 68, Lubbock, Ta.

Patterson, C. B. (1981), Perikles' Citizenship Law of 451 – 50 B. C., New York.

Patterson, O. (2008), "Slavery, Gender, and Work in the Pre-modern World and Early Greece: A Cross-cultural Analysis", in dal Lago, E. & C. Katsari (eds), Slave systems ancient and modern, 32 - 69, Cambridge.

Paulakes, G. E. (1996), He diamorphosssi ton nomon sten archaia Ellada, Peiraias.

Pauley, M. A. (1994), "The Jurisprudence of Crime and Punishment from Plato to Hegel", *American Journal of Jurisprudence* 39, 97 - 152.

Paulsen, Th. (1999), Parapresbeia-Reden des Demosthenes und des Aischines. Kommentar und Interpretation zu Demosthenes, or. XIX und Aischines or. II, Trier.

Pease, A. S. (1907), "Stoning among the Greeks and the Romans", TAPhA 38, 5 - 18.

Pecirka, J. (1966), The Formula for the Grant of Enktesis in Attic Inscriptions, Praha.

Pecirka, J. (1966), "A Note on Aristotle's Conception of Citizenship and the Role of Foreigners in Fourth Century Athens", *Eirene* 6, 23 - 26.

Pecirka, J. (1964), "Land Tenure and the Right of Enktesis in Athens", in Neue Beiträge zur Geschichte der alten Welt I. Alter Orient und Griechenland, 239 - 246, Berlin.

Pecorella Longo, C. (2011), "Il reato di empieta nel diritto attico", in Cecconi, G. A. & Ch. Gabrielli (eds), Politiche religiose nel mondo antico e tardoantico. Poteri e indirizzi, forme del controllo, idee e prassi di tolleranza (Atti del convegno internazionale di studi, Firenze, 24 - 26 settembre 2009), 43 - 56, Bari.

Pecorella Longo, C. (2010), "Il coinvolgimento dei discendenti nella condanna del reo nel diritto attico", Prometheus 36, 23 - 42 & 123 - 140.

Pecorella Longo, C. (2007), "La richiesta della pena nella probole e nei processi publici nel diritto attico", Prometheus 33, 124 - 136.

Pecorella Longo, Ch. (2004), "Il decreto di Demofanto e il nomos eisaggeltikos: due provvedimenti a confronto", Sileno 30, 11 - 27.

Pecorella Longo, C. (2004), "Il condono della pena in Atene in età classica", Dike 7, 85 - 111.

Pecorella Longo, C. (2002), "Aristofane e la legge sull'eisangelia", Prometheus 28, 222 - 228.

Pecorella Longo, C. (1988), "Sulla legge 'soloniana' contro la neutralità", Historia 37, 374 - 379.

Pecorella Longo, C. (1981), "Graphe traumatos o dike traumatos", SIFC 53, 246-261.

Pecorella Longo, C. (1980), "La Bule e la procedura dell'ostracismo: considerazioni su Vat. Gr. 1144", Historia 29, 257-281.

Pecorella Longo, C. (1971), «Eterie» e gruppi politici nell'Atene del Ⅳ sec. a. C., Firenze.

Pelling, Chr. (2002), "Speech and Action: Herodotus' Debate on the Constitutions", PCPS 48, 123-158.

Pepe, Laura (2012), Phonos. L'omicidio da Draconte all'età degli oratori, Milano.

Pepe, Laura (2012), « Processo a un'avvelenatrice: la prima orazione di Antifonte », Index 40, 131-145.

Pepe, Laura (2011), "Quali, altri'? le vittime della tortura ad Atene tra il Ⅴ e Ⅳ secolo", in Maffi, A. & L. Gagliardi (eds), I diritti degli altri in Grecia e a Roma, 218-235, Sankt Augustin.

Pepe, Laura (2008), "Osservazioni su phonos akousios e phonos dikaios nell' Atene del Ⅴ e Ⅳ secolo a. C.", Dike 11, 139-166.

Pepe, Laura (2007), "A proposito di una legge siceliota sull'omicidio", in Symposion 2005, 23-54.

Pepe, Laura (2007), "I Sette contro Tebe e la spartizione dell'eredità di Edipo", in Eva Cantarella, & L. Gagliardi (eds), Diritto e teatro in Grecia e a Roma, 31-67, Milano.

Pepe, Laura (2004), "Furto e giustizia privata nelle Ⅻ Tavole e nel diritto attico: un'indagine comparativa", in Scritti in ricordo di Barbara Bonfiglio, 273-310, Milano. (Pubblicazioni dell'Istituto di diritto Romano. Università degli Studi di Milano 39)

Perlman, P. (2002), "Gortyn. The First Seven Hundred Years. Part Ⅱ: The Laws from the Temple of Apollo Pythios", in Heine Nielsen, Th. (ed), Even more studies in the ancient Greek polis (Papers from the Copenhagen Polis Centre 6), 187-227, Stuttgart. (Historia Einzelschriften 162)

Perlman, S. (1976), "On bribing Athenian ambassadors", GRBS 17, 223-233.

Perlman, S. (1958), "A Note on the Political Implications of Proxenia in the

Fourth Century B. C. ", *CQ* 8, 184 – 191.

Peters, E. M. (1995), "Prison before the Prison: The Ancient and Medieval Worlds", in Morris, N. & D. J. Rothman (eds), The Oxford History of the Prison. The Practice of Punishment in Western Society, 1 – 48, New York.

Petersen, Chr. (1860), "Ursprung und Auslegung des heiligen Rechts bei den Griechen", Philologus 1, 155 – 212.

Petit, S. (1738 – 1741), Leges atticae2, Leyden. (Jurisprudentia romana et attica 3) de Philippo, G. & P. Mitsis (1994), "Socrates and Stoic Natural Law", in van der Waerdt, P. (ed), The Socratic Movement, 252 – 71, Ithaca.

Philippi, Adolf (1879), "Kleine Bemerkungen zu griechischen Rednern", RhM 34, 609 – 613.

Philippi, Adolf (1878), Adnotiunculae ad legum formulas quae in Demosthenis Midiana extant nonnullae, Giessen.

Philippi, Adolf (1874), Der Areopag und die Epheten. Ein Untersuchung zur athenischen Verfassungsgeschichte, Berlin.

Philippi, Adolf (1874), "Amnestiegesetz des Solon und die Prytanen der Naukraren zur Zeit des kylonischen Aufstandes", RhM 29, 1 – 12.

Philippi, Adolf (1871), Symbolae ad doctrinam juris attici de syngraphis et de ousias notione, Leipzig.

Philippi, Adolf (1870), Beiträge zu einer Geschichte des attischen Bürgerrechtes, Berlin.

Philippi, Adolf (1867), "Das Fragment der demosthenischen Rede gegen Zenothemis", NJ 95, 577 – 593.

Philippi, Adolf (1866), "Zu Demosthenes gegen Apaturios § 10", NJ 93, 825 – 827.

Philippi, Adolf (1866), "Über die demosthenische Rede gegen Timotheos", NJ 93, 611 – 620.

Phillips, D. D. (2009), "Hypereides 3 and the Athenian Law of Contracts", *TAPhA* 139, 89 – 112.

Phillips, D. D. (2008), Avengers of Blood. Homicide in Athenian Law and Custom from Draco to Demosthenes, Stuttgart. (Historia Einzelschriften 202)

Phillips, D. D. (2007), "Trauma ek pronoias in Athenian Law", *JHS* 127, 74 –

137.

Phillips, D. D. (2006), "Why was Lycophron Prosecuted by Eisangelia", *GRBS* 46, 375 – 394.

Phillips, D. G. (1982), "Ancient ostracism", in Hellenika: Essays, 21 – 44.

Phillips, J. – O. (2011), "Law, Compulsion, and Community in Plato's Republic", Polis 28, 108 – 125.

Phillipson, C. (1911), The International Law and Custom of Ancient Greece and Rome, London.

Philippson, R. (1910), "Die Rechtsphilosophie der Epikureer", AGPh 23, 289 – 337.

Photiades, P. S. (1928), "Eisiterios logos eis ten didaskalian tes historias tou hellenikou dikaiou", AG 104, 238 – 244.

Photiades, P. S. (1925), He apokeryxis en to archaio elleniko dikaio, Athenai.

Photiades, P. S. (1925), "Diorthotika eis Isaion", Athena 35, 54 – 66.

Photiades, P. S. (1924), "Attikon dikaion. Nomike hermeneia tes Demosthenous p. Zenothemin paragraphes", Athena 36, 109 – 132.

Photiades, P. S. (1924), "Attikon dikaion. Hermeneutika kai diorthotika eis Isaion", Athena 36, 3 – 78.

Photiades, P. S. (1920), "Peri tes eggues pros gamon kai ton synaphon aute nomon", Athena 32, 100 – 154.

Photiades, P. S. (1914), "Symplerosis aristotelikou choriou tes Athenaion Politeias", Athena 26, 267 – 270.

Photiades, P. S. (1908), "Hermeneutika eis Aristotelous Athenaion Politeia", Athena 18, 67 – 106.

Photiades, P. S. (1907), "Peri tou etesiou kerugmatos tou archontos en Athenais", Athena 17, 154 – 159.

Photiades, P. S. (1907), "Paratereseis eis ten Aristotelous Athenaion Politeia", Athena 17, 150 – 153.

Photiades, P. S. (1906), "Lysiakou choriou hermeneia kai diorthosis", Athena 16, 631 – 634.

Photiades, P. S. (1904), "Diorthossis kai hermeneia demosthenikou choriou", Athena 14, 364 – 366.

Photiades, P. S. (1904), "Peri kleroseos kai pleroseos ton heliastikon dikasterion kata ten Aristotelous Athenaion Politeian", Athena 14, 241 – 282.

Photiades, P. S. (1904), "Hermeneutika kai diorthotika eis tina choria tes Aristotelous Athenaion Politeian (Prosthekai)", Athena 14, 225 – 231.

Photiades, P. S. (1904), "Hermeneutika kai diorthotika eis tina choria tes Aristotelous Athenaion Politeian", Athena 14, 65 – 74.

Photiades, P. S. (1904), "Symbolai eis to attikon dikaion e diorthotika kai hermeneutika eis to Rhetorikon Kantabrigiakon Lexikon", Athena 14, 3 – 46.

Photiades, P. S. (1901 – 1902), "Symbolai eis to attikon dikaion e diorthotika kai hermeneutika eis to Rhetorikon Kantabrigiakon Lexikon", Athena 13, 3 – 64; 14, 75 – 122.

Photiades, P. S. (1899), "Parateresseis eis ten Aristotelous Athenaion Politeia", Athena 11, 361 – 377.

Photiades, P. S. (1899), "Symbolai eis to attikon dikaion e diorthotika kai hermeneutika eis to Rhetorikon Kantabrigiakon Lexikon", Athena 11, 3 – 116.

Photiades, P. S. (1899), "Paratereseis eis tina choria tou peri tou Kleonumou klerou logou tou Isaiou", Athena 9, 58 – 64.

Photiades, P. S. (1898), Eikasiai peri tinon ephtharmenon aristotelikon chorion tes Athenaion iccirilli, L. (2002) L'invenzione della diplomazia nella Grecia antica, Roma.

Piccirilli, Luigi (2001), "La diplomazia nella Grecia antica: temi del linguaggio e caratteristiche degli ambasciatori", MH 58, 1 – 31.

Piccirilli, Luigi (1999), "I symbouloi spartani", QS 49, 261 – 266.

Piccirilli, Luigi (1996), "La confisca dei beni nel diritto attico del Ⅳ secolo a. C.: una pena aggiuntiva?", SIFC 14, 53 – 55.

Piccirilli, Luigi (1996), "L'ostracismo di Callia, figlio di Didimia", Klio 78, 325 – 328.

Piccirilli, Luigi (1989), "Il processo di Callia", Serta historica antica 2, 27 – 36.

Piccirilli, Luigi (1983), "Eisangelia e condanna di Temistocle", CivClCr 4, 353 – 363.

Piccirilli, Luigi (1981), "Nomoi cantati e nomoi scritti", CivClCr 2, 7 – 14.

Piccirilli, Luigi (1977), "La legge di Solone sulla dote (Plut. 20, 6)", in

Gasperini, L. (ed), Scritti storico-epigrafici in onore di M. Zambelli, 321 – 324, Macerata.

Piccirilli, Luigi (1976), "Aristotele e l'atimia", ASNP 6, 739ff.

Piccirilli, Luigi (1973), "Prodikazein e prodikasia", ASNP 3, 1021 – 1025.

Piccirilli, Luigi (1972), "Aspetti storico-giuridici dell'anfizionia delfica e suoi rapporti con la colonizzazione greca", ASNP 2, 35 – 61.

Piccirilli, Luigi (1969), "Sull'arbitrato fra Calcide e Andro e alcuni aspetti del diritto coloniale greco", BIDR 72, 1 – 8.

Piérart, M. (2005), "Retour sur les Lois de Platon", in Le législateur et la loi, 37 – 48.

Piérart, M. (2004), "Qu'est-ce qu'être Argien? Identité civique et régime démocratique à Argos au Ve s. avant J. -C.", in Poleis e politeiai, 167 – 185.

Piérart, M. (2000), "Qui étaient les nomothétes à Athènes à l'époque de Demosthène?", in La codification, 229 – 256.

Piérart, M. (1994), "Hairesis and klerosis chez Platon et Aristote", in Aristote et Athènes, 119 – 138.

Piérart, M. (1974), Platon et la cité grecque: theorie et realité dans la constitution des Lois, Brussels. (Acad. Roy. Belg., Mem. de la Classe des Lettres 62(3))

Piérart, M. (1974), "A propos de l'election des strateges atheniens", BCH 98, 51 – 94.

Piérart, M. (1973), "Note sur la 'prorrhesis' en droit attique", AC 42, 427.

Piérart, M. (1971), "Les euthynoi atheniens AC 40, 526 – 573. Politeias", Athena 10, 149 – 157.

Plascia, J. (1970), The oath and perjury in ancient Greece, Tallahassee.

Poddighe, E. (2010), "Riflessioni sul fondamento etico-legale e sul carattere finanziario dell'eisphora ateniese tra V e IV sec. A. C.", in Cataudella, M. R., Greco, A. & G. Mariotta (eds), Strumenti e techniche della riscossione die tributi nel mondo antico (Atti del convegno nazionale, Firenze 6 – 7 dicembre 2007), 97 – 118, Padova.

Poddighe, E. (2010), "Mescolanza o purezza? Il diapsephismos tra i Pisistratidi e la riforma di Clistene", Klio 92, 285 – 304.

Poddighe, E. (2006), "Ateniesi infami (atimoi) ed ex Ateniesi senza i requisiti (apepsephismenoi): nuove osservazioni in margine al fr. 29 Jensen di Iperide sulle diverse forme di esclusione dal corpo civico di Atene", AFLC 24, 5 – 24.

Poddighe, E. (2003), "I termini giuridici del decreto di Iperide sulla concessione di privilegi in cambio della disponibilità a combattere per Atene", AFLC 21, 43 – 68.

Poddighe, E. (2001), "L'atimia nel diagramma di Cirene. La definizione della cittadinanza tra morale e diritto alla fine del Ⅳ secolo a. C.", Aevum 75, 37 – 56.

Poddighe, E. (1997 – 1998), "Il diagramma di Poliperconte e la politica in Grecia nell'anno 319 a. C.", AFLC 16, 15 – 59.

Poddighe, E. (1993), "La condition juridique des citoyens Atheniens frappés par le décret du 322: Atimoi ou phygades?", Mètis 8, 271 – 283.

Podlecki, A. J. (1993), "The hybris of Oedipus: Sophocles Oed. Tyr. 873 and the genealogy of tyranny", Eirene 29, 7 – 30.

Pomeroy, S. B. (2004), "Xenophon's Spartan Women", in Tuplin, Chr. (ed), Xenophon and His World (Papers from a conference held in Liverpool in July 1999), 201 – 214, Stuttgart. (Historia Einzelschriften 172)

Pomeroy, S. B. (1997), Families in Classical and Hellenistic Greece, Oxford.

Preus, A. (2005), "Citizenship and Participation in Government in Classical Greek Political Thought", *Skepsis* 16, 150 – 163.

Price, A. W. (2011), "Reasoning about justice in Plato's Republic", in Anagnostopoulos, G. (ed), Socratic, Platonic and Aristotelian Studies: Essays in Honor of G. Santas, 245 – 54, New York.

Pringsheim, F. (1957), "Some Causes of Codification", *RIDA* 4, 301 – 311.

Pringsheim, F. (1955), "The Transition from Witnessed to Written Transactions in Athens", in Aequitas und bona fides. Festgabe A. Simonius, 287 – 297, Bale.

Pringsheim, F. (1950), The Greek Law of Sale, Weimar.

Pringsheim, F. (1949), "The Greek Sale by Auction", in Scritti Ferrini 4, 284 – 343. (= Gesammelte Ⅱ, 262 – 329)

Pritchett, W. K. (1977), "Loans of Athena in 407 B. C.", AncSoc 8, 33 – 49.

Pritchett, W. K. (1956), "The Attic stelai. Part 2", Hesperia 25, 178 – 317.

Pritchett, W. K. (1953), "The Attic stelai. Part 1", Hesperia 22, 225 – 299.

Pritchett, W. K. (1940), "The Term of Office of Attic Strategoi", *AJPh* 61, 469 – 474.

Proffitt, L. (2011), " Family, Slavery and Subversion in Menander's

Epitrepontes", in Alston, R., Hall, E. & L. Proffitt (eds), Reading Ancient Slavery, 152 - 174, London.

Q

Quass, F. (1979), "Zur Verfassung der griechische Städte im Hellenismus", Chiron 9, 37 - 52.

Quass, F. (1971), Nomos und Psephisma. Untersuchungen zum griechischen Staatsrecht, München. (Zetemata 55)

Quillin, J. M. (2002), "Achieving Amnesty: The Role of Events, Institutions, and Ideas", *TAPhA* 132, 71 - 108.

Quinn, M. (1990), "Aristotle on Justice, Equality and the Rule of Law", Polis 9, 170 - 186.

R

Raaflaub, K. A. (2003), "The Ostracism of Damon", in Gestures, 317 - 331.

Raaflaub, K. A. (2003), "Stick and Glue: The Function of Tyranny in Fifth-century Athenian Democracy", in *Popular Tyranny*, 59 - 94.

Raaflaub, K. A. (2000), "Poets, Lawgivers and the Beginnings of the Political Reflection in Archaic Greece", in Rowe, C. & M. Schofield (eds) The Cambridge History of Political Thought, 23 - 60, Cambridge.

Raaflaub, K. A. (1983), "Democracy, oligarchy and the concept of free citizen in the latefifth-century Athens", Political Theory 11, 517 - 544.

Radin, M. (1934), "Early Greek Concepts of Equity", in Vallindas, P. G. (ed), Mnemosyna Pappoulia, 213 - 220, Athenai.

Radin, M. (1927), "Freedom of Speech in Ancient Athens", *AJPh* 48, 215 - 230.

Radin, M. (1910), "Greek Law in Roman Comedy", *CPh* 5, 365 - 367.

Radin, M. (1909), Legislation of the Greeks and Romans on Corporations, diss. New York.

Rahe, P. A. (1980), "The Selection of Ephors at Sparta", *Historia* 29, 385 - 401.

Rakover, N. (1988), "Law and Equity in Aristotle and Maimonides", in

Zarcone, Th. (ed), Individu et société. L'influence d'Aristote dans le monde méditerranéen (Actes du colloque d'Istanbul, Palais de France, 5 - 9 janvier 1986), 69 - 76, Istanbul.

Ranulf, S. (1933 - 1934), The Jealousy of the Gods and Criminal Law at Athens. A Contribution to the Sociology of Moral Indignation, London.

Raubitschek, A. E. (1975), "Nomos and Ethos", in Brannan, P. T. (ed), Classica and Iberica. A Festschrift in Honor of J. M. F. Marique, 273, Worcester, MA.

Raubitschek, A. E. (1965), "A note on the Themistokles decree", in Studi in onore di L. Banti, 285 - 287, Roma.

Raubitschek, A. E. (1958), "Theophrastos on ostracism", ClassMed 19, 73 - 109. (= The School of Hellas, 81 - 107)

Raubitschek, A. E. (1953), "Ostracism: The Athenian Ostraka", in Actes du IIe congrés internationale d'épigraphie grecque et latine, 59 - 74. (= The School of Hellas, 53 - 64)

Raubitschek, A. E. (1952), "Athenian Ostracism", *CJ* 48, 113 - 122.

Raubitschek, A. E. (1951), "The Origin of Ostracism", *AJA* 55, 221 - 229. (= The School of Hellas, 65 - 76)

Raubitschek, A. E. (1948), "The Case Against Alcibiades (Andocides Ⅳ)", *TAPhA* 79, 191 - 210. (= The School of Hellas, 116 - 131)

von Reden, S. (1997), "Money, Law, and Exchange: Coinage in the Greek Polis", *JHS* 117, 154 - 175.

Reduzzi Merola, Fr. (2007 - 2008), "Il giudizio di costituzionalità nell'esperienza greco-romana", ASGP 52, 41 - 51.

Reed, C. (2003), Maritime traders in the ancient Greek world, Cambridge.

Reger, G. (1992), "Private property and private loans on independent Delos", Phoenix 46, 322 - 341.

Reichardt, T. (2003), Recht und Rationalität im frühen Griechenland, Würzburg. (Contradictio. Studien zur Philosophie und ihrer Geschichte 4)

Reichenstein, S. (1881), Demosthenes tertiam contra Aphobum orationem esse genuinam, Würzburg.

Reinhardt, T. (2007), "Techniques of Proof in 4th Century Rhetoric: Ar. Rhet. 2.23 - 24 and Pre-Aristotelian Rhetorical Theory", in Mirhady, D. C. (ed),

Influences on Peripatetic Rhetoric. Essays in Honor of W. W. Fortenbaugh, 87 – 104, Leiden. (Philosophia Antiqua 105)

Remow, G. (2008), "Aristotle, Antigone and natural justice", History of Political Thought 29, 585 – 600.

Reynolds, N. B. (1988), "Plato's Defense of Rule of Law", in *Philosophy of Law*, 16 – 21.

Rhodes, P. J. (2011), "The Erxadieis inscription (SEG xxvi 461; Meiggs-Lewis 1998 reissue, 67bis; Nomima i 55)", Acta Antiqua 51, 9 – 15.

Rhodes, P. J. (2009), "Hyperides' Against Diondas: Two Problems", *BICS* 52, 223 – 228.

Rhodes, P. J. (2009), "Civic Ideology and Citizenship", in *Greek and Roman Political Thought*, 57 – 69.

Rhodes, P. J. (2009), "State and Religion in Athenian Inscriptions", *G & R* 56, 1 – 13.

Rhodes, P. J. (2008), "Making and Breaking Treaties in the Greek World", in de Souza, Ph. & S. J. France (eds), War and Peace in Ancient and Medieval History, 6 – 27, Cambridge.

Rhodes, P. J. (2007), "Dioikesis", *Chiron* 37, 349 – 362.

Rhodes, P. J. (2007), "Oaths in Political Life", in *Horkos*, 11 – 25.

Rhodes, P. J. (2006), "The Reforms and Laws of Solon: An Optimistic View", in *Solon of Athens*, 261 – 275.

Rhodes, P. J. (2004), "The Laws of Athens in the Aristotelian Athenaion Politeia", in Nomos. Direito e sociedade, 75 – 90.

Rhodes, P. J. (2004), "Keeping to the Point", in *The Law and the Courts*, 137 – 158.

Rhodes, P. J. (2003), "Sessions of Nomothetai in Fourth-century Athens", *CQ* 53, 124 – 129.

Rhodes, P. J. (2002), "Oligarchs in Athens", in Alternatives to Athens, 119 – 136.

Rhodes, P. J. (2001), "Public Documents in the Greek States: Archives and Inscriptions", *G & R* 48, 33 – 44; 136 – 153.

Rhodes, P. J. (1997), "Deceleans and Demotionidae Again", *CQ* 47, 109 – 120.

Rhodes, P. J. (1995), "Epigraphical Evidence: Laws and Decrees", in *Hansen*, *Sources*, 91 – 112.

Rhodes, P. J. (1995), "Judicial Procedures in Fourth-century Athens: Improvement or Simply Change?", in Die athenische Demokratie, 303 – 320.

Rhodes, P. J. (1994), "The Ostracism of Hyperbolus", in *Ritual*, *Finance*, *Politics*, 85 – 98.

Rhodes, P. J. (1993), "The Greek poleis: demes, cities and leagues", in Hansen, M. H. (ed), The Ancient Greek City-state, 161 – 182, Copenhagen.

Rhodes, P. J. (1991), "The Athenian Code of Laws, 410 – 399 BC", *JHS* 111, 87 – 100.

Rhodes, P. J. (1987), "Nomothesia in Classical Athens", in L'educazione giuridica V(ii), 5 – 26.

Rhodes, P. J. (1984), "Nomothesia in Fourth-century Athens", *CQ* 35, 55 – 60.

Rhodes, P. J. (1981), "The Selection of Ephors at Sparta", *Historia* 30, 498 – 502.

Rhodes, P. J. (1981), A Commentary on the Aristotelian Athenaion Politeia, Oxford.

Rhodes, P. J. (1979), "Eisangelia in Athens", *JHS* 99, 103 – 114.

Rhodes, P. J. (1978), "Bastards as Athenian Citizens", *CQ* 28, 89 – 92.

Rhodes, P. J. (1972), The Athenian Boule, Oxford.

Rhodes, P. J. & D. M. Lewis. (1997), The Decrees of the Greek States, Oxford.

Rhodes, P. J. & R. Osborne(eds) (2003), Greek Historical Inscriptions 404 – 323 BC, Oxford.

Riano Rufilanchas, D. (2003), "Carcer y encarcelamiento en la Grecia clasica", in Torallas Tovar, S. & I. Perez Martin(eds), Castigo y reclusion en el mundo antigo, 73 – 94, Madrid.

Ribeiro Ferreira, J. (2004), "Proxeno e proxenia", in Nomos. Direito e sociedade, 227 – 240.

Rice, D. (1997), "Litigation as a Political Weapon: The Case of Timotheus of Athens", in Hamilton, Ch. D. & P. Krentz(eds), Polis and Polemos. Essays on Politics, War, and History in Ancient Greece in Honor of D. Kagan, 229 – 240, Claremont CA.

Richardson, M. B. (2000), "The Location of Inscribed Laws in Fourth-century

Athens. IG II2 244, on Rebuilding the Walls of Peiraeus (337/6 BC)", in *Polis and Politics*, 601 – 616.

Richardson, W. F. (1970), "Dike in Aristophanes' Clouds", in Harris, B. F. (ed), Auckland Classical Essays Presented to E. M. Blaiklock, 59 – 67, Auckland.

Richer, N. (2001), "'Eunomia' et 'eudaimonia' à Sparte", Dike 4, 13 – 38.

Richter, C. G. (1790), Animadversionum de veteribus legum latoribus ad I. A. Fabricii Bibliothecam graecam specimen I, Hamburg.

Richter, G. M. A. (1945), "Peisistratos' Law Regarding Tombs", *AJA* 49, 152.

Richter, W. (1966), Recht und Ethos. Versuch einer Ortung des weisheitlichen Manspruches, München.

Ricl, M. (2011), "Neokoroi in the Greek world", Belgrade Historical Review 2, 7 – 26.

Ricoeur, P. (2002), "Le droit de punir", in Buchheim, Th. et al. (eds), Die Normativität des Wirklichen. Über die Grenze zwischen Sein und Sollen, 439 – 457, Stuttgart.

Riehemann, J. (1866), De litis instrumentis quac exstant in Demosthenis quae fertur oratione adversus Neaeram, Leipzig.

Ries, G. (1983), Prolog und Epilog in Gesetzen des Altertums, München. (MBPaR 76)

Riess, W. (2012), Performing interpersonal violence. Court, curse, and comedy in fourth-century BCE Athens, Berlin.

Riess, W. (2008), "Private Violence and State Control. The Prosecution of Homicide and its Symbolic Meanings in Fourth-century BC Athens", in Brélaz, C. & P. Ducrey (eds), Sécurité collective et ordre public dans les sociétés anciennes, 1 – 39, Genève. (Entretiens sur l'antiquité classique 54)

Riess, W. (2006), "How Tyrants and Dynasts Die: The Semantics of Political Assassination in Fourth Century Greece", in Urso, G. (ed), Terror e pavor: violenza, intimidazione, clandestinità nel mondo antico (Atti del convegno internazionale, Cividale dei Friuli, 22 – 24 settembre 2005), 65 – 88, Pisa.

Rigsby, K. (2009), "Notes on Sacred Laws", ZPE 170, 73 – 80.

Rihll, T. E. (1989), "Lawgivers and Tyrants (Solon, Frr. 9 – 11 West)", *CQ* 39, 277 – 286.

Rihill, T. E. (1991), "Hektemoroi: Partners in Crime?", *JHS* 111, 101 - 127.

Robb, K. (1991), "The Witness in Heraclitus and Early Greek Law", The Monist 74, 638ff.

Robert, C. (1876), "Proxeniedekrete aus Tanagra", Hermes 11, 97 - 103.

Roberts, J. T. (1987), "Plato on the Causes of Wrongdoing in the Laws", *AncPh* 7, 23 - 37.

Roberts, J. T. (1982), Accountability in Athenian Government, Madison, Wisc.

Roberts, J. T. (1980), "The Athenian Conservatives and the Impeachment Trials of the Corinthian War", *Hermes* 108, 100 - 114.

Roberts, J. T. (1977), "Arginusae once again", CW 71, 107 - 111.

Robertson, B. (2000), "The Scrutiny of New Citizens at Court", in *Law and Social Status*, 149 - 174.

Robertson, H. G. (1928), "The Administration of Justice in the Second Athenian Confederacy", *CPh* 23, 30 - 33.

Robertson, H. G. (1924), The Administration of Justice in the Athenian Empire, diss. Toronto.

Robertson, N. (2010), Religion and Reconciliation in Greek Cities: The Sacred Laws of Selinous and Cyrene, Oxford.

Robertson, N. (1998), "Phratries and Trittyes: The Early Organization of Attica", in Hillard, T. W. et als(eds) Ancient History in a Modern University, I, 111 - 120, Toronto.

Robertson, N. (1990), "The laws of Athens, 410 - 399 BC: The Evidence for Review and Publication", *JHS* 110, 43 - 75.

Robertson, N. (1986), "Solon's Axones and Kyrbeis and the Sixth-century Background", *Historia* 35, 147 - 176.

Robertson, N. (1982), "The Decree of Themistokles in its Contemporary Setting", *Phoenix* 36, 1 - 44.

Robinson. jr, C. A(1952), "Cleisthenes and Ostracism", *AJA* 56, 23 - 26.

Robinson, D. M. (1950), "A New Mortgage Inscription from Ikaria", *Hesperia* 19, 23 - 24.

Robinson, D. M. (1935), "A New Fragment of the Athenian Decree on Coinage", *AJPh* 56, 149 - 154.

Robinson, D. M. (1928), "A Deed of Sale at Olynthus", *TAPhA* 59, 225 – 232.

Robinson, E. (2011), Democracy Beyond Athens: Popular Government in the Greek Classical Age, Cambridge.

Robinson, E. (2000), "Democracy in Syracuse, 466 – 412 BC", *HSCP* 100, 189 – 206.

Robinson, Th. (2000), "State and individual in Plato's Laws", in Lisi, F. (ed), Plato's Laws and its historical significance. Selected papers from the I International congress on ancient thought (Salamanca 1998), 115 – 123, Sank Augustin.

Robiou de la Trehonnaus, F. M. L. J. (1880), Questions de droit attique, politique, administratif et privé, Paris.

Robles Velasco, L. M. (2006), "El comercio maritime y sua influencia en las formas de garantia", Nuevos Estudios Juridicos 11, 375 – 384.

Roby, H. J. (1886), "The Twelve Tables of Gortyn", *Law Quarterly Review* 2, 135 – 152.

Rochette, D. R. (1827), "Sur la forme et l'administration de l'État fédératif des Boeotiens", AIB 8, 214 – 249.

Rochette, D. R. (1815), Histoire critique de l'etablissement des colonies grecques, Paris.

Rockwell, K. A. (1972), "The Slave Against His Master", *CB* 48, 64.

Rodgers, R. S. (1985), "The Wasps in Court: Argument and Audience in the Athenian Dicasteries", *American Journal of Legal History* 28, 147ff.

Rodgers, V. A. (1971), "Some Thoughts on Dike", *CQ* 21, 289 – 301.

Rodolakis, G. E. (1994), "He Themis kai he Pandora. To dikaio, oi thees tou kai I thessi tes gunaikas", in Ai archaiai imon progonoi. Ena aphieroma stis agnostes archaies Ellenides gunaikes meteres olon mas (Athina, 18 Apriliou 1994), Athina.

Rodriguez Somolinos, H. (1996), "The Commercial Transaction of the Pech Maho Lead. A New Interpretation", *ZPE* 110, 74 – 78.

Roebuck, C. A. (1980), "Stasis in Sicily in the Seventh Century B. C.", in Studi Manni 4, 1921 – 1930.

Roebuck, C. (1948), "The Settlement of Philip II with the Greek states in 338 B. C.", *CPh* 43, 73ff.

Roebuck, D. (2001), Ancient Greek Arbitration, Oxford.

Roebuck, D. (2000), "'Best to Reconcile'. Mediation and Arbitration in the Ancient Greek World", *Arbitration* 66, 275 – 287.

Rogers, R. V. (1899), "Legal Position of Women in Ancient Greece", Green Bag 11, 209 – 219.

Rohde, E. (1921), Psyche. Seelencult und Unsterblichkeitsglaube der Griechen, 8 vols. Tübingen.

Roisman, J. (2003), "The Rhetoric of Courage in the Athenian Orators" in Rosen, R. M. & I. Sluiter (eds), Andreia. Studies in Manliness and Courage in Classical Antiquity, 127 – 144, Leiden. (Mnemosyne Suppl. 238)

Roisman, J. (1984 – 1986), "The Image of the Political Exile in Archaic Greece", AncSoc 15 – 17, 23 – 32.

Romano, D. G. (2007), "Judges and Judging at the Ancient Olympic Games", in Schauss, G. P. & S. R. Wenn (eds), Onward to the Olympics. Historical Perspectives on the Olympic Games, 95 – 113, Waterloo, Ont.

Romer, F. E. (1982), "The Aisymneteia: A Problem in Aristotle's Historic Method", *AJPh* 103, 25 – 46.

de Romilly, J. (1973), "Religion et droit dans la Grèce ancienne. Dimensions religieuses du droit", APhD 18, 5 – 16.

Rosivach, V. J. (2010), "The Oaths of the Athenians at the Ratification of Solon's Reforms", *Phoenix* 64, 223 – 37.

Rosivach, V. J. (1999), "Drama in the Athenian Courts", *AHB* 13, 157 – 162.

Rosivach, V. J. (1999), "Enslaving Barbaroi and the Athenian Ideology of Slavery", *Historia* 48, 129 – 157.

Rosivach, V. J. (1992), "Redistribution of Land in Solon frg. 34West", *JHS* 112, 153 – 157.

Rosivach, V. J. (1984), "Aphairesis and Apoleipsis. A Study of the Sources", *RIDA* 31, 193 – 230.

Rossetti, L. (2004), "Materiali per una storia della letteratura giuridica greca", in Nomos. Direito e sociedade, 51 – 74.

Rossetti, L. (2002), "Non solo dottrine politiche. L'apporto di Platone, Aristotele, Teofrasto e altri peripatetici alla cultura giuridica", in Migliori, M. (ed), Gigantomachia. Convergenze e divergenze tra Platone e Aristotele, 357 – 377, Brescia.

Rossetti, L. (2001), "Le Leggi di Platone nel contesto della cultura e della letteratura giuridica attica", in Lisi, F. (ed), Plato's Laws and its historical significance (Selected papers of the I international congress on ancient thought, Salamanca 1998), 203 – 220, Sankt Augustin.

Rossetti, L. (1999), "Aristotele, Teofrasto e la letteratura giuridica attica del Ⅳ secolo a. C.", RIFD 76, 651 – 681.

Rossetti, L. (1998), "El atheismo considerado como delito extreme an las Leyes de Platon", Theoria 6, 75 – 86.

Rossetti, L. (1994), "Processo ed istituzioni giudiziarie nelle Leggi di Platone", in Giuliani, A. & N. Picardi (eds), L'educazione giuridica Ⅵ: Modelli storici della procedura conlinentale (Atti del 60 Seminario internazionale sull'educazione giuridica), 1, 3 – 26, Napoli.

Rossetti, L. (1991 – 1992), "Il recorso alla pena detentiva nelle Leggi di Platone", in Diliberto, O. (ed), Il problema della pena criminale fra filosofia greca e diritto romano (Actes du deuxième colloque de philosophie pénale, Cagliari, 20 – 22 Aprile 1989), 347 – 369, Napoli. (Studi Economico – Giuridici 54)

Rossetti, L. (1989), "La filosofia penale di Ippodamo e la cultura giuridica dei Sofisti", RIFD 66, 315 – 335.

Rossetti, L. (1987), "La riforma delle istituzioni tra legislazione ed educazione in Platone", in Giuliani, A. & N. Pirandi (eds), L'educazione Giuridica V: Modelli di legislatore e scienza della legislazione, I, Filosofia e scienza della legislazione, 29 – 56, Perugia.

Rossetti, L. (1985), "Come instaurare un nuovo assetto costituzionale secondo Platone (La 'spiacevole necessiti': chi, si non il demos?)", Gerion 3, 63 – 77.

Rossetti, L. (1982), "Dikastai anypeuthynoi", QS 15, 181 – 202.

Rossetti, L. (1981), "Le magistrature nell'Atene classica. Forme di controllo e forme di responsabilitò", in Giulane, A. & N. Picardi (eds), L'educazione giuridica. Il pubblico funzionaria, 1 – 42, Perugia.

Rossetti, L. (1980), "Como instaurare un nuovo assetto costituzionale secondo Platone", Gerion 3, 63 – 78.

Rossetti, L. (1980), "Tre studi sui dissoi logoi", Studi Filos. Napoli Istituto Universitario Orientale 3, 27 – 54.

Rowe, G. O. (1995), "The Charge Against Meidias", *Hermes* 122, 55 - 63.

Rowe, G. O. (1993), "The Many Facets of Hybris in Demosthenes' Against Meidias", *AJPh* 114, 397 - 406.

Roy, J. (2002), "Problems of Democracy in the Arcadian Confederacy", in *Alternatives to Athens*, 308 - 326.

Roy, J. (1991), "Traditional Jokes about the Punishment of Adulterers in Ancient Greek Literature", *LCM* 16, 73 - 76.

Rubinstein, L. (2010), "Praxis: The Enforcement of Penalties in the Late Classical and Early Hellenistic Periods", in Thür, G. (ed), Symposion 2009. Vorträge zur griechischen und hellenistischen Rechtsgeschichte (Seggau, 25. - 30. August 2009), 193 - 216, Wien. (with a response by F. Mitthof)

Rubinstein, L. (2009), "Legal Argumentation in Hypereides' Against Timandros", *BICS* 52, 149 - 160.

Rubinstein, L. (2009), "Ateleia Grants and Their Enforcement in the Classical and Early Hellenistic Periods", in Greek History and Epigraphy, 115 - 144.

Rubinstein, L. (2007), "Arai in Greek Laws in the Classical and Hellenistic Periods: Deterrence or Concession to Tradition?", in Symposion 2005, 269 - 286.

Rubinstein, L. (2007), "Arguments from Precedent in the Attic Orators", in *The Attic Orators*, 359 - 371.

Rubinstein, L. (2005), "Main Litigants and Witnesses in the Athenian Courts: Procedural Variations", in Symposion 2001, 99 - 120. (with a reply by G. Thür, 121 - 124)

Rubinstein, L. (2005), "Differentiated Rhetorical Strategies in Athenian Courts", in *The Cambridge Companion*, 129 - 145.

Rubinstein, L. (2004), "Stirring up Dicastic Anger", in *Law, Rhetoric, and Comedy*, 1 - 14.

Rubinstein, L. (2003), "Synêgoroi: Their Place in our Reconstruction of the Athenian Legal Process", in Symposion 1999, 193 - 208.

Rubinstein, L. (2003), "Volunteer Prosecutors in the Greek World", Dike 6, 87 - 114.

Rubinstein, L. (2000), Litigation and Cooperation. Supporting Speakers in the Courts of Classical Athens, Stuttgart. (Historia Einzelschriften 147)

Rubinstein, L. (1999), "Adoption in Classical Athens", in Corbier, M. (ed), Adoption et fosterage, 45 – 62, Paris.

Rubinstein, L. (1993), Adoption in IVth Century Athens, Copenhagen. (Opuscula Graeco Latina 34)

Rupprecht, H. – A. (2005), "Greek Law in Foreign Surroundings: Continuity and Development", in *The Cambridge Companion*, 328 – 342.

Rydberg – Cox, J. A. (2003), "Oral and Written Sources in Athenian Forensic Rhetoric", *Mnemosyne* 56, 652 – 66.

Ruschenbusch, Eberhard (2010), Solon: Das Gesetzeswerk-Fragmente, Stuttgart. (Historia Einzelschriften 215)

Ruschenbusch, Eberhard (2002), "Platons Gesetze als Beispiel für ein griechisches Gesetzbuch", in Mélanges Dimakis, 565 – 568.

Ruschenbusch, Eberhard (2001), Ein altgriechisches Gesetzbuch: aus dem Kontext von Platons Gesetzen, München.

Ruschenbusch, Eberhard (1997), "Drei Beiträge zum Strafrecht Athens", in Symposion 1995, 167 – 171. (= Ruschenbusch, Kleine Schriften, 231 – 235)

Ruschenbusch, Eberhard (1993), "Wortlaut und Aufbau des Friedensvertrages vom Jahre 446/5 v. Chr. (Der Dreissigjährige Friede) (Bengtson, Die Staatsverträge des Altertums (StV) Nr. 156)", ZPE 97, 207 – 212.

Ruschenbusch, Eberhard (1991), "Die verheiratete Frau als Erbtochter im Recht von Gortyn?", ZRG 108, 287 – 289. (= Ruschenbusch, Kleine Schriften, 201 – 203)

Ruschenbusch, Eberhard (1990), "Die Grenze im athenischen Recht", in Olshausen, E. & H. Sonnabend (eds) Stuttgarter Kolloquium zur historischen Geographie des Altertums 4, 303 – 308, Amsterdam. (= Ruschenbusch, Kleine Schriften, 197 – 200)

Ruschenbusch, Eberhard (1989), "Über die rechte Art, das Recht Athens zu studieren", in Symposion 1985, 293 – 299. (= Ruschenbusch, Kleine Schriften, 185 – 187)

Ruschenbusch, Eberhard (1989), "Drei Beitrage zur öffentlichen Diaita in Athen", in Symposion 1982, 31 – 40. (= Ruschenbusch, Kleine Schriften, 172 – 178)

Ruschenbusch, Eberhard (1988), "Das Vergehen und dessen Ahndung im griechischen Recht", Gymnasium 95, 369 – 374. (= Ruschenbusch, Kleine Schriften,

188 – 192)

Ruschenbusch, Eberhard (1982), "Die Diaitetenliste IG II/III2 1927. Zugleich ein Beitrag zur sozialen Herkunft der Schiedsrichter und zur Demographie Athens", ZPE 49, 267 – 281. (= Ruschenbusch, Kleine Schriften, 159 – 171)

Ruschenbusch, Eberhard (1982), "Stasis und politischer Umsturz in Rhodos", Hermes 110, 495 – 498.

Ruschenbusch, Eberhard (1982), "Die Polis und das Recht", in Symposion 1979, 303 – 326. (= Ruschenbusch, Kleine Schriften, 141 – 158)

Ruschenbusch, Eberhard (1982), "Der Ursprung des gerichtlichen Rechtsstreits bei den Griechen", in Symposion 1977, 1 – 8. (= Ruschenbusch, Kleine Schriften, 135 – 140)

Ruschenbusch, Eberhard (1975), "Die Verträge Athens mit Leontinoi und Rhegion vom Jahre 433/2 v. Chr.", ZPE 19, 225 – 232.

Ruschenbusch, Eberhard (1975), "Die Quellen zur älteren griechischen Geschichte. Ein Überblick den Stand deuellenforschung unter besonderer Berücksichtigung der Belange des Rechtshistorikers", in Symposion 1971, 67 – 78.

Ruschenbusch, Eberhard (1972), "Über das Bodenrecht im archaischen Athen", Historia 21, 753 – 755. (= Ruschenbusch, Kleine Schriften, 131 – 134)

Ruschenbusch, Eberhard (1969), "Dike kata tinos und pros tina", ZRG 86, 386 – 394. (= Ruschenbusch, Kleine Schriften, 124 – 130)

Ruschenbusch, Eberhard (1968), Untersuchungen zur Geschichte des athenischen Strafrechts, Köln. (Gräzistische Abhandlungen 4) (= Ruschenbusch, Kleine Schriften, 75 – 123)

Ruschenbusch, Eberhard (1966), Solonos Nomoi. Die Fragmente des solonische Gesetzeswerkes mit einer Text-und Überlieferungsgeschichte, Wiesbaden. (Historia Einzelschriften 9)

Ruschenbusch, Eberhard (1965), "Hybreos Graphe. Ein Fremdkorper im athenischen Recht des 4. Jahrhunderts v. Chr.", ZRG 82, 302 – 309. (= Ruschenbusch, Kleine Schriften, 67 – 74)

Ruschenbusch, Eberhard (1965), "Heliaia. Die Tradition über das solonische Volksgericht", Historia 14, 381 – 384. (= Ruschenbusch, Kleine Schriften, 63 – 66)

Ruschenbusch, Eberhard (1962), "Diatithesthai ta heautou. Ein Beitrag zum sogennanten Testamentgesetz des Solon", ZRG 79, 307 – 311. (= Ruschenbusch, Kleine Schriften, 59 – 62)

Ruschenbusch, Eberhard (1961), "Ephesis. Ein Beitrag zur griechischen Rechtsterminologie", ZRG 78, 386 – 390. (= Ruschenbusch, Kleine Schriften, 54 – 58)

Ruschenbusch, Eberhard (1960), "Phonos. Zum Recht Drakons und seiner Bedeutung für das Werden des athenischen Staates", Historia 9, 129 – 154. (= Ruschenbusch, Kleine Schriften, 32 – 53)

Ruschenbusch, Eberhard (1958), "Patrios politeia. Theseus, Drakon, Solon und Kleisthenes in Publizistik und Geschichtsschreibung des 5. u. 4. Jh. v. Chr. ", Historia 7, 398 – 424.

Ruschenbusch, Eberhard (1957), "Dikasterion panton kurion", Historia 6, 257 – 274. (= Ruschenbusch, Kleine Schriften, 17 – 31)

Ruschenbusch, Eberhard (1956), "Der sogenannte Gesetzescode vom Jahre 410 v. Chr. ", Historia 5, 123 – 128. (= Ruschenbusch, Kleine Schriften, 11 – 16)

Ruzé, Fr. (2012), "Tyrannie grecque et royautés orientales", in Legras, B. (ed), Transferts culturels et droits dans le monde grec et hellénistique (Actes du colloque international, Reims, 14 – 17 mai 2008), 79 – 98, Paris.

Ruzé, Fr. (2006), "En Grèce archaique: la législation au secours des plus faibles", in Les régulations sociales, 171 – 188.

Ruzé, Fr. (2005), "Lycurgue de Sparte et ses collègues", in Le législateur et la loi, 151 – 160.

Ruzé, Fr. (2001), "La loi et le chant", in Brun, J. -P. & Ph. Jockey (eds), Technai. Techniques et sociétés en Méditerranée. Hommage à M. -Cl. Amouretti, 708 – 719, Paris. (= Eunomia, 183 – 207)

Ruzé, Fr. (2000), "Les premières manifestations de la citoyenneté en Grèce", in Sampy, J. (ed), Invention et ré-invention de la citoyenneté, 19 – 28, Pau.

Ruzé, Fr. (1997), Délibération et pouvoir dans la cité grecque de Nestor à Socrate, Paris.

Ruzé, Fr. (1993), "Les oligarques et leurs 'constitutions' dans l'Athenaion Politeia", in Aristote et Athènes, 185 – 201. (= Eunomia, 139 – 152)

Ruzé, Fr. (1993), "Les inférieurs libres à Sparte: exclusion ou intégration?", in

Mélanges Levêque 7,93 – 106. (= Eunomia,93 – 106)

Ruzé, Fr. (1991), "Le Conseil et l'Assemblée dans la Grande Rhètra de Sparte", REG 104,15 – 30. (= Eunomia,125 – 138)

Ruzé, Fr. (1989), "Basileis, tyrans et magistrats", Metis 4,211 – 231. (= Eunomia,107 – 124)

Ruzé, Fr. (1974), "La fonction des probouloi dans le monde grec antique", in Mélanges Seston,443 – 462. (= Eunomia,11 – 30)

S

Sakurai, M. (1995), "A new reading in P. Oxy. XIII 1606 (Lysias, Against Hippotherses)", ZPE 109,177 – 180.

Sakurai, M. (1992), Ancient Greek Women: Athenian Ideals and Reality, Tokyo.

Sakurai, M. (1986), "A Note on the Athenian Law of Adultery", Bulletin of Tokyo Gakugei University Ⅲ Social Sciences 38,119 – 134.

Sakurai, M. (1981), "The Epiklerate in Classical Athens and Preservation of the Oikos", Shicho (Current of History) 9,61 – 80.

Sakurai, M. (1977), "The Social Position of Women and Their Property Rights in Classical Athens, Mainly on the Law in Isaios X. 10", in Yuge, T. & S. Ito (eds), State and Society in Classical Antiquity, 183 – 221, Tokyo.

Salehi-Esfahani, H. (2008), "Rule of Law: A Comparison between Ancient Persia and Ancient Greece", *Iranian Studies* 41,629 – 644.

Samaras, Th. (2010), "Family and the Question of Women in the Laws", in Bobonich, Chr. (ed), Plato's Laws. A Critical Guide, 172 – 196, Cambridge.

Samaras, Th. (2007), "Who believes in Socrates' innocence? The religious charge against Socrates and the Intentional Audience of Plato's Apology", Polis 24,1 – 11.

Samberg, M. (1993), "Law and politics in Plato's 'Statesman'", Polis 12, 204 – 212.

Sanada, Y. (1974), "The Arbitration System in Athens", Hikakuho Zasshi (*Comparative Law Review*) 8,1 – 92.

Santas, G. (2006), "Justice, law, and women in Plato's Republic", Philosophical Inquiry 27,91 – 103.

Santas, G. (2002), "Legalité, justice et femmes dans la Republique et les Lois de Platon", RFHIP 16, 309 - 330. (= "Justice and Gender in the Laws and the Republic" in Plato's Laws: From Theory into Practice, 237 - 242)

Sardemann, W. (1914), Eleusinische Übergabeurkunden aus dem v. Jahrhundert, Marburg.

Saripolos, N. I. (1860), "Melete peri ton aition, di'a he archaia Hellas den paregage nomikous", Solon 1, 3ff.

Sarrazin, A. (1909), Etudes sur les fondations dans l'antiquité, Paris.

Sartori, Cr. (1999), "I tamiai di Delfi", MEP 2, 157 - 176.

Saunders, T. J. (1998), "Plato on the Treatment of Heretics", in *Law in its Political Setting*, 91 - 100.

Saunders, T. J. (1997), "Plato on Women in the Laws", in Powell, A. (ed), The Greek World, 591 - 609, London.

Saunders, T. J. (1991 - 1992), "Plutarch's De sera numinis vindicta in the tradition of Greek penology", in Diliberto, O. (ed), Il problema della pena criminale fra filosofia greca e diritto romano (Actes du deuxième colloque de philosophie penale, Cagliari, 20 - 22 Aprile 1989), 63 - 94, Napoli. (Studi Economico-Giuridici 54)

Saunders, T. J. (1991), Plato's Penal Code. Tradition, Controversy, and Reform in Greek Penology, Oxford.

Saunders, T. J. (1990), "Plato and the Athenian Law of Theft", in *Nomos*, 63 - 82.

Saunders, T. J. (1982), "Talionic and mirroring punishments in Greek culture", Polis 4, 1 - 16.

Saunders, T. J. (1981), "Protagoras and Plato on Punishment", in Kerford, G. B. (ed), The Sophists and Their Legacy, 129 - 141, Wiesbaden.

Saunders, T. J. (1975 - 1976), "Plato's Clockwork Orange", *Durham University Journal* 37, 113 - 117.

Saunders, T. J. (1973), "Plato on Killing in Anger: A Reply to Professor Woozley", *PhilosQ* 23, 350 - 356.

Saunders, T. J. (1973), "Penology and Eschatology in Plato's Timaeus and Laws", *CQ* 23, 232 - 244.

Saunders, T. J. (1963), "Two Points in Plato's Penal Code", *CQ* 13, 194 – 199.

Saunders, T. J. (1962), The Metic in Plato's Laws, diss. Cambridge.

Sautel, G. (1963), Introduction bibliographique à l'histoire du droit et à l'ethnologie juridique: A/7 Grèce, Bruxelles.

Savage, C. A. (1907), The Athenian Family; a Sociological and Legal Study, Based Chiefly on the Works of the Attic Orators, Baltimore.

Savage, C. A. (1902), "The Athenian in His Relations to the State", in Studies in Honour of Basil L. Gildersleeve, 87 – 94, Baltimore.

Sawada, N. (1996), "Athenian Politics in the Age of Alexander the Great: A Reconsideration of the Trial of Ctesiphon", *Chiron* 26, 57 – 84.

Saxonhouse, A. (2006), Free Speech and Democracy in Ancient Athens, Cambridge.

Sbordone, F. (1970), "Due note sul nuovo Menandro", Rendiconti dell' Accademia di Archeologia, Lettere e Belle Arti, Napoli 45, 41 – 56.

Scafuro, A. C. (2011), Demosthenes, Speeches 39 – 49, Austin, Tx. (The oratory of classical Greece 13)

Scafuro, A. C. (2010), "Conservative Trends in Athenian Law: IE 138, a Law Concerning the Mysteries", in Thür, G. (ed), Symposion 2009. Vorträge zur griechischen und hellenistischen Rechtsgeschichte (Seggau, 25. – 30. August 2009), 23 – 46, Wien. (with a response by A. Maffi)

Scafuro, A. (2009), "Eudikos' Rider (IG I3 102. 38 – 47)", in Themos, A. A. & N. Papazarkadas (eds), Attika Epigraphika. Meletes pros timen tou Chr. Habicht, 47 – 67, Athenai.

Scafuro, A. C. (2006), "Magistrates with Hegemony in the Courts of Athens", in Symposion 2003, 27 – 56.

Scafuro, A. C. (2006), "Identifying Solonian Laws", in Solon of Athens, 175 – 196.

Scafuro, A. (2005), "Parent Abusers, Military Shirkers, and Accused Killers: The Authenticity of the Second Law Inserted at Dem. 24. 105", in Symposion 2001, 51 – 70. (with a reply by D. C. Mirhady, 71 – 78)

Scafuro, A. (2004), "Lokale Gerichtsbarkeit in den attischen Demen", *ZRG* 121, 94 – 109.

Scafuro, A. (2004), "The Role of the Prosecutor and Athenian Legal Procedure (Dem. 21. 10)", Dike 7, 113 - 133.

Scafuro, A. (2003), "IG II2 204: Boundary Setting and Legal Process in Classical Athens", in Symposion 1999, 123 - 144.

Scafuro, A. (1997), The Forensic Stage: Settling Disputes in Graeco-Roman New Comedy, Cambridge.

Scafuro, A. (1994), "Witnessing and False Witnessing: Proving Citizenship and Kin Identity in Fourth-century Athens", in *Athenian Identity*, 156 - 198.

Scallen, E. A. (1995), "Classical Rhetoric, Practical Reasoning, and the Law of Evidence", *American University Law Review* 44, 1717 - 1816.

Scanlon, T. F. (1994), "Echoes of Herodotus in Thucydides: Self-sufficiency, Admiration and the Law", *Historia* 43, 143ff.

Schaps, D. M. (2001), "[Demosthenes] 35: Little Brother Strikes out on His Own", *Laverna* 12, 67 - 85.

Schaps, D. M. (1998), "What was Free about a Free Athenian Woman", *TAPhA* 128, 161 - 188.

Schaps, D. M. (1996), "Builders, Contractors, and Power: Financing and Administering Building Projects in Ancient Greece", in Katzoff, R., Petroff, Y. & D. Schaps (eds), Classical Studies in Honor of D. Sohlberg, 77 - 90, Ramat Gan.

Schaps, D. M. (1979), Economic Rights of Women in Ancient Greece, Edinburgh.

Schaps, D. M. (1976), "A Disputed Slave in Boeotia", *ZPE* 20, 63 - 64.

Schaps, D. M. (1975), "Women in Greek Inheritance Law", *CQ* 25, 53 - 57.

Scheibelreiter, Ph. (2012), "Pharmakos, aries und talio. Rechtsvergleichende Überlegungen zum frühen römischen und griechischen Strafrecht", in Rollinger, R., Lang, M. & H. Barta (eds), Strafe und Straferecht in den antike Welten. Unter Berücksichtigung von Todesstrafe, Hinrichtung und peinlicher Befragung, 23 - 48, Wiesbaden.

Scheibelreiter, Ph. (2010), "'Die gleichen für Freunde und Feinde halten': Rechtsvergleichende Untersuchungen zur Geschichte der Freund-Feind Klausel", in Lang, M., Barta, H. & R. Rollinger (eds), Staatsverträge, Völkerrecht und Diplomatie im alten Orient und in der griechisch-römischen Antike, 51 - 70, Wiesbaden.

Scheibelreiter, Ph. (2008), "Der ungetreue Verwahrer in Herodot 6. 86", ZRG 125, 189 - 213.

Scheibelreiter, Ph. (2008), "Der peri tou ostrakismou nomos in einem Scholion zu Aristophanes Equites 855B? Überlegungen zum Ostrakismos-Gesetz", Dike 11, 111 - 138.

Scheibelreiter, Ph. (2008), "Rechtspraktiken im Kontext des delisch-attischen Seebundes: Die Besicherung des Seebundvertrages-mydroi", in Rollinger, R., H. Barta & M. Lang (eds), Recht und Religion. Menschliche und göttliche Gerechtigkeitsvorstellungen in den antiken Welten, 169 - 190, Wiesbaden.

Scheid-Tissinier, Ev. (2011), "Les démes, lieux de citoyenneté, lieux de conflits", in Azoulay, V. & P. Ismard (eds), Clisthène et Lycurgue d'Athènes. Autour du politique dans la cité classique, 275 - 294, Paris.

Scheid-Tissinier, Ev. (2011), "Du bon usage des amis et des ennemis dans les plaidoyers attiques", in Peigney, J. (ed), Amis et ennemis en Grèce ancienne, 165 - 178, Bordeaux.

Scheid-Tissinier, Ev. (2010), "L'énoncé des normes dans le monde homérique et leur application", Mètis 8, 21 - 38.

Scheid-Tissinier, Ev. (2008), "Jean Rudhardt et la dike", Kernos 21, 173 - 184.

Scheid-Tissinier, Ev. (2007), "La colère des jurés dans les tribunaux athéniens", in Athènes et le politique, 179 - 198.

Scheid-Tissinier, Ev. (2006), "Les revendications de la vengeance dans les plaidoyers attiques", in Les régulations sociales, 97 - 114.

Scheid, Ev. (2005), "Remarques sur les fondements de la vengeance en Grèce archaique et classique", in La violence, 395 - 412.

Scheid-Tissinier, Ev. (2002), "Laos et démos, le people de l'épopée", AC 71, 1 - 26.

Schaps, D. M. (1979), Economic Rights of Women in Ancient Greece, Edinburgh.

Schaps, D. M. (1976), "A Disputed Slave in Boeotia", *ZPE* 20, 63 - 64.

Schaps, D. M. (1975), "Women in Greek Inheritance Law", *CQ* 25, 53 - 57.

Schaube, A. (1886), "Objekt und composition der Rechtsaufzeichnung von Gortyn", Hermes 21, 213 - 239.

Schils, G. (1991), "Solon and the hektemoroi", AncSoc 22, 75 - 90.

Schipp, G. P. (1966), "Divine and Natural Law in Greece", in Melbourne, K. M. (ed), For Service to Classical Studies. Essays in Honor of Francis Letters, 149 - 152, Cheshire.

Schmidt, L. V. (1876), Commentatio de auctoritate probouleúmatos in re publica Atheniensium, Marburg.

Schmink, A. (1994), "Apo to 'nomo' ston 'nomo'. O Photios kai he ennoia tou nomou sten archaioteta", Symboles II, 61 - 72.

Schmitt, H. H. (1994), "Überlegungen zur Sympolitie", in Symposion 1993, 35 - 44.

Schmitz, Th. A. (2000), "Plausibility in the Greek Orators", *AJPh* 121, 47 - 77.

Schofield, M. (2006), "Law and Absolutism in the Republic", Polis 23, 319 - 327.

Schöll, R. (1887), "Athenische Fest-commissionen", SBAW I, 1 - 24; 170.

Schöll, R. (1886), "Über attische Gesetzgebung", SBAW, 83 - 139.

Schöll, R. (1879), "De communibus et collegiis quibusdam Graecorum", in Sauppe, H. (ed), Satura philologa, 167 - 180, Berlin.

Schöll, R. (1877), "De extraordinariis quibusdam magistratibus Atheniensium", in Commentationes philologae in honorem Theodori Mommseni, 451 - 470, Berlin.

Schöll, R. (1875), "De synegoris atticis commentatio", in Adolfo Schoellio patri optimo natalem septuagesimum pie gratulantor Rudolfus et Fridericus Schoellii, 1 - 35, Jena.

Schöll, R. (1873), Quaestiones fiscales iuris attici ex Lysiae orationibus illustratae, Berlin.

Schömann, G. F. (1897 - 1902), Griechische Alterthülmer, Berlin.

Schömann, G. F. (1876), "Der Kranz des Basileus und der stimmstein der Athena. Die Basileis und ihre Kompetenz in den Blutgerichten", NJ 113, 12 - 20.

Schömann, G. F. (1875), "Die Epheten und der Areopag", NJ 111, 153 - 165.

Schömann, G. F. (1869), "Zu Demosthenes", NJ 99, 755 - 757.

Schömann, G. F. (1866), "Die solonische Heliäa und der Staatsstreich des Ephialtes", NJ 93, 585 - 594.

Schömann, G. F. (1857), De exteris religionibus apud Athenienses, Greifswald.

(= Schoemann, Opuscula, 3, 428 - 441)

Schömann, G. F. (1855), Recognitio quaestionis de Spartanis homoeis, Greifswald.

Schömann, G. F. (1855), De causa Leptinea, Greifswald. (= Schoemann, Opuscula, 1, 237 - 246)

Schömann, G. F. (1855), Dissertatio de reddendis magistratuum gestorum rationibus apud Athenienses, Gryphiswaldia.

Schömann, G. F. (1854), Animadversiones de nomothetis, Greifswald. (= Schoemann, Opuscula, 1, 247 - 259)

Schömann, G. F. (1854), Die Verfassungsgeschichte Athens nach Grote's History of Greece. Kritisch geprüft, Leipzig.

Schömann, G. F. (1847), "Über die Probole im attischen Process", Philologus 2, 593 - 607.

Schömann, G. F. (1847), Animadversiones de judiciis heliasticis, Greifswald.

Schömann, G. F. (1842), De causa hereditaria in Isaei or. de Philoctemon Hereditate, Greifswald. (= Schoemann, Opuscula, 1, 272 - 284)

Schömann, G. F. (1839), De iudiciorum suffragiis occultis, Greifswald. (= Schoemann, Opuscula 1, 260 - 271)

Schömann, G. F. (1838), Antiquitates iuris publici Graecorum, Greifswald.

Schömann, G. F. (1836), De ecclesiis Lacedaemoniorum, Greifswald. (= Schoemann, Opuscula, 1, 87 - 107)

Schömann, G. F. (1831), Isaei orationes xi cum aliquot deperditarum fragmentis, Greifswald.

Schömann, G. F. (1830), De cognatorum qui collaterales dicuntur hereditatibus, Greifswald.

Schömann, G. F. (1820), De sortitione iudicum apud Athenienses, Greifswald. (= Schoemann, Opuscula, 1, 200 - 229)

Schömann, G. F. (1819), De comitiis Atheniensium, libri tres, Greifswald.

Schöpsdau, K. (2012), "Strafen und Strafrecht bei griechischen Denkern des 5. und 4. Jahrhunderts", in Rollinger, R., Lang, M. & H. Barta (eds), Strafe und Straferecht in den antike Welten. Unter Berücksichtigung von Todesstrafe, Hinrichtung und peinlicher Befragung, 1 - 22, Wiesbaden.

Schöpsdau, K. (2008), "Platon als Reformer des Strafrechts. Zu den Strafgesetzen in den Nomoi", Politisches Denken Jahrbuch 2008, 185 – 206.

Schöpsdau, K. (2005), "Der soziale und rechtliche Status der Fremden in Staatsentwurf der platonischen Nomoi", in Riemer, U. & P. Riemer (eds), Xenophobie-Philoxenie. Vom Umgang mit Fremden in der Antike, 115 – 129, Stuttgart.

Schöpsdau, K. (2004), "Die soziale und rechtliche Stellung der Fremden in Platons Nomoi", in Riemer, U. & P. Riemer (eds), Xenophobie-Philoxenie. Vom Umgang mit Fremden in der Antike, 115 – 129, Stuttgart.

Schöpsdau, K. (2004), "Richten und Strafen. Zum Strafrecht in Platons Nomoi", Études Platoniciennes 1, 51 – 72.

Schöpsdau, K. (2000), "Die Regelung des Sexualverhaltens (Ⅷ 835c1 – 842a10) als ein Exempel platonischer Nomothetik", in Lisi, F. (ed), Plato's Laws and its historical significance. Selected papers from the I International congress on ancient thought (Salamanca 1998), 179 – 192, Sank Augustin.

Schöpsdau, K. (2000), "Zur Wahl der Gesetzeswaechter in Platons 'Nomoi'", ZPE 131, 243 – 250.

Schöpsdau, K. (1984), "Zum Strafrechtsexkurs in Platons Nomoi", RhM 127, 97 – 132.

Schroeder, D. N. (1981), "Aristotle on law", Polis 4, 17 – 31.

Schröder, O. (1917), "Nomos ho panton basileus", Philologus 74, 195 – 204.

Schuchman, Ph. (1963), "Comments on the Criminal Code of Plato's Laws", *Journal of the History of Ideas* 24, 25 – 40.

Schuchman, Ph. (1962), "Aristotle's Conception of Contract", *Journal of the History of Ideas* 23, 257 – 264.

Schulthess, O. (1921), Das attische Volksgericht, Bern.

Schulthess, O. (1899), Die Vormundschaftsrechnung des Demosthenes, epikritische Beiträge zur Erklärung der Vormundschaftsreden des Demosthenes, Frauenfeld.

Schulthess, O. (1886), Vormundschaft nach attischem Recht, Freiburg.

Schulze, E. R. (1878), Prolegomenon in Demosthenis quae fertur orationem adversus Apaturium capita duo, Leipzig.

Schulze, W. (1918), "Beiträge zur Wort-und Sittengeschichte", SPA, 320 – 332 & 481 – 511. (= Kleine Schriften, 160 – 189, Berlin 1934)

Schuster, St. (2005), Das Seedarlehen in den Gerichtsreden des Demosthenes: mit einem Ausblick auf die weitere historische Entwicklung des Rechtsinstitutes: daneion nautikon, fenus nauticum und Bodenerei, Berlin. (Freiburger rechtsgeschichtliche Abhandlungen n. F. 49)

Schütrumpf, E. (2004), "Imperfect Regimes for Imperfect Human Beings: Variations of Infractions of Justice", Mélanges de l'Université Saint-Josephe (Beyruth) 57, 13 – 36.

Schuurmans-Stekhoven, J. H. (1846), De civium atticorum recogn. sive diapsephisei, Leyden.

Schwab, G. (1818), Num quod Areopagus in plebiscita aut confirmanda aut rejicienda jus exercuerit, Stuttgart.

Schwartzberg, M. (2004), "Athenian Democracy and Legal Change", *American Political Science Review* 98, 311 – 325.

Schwebsch, K. A. H. (1878), De oratione quae contra Leocharem a Demosthene scripta fertur, Berlin.

Schwenn, Fr. (1915), Die Menschenopfer bei den Griechen und Römern, Giessen. (Religionsgeschichtliche Versuche und Vorarbeiten 15(3))

Sciascia, G. (1965), "Il collegio dei nomofilaci garanzia costituzionale delle repubbliche elleniche", in Studi Biondi I, 633 – 646.

Scodel, R. (1993), "Meditations on Lysias 1 and Athenian adulter", Electronic Antiquity 1(2), http://scholar.lib.vt.edu/ejournals/ElAnt/V1N2/scodel.html.

Scott, A. G. (2011), "Plural Marriage and the Spartan State", *Historia* 60, 413 – 424.

Scott, R. (1838), The Athenian ballot and secret suffrage, Oxford.

Scott, J. A. (1919 – 1920), "Why Meletus Demanded the Death Penalty for Socrates", *CJ* 15, 436 – 437.

Seaford, R. (2003), "Tragic tyranny", in Morgan, K. A. (ed), Popular Tyranny: Popular Sovereignty and its Discontents in Ancient Greece, 95 – 115, Austin, Tx.

Seaford, R. (1990), "The Imprisonment of Women in Greek Tragedy", *JHS* 110, 76 – 90.

Seager, R. (1967), "Alcibiades and the Charge of Aiming at Tyranny", *Historia* 16, 6 – 18.

Seager, R. (1966), "Lysias Against the Corndealers", *Historia* 15, 172 – 184.

Sealey, R. (2009), "The Drakontian Law of 409/8 BC", *AHB* 23, 32 – 37.

Sealey, R. (2006), "Aristotle, Athenaion Politeia 57. 4: Trial of Animals and Inanimate Objects for Homicide", *CQ* 56, 475 – 485.

Sealey, R. (1994), The Justice of the Greeks, Ann Arbor.

Sealey, R. (1991), "Ath. Pol 25. 2 and Lys. fr. 178: Additional Functions of the Areopagite Council", *JHS* 111, 210.

Sealey, R. (1990), Women and Law in Classical Greece, Princeton.

Sealey, R. (1987), The Athenian Republic: Democracy or the Rule of Law?, London.

Sealey, R. (1984), "On Lawful Concubinage in Athens", ClAnt 3, 111 – 133.

Sealey, R. (1984), "The Tetralogies Asribed to Antiphon", TAPhA 114, 71 – 85.

Sealey, R. (1983), "The Athenian Courts for Homicide", *CPh* 78, 275 – 296.

Sealey, R. (1983), "How Citizenship and the City Began in Athens", *AJAH* 8, 97 – 129.

Sealey, R. (1982), "On the Athenian Concept of Law", CJ 77, 289 – 302.

Sealey, R. (1981), "Ephialtes, Eisangelia, and the Council", in G. S. Schrimpton & D. J. McGargar (eds), Classical Contributions. Studies in Honour of Malcolm Francis MacGregor, 125 – 134, New York. (= Rhodes, P. J. (ed) (2004), Athenian democracy, 310 – 326, Edinburgh)

Sealey, R. (1978), "Zum Datum der solonischen Gesetzgebung", Historia 28, 238 – 241.

Sealey, R. (1969), "Probouleusis and the Sovereign Assembly", *CSCA* 2, 247 – 269.

Sealey, R. (1964), "Ephialtes", *CPh* 59, 11 – 22.

Sealey, R. (1958), "On Penalizing Areopagites", *AJPh* 79, 71 – 73. (= R. Sealey, Essays in Greek Politics, 183 – 185, New York 1967)

Sealey, R. (1957), "IG II2 1609 and the Transformation of the Second Athenian Sea-league", *Phoenix* 11, 95 – 111.

Sedley, D. (2003), "The nomothetes in Plato's Cratylus", The Studia Philonica Annual 15, 5 – 16.

Seel, G. (2011), "The Citizen is a Ruler", in Moutsopoulos, E. & M. Protopappas-Marnelli (eds), The Notion of Citizenship in Greek Philosophy (Proceedings of the 2nd International Conference of Philosophy, Alexandria, 4 - 6 March 2010), 100 - 112, Athens.

Seel, G. (1990), "Die Rechtfertigung von Herrschaft in der 'Politik' des Aristoteles", in Patzig, G. (ed), Aristoteles' "Politik" (Akten des XI Symposium Aristotelicum, Friedrichschafen/Bodensee, 25. 8. - 3. 9. 1987), 58 - 61, Göttingen.

Segal, Ch. (1989), "Law and Universal in Euripides' Hecuba", in Viljamaa, T., Jaekel, S. & K. Nyholm (eds), Sprachaspekte als Experiment. Beiträge zur Literaturkritik in Antike und Neuzeit, 63 - 82, Turku. (Annales Univers. Turkuensis ser. B, 187)

Seimiya, S. (1985), "A Reconsideration of Drakon's Law on Homicide", SeiyoShigaku (Studies in Western History) 136, 54 - 66.

Seimiya, S. (1983), "Drakon's Law on Homicide: Some Comments on the Recent Work of M. Gagarin", *Rekishi* (*Tohoku Historical Journal*) 60, 60 - 72.

Sekunda, N. V. (2002), "Land-use, Ethnicity and Federalism in West Crete", in *Alternatives to Athens*, 327 - 348.

Sens, Al. (1991), Not I, but the Law: Juridical and Legislative Language in Aristophanes' Ecclesiazusae, diss. Harvard University.

Shear, J. L. (2011), Polis and Revolution: Responding to Oligarchy in Classical Athens, Cambridge.

Sheets, G. A. (1994), "Conceptualising International Law in Thucydides", *AJPh* 115, 51 - 73.

Sheld, E. R. (2002), Law, Virtue and Justice in Aristotle's Politics, diss. Boston University.

Sheppard, St. (2005), "The Laws of War in the Pre-dawn Light: Institutions and Obligations in Thucydides' Peloponnesian War", *Columbia Journal of Transnational Law* 43, 905 - 926.

Shibakawa, O. (1979), "The Areopagus before Solon", SeiyoShigaku (*Studies in Western History*) 112, 53 - 66.

Shinmura, Y. (1968), "On the addenda to the Great Rhetra", SeiyoShigaku (*Studies in Western History*) 80, 1 - 17.

Shinmura, Y. (1964), "A Few Problems on the Spartan Great Rhetra", Seiyo Kotengaku Kenkyu(*Journal of Classical Studies*)12,27 – 39.

Shinmura, Y. (1963), "Ephoroi in Sparta: Its Origin and the Process of Getting Its Right", SeiyoShigaku(*Studies in Western History*)57,1 – 18.

Shimron, B. (1965), "The Original Task of the Spartan Patronomoi. A Suggestion", *Eranos* 63,155 – 158.

Shinozaki, M. (1977), "Communal Landownership in Attica of the Classical Ages: An Analysis of Lease Inscriptions", in Yuge, T. & S. Ito (eds), State and Society in Classical Antiquity,69 – 106,Tokyo.

Shipton, K. M. W. (2008), "Bankers as Money Lenders: The Banks of Classical Athens", in Verboven, K., Vandorpe, K. & V. Chankowski (eds), Pistoi dia ten technen. Bankers, loans, and archives in the ancient world. Studies in honour of R. Bogaert,93 – 114,Leuven. (Studia Hellenistica 44)

Shipton, K. M. W. (2000), Leasing and Lending in Fourth Century Athens, London. (BICS Suppl. 74)

Shipton, K. M. W. (1997), "The Private Banks in Fourth-century B. C. Athens: A Reappraisal", *CQ* 47,396 – 422.

Shortridge, A. (2008), "Law Against Nature?", in O'Grady, P. (ed), The Sophists. An Introduction,194 – 203,London.

Shortridge, A. (2007), "Law and nature in Protagoras' great speech", Polis 24, 12 – 25.

Sickinger, J. P. (2009), "Indeterminacy in Greek Law: Statutory Gaps and Conflicts", in Symposion 2007,99 – 112.

Sickinger, J. P. (2007), "Rhetoric and the Law", in Worthington, I. (ed), A companion to Greek rhetoric,286 – 302,Oxford.

Sickinger, J. P. (2004), "The Laws of Athens: Publication, Preservation, Consultation", in *The Law and the Courts*,93 – 110.

Sickinger, J. P. (2002), "Literacy, Orality, and Athenian Legislative Procedure", in Worthington, I. & J. M. Foley (eds), Epea and Grammata. Oral & Written Communication in Ancient Greece,147 – 169,Leiden.

Sickinger, J. P. (1999), Public Records and Archives in Classical Athens, Chapel Hill, NC.

Sickinger, J. P. (1991), "A Note on Wasps 349", *CQ* 41, 529 - 532.

Siewert, P. (2005), "Föderalismus in der griechischen Welt bis 338 v. Chr.", in Siewert, P. & L. Aigner-Foresti (eds), Föderalismus in der griechischen und römischen Antike, 17 - 42, Frankfurt.

Siewert, P. (2005), "'Richter über der Hellenen' (Hellanodikas) und andere überstaatliche Gemeinschaftsbezeichnungen in Olympia", in Il cittadino, lo straniero, 93 - 104.

Siewert, P. (ed) (2002), Ostrakismos-Testimonien I. Die Zeugnisse antiker Autoren, der Inschriften und Ostraka über das athenische Scherbengericht aus vorhellenistischer Zeit (487 - 322 v. Chr.), Stuttgart. (Historia Einzelschriften 155)

Siewert, P. (2000), "Due iscrizioni giuridiche della cittd di Elide", MEP 3, 19 - 38.

Siewert, P. (1994), "Symmachien in neuen Inschriften von Olympia. Zu den sogenannte Periöken der Eleer", in Federazioni e federalismo, 257 - 264.

Siewert, P. (1994), "Eine archäische Rechtsaufzeichung aus der antiken Stadt Elis", in Symposion 1993, 17 - 32.

Siewert, P. (1992), "The Olympic Rules", in Coulson, W. & H. Kyrieleis (eds), Proceedings of Aninternational Symposium on the Olympic Games (5 - 9 September 1988), 113 - 117, Athens.

Siewert, P. (1991), "Accuse contro i 'candidati' all'ostracismo per la loro condotta politica e morale", in Sordi, M. (ed), L'immagine dell'uomo politico: vita pubblica e morale nell'antichitd, 3 - 13, Milano. (CISA 17)

Siewert, P. (1981), "Eine Bronze-Urkunde mit elischen Urteilen über Böoter, Thessaler, Athen und Thespiai", in Olympia Berichte 10, 228 - 248, Berlin.

Siewert, P. (1978), "Die angebliche Übernahme solonischer Gesetze in die Zwölftafeln. Ursprung und Ausgestaltung einer Legende", Chiron 8, 331 - 344.

Silcox, H. M-M. (2011), "The evolution of justice in The Oresteia", Analecta Husserliana 109/2, 33 - 41.

Silva, M. (2010b), "Crimes no feminino nas Historias de Herodoto", in Cortes Gabaudan, F. & J. V. Mendez Dosuna (eds), Dic mihi, Musa, virum. Homenaje al profesor A. Lopez Eire, 645 - 652, Salamanca.

Silva, M. (2010), "Euripides' Orestes: The chronicle of a trial", in Law and drama in ancient Greece, 77 – 93.

Silver, M. (2009), "The Role of International Trade in the Transformation of Attica's Agricultural Organization: From Solon to Socrates", MBAH 27, 95 – 163.

Silverthorne, M. J. (1975), "Laws, Preambles and the Legislator in Plato", *Humanities Association Review* 26, 10 – 20.

Simonsen, K. (2008), "IG II2 1622 and the Collection of Naval Debts in the 340s", in Epigraphy and the Greek historian, 68 – 78.

Simpson, P. (2006), "Aristotle's Defensible Defense of Slavery", *Polis* 23, 95 – 115.

Singer, H. (2009), "War and international relations", in Raaflaub, K. A. & H. van Wees (eds), A companion to archaic Greece, 585 – 603, Oxford.

Sinou, Chr. (2009), "Aristotle on Woman as a Citizen", in The Notion of Citizenship, 190 – 202. (in Greek)

Sisova, I. A. (1970), "The reforms of Philolaus", VDI 114, 64 – 72. (in Russian)

Skoczylas Pownall, F. (2000), "Shifting Viewpoints in Xenophon's Hellenica: The Arginusae Episode", *Athenaeum* 88, 499 – 513.

Slater, W. J. (1995), "The Theatricality of Justice", *CB* 71, 143 – 157.

Slings, S. R. & É. de Strycker (1994), Plato's Apology of Socrates: A Literary and Philosophical Study with Running Commentary, Leiden.

Small, D. B. (1995), "Monuments, Laws and Analysis: Combining Archaeology and Text in Ancient Athens", in Small, D. B. (ed), Methods in the Mediterranean. Historical and Archeological Views on Texts and Archaeology, 143 – 176, Leiden.

Smith, F. D. (1921), Athenian Political Commissions, Chicago.

Smith, G. (1957), "Cretan Law and Common Tendencies in Archaic Greek Law", in Hoeg, C., Krarup, P., Rils, J. P. & I. Magnussen (eds), Acta Congressus Madvigiani (Proceedings of the second international congress of classical studies) I, 235 – 249, Kopenhagen.

Smith, G. (1956), "More Recent Theories on the Origin and the Interrelation of the First Classifications of Greek Laws", Cahiers d'Histoire Mondiale 3, 173 – 195.

Smith, G. (1927), "The jurisdiction of Areopagus", *CPh* 22, 61 – 79.

Smith, G. (1924), "Dicasts in the Ephetic Courts", *CPh* 19, 353 – 358.

Smith, G. (1924), The Administration of Justice from Hesiod to Solon, Chicago.

Smith, G. (1922), "Early Greek Codes", *CPh* 17, 187 - 201.

Smith, G. (1921), "The Prytaneum in the Athenian Amnesty Law", *CPh* 16, 345 - 353.

Smith, M. S. (1967), "Greek Adoptive Formulae", *CQ* 17, 302 - 310.

Smith, N. D. & T. C. Brickhouse (1984), "Socrates and the Obedience to the Law", *Apeiron* 18, 10 - 18.

Smith, S. B. (1925), "The Establishment of Public Courts at Athens", *TAPhA* 56, 106 - 119.

Smyrniades, Bi. (1952), He eisaggelia en tei Athenaion Politeia, Athenai.

Sokolowski, Fr. (1976), "The Athenian Law Concerning Silver Currency (375/4 B. C.)", *BCH* 100, 511 - 515.

Solum, L. B. (1988), "The Virtues and the Vices of a Judge: An Aristotelian Guide to Judicial Selection", *Southern California Law Review* 61, 1735 - 1756.

Sommer, St. (2001), Das Ephorat: Garant des spartanischen Kosmos, St. Katharinen. (Mainzer althistorische Studien 2)

Sommerstein, A. H. (2010), "Orestes' trial and Athenian homicide procedure", in Law and drama in ancient Greece, 25 - 38.

Sommerstein, A. H. (2006), "Rape and Consent in Athenian Tragedy", in Cairns, D. & V. Liapis (eds), Dionysalexandros. Essays on Aeschylus and his fellow tragedians in honour of A. F. Garvie, 233 - 252, Swansea.

Sondhaus, K. (1909), De Solonis legibus, Jena.

Sonne, E. E. (1888), De arbitris externis, quos Graeci adbibuerunt ad lites et intestinas et peregrinas componendas, quaestiones epigraphicae, Göttingen.

Soraci, R. (2003), "Il 'codice' di Caronda e l'obbedienza alle leggi", Quaderni catanesi di studi antichi e medievali 2, 5 - 58.

Sordi, M. (2006), "Atene e l'unione fra Argo e Corinto", in Bearzot Cinzia, & F. Landucci (eds), Argo. Una democrazia diversa, 299 - 310, Milano.

Sordi, M. (1997), "La fortuna dell'amnistia del 403/2 a. C.", in Amnistia, perdono, 79 - 90.

Sordi, M. (1994), "Il federalismo greco nell'etǎ classica", in Federazioni e federalismo, 3 - 22.

Sordi, M. (1991), "Il trattato fra Sparta e gli Etoli e la guerra d'Elide", Aevum 65, 35 - 38.

Sordi, M. (1989), "Il decreto di Eucrate e la liceità del tirannicidio", GFF 9, 59 - 63.

Sordi, M. (1988), "Il dibattito sulle costituzioni nella Grecia dell'età classica e la tirannide", in Per i 40 anni della costituzione, 9 - 23, Milano.

Sordi, M. (1983), "Citta e stati federali nel mondo greco", in La città antica come fatto di cultura, 185 - 193, Como.

Sordi, M. (1981), "Teramene e il processo delle Arginuse", Aevum 55, 3 - 12.

Sordi, M. (1973), "La restaurazione della lega beotica nel 479 - 477 a. C.", Athenaeum 51, 79 - 91.

Sordi, M. (1968), "Aspetti del federalismo greco arcaico. Autonomia e egemonia nel koinon Beotico", A & R 13, 66 - 75.

Sordi, M. (1958), La lega tessala fino ad Alessandro Magno, Roma.

Sordi, M. (1955), "A proposito di uno scritto del 410 - 400 a. C.: il Peri Politeias dello Pseudo Erode", *RFIC* 33, 175 - 198.

Sosin, J. D. (2002), "Two Attic endowments", *ZPE* 138, 123 - 128.

Spatharas, D. (2006), "Wounding, rhetoric and the law in Lysias Ⅳ", *RIDA* 53, 87 - 106.

Spencer, M. E. (1978 - 1979), "Plato and the Anatomy of Constitutions", *Social Theory and Practice* 5, 95 - 130.

Spencer, N. (2002), "Exchange and stasis in archaic Mytilene", in Alternatives to Athens, 68 - 81.

Spina, L. (1986), Il cittadino alla tribuna. Diritto e libertà di parola nell'Atene democratica, Napoli. (Forme materiali e ideologie del mondo antico 25)

Spyridakis, St. (1969), "Aristotle on the election of kosmoi", PdP 24, 265 - 268. (= Cretica. Studies on ancient Crete, 149 - 152, New York 1992)

Stafford, E. J. (1997), "Themis. Religion and Order in the Archaic Polis", in *The Development of the Polis*, 158 - 167, New York.

Stalley, R. F. (2006), "Law and Justice in Plato", in Herrmann, F. -G. (ed), New essays on Plato. Language and thought in fourth-century Greek philosophy, 1 - 20, Swansea.

Stalley, R. F. (2002), "La justice dans les Lois de Platon", RFHIP 16, 229 - 246. (= "Justice in Plato's Laws" in Plato's Laws: From theory into practice, 174 - 186)

Stalley, R. F. (1995), "Punishment in Plato's Laws", History of Political, Theory 16, 469 - 487.

Stalley, R. F. (1995), "Punishment in Plato's Protagoras", Phronesis 46, 1 - 18.

Stanley, Ph. V. (1998), "The Hektemoroi and Land Usage in Ancient Athens", *Laverna* 9, 19 - 45.

Stanley, Ph. V. (1990), "The Purpose of Loans in Ancient Athens. A Reexamination", *MBAH* 9, 57 - 73.

Stanley, Ph. V. (1979), "Agoranomoi and Metronomoi: Athenian Market Regulations and Officials", AncW 1, 72 - 9.

Stanton, G. R. (1982), "Federalism in the Greek World: An Introduction", in Hellenika. Essays, 183 - 190.

Stanton, G. R. (1970), "The Introduction of Ostracism and Alcmeonid Propaganda", *JHS* 90, 180 - 183.

Stears, K. (2000), "Losing the Picture: The Funerary Legislation of Demetrios of Phaleron", in Rutter, N. K. & B. A. Sparkes (eds), Word and image in ancient Greece, 206 - 227, Edinburgh.

Stecchini, L. C. (1950), Athenaion Politeia. The Constitution of Athens by the old oligarchs and by Arlstotle, Glencoe.

Steinbock, B. (2011), "A Lesson in Patriotism: Lycurgus' Against Leokrates, the Ideology of the Ephebeia, and Athenian Social Memory", ClAnt 30, 279 - 317.

Steiner, D. T. (1994), The Tyrant's Writ: Myths and Images of Writing in Ancient Greece, Princeton.

Stephens, J. (1985), "Socrates on the Rule of Law", *History of Philosophy Quarterly* 2, 3 - 10.

Stergiopoulos, K. D. (1978), "Peri ten dioikesin ton archaion Athenon", in Mneme. Mélanges à la mémoire de Michel A. Dendias, 1193 - 1236, Athénes-Paris.

Stevenson, G. H. (1936), "The Constitution of Theramenes", *JHS* 56, 48 - 57.

Stone, I. F. (1988), The Trial of Socrates, London.

Stratton, J. (1980), "The Concept of Law in Ancient Greece", Visible Language

14,99 – 121.

Straus, B. S. (1985), "The Cultural Significance of Bribery and Embezzlement in Athenian Politics: The Evidence of the Period 403 – 386 BC", AncW 11,67 – 74.

Striker, G. (1990), "Origins of the Concept of Natural Law", Proceedings of the Boston Area Colloquium in Ancient Philosophy 2,79 – 94.

Stroud, R. S. (1998), The Athenian Grain-tax Law of 374/3 B. C., Princeton. (Hesperia Suppl. 29)

Stroud, R. S. (1993), "Aristotle and the Athenian Homicide", in Aristote et Athenes, 203 – 221.

Stroud, R. S. (1979), The Axones and Kyrbeis of Drakon and Solon, Berkeley. (University of California Publications in classical studies 19)

Stroud, R. S. (1974), "An Athenian Law on Silver Coinage", *Hesperia* 43, 157 – 188.

Stroud, R. S. (1972), "A Law of the Athenian Nomothetai", *AJA* 76,221.

Stroud, R. S. (1971), "Theozotides and the Athenian Orphans", *Hesperia* 40, 280 – 301.

Stroud, R. S. (1968), Dracon's Law on Homicide, Berkeley. (University of California Publications in Classical Studies 3)

Suarez, M. A. & M. B. Alvarez (2007), "La in ius vocatio en Plauto: entre lo griego y lo romano", Faventia 29,9 – 19.

Suarez de la Torre, E. (2003 – 2004), "On some Linguistic Features of Solon's Laws", Ploutarchos 1,97 – 106.

Sullivan, J. (2003), "Demosthenes' Areopagus Legislation-yet Again", *CQ* 53, 130 – 134.

Sullivan, J. (2002), "'Second' thoughts on Aiskhines 3.252", *G &R* 49,1 – 7.

Sundahl, M. J. (2009), "The Living Constitution of Ancient Athens: A Comparative Perspective on the Originalism Debate", *The John Marshall Law Review* 42,463 – 504.

Sundahl, M. J. (2005), "When Literature becomes Law: An Example from Ancient Greece", *Texas Wesleyan Law Review* 12,331 – 343.

Sundahl, M. J. (2003), "The Rule of Law and the Nature of the Fourth-century Athenian Democracy", *ClassMed* 54,127 – 156.

Surikov, I. E. (2007), "Pre-Solonian 'Sixth Partners' and Debt Question in Archaic Athens", *VDI* 262, 28 – 46. (in Russian)

Surikov, I. E. (2005), "Alcuni problemi della storia della Eliea di Atene", Ius antiquum 16, 8 – 20.

Surikov, I. E. (2004), "Functions of Ostracism and Athenian Political Elite", *VDI* 248, 3 – 30. (in Russian)

Surikov, I. E. (1995), "The Areopagos in the First Half of the Fifth Century B. C.", VDI 212, 23 – 40. (in Russian)

Szegedy-Maszak, A. (1978), "Legends of the Greek Lawgivers", *GRBS* 19, 199 – 209.

Swoboda, H. (1924), Zwei Kapitel aus dem griechischen Bundesrecht, Wien. (SAW. Philosophisch-historische Klasse 199(2))

Swoboda, H. (1918), "Skytalismós", Hermes 53, 94 – 101.

Swoboda, H. (1914), Die griechischen Bünde und der moderne Bundesstaat, Prag.

Swoboda, H. (1912), "Studien zu den griechischen Bünden", Klio 12, 17 – 50.

Swoboda, H. (1912), "Die ätolische Komenverfassung", WS 34, 37 – 42.

Swoboda, H. (1911), "Studien zu den griechischen Bünden", Klio 11, 450 – 463.

Swoboda, H. (1910), "Studien zur Verfassung Boiotiens", Klio 10, 315 – 334.

Swoboda, H. (1905), "Beiträge zur griechischen Rechtsgeschichte", ZRG 26, 149 – 284.

Swoboda, H. (1898), "Zum griechischen Staatsrecht", in Festgaben zu ehren Max Büdinger, 53 – 67, Innsbruck.

Swoboda, H. (1894), "Der hellenische Bund des Jahres 371 v. Chr.", RhM 49, 321 – 352.

Swoboda, H. (1893), "Über den Process des Perikles", Hermes 28, 536 – 598.

Swoboda, H. (1890), Die griechischen Volksbeschlüsse, epigraphische Untersuchungen, Leipzig.

Swoboda, H. (1888 – 1889), "Über griechische Schatzverwaltung", WS 10, 278 – 307; 11, 65 – 87.

Szanto, E. (1902), "Freilassungstermine", WS 24, 582 – 585. (= Ausgewählte

Abhandlungen,138 – 142)

Szanto, E. (1901), Die griechischen Phylen, Wien. (SAW 145 (5)) (= Ausgewählte Abhandlungen II,15 – 288)

Szanto,E. (1896), "Zur antiken Wirtschaftsgeschichte", in Serta Harteliana, 113 – 116,Vienna.

Szanto,E. (1893), "Zum attischen Budgetrecht", in Eranos Vindobonensis, 103 – 107,Vienna. (= Ausgewählte Abhandlungen,108 – 113)

Szanto,E. (1892),"Die kleisthenischen Trittyen",Hermes 27,312 – 315.

Szanto,E. (1892),Das griechische Bürgerrecht,Freibourg im Br.

Szanto,E. (1891),"Die Verbalinjurie im attischen Process",WS 13,159 – 163. (= Ausgewählte Abhandlungen,103 – 108)

Szanto,E. (1891),"Zum Gerichtswesen der attischen Bundesgenossen",MDAI 16,30 – 45. (= Ausgewählte Abhandlungen,163 – 177)

Szanto,E. (1887),"Hypothek und Scheinkauf im griechischen Rechte",WS 9, 279 – 296. (= Ausgewählte Abhandlungen,74 – 92)

Szanto,E. (1885 – 1886),"Anleihen griechischer Staaten",WS 7,232 – 252; 8,1 – 36. (= Ausgewäblte Abhandlungen,11 – 73)

Szanto,E. (1885),"Zur attischen Phratrien-und Geschlechterverfassung",RhM 40,506 – 520.

Szanto,E. (1881),"Die Abstimmung in den attischen Geschworenengerichten", WS 3,24 – 31. (= Ausgewählte Abhandlungen,3 – 11)

Szanto,E. (1881),Untersuchungen über das attische Bürgerrecht,Vienna.

T

Tadashi,I. (2004),"Did the Hektemoroi Exist?",*PdP* 59,241 – 247.

Takabatake,S. (2000),"Foreigners and Lawcourts in the Athenian Empire: A Reading the Fifth Oration of Antiphon",Shigaku Zasshi 109,43 – 70.

Takabatake, S. (1989), "Funeral Laws and Athens", Shicho (*Journal of History*)25,83 – 95. (= Kodai 3(1992)1 – 13)

Takabatake,S. (1988),"The idea of xenos in classical Athens: its structure and peculiarities",in Yuge,T. & M. Doi (eds),Forms of control and subordination in antiquity,449 – 455,Leiden.

Takahashi, S. (1984), "So Called 'stasis' Law Enacted by Solon", Seiyoshi Kenkyu(*Study of European and American History*) 19, 83 - 106.

Takayama, K. (1957), "On hektemoroi", Hiroshima University Studies(Faculty of Letters) 12, 278 - 297.

Talamanca, Mario (2008), "Ethe e nomos agraphos nel 'Corpus oratorum atticorum'", in Bove, L. (ed), Prassi e diritto. Valore e ruolo della consuetudine, 3 - 104, Napoli.

Talamanca, Mario (2001), "L'antichità e i 'diritti dell' uomo", in Atti dei convegni dei Lincei in onore di P. Barile in occasione del 50o della Convezione europea per la protezione dei diritti umani e delle libertà fondamentali, 41 - 89, Roma.

Talamanca, Mario (1999), "Diritto e prassi nel mondo antico", in Règle et pratique, 105 - 211.

Talamanca, Mario (1992), "Oi spoudes tou archaiou ellenikou dikaiou apo to dekato enato aiona os simera", Symboles I, 25 - 46. (= "Gli studi di diritto greco dall'inizio dell'ottocento ai nostri giorni" in Studi in memoria di Gino Gorla, 889 - 949, Milano 1994)

Talamanca, Mario (1984), "Politica, equità e diritto nella pratica giudiziaria attica", in Mneme Petropoulou II, 333 - 356.

Talamanca, Mario (1981), "Il diritto in Grecia", in Bretone, M. & M. Talamanca (eds), Il diritto in Grecia e a Roma, 5 - 17, Bari.

Talamanca, Mario (1979), "'Dikazein' e 'krinein' alle origini dell'attivita giurisdizionale in Grecia", in Symposion 1974, 103 - 133.

Talamanca, Mario (1975), "La legge di Dem., 'Or.', 21, 94 e l'appellabilità delle pronuncedell' arbitro privato in diritto attico", BIDR 17, 93 - 159.

Talamanca, Mario (1975), "Giudizio paragrafico e amissibilità dell'azione nel sistema processuale attico", in Symposion 1971, 125 - 131.

Talamanca, Mario (1973), "Qualche osservazione sull or. 17 di Lisia", in Xenion Zepos 1, 599 - 632.

Talamanca, Mario (1971), "L'oggetto dell'azione di Apollodoro contro Formione. Contributi allo studio di Demostene, 'or.' 36 e 45", in Scritti A. Raselli, II, 1509ff, Milano.

Tarbell, F. B. (1889), "The Decrees of the Demotionidai. A Study of the Attic Phratry", *AJA* 5, 135 – 153.

Tarbell, F. B. (1889), "The Relations of Psephismata to Nomoi at Athens in the Fifth and Fourth Centuries", *AJPh* 10, 79 – 83.

Taubenschlag, R. (1938), "The Ancient Greek City Laws in Ptolemaic Egypt", in Actes du Ie Congrés International de Papyrologie 1937, 471 – 489, Bruxelles. (= Taubenschlag, Opera, 601 – 622)

Taubenschlag, R. (1936), "Die Geschichte der Rezeption des griechischen Privatrechts in Ägypten", in Atti del Ⅳ congresso internazionale di Papirologia (Firenze, 28 aprile – 2 maggio 1935), 259 – 282, Milano.

Taylor, Cl. (2007), "From the Whole Citizen Body? The Sociology of Election and Lot in the Athenian Democracy", *Hesperia* 76, 323 – 346.

Taylor, Cl. (2001), "Bribery in Athenian Politics: Accusations, Allegations and Slander", *G & R* 48, 53 – 66; 154 – 172.

Taylor, E. S. (1892), "On the Age of the Diaitetai", *CR* 6, 182.

Te Riele, G. J. and M. J. Te Riele (1987), "Hélisson entre en sympolitie avec Mantinée: une nouvelle inscription d'Arcadie", BCH 111, 167 – 190.

Tébar Megías, E., R. M. Tébar Megías (1998), "El epiclerato en la Grecia clǿsica", in Alfaro Giner, C. & A. Noguera Borel (eds), La mujer en la Antigüedad 1 (Actas del primer seminario de estudios sobre la mujer en la Antigüedad (24 – 25 abril 1997), 45 – 62, Valencia.

Tedeschi, G. (1986), "Un problema ancora aperto: la pseudosenofontea Costituzione degli Ateniesi", Il pensiero politico 19, 81 – 85.

Telfy, J. B (1868), Synagoge ex attikon nomon: Corpus Juris Attici, e fontibus composuit, commentariis indicibusque, Leipzig.

Telò, M. (2004), "Eupoli, Solone e l'adulterio: una proposta per la 'persona loquens' di Eup. fr. 101 K. -A. (= P. Oxy. 863)", ZPE 146, 1 – 12.

Telschow, K. (1953), Die griechischen Flüchtlinge und Verbannten von der archaischen Zeit bis zum Restitutionsedikt Alexanders des Großen (324), diss. Kiel.

Thalheim, Th. (1888), "Der Prozess des Chrysippos gegen Phormion", in Philologische Abhandlungen für Martin Hertz, 58 – 68, Berlin.

Thalheim, Th. (1920), "Adoption und Testament in Attika", BPh 40, 1103 –

1104.

Thalheim, Th. (1910), "Testament, Adoption und Schenkung auf den Todesfall", ZRG 31, 398 - 401.

Thalheim, Th. (1906), "Der Eid der Schiedsrichter in Athen", Hermes 41, 152 - 156.

Thalheim, Th. (1906), "Eisangeliegesetz in Athen", Hermes 41, 304 - 309.

Thalheim, Th. (1904), "Gesetz von Samos, über Getreideankauf und-vertheilung", Hermes 39, 604 - 610.

Thalheim, Th. (1903), "Zu Isaios", Hermes 38, 456 - 467.

Thalheim, Th. (1902), "Zur Eisangelie in Athen", Hermes 37, 339 - 352.

Thalheim, Th. (1892 - 1894), Zu den griechischen Rechtsalterthümern, Hirschberg-Schneidemühl.

Thalheim, Th. (1889), Quaestiones Demosthenicae, Schneidemühl.

Thalheim, Th. (1888), "Der Prozess Demons gegen Zenothemis", Hermes 23, 202 - 210.

Thalheim, Th. (1888), "Der Prozess des Androkles gegen Lakritos und seine Urkunden", Hermes 23, 333 - 345.

Thalheim, Th. (1884), "Die Antidosis", Hermes 19, 80 - 91.

Thalheim, Th. (1879), "Die dokimasie der Beamten in Athen", NJ 119, 601 - 608.

Thalheim, Th. (1878), "Zur dokimasie der Beamten in Athen", Hermes 13, 366 - 372.

Thalheim, Th. (1878), "Zu Lysias", NJ 117, 545 - 561.

Thalheim, Th. (1877), "Zu Lykurgos", NJ 115, 673 - 683.

Thalheim, Th. (1877), "Die Antidosis", NJ 115, 613 - 618.

Thalheim, Th. (1877), "Das attische Militärstrafgesetz und Lysias 14, 7", NJ 115, 269 - 272.

Thalheim, Th. (1876), Des Lysias Rede für Polystratos, Breslau.

Thomas, C. G. (1984), "Mycenaean Law in its Oral Context", Studi Micenei ed Egeo-Anatolici 25, 247 - 253.

Thomas, C. G. (1977), "Literacy and the Codification of Law", *SDHI* 43, 455 - 458.

Thomas, C. G. (1974), "On the Role of the Spartan Kings", *Historia* 23, 257 - 270.

Thomas, R. (2005), "Writing, Law, and Written Law", in *The Cambridge Companion*, 41 - 60.

Thomas, R. (1998), "Written in Stone? Liberty, Equality, Orality and the Codification of Law", in *Law in Its Political Setting*, 9 - 32. (= BICS 40(1995) 59 - 74).

Thomas, R. (1994), "Law and Lawgiver in the Athenian Democracy", in *Ritual, Finance, Politics*, 119 - 133.

Thomas, R. (1989), Oral Tradition and Written Record in Classical Athens, Cambridge.

Thompson, C. V. (1894), "Slave Torture in Athens", *CR* 8, 136.

Thompson, W. E. (1986), "The Stasis at Corinth", *SIFC* 79, 155 - 171.

Thompson, W. E. (1982), "Athenian Marriage Patterns: Remarriage", *CSCA* 5, 211 - 225.

Thompson, W. E. (1981), "Apollodoros v. Phormion: The Computation of Damages", *RIDA* 28, 83 - 94.

Thompson, W. E. (1980), "An Athenian Commercial Case: Demosthenes 34", *TR* 48, 137 - 149.

Thompson, W. E. (1979), "A View of Athenian Banking", *MH* 36, 224 - 241.

Thompson, W. E. (1976), De Hagniae Hereditate: An Athenian Inheritance Case, Leiden. (Mnemosyne Suppl. 44)

Thompson, W. E. (1970), "Some Attic kinship terms", Glotta 48, 75 - 81.

Thompson, W. E. (1968), "An Interpretation of the Demotionid Decrees", SO 42, 51 - 68.

Thompson, W. E. (1967), "The Marriage of First Cousins in Athenian Society", Phoenix 21, 273 - 282.

Thompson, W. E. (1965), "The Demes in Plato's Laws", Eranos 63, 13 - 46.

Thomsen, R. (1972), The Origin of Ostracism, Kopenhagen. (Humanitas 4)

Thomsen, R. (1964), Eisphora. A Study of Direct Taxation in Ancient Athens, Kopenhagen. (Humanitas 3)

Threatt, T. (2009), "Legally Speaking: Rape and Seduction in Athenian Law",

Rhetoric Review 28,87 - 88.

Thür, G. (2012), "Rechtstransfer aus dem Vorderen Orient im archaischen griechischen Prozess", in Legras, B. (ed), Transferts culturels et droits dans le monde grec et hellénistique (Actes du colloque international, Reims, 14 - 17 mai 2008), 47 - 62, Paris.

Thür, G. (2009), "Ownership and Security in Macedonian Sale Documents", in Symposion 2007, 173 - 187.

Thür, G. (2008), "Zu misthosis und phasis oikou orphanikou in Hypereides, Gegen Timandros", AAntHung 48, 125 - 137.

Thür, G. (2008), "Ounē katochos und (ta) katochima" (SEG 38, 671, 2, Stolos?; IK 34, 109, 8 Mylasa), in Mauritsch, P., Petermandl, W., Rollinger, R. & Chr. Ulf (eds), Antike Lebenswelten, Konstanz-Wandel-Wirkungsmacht. Festschrift für Ingomar Weiler zum 70. Geburtstag, 465 - 474, Wiesbaden. (Philippika 25)

Thür, G. (2008), "Zur phasis in der neu entdeckten Rede Hypereides' gegen Timandros", ZRG 125, 645 - 663.

Thür, G. (2007), "Die Einheit des 'Griechischen Rechts'. Gedanken zum Prozessrecht in den griechischen Poleis", Etica & Politica 9, 25 - 54. (= Dike 9 (2006) [2008] 23 - 62)

Thür, G. (2007), "Elemente der Vergleichbarkeit von Gesetzgebung. Bemerkungen zur Grossen Gesetzinschrift von Gortyn", in Gesetzgebung in antiken Gesellschaften, 77 - 85.

Thür, G. (2007), "Der Reinigungseid im archaischen griechischen Rechtsstreit und seine Parallelen im alten Orient", in Rollinger, R., Barta, H., & Lang, M. (eds), Rechtsgeschichte und Interkulturalität: zum Verhältnis der östlichen Mittelmeerraums und 'Europas' im Altertum, Wiesbaden, 179 - 195.

Thür, G. (2007), "Das Prinzip der Fairness im attischen Prozess: Gedanken zu Echinos und Enklema", in Symposion 2005, 131 - 151. (= "The principle of fairness in Athenian legal procedure: Thoughts on the echinos and enklema", Dike 11 (2008) 51 - 74)

Thür, G. (2006), "Neues zur Basanos", in Gamauf, R. (ed), Festschrift für H. Hausmaninger zum 70. Geburtstag, 287 - 291, Wien.

Thür, G. (2005), "Rechtsstreit im archaischen Griechenland", in Witte, M. & M.

Th. Fögen(eds),Kodifizierung und Legitimierung des Rechts in der Antike und im alten Orient,29 – 43,Wiesbaden.

Thür,G. (2005),"The Role of Witnesses in Athenian Law",in The Cambridge Companion,146 – 169.

Thür,G. (2005),"Gab es 'Rechtscorpora' im archaischen Griechenland?",in Witte,M. & M. -Th. Fögen(eds),Kodifizierung und Legitimierung des Rechts in der Antike und im alten Orient,9 – 27,Wiesbaden.

Thür,G. (2004),"Pachtzins und Vergabe der Silberminen im Laureion",in Ruscu,L. et als. (eds),Orbis Antiquus. Studia in honorem Ioannis Pisonis,159 – 163,Cluj-Napoca.

Thür,G. (2004),"Law of Procedure in Attic Inscriptions",in *Law,Rhetoric,and Comedy*,33 – 50.

Thür,G. (2004),"Prospektion und Bergregal in IG II2 411",in Matthaiou,A. P. (ed),Attikai epigraphai. Praktika symposiou eis mnemen Adolf Wilhelm(1864 – 1950),175 – 184,Athena. (= Annals of the Faculty of Law,Belgrade University 2007(1))

Thür,G. (2003),"Die Listen der Poletai in Athen. Versteigerung konfiszierten Vermögens,Verpachtung von Silberminen und von Steuereintreibung",*Balkans Law Review* 6(16),3 – 6.

Thür,G. (2003),"Sachverfolgung und Diebstahl in den griechischen Poleis (Dem. 32,Lys. 23,IC IV 72 I,IPArk 32 u. 17)",in Symposion 1999,57 – 96.

Thür,G. (2003),"Recht im antiken Griechenland",in Manthe,U. (ed),Die Rechtskulturen der Antike. Vom alten Orient bis zum römischen Reich,191 – 230,München.

Thür,G. (2003),"Gerichtliche Kontrolle des Asylanspruchs",in Das antike Asyl,23 – 36.

Thür,G. (2002),"Gedanken zu 'Bergregal' und 'Bergfreiheit' in der griechisch-römischen Antike",in Valentinitsch,H. & M. Steppan(eds),Festschrift für Gernot Kocher zum 60. Geburtstag,317 – 329,Graz.

Thür,G. (2002),"Two 'Curses' from Mantineia(IPArk 8,IG V2,262),prayers for justice and oaths",in Demokratie,Recht und soziale Kontrolle,109 – 114.

Thür,G. (2002),"IG II2 411:Pacht oder Werkvertrag?",in Schermaier,M. J.,

Rainer, J. M. & L. C. Winkel (eds), Iurisprudentia universalis. Festschrift für Theo Mayer-Maly zum 70. Geburtstag, 779 – 784, Köln.

Thür, G. (2002), "Eigentumsstreit und Statusprozess in der grossen Gesetzesinschrift aus Gortyn", Dike 5, 95 – 110.

Thür, G. (2002), "Gesetzeskodizes im archaischen und klassischen Athen", in Mélanges Dimakis, 631 – 640.

Thür, G. (2002), "Entscheidung in Bausachen aus Kerkyra (IG IX 12, 4, 794)", ZRG 119, 326 – 339.

Thür, G. (2001), "Neues über eine alte Inschrift (IPArk 8; IG V (2) 262, Mantineia um 460 v. Chr.)", in Mitsopoulos-Leon, V. (ed), Forschungen in der Peloponnes, 207 – 212, Athen.

Thür, G. (2000), "Das Gerichtswesen Athens im 4. Jahrhundert v. Chr.", in Große Prozesse, 30 – 49. (= Acta Juridica et Politica 65 (20) (2004) 369 – 389 (in Hungarian))

Thür, G. (2000), "Biscardi Arnaldo e il diritto greco. Riflessioni sul prestito maritimo SB VI 9571", Dike 3, 177 – 186.

Thür, G. (2000), "Rechtsvorschriften und Rechtsanwendung in Athen (5./4. Jh. v. Chr.)", in Timai Triantaphyllopoulou, 89 – 100.

Thür, G. (1999), "Stipulation und Bauvertrag", in Gerkens, J.-F. (ed), Mélanges Fritz Sturm I, 477 – 492, Liège.

Thür, G. (1998), "Oaths and Dispute Settlement in Ancient Greek Law", in *Law in Its Political Setting*, 57 – 72.

Thür, G. (1998), "IPArk 8: 'Gottesurteil' Oder 'Amnestiedekret'? (Nochmals zu IG V 2, 262)", Dike 1, 13 – 26.

Thür, G. (1998), "Gedanken zum Schicksal der Inscriptiones Graecae", ZRG 115, 404 – 408.

Thür, G. (1997), "Der Rechtsgewährungsvertrag aus Stymphalos (IPArk 17; IG V2, 357)", in Symposion 1995, 173 – 178.

Thür, G. (1997), "Rechtsfragen des Weinkaufs", in Kramer, B. (ed), Akten des 21. Internationalen Papyrologenkongresses, 967 – 975, Berlin. (Archiv für Papyrusforschung, Beiheft 3)

Thür, G. (1997), "Prozessrechtliches in der Gründungsurkunde des Hellenenbundes",

BIDR 39,219 – 232.

Thür, G. (1995), "Zu den Hintergründen des Rechtsgewährungsvertrags zwischen Stymphalos und Demetrias (IPArk 17)", in Ch. Schubert & K. Brodersen (eds), Rom und der griechische Osten. Festschrift für H. H. Schmitt zum 65. Geburtstag,262 – 272, Stuttgart.

Thür, G. (1995), "Die athenischen Geschworengerichte-eine Sackgasse?", in Die athenische Demokratie,321 – 336.

Thür, G. (1994), "Die Aestimationsabrede im Seefrachtvertrag", in Symposion 1993,267 – 271.

Thür, G. (1993), "Fides. Zur Haftung des Kriegsgefangenen für sein Lösegeld in der Antike und in den Türkenkriegen", in Zlinszky, J. (ed), Questions de responsabilité (XLVe Session de la Société Internationale "Ferdinand de Visscher" pour l' Histoire des Droits de l' Antiquité),371 – 382, Miskolc – Eger.

Thür, G. (1992), "Prozeßformeln im griechischen Recht?", Acta Juridica et Politica 41(34),521 – 531. (in Hungarian)

Thür, G. (1992), "Armut. Gedanken zu Ehegüterrecht und Familienvermögen in der griechischen Polis", in Eherecht und Familiengut,121 – 132.

Thür, G. (1991), "The Jurisdiction of the Areopagos in Homicide Cases", in Symposion 1990,53 – 72.

Thür, G. (1990), "Nachträge zum Urteil aus Mantineia (IG V 2. 262)", in Symposion 1988,277 – 282.

Thür, G. (1989), "Sechs Todesurteile und zwei plattierte Hemidrachmen aus Dyme. Teil I", Tyche 4,171 – 180. (= "Oi exi thanatikes katadikes apo ti Dyme (sto Syll3 530)" in Rizakis, A. D. (ed), Achaia und Elis in der Antike (Akten des 1. internationalen Symposiums, Athen 19 – 21 Mai 1989), 115 – 122, Athen 1991 (Meletemata 13))

Thür, G. (1989), "Quittung oder Schuldschein? Zu einem Bleitaefelchen aus Hyampolis", ZRG 106,545ff.

Thür, G. (1989), "Zum dikazein im Urteil aus Mantineia (IG V. 2,262)", in Symposion 1985,55 – 71.

Thür, G. (1988), "Smrtna kazna za ubistvo u antitschkoj Atini (Komentar zu dikazein u IG I3 104,11 – 13; Dem. 23,22; Aristot. AP 57,4)", Anali Pravnog

Fakulteta u Beogradu 36, 213 - 223. (= "Die Todesstrafe im Blutprozess Athens (Zum dikazein in IG i3 104. 11 - 13; Dem. 23. 22; Aristot. AP 57. 4)" JJP 20 (1990) 143 - 156)

Thür, G. (1988), "Das Recht der altgriechischen und hellenistischen Staaten. Ein Überblick", in Gigon, M. W. O. & M. W. Fischer (eds), Antike Rechts-und Sozialphilosophie, 251 - 257, Frankfurt. (Salzburger Schriften zur Rechts-, Staats-und Sozialphilosophie 6)

Thür, G. (1987), "Neuere Untersuchungen zum Prozessrecht der griechischen Poleis. Formen des Urteils", in Simon, D. (ed), Akten des 26. Deutschen Rechthistorikertages, 467 - 484, Frankfurt.

Thür, G. (1986), "IG V/2, 159: Testament oder Orakel", in Festschrift Kränzlein, 69 - 82.

Thür, G. (1985), "Bemerkungen zum altgriechischen Werkvertrag. (Die Bauvergabeordnung aus Tegea, IG V/2, 6A)", in Studi Biscardi 5, 471 - 514.

Thür, G. (1985), "Prozessrechtliches in der Mauerbauinschrift IG II2 244", in E. Plöckinger, M. Bietak et al. (eds), Lebendiges Altertumswissenschaft. Festgabe zur Vollendung des 70. Lebensjahres von H. Vetters, 66 - 99, Wien.

Thür, G. (1983), "Bemerkungen zum Zeugenbeweis im Rechtshilfevertrag aus Stymphalos (IG 5. 2 357)", in Symposion 1979, 327 - 342.

Thür, G. (1982), "Kannte das altgriechische Recht die Eigentumsdiadikasie?", in Symposion 1977, 55 - 70.

Thür, G. (1981), "Apophasi kai apodeixe sto dikaio tes Gortynas", Amaltheia 47, 161 - 168.

Thür, G. (1979), "Die Proklesis zur basanos", in Symposion 1974, 153 - 173.

Thür, G. (1977), Beweisführung vor den Schwurgerichtshöfen Athens: die Proklesis zur Basanos, Wien. (Sitzungsberichte der Österreichischen Akademie der Wissenschaften, Phil. -hist. Klasse 317)

Thür, G. (1975), "Komplexe Prozessführung. Dargestellt am Beispiel des Trapezitikos (Isokr. 17)", in Symposion 1971, 157 - 188.

Thür, G. (1972), "Die Streit über den Status des Werkstättenleiters Milyas (Dem. Or. 29)", RIDA 19, 151 - 177. (= revised version in Schindler, U. (ed) (1987), Demosthenes, 403 - 430, Darmstadt)

Thür, G. (1970), "Zum dikazein bei Homer", ZRG 87, 426 – 444.

Thür, G. & Chr. Koch. (1981), "Prozessrechtliche Inschriften der griechischen Poleis. Sonderheft B. Prozessrechtlicher Kommentar zum Getreidegesetz aus Samos", AAWW 118, 61 – 88.

Thür, G. & H. Taeuber (1994), Prozeßrechtliche Inschriften der griechischen Poleis: Arkadien, Wien. (Sitzungsberichte der Österreichischen Akademie der Wissenschaften, phil. -hist. Klasse 607)

Thür, G. & H. Taeuber. (1978), "Prozessrechtliche Inschriften der griechischen Poleis. Sonderheft A. Prozessrechtlicher Kommentar zur Krämerinschrift auf Samos", AAWW 115, 205 – 225.

Tillyard, H. J. W. (1904 – 1905), "Boundary and mortgage stones from Attica", BSA 11, 63 – 71.

Tindemans, Kl. (2010), "Antigone and the Law: Legal Theory and the Ambiguities of Performance", in Wilmer, S. E. & Au. Zukauskaite (eds), Interrogating Antigone in postmodern philosophy and criticism, 185 – 196, Oxford.

Tod, M. N. (1933 – 1948), A selection of Greek historical inscriptions, 2 Vols, Oxford.

Tod, M. N. (1932), "Inter-state Arbitration in the Greek World", in Ancient Inscriptions: Sidelights on Greek History, 39 – 68, Oxford.

Tod, M. N. (1932), "Clubs and Societies in the Greek World", in *Ancient Inscriptions: Sidelights on Greek History*, 69 – 93, Oxford.

Tod, M. N. (1913), International Arbitration Amongst the Greeks, Oxford.

Tod, M. N. (1906 – 1907), "A Statute of an Attic Thiasos", *BSA* 13, 328 – 338.

Tod, M. N. (1902 – 1903), "An Unpublished Attic Decree", *BSA* 9, 154 – 175.

Todd, S. C. (2010), "The Athenian procedure(s) of dokimasia", in Thür, G. (ed), Symposion 2009. Vorträge zur griechischen und hellenistischen Rechtsgeschichte (Seggau, 25. – 30. August 2009), 73 – 98, Wien. (with a response by L. Gagliardi)

Todd, S. C. (2007), A Commentary on Lysias, Speeches 1 – 11, Oxford.

Todd, S. C. (2006), "Some Notes on the Regulation of Sexuality in Athenian Law", in Symposion 2003, 93 – 120.

Todd, S. C. (2005), "Law and Oratory at Athens", in *The Cambridge Companion*, 97 – 111.

Todd, S. C. (2005), "Law, Theatre, Rhetoric and Democracy in Classical Athens", *European Review of History* 12, 63 – 79.

Todd, S. C. (2003), "Lysias on Abortion", in Symposion 1999, 235 – 256.

Todd, S. C. (2002), "Advocacy, Logography and Erotesis in Athenian Lawcourts", in McKechnie, P. (ed), Thinking like a lawyer. Essays on legal history and general history for J. Crook on his eightieth birthday, 151 – 166, Leiden. (Mnemosyne Suppl. 231)

Todd, S. C. (2000), "The Language of Law in Classical Athens", in Coss, P. (ed), The Moral World of the Law, 17 – 36, Cambridge.

Todd, S. C. (2000), Lysias, Austin, Tx. (The oratory of classical Greece 2)

Todd, S. C. (2000), "How to Execute People in Fourth-century Athens", in *Law and Social Status*, 31 – 51.

Todd, S. C. (1998), "Lysias Against Nikhomakhos: The Fate of the Expert in Athenian Law", in *Law in its Political Settng*, 110 – 131.

Todd, S. C. (1994), "Status and Contract in Fourth-century Athens", in Symposion 1993, 125 – 140. (with a reply by E. E. Cohen, 141 – 152)

Todd, S. C. (1993), The Shape of Athenian Law, Oxford.

Todd, S. C. (1992), "Writing the Law in Early Greece", *Polis* 11, 28 – 39.

Todd, S. C. (1990), "Law, Society and Athens", in Nomos, 1 – 18.

Todd, S. C. (1990), "The Purpose of Evidence in Athenian Courts", in Nomos, 19 – 40.

Todd, S. C. (1990), "Lady Chatterley's Lover and the Attic Orators: The Social Composition of the Athenian Jury", *JHS* 110, 146 – 173. (= The Attic Orators, 312 – 358)

Todescan, F. (1968), "Considerazioni sulla genesi dell'idea di giustizia in un frammento di Anassimandro", RIFD 45, 414 – 428.

Toepffer, J. (1891), "Koisches Sakralgesetz", MDAI 16, 411 – 432.

Toher, M. (1991), "Greek Funerary Legislation and the Two Spartan Funerals", in Flower, M. A. & M. Toher (eds), Georgica. Greek studies in honour of George Cawkwell, London, 159 – 175. (BICS Suppl. 58)

Tondo, S. (1976), "Diritto Ateniese a Roma", AATC 41, 52 – 103.

Too, Y. L. (2008), A Commentary on Isokrates' Antidosis, Oxford.

Too, Y. L. (2001), "Legal Instructions in Classical Athens", in Too, Y. L. (ed), Education in Greek and Roman Antiquity, 111 – 132, Leiden.

Toogood, N. (1997), "'Athens Aids Eretria': A State's Jurisdiction over its Citizens' Actions", *CQ* 47, 295 – 297.

Toumbouros, G. (1959), The Laws of Ancient Greece, Munich.

Tourraix, A. (2005), "Déiocès, législateur de modèle grec ou fondateur souverain iranien?", in Le législateur et la loi, 161 – 168.

Tourraton, E. (1911), Le magistrat athénien dans le theâtre d'Aristophane, Toulouse.

Tracy, S. V. (1991), "To Me Dis Archein", CPh 86, 210 – 204.

Travis, A. H. & St. Dow. (1943), "Demetrios of Phaleron and His Lawgiving", *Hesperia* 12, 144 – 165.

Travlos, J. (1974), "The Lawcourt epi Palladioi", Hesperia 43, 500 – 511.

Traulsen, Chr. (2004), Das sakrale Asyl in der alten Welt. Zur Schutzfunktion des Heiligen von König Salomo bis zum Codex Theodosianus, Tübingen. (Jus Ecclesiasticum 72)

Tréheux, J. (1989), "Sur les probouloi en Grèce", BCH 113, 241 – 247.

Trelawny-Cassity, L. (2010), "Ten Tou Aristou Doxan: On the Theory and Practice of Punishment in Plato's Laws", *Polis* 27, 222 – 239.

Treston, H. J. (1923), Poine. A Study in Ancient Greek Blood-vengeance, London.

Trevett, J. C. (2011), Demosthenes, speeches 1 – 17, Austin, Tx. (The oratory of classical Greece 14)

Trevett, J. C. (1996), "Aristotle's Knowledge of Athenian Oratory", *CQ* 46, 371 – 379.

Trevett, J. C. (1992), Apollodoros, the Son of Pasion, Oxford.

Triantaphyllopoulos, J. K. (1994), "Greek Laws in Cicero", Index 22, 409 – 418.

Triantaphyllopoulos, J. K. (1991), "Le droit romain dans le monde grec", JJP 21, 75 – 85.

Triantaphyllopoulos, J. K. (1990), "Méthodologie juridique d'Aristote et méthodologie historique de Thucydide", SO 65, 19 – 29.

Triantaphyllopoulos, J. K. (1989), "Griechische Parallelen zur lex Aquilia", in Symposion 1985, 415 - 425.

Triantaphyllopoulos, J. K. (1986), "La tradition dans les droits antiques", in Festschrift Kränzlein, 137 - 141.

Triantaphyllopoulos, J. K. (1985), "Graphe paranomon fuori di Atene", in Xenia. Scritti in onore di Piero Treves, 219 - 221, Roma.

Triantaphyllopoulos, J. K. (1985), Das Rechtsdenken der Griechen, München. (MBPaR 78)

Triantaphyllopoulos, J. K. (1983), "Cantar le leggi", Atti dell'Academia Mediterranea delle Scienze Catania 1, 27 - 34.

Triantaphyllopoulos, J. K. (1975), "Rechtsphilosophie und positives Recht in Griechenland", in Symposion 1971, 23 - 66. (= Xenion Zepos 1, 647 - 692)

Triantaphyllopoulos, J. K. (1968), "Ta pragmatika elattomata tou polethentos kata ta archaia hellenika dikaia exairesei ton papyron", Ephemeris Hellenon Nomikon 35, 1 - 11. (= Triantaphyllopoulos, J. (1971), "Les vices cachés de la chose vendue d'après les droits grecs à l'exception des papyrus", in Studi Volterra 5, 697 - 719)

Triantaphyllopoulos, J. K. (1966), "L'amministrazione della giustizia", in Tutto su Atene classica, 237 - 246, Firenze.

Triantaphyllopoulos, J. K. (1966), "Gesetze und Gerichte", in Athen und seine grosse Zeit, 237 - 246, Würzburg.

Triantaphyllopoulos, J. K. (1963), "Ta kena tou nomou en to archaio helleniko dikaio", EEN 30, 753 - 758.

Triantaphyllopoulos, J. K. (1961), "Eisagoge eis to mathema tes historias tou dikaiou kai eidikoteron tou archaiou hellenikou dikaiou", Ephemeris Hellenon Nomikon 28, 257 - 263.

Triantaphyllopoulos, J. K. (1960), "Graphe paranomon", Neon Dikaion 16, 229ff.

Triggiano, A. (2009), "Evidence given under Torture in Aristotle and Cicero", Teoria e storia del diritto romano 2, 17 - 36.

Tritle, L. A. (1993), "Continuity and Change in the Athenian Strategia", *AHB* 7 (3/4), 125ff.

Tritle, L. A. (1992), "Virtue and Progress in Classical Athens: The Myth of the

Professional General", *AncW* 23,71 – 89.

Tronson, A. (1991), "The Hellenic League of 480 B. C. Fact or Ideological Fiction?", AClass 34,93 – 110.

Tsames, A. D. (1968), Archaion ellenikon dikaion, Athens.

Tschernetska, N. (2005), "New Fragments of Hyperides from the Archimedes Palimpsest", *ZPE* 154,1 – 6.

Tschernetska, N. T., Handley, E. N., Austin, C. F. L. & L. Horvath (2007), "New Readings in the Fragment of Hyperides's Against Timandros from the Archimedes palimpsest", *ZPE* 162,1 – 4.

Tsitsiklis, M. I. (1984), "He katagoge tou attikou dikasteriou ton epheton", in Mneme Petropoulou II,369 – 382.

Tsitsiklis, M. I. (1979), "Alphano, alphestes, alphesiboia. Contribution à l'étude de la prehistoire du droit grec des contrats", Hellenika 31,3 – 43.

Tsitsiklis, M. I. (1979), "He melete tes istorias tou hellenikou dikaiou", Armenopoulos 33,237ff.

Tsitsiklis, M. I. (1978), O gamos di'agoras tes suzugou eis ten proklasiken Hellada; sumbole eis ten dikaiiken anatomian tes ellenikes politeiakes koinonias, Thessalonike.

Tsitsiklis, M. I. (1969), "Histor. Symbole eis ten ereunan tes proistorias tou hellenikou poinikou dikaiou", in Charmosynon Demetrio I. Karanika III,753 – 770, Thessaloniki. (EES NOE 14)

Tsitsiklis, M. I. (1960), "Eednoomai-eednotes", Hellenika 17,24 – 39.

Tsitsiklis, M. I. (1960), "Cherostai. Sumbole eis ten proistorian tou hellenikou kleronomikou dikaiou", in Mnemosynon Bisoukidou II,149 – 172.

Tsopanakis, A. G. (1971), "Moral and Legal Aspects of Aggression and Defence in Homer", Epistemonike Epeteris Philosophikes Scholes Aristoteleiou Panepistemiou Thessalonikes 11,335 – 352.

Tuci, P. A. (2007), "Boule e assemblea ateniesi in Polluce, Onomasticon VIII", in L'Onomasticon,69 – 102.

Tulin, A. (1999), "Slave witnesses in Antiphon 5,48", SCI 18,21 – 24.

Tulin, A. (1996), Dike Phonou: The Right of Prosecution and Attic Homicide Procedure, Stuttgart.

Tuplin, C. J. (1986), "Sumpriasthai in Lysias 'Against the Corndealers'", Hermes 114, 495 - 498.

Turasiewicz, R. (2001), "The Trial of the Athenian Strategoi in 406 BC: Legal and Moral Issues", in Korpanty, J. & J. Styka (eds), Freedom and Democracy in Greek literature, 41 - 62, Kraków. (Classica Cracoviensia 6) (in Polish)

Turasiewicz, R. (1965), "The Factor of Mercy in Athenian Courts", Meander 20, 35 - 41. (in Polish)

U

Usher, S. (1999), Greek Oratory: Tradition and Originality, Oxford.

Usher, S. (1976), "Lysias and His Clients", *GRBS* 17, 31 - 40 (= The Attic Orators, 27 - 36).

V

Valdes Guia, M. (2009), "Bouzyges nomothetes: purification et exégèse des lois sacrées à Athènes", in La norme, 293 - 320.

Valdés Guia, M. (2008), "Zeus Eleutherios/Zeus Soter y la liberación de esclavos-dependientes en el Peloponeso", in Hommage à J. Annequin, 77 - 87.

Valdés Guia, M. (2007), "La situación de las mujeres en la Atenas del s. VI a. C.: ideología y práctica de la ciudadania", Gerion extra vol., 207 - 214.

Valdés Guia, M. (2007), "Peur et contrainte des dependants ratifiées par les pratiques judiciaires et religieuses: les paysans atimoi de l'Attique archaïque", in Fear of slaves, 99 - 114.

Valdés Guía, M. (2006), "La tierra 'esclava' del Ática en el s. VII a. C.: campesinos endeudos y hectémoros", Gerion 24, 143 - 161.

Valdés Guia, M. (2005), "El modelo politico de Solón: la aplicación de 'Dike' y la participación del 'demos' en la 'politeia'", Studia Historica. Historia Antigua 23, 57 - 74.

Valdés Guia, M. (2004), "Sinecias, basileis y ley de Dracón: preeminencia eupátrida en los cultos politicos y control aristocrático de las fratrías en el s. VII a. C. en Atenas", Polifemo 4, 62 - 78.

Valdés Guia, M. (2003), "El culto a Zeus Eleutherios en epoca arcaica:

Liberacion de esclavos/dependientes y constitucion de ciudadanias", in Garrido-Hory, M. & A. Gonzales (eds), Histoire, espaces et marges de l'Antiquité Ⅱ. Hommage à Monique Clavel-Levêque, 291 – 323, Besançon.

Valdés Guía, M. (2003), "Entre el Consejo de Solon y el de Clistenes: Heliea en epoca de Pisistrato?", Gerioń 21, 73 – 91.

Valdés Guía, M. (2002), "La exégesis en Atenas en época arcaica y clásica", MedAnt 5, 185 – 245.

Valdes, M. (1999), "La sisactia de Solon y el juramento de los heliastas", Arys 2, 35 – 48.

Valdes, M. (1998), "Las restricciones funerarios en la legislacion ateniese del siglo Ⅵ: El papel de la mujer", Arys 1, 51 – 62.

Vamvoukos, A. (1979), "Fundamental Freedoms in Athens of the Fifth Century", *RIDA* 26, 89 – 124.

Vanderpool, E. (1980), "The State Prison in Ancient Athens", in DeVries, K. (ed), From Athens to Gordion. The Papers of a Memorial Symposiom for R. S. Young, 17 – 31, Philadelphia.

Vanderpool, E. & W. P. Wallace (1964), "The Sixth Century Laws from Eretria", Hesperia 33, 381 – 391.

Van Effenterre, Henri (2003), "Un mort parle toujours", in Symposion 1999, 21 – 26.

Van Effenterre, Henri (2000), "Sanction contre un juge", in Timai Triantaphyllopoulou, 69 – 76.

Van Effenterre, Henri (1993), "Modernité du droit grec: un patrimoine", in Cahiers Glotz 4, 1 – 11.

Van Effenterre, Henri (1991), "Criminal Law in Archaic Crete", in Symposion 1990, 83 – 86.

Van Effenterre, Henri (1989), "Les degrés de la liberté dans les cités grecques", Recueils de la société Jean Bodin 46 (L'individu face au pouvoir) I, 97 – 104.

Van Effenterre, Henri (1989), "Droit et prédroit en Grèce depuis le dechiffrement du Linéaire B", in Symposion 1985, 3 – 7.

Van Effenterre, Henri (1989), "Préliminaires épigraphiques aux études d' histoire du droit grec", in Symposion 1982, 1 – 8. (= Cretica selecta, 819 – 826)

Van Effenterre, Henri (1985), "Damos, damioi et damiorgoi", in Pepragmena tou 9ou Diethnous Kretologikou Synedriou, I, 385 - 396, Herakleio.

Van Effenterre, Henri (1984), "Problèmes d' épigraphie juridique grecque", RHDFE 62, 47 - 52.

Van Effenterre, Henri (1982), "Les epiballontes", in Studi Biscardi 3, 459 - 462.

Van Effenterre, Henri (1982), "Le droit et la langue. A propos du code de Gortyne", in Symposion 1979, 113 - 128. (= Epeteris Panteiou Panepistemiou 1981, 115 - 128 and Cretica selecta, 663 - 676)

Van Effenterre, Henri (1982), "Andichazo dans le traité Oiantheion-Chaleion", in Symposion 1977, 85 - 97.

Van Effenterre, Henri (1980), "La fondation de Paestum", PdP 35, 161 - 175.

Van Effenterre, Henri (1974), "Thémistodikè", in Mélanges Seston, 481 - 488.

Van Effenterre, Henri (1973), "Le contrat de travail du scribe Spensithios", BCH 97, 31 - 46. (= Cretica selecta, 619 - 634)

Vartsos, I. A. (2008), "Fifth Century Athens, Citizens and Citizenship", Parnassos 50, 65 - 74.

Vatin, Cl. (1984), Citoyens et non-citoyens dans le monde grec, Paris.

Velissaropoulos-Karakostas, J. (2010), "Lois sacrées et biens sacrés dans la Grèce ancienne", in Timetikos tomos Mich. P. Stathopoulos II, 3103 - 3122, Athena-Komotini.

Velissaropoulou-Karakosta, J. (2010), "Demosia daneia sten ellenike arxhaioteta", in Pneumatos dorema Georgio. P. Nako, 119 - 134, Thessaloniki.

Velissaropoulou-Karakosta, J. (2006), "Stergein tous kata pistin sunallaxantas kai pacta conventa servabo", in Genethlion Apostolou S. Georgiadou, II, 2339 - 2358, Athena.

Vélissaropoulos-Karakostas, J. (2006), "Une inscription inédite de Corfou", in Symposion 2003, 285 - 293.

Vélissaropoulos-Karakostas, J. (2006), "Dire le droit dans la Grèce archaique", in Anagnostou-Canas, B., R. Carvais, S. Daubresse & L. de Carbonnieres (eds), Dire le droit: normes, juges, jurisconsultes, 45 - 56, Paris.

Vélissaropoulos-Karakostas, J. (2005), "Codes oraux et lois écrites. La grande rhètra et les sources du droit à l'époque archaïque", in Le législateur et la loi, 109 -

118.

Velissaropoulos-Karakosta, J. (2004), "Dōrophagoi basilēes", in Symmeikta G. Koumantou, 63 – 72, Athens-Komotini. (= Velissaropoulou-Karakosta, Archaioellenika, 67 – 78).

Vélissaropoulos, J. (2003), "Homère et Anaximandre de Milet. Aux origines de la justice grecque", in Symposion 1999, 3 – 20. (= Velissaropoulou-Karakosta, Archaioellenika, 5 – 24)

Velissaropoulos-Karakostas, J. (2002), "Merchants, Prostitutes and the 'New Poor': Forms of Contract and Social Status", in Cartledge, P., Cohen, E. E. & L. Foxhall (eds), Money, labour and land. Approaches to the economies of ancient Greece, 130 – 139, London. (= Velissaropoulou-Karakosta, Archaioellenika, 161 – 172)

Velissaropoulou-Karakosta, I. (2002), "Kodikopoieseis sten archaike Ellada", EHHD 36, 301 – 322. (= Velissaropoulou-Karakosta, Archaioellenika, 43 – 66)

Velissaropoulos-Karakostas, J. (2001), "Remarques sur la clause kyria he syngraphe", in Symposion 1997, 103 – 115. (= Velissaropoulos-Karakosta, Archaioellenika, 195 – 210)

Vélissaropoulos-Karakostas, J. (2000), "L'arbitrage dans la Grèce antique. Époque archaïque et classique", Revue de l'arbitrage 46, 3 – 26. (= Velissaropoulou-Karakosta, Archaioellenika, 135 – 154)

Vélissaropoulos-Karakostas, J. (1998), "Remarques sur la responsabilité civile en Grèce", Cahiers Glotz 9, 71 – 82. (= Velissaropoulou-Karakosta, Archaioellenika, 173 – 186)

Vélissaropoulos-Karakostas, J. (1996), "'Pacta conventa servabo' et Aristote", RHDFE 74, 185 – 194. (= Velissaropoulou-Karakosta, Archaioellenika, 279 – 294)

Vélissaropoulos-Karakostas, J. (1994), "Altgriechische pistis und Vertrauenshafung", in Symposion 1993, 185 – 190. (= Velissaropoulou-Karakosta, Archaioellenika, 187 – 194)

Vélissaropoulos-Karakostas, J. (1991), "Nepoinei tethnanai", in Symposion 1990, 93 – 105. (= Velissaropoulou-Karakosta, Archaioellenika, 211 – 224) (with a reply by Carawan, E. M., 107 – 114)

Velissaropoulos-Karakostas, J. (1990), "Sunepainountes. Aux origines du droit de preemption", in Symposion 1988, 413 – 424. (= Velissaropoulou-Karakosta, Archaioellenika, 265 – 278)

Velissaropoulos-Karakostas, J. & H. van Effenterre (1991), "Une affaire d' affrètement. A propos du 'plomb de Pech Maho'", RHDFE 69, 217 – 226. (= Velissaropoulos-Karakosta, Archaioellenika, 95 – 106)

Veltman, A. (2005), "The justice of the ordinary citizen in Plato's Republic", Polis 22, 45 – 59.

Veneciano, G. (2010), "Construccion y legitimacion de la polis como agente de la enunciacion legal", Mètis 8, 143 – 166.

Versnel, H. S. (2002), Writing mortals and reading gods. Appeal to the gods as a dual strategy in Social Control. In: Cohen D (Hrsg.) Demokratie, Recht und Soziale Kontrolle im klassischen Athen, München, 37 – 76.

Versteeg, R. (2010), The Essentials of Greek and Roman Law, Durham, NC.

Versteeg, R. (2002), Law in the Ancient World, Durham, NC.

Versteeg, R. (1998), "A Contract Analysis of the Trojan War", *Arizona Law Review* 40, 173 – 196.

Vial, Cl. (1992), "Mariages mixtes et statut des enfants. Trois exemples en Egée orientale", in L'étranger, 287 – 296.

Vinogradoff, P. (1922), "The legal background of Demosthenes' speech in Zenothemis v. Demon", TR 3, 163 – 174. (= Collected Papers: with a memoir. 24ff, Oxford 1964)

Vlassopoulos, K. (2011), "Greek Slavery: From Domination to Property and Back Again", JHS 131, 115 – 130.

Vlassopoulos, K. (2009), "Slavery, Freedom, and Citizenship in Classical Athens: Beyond Legalistic Approach", *European Review of History* 16, 347 – 363.

Vlassopoulos, K. (2007), "Free Spaces: Identity, Experience and Democracy in Classical Athens", *CQ* 57, 33 – 52.

Vlastos, G. (1978), "The rights of persons in Plato's conceptions of the foundations of justice", in Englehardt, H. T. & D. Callahan (eds), Morals, science and society, 172 – 201, New York (= Studies in Greek philosophy. II. Socrates, Plato and their tradition, 104 – 25, Princeton 1995)

Vlastos, G. (1953), "Isonomia", AJPh 74, 337 – 360.

Vlastos, G. (1952), "The Constitution of the Five Thousand", *AJPh* 73, 189 – 198.

Vlastos, G. (1946), "Solonian Justice", *CPh* 41, 65 – 83.

Vlastos, G. (1941), "Slavery in Plato's Thought", *Philosophical Review* 50, 289 – 304.

van der Vliet, E. Ch. L. (2003), "Justice and Written Laws in the Formation of the Polis", in Feldbrugger, F. J. M. (ed), The Law's Beginnings, 23 – 44, Leiden.

Volonaki, E. (2001), "The Republication of the Athenian Laws in the Last Decade of the Fifth Century B. C.", Dike 4, 137 – 168.

Volonaki, E. (2000), "'Apagoge' in Homicide Cases", Dike 3, 147 – 176.

W

Wade-Gery, H. T. (1958), "The Judicial Treaty with Phaselis and the History of the Athenian Courts", in Wade-Gery, Essays, 180 – 200.

Wade-Gery, H. T. (1944), "The Spartan Rhetra in Plutarch Lycurgus VI. B. The Eunomia of Tyrtaios, C. What is the Rhetra", *CQ* 38, 1 – 9, 115 – 126. (= Wade-Gery, Essays, 37 – 85)

Wade-Gery, H. T. (1943), "The Spartan Rhetra in Plutarch Lycurgus VI. A. Plutarch's Text", CQ 36, 57 – 78.

Wade-Gery, H. T. (1940), "Themistokles' archonship", in Athenian studies presented to W. S. Ferguson, 121 – 136, Cambridge, Mass. (HSCP Suppl. 1) (= Wade-Gery, Essays, 171 – 179)

Wade-Gery, H. T. (1933), "Studies in the Structure of Athenian Society II. The Laws of Kleisthenes", *CQ* 27, 17 – 29. (= Wade-Gery, Essays, 135 – 154 as "The laws of Kleisthenes")

Wade-Gery, H. T. (1931), "Studies in the Structure of Athenian Society I. Demotionid Decree", *CQ* 25, 129 – 143. (= Wade-Gery, Essays, 116 – 134 as "Demotionidai")

Walbank, F. W. (1976 – 1977), "Were there Greek Federal States?", *SCI* 3, 27 – 51. (= Selected papers. Studies in Greek and Roman history and historiography, 20 – 37, Cambridge 1985)

Walbank, F. W. (1966), "The Spartan Ancestral Constitution in Polybius", in

Ancient Society and Institutions,303 – 312.

Walbank,M. B. (2010),"New Grants of Athenian Citizenship,from the Fourth to the Second Century B. C. ",in Philathenaios,55 – 63.

Walbank,M. B. (1989),"A Proxeny-decree of 353/2 B. C. (IG II2 139 + 289)",AHB 3,119 – 122.

Walbank,M. B. (1982),"The Confiscation and Sale by the Poletai in 402/1 B. C. of the Property of the Thirty Tyrants",*Hesperia* 51,74 – 98.

Walcot,P. (1963),"Hesiod and the Law",*SO* 38,5 – 21.

Wallace,M. B. (1976),"'Emprunts Publics à Karystos'-Discussion",Phoenix 30,42 – 45.

Wallace,M. B. (1970),"Early Greek Proxenoi",Phoenix 24,189 – 208.

Wallace,R. W. (2011),"Plato's Socrates on obeying the laws of democratic Athens",Philosophia 41,87 – 96.

Wallace, R. W. (2010), "Socrates and democratic law: Plato's Crito and Apology", in Thür, G. (ed), Symposion 2009. Vorträge zur griechischen und hellenistischen Rechtsgeschichte(Seggau,25. – 30. August 2009),109 – 16,Wien.

Wallace,R. W. (2009),"Personal Freedom in Greek Democracies,Republican Rome and Modern Liberal States",in *Greek and Roman Political Thought*,164 – 177.

Wallace, R. W. (2007), "Nomos/phusis: The Antidemocratic Context", in Pierris,A. L. (ed),Phusis and Nomos. Power,justice and the agonistical ideal of life in high classicism,23 – 44,Patras.

Wallace,R. W. (2007),"Law's Enemies in Ancient Athens", in Symposion 2005,183 – 196.

Wallace,R. W. (2006),"Freedom,Community,and Law in Classical Athens", in Anagnostopoulos,Y. (ed),Law and Rights in the Ancient Greek Tradition,57 – 78,Thessaloniki.

Wallace,R. W. (2006),"The Legal Regulation of Conduct at Athens. Two Controversies on Freedom",Dike 9,107 – 128. (= Etica e Politica 9(2007)155 – 171)

Wallace,R. W. (2006),"Withdrawing Graphai in Ancient Athens-A Case Study in 'Sycophancy' and Legal Idiosyncrasies",in Symposion 2003,57 – 72.

Wallace,R. W. (2006),"Law and Rhetoric: Community Justice in Athenian

Courts", in Kinzl, K. H. (ed), A Companion to the Classical Greek World, 416 - 431, Oxford.

Wallace, R. W. (2005), "'Listening to' the Archai in Democratic Athens", in Symposion 2001, 147 - 157.

Wallace, R. W. (2005), "Law, Attic Comedy, and the Regulation of Comic Speech", in *The Cambridge Companion*, 357 - 373.

Wallace, R. W. (2004), "The Power to Speak-and not to Listen-in Ancient Athens", in *Free Speech*, 221 - 232.

Wallace, R. W. (2003), "Phainein in Athenian Laws and Legal Procedures", in Symposion 1999, 167 - 183.

Wallace, R. W. (2001), "Diamarturia in Late Fourth-century Athens: Notes on a 'Cheese Pot' (SEG XXXVI 296)", in Symposion 1997, 89 - 102.

Wallace, R. W. (2000), "Investigations and Reports' by the Areopagos Council and Demosthenes' Areopagos Decree", in *Polis and Politics*, 581 - 596.

Wallace, R. W. (1999), "The Structure of Aristotle's Athenaion Politeia", in Mellor, M. & L. Tritle (eds), Text and tradition. Studies in Greek history and historiography in honor of M. Chambers, 239 - 257, Claremont, Cal.

Wallace, R. W. (1998), "Unconvicted or Potential Atimoi in Ancient Athens", Dike 1, 63 - 78.

Wallace, R. W. (1997), "On not Legislating Sexual Conduct in Fourth-century Athens", in Symposion 1995, 151 - 166.

Wallace, R. W. (1996), "Law, Freedom, and the Concept of Citizen's Rights in Democratic Athens", in Ober, J. & Ch. Hedrick jr (eds), Demokratia. A Conversation on Democracies, Ancient and Modern, 105 - 119, Princeton.

Wallace, R. W. (1994), "The Athenian Laws on Slander", in Symposion 1993, 109 - 124.

Wallace, R. W. (1994), "Democratic Justice-no Lawyers", in A Challenge to Democracy, 69 - 80, Washington D. C.

Wallace, R. W. (1993), "Personal Conduct and Legal Sanction in the Democracy of Classical Athens", in Zlinsky, J. (ed), Questions de responsabilité (XLVe Session de la Société Internationale "Ferdinand de Visscher" pour l' Histoire des Droits de l' Antiquité), 397 - 413, Miskolc-Eger.

Wallace, R. W. (1993), "La politeia aristotelica e l' Athenaion Politeia", in Cresci, L. R. & L. Piccirilli (eds), L'Athenaion Politeia di Aristotele, 25 – 52, Genova.

Wallace, R. W. (1992), "Aristotelian Politeiai and Athenaion Politeia 4", in Nomodeiktes, 269 – 286.

Wallace, R. W. (1989), The Areopagus Council to 307 B. C., Baltimore-London.

Wallace, R. W. (1986), "The Date of Isokrates' Areopagitikos", *HSCP* 90, 77 – 84.

Wallace, R. W. (1983), "The Date of Solon's Reforms", *AJAH* 8, 81 – 95.

Wallace, R. W. (1974), "Ephialtes and the Areopagus", *GRBS* 15, 259 – 269.

Wallace, W. (1936), "An Eretrian Proxeny Decree of the Early Fifth Century", *Hesperia* 4, 273 – 284.

Wallace, W. P. (1962), "Loans to Karystos", Phoenix 16, 15 – 28.

Wallon, H. A. (1879), Histoire de l' esclavage dans l'antiquité2, Paris.

Wallon, H. A. (1850), Explication d' un passage de Plutarque sur une loi de Lycurgue nominée la cryptie, Paris.

Wallon, H. A. (1837), Du droit d'asile, Paris.

Walser, A. V. (2008), Bauern und Zinsnehmer. Politik, Recht und Wirtschaft im frühhellenistischen Ephesos, München.

Wankel, H. (1991), "'The Hypereides principle'? Bemerkungen zur Korruption in Athen", ZPE 85, 34 – 36.

Waterfield, R. (2009), Why Socrates died. Dispelling the myths, London.

Watson, G. (1971), "The Natural Law and Stoicism", in Long, A. A. (ed), Problems in Stoicism, 216 – 238, London.

Watson, J. (2010), "The Origin of Metic Status in Athens", *PCPS* 56, 259 – 276.

Waugh, J. B. (2001), "Oral Preambles and Written Laws. The Dialogical Character of the Laws and Lawfulness", in Lisi, F. (ed), Plato's Laws and Its Historical Significance (Selected Papers of the I International Congress on Ancient Thought), 27 – 31, Sankt Augustin.

Weber, C. G. (1791), Animadversionum de scriptoribus juris attici ad I. A. Fabricii bibliothecam graecam specimen II, Hamburg.

Weber, Gr. (2010), Pseudo-Xenophon. Die Verfassung der Athener, Darmstadt.

Weber, H. V. (1908), Attisches Prozessrecht in den attischen Seebundsstaaten, Paderborn. (Studien zur Geschichte und Kultur des Altertums I. 5)

van Wees, H. (2011), "The 'Law of Hybris' and Solon's Reform of Justice", in Lambert, St. (ed), Sociable man: Essays on ancient Greek social behaviour in honour of N. Fisher, 117 – 144, Swansea.

van Wees, H. (2008), "'Stasis, Destroyer of Men'. Mass, Elite, Political Violence and Security in Archaic Greece", in Brélaz, C. & P. Ducrey (eds), Sécurité collective et ordre public dans les sociétés anciennes, 1 – 39, Genève. (Entretiens sur l' antiquité classique 54)

van Wees, H. (2002), "Tyranny, Oligarchy, and Citizen Militias", in Chaniotis, A. & P. Ducrey (eds), Army and Power in the Ancient World, 61 – 82, Stuttgart.

van Wees, H. (1999), "Tyrtaeus' eunomia: Nothing to do with the Great Rhetra", in Hodkinson, St. & A. Powell (eds), Sparta. New perspectives, 1 – 41, London.

Weingast, B. (1997), "The Political Foundations of Democracy and the Rule of Law", *American Political Science Review* 91, 245 – 263.

Weinrib, E. J. (1989), "Law as Myth: Reflections on Plato's Gorgias", *Iowa Law Review* 74, 787 – 806.

Weirnick, D. (1998), Law in Aristotle's Ethical-political Thought, diss. Rice University, Houston.

Weise, C. H. (1823), Diversa naturae et rationis in civitatibus constituendis indoles e Graerorum historia illustrata, Leipzig.

Welton, W. A. (2006), "Thrasymachus vs. Socrates. What counts as a good answer to the question 'what is justice?' (Republic 396b – 399b)", Apeiron 39, 293 – 317.

Welton, W. A. (1995), "Divine Inspiration and the Origin of the Laws in Plato's Laws", *Polis* 14, 53 – 58.

Welwei, Karl-Wilhelm (2010), "Eine Tyrannis als Vorstufe der Demokratie? Überlegungen zur Tyrannis des Peisistratos", in Linke, B., Meier, M. & M. Strothmann (eds), Zwischen Monarchie und Republik. Gesellschaftliche Stabilisierungsleistungen und politische Transformationspotentiale in den antiken Stadtstaaten, 51 – 66, Stuttgart.

(Historia Einzelschriften 217)

Welwei, Karl-Wilhelm (2008), "Neuere Forschungen zur Rechtsstellung der Penesten", in Mauritsch, P., Petermandl, W., Rollinger, R. & Chr. Ulf (eds), Antike Lebenswelten, Konstanz-Wandel-Wirkungsmacht. Festschrift für Ingomar Weiler zum 70. Geburtstag, 393 – 412, Wiesbaden. (Philippika 25)

Welwei, Karl-Wilhelm (2000), "Die Entwicklung des Gerichtswesens im antiken Athen. Vom Solon bis zum Ende des 5. Jahrhunderts v. Chr.", in Große Prozesse, 15 – 29.

Welwei, Karl-Wilhelm (1997), "Apella oder Ekklesia? Zur Bezeichnung der spartanischen Volksversammlung", RhM 140, 242 – 249.

Welwei, Karl-Wilhelm (1983), Die griechische Polis. Verfassung und Gesellschaft in archaischer und klassischer Zeit, Stuttgart.

Welwei, Karl-Wilhelm (1967), "Der Diapsephismos nach dem Sturz der Peisistratiden", Gymnasium 74, 423 – 437.

Wenger, L. (1937), "Ancient Legal History", in Independence, Convergence and Borrowing in Institutions, Thought and Art, 62 – 79, Cambridge, Mass.

Werhan, K. (2008), "The Classical Athenian Ancestry of American Freedom of Speech", Supreme Court 2008, 293 – 347.

Werhan, K. (2007), "Athens and America. Constitution Making as an Act of Democratic Justice", in Justice in particular. Festschrift in honour of Professor P. J. Kozyris, 521 – 556, Athens-Komotini.

West, W. C. (1995), "The Decrees of Demosthenes' Against Leptines", *ZPE* 107, 237 – 247.

Westbrook, R. (2009), "Drakon's Homicide Law", in Symposion 2007, 3 – 16.

Westbrook, R. (2005), "Penelope's Dowry and Odysseus' Kingship", in Symposion 2001, 3 – 24. (with a reply by E. Cantarella, 25 – 32).

Westbrook, R. (1992), "The Trial Scene in the Iliad", *HSCP* 94, 53 – 76.

Westerholm, S. (1986), "Torah, Nomos, and Law. A Question of Meaning", *Studies in Religion* 15, 327 – 336.

Westermann, W. L. (1955), The Slave Systems of Greek and Roman Antiquity, Philadelphia, PA.

Westermann, W. L. (1946), "Two Studies in Athenian Manumission", *Journal of Near Eastern Studies* 5,92 – 104.

Westgate,R. (2007),"The Greek house and the ideology of citizenship",World Archaeology 39,229 – 245.

Wexter,St. & A. Irvine(2006),"Aristotle on the rule of law",Polis 23,116 – 139.

Whibley,L. (1896), Greek Oligarchies; Their Character and Organization, London.

Whitaker,F. E. (1912),"A chapter from old Greek probate law",Green Bag 24,129 – 134.

Whitby,M. (1998),"Athenian grain trade in the fourth century B. C.", in Parkins,H. & C. Smith(eds),Trade,traders and the ancient city,102 – 128,London.

Whitby,M. (1984),"The Union of Corinth and Argos:A Reconsideration", *Historia* 33,295 – 308.

White,J. B. (1983),"The Ethics of Argument:Plato's Gorgias and the Modern Lawyer",*University of Chicago Law Review* 50,849 – 895.

White,M. (1955),"Greek Tyranny",*Phoenix* 9,1 – 18.

Whitehead,D. (2009),"Hypereides' Timandros:Observations and Suggestion", *BICS* 52,135 – 148.

Whitehead,D. (2009),"Athenian Juries in Military Graphai", in Symposion 2007,23 – 36.

Whitehead,D. (2007),"'Theft' in Greek Oratory",*CQ* 57,70 – 76.

Whitehead,D. (2006), "Absentee Athenians: Lysias Against Philon and Lycurgus Against Leocrates",MH 63,132 – 151.

Whitehead,D. (2005),"Ephorus on the Spartan Constitution", *CQ* 55,299 – 300.

Whitehead,D. (2004),"Isokrates for Hire. Some Preliminaries to a Commentary on Isokrates 16 – 21",in *Law,Rhetoric,and Comedy*,1 – 14.

Whitehead,D. (2002),"Athenian Law and Lawsuits in the Late Fifth Century BC",*MH* 59,71 – 96.

Whitehead,D. (2000),Hypereides. The Forensic Speeches,Oxford.

Whitehead,D. (1997),"Oion to mnas Lytrousthai",in Hommage Garlan,139 – 146.

Whitehead, D. (1995), "The Impeachment of Philon (Hypereides, Pro Euxenippos 1)", *AHB* 9, 64 - 67.

Whitehead, D. (1991), "Norms of Citizenship in Ancient Greece", in Molho, A., Raaflaub, K. & J. Emlen (eds), City-states in Classical Antiquity and Medieval Italy, 135 - 154, Stuttgart.

Whitehead, D. (1986), "Women and Naturalization in Fourth-century Athens: The Case of Archippe", *CQ* 36, 109 - 114.

Whitehead, D. (1986), "The Ideology of the Athenian Metic: Some Pendants and a Reappraisal", *PCPS* 212, 145 - 158.

Whitehead, D. (1986), The Demes of Attica (508/7 - ca. 250 B. C.). A Political and Social Study, Princeton.

Whitehead, D. (1984), "A Thousand New Athenians", *LCM* 9, 8 - 10.

Whitehead, D. (1977), The Ideology of the Athenian Metic, Cambridge. (Cambridge Philological Society Suppl. 4)

Whitehorn, J. (1989), "Punishment under the Decree of Cannonus", in Symposion 1985, 89 - 99.

Whitley, J. (1997), "Cretan Laws and Cretan Literacy", *AJA* 101, 633 - 661. (= "Literacy and law-making. The case of archaic Crete" in Fisher, N. R. E. & H. van Wees (eds) Archaic Greece. New approaches and new evidence, 311 - 332, London 1998 abridged)

Wichmann, O. (1753), Commentatio academica qua mos Graecorum infantes exponendi ex variis scriptoribus antiquis, maxime Euripidis Ione, illustratur, Wittenberg.

Wickert, K. (1961), Der peloponnesische Bund von seiner Entstehung bis zum Ende des archidamischen Krieges, diss. Erlangen-Nürnberg.

Wiegand, H. (1888), Die Platäer in Athen, Ratzeburg.

Wiegand, Th. & U. von Wilamowitz-Möllendorff (1904), "Ein Gesetz von Samos über die Beschaffung von Brotkorn aus öffentlichen Mitteln", SPA, 917 - 931.

von Wilamowitz-Möllendorff, U. (1919), Der griechische und der platonische Staatsgedanke, Berlin.

von Wilamowitz-Möllendorff, U. (1904), "Satzungen einer milesischen Sängergilde", SPA, 619 - 640.

von Wilamowitz-Möllendorff, U. (1900), "Die sechste Rede des Antiphon", SPA,398 – 416.

von Wilamowitz-Möllendorff, U. (1898), "Die lebenslänglichen Archonten Athens", Hermes 33,119 – 129.

von Wilamowitz-Möllendorff, U. (1893), Aristoteles und Athen, Berlin.

von Wilamowitz-Möllendorff, U. (1887), "Demotika der attischen Metöken", Hermes 22,107 – 128,211 – 259.

von Wilamowitz-Möllendorff, U. (1880), "Der Markt von Kekrops bis Kleisthenes", PhU 1,195 – 212.

von Wilamowitz-Möllendorff, U. (1880), "Burg und Stadt von Kekrops bis Perikles", PhU 1,97 – 172.

von Wilamowitz-Möllendorff, U. (1880a), "Von des attischen Reiches Herrlichkeit", PhU 1,1 – 96.

von Wilamowitz-Möllendorff, U. (1879), "Grammateus tes poleos", Hermes 14, 148 – 152.

von Wilamowitz-Möllendorff U. & B. Niese (1910), Staat und Gesellschaft der Griechen und Römer, Berlin. (Kultur der Gegenwart, 2. 4,1)

Wilhelm, A. (1951), Griechische Inschriften rechtlichen Inhalts, Athenai. (Pragmateiai Akademias Athenon 17 (1)) (= Akademieschriften zur griechischen Inschriftenkunde(1895 – 1951)3,391 – 506, Leipzig 1974)

Wilhelm, A. (1943 – 1947), "Zu Lykurgos' Rede gegen Leokrates", WS 61 – 62,68 – 70. (= Kleine Schriften II. 5,462 – 464, Wien 2003)

Wilhelm, A. (1935), "Attische Pachturkunden", AfP 11,189 – 217. (= Kleine Schriften II. 3,265 – 293, Wien 2000)

Wilhelm, A. (1933), "Die Pachturkunden der Klytidai", JÖAI 27,197 – 212. (= Abhandlungen und Beiträge zur griechischen Inschriftenkunde in den JÖAI(1898 – 1948)1,719 – 743, Leipzig 1984)

Wilhelm, A. (1925), "Zu Xenophons Lakedaimonion Politeia", WS 44,154 – 159. (= Kleine Schriften II. 5,328 – 334, Wien 2003)

Wilhelm, A. (1914), "Bürgerrechtsverleihungen der Athener", MDAI 39,257 – 315. (= Kleine Schriften II. 3,575 – 634, Wien 2000)

Wilhelm, A. (1909), "Urkunden des attischen Reiches", AAWW,41 – 58 (=

Akademieschriften zur griechischen Inschriftenkunde (1895 – 1951) 1, 1 – 18, Leipzig).

Wilhelm, A. (1909), Beiträge zur griechischen Inschriftenkunde mit einem Anhange über die öffentliche Aufzeichnung von Urkunden, Wien. (Sonderschriften des österreichisches archäologischen Institutes 7)

Wilhelm, A. (1901), "Nochmals die Bundesurkunde aus Argos", RhM 56, 571 – 586. (= Kleine Schriften II. 5, 51 – 66, Wien 2003)

Wilhelm, A. (1900), "Inschrift der Akropolis betr. Erlass der Metökensteuer für die Flülchtlinge aus Olynth", AIB 44, 524ff.

Willetts, R. F. (1982), "Cretan Laws and Society", in Cambridge Ancient History Ⅲ/3: The Expansion of the Greek World, Eighth to Sixth Centuries B. C., 234 – 248.

Willets, R. F. (1973), "Cretan Law and Early Greek Society", in Antichita cretesi. Studi in onore di Doro Levi Ⅱ, 22 – 31, Catania. (Cronache di Archeologia. Universita di Catania. Istituto di Archeologia 12 – 13) (= Selected papers I, 251 – 260)

Willetts, R. F. (1967), The Law Code of Gortyn, Berlin. (Kadmos Supplement I) (= Selected papers I, 33 – 162)

Willetts, R. F. (1966), "The Rights of Epiballontes", Eirene 5, 5 – 16.

Willetts, R. F. (1965), "Marriage and Kinship at Gortyn", *PCPS* 2, 50 – 61.

Willetts, R. F. (1961 – 62), "Cretan Kadestas", *Kretika Chronika* 15 – 16, 241 – 247.

Willetts, R. F. (1955), Aristocratic Society in Ancient Crete, London.

Willetts, R. F. (1954), "Freedmen at Gortyn", *CQ* 4, 216 – 219.

Willetts, R. F. (1952), "The Historical Importance of the Gortyn Laws", *University of Birmingham Historical Journal* 3, 95 – 118.

Williams, A. (2011), "Leasing of Sacred Land in 4th-century Athens. A Reassessment of Six Inscribed Fragments", *Hesperia* 80, 261 – 86.

Williams, A. (2008), "The Law Concerning the Little Panathenaia and the Leasing of the Nea Kata Diklerian", *ZPE* 167, 33 – 36.

Williams, J. (1997), "Ideology and Constitution of Demetrius of Phalerum", in Hamilton, Ch. D. & P. Krentz (eds), Polis and Polemos. Essays on Politics, War, and

History in Ancient Greece in Honor of D. Kagan,327 - 346,Claremont,CA.

Wilsdorf,H. (1952),Bergleute und Hüttenmänner im Altertum bis zum Ausgang der Republik,ihre wirtschaftliche,soziale und juristische Lage,Berlin.

Wilson,J. R. S. (1980 - 1981),"Thrasymachus' theory of justice",Polis 3,1 - 13.

Wilson,P. (1992),"Demosthenes 21 (Against Meidias): Democratic Abuse", PCPS 37,164 - 195.

Wilutsky,P. (1903),Vorgeschichte des Rechts,Breslau.

Winckler,G. Z. (1744),De concubinatu,Leipzig.

Winton,R. I. (2004),"Thucydides 2,37,1: Pericles on Athenian Democracy", RhM 147,26 - 34.

Winton,R. I. (1980),"Philodikein Dokoumen: Law and Paradox in the Athenian Empire",*MH* 37,89 - 97.

Wohl,V. (2010b),"A Tragic Case of Poisoning: Intention between Tragedy and the Law",*TAPhA* 140,33 - 70.

Wohl, V. (2010), Laws' Cosmos. Juridical Discourse in Athenian Forensic Oratory,Cambridge.

Wolf,E. (1970),Griechisches Rechtsdenken,4 vols,Frankfurt.

Wolf,E. (1953),"Mass und Gerechtigkeit bei Solon",in D. S. Constantopoulos & H. Wehberg (eds), Gegenwartsprobleme des intenationalen Rechtes und der Rechtsphilososphie. Festschrift für Rudolph Laum zu seinem siebzigsten Geburtstag, 449 - 464,Hamburg.

Wolf,E. (1949),"Dike bei Anaximander und Parmenides",Lexis 2,16 - 24.

Wolf,F. A. (1789),Praefatio orationis adversus Leptinem,Halle.

Wolf,Osw. (1882),Quaestiones Iophonteae,Meissen.

Wolff, H. J. (1983), "Zum Problem der dogmatischen Erfassung des altgriechischen Rechts",in Symposion 1979,7 - 20.

Wolff,H. J. (1982),"Sammlung griechischer Rechtsinschriften",ZPE 45,123 - 126.

Wolff,H. J. (1980),"Vorgeschichte und Entstehung des Rechtsbegriffs in fruhen Griechentum", in W. Fikentscher, H. Franke & O. Kohler (eds), Entstehung und Wandel rechtlicher Traditionen, 557 - 579, Freiburg. (= "Preistoria ed origine del concetto di diritto nell' esperienza greca arcaica" Studi Sanfilippo Ⅱ, 759 – 780, Roma 1982)

Wolff, H. J. (1979), Das Problem der Konkurrenz von Rechtsordnungen in der Antike, Heidelberg. (Sitzungsberichte der Heidelberger Akademie der Wissenschaften, Philos. -Histor. Klasse 5)

Wolff, H. J. (1975), "Greek Legal History-Its Functions and Potentialities", *Washington University Law Quarterly*, 395 – 408. (= Revista de Estudios Historico-Juridicos 1 (1976) 136 – 148)

Wolff, H. J. (1975), "Juristische Gräzistik-Aufgaben, Probleme, Möglichkeiten", in Symposion 1971, 1 – 22.

Wolff, H. J. (1973), "Das Recht als Komponente des griechischen Erbes", in Gehrig, H. (ed), Der Lebenswert des Griechischen, 29 – 41, Karlsruhe. (Veröffentlichungen der Katholischen Akademie der Erzdioezese Freiburg 29) (= Opuscula, 1 – 13)

Wolff, H. J. (1973), "Zur Bedeutung der altgriechischen Rechtsgeschichte für die Rechtswissenschaft", in Xenion Zeppos, 757 – 763.

Wolff, H. J. (1973), "Die Bedeutung der Epigraphik für die griechische Rechtsgeschichte", in Akten des 6. Internationalen Kongresses, 131 – 144.

Wolff, H. J. (1972), "Normenkontrolle im klassischen Athen: Die graphe paranomon", in Tomos aphieromenos eis ton omotimon kathegeten Pan. Perdika, 127 – 139, Athenai.

Wolff, H. J. (1971), "Methodische Grundsatzfragen der rechtsgeschichtlichen Verwendung attischer Gerichtsreden", in La critica del testo Ⅱ (Atti del Ⅱ Congresso Internazionale della Società Italiana di Storia del Diritto, Venezia, 18 – 22 settembre 1967), 1123 – 1135, Florence. (= Opuscula 27 – 39)

Wolff, H. J. (1971), "Neue juristische Urkunden, IV: Eigentumsbindung nach griechischen Recht", ZRG 88, 329 – 339.

Wolff, H. J. (1970), Normenkontrolle und Gesetzesbegriff in der athenischen Demokratie. Untersuchungen zur graphe paranomon, Heidelberg. (Sitzungsberichte der Heidelberger Akademie der Wissenschaften, Philos. -Histor. Klasse 2)

Wolff, H. J. (1970), "Griechische Rechtsgeschichte als Anliegen der Altertumswissenschaft und der Rechtswissenschaft", Ellenike Anthropistike Hetaireia

20,152 – 162. (= Opuscula 15 – 24)

Wolff, H. J. (1968), Demosthenes als Advokat, Berlin. (Schriftenreihe der iuristischen Gesellschaft 30) (= "O Demosthenes hos dikegoros" Ephemeris Ellenon Nomikon 36(1969)305 – 314, translated as "Demosthenes as advocate: The functions and methods of legal consultants in classical Athens" with an epilogue by G. Thür in The Attic Orators, 91 – 115)

Wolff, H. J. (1967), "Der Rechtshistoriker und die Privatrechtsdogmatik", in Festschrift für Fritz von Hippel, Tübingen, 687 – 710. (= Opuscula, 41 – 64)

Wolff, H. J. (1966), Die attische Paragraphe: ein Beitrag zum Problem der Auflockerung archaischer Prozessformen, Weimar.

Wolff, H. J. (1966), "Debt and assumpsit in the light of comparative legal history", The Irish Jurist 1, 316 – 327. (= Opuscula, 123 – 134)

Wolff, H. J. (1966), "La structure de l'obligation contractuelle en droit grec", RHDFE 44, 569 – 583.

Wolff, H. J. (1964), "Rechtsexperten in der griechischen Antike", in Festschrift für den 45. deutschen Juristentag, 1 – 22, Karlsruhe. (= Opuscula, 81 – 102)

Wolff, H. J. (1963), "Verjährung von Ansprüchen nach attischem Recht", in Eranion Maridaki, 87 – 109.

Wolff, H. J. (1962), "Gewohnheitsrecht und Gesetzesrecht in der griechischen Rechtsauffassung", in Deutsche Landesreferate zum VI. Intern. Kongress für Rechtsvergleichung in Hamburg, 99 – 120, Berlin. (= Zur griechischen Rechtsgeschichte, 99 – 120, and as "Ethimikon dikaion kai nomoi tethemenou dikaiou kata tas peri dikaiou antilepseis ton archaion Ellenon" Ephemeris Ellenon Nomikon 29 (1962)649 – 678)

Wolff, H. J. (1957), "Die Grundlagen des griechischen Vertragsrechts", ZRG 74, 26 – 72. (= Zur griechischen Rechtsgeschichte, 483 – 533)

Wolff, H. J. (1954), "Prozessrechtliches und materiellrechtliches Denken in rechtsgeschichtlicher Beleuchtung", in Studi in memoria di Paolo Koschaker II, 405 – 423, Mailand.

Wolff, H. J. (1954), "Das attische Apotimema", in Festschrift Rabel II, 293 – 333.

Wolff, H. J. (1953), "Verpachtung von Mundelvermogen in Attika", in

Festschrift Lewald, 201 – 208.

Wolff, H. J. (1952), "Die Grundlagen des griechischen Eherechts", RHDFE 20, 1 – 29 and 157 – 181. (= Atti del Terzo Congresso di Diritto Comparato I, 213 – 257, Rome 1953 and in Zur griechischen Rechtsgeschichte, 620 – 654)

Wolff, H. J. (1950), "Nochmals zum Schild des Achilles", Iura 1, 272 – 275.

Wolff, H. J. (1950), "The Science of Ancient Legal History", *Law Guild Review* 10, 47 – 51.

Wolff, H. J. (1946), "The Origin of Judicial Litigation among the Greeks", *Traditio* 4, 31 – 87. (= Beiträge, 1 – 90)

Wolff, H. J. (1944), "Marriage Law and Family Organisation in Ancient Athens", *Traditio* 2, 43 – 95. (= Beiträge, 155 – 242)

Wolff, H. J. (1943), "The Dike Blabes in Demosthenes, or. 51", AJPh 64, 316 – 324. (= Beiträge, 91 – 101)

Wolicki, Al. (2007), "Moicheia: Adultery or Something More?", *Palamedes* 2, 131 – 142.

Wolpert, A. (2003), "Addresses to the Jury in the Attic Orators", AJPh 124, 537 – 555.

Wolpert, A. (2002), Remembering defeat. Civil War and Civic Memory in Ancient Athens, Baltimore.

Wolpert, A. (2002), "Lysias 18 and the Athenian Memory of Civil War", *TAPhA* 132, 109 – 126.

Wolpert, A. (2001), "Lysias 1 and the Politics of the Oikos", *CJ* 96, 415 – 424.

Wolpert, A. & K. Kapparis (eds) (2011), Legal speeches of democratic Athens, Sources for Athenian history, Indianapolis.

Woodhead, A. G. (1997), Inscriptions. The Decrees, Princeton, NJ. (The Athenian Agora 16)

Woodhead, A. G. (1967), "Isegoria and the Council of 500", *Historia* 16, 129 – 140.

Woodhead, A. G. (1959), "The Institution of the Hellenotamiae", *JHS* 79, 149 – 152.

Woodhead, A. G. (1949), "I. G., I2, 95, and the Ostracism of Hyperbolus", Hesperia 18, 78 – 83.

Woozley, A. D. (1979), Law and Obedience. The Argument of Plato's Crito, Chapel Hill.

Woozley, A. D. (1972), "Platon Killing in Anger", *PhilosQ* 22, 303 – 317.

Woozley, A. D. (1969 – 1971), "Socrates on Disobeying the Law", in Vlastos, G. (ed) The Philosophy of Socrates. A Collection of Critical Essays, 299 – 318, New York.

Worrle, M. (2003), "Inschriften von Herakleia am Latmos Ⅲ. Der Synoikismos der Latmioi mit den Pidaseis", Chiron 33, 121 – 143.

Wormuth, F. D. (1948), "Aristotle on Law", in Konvitz, M. R. & A. E. Murphy (eds), Essays in Political Theory Presented to G. H. Sabine, 45 – 61, Ithaca, N. Y.

Woronoff, M. (2006), "L' étranger dans les poèmes homériques", in Mélanges Casevitz, 37 – 44.

Worthigton, I., Cooper, C. & E. M. Harris (2001), Dinarchus, Hyperides & Lycurgus, Austin, Tx. (The oratory of classical Greece 5)

Worthington, I. (2006), Demosthenes: Speeches 60 – 61, Prologues, Letters, Austin, Tx. (The oratory of classical Greece 10)

Worthington, I. (2003), "The Length of an Athenian Public Trial. A Reply to Professor MacDowell", Hermes 131, 364 – 371.

Worthington, I. (2000), "The Date of Chaerephilus' Citizenship", *ZPE* 130, 296 – 298.

Worthington, I. (1994), "The Canon of Ten Attic Orators", in Worthington, I. (ed), Persuasion: Greek Rhetoric in Action, 244 – 263, London.

Worthington, I. (1989), "The Duration of an Athenian Political Trial", *JHS* 109, 204 – 207.

van't Wout, P. E. (2011), "From oath-swearing to entrenchment clause: the introduction of atimia-terminology in legal inscriptions", in Lardinois, A. P. M. H., Blok, J. H. & M. G. M. van der Poel (eds), Sacred words: Orality, literacy and religion, 143 – 60, Leiden. (Orality and literacy in the ancient world 8) (Mnemosyne Suppl. 332)

van't Wout, P. E. (2011), "Neglected evidence for the nature of atimia. Agora P 17615 and DIA 107", ZPE 176, 126 – 134.

van't Wout, P. E. (2010), "Visibility and social evaluation in Athenian litigation", in Rosen, R. M. & I. Sluiter (eds), Valuing others in classical antiquity, 113 – 136, Leiden. (Mnemosyne Suppl. 323)

van't Wout, P. E. (2010), "Solon's Law on Stasis: Promoting Active Neutrality", *CQ* 60, 289 – 301.

Wrenhaven, K. L. (2009), "The Identity of the 'wool-workers' in the Attic Manumissions", *Hesperia* 78, 367 – 86.

Wüst, F. R. (1954), "Amphiktyonie, Eidgenossenschaft, Symmachie", *Historia* 3, 129 – 153.

Wurm, M. (1972), Apokeryxis, Abdicatio und Exheredatio, München. (MBPaR 60)

Wycherley, R. E. (1954), "Euboulos 74, Markets and Law Courts", *Proceedings of the Classical Association* 51, 54 – 55.

Wyse, W. (1916), "Law", in Whibley, L. (ed), A companion to Greek studies, 461 – 490, Cambridge.

Wyse, W. (1904), The Speeches of Isaeus, Cambridge.

Wysocki, L. (1988), "The So Called Demotionid Decrees", *Eos* 76, 34 – 46.

Y

Yamauchi, A. (2005), "Oaths and Disputes in Fourth-century Athenian Society", *Journal of Classical Studies* 53, 59 – 67.

Yamauchi, A. (1998), "Religious Procedures and the Process of Identification of Civic Status in Classical Athens", Shirin (*Journal of History*) 81, 1 – 34.

Yiannopoulos, A. N. (1996), "The Hellenic Legal Tradition in the United States", *Loyola Law Review* 42, 193 – 214.

Yasunaga, S. (1993), "Citizenship Law and the Position of Women in Classical Athens", in Ito, T., Katsura, M. & Yasunaga, S. (eds), The Ancient Mediterranean World: Greek and Roman Studies Presented to Ichiro Miura on his 80th birthday, 50 – 77, Tokyo.

Yasunaga, S. (1992), "Athenian Marriage Pattern in the Fourth Century B. C.", Seiyoshigaku Ronshu (*Journal of Western History*) 30, 1 – 14.

Yasunaga, S. (1990), "Citizenship of Women in Classical Athens", Bulletin of the College of Liberal Arts (Kyushu Sangyo University), 27, 87 – 109.

Yasunori, K. (2010), "A space for epieikeia in Greek law", in Thür, G. (ed), Symposion 2009. Vorträge zur griechischen und hellenistischen Rechtsgeschichte (Seggau, 25. -30. August 2009), 117 -26, Wien.

Yates, D. C. (2005), "The Archaic Treaties between the Spartans and Their Allies", *CQ* 55, 65 -76.

Yiftach-Firanko, U. (2003), Marriage and Marital Arrangements. A History of the Greek Marriage Document in Egypt (4th century BCE - 4th century CE), München. (MBPaR 93)

Yoshizawa, K. (2007), "Concerning the legal terms in Plato's Hippias Major", Methodos 39, 16 -27. (in Japanese with English summary)

Young, S. (1939), "An Athenian Clepsydra", Hesperia 8, 274 -284.

Youni, M. S. (2011), He geneses tou graptou nomou ste dorike Krete, Thessalonike.

Youni, M. S. (2011), "L'imprécation et la loi: châtiment divine et sanctions pénales dans la polis grecque", in Helmis, A. (ed), Vertiges du droit. Mélanges Franco-Héllénique à la mémoire de Jacques Phytilis, 393 -404, Paris.

Youni, M. S. (2010), "Polis and legislative procedure in early Crete", in Thür, G. (ed), Symposion 2009. Vorträge zur griechischen und hellenistischen Rechtsgeschichte (Seggau, 25. -30. August 2009), 151 -68, Wien.

Youni, M. S. (2010), "Lex est quod invenimus. Oi peripeteies enos nomou", in Pneumatos dorema Georgio P. Nako, 147 - 158, Thessaloniki.

Youni, M. S. (2008), "Sur le statut juridique de l' affranchi grec dans le monde gréco-romain", in Hommage à J. Annequin, 161 - 174.

Youni, M. S. (2007), "An Inscription from Teos Concerning Abdera", in Thrace in the Graeco-Roman World (Proceedings of the 10th International Congress of Thracology, Komotini-Alexandroupolis 18 -23 October 2005), 724 -736, Athens.

Youni, M. S. (2006), Nomos poleos. Dikaiosyne kai nomothesia sten archaia ellenike polin, Thessaloniki.

Youni, M. S. (2005), "Oi periousiakes schesseis ton syzygon sto dikaio tes Gortynas", in La grande iscrizione, 191 -213.

Youni, M. S. (2003), "Archaia hellenika dikasteria", Historika 183, 12 -17.

Youni, M. S. (2001), "Ennemis ou amis: traités entre poleis de l' antiquité grecque", Méditerranées 29, 29 – 37.

Youni, M. S. (2001), "The Different Categories of Unpunished Killing and the Term Atimos in Ancient Greek Law", in Symposion 1997, 117 – 137.

Youni, M. S. (2000), "Hetaireiai. He ensomatose ton neon politon sten archaike Krete", Digesta 3, 45 – 54.

Youni, M. S. (1998), Atimos esto-Atimos tethnato. Symbole ste meleti tes poines tes atimias kai tes thessis ektos nomou sto attiko dikaio, Thessaloniki.

Youni, M. S. (1997), "Individu, pouvoir et pénalité en droit attique", Méditerranées 12, 49 – 57.

Youni, M. S. (1996), "À propos de quatre inscriptions olynthiennes. Quelques remarques sur la surété rèelle au 4eme siècle av. J. -C. ", Tekmeria 2, 135 – 153.

Youni, M. S. (1991), "Onai Makedonias I. Agorapolesies akineton se makedonikes epigraphes tou 4ou kai 3ou p. Ch. aiona", Epistemoniki Epeterida D. S. Th. Armenopoulos 12, 25 – 50.

Yunis, H. (2010), "The Rhetoric of Law in Plato's Apology of Socrates and Isocrates' Antidosis", in Yunis, H. (2007), "Politics as literature: Demosthenes and the burden of the Athenian past", in The Attic Orators, 372 – 390.

Yunis, H. (2005b), "The Rhetoric of Law in Fourth-century Athens", in *The Cambridge Companion*, 191 – 208.

Yunis, H. (2005a), Demosthenes: Speeches 18 – 19, Austin, Tx. (The oratory of classical Greece 9)

Yunis, H. (2001), Demosthenes: On the Crown, Cambridge.

Yunis, H. (1988), "Law, Politics, and the Graphe Paranomon in Fourth-century Athens", *GRBS* 29, 361 – 382.

Z

Zachos, G. (2007), "Interference of the City in the Elateian Manumissions", in Fear of slaves, 115 – 124.

Zelnick-Abramovitz, R. (2011), "The guardian of the land: The Areopagos council as a symbol of stability", in Herman, G. (ed), Stability and crisis in the Athenian democracy, 103 – 26, Stuttgart. (Historia Einzelschriften 220)

Zelnick-Abramovitz, R. (2009), "Freed Slaves, Their Status and State Control in

Ancient Greece", *European Review of History* 16, 303 - 318.

Zelnick-Abramovitz, R. (2005), "The Phrase Xenike Lysei in Manumission Inscriptions", *ZPE* 153, 108 - 112.

Zelnick-Abramovitz, R. (2005), Not Wholly Free: The Concept of Manumission and the Status of Manumitted Slaves in the Ancient Greek World, Leiden. (Mnemosyne Suppl. 266)

Zelnick-Abramovitz, R. (2004), "The Proxenoi of Western Greece", *ZPE* 147, 93 - 106.

Ziebarth, E. (1929), Beiträge zur Geschichte des Seeraubs und Seehandels im alten Griechenland, Hamburg.

Ziebarth, E. (1917), "Delische Stiftungen", *Hermes* 52, 425 - 441.

Ziebarth, E. (1900), "Zu den griechischen Vereinsinschriften", *RhM* 55, 501 - 519.

Ziebarth, E. (1898), "Neue attische Grenzsteine", SPA, 776 - 784.

Ziebarth, E. (1897), "Popularklagen mit Delatorenprämien nach griechischem Recht", *Hermes* 32, 609 - 628.

Ziebarth, E. (1897), "Neue attische Hypothekeninschriften", SPA, 664 - 675.

Ziebarth, E. (1896), Das griechische Vereinswesen, Leipzig.

Ziebarth, E. (1892), De iureiurando in iure Graeco quaestiones, Göttingen.

Ziebarth, E. (1885), "Der Fluch im griechischen Recht", Hermes 30, 57 - 70.

Zimet, B. T. R. (1973), "Ancient Athenian Procedural Due Process: A Reflection of Societal Values", *American University Law Review* 23, 485 - 511.

后 记

2012 年 9 月至 2013 年 3 月，我有幸在北京大学黄洋教授推荐下，赴英国伦敦大学国王学院古典系进修半年，并在此期间收集了大量古希腊法研究资料。由英国带回的资料不但数量众多，而且纷繁复杂，如何分类整理进而深入研究是一件颇费心思的事情。由于先前有出版古希腊法专著的基础和相应的研究成果，思虑再三，决定仍按照法系的标准，以专题研究的形式对新收集的外文资料进行部分整理分类，并结合已有成果对一些重点问题进行研究，本书即这一研究思路的阶段性成果。

本书的初衷是想在整体展示英美国家古希腊史研究成果的基础上，重点介绍国外学者对该领域的研究成果和最新的原始资料发掘整理情况，特别是碑刻铭文所记载的古希腊相关立法的原貌，但限于个人能力和写作时间的紧迫，好多原来的设想没有完成。本书借鉴了众多国内外学者的最新研究成果，限于篇幅未能一一注明，在此一并表示感谢。书末附录了国外古希腊法研究的扩展性参考文献，希望能为有志于深入研究该领域的学者提供些许便利。

赴英进修期间收获良多，特别感谢北京大学黄洋教授的大力推荐和华东政法大学何勤华教授的全力支持。感谢赴英学习期间黄洋教授的英国导师多米尼克·拉斯伯恩教授的热心指导和悉心照顾，以及几位前辈的无私帮助。最后，还要感谢法律出版社法治与经济分社社长沈小英女士、责任编辑刘晓萌女士,以及为此书付出辛苦工作但不曾谋面的其他编校工作者,没有他们的支持,本书不会顺利出版。

本书的出版得到华东政法大学外国法与比较法研究院、法律文明史研究院以及国家重点学科华东政法大学法律史学科的经费支持,也是国家社科重大项目“法律文明史”(批准号:11&ZD081)的阶段性成果之一。

胡骏

2022年5月15日

于上海松江寓所